FEDERAL INCOME TAX

By

ROBERT G. POPOVICH
Pepperdine University School of Law

Exam Pro

WEST
GROUP

A THOMSON COMPANY

To my two sons, Mark and Brian
The happiness and pride that you bring to my life is immeasurable;
as is my love for you.

COPYRIGHT © 2002 By WEST GROUP
610 Opperman Drive
P.O. Box 64526
St. Paul, MN 55164–0526
1–800–328–9352

ISBN 0–314–25997–X

TEXT IS PRINTED ON 10% POST CONSUMER RECYCLED PAPER

FEDERAL INCOME TAX
PREFACE

TO THE STUDENT:

This book is the Federal Income Tax contribution to West Group's *Exam Pro* series. I love teaching Federal Income Tax; the course material is always fun as well as challenging. It is my sincere hope that you find the book helpful to your understanding of Federal Income Tax.

This book consists of eight examinations in Federal Income Tax, containing a total of 200 OBJECTIVE QUESTIONS. Virtually all of these questions are *actual, final exam questions* (many originally in essay form) which are being released for the first time. You will probably find most of the questions to be "challenging." Many of the questions contain multi-faceted fact patterns that are designed to raise multiple diverse and overlapping Federal Income Tax issues. The questions are designed to prepare you for whatever questions you see on your exams – whether they be multiple-choice or essay.

Each exam consists of twenty-five objective problems, followed by four or five multiple-choice answers. In the back of this book, there are tear-out answer sheets to allow you to take each exam under simulated examination conditions. As indicated, many of the questions are "challenging," and each exam may take more than one hour to complete (many of the questions can easily be split into simpler questions on an actual exam). If your professor permits you to use other materials during your exam, then use these as well in answering the questions in this book.

Each exam has an answer key with a thorough discussion of the relevant issues and a step-by-step, detailed explanation of the analysis for the problem. The answer key explains why the *best* answer is the best choice, and it explains why the other proposed answers are incorrect, or not the best possible choice. The answer key also identifies "red herring" answers that are intended to lure you into appropriate-sounding, but incorrect, responses. Some of the question explanations are quite lengthy, but they are designed to assist you in a better understanding of the subject matter, and to illuminate other testable issues not specifically asked in the respective question. Federal Income Tax is a very "real-world" subject, and I have tried to reflect this in the questions, and the answer key discussions.

The study of Federal Income Tax does involve some math and many of the questions contain numbers (primarily for the purpose of more clearly defining the facts). However, the math utilized is <u>very basic</u> and should not be a source of concern for those of you who do not get excited at the sight of numbers. Actually, the only math skills necessary are those from the four basic "arithmetic" food groups: addition, subtraction, multiplication, and division. Appendix C contains a discussion of "Code" math, and explains almost everything you need to know about how tax math.

In addition to the thorough answer key explanations, for each answer, the text provides relevant citations to Internal Revenue Code Sections, Treasury Regulations, Revenue Rulings, Internal Revenue Service Publications, Case law, and the like. Additionally, specific relevant citations are provided to the West Group's "hornbook" series: FEDERAL INCOME TAXATION OF INDIVIDUALS (5th ed. 2000), by Daniel Q. Posin.

The breadth and depth of topics covered in Federal Income Tax courses can vary dramatically. In addition, courses in Federal Income Tax vary in credit hours from a single 2-credit course, to a multiple-part course in excess of 5-credits. I have attempted to cover most of the issues that are typically addressed in the basic Federal Income Tax course. As your study in Federal Income Tax progresses, however, you will quickly come to realize that 200 objective questions could be supplied for almost any one of the subjects covered in a typical Federal Income Tax course. Writing a study aid under such conditions is a challenge. To facilitate your use of this book, and to maximize your benefit from this book, following this PREFACE is an ORGANIZATION OF MATERIAL section which is designed to assist you: (1) in understanding the organization of the subject matter coverage in this book, and (2) in locating particular Federal Income Tax topics as they appear in the problems in the exams. No matter how many credit hours your Federal Income Tax course has, which textbook book you use, or who your professor is, the problems in this book should provide you with a better understanding of Federal Income Tax, and help prepare you for your exam.

Federal Income Tax is also challenging from the standpoint that the tax laws seem to sometimes be in a constant state of flux. Changes to tax law made by the *Economic Growth and Tax Relief Reconciliation Act of 2001* (the "2001 Tax Act"), were extensive, and included a host of provisions that "phase-in," "phase-out," appear, and then disappear over a period of many years. To add a further challenge to the understanding of Federal Income Tax, as enacted (and as of this writing), the entire 2001 Tax Act is subject to a *sunset clause*. Unless affirmatively changed by Congress and enacted into law, all changes made and provisions enacted by the 2001 Tax Act will disappear after December 31, 2010, and tax laws will revert to their status immediately prior to the enactment of the 2001 Tax Act. As of this writing, there have been discussions in Congress about altering some aspects of the scheduled changes. However, as of this writing, nothing has been enacted to that effect. This book contains up-to-date material from the 2001 Tax Act as well as tax provisions added by the *Job Creation and Worker Assistance Act of 2002*.

This book could not have been written without the assistance of Ms. Melinda van Hemert, who spent long hours proofing countless drafts of the manuscript. I wish to offer my sincerest heartfelt thanks and gratitude for her painstaking attention to detail. I am forever indebted. Moreover, I would also like to thank two of my former Federal Income Tax students; Annie Krikorian, and Peter Weiner, who provided me with invaluable assistance in the early stages of the manuscript. In addition, I would like to thank my students, without whom I would not have the privilege of teaching Federal Income Tax.

I have been an enthusiastic user of Westlaw's student online education network (TWEN) for many years, and use it for all of my law school courses. In the near future, I hope to have a TWEN site dedicated exclusively to all users of this *Exam Pro* for Federal Income Tax. This TWEN site will provide a convenient forum for your questions about the material in this book. In addition, in the event of tax law changes, I can easily update the questions and answers in this book to keep the material "current." In the meantime, if you wish to discuss any of the questions in further detail, feel free to E-mail me (with "Exam Pro" in the subject line) at: <robert.popovich@pepperdine.edu>.

Thank you, and I hope that you enjoy this book as much as I enjoy teaching Federal Income Tax.

PROFESSOR ROBERT G. POPOVICH
PEPPERDINE UNIVERSITY SCHOOL OF LAW
JULY 2002

FEDERAL INCOME TAX

ORGANIZATION OF MATERIAL

I. Organization By Exams

The breadth and depth of topics covered in Federal Income Tax courses can vary dramatically. In addition, courses in Federal Income Tax vary in credit hours from a single 2-credit course, to multiple-part courses in excess of 5-credits. Exams I through VI focus primarily on the classic components that make up most Federal Income Tax courses: issues of income and exclusions, deductions, gains and losses, and the like (see detail below). Exam VII contains questions in which all of these elements are put together in the concepts of adjusted gross income and taxable income. Exam VIII's focus is on tax computation, tax credits, tax doctrines, procedural and constitutional matters.

EXAM I .... PRIMARILY ISSUES OF INCOME
GENERAL SCOPE OF INCOME
SPECIFIC INCLUSIONS IN INCOME
SPECIFIC EXCLUSIONS FROM INCOME

EXAM II .... PRIMARILY ISSUES OF DEDUCTIONS
BUSINESS DEDUCTIONS
NONBUSINESS DEDUCTIONS

EXAM III .... OVERLAPPING AND COMBINED ISSUES
INCOME & EXCLUSIONS
DEDUCTIONS
GAINS/LOSSES

EXAMS IV AND V .... OVERLAPPING AND COMBINED ISSUES
INCOME & EXCLUSIONS
DEDUCTIONS
GAINS/LOSSES
CAPITAL GAINS/LOSSES
BARTER TRANSACTIONS

EXAM VII .... PUTTING IT ALL TOGETHER
ADJUSTED GROSS INCOME
TAXABLE INCOME
OVERLAPPING QUESTIONS

EXAM VIII .... TAX COMPUTATION
TAX CREDITS
TAX DOCTRINES
TAX PROCEDURE
CONSTITUTIONAL ISSUES

II.   Table of Exam Topics

DEDUCTIONS

INCOME

TAXABLE INCOME & ADJUSTED GROSS INCOME

FEDERAL INCOME TAX
TABLE OF CONTENTS

EXAM I

FEDERAL INCOME TAX
MULTIPLE-CHOICE OBJECTIVE QUESTIONS
EXAM I

1. Melinda is the sole shareholder of ABC, Incorporated ("ABC"). Melinda is also the sole employee of ABC. Two years ago, ABC obtained a loan from a bank upon the condition that some of Melinda's property be transferred to ABC as additional security for the loan. Pursuant to this condition, Melinda transferred ownership of her personal Ferrari automobile to ABC two years ago. At all times subsequent to this transfer, Melinda has continued to use the Ferrari for her personal use – totally unrelated to any matter or activity involving ABC. **For the current year, Melinda will most likely:**

    (a)   Not be required to recognize any income because such use is an excludable fringe benefit pursuant to IRC § 132.

    (b)   Not be required to recognize any income because as sole shareholder of ABC, Melinda is effectively using her own car and there is no net economic benefit or accession to wealth.

    (c)   Be required to recognize income in the form of compensation from ABC because as an employee, she has experienced a net economic benefit (or net accession to wealth).

    (d)   Not be required to recognize any income this year because income, if any, should have been recognized two years ago when she transferred the automobile to ABC.

2. Tricia purchased her home a few years ago. Late last year, something unexpected happened. While excavating a portion of her backyard to build a swimming pool, an unmarked bag containing old coins worth $6,000 was unearthed. The pool contractor, the previous owners of their house, and Tricia all claimed ownership. A week ago, a court with competent authority declared Tricia the unequivocal legal owner of the coins (still worth $6,000). **As a result of the foregoing, Tricia most likely:**

    (a)   Has $6,000 of income in the current year.

    (b)   Has no income in the current year, but will have income when, and if, she sells the coins.

    (c)   Has no income because the coins were not the result of her labor, invested capital, or from both combined.

    (d)   Has no income in the current year, but should have reported $6,000 of income either years ago when she purchased the house, or last year when the coins were discovered.

3. John, a U.S. citizen domiciled in Florida, receives interest from three sources: 1) a ten-year U.S. government note, 2) a savings account at First Bank of the Alps (A Swiss bank with all accounts and offices located in Switzerland), and 3) a thirty-year general obligation bond of the state of Maine (in registered form and not of a "private activity" or "arbitrage" nature). **For federal income tax purposes, John's gross income most likely will include:**

    (a) The interest from all three sources.

    (b) The interest from the U.S. note, but not the interest from the Swiss bank account or the Maine government bond.

    (c) The Interest from the U.S. note and the Swiss bank account, but not the interest from the Maine government bond.

    (d) None of the interest from all three sources.

    (e) The interest from the Swiss bank account, but not the interest from the U.S. note or the Maine government bond.

4. Paul, while attending his brother's funeral, was shocked when he discovered that the funeral director had purposefully disfigured his brother's body. Paul suffered severe emotional trauma, so much so that he ultimately became physically ill and required hospitalization. He sued the funeral director based on the tort of "intentional infliction of emotional distress" and reached an out-of-court settlement, with Paul receiving a total of $100,000. Of this total, $50,000 was designated for Paul's physical pain and suffering, $10,000 for Paul's mental and emotional pain, $15,000 to cover Paul's hospital bills, and $25,000 to compensate Paul for wages lost as a result of missing work because of the incident. **With respect to the foregoing, Paul will, most likely, have to recognize:**

    (a) $25,000 of income.

    (b) $35,000 of income.

    (c) No income.

    (d) $100,000 of income.

    (e) None of the above answers is correct.

5. This fall, Amy will be starting law school at an ABA and AALS accredited university. Because of both her outstanding LSAT score and undergraduate GPA, the law school is awarding her a $30,000 scholarship for her first year of study. The scholarship benefits are specifically identified as follows:

- $20,000 applied to fully offset her law school tuition.
- $500 for books required for her first-year classes.
- $5,000 applied to offset some of her on-campus housing costs.
- $4,500 in cash for her to use as she chooses with precatory language that the monies be used for food and other living costs.

How much of this scholarship, if any, will be taxable to Amy?

(a) $9,500, representing the $5,000 to be applied towards housing plus the $4,500 cash to be received. The balance will qualify as excludable scholarship benefits pursuant to IRC § 117.

(b) $4,500, representing the amount of cash to be received. The balance will qualify as excludable scholarship benefits pursuant to IRC § 117.

(c) None of the benefit received will be taxable. The entire $30,000 is designated as a scholarship that, pursuant to IRC § 117, is fully excludable from gross income.

(d) $10,000 representing the $500 and $5,000 to be applied towards books and housing, respectively, plus the $4,500 cash to be received. The $20,000 being used for tuition will qualify as an excludable scholarship pursuant to IRC § 117.

(e) A currently indeterminable amount. The total amount that she can exclude from gross income will depend on how much of the $4,500 cash she uses for food and living costs.

6. Amy, from problem 5, above, discovered that all of her professors for her first-year courses utilize Westlaw's student online education network (TWEN). During her free online registration for TWEN, she entered West's "welcome to law school" giveaway. To her delight, she was selected (at random from all entrants) as the winner of the grand prize: a top-of-the-line laptop computer worth $3,000. **Which of the following statements best describes the income tax ramifications to Amy as a result of the foregoing?**

   (a) She will have gross income of $3,000 (the value of the computer) unless, before actually receiving the computer, she designates that it be transferred directly to a qualified charitable organization.

   (b) She will have gross income equal to West's cost of the computer. This will be included in her gross income regardless of any recipient designation.

   (c) She will have gross income of $3,000 (the value of the computer). This will be included in her gross income regardless of any recipient designation.

   (d) She will have no gross income because such prizes are excluded pursuant to IRC § 74.

   (e) While normally such a prize would constitute gross income, Amy will be able to exclude it therefrom because she can properly classify the benefit as part of a "scholarship."

7. Wendy was the owner/insured of a $100,000 (face amount) life insurance policy and husband Hank was the beneficiary. Wendy died unexpectedly in December of last year, and Hank decided not to receive the full $100,000 presently. Rather, he selected a payment option that allows him to leave all of the insurance proceeds with the insurer (insurance company) for as long as he wants and they will pay him interest until he withdraws the proceeds. At the time of Wendy's death, Hank had a 50-year life expectancy and he planned to leave all of the insurance proceeds with the insurer for 20 years. In the current year, Hank does not plan to withdraw any of the original $100,000 proceeds, but will receive $8,000 in interest from the insurer. **In the current year, as a result of the foregoing, Hank must recognize:**

   (a) The full $8,000 as income.

   (b) $6,000 of income – the difference between the $8,000 received and $2,000 ($100,000 divided by 50 years).

   (c) $3,000 of income – the difference between the $8,000 received and $5,000 ($100,000 divided by 20 years).

   (d) No income.

8.   Brian, a recent college graduate, was hired as a design engineer for a company that makes very sophisticated, and expensive, metal die-cast scale models of automobiles, airplanes and boats. The company has only one place of business, a large multi-building facility located on many acres of land. The company prides itself on uncompromising quality in its products and in its workforce. To this end, the company operates, on the business premises, an impressive dining facility featuring one of the finest chefs in the state. All employees are entitled, but not required, to eat lunch at this dining facility. Employees eating at the facility are required to pay something for their lunches, but it is **much less** than what they would have to pay for such a quality meal in an "outside" restaurant. Brian eats lunch almost every day at this company dining facility. **Which of the following statements is the most accurate?**

    (a)   Brian has no income resulting from this benefit because the dining facility is available to all of the company employees.

    (b)   Brian has income equal to the difference between the value of the meals received (measured by what they would cost in a normal restaurant) and the price that he pays for the meals.

    (c)   The difference between the value of the meals Brian receives (measured by what they would cost in a normal restaurant) and the price that he pays for them will not be income to him but only if the employer deems it necessary that employees remain on the business premises during lunch.

    (d)   Brian has no income resulting from this benefit assuming that the price employees pay for the lunches covers the employer's cost for the food and other direct operating costs of the facility.

9.   Malcolm's regular job is that of a financial consultant. Malcolm also has a penchant for gambling and has won a substantial amount from this activity. In addition, he occasionally earns some extra cash working as a prostitute. **Which answer best describes what should be included in Malcolm's gross income?**

    (a)   Amounts earned from his regular job. The amounts earned from his gambling and prostitution are included in gross income only if, and to the extent, that such activities are lawful.

    (b)   Amounts earned from all of these sources.

    (c)   Amounts earned from his regular job only. His other sources of earnings are excluded from income.

    (d)   Amounts earned from his regular job and amounts earned from prostitution (regardless of its legality). Amounts earned from gambling, however, are excluded from income.

10.   Sally is sixty-six (66) years old, retired and receiving regular Social Security retirement benefits. **With respect to the Social Security benefits received, Sally:**

   (a)   May be taxed on them at rates up to 50% depending on the extent of her other income.

   (b)   May be taxed on them at rates up to 85% depending on the extent of her other income.

   (c)   Will not be taxed on any of these benefits regardless of her level of income. Historically, they were fully includible in gross income, but changes in tax laws over the past couple of decades have eliminated their inclusion.

   (d)   Must include all of them in gross income regardless of her level of other income. Historically, they were fully excluded from gross income, but changes in tax laws over the past couple of decades have eliminated their exclusion.

   (e)   None of the above responses is correct.

11.   Laura purchased some United States Savings Bonds (Series EE) that mature many years in the future. Series EE U.S. Savings Bonds are purchased at a discount from their stated face amount and pay the stated face amount upon maturity. **Which of the following statements is the most accurate?**

   (a)   The difference between the price for which Laura purchased the bonds and their stated face amount represents interest, all of which is excluded because it is interest from an obligation of the United States.

   (b)   The difference between the price for which Laura purchased the bonds and their stated face amount represents taxable interest income, all of which is recognized in the year the bonds mature, unless Laura elects to recognize the interest in each year as it effectively accrues.

   (c)   The difference between the price for which Laura purchased the bonds and their stated face amount represents taxable interest income. It is recognized in each year as it effectively accrues, unless Laura elects to defer it, in which case it will all be recognized in the year the bonds mature.

   (d)   The difference between the price for which Laura purchased the bonds and their stated face amount represents taxable interest income that must be recognized in each year as it effectively accrues.

12. Debra died and in her will she devised $10,000 to her nephew Nathan. While the devise to Nathan was not qualified in any way in Debra's will, she owed Nathan $10,000 at the time of her death. Prior to Debra's death, the two orally agreed that the debt would be paid to Nathan at Debra's death by way of devise (this debt involved no interest). **With respect to the $10,000, Nathan received, he:**

(a) Can exclude it from income as a "gift, bequest or devise" pursuant to IRC § 102.

(b) Must include it in his gross income because it does not qualify as a devise for purposes of IRC § 102.

(c) Can exclude it from income because Nathan did not derive an economic benefit or a "net accession to wealth."

(d) Must include it in his gross income because it is a "net accession to wealth."

13.　Paulette and Dave are the sole shareholders of SewaClean, Incorporated ("The Corporation"). The Corporation owns and operates a private sewage treatment facility that serves the sewage treatment needs of a moderately sized city. Paulette and Dave are the respective president and general manager of The Corporation. The sewage treatment plant occupies a fair amount of land, which The Corporation leases from the city. A small two-bedroom bungalow is located at one end of the property (as far away from the open sewage pits as possible) and Paulette and Dave reside there, paying no rent to The Corporation. Paulette wrote her and Dave's employment contracts on behalf of The Corporation, and as a condition of their employment, their contracts state that they must live in the bungalow located on the plant premises. The Corporation employs many individuals, but Paulette and Dave are the only employees who live on the premises and are there during "off-hours." **Relating to the couple's residency in the bungalow, they will:**

(a)　Be required to include in their income, the fair rental value of their lodging. Even if it is necessary for the couple to be on the premises during off-hours, the fact that Paulette essentially "required" herself and Dave to live on the premises as a condition of their employment precludes any exclusion.

(b)　Not be required to include anything in income with respect to the lodging because The Corporation is effectively the same person as Paulette and Dave by virtue of their 100% ownership of The Corporation. Income, for tax purposes, is not imputed to "themselves."

(c)　Not be required to include the value of the lodging in their income if, by objective standards, it is important that the couple be on the premises during off-hours.

(d)　Be required to include in their income the fair rental value of the lodging because even if it is necessary that the couple be on the premises during off-hours, The Corporation does not own the land on which the bungalow is situated.

14. Patricia is a highly acclaimed physician and is employed by a well-known medical school as a teaching physician. Patricia's employment contract, which she negotiated, is unusual in that it requires that her employer pay one-third of her monthly salary directly to her daughter, Denise. In a totally unrelated matter, the medical school operates an active "outreach" program where Patricia spends a fair amount of time each month caring for the medical needs of indigent patients. Sometimes, she receives fees, in accordance with applicable state statute, for these services. Pursuant to the standard employment contract with the university, she (as well as all other employees) is required to immediately remit any such fees received to the university. **With respect to the foregoing, which of the following statements is most accurate?**

    (a)   Patricia must include, in her gross income, all of her salary (including the one-third paid to her daughter) as well as the fees that she receives from her work with indigent patients. She cannot assign this income to others.

    (b)   Patricia must include, in her gross income, all of her salary (including the one-third paid to her daughter) as she cannot assign any of this income to others. She will not, however, be required to include in her income the fees that she receives relating to her work with indigent patients.

    (c)   Patricia's assignment of one-third of her salary to Denise is valid as an "anticipatory" assignment, and Patricia need not include that portion of her salary in her gross income. She will also not be required to include in her income the fees that she receives relating to her work with indigent patients.

    (d)   Patricia's assignment of one-third of her salary to Denise is valid as an "anticipatory" assignment, and Patricia need not include that portion of her salary in her gross income. She must include, in her gross income, the fees that she receives from her work with indigent patients, but will be entitled to a corresponding charitable contribution deduction.

15.   Tad hired contractor Carl to repair earthquake damage to his house. Tad claims that Carl originally told him that the total cost of the job would be $10,000. Carl completed the work and billed Tad $15,000 ($10,000 for labor and $5,000 for materials). Carl claims that he originally told Tad that the $10,000 was the total cost for his labor, and that materials costs would be added thereto. After much arguing, Carl reluctantly agreed to compromise his bill and accept $12,000 as payment, in full, for the job. Tad then paid Carl $12,000. **As a result of the foregoing, Tad will most likely:**

(a)   Realize and recognize the entire $3,000 debt reduction as income from discharge of indebtedness, unless Tad was insolvent at the time the debt was forgiven.

(b)   Not realize or recognize any income from discharge of indebtedness.

(c)   Realize and recognize the entire $3,000 debt reduction as income, but Tad will be able to add this amount to the adjusted basis of his home.

(d)   Not realize or recognize any income from discharge of indebtedness, but will realize and recognize $12,000 in income as compensation for services.

16.   A car hit Dave while he was crossing the street. Dave sued the driver of the car alleging that the driver was negligent. The parties reached an out-of-court settlement and Dave received $100,000. Of this total, $50,000 was designated for pain and suffering, $10,000 for negligent infliction of emotional distress, $15,000 for medical expenses (of which $5,000 were for medical expenses arising out of the emotional distress), and $25,000 to compensate Dave for wages lost because of the accident. **Of the amount received, Dave will, most likely, have to recognize:**

(a) $25,000 of income.

(b) $35,000 of income.

(c)   No income.

(d) $50,000 of income.

(e)   None of the above responses is correct.

17. Taxpayer entered into an annuity contract with a well-known life insurance company. In exchange for a substantial one-time payment to the insurance company, Taxpayer was guaranteed to receive a specified dollar amount every month until her death. **Which of the following answers best describe the income tax treatment to Taxpayer with respect to the monthly payments to her?**

(a) The payments received will be fully tax-free until the cumulative benefits received reach the amount Taxpayer originally paid to the insurance company. Payments received thereafter will be fully taxable.

(b) A portion of each payment received will be tax-free until the cumulative tax-free amount equals the amount Taxpayer originally paid to the insurance company. Payments received thereafter will be fully taxable.

(c) A portion of each payment received will be tax-free regardless of how long Taxpayer lives or the amount of benefits Taxpayer receives pursuant to the contract.

(d) All payments received by Taxpayer will be totally tax-free because the benefits are paid pursuant to a contract with a life insurance company.

18. Cheryl's principal residence in Indiana is located close to the Indianapolis Motor Speedway. Not a big motor racing fan, she prefers not to be in town during the three major racing events held at the speedway: the Indianapolis 500, the U.S. Formula One Grand Prix, and NASCAR's Brickyard 400. She takes her absences as opportunities to rent her home to race fans. Last year, she rented her home for three, four-day racing weekends (twelve days total) and received aggregate rents of $18,000 (the Grand Prix event was especially lucrative renting her home to the Ferrari team's support staff). Other than these racing weekends (never exceeding twelve days in the aggregate), Cheryl does not rent out her home. **Which of the following statements is most accurate with respect to the foregoing?**

(a) Cheryl must include the $18,000 in her gross income. She can, however, offset this income to the extent of her actual "out-of-pocket" home-related expenses associated with the rental periods.

(b) Cheryl must include the $18,000 in her gross income. She can, however, deduct (offsetting this income) a fraction of her total "out-of-pocket" home-related expenses for the entire year. The numerator of this fraction is the number of days she rented her house and the denominator is the total number of days in the year, or $^{12}/_{365}$ in this case.

(c) Cheryl must include the $18,000 in her gross income. She can, however, deduct (offsetting this income) her actual "out-of-pocket" home-related expenses and properly determined "depreciation" expenses for the rental periods.

(d) Cheryl can exclude the entire $18,000 from her gross income. She is not entitled to extra deductions associated with renting her house.

(e) Because of the amount of rent Cheryl received, she can exclude only a portion of it from her gross income. She may be entitled to some extra deductions associated with renting her house.

Questions 19 through 21 are based on the following facts:

Tillie, a successful businesswoman, owns and operates a chain of small, very expensive boutique hotels located in major cities throughout the United States. She provides certain benefits to her employees.

19. Tillie employs, at each hotel, a manager who is required to live at that hotel and be "on call" 24 hours a day (to handle problems that might arise). Each hotel manager is provided, free of charge, a simple one-bedroom unit in the hotel. Tillie's son, Sid, is the manager of her hotel in Chicago and she provides him with a luxurious three-bedroom penthouse suite in the hotel (at no cost to Sid). When asked by her accountant about this arrangement regarding her son, Tillie said only that, "she loves him dearly and would do almost anything for him." **Regarding the accommodations furnished to Sid, he most likely will have to include in his gross income:**

   (a)   Nothing. The value of the lodging is excludable because his lodging is furnished on the hotel premises, it is a requirement of his employment, and it is for the convenience of his employer.

   (b)   The full value of his lodging because the benefit discriminates in his favor when compared with the benefit given to the managers of Tillie's other hotels.

   (c)   A portion of the value of the lodging received. This amount is the difference between the value of his luxurious accommodations and the value of the standard lodging provided to the managers of Tillie's other hotels.

   (d)   Nothing. An amount equal to the value of standard lodging furnished to the managers of Tillie's other hotels is excludable, because his lodging is furnished on the hotel premises, it is a requirement of his employment, and it is for the convenience of his employer. The additional value of his luxury accommodations is excludable as a gift.

20. One of the benefits that Tillie provides to all of her full-time employees, free lodging at any of her hotels as long as there are vacancies. Tillie extends this benefit to the families (defined as spouses and dependent children) of all full-time employees regardless of whether they are accompanied by such employee. Sid's wife and dependent children recently stayed two nights, free of charge, at Tillie's Beverly Hills hotel while vacationing in the area. Sid did not accompany them on this particular trip. **Which of the following answers best describes the income tax ramification to Sid as a result of the foregoing?**

    (a) Sid recognizes no income because the value of the lodging provided to his family qualifies as an excludable IRC § 132 "no-additional-cost service" fringe benefit.

    (b) Sid must include, in his gross income, the entire value of the lodging because his family staying at the hotel was not "for the convenience of" Sid's employer.

    (c) Sid must include the value of the lodging in his gross income because Sid was not present.

    (d) Sid can exclude the value of the lodging from his gross income, if he can show that his wife (or children) had a legitimate business reason for being in Beverly Hills or for staying at the hotel.

    (e) Sid will have to include the value of the lodging in his gross income assuming that he is considered a "highly compensated employee" for purposes of IRC § 132.

21. In addition to the benefit addressed in question 20, above, Tillie also allows all of her full-time employees to stay, free of charge, four nights per year in any of her hotels even if they take the place of a paying customer (i.e., they can "bump" a paying customer). Recently, one of her Boston hotel employees, Emmy, spent her four free nights at Tillie's fully-booked New York hotel (i.e., Emmy took the place of a paying customer). **Emmy most likely:**

    (a) Will have to include the full value of the four nights lodging in her gross income.

    (b) Will be able to exclude the value of the four nights lodging because this fringe benefit does not discriminate in favor of "highly compensated employees."

    (c) Will have to include 80% of the value of the four nights lodging in her gross income. The remaining 20% is excludable as a qualified employee discount.

    (d) Will be able to exclude a portion of the value of the four nights lodging equal to the "gross profit percentage" of Tillie's hotel business.

Questions 22 through 24 are based on the following facts:

Brandon operates a construction business as an unincorporated sole proprietor and has experienced severe financial difficulties. Hoping to keep Brandon in business and to assure his future patronage, one of Brandon's major sub-contractors agreed to "write off" $25,000 of an uncontested $50,000 debt that Brandon owed for services received. This happened on April 1 of this year. Just prior to this partial cancellation of the debt, Brandon's total liabilities were $350,000 and the aggregate adjusted bases of his assets were $340,000. At such time, the aggregate fair market values of such assets were $320,000.

22. **As a result of the foregoing, how much income, if any, must Brandon recognize this year?**

   (a) No income pursuant to IRC § 108(e)(5) since the sub-contractor (the provider of services) was also the creditor.

   (b) $15,000, representing the difference between the $25,000 cancellation and the $10,000 amount by which Brandon was insolvent immediately before the debt cancellation.

   (c) No income since at the time of the cancellation, Brandon was insolvent by more than the amount of the debt canceled.

   (d) Currently an indeterminable amount of income since we do not yet know the degree to which Brandon will be insolvent at the end of this tax year.

   (e) None of the above responses is correct

23. Brandon has a $5,000 net operating loss carryover (NOL) from a prior year, but has no business or minimum tax credits, or capital losses or carryovers. **Assuming no special elections are made, what are the tax ramifications (other than inclusion or exclusion from income) of the partial cancellation of the debt?**

   (a) The adjusted basis of his assets will be reduced by $25,000.

   (b) The net operating loss carryover (NOL) will be eliminated, and the basis of his assets will be reduced by $20,000.

   (c) The net operating loss carryover (NOL) will be eliminated, but the basis of his assets will not be reduced.

   (d) The net operating loss carryover (NOL) will be eliminated, and the basis of his assets will be reduced by $10,000.

   (e) None of the above responses is correct.

24. For this question only, assume that later in the current year, Brandon satisfies the $25,000 remaining debt with the major sub-contractor not by paying $25,000 in cash but, rather, by performing services for the sub-contractor that were worth $25,000. **As a result, Brandon:**

   (a) Does not have realization of income, since he is merely repaying a debt.

   (b) Will realize $25,000 of income.

   (c) Will realize income only to the extent Brandon is solvent at the time of the satisfaction of the debt.

   (d) Does not have realization of income, because this is a nontaxable "barter" type exchange of equal value.

   (e) None of the above responses is correct.

25. In December 2001, Professor P, a U.S. citizen and professor at a California University, left his Malibu, California home to go to England where he was hired to teach tax courses at Oxford University. He taught classes in their spring 2002 term and plans to teach courses in their fall 2002 term (which ends in November 2002). He has been living in England since his arrival last December. He did not teach during the summer of 2002, but, rather, traveled extensively for pleasure. He returned to California for two weeks in July to visit friends. For the balance of the summer, he traveled throughout Western and Eastern Europe spending most of the time outside of England. At the end of the fall 2002 term, Professor P will remain in England until his ultimate return to Malibu in January 2003, to resume teaching at his "regular" California University. **For U.S. federal income tax purposes for the year 2002, Professor P will most likely be able to exclude:**

   (a) Up to $80,000 of "earned" income derived outside of the U.S. (i.e., the payments for his work at Oxford University in England), but only if he qualifies as a "bona fide resident" of England pursuant to IRC § 911(d)(1)(A). He most likely will not meet the "physical presence" test of IRC § 911(d)(1)(B) for 2002, because of the number of days he will spend outside of England.

   (b) All income from sources outside of the U.S. regardless of the status of his English residency or the number of days spent outside of the U.S.

   (c) All "earned" income derived outside of the U.S. (i.e., the payments for his work at Oxford University in England) and up to $80,000 of other income derived from sources outside of the U.S. as long as he meets either the foreign "bona fide resident" or "physical presence" test of IRC § 911(d)(1).

   (d) None of the above responses is correct.

END OF EXAMINATION QUESTIONS

EXAM II

FEDERAL INCOME TAX
MULTIPLE-CHOICE OBJECTIVE QUESTIONS
EXAM II

1. Alfred suffers from severe arthritis. At the insistence of his physician, he installed an elevator in his three-story house in an effort to help alleviate the discomforts caused by his condition. The elevator was installed last year at a cost of $20,000 and it increased the value of his home by $15,000. With respect to the elevator, Alfred paid $1,000 for maintenance of the elevator last year. In addition, last year Alfred paid $200 in over-the-counter (non-prescription) medicines that were recommended by his doctor. **Assuming Alfred was not reimbursed through insurance for any of the above costs, what amount will qualify as expenses paid for medical care for purposes of IRC § 213(a) <u>before</u> applying the "7.5% of adjusted gross income (AGI) floor?"**

   (a) $5,250.

   (b) $6,000.

   (c) $20,000.

   (d) $21,000.

   (e)   None of the above is correct.

Questions 2 and 3 are based on the following facts:

Tom is an associate lawyer (employee) in the prestigious Philadelphia firm of Hungadinger, Hungadinger, and Hungadinger. During the year, Tom had various expenditures as discussed below. The firm is prestigious, but is also "thrifty" (i.e., cheap) and did <u>not</u> reimburse him for any of his expenditures.

2.   Tom has friends in Providence, Rhode Island, and after earning a few days off, he decided to fly up for a visit. Prior to leaving, Tom's boss asked him to handle a business matter with one of the firm's Providence clients while he was up there. He arrived in Providence early on Tuesday and returned to Philadelphia early on Sunday. He ended up meeting with the client for twelve hours on Friday. He spent the rest of the trip visiting with friends. He originally had planned on leaving early Saturday, but decided to stay over Saturday night because he then qualified for a reduced airfare. By staying Saturday, he saved more in airfare than it cost him for the extra lodging, meals and incidentals. **Assuming that all of Tom's expenditures for travel, lodging, meals and incidentals were reasonable in amount, how much will probably qualify as "IRC § 162" business expenses?**

(a)   All of his transportation costs to/from Providence and his meals (at 50%), lodging and incidentals for Friday, and as many extra days to equal the amount of airfare saved by staying over Saturday.

(b)   All of his transportation costs to/from Providence, and his meals (at 50%), lodging, and incidentals for Friday only.

(c)   None of his transportation costs to/from Providence, but his meals (at 50%), lodging, and incidentals for Friday will qualify.

(d)   None of his transportation costs to/from Providence, but his meals (at 50%), lodging, and incidentals for Friday and Saturday will qualify.

(e)   None of his costs because the trip was primarily for pleasure and not for business.

3. A few years ago, Tom purchased a computer that he uses exclusively at his office for firm-related business. He obtained an unsecured bank loan to purchase the computer. In the current year, he paid interest on this loan. **With respect to the interest paid on this loan in the current year, Tom will most likely:**

    (a) Be entitled to an "above the line" deduction as an IRC § 162 trade/business expense.

    (b) Be entitled to a "below the line" deduction as an IRC § 162 trade/business expense but this, along with other "miscellaneous itemized deductions," will, in the aggregate, be subject to a two percent (2%) of adjusted gross income (AGI) nondeductible floor.

    (c) Not be entitled to deduct this interest.

    (d) Not be entitled to deduct this interest, unless he owns a house and had, at the time of the loan, equity in the amount equal to or greater than the amount borrowed for the computer.

4. **Can an individual, who is not engaged in the business of gambling, deduct gambling losses?**

    (a) No, losses from gambling are not deductible.

    (b) Yes, an individual can use gambling losses to offset gambling winnings, and report as income, only the net amount of any winnings. If the net amount is a loss, it is not deductible.

    (c) Yes, an individual can deduct, as a "miscellaneous itemized deduction," gambling losses, but only to the extent that he or she has gambling winnings.

    (d) Yes, an individual can deduct gambling losses as a "miscellaneous itemized deduction."

Questions 5 and 6 are based on the following facts:

Some years ago, Tim purchased his principal residence for $400,000, paying $200,000 down and borrowing $200,000 (evidenced by a mortgage secured by the house). The value of his home has risen substantially, and in the current year he decided to "tap into the equity" in his home and borrow against it. He took out a second mortgage or "home equity loan" (also secured by the home) in the amount of $160,000. He used $80,000 of these funds to add a bedroom to his home. He used the remaining $80,000 to purchase some stocks for investments and pay for a luxury cruise. Assume that his first mortgage remains undiminished at $200,000. Also in the current year, he bought a vacation cabin (used exclusively for personal purposes and not rented out), borrowing $100,000 in a separate mortgage loan (secured by the cabin). Tim owns no other real property.

5. **For the current year, Tim should be entitled to a deduction for the interest paid with respect to:**

    (a)   The full amount of all of the loans.

    (b)   Both the original $200,000 loan and the $100,000 cabin loan as "acquisition indebtedness," and a maximum of $100,000 of the home equity loan as "home equity indebtedness."

    (c)   Only the original $200,000 loan as "acquisition indebtedness," and an aggregate maximum of $100,000 from the home equity and the cabin loans as "home equity indebtedness."

    (d)   Both the original $200,000 loan and $80,000 of the home equity loan as "acquisition indebtedness," and an aggregate maximum of $100,000 from the remaining home equity loan and the cabin loan as "home equity indebtedness."

6. For this question only, assume that Tim had to pay the applicable lender one (1) "point" to obtain each of the two loans obtained in the current year (the second mortgage on his home and the cabin loan). **In the current year, Tim will be entitled to deduct:**

   (a) One percent of the full amount of both loans.

   (b) One percent of both the cabin loan and $80,000 of the home equity loan. The points paid with respect to the balance of the home equity loan must be amortized (deducted pro-rata) over the life of that loan.

   (c) One percent of only the cabin loan. The points paid with respect to the home equity loan must be amortized (deducted pro-rata) over the life of that loan.

   (d) One percent of only $80,000 of the home equity loan. The points paid with respect to the balance of the home equity loan and the entire cabin loan must be amortized (deducted pro-rata) over the respective lives of the loans.

   (e) None of the above responses is correct.

7. Since graduating from law school a couple of years ago, Ben has been employed as an associate in a law firm specializing in personal injury law representing plaintiffs in tort actions. Having not taken "federal income tax" in law school, but realizing it was important to know something about the subject, Ben recently attended a two-day state bar sponsored "basic taxation for lawyers" seminar (six hours of classroom time for each day). The seminar was in Neighborville (some 30 miles from his residence and office in Centerville) and it cost him $500 in course fees. In addition, he spent $100 in lodging (he stayed the night between the two seminar days at the conference hotel because they offered a special seminar room rate), $100 in meals for both days, and $50 in transportation costs to and from the seminar. Ben's employer did not reimburse him for any of these costs. **To what extent do these costs qualify as trade or business expenses to Ben?**

   (a) The $500 course fee, the $100 for lodging, and the $50 in transportation costs.

   (b) The $500 course fee, and the $50 in transportation costs.

   (c) The $500 course fee, the $100 for lodging, the $50 in transportation costs, and one-half of the $100 spent for meals.

   (d) Only the $500 course fee.

   (e) None of these costs qualify as trade or business expenses to Ben.

8.   Abigail operates a very substantial light manufacturing business as an unincorporated sole proprietorship. Early in the year, she constructed a new warehouse on property that she already owned, and purchased a few very expensive machines (each costing well in excess of $100,000) used in her manufacturing business. **Which of the following statements is most accurate with respect to the income tax ramifications to Abigail with respect to these expenditures?**

   (a)   She can deduct the full cost of the equipment purchases in the current year as business expenses. The cost of the warehouse represents a capital expenditure and is not deductible, in full, in the current year but, rather, is "expensed" over more than one year in the form of depreciation deductions.

   (b)   Both the warehouse and equipment costs represent capital expenditures and she cannot deduct their full cost as an expense in the current year. Rather, their cost will be "expensed" over more than one year in the form of depreciation deductions.

   (c)   Because Abigail operates her business as an unincorporated sole proprietorship, as opposed to a corporation, she is entitled to deduct the full cost of the warehouse and equipment in the current year as business expenses.

   (d)   Both the warehouse and equipment costs are not deductible in full in the current year. Rather, they are capitalized expenditures and she can elect, pursuant to IRC § 195, to deduct them over a period of no less than five years.

9.   Abigail, in question 8, above, has a manufacturing building (different from the newly constructed warehouse) for which she originally paid $1million (this included the cost of the underlying land) some years ago. She has not made any major improvements to this building since purchasing it. This manufacturing building is the type of asset for which depreciation deductions would be allowed. Abigail's business has always been very successful and her taxable income, for all years that she has had the business, has been substantial in amount. **Which of the following statements is most accurate with respect to Abigail's basis (adjusted basis or AB) in this building at the beginning of the current year (or at the end of the previous year)?**

(a)   Her basis (AB) in the property is her "cost" basis of $1 million.

(b)   Assuming Abigail actually claimed depreciation deductions allowed with respect to this building, her basis (AB) in the property is $1 million less the depreciation deductions actually taken.

(c)   Her basis (AB) in the property is the $1 million cost less the amount of depreciation deductions allowable to her regardless of whether or not she actually claimed the deductions.

(d)   Her basis (AB) in the property is <u>not</u> the $1 million less the amount of depreciation deductions allowable to her, because part of the original $1 million purchase price represented the cost of the underlying land (and land is generally not a depreciable asset).

Questions 10 through 12 are based on the following facts:

Wendy is self-employed and operates a business as an unincorporated sole proprietorship. Wendy's husband, Hank, is an elementary school teacher at a local public school and is not involved in her business. They live together in their house on the beach in Santa Monica, California (which is located immediately west of Downtown Los Angeles, California). Wendy owns and operates two retail stores that sell men's suits exclusively (very "high-end" Italian and custommade). One store is in Malibu, California (approximately ten miles up the coast from their Santa Monica home) and the other store is in Downtown Los Angeles (about fifteen miles east/inland from their Santa Monica home). Most days she goes to both stores and while her routine varies, her normal pattern is to drive to the Los Angeles store in the morning from home, then drive directly to the Malibu store, and then drive home in the early evening. On occasion, she also drives to the homes or offices of "special" customers. Wendy drives her own car and keeps meticulous records of her miles. Last year, her total miles driven break down as follows: 30% for driving to/from home to either store, 25% for driving between the Los Angeles and Malibu stores, 15% for driving to/from special customers (sometimes directly from home and sometimes from one of her stores), and the remaining 30% driving for purely personal purposes.

10.   **What percent of Wendy's miles driven will qualify as "business miles" for purposes of determining her deduction for business transportation costs?**

(a)   15 percent.

(b)   25 percent.

(c)   Between 25 and 40 percent. The exact percentage will depend on what portion of the 15 percent of miles driven to special customers originated from or terminated with either store location.

(d)   40 percent.

(e)   None of the above response is correct.

11. Wendy and Hank are planning to fly up to Seattle for a two-week trip. Wendy says that she will be "combining business with pleasure." They vacation often in the Seattle area and for their upcoming trip, they plan to spend most of their time enjoying the sights. Wendy has seriously been thinking of opening a small boutique in Seattle, and she states that one purpose of the upcoming trip is to search out store locations, make business contacts and talk to suppliers in the area. This contemplated store will, however, be quite a departure for Wendy – no men's suits but, rather, "clothing" exclusively for pets (dogs, cats, etc.). **Which of the following statements best describes the income tax consequences, if any, to Wendy with respect to the planned two-week trip?**

(a) It is unlikely that any of Wendy's airfare will qualify as a trade or business expense pursuant to IRC § 162. However, some of her costs for lodging, meals and incidentals while in Seattle may qualify as § 162 trade/business deductions, if retail "pet clothing" sales is considered the same business as her current business (or a logical extension thereof).

(b) It is unlikely that any of Wendy's airfare will qualify as a trade or business expense pursuant to IRC § 162. Additionally, she will not be entitled to deduct any of her costs for lodging, meals and incidentals while in Seattle, even if retail selling of pet clothing is considered the same trade/business as her current business.

(c) If the business of retail sales of pet clothing is considered the same trade or business as is Wendy's current business (or a logical extension thereof), then a portion of her airfare and some of her costs for lodging, meals and incidentals will qualify as business deductions pursuant to IRC § 162.

(d) If the business of retail sales of pet clothing is considered the same trade or business as is Wendy's current business (or a logical extension thereof), then all of her airfare and some of her costs for lodging, meals and incidentals will qualify as business deductions pursuant to IRC § 162.

(e) If the business of retail sales of pet clothing is considered the same trade or business as is Wendy's current business (or a logical extension thereof), then all of the cost for her airfare, lodging, incidentals, and 50% of the cost of her meals will qualify as business deductions pursuant to IRC § 162.

12.   Assume the same facts as in question 11, above, except that for this question, Wendy is not contemplating any type of future business in Seattle. However, for this question, please assume that Hank indicates a business purpose for the upcoming Seattle trip. He will visit sites, take pictures and gather data on American Indian tribes indigenous to the area, thereby better educating himself on the subject. Hank plans to utilize the information that he learns in his classroom teaching. **Most likely, will Hank be entitled to deduct, as business expenses, any of his costs associated with this trip?**

(a)   No, but only because he is an employee and not self-employed.

(b)   No, regardless of whether he is an employee or self-employed.

(c)   Yes, but only the costs for his lodging, incidentals and meals (at 50%) for the days actually spent on the above-described activities.

(d)   Yes, most likely he will be able to deduct the cost of his airfare. In addition he should be entitled to a deduction for the cost of his lodging, incidentals and meals (at 50%) for the days actually spent on the above-described activities.

13. Chad is overweight and has been diagnosed by his physician as suffering from obesity. Donna suffers from hypertension and her physician has directed her to lose weight as a treatment for the disease. Both Chad and Donna join a commercial weight-loss program requiring them to pay an initial fee and additional fees to attend periodic meetings. The program meetings consist of developing diet plans, learning about nutritional information, and group discussions about the participants' challenges encountered in dieting. This weight-loss program also sells their own line of special diet foods that participants are encouraged to purchase. Chad and Donna both purchase the weight-loss program's food items. **Assuming neither Chad nor Donna are reimbursed through insurance for any of these costs, what will qualify as expenses paid for medical care for purposes of IRC § 213(a) <u>before</u> applying the "7.5% of adjusted gross income (AGI) floor?"**

(a) Only Donna's weight-loss program fees (initial fee plus fees for meetings) qualify as medical care expenses. Chad's program/meeting fees do not qualify as medical care expenses. The costs of the program's diet foods do not qualify as medical care expenses for either Donna or Chad.

(b) Both Chad's and Donna's weight-loss program fees (initial fee plus fees for meetings) qualify as medical care expenses. However, the costs for the program's diet foods do not qualify as medical care expenses for either Donna or Chad.

(c) Both Chad's and Donna's weight-loss program fees (initial fee plus fees for meetings) qualify as medical care expenses. The costs for the program's diet foods also qualify as medical care expenses for both Chad and Donna.

(d) Donna's weight-loss program fees (initial fee plus fees for meetings) and the cost of her special program foods qualify as medical care expenses. Chad's program/meeting fees and the special program food costs do not qualify as medical care expenses.

(e) None of the above responses is correct.

14.   Shirin graduated from law school last spring and recently began work as an associate (an employee) in a prestigious Chicago law firm. This was Shirin's first full-time job and she had few "professional" clothes. After working for the firm for about a month and "getting by" with frequent rotation of the few business clothes that she owned, she realized that major additions to her wardrobe were in order. She purchased several items including business suits, blouses, scarves, dress shoes, and the like. Shirin's employer requires that she wear professional attire at work and for most work related functions. Outside of work or work related functions, she rarely wears business attire. **In all likelihood, will Shirin's recent clothes expenditures qualify as a deductible IRC § 162 business expense?**

(a)   No, because she has just started working, and has not worked long enough in her job as a lawyer to be considered engaged in that trade or business.

(b)   Yes, but only if she can show that she does not wear these business clothes outside of work.

(c)   No, because the business clothes are considered adaptable to normal street wear.

(d)   Yes, because her employer requires that she wear professional business attire at work and most work related functions.

(e)   No, because IRC § 162 deduction is allowed, but she can elect, pursuant to IRC § 195, to amortize their cost over a period not less than five years.

15.   Shirin, in question 14, above, takes good care of her business wardrobe. It did not take her long, however, to discover how costly regular maintenance (e.g., dry cleaning) of a business wardrobe could be. **Which of the following statements most likely describes the deductibility of these maintenance costs?**

(a)   A percentage of these costs qualify as a legitimate business expense equal to the percentage of time that they are worn for business purposes. This deduction is allowed even though the cost of her clothes did not give rise to a deduction.

(b)   All of these costs will qualify as a legitimate business expense because the cost of the clothes qualified as deductible under either IRC § 162 or IRC § 195.

(c)   None of these costs will qualify as a legitimate business expense because the cost of the clothes did not qualify as deductible under either IRC § 162 or IRC § 195.

(d)   Regardless of whether or not the cost of the clothes gave rise to any business related deduction, maintenance costs do not qualify as a legitimate business expense.

16. Janet operates her home remodeling business as an unincorporated sole proprietorship. Recently, she rented a piece of construction equipment for a two-day job, costing her $2,000 plus sales tax of $160 (her state charges sales tax on rentals). In a totally unrelated transaction, she also recently purchased a new car used solely for purposes, totally unrelated to her business. She paid $30,000 for the car plus she had to pay sales tax of $2,400. **Which of the following statements is most accurate?**

   (a) The $2,000 equipment rental cost gives rise to a deduction, but the sales tax on both the equipment rental and car purchase is nondeductible taxes pursuant to IRC § 164.

   (b) The $2,160 total paid for the equipment rental (rental plus sales tax thereon) is deductible as a business expense, but her sales tax on the car is not a deductible tax pursuant to IRC § 164.

   (c) The $2,000 paid for the equipment rental is deductible as a business expense and the sales tax on both the equipment rental and car purchase is deductible pursuant to IRC § 164 because they are imposed by a state.

   (d) None of these expenditures qualify for a deduction.

17. Rachael "lives" with her family in Los Angeles, but works as an employee of Bank of America in San Francisco, where she stays in a hotel and eats in restaurants during the week. She returns to Los Angeles every weekend. She usually travels back and forth (approximately 400 miles each way) by airplane, but occasionally she drives her car. Her employer does not reimburse her for any of these expenditures. **Which of the following statements is most accurate?**

   (a) Pursuant to the I.R.S., Rachael's "tax home" is San Francisco and her expenses associated with her trips to Los Angeles are qualified business expenses because she is "traveling away from home."

   (b) Pursuant to some court decisions, Rachael's home is in Los Angeles and her expenses associated with her trips to San Francisco are qualified business expenses because she is "traveling away from home."

   (c) Answers (a) and (b) are both correct.

   (d) Answers (a) and (b) are both incorrect.

18.   Takuma is a self-employed Denver lawyer operating his business as an unincorporated sole proprietor and specializing in estate planning. Takuma invited a prospective client, Christina, to a Colorado Rockies baseball game. While, at times, it was a bit difficult to talk during the ballgame, Takuma was able to make an effective "pitch" for why he could best serve Christina's estate planning needs. Christina was impressed, and during the game's "seventh inning stretch," they shook hands with Christina agreeing to meet with Takuma the following week to go over her estate plan. During the game's last couple of innings, they even discussed some of the pertinent issues relating to Christina's estate. Takuma paid for the tickets to the game as well as for lunch and snacks at the ballgame. Other than their planned meeting next week, Takuma and Christina have had no formal business meetings either before or after the game. **Which of the following statements best describes the tax implications to Takuma as a result of the foregoing?**

(a)   He will not be entitled to any deduction for the cost of the tickets or food because these are considered entertainment activities. While the cost of entertainment activities may be deductible if the taxpayer establishes that the activity was directly related to the active conduct of a trade or business, the regulations provide that a sporting event is an environment that precludes this.

(b)   He will not be entitled to any deduction for the cost of the tickets or food because these are considered entertainment activities. Had he and Christina met in his office for a bona fide business meeting either immediately preceding or following the ballgame, some deduction would have been allowed.

(c)   He will be entitled to some deduction for the cost of the tickets and food even though these were considered entertainment activities. Takuma most likely will be able to establish that the activity was directly related to the active conduct of a trade or business notwithstanding the regulation's presumptive conclusion to the contrary.

(d)   He will be entitled to some deduction for the cost of the tickets and food even though these are considered entertainment activities. Because he and Christina agreed to meet the following week, the ballgame is considered a legitimate entertainment activity that is "associated with" the active conduct of a trade or business.

19. Assume for this question that Takuma, in question 18, above, is not self-employed but, rather, is an associate lawyer (employee) in a Denver estate planning firm. Also assume that his firm did not reimburse him for the ticket or food costs he incurred. **Which of the following statements is most accurate?**

(a) The requirements for deductibility of entertainment related expenses are more restrictive for an employee versus a self-employed individual.

(b) The requirements for deductibility of entertainment related expenses are the same for an employee and a self-employed individual as is the 50% reduction pursuant to IRC § 274(n). However, in most instances the actual amount deductible by an employee is less or is less valuable.

(c) The requirements for deductibility of entertainment related expenses are the same for an employee and a self-employed individual. However, the 50% reduction required by IRC § 274(n) applies only to employees.

(d) The requirements for deductibility of entertainment related expenses are the same for an employee and a self-employed individual. For both, the full cost of the ticket (at the stated ticket price) will qualify for a deductible expense, but only 50% of the meals will qualify.

(e) Entertainment related expenses incurred by self-employed individuals could qualify for deductions to some degree. However, such expenses do not qualify for deductions if incurred by an employee.

20. Monet, a very successful and well-known self-employed business consultant, is planning a trip to France. Her principal reason for the trip is to meet with one of her corporate clients in Paris to negotiate a complex merger involving the company. After concluding her business related work in Paris, she plans to take some time off, vacationing in the French countryside before returning home to New York. She expects the trip's duration to total six weeks with about one-third (33.33%) of this time spent on pleasure travel. **With respect to the cost of her round-trip transportation from New York to France, which of the following statements is most accurate?**

(a) She will be entitled to deduct approximately two-thirds (66.67%) of the transportation costs.

(b) Because the trip is primarily for business, she will be entitled to deduct 100% of the transportation costs.

(c) She will not be entitled to deduct any portion of her transportation costs. Although the trip is primarily for business, because this is "foreign travel" and she plans to spend more than twenty-five percent (25%) of the time for pleasure travel, the statute precludes any deduction for the transportation costs.

(d) She will not be entitled to deduct any portion of her transportation costs. Although the trip is primarily for business, the statute precludes any deduction for her transportation costs because: this is "foreign travel," the trip will last longer than one week, and she plans to spend more than twenty-five percent (25%) of the time for pleasure travel.

21. Jeremy, a single individual, is a full-time tenth grade science teacher at a financially strapped public high school. He has been a high school science teacher for many years. During 2002, he purchased $1,000 of much needed supplies and software for use in his classroom. Jeremy's employer does not reimburse teachers for such expenditures. **Which of the following statements best describes the income tax ramifications to Jeremy as a result of the foregoing?**

   (a) Jeremy is entitled to deduct $250 in computing his adjusted gross income (AGI). The remaining $750 is considered a "miscellaneous itemized deduction" which is deductible only to the extent that the aggregate of such category of deductions exceeds 2% of his AGI.

   (b) Jeremy is entitled to deduct the entire $1,000 in computing his adjusted gross income (AGI).

   (c) Jeremy is not entitled to deduct any portion of the $1,000 because he is an employee. Had he been "self-employed," he would have been entitled to deduct the full $1,000 in computing his adjusted gross income (AGI).

   (d) The entire $1,000 is considered a "miscellaneous itemized deduction" which is deductible only to the extent that the aggregate of such category of deductions exceeds 2% of his AGI.

22. Teresa graduated from law school in May of 2002. She financed most of her legal education with student loans ("normal" school-arranged type – Stafford, Perkins, etc.). In 2003, she expects to pay interest of $2,800 on these loans. Teresa is employed as a lawyer and in 2003, she expects to have gross income of $105,000. **Which of the following statements is most accurate in describing Teresa's deductibility of interest in 2003 pursuant to IRC § 221?**

   (a) She will not be entitled to any deduction.

   (b) She will be entitled to a deduction, but it will be limited to $2,500.

   (c) Teresa will be entitled to at least some deduction, but only if she is married (and files a joint return).

   (d) Teresa may be entitled to a deduction even if she is single, but this depends on the type and the scope of other deductions that she might have.

23. Bill and Wilma, husband and wife, will file a joint return for 2002. Assume that at the end of 2002, they will have three unmarried children: Jeremy (age 10), Heidi (age 19) and Marsha (age 27). In 2002, Jeremy will have a total income of $3,200 – earnings from acting in a television commercial. Heidi's total income in 2002 will be $8,200, all in the form of interest. Marsha will have only $2,950 of income in 2002, all from wages from a part-time job. For all of 2002, Jeremy will be in grade school, Heidi a full-time student at UCLA, and Marsha a full-time student at USC. Other than Jeremy, none of the kids will live with Bill and Wilma during 2002. However, Bill and Wilma will provide more than one-half of each child's support. **For 2002, how many exemption deductions will Bill and Wilma be entitled to claim pursuant to IRC § 151?**

   (a)   Two.

   (b)   Three.

   (c)   Four.

   (d)   Five.

24. Ida, a landscape architect, started investing in the stock market last year. She bought most of her stocks on "margin" (paying only a percentage of the stock's actual price and borrowing the balance of the purchase price from the brokerage firm). Last year, she paid $3,000 in interest on these "margin" loans. Other than her stock market activities, her other investments consist only of money deposited in interest bearing savings accounts at various banks. Last year, her stocks paid (to her), a total of $500 in dividends, and she sold none of the stocks in her portfolio. Also last year, she received $300 in interest from her savings accounts. **Which of the following statements is most accurate with respect to Ida's deduction for the "margin" interest that she paid?**

   (a)   She could not deduct any of the $3,000 in interest because it represented "personal interest."

   (b)   She could deduct, last year, all of the $3,000 interest because the interest related to investments and not to funds borrowed for the purchase of personal-use assets.

   (c)   She could deduct, last year, only $500 of the $3,000 interest that she paid. The excess not deducted ($2,500), is carried forward to future years and deducted to the extent that she has net income from her stock investments.

   (d)   She could deduct, last year, only $800 of the $3,000 interest that she paid. The excess not deducted ($2,200) is not available for any future deductions.

   (e)   She could deduct, last year, only $800 of the $3,000 interest that she paid. The excess not deducted ($2,200) is carried forward to future years and deducted to the extent that she has net income from her investments.

25. Bonnie, a recent law school graduate, is employed full-time at a large law firm. Throughout her life, Bonnie has had a love for horses and horseback riding. A few years ago, she purchased a horse and boards it at a local stable. The recurring costs of caring for her horse are rather high and include such things as food, veterinary care, boarding/stable fees, equipment, and the like. Having taken federal income tax in law school, she recognizes that none of these costs are deductible because she uses her horse for purely recreational purposes (going on rides in the late afternoons and on weekends and holidays). She also remembers from her tax course that "business expenses" are deductible and has come up with an idea that she believes will convert her substantial amount of horse related costs from non-deductible to deductible expenses. She is thinking of renting out her horse for others to ride about once every month or so, generating income to her. She would then claim that she is operating a business which she then believes would enable her to claim all of her horse related costs as business deductions. This "business" would generate substantial operating losses (the costs far exceeding the revenue) which she would like to use for tax purposes to help offset some of her salary and other income. **Most likely, will Bonnie's plan succeed for income tax purposes?**

(a) Yes. Assuming that she gets a business license (if necessary), advertises and keeps adequate financial records, this activity could qualify as a business, and she could deduct all of her horse related expenses.

(b) No. No matter to what degree she conducts herself as a business, as long as she derives some personal benefit from the activity, it will not be considered a business (and she cannot deduct any of her horse related expenses).

(c) No. She would not be entitled to deduct all of her horse related expenses, generating business losses therefrom. However, she would probably be entitled to deduct her horse related expenses up to the amount of the income that she derives from the activity.

(d) No. The statute contains objective criteria for determining whether an activity constitutes engaging in a business for profit (the requirement to deduct any "business" expenses). To be so classified, a taxpayer must generate a profit, in a certain number of years, in a given period of time.

END OF EXAMINATION QUESTIONS

EXAM III

FEDERAL INCOME TAX
MULTIPLE-CHOICE OBJECTIVE QUESTIONS
EXAM III

Questions 1 through 6 are based on the following facts:

Ann and Bob, a married couple both sixty years of age, lived in Centerville for many years. Ann managed the frozen foods section of a warehouse type market in Nearbyville (ten miles from their Centerville home) until September of last year. Bob was employed for many years as an engineer at a company in Otherville (thirty miles from their Centerville home), but was laid-off five years ago in a company "downsizing." In September of last year, Ann was involved in a horrible accident. As she was entering the store's freezer, a store employee driving a forklift, hit the freezer door, crushing Ann. Ann suffered severe spinal injuries and is now confined to a wheelchair.

1. As a result of the freezer incident, Ann filed a lawsuit against the market claiming negligence. The case went to trial and in November of last year, a jury found in Ann's favor and awarded her compensatory damages, specifically identifying amounts for pain and suffering, medical costs, lost wages, and emotional distress suffered as a result of the incident. **With respect to the foregoing, Ann:**

    (a)   Can exclude from gross income only the amount of the award identified for pain and suffering, and medical costs. She cannot exclude from income the amount of the award compensating her for lost wages or emotional distress.

    (b)   Can exclude from gross income the entire amount of this award.

    (c)   Cannot exclude from gross income the amount of the award compensating her for lost wages. She can, however, exclude from gross income, the balance of the award.

    (d)   Cannot exclude from gross income the amount of the award identified as compensating her for emotional distress. She can, however, exclude from gross income, the balance of the award.

    (e)   Must include in gross income, the entire amount of the award since they represent "compensatory" damages.

2. In addition to the compensatory damages awarded to Ann in question 1, above, the jury found the market's actions to be particularly egregious and awarded her punitive damages. **Which of the following statements is most accurate?**

    (a) The punitive damages received can be excluded from gross income because they stem from a physical injury.

    (b) The punitive damages received can only be excluded from gross income if state law expressly permitted the awarding of such damages, and such law was in effect on September 13, 1995.

    (c) The punitive damages received must be included in gross income because a portion of the underlying compensatory award included amounts for lost wages or emotional distress.

    (d) The punitive damages received must be included in gross income regardless of the foundation or composition of Ann's underlying award or the application of any state law.

3. Bob, who was visiting Ann at work the day of the freezer incident, witnessed, in horror, his wife being injured. As a result, he suffered severe emotional trauma, manifesting into actual physical sickness requiring medical treatment. In a separate action, Bob sued the market claiming negligent infliction of emotional distress. The market settled this lawsuit for a substantial sum, specifically identifying amounts for emotional pain/suffering, physical pain/suffering, and payments for medical costs incurred. **Must Bob include all or any part of this settlement in gross income?**

    (a) Yes, he must include all but the amount representing payment for his medical costs.

    (b) No, he is entitled to exclude the entire amount received because the cause of action was "tort or tort-like."

    (c) Yes, he must include the entire amount received because the cause of action was based on emotional distress.

    (d) No, he is entitled to exclude the entire amount received because even though the cause of action was emotional distress, it manifested into an actual physical injury thereby allowing for full exclusion.

4.   Following the freezer incident, Ann discovered that Mike, the market's manager, had been talking to employees and customers about the incident, and had repeatedly said: "the whole thing was probably Ann's own fault. That old lady was probably half asleep or drunk at the time." Ann filed a separate defamation lawsuit against Mike, claiming that both her personal and business reputation had been injured as a result of his statements. Ann was neither asleep nor drunk at the time of the incident and the lawsuit was settled before going to trial with Ann receiving a substantial sum of money. **Which of the following statements is most accurate?**

(a)   If Ann can show that the primary component of her defamation claim was the injury to her personal reputation, she may be entitled to exclude the settlement from gross income.

(b)   If Ann can show that the primary component of her defamation claim was the injury to her business reputation, she may be entitled to exclude the settlement from gross income.

(c)   Ann cannot exclude the settlement from gross income regardless of whether the primary component of her claim was injury to her personal or business reputation.

(d)   Ann can exclude the settlement from gross income regardless of whether the primary component of her claim was injury to her personal or business reputation.

5.   In November of last year, Ann and Bob purchased a home in Awayville, and moved there. They paid a moving company a significant amount to move their belongings. Within weeks of this move, both Ann and Bob obtained full-time jobs in the area: Ann as a clerk at an electronics store and Bob as an engineer for a company. Both of these jobs were about fifty-five miles from their old Centerville home. Ann found her new job too tiring and in March of this year, she quit (not intending to get a new job). Bob also quit his engineering job in March of this year, but immediately found a new full-time job as a clerk at a home improvement store just across the street. **Most likely, will they be entitled to a deduction for the amount paid to the moving company?**

(a)   No, because moving costs are personal expenses and, pursuant to IRC § 262, are not deductible.

(b)   No, because Bob's places of work are not located far enough from their old home in Centerville. Subtracting thirty miles (distance from his old home to his old job) from fifty-five miles (distance from his old home to his new job(s)), does not meet the minimum statutory requirement of fifty miles.

(c)   No, because subsequent to their move, Bob voluntarily changed jobs.

(d)   Yes, because only one spouse must meet the requirements of IRC § 217 to deduct moving costs, and here Ann meets all of the requirements. Although she did not (or will not) work for thirty-nine weeks in Awayville during the twelve-month period immediately following their move, she is excused from this requirement because she is disabled.

(e)   Yes, assuming that Bob works an aggregate of thirty-nine weeks in Awayville during the twelve-month period immediately following their move there last November. He can combine the time worked at both jobs to make this determination.

6. When Ann and Bob purchased their new home in Awayville in November of last year, it soon became apparent that extensive modifications to the house would be necessary for wheelchair accessibility. They spent a substantial amount of money widening doorways and installing ramps, grab bars and railings. In addition, at this time Ann spent a considerable amount of money to purchase a new motorized wheelchair. **With respect to these house modification and wheelchair expenditures, which statement best describes their qualification as "expenses for medical care" for purposes of IRC § 213?**

 (a) All of the expenditures will qualify as medical care expenses notwithstanding that they appear to be nondeductible capital expenditures pursuant to IRC § 263.

 (b) The cost of the wheelchair will qualify as a medical care expense. However, the cost of the home modifications will qualify as medical care expenses only to extent that the costs exceed the increase in the value to their home as a result of the modifications. In the present case, this will most likely result in a substantial amount of the home modification expenditures not qualifying as medical care expenses.

 (c) Neither the expenditures for the wheelchair nor the home modifications will qualify as medical care expenses because they represent capital expenditures that, pursuant to IRC § 263, are nondeductible.

 (d) None of these expenditures will qualify as medical care expenses unless specifically prescribed by her doctor.

Questions 7 through 11 are based on the following facts:

Larry, a single individual, age 28 and a recent law school graduate, started work in August of last year, as an associate (employee) in his Mother's law firm. To date, Larry's work at the firm has been exemplary. Unbeknownst to his mother, Larry, while in law school, borrowed $15,000 from his grandmother, Glenda, and used the money to pay tuition. Larry, wanting everything to be "above board," gave Glenda a promissory note for the amount borrowed. The note provided that Larry would pay her interest only (monthly at a fair market rate) until such time, after graduating law school, when he obtained a job – at which time he would re-pay the full $15,000 principal.

7. **Pursuant to the promissory note, Larry paid $1,100 in interest to his grand-mother, Glenda. Most likely, the interest that he paid is:**

    (a)   Nondeductible personal interest.

    (b)   Deductible as investment interest.

    (c)   Deductible pursuant to IRC § 221 assuming that the level of Larry's in-come is not sufficient to reduce or eliminate the deduction.

    (d)   Nondeductible because no interest deductions are allowed on loans be-tween "related" individuals.

    (e)   Deductible as "regular" interest.

8. Please assume **for this question only** that instead of borrowing the $15,000 from his grandmother Glenda, Larry borrowed the money from his aunt, Ann. **Pursu-ant to the promissory note, Larry paid $1,100 in interest to Ann. Most likely, the interest that he paid is:**

    (a)   Nondeductible personal interest.

    (b)   Deductible as investment interest.

    (c)   Deductible pursuant to IRC § 221 assuming that the level of Larry's in-come is not sufficient to reduce or eliminate the deduction.

    (d)   Nondeductible because no interest deductions are allowed on loans be-tween "related" individuals.

    (e)   Deductible as "regular" interest.

9. **Back to our original facts (Larry borrowed money from Glenda), as to Glenda, which of the following statements most accurately describes the income tax consequences with respect to the interest received from her grandson Larry?**

    (a) It is excludable from gross income as a gift between family members.

    (b) Its inclusion or exclusion from gross income depends on the deductibility or non-deductibility of the interest, respectively, as to Larry.

    (c) It is included in gross income.

    (d) It is included in gross income unless Glenda's other income is not sufficient to generate an income tax liability.

10. In August of last year, shortly after Larry began working, he realized that he was not in adequate financial shape to repay the $15,000 loan to Glenda as promised. Reluctantly, he told his grandmother that he could not pay her the principal at that time, but would continue to pay her interest and hoped to be in the position to pay her the principal within a few months. Without hesitation, Glenda told Larry, her favorite grandchild, not only to take as long as he needed to pay her back, but that she was forgiving $5,000 of the loan principal because she was so proud of him. **As a result of this compromise of debt principal, is it likely that Larry has taxable income?**

    (a) No, the $5,000 debt discharged would be excluded from income.

    (b) Yes, the $5,000 debt discharged represents income.

    (c) No but only if Larry, immediately before the $5,000 forgiveness, was insolvent by at least that amount. Otherwise, some or all of the $5,000 is taxable to Larry.

    (d) Yes, the $5,000 debt discharged is income assuming Larry considered the loan a bona fide debt.

11. In October of last year, Larry's dad found out about Glenda's loan to Larry. Larry's dad felt somewhat embarrassed that his son borrowed the money from Glenda, and a bit hurt that Larry did not ask him for the money. Also proud of his son, Larry's dad paid the remaining $10,000 Larry owed to Glenda, renouncing any claim to repayment by Larry. **Which of the following statements is most accurate with respect to the income tax ramifications to Larry as result of the foregoing?**

   (a)   Larry has $10,000 of income from discharge of indebtedness.

   (b)   Larry has $10,000 of income in the form of compensation (albeit indirectly) because his employer (his father) paid this obligation.

   (c)   Larry can exclude some or all of the $10,000 from income if, immediately before his dad paid off the loan, he was insolvent.

   (d)   Larry can exclude the $10,000 from income if he can show that his father was acting out of "detached and disinterested generosity" in paying off the debt of his son.

Questions 12 through 15 are based on the following facts:

Harold and Wanda were divorced on June 1st of last year, and have not lived together at any time subsequent to the divorce. They have one child, Charles, who is in Wanda's custody. Neither Harold nor Wanda has remarried. For these questions, you are to assume that applicable state law has no provision regarding cessation of support obligations upon the death of a spouse receiving support payments.

12. For this question only, assume that the divorce decree requires that Harold pay Wanda $20,000 "alimony" per year for life or until she remarries. While Harold and Wanda are no longer that fond of each other, they are both less fond of the I.R.S. Also assume for this question that in a plot to "cheat the tax man," their divorce decree provides that the yearly payments are not income to Wanda (and not deductible by Harold), this despite the fact that the payments are labeled as "alimony." **Assuming that all such "alimony" will be paid for the current year:**

   (a) Wanda does not have to recognize any of the $20,000 as income, and Harold is not entitled to a deduction.

   (b) Wanda has to recognize $20,000 as income, and Harold is entitled to a corresponding $20,000 "above the line" deduction – they can affirmatively decide what **is** alimony but they cannot treat the payments as not being alimony if they otherwise qualify.

   (c) Wanda has to recognize $20,000 as income, but Harold is not entitled to a deduction – Wanda has a net accession to wealth and the agreement that the payments "are not alimony" is effective only as to Harold.

   (d) Wanda has to recognize $20,000 as income, and Harold is entitled to a corresponding $20,000 "below the line" deduction – they can affirmatively decide what **is** alimony but they cannot treat the payments as not being alimony if they otherwise qualify.

13. For this question only, assume that the divorce decree requires that Harold pay Wanda $20,000 "alimony" per year for ten years or until she remarries. Also assume, for this question only, that the decree provides that the alimony is to be reduced by $2,000 per year when Charles reaches age eighteen, dies or marries prior to reaching eighteen. Assume that Wanda receives the full $20,000 in the current year, and Charles is alive, unmarried and under age eighteen. **For the current year, Harold is entitled to:**

   (a) A $20,000 deduction because the divorce decree labels the entire payment as "alimony."

   (b) An $18,000 deduction because of the provision regarding Charles.

   (c) A $2,000 deduction because of the provision regarding Charles.

   (d) No deduction.

14. For this question only, assume that the divorce decree gave each spouse a one-half "tenant in common" interest in the couple's residence and allows Wanda to remain living there (Harold is not living there). Also assume that the decree requires Harold to pay 100% of the house insurance and gardening expenses for as long as Wanda remains living there, remarries or dies, whichever is sooner. **Which of the following statements is most accurate?**

(a) Harold can deduct, as alimony, one-half of both the house insurance and gardening expenses.

(b) Harold cannot deduct, as alimony, any portion of either expense.

(c) Harold can deduct, as alimony, all of his expenditures for house insurance and gardening.

(d) Harold can only deduct, as alimony, one-half of the house insurance expense. None of the gardening expense is deductible as alimony.

15. The couple's divorce decree awarded certain shares of XYZ Co. stock to Harold (the couple had purchased the stock many years ago for $5,000). In April of this year, Wanda heard a tip that XYZ Co. was going to be acquired by another company, and that the price of the stock was going to skyrocket as a result. Harold was unaware of this rumor but, coincidentally, was desperately in need of cash at about the same time.   Wanda offered to buy the stock from Harold for $50,000 (its then current fair market value), and he accepted, selling the stock to her in April of this year. Shortly thereafter, the news about the acquisition came out and the stock price of XYZ increased dramatically. Wanda sold these same XYZ shares for $150,000 in May of this year. **As a result of selling these shares, Wanda should have to:**

(a) Recognize a $100,000 short-term capital gain because Wanda's purchase of the shares from Harold did not relate to the cessation of their marriage.

(b) Recognize a $145,000 short-term capital gain – Wanda's purchase of the shares from Harold was incident to their divorce.

(c) Recognize a $145,000 long-term capital gain – Wanda's purchase of the shares from Harold was incident to their divorce.

(d) Recognize no gain or loss – Wanda's purchase, and sale, of the shares were incident to their divorce.

(e) None of the above responses is correct.

incident = happening w/in 1yr of the divorce.

Questions 16 through 19 are based on the following facts:

Philip is a general contractor in the business of building and remodeling single-family homes. His business is very successful and he has a strong conviction that philanthropy is an obligatory moral companion of success. To this end, he actively contributes his time and wealth to eleemosynary causes. For purposes of this series of questions, please treat each as a separate and independent question.

16. Philip made a substantial cash gift to the American Red cross in the current year. Also, almost every day he gave various amounts of cash to homeless individuals that he encountered. **Assuming that the foregoing represents all gifts made by Philip in the current year, he:**

    (a)   Will be entitled to a charitable contribution deduction pursuant to IRC § 170 for all of the above cash gifts. However, such deduction cannot exceed, in the current year, 50% of his "contribution base" as defined in IRC § 170(b)(1)(F).

    (b)   Will be entitled to a charitable contribution deduction pursuant to IRC § 170 for all of the above cash gifts. However, the deductions for the gifts to the American Red cross and his cash gifts to the homeless individuals cannot exceed 50% and 30%, respectively, of his "contribution base" as defined in IRC § 170(b)(1)(F).

    (c)   Will be entitled to a charitable contribution deduction pursuant to IRC § 170 only for his cash gift to the American Red cross. However, such deduction cannot exceed, in the current year, 50% of his "contribution base" as defined in IRC § 170(b)(1)(F).

    (d)   Will be entitled to a charitable contribution deduction pursuant to IRC § 170 only for his cash gift to the American Red cross. However, such deduction cannot exceed, in the current year, 30% of his "contribution base" as defined in IRC § 170(b)(1)(F).

---

17. Philip is very active in the Habitat for Humanity organization (a qualified public charity) helping to construct homes for qualifying individuals. During the year, he spent most of his weekends working on building projects for this organization. His contributed labor, had he charged for it in the context of his normal business operations, would have been worth $20,000. For the year, in the aggregate, he drove thousands of miles from his home to (and back from) the various Habitat for Humanity building projects. **Which of the following statements is most accurate in describing the extent of Philip's charitable deduction with respect to the foregoing?**

(a) While he cannot deduct the value of his services, he can deduct his transportation costs from his home to (and back from) the building projects. The amount of the charitable deduction for these transportation costs is the greater of his actual costs of driving or the statutory per-mile rate specified in IRC § 170.

(b) He can deduct $20,000 for his services because this amount, as in a barter transaction, represents the fair value of his services. He is also entitled to deduct his transportation costs from his home to (and back from) the building projects using the greater of his actual costs of driving or the statutory per-mile rate specified in IRC § 170.

(c) He cannot deduct the value of his services or his transportation costs from his home to (and back from) the building projects. Both of these do not represent qualified charitable contributions as defined in IRC § 170.

(d) He can deduct $20,000 for his services because he is in the construction business. However, he cannot deduct his transportation costs unless his "home" is considered his "office" for his normal business operations.

(e) He cannot deduct the $20,000 value of his services. In addition, he cannot deduct his transportation costs unless his "home" is considered his "office" for his normal business operations.

18. Philip gave to the American Red Cross (a qualified public charity), his car that he used solely for personal purposes, totally unrelated to his business. He originally paid $30,000 for the car a few years ago, but it was worth only $10,000 when he gave it to the American Red Cross. In addition, he gave shares of General Motors Corporation common stock worth $20,000 to the American Red Cross (he originally purchased these shares two years earlier for $12,000). Lastly, Philip attended a special American Red Cross "Cirque du Soleil" gala event, a special fund-raising performance benefiting the American Red Cross. The ticket for this event cost $500 with all of the proceeds going to the American Red Cross. Tickets for regular performances of Cirque du Soleil cost $100. **Assuming that any required documentation was obtained, which statement best describes the extent of Philip's charitable deduction with respect to the foregoing?**

(a) Subject to certain "percent of contribution base" limits, Philip can deduct the $10,000 value of the car, the $12,000 cost of the General Motors stock, and the $500 paid for the fundraising tickets.

(b) Subject to certain "percent of contribution base" limits, Philip can deduct the $10,000 value of the car, the $12,000 cost of the General Motors stock, but only $400 for the fundraising event (the difference between the $500 paid and the $100 representing the value of the benefit received as evidenced by the regular ticket price).

(c) Subject to certain "percent of contribution base" limits, Philip can deduct the $10,000 value of the car, the $20,000 value of the General Motors stock, but only $400 for the fundraising event (the difference between the $500 paid and the $100 representing the value of the benefit received as evidenced by the regular ticket price).

(d) Subject to certain "percent of contribution base" limits, Philip can deduct the $30,000 original cost of the car, the $20,000, the value of the General Motors stock, but only $400 for the fundraising event (the difference between the $500 paid and the $100 representing the value of the benefit received as evidenced by the regular ticket price).

(e) None of the above responses is correct.

---

19. Samantha, Philip's daughter, was recently accepted as a beginning undergraduate student at a private university. Tuition at this university is substantial, but Philip has "taken care" of it. Philip recently made a cash contribution to this university (a qualified public charity) equal to the amount of a student's tuition with explicit instructions that it be used as a "scholarship" awarded to Samantha covering the full amount of her tuition. The university accepted the money under these terms, and awarded a "full scholarship" to Samantha. **Which of the following answers is most accurate?**

(a) Philip will be entitled to a charitable deduction for the amount contributed. Samantha will be able to exclude the scholarship from income under IRC § 117.

(b) Philip will not be entitled to a charitable deduction for the amount contributed. Samantha will have to include the "scholarship" in her gross income.

(c) Philip will be entitled to a charitable deduction for the amount contributed. Samantha will have to include the "scholarship" in her gross income unless it can be determined that this was a "gift" excludable from gross income under IRC § 102.

(d) Philip will not be entitled to a charitable deduction for the amount contributed. Samantha will not have to include the "scholarship" in her gross income.

Questions 20 through 22 are based on the following facts:

Kathy is an officer of XYZ Industries ("XYZ"), a conglomerate with operations in various businesses including passenger airline, hotel, consumer electronics and life insurance. She has worked for XYZ for more than 25 years and is very well liked by all of the other officers (she is not related to anyone at XYZ). Kathy performs a substantial amount of work in all areas of company operations and she is considered a "highly compensated employee" for purposes of IRC § 132.

20. Kathy was involved in an automobile accident while on vacation. While she was not hurt in the accident, her child suffered some injuries and her car was "totaled." In a gesture of kindness and compassion, XYZ made a gift to Kathy of $5,000 in cash and a new automobile worth $25,000. **As a result of the foregoing, Kathy will most likely:**

    (a) Not be required to recognize any amount as income if she can show that XYZ was acting with "detached and disinterested generosity."

    (b) Be required to recognize $5,000 (cash received) as income, but not be required to recognize any income with respect to the automobile assuming that she can show that XYZ was acting with "detached and disinterested generosity."

    (c) Be required to recognize as income both $5,000 (cash received) and $25,000 (the value of the automobile) regardless of XYZ's motive for making the gift.

    (d) Be required to recognize as income $5,000 (cash received) plus 80% of the $25,000 value of the automobile regardless of XYZ's motive in making the gift.

21. Kathy, as well as all full-time employees of XYZ, is entitled to obtain a personal life insurance policy at a substantial discount when compared to the cost at which XYZ offers such policies to the general public. The available discount is 40%, which equals XYZ's "gross profit percentage" in the life insurance portion of its business. Assume that in the current year, only Kathy and one other officer took advantage of this insurance deal. Kathy obtained a life insurance policy at a cost of $6,000 (a 40% savings off the regular $10,000 cost to the public). **With respect to the foregoing, Kathy must include in gross income:**

    (a) None of the discount.

    (b) $2,000.

    (c) $4,000.

    (d) $6,000.

22. As a matter of company policy, XYZ pays professional association dues and subscription fees to professional periodicals for all "highly compensated employees" of XYZ. XYZ does not pay for these items for other XYZ employees. During the year, XYZ paid Kathy's $700 annual dues to the American Society of Corporate Officers and $400 in annual subscription fees to various professional periodicals that directly related to her job function at XYZ. **How much income must Kathy recognize with respect to XYZ's payment of these items?**

(a) No income need be recognized.

(b) $1,100, because the benefit is discriminatory.

(c) $880 (80% of $1,100), because even though it doesn't qualify as a "no additional cost fringe," at least 20% will be excluded as a "qualified employee discount."

(d) $400, representing the cost of the periodical subscriptions.

Questions 23 through 25 are based on the following facts:

For years, Martha has owned an apartment building as an investment. A tenant in the building was the on-site manager, taking care of all maintenance and collection of rents. At the end of each month, the manager would remit to Martha, all of the money representing rents for the month then ended. On April 16th of this year, Martha made a gift of the apartment building to Steve, her son (legally transferred ownership). On April 30th, the apartment manager remitted the rent money to Steve, the then legal owner. On May 1st of this year, the apartment building was sold to Peter, an unrelated purchaser, resulting in a substantial gain.

23. **With respect to the April rent and the gain from the sale of the property, which of the following statements is most accurate?**

(a) Steve will recognize the rental income as legal owner, but Martha will have to recognize the gain assuming the sale deal was in the works at the time the property was given to Steve.

(b) Martha and Steve will each recognize one-half of the rental income, but Steve will recognize the gain from the sale assuming the sale was Steve's idea and he made the deal after receiving the property.

(c) Martha and Steve will each recognize one-half of the rental income, but Martha will have to recognize the gain from the sale since she cannot effectively assign the gain to anyone other than herself.

(d) Martha will recognize the rental income (she cannot assign this to Steve), but Steve will recognize the gain from the sale assuming that the sale was his idea and he made the deal after receiving the property.

24. For this question, assume that Peter, the purchaser of the apartment building, is an attorney who also plans to hold the apartment building as investment property for many years to come. County real property taxes are assessed on a calendar year basis and are payable in advance, on January 1st, for each year. On January 1st of this year, Martha paid $12,000 in property taxes for the apartment building. **How much of this property tax, if any, will Peter most likely be entitled to deduct this year?**

    (a)   No deduction will be allowed because Peter was not the legal owner on January 1st.

    (b)   Approximately $8,000, but only if Steve and Peter actually apportioned the tax, and Peter reimbursed Steve (or Martha) for this amount.

    (c)   Approximately $8,000 regardless of whether Steve and Peter actually apportioned the tax or whether Peter reimbursed any of it to Steve (or Martha).

    (d)   No deduction will be allowed because real property taxes are not deductible.

    (e)   The lesser of: 1) an apportioned amount of the $12,000 tax for the total based upon the date that Peter purchased the property, or 2) the actual amount of the tax that Peter reimbursed to Steve (or Martha).

25. Assume on January 1st of next year, that Peter pays the real property tax for the full year on the apartment building. Also assume that he continues to hold the property as an investment. **Which of the following statements best describes the income tax consequences to Peter with respect to the payment of these property taxes?**

    (a)   He will be entitled to a deduction for the amount of tax paid, and it will be allowed as an "above the line" deduction in computing his adjusted gross income (AGI).

    (b)   He will be entitled to a deduction for the amount of tax paid, and it will be allowed as a "below the line" deduction (part of the *itemized deductions* group) in computing his taxable income.

    (c)   The payment of property taxes will generate no income tax deduction but, rather, will be added to Peter's basis in the property.

    (d)   He will be entitled to an exclusion, against his rental income from the property, for the amount of tax paid.

END OF EXAMINATION QUESTIONS

EXAM IV

FEDERAL INCOME TAX
MULTIPLE-CHOICE OBJECTIVE QUESTIONS
EXAM IV

Questions 1 and 2 are based on the following facts:

Roger is a self-employed computer consultant and operates his very profitable consulting business as an "unincorporated sole proprietorship." This year, Cassandra (a CPA) rendered tax advice to Roger. This tax advice related solely to Roger's consulting business and Roger was billed $4,000. Both Roger and Cassandra collect baseball cards for a hobby and just as Roger was about to pay Cassandra's bill, Cassandra inquired about a particular rare baseball card in Roger's collection. The card had a value of $4,000 and Cassandra asked whether Roger would consider making an even trade (the card in exchange for discharging the bill). Roger agreed to the exchange, which then took place. Roger was happy with the deal because he had purchased the card some three months earlier for only $2,500. Both Roger and Cassandra operate their respective businesses on a "cash basis."

1. **Which answer best describes the income tax ramifications to <u>Cassandra</u> as a result of the facts presented?**

    (a) There are no income tax ramifications to her because this was a barter transaction in which no cash changed hands.

    (b) She has $4,000 of gross income from services rendered, but has an offsetting $4,000 business deduction.

    (c) She has no immediate income tax consequences because, in effect, she merely purchased the baseball card. She may have a gain or loss if she subsequently sells the card.

    (d) She has $4,000 of gross income from services rendered. In addition, her adjusted basis in the card, for purposes of determining gain or loss on any subsequent sale, is zero.

    (e) None of the above responses is correct.

2. **Which answer best describes the income tax ramifications to <u>Roger</u> as a result of the facts presented?**

    (a) He has gross income of $4,000 because this is a taxable barter type transaction.

    (b) He has no gross income because he was not the party providing services, but he is entitled to a $2,500 deduction.

    (c) He has a realized gain of $1,500 and a $2,500 deduction pursuant to IRC § 162.

    (d) He has a realized gain of $1,500 and a $4,000 deduction pursuant to IRC § 212.

    (e) He has a realized gain of $1,500 and a $4,000 deduction pursuant to IRC § 162.

Questions 3 through 5 are based on the following facts:

In March of this year, Tom's grandmother, Gloria, died and Tom received shares of XYZ Co. stock from her as a devise (bequest). Gloria had purchased these shares for $50,000 just one month prior to her death. While the value of these shares had declined to $35,000 at the time of her death, their price rebounded some, and Tom sold them for $40,000 in May of this year.

3.   **When Tom received the XYZ Co. shares from Gloria, he:**

(a)   Realizes a net accession to wealth of $35,000, but can exclude it from his gross income pursuant to IRC § 102.

(b)   Realizes a net accession to wealth of $35,000, and, because this was not an inter vivos gift, he must recognize this amount in his gross income.

(c)   Has no gain or loss realized or recognized because transfers between family members are "tax free."

(d)   Has no gain or loss realized or recognized because of the value of the shares at the time of the devise, and the price for which Tom subsequently sold them.

4.   **When Tom subsequently sells the XYZ Co. shares, he:**

(a)   Realizes a gain of $5,000.

(b)   Realizes a loss of $10,000.

(c)   Realizes neither a gain nor a loss because the fair market value of the shares at the time of the transfer to Tom was less than Gloria's basis, and Tom subsequently sold them for a price in between these two values.

(d)   Realizes neither a gain nor a loss because the value of these shares is excluded from his gross income pursuant to IRC § 102.

5. **What is the extent and character of gain or loss recognized by Tom when he sells the XYZ Co. shares?**

   (a) There is no recognition of gain or loss because Tom realizes no gain or loss when he sells the shares. Characterization of a recognized gain or loss, therefore, is moot.

   (b) Tom has $5,000 of recognized gain. This gain is a short-term capital gain because although, pursuant to IRC § 1223(2) he can tack onto his holding period that of Gloria, the combined holding period is less than one year.

   (c) Tom has ($10,000) of recognized loss. This loss is a long-term capital loss because, pursuant to IRC § 1223(2) he can tack onto his holding period that of Gloria.

   (d) Tom has ($10,000) of recognized loss. This loss is a short-term capital loss because although, pursuant to IRC § 1223(2) he can tack onto his holding period that of Gloria, the combined holding period is less than one year.

   (e) None of the above responses is correct.

6. Brad purchased his house four years ago for $200,000. Three years ago Gail, his girlfriend, moved into Brad's house and has been living with him ever since. Brad is going to sell his house, with he and Gail, still unmarried, moving overseas together. Gail has no ownership interest in this or any other house. **Assuming Brad sells his house to an unrelated individual at a gain, he:**

   (a) Will be able to exclude up to $250,000 of such gain pursuant to IRC § 121 because he meets both the "use" and "ownership" requirements contained therein.

   (b) Will not have to recognize any such gain because he has used the house as his principal residence. Had he been renting out the house, instead of living in it, then some or all of the gain would have been recognized.

   (c) Will be able to exclude up to $500,000 of such gain pursuant to IRC § 121 because he meets the "ownership" requirement, and both he and Gail meet the "use" requirement contained therein.

   (d) Will not have to recognize any such gain, regardless of the amount, assuming that within a two-year period, he buys (and occupies) a new house.

   (e) Will not have to recognize any such gain, regardless of the amount, assuming that his overseas move is work related.

7.   **Would your answer to question 6, above, be different if, at the time of the sale, Brad and Gail had been married for six months?**

(a)   Yes. The maximum excludable gain would be $500,000, assuming that Gail had some ownership interest in the house at the time of the sale.

(b)   No, because they had not been married for a long enough period at the time of the house sale.

(c)   No, because the maximum amount of gain excludable pursuant to IRC § 121 would be the same in this scenario.

(d)   Yes. The maximum excludable gain would be $312,500 assuming that they file a joint return for the year in which the sale occurred.

(e)   Yes. The maximum excludable gain would be $500,000 assuming that they file a joint return for the year in which the sale occurred.

Questions 8 through 12 are based on the following facts:

Sonia was both the original owner and the insured of a $100,000 life insurance policy. Richard, her husband, was the named beneficiary of the policy. Sonia died in December of last year. The total of all premiums paid on the policy up to the time of Sonia's death was $15,000.

8.   In January of this year, Richard, as policy beneficiary, received a check for $100,000 from the insurance company. **With respect to this insurance benefit, Richard must recognize:**

(a) $85,000 of income pursuant to § 1001 – the difference between the "amount realized" and the "adjusted basis" in the policy.

(b)   No income pursuant to § 101(a).

(c) $100,000 of income as an "accession to wealth."

(d) $15,000 of income because this amount represents Richard's "tax cost" of the policy.

9. Same as Question 8, above, except that instead of receiving a lump sum, Richard selected a payout option in which the insurance company promises to pay him $10,000 a year for the rest of his life. The insurance company estimated that Richard had a 40-year life expectancy. During the current year, Richard received his first $10,000 payment. **As a result, the amount of income Richard can exclude from this is:**

   (a) $10,000.
   (b) $7,500.
   (c) $2,500.
   (d) Zero.

10. Same as Question 9, above, except that it is now forty-one years later (the tax laws have remained unchanged) and Richard is still alive, and he receives his forty-first annual $10,000 payment from the insurance company. **As a result, the amount of income Richard must recognize is:**

   (a) $10,000 because Richard has fully recovered the otherwise tax-free amount of life insurance benefits.
   (b) Zero because Richard has outlived his life expectancy.
   (c) $7,500.
   (d) $2,500.

11. Same as Question 8, above, except that in January 2000, Sonia and Richard were divorced. In May 2001, Sonia transferred the policy to Richard in exchange for $30,000 worth of his property. This transfer was not pursuant to any written or oral agreement relating to the divorce. Subsequent to this exchange, but prior to Sonia's death, Richard paid $3,000 in insurance premiums on the policy. The aggregate sum of all premium payments made by Richard and Sonia (by either or both of them) remained the same at $15,000. Richard remained as policy beneficiary. **With respect to the $100,000 insurance benefit received by Richard in the current year, Richard will most likely be able to exclude:**

(a) $30,000, representing the consideration paid, because the transfer to Richard was not incident to the divorce.

(b) $33,000, representing the sum of the consideration paid plus premiums paid subsequent to the transfer. This is because the transfer to Richard was not related to the cessation of the marriage.

(c) Nothing, because the amounts received by Sonia in 2001 were not by reason of the death of the insured.

(d) $100,000, representing the entire insurance proceeds. This is because transfers within six years of divorce are considered related to the cessation of the marriage.

(e) Nothing, because life insurance proceeds received by reason of the death of the insured are fully excluded from income pursuant to IRC § 101(a).

12.   Assume the same facts as in question 11, above, except that Richard and Sonia were divorced in January of 2001. **Which of the following answers is most accurate with respect to the $100,000 insurance benefit received by Richard in the current year?**

(a)   Richard can exclude, from gross income, $30,000 representing the consideration that he paid to Sonia. The $70,000 balance is included in his gross income. This is because the transfer of the policy to Richard was <u>not</u> pursuant to their divorce decree and, therefore, not incident to the divorce.

(b)   Richard can exclude, from gross income, $33,000 representing the sum of the consideration paid plus premiums paid subsequent to the transfer. The $67,000 balance is included in his gross income. This is because the transfer of the policy to Richard was <u>not</u> pursuant to their divorce decree and, therefore, not incident to divorce.

(c)   Richard can exclude, from gross income, the entire $100,000 received because life insurance proceeds received by the death of the insured are always excludable pursuant to IRC § 101.

(d)   Richard can exclude, from gross income, the entire $100,000 received. This is because transfers within six years of divorce are considered related to the cessation of the marriage.

(e)   Richard can exclude, from gross income, the entire $100,000 received. This is because the transfer of the policy to Richard was incident to divorce.

Questions 13 through 15 are based on the following facts:

Earlier this year, Roxanne received a gift of jewelry from Martha, her aunt (no gift tax resulted from this transfer). Martha had originally purchased the jewelry years ago for $20,000. It was worth $60,000 at the time of the gift. Later in the year, Roxanne became desperate for cash and sold the jewelry for $42,000, its then current fair market value.

13.   **How much gain or loss did Roxanne realize from the sale of the jewelry?**

(a)   Neither a gain nor a loss because Roxanne sold it for a price that was between Martha's basis and the fair market value at the time of the gift.

(b)   A loss of $18,000.

(c)   A gain of $22,000.

(d)   A gain of $42,000 because Roxanne paid nothing for the stock (and, therefore had a basis of $0).

14.   For this question only, assume that Roxanne did not receive cash in exchange for her "sale" of the jewelry. Rather, she gave the jewelry to Carl, an individual to whom she owed $40,000. Upon receipt of the jewelry, Carl discharged this debt. However, since the jewelry was worth $42,000, Carl, a dentist, also agreed to render $2,000 worth of dental services to Roxanne (which he did). **Does Roxanne realize any income as a result of the foregoing?**

(a)   Yes, she realized $42,000 in income: $40,000 of which was income from discharge of indebtedness.

(b)   Yes, she realized $40,000 income from discharge of indebtedness. The $2,000 value of services received is not income because this was not part of the debt discharged.

(c)   Yes, she realized no income from discharge of indebtedness, but did realize a gain of $22,000 from the disposition of the jewelry.

(d)   She realized no income from discharge of indebtedness, but did realize a gain of $20,000 from the disposition of the jewelry. The $2,000 services received is not part of the gain calculation but, rather, is income to her under the concept of a "net accession to wealth."

15.   Assume that the $40,000 Roxanne originally owed Carl in question 14, above, was not related to Carl's dental practice (i.e., it was a personal loan to Roxanne outside of the context of Carl's business). **Referring to question 14, above, what are the income tax consequences to Carl?**

(a)   Carl has $2,000 of gross income from the performance of services.

(b)   Carl has gross income in the amount of $42,000: $2,000 from the performance of services and $40,000 because of the discharge of the debt.

(c)   Carl has no income from the transaction, as he was simply being repaid amounts owed to him.

(d)   Carl has no income but, rather, was merely "purchasing" the jewelry for $42,000.

(e)   Carl has $2,000 of gross income from the performance of services and a "bad debt" deduction of the $40,000 debt discharged.

16.   This past year has been a particularly bad year for Donald, a single individual. His bad year started in January, when he was fired from his engineering job of five years. During the two months following his termination, he received a total of $3,000 in regular "unemployment" benefits from his state's governmental unemployment compensation insurance program. **For income tax purposes the $3,000 in unemployment benefits:**

(a)   Are excludable from Donald's gross income because they represent government affiliated welfare benefits.

(b)   Are excludable from Donald's gross income pursuant to IRC § 104.

(c)   Are fully included in Donald's gross income because they represent taxable unemployment compensation.

(d)   Are fully included in Donald's gross income because they are represent taxable employer fringe benefits.

17. Donald, in question 16 above, had more financial woes last year. Frustrated, out of work, and low on funds, he sold his personal residence. His timing, however, could not have been worse. He had purchased the house five years ago at the peak of a real estate boom for $400,000, hoping that it would be a good investment. His instincts and timing, however, proved to be poor as he sold the house in March of last year just after the real estate bubble in his area had burst. Receiving only $360,000 from the sale, he was disappointed that the house did not prove to be a better investment. He lived in the house at all times during his ownership thereof. This house was the first, and only, house he has owned and, while he is currently employed, he is undecided as to whether he will buy another home in the near future. **With respect to the sale of the house in March of last year, Donald:**

(a) Realized a loss of $40,000. Because the house is a capital asset, this loss is a recognized long-term capital loss.

(b) Realized a loss of $40,000. While the house is a capital asset, the loss is not recognized for income tax purposes.

(c) Realized a loss of $40,000. Because the house is not a capital asset, this loss is recognized as an "ordinary" loss for income tax purposes.

(d) Realized a loss of $40,000. While this loss is not recognized, the cost basis of any principal residence that is purchased (and occupied) within two years will be increased by $40,000.

(e) None of the above responses is correct.

18. The bad year for Donald, in questions 16 and 17 above, continued to worsen. To add insult to injury, in July of last year, his prior years' Federal and State income tax returns were audited (by the I.R.S. and applicable State authorities, respectively). He paid a CPA $1,000 to handle the audits. Even this did not turn out well, because as a result of the audits, he had to pay additional Federal and State income taxes of $2,000 and $750, respectively (no penalties or interest were assessed). **With respect to the foregoing, which of the following statements is most accurate?**

(a) None of these items give rise to possible deductions for income tax purposes.

(b) He is entitled to deduct, as part of his "itemized deductions," the $750 in State income taxes. None of the other items give rise to possible deductions for income tax purposes.

(c) He is entitled to deduct, as part of his "itemized deductions," the $1,000 paid to his CPA and the $750 in State income taxes. The $2,000 in Federal taxes does not give rise to a deduction for income tax purposes.

(d) He is entitled to deduct, as part of his "itemized deductions," the $1,000 paid to his CPA to the extent that the aggregate of it, and any other "miscellaneous" itemized deductions, exceed 2% of his adjusted gross income (AGI), and the $750 in State income taxes. The $2,000 in Federal taxes does not give rise to a deduction for income tax purposes.

(e) All of the above items give rise to possible deductions for income tax purpose.

19. Mark is an officer in Little Cub, Inc., the offices of which are located in a high-rise building in downtown Los Angeles. He is considered a "highly compensated employee" for purposes of IRC § 132. Little Cub pays for Mark's parking in the building. **With respect to this parking for 2002, Mark must include in income:**

    (a) Nothing for 2002, even if parking was not furnished to other employees of Little Cub.

    (b) Nothing for the value of parking up to $185 per month for 2002. This is true even if parking was not furnished to other employees of Little Cub.

    (c) Nothing for the value of parking up to $185 per month for 2002 unless this benefit was discriminatory in favor of a "highly compensated class of employees" in which case the entire value of the parking would be included.

    (d) Nothing for the value of parking up to $185 per month for 2002 unless this benefit was discriminatory in favor of a "highly compensated class of employees" in which case the value of the parking received in excess of that received by all employees would be included.

    (e) None of the above responses is correct.

20. In April of this year, Tom sold a diamond Rolex watch for $23,000. He received it as a gift from his aunt in 1975 upon graduating college. Tom's aunt originally paid $18,000 for the watch in 1973, it had appreciated in value to $21,000 at the time of her gift to Tom. She incurred, and paid, gift taxes of $7,000 with respect to this gift. Tom wore the watch daily (i.e. it was not an investment). **As a result of selling the watch, Tom realized:**

    (a) A loss of $2,000.

    (b) A gain of $4,000.

    (c) A gain of $2,000.

    (d) A gain of $5,000.

    (e) None of the above responses is correct.

Questions 21 and 22 are based on the following facts:

Grant, Taylor's grandfather, had been quite ill for some time and, unfortunately, not in the best financial health either. In March of last year, Taylor made a gift to Grant of shares of stock in XYZ Co. with the hope that he would sell the stock and use the proceeds for his medical/living needs. These shares were worth $40,000 at the time of the gift (Taylor originally paid $15,000 for them two years ago) and no gift tax resulted from this gift. Unfortunately, Grant died in November of last year. In addition to the sadness Taylor experienced from the loss of her grandfather, she was also quite sad to learn that he never did sell or use the stock that she had given him to help ease his situation. These shares were worth $50,000 at the time of Grant's death. Grant's estate was not of sufficient size to incur any estate tax liability.

21.   For this question, assume that Grant died with a will containing the following language: "In recognition of my beloved granddaughter Taylor's selfless caring for me and the profound help that she has given me, I hereby give to her the shares of XYZ Co. stock." These shares of XYZ Co. stock were the same shares that she had given to him in March of last year. **What is the most likely income tax consequence to Taylor as a result of receiving these shares?**

(a)   She will not have to recognize any income.

(b)   She will have $50,000 of gross income.

(c)   She will have $10,000 of gross income.

(d)   She will have gross income equal to the lesser of: $50,000, or the value of the services that she rendered to Grant in caring for him.

22.   For this question, assume that Grant died intestate (without a will) and, pursuant to the applicable state intestate succession statute, Taylor was the sole beneficiary of Grant's estate. **Taylor's basis in the XYZ Co. shares that she receives as intestate beneficiary of Grant's estate is:**

(a) $50,000.

(b) $40,000.

(c) $15,000.

(d)   None of the above responses is correct.

23. Jonathan, a California domiciliary, recently incorporated his plumbing business in Nevada (as a Nevada corporation) after hearing advertisements extolling numerous benefits by doing so. The benefits that he believes he heard advertised include: no state corporate income taxes, the ability to establish large amounts of corporate credit, the ability to have the corporation buy, for his personal-use, items such as houses, cars, house furniture, sporting equipment, etc. In addition, he believes that he heard that he can use the corporation to pay, and deduct, all or most of his purely personal expenses such as his home mortgage, property taxes on his house and personal automobile (state registration fees), vacations, and the like. Jonathan is the sole shareholder and employee of his new Nevada corporation. **If Jonathan's Nevada corporation does buy, on his behalf, personal-use assets and pays for his personal expenses, Jonathan, the individual:**

   (a) Will have income equal to the amount of his personal expenses paid by the corporation, but not for the personal-use assets bought by the corporation on his behalf.

   (b) Will have no income because these items are not in relation to the corporation's business and Jonathan is the sole owner of the corporation.

   (c) Will have income equal to the value of the personal-use assets purchased on his behalf and the amount of his personal expenses paid by the corporation.

   (d) Will have income only because he is domiciled in a state other than Nevada.

24. Marshall is an engineer and is employed by a large computer chip manufacturing company. All full-time employees qualify to participate in the company's "401(k)" plan (a qualified retirement/pension plan). The company, concerned about the financial well being of its employees, recently introduced a new service to all of its employees participating in the company's 401(k) plan. Each such employee is entitled to receive, free of charge, professional financial consulting services covering information about the company's 401(k) plan as well as advice and information on retirement income planning and how the company's 401(k) plan fits into the employee's retirement income plan. Company employees, expert in financial planning matters, will provide these services. Marshall took advantage of this new service and received valuable retirement planning advice. The services Marshall received were worth in excess of $800. **Is Marshall required to include in gross income the value of the services received?**

   (a)   No, because most likely this would be considered a tax-free "de minimis" fringe benefit.

   (b)   No, but only if this service qualifies as an educational assistance program pursuant to IRC § 127.

   (c)   No, because most likely this would qualify as a tax-free "working condition" fringe benefit.

   (d)   Yes, because most likely this would be considered additional compensation not qualifying for exclusion.

   (e)   None of the above responses is correct.

25. A few years ago, when Ara was 26 years old, he purchased some United States Series EE Savings Bonds. While he originally planned on holding them until they matured, he recently cashed them in (redeemed them). Ara is going to attend a state funded vocational school to become a certified air conditioning repairman. **The interest earned from the U.S. Savings Bonds that he recently cashed-in is fully:**

- (a) Includible in his gross income because he cashed in the bonds prior to their maturity,

- (b) Excludable from gross income because the interest is from an obligation of the United States.

- (c) Excludable from gross income if, 1) he uses, for his tuition, the entire amount of the bond proceeds constituting interest, and 2) his adjusted gross income, as modified, is below certain statutory thresholds.

- (d) Excludable from gross income if, 1) he uses, for his tuition, the entire amount of the bond proceeds, and 2) his adjusted gross income, as modified, is below certain statutory thresholds.

- (e) Includible in his gross income in this case because he is not attending an undergraduate or graduate college or university.

END OF EXAMINATION QUESTIONS

EXAM V

Questions 1 through 3 are based on the following facts:

Exactly four years ago, Tom and his wife Edna purchased a house for $400,000, taking title as joint tenants. Shortly after buying it, they spent $110,000 on major additions/improvements to the house. They bought the house strictly for investment purposes, but decided to use it as their residence while the additions/improvements were being made (fully intending to move out and either sell it or rent it thereafter). Unfortunately the cost of these additions/improvements was much more than the value that they added to the house (it was worth only $450,000 after the work was completed). It was after this work was completed that their marriage began to falter and they continued living together, albeit unhappily, in the house. Tom and Edna's marriage ended in divorce exactly two years ago and, pursuant to their divorce decree, Tom received 100% of the house.

1. **Immediately after the improvement/addition work had been completed, the couple's "adjusted basis" in the house was:**

   (a) $400,000.

   (b) $450,000.

   (c) $510,000.

   (d) None of the above responses is correct.

2. For this question only, assume that the $110,000 used for improvements/additions came from a second mortgage loan secured by the house. **The income tax ramifications of this loan are:**

   (a) The $110,000 represents income. The interest that they pay on this loan will not qualify as deductible interest because the loan exceeds the $100,000 limit for qualified home equity indebtedness.

   (b) The $110,000 is not income. Assuming that they have no other loans outstanding, the interest that they pay on only $100,000 of the loan, the limit for home equity indebtedness, will qualify as deductible interest.

   (c) The $110,000 is not income. Assuming that they have no other loans outstanding, the interest that they pay on the entire loan will qualify as deductible interest because the loan does not exceed $1 million.

   (d) The $110,000 represents income. Assuming that they have no other loans outstanding, the interest that they pay on the entire loan will qualify as deductible interest because the loan does not exceed $1 million.

   (e) None of the above responses is correct.

3.   Assume for this question, that the value of the house had declined to $350,000 when it was transferred to Tom two years ago pursuant to their divorce decree. After the divorce, Tom, still hoping that the house would prove to be a good investment, continued living there until he sold it today for $380,000. **Which answer best describes the income tax consequences to Tom resulting from the house sale?**

(a)   Tom has a realized and recognized loss of $130,000. This loss qualifies as a long-term capital loss.

(b)   Tom has a realized and recognized gain of $30,000. This gain qualifies as a long-term capital gain.

(c)   Tom realizes neither a gain nor a loss from the sale of the house.

(d)   Tom has a realized and recognized loss of $70,000. This loss does not qualify as a capital loss.

(e)   None of the above responses is correct.

Questions 4 through 8 are based on the following facts:

Todd is an employee in his mother's music company. In January of this year, following a financially great year, Todd's mother gave each of her thirty employees, including her son Todd, a "mint condition" commemorative plate that had been made for the company many years earlier to celebrate their then twentieth year in business. The company had commissioned the then unknown artist Andy Warhol to design the plates which, including the design fee, cost the company $50 each. These plates, of course, became rare collector's items and were worth $20,000 each when given to the employees in January and were in addition to their regular salaries.

4. **Not considering Todd for this question, will the receipt of the commemorative plate by company employees result in the recognition of gross income?**

    (a)   No, because transfers of property to employees must be in the form of cash to be considered compensation/income when received. The employee's receipt of the plate results in the realization of income, but no income is recognized until the employee sells the plate.

    (b)   No, assuming that this was a "gift" made by the company acting with "detached and disinterested generosity." Gifts are specifically excluded from gross income.

    (c)   No, because this represents an excludable "de minimis" fringe benefit. This is because the cost of the plate to the employer is so small and this was a one-time transfer to employees.

    (d)   Yes, regardless of the company's motive for giving the plates to their employees. The $20,000 value of the plate is considered compensation to the employee.

    (e)   Yes, regardless of the company's motive for giving the plate to their employees. The employee has compensation of $50, representing the employer's cost of the plate.

5. **Specifically with respect to Todd, which statement most likely describes the income tax consequences of his receipt of the commemorative plate?**

    (a)   Todd has $20,000 of gross income in the form of compensation.

    (b)   Todd has $50 of gross income in the form of compensation

    (c)   Todd has no gross income because for him, as opposed to the other employees, this will be considered a gift.

    (d)   Todd has no gross income because for tax purposes here, he is treated like the other employees.

6. Notwithstanding Todd, all of the company employees took great care of the commemorative plates received and held onto them as an investment. In March of this year, however, one of the company employees, Marcia, sold her commemorative plate to an art dealer for $23,000. **To what extent does Marcia have a realized gain as a result of this sale?**

    (a) She has a realized gain of $22,950, the difference between the $23,000 selling price and her basis in the plate of $50.

    (b) She has a realized gain of $3,000, the difference between the $23,000 selling price and her basis in the plate of $20,000.

    (c) She has a realized gain of $23,000, the difference between the $23,000 selling price and her basis in the plate of zero.

    (d) She has no realized gain because the receipt of the plate was properly classified as either a gift or de minimis fringe benefit.

7. **As to Marcia's sale of the commemorative plate in question 6, above, which answer best describes the recognition and character of such gain?**

    (a) Because there was no realized gain, there is no recognition of gain. The "character" of such gain, therefore, is moot.

    (b) The realized gain is recognized and will be a long-term capital gain.

    (c) The realized gain is recognized and will be a short-term capital gain.

    (d) The realized gain is recognized and will be a "qualifying 5-year" long-term capital gain.

    (e) The realized gain is not recognized and, therefore, its character is irrelevant.

8. Todd, unlike other employees, did not take good care of his commemorative plate nor treat it as an investment. Rather, Todd used his plate as everyday dinnerware and it soon became scratched and nicked from daily use. In November of this year, Todd sold his "used" plate on an Internet auction site, receiving $14,000 for it. **Most likely Todd:**

    (a) Will have a recognized gain.

    (b) Will have a recognized loss.

    (c) Will have a realized gain which, however, will not be recognized.

    (d) Will have a realized loss which, however, will not be recognized.

    (e) Will have neither a realized nor recognized gain or loss.

9.   Recently, Mark made a "gift" of a parcel of real property to his brother Brian. There was a loan secured by the property, but Brian did not assume it. Rather, Brian took the property "subject to" the loan. At time of the gift to Brian, the amount of the loan was less than the fair market value of the property. There was no gift tax on the transfer. **In order to determine whether Mark realized any gross income from this transfer, which of the following variables must we know?**

       I.   Mark's adjusted basis in the property.
      II.   The fair market value of the property at the time of the gift.
     III.   The amount of the loan on the property.
     IV.   Whether Mark was personally liable on the loan.

(a)   I, II, III and IV.

(b)   I, II, III but not IV.

(c)   I and II only.

(d)   I and III only.

(e)   None of the above responses is correct.

10. **With respect to Brian in question 9, above, which of the following statements is most accurate?**

(a) Because of the broad definition given to gross income, Brian has gross income equal to the value of the real property at the time of the gift. Brian's basis in the real property is equal to the amount of gross income realized as a result of the gift.

(b) Gross income is broadly defined and Brian must include, in gross income, an amount equal to the value of the real property at the time of the gift less the amount of the loan to which he took the property "subject to." This amount of gross income also represents Brian's resulting basis in the real property.

(c) While gross income is broadly defined, Brian has no gross income as a result of his receipt of the real property. Brian's basis in the real property is equal to his brother Mark's basis (or adjusted basis) in the property at the time of the gift.

(d) While gross income is broadly defined, Brian has no gross income as a result of his receipt of the real property. Brian's basis in the real property is equal to the amount of the loan to which he took the property "subject to."

(e) While gross income broadly defined, Brian has no gross income as a result of his receipt of the real property. Brian's basis in the real property is equal to the greater of his brother Mark's basis (or adjusted basis) in the property at the time of the gift, or the amount of the loan to which he took the property "subject to."

Questions 11 through 13 are based on the following facts:

This has been a rather bad year for Dan. In January, he purchased a diamond engagement ring intending to propose marriage to Carol later in the year. In March, the day before proposing to Carol, Dan's apartment was burglarized and the ring was stolen. Unfortunately, there is no chance of its recovery and he was not insured against its loss. He paid $20,000 for the ring in January, and it had increased in value to $25,000 at the time of its theft in March. Undeterred by the theft he proposed, as planned, to Carol. Not only did she say "no," when he returned, dejected, to where his car had been parked, it was not there. An errant, uninsured motorist had plowed into his car pushing it over a railing and into the river below. To make matters worse, Dan's auto insurance had lapsed and he recovered nothing from its loss (there was no salvage value either). Dan had purchased the car, which he used for non-business purposes only, less than six months ago for $30,000 and its value at the time of the accident was $25,000.

11.   **As a result of the foregoing, which of the following statements is most accurate?**

   (a)   Both the theft of the ring and the loss of the car are considered "casualty losses." For casualty loss purposes, the valuation of the losses is $20,000 for the ring and $25,000 for the car.

   (b)   Both the theft of the ring and the loss of the car are considered "casualty losses." For casualty loss purposes, the valuation of the losses is $25,000 for the ring and $30,000 for the car.

   (c)   The theft of the ring is considered a "casualty loss" and its valuation for such purposes is $20,000. The loss of the car does not qualify as a "casualty loss."

   (d)   Both the theft of the ring and the loss of the car are considered "casualty losses." For casualty loss purposes, the valuation of the losses is $25,000 for the ring and $25,000 for the car.

   (e)   Neither the theft of the ring nor the loss of the car constitutes a "casualty loss."

12. **In general, assuming an individual has no "casualty gains," the deduction for personal casualty losses is:**

(a) The correctly determined aggregate amount of the loss, less $100 per casualty.

(b) The correctly determined aggregate amount of the loss, less $100.

(c) The correctly determined aggregate amount of the loss, less $100 per casualty. This result is then deductible only to the extent that it exceeds 7.5% of the taxpayer's adjusted gross income (AGI).

(d) The correctly determined aggregate amount of the loss, less $100. This result is then deductible only to the extent that it exceeds 10% of the taxpayer's adjusted gross income (AGI).

(e) The correctly determined aggregate amount of the loss, less $100 per casualty. This result is then deductible only to the extent that it exceeds 10% of the taxpayer's adjusted gross income (AGI).

13. For this question only, assume that Dan used the car exclusively for business purposes, and that the uninsured loss arising from its plunge into the river occurred when parked while he was attending a business meeting. **Which of the following answers is most accurate in stating the change in income tax consequences, if any, resulting from these changed facts?**

(a) The loss would now qualify as a casualty loss.

(b) Although already qualified as a casualty loss, the amount of loss would equal the adjusted basis (AB) of the car at the time of the loss.

(c) Although already qualified as a casualty loss, the amount of loss would equal the greater of the car's fair market value or its adjusted basis (AB) of the car, both measured at the time of the loss.

(d) Although already qualified as a casualty loss, the determination of the deduction would not require that it exceed any particular percentage of the taxpayer's adjusted gross income (AGI). However, the first $100 of this loss would still not be deductible.

(e) There would be no change in income tax consequences to Dan as a result of these changed facts.

14. In March of last year, Thelma received a "gift" of some shares of XYZ Co. stock from her father, Frank. At the time of the gift, the stock was worth $4,000. This was less than the $5,000 Frank paid for the stock some two years earlier. Frank incurred, and paid, $2,000 in gift taxes on this transfer. By November of last year, these shares had increased in value and Thelma sold them for $6,000. **As a result of Thelma's sale, she realized:**

   (a) A gain of $2,000.

   (b) A gain of $1,000.

   (c) A loss of ($1,000).

   (d) Neither a gain nor loss.

   (e) None of the above responses is correct.

15. A California domiciled husband and wife purchased a vacant parcel of real estate (i.e., raw land) many years ago hoping that it would appreciate in value. Fortunately, the parcel has steadily increased in value over the years, and it is anticipated that it will continue to appreciate in the future. When the first spouse dies, they want the surviving spouse to own 100% of the land. **For income tax purposes, is it better for them to own the property as *community property* (with the first spouse to die devising his/her one-half share to the surviving spouse) or as *joint tenancy* (with right of survivorship)?**

   (a) *Community property* is better because of the "double step-up" in basis pursuant to IRC §§ 1014(b)(6) and 1014(a).

   (b) *Joint tenancy* is better because there will be a gain with respect to the property and the non-recognition of gain/loss rule of IRC § 1041(a) does not apply to joint tenancy.

   (c) *Joint tenancy* is better because the special rule of IRC § 1014(b)(6) does not apply.

   (d) Neither is better – *joint tenancy* and *community property* will produce the same income tax consequences in their situation.

16. A California domiciled husband and wife purchased a vacant parcel of real estate (i.e., raw land) many years ago hoping that it would appreciate in value. Unfortunately, its value has steadily declined over the years and it is not expected to regain its original value. When the first spouse dies, they want the surviving spouse to own 100% of the land. **For income tax purposes, is it better for them to own the property as** *community property* **(with the first spouse to die devising his/her one-half share to the surviving spouse) or as** *joint tenancy* **(with right of survivorship)?**

   (a) *Community property* is better because of the "double step-up" in basis pursuant to IRC §§ 1014(b)(6) and 1014(a).

   (b) *Joint tenancy* is better because there will be a loss with respect to the property and the non-recognition of gain/loss rule of IRC § 1041(a) does not apply to joint tenancy.

   (c) *Joint tenancy* is better because the special rule of IRC § 1014(b)(6) does not apply.

   (d) Neither is better – *joint tenancy* and *community property* will produce the same income tax consequences in their situation.

17. A few years ago, Sean purchased a parcel of raw land for investment purposes. Unfortunately, it did not prove to be a good investment as it declined substantially in value. Sean's mother, Marta, felt sorry for her son and offered to buy the property. While somewhat reluctant, Sean, financially strapped, sold the land to his mother Marta at its then current fair market value (which was substantially less than he originally paid for it). **Which of the following statements best describes the income tax consequences to Sean as a result of this sale to Marta?**

   (a) Sean's loss will not be recognized because the transaction is automatically considered to be a gift.

   (b) Sean's loss will not be recognized because the sale was to his mother.

   (c) Sean's loss will be recognized because it was the sale of investment property.

   (d) Sean's loss will be recognized assuming that Marta did not purchase the property out of a sense of "detached and disinterested generosity."

18. Sean, in question 17, above, owned another undeveloped parcel of raw land that he purchased a few years ago (This was also purchased and held for investment purposes). This property also suffered a substantial decline in value since he purchased it. Sean's brother-in-law Bob (his wife's brother), an individual for whom Sean holds little respect, inquired about the property. While not making false or fraudulent statements about the future prospects for the property, Sean "enhanced" its attributes just a bit. Bob bought the property for its then current fair market value (which was substantially less than Sean originally paid for it). **Which of the following statements best describes the income tax consequences to Sean as a result of this sale to Bob.**

(a) Sean's loss is a recognized capital loss because the property was held for investment purposes.

(b) Sean's loss is not recognized because he sold the property to his brother-in-law.

(c) Sean's loss is recognized, but is an ordinary loss because the property was held for investment purposes.

(d) Sean's loss is not recognized because the property was held for investment purposes and was not the result of a "casualty."

19. Winnie has owned and lived in her house for five years (she purchased it for $300,000). Exactly two years ago, she married Herb and he moved into her house. Unfortunately, the couple divorced exactly one year ago and Herb immediately moved out of the house at that time. Pursuant to their divorce decree, however, Herb was awarded a one-half interest in Winnie's house. Also pursuant to the divorce decree, Winnie continued to live in the house by herself. Today, they each sold their one-half interest in the house to an unrelated buyer for a combined total of $500,000 (Herb and Winnie splitting the proceeds). **Which answer best describes the tax consequences to Winnie and Herb?**

   (a) Each will realize a $100,000 gain. Winnie's gain is fully excluded pursuant to IRC § 121. Herb, however, can exclude only a pro-rata one-half amount of the gain ($50,000) assuming a divorce (moving out and then selling his interest) is considered an "unforeseen circumstance."

   (b) Each will realize a $100,000 gain, and both can exclude all of it pursuant to IRC § 121.

   (c) Each will realize a $100,000 gain, and both can exclude all of it pursuant to IRC § 1041 because the sale was within one year of the divorce.

   (d) Winnie will realize a $200,000 gain, all of which will be fully excluded pursuant to IRC § 121. Herb has no gain because the transfer was incident to divorce.

   (e) Each will realize a $100,000 gain. Winnie can fully exclude her gain pursuant to IRC § 121. Herb, however, must recognize all of his gain even if his divorce (moving out and then selling his interest) is considered an "unforeseen circumstance."

20. In April of this year, Tom sold a diamond Rolex watch for $23,000. He received it as a gift from his aunt in 1990 upon graduating college. Tom's aunt originally paid $18,000 for the watch in 1985, and it had appreciated in value to $21,000 at the time of her gift to Tom. She incurred, and paid, gift taxes of $7,000 with respect to this gift. Tom wore the watch daily (i.e. it was not an investment). **As a result of selling the watch, Tom realized:**

   (a) A loss of $2,000.

   (b) A gain of $4,000.

   (c) A gain of $2,000.

   (d) A gain of $5,000.

   (e) None of the above responses is correct.

Questions 21 and 22 are based on the following facts:

Alicia, a lawyer, makes occasional investments in stocks. In March of last year, she bought 500 shares of XYZ Co. for $10,000. Shortly after buying the stock, it started to decline in value. Thinking that her hopes of rebound would never materialize, she gave up and sold the shares on December 27th of last year for $4,000. Casually discussing XYZ Co. with an investment professional at a party on January 1 of this year, she learned that the company was introducing a new line of products that would turn the company around. While reluctant to get involved with the stock again (it had continued to decline in price since her December sale), on January 5 of this year, she purchased 500 shares of XYZ Co for $3,500. The company experienced a dramatic turnaround and now that her 500 shares are worth $15,000, she is contemplating selling them.

21. **The loss Alicia realized as a result of her December sale of the XYZ Co. shares will:**

   (a) Not be recognized in December when sold but, rather, when, and if, she sells the shares purchased in January of this year.

   (b) Be recognized and because it was a sale of a capital asset, it was a capital loss. However, this capital loss (and any other capital losses recognized) can only be used to offset capital gains for that year, with any excess loss deductible up to $3,000.

   (c) Be recognized because these shares were sold in a year (last year) different from that in which she again purchased the XYZ Co. shares (this year).

   (d) Be recognized because even though she repurchased XYZ Co. shares, she did not have the requisite intent for this to be considered a "wash sale."

   (e) Not be recognized because of her purchase of XYZ Co. stock in January of this year.

22. Assume that Alicia decides to sell her 500 shares of XYZ Co. stock for their current fair market value of $15,000. **For purposes of computing her gain or loss realized from this sale, her adjusted basis (AB) in the stock is:**

   (a) $3,500.

   (b) $4,000.

   (c) $9,500.

   (d) $10,000.

   (e) None of the above answers is correct.

23. Derrick made a gift of highly appreciated shares of stock to his favorite grand-daughter Gail, on the condition that she pay the gift tax resulting from the transfer. Gail gladly did so, as the tax was much less than the value of the shares. **Which of the following statements is most accurate?**

   (a) Derrick's gift to Gail may result in the realization, and recognition, of a gain because he received consideration from Gail.

   (b) Derrick has gross income equal to the amount of the gift tax Gail paid because the gift tax was Derrick's obligation.

   (c) Gail will not be entitled to a deduction for the tax paid because she was not the obligor. Most likely, however, Derrick will be entitled to the deduction.

   (d) Gail is not entitled to exclude any portion of the gift pursuant to IRC § 102 because she is deemed to have paid consideration.

24. Two years ago, Brenda invested a substantial amount of money in the stock market purchasing shares in a large, publicly-traded biopharmaceutical company, paying well over $100 per share for the company's common stock. Recently, the company has been rocked by two major scandals: accounting improprieties that substantially misrepresented the company's financial situations, and the falsification of research and patient data in applications made to the FDA as part of the approval process for major new medications. As a result the company is in shambles and its common stock is currently trading at around 7¢ per share. Financial pundits hold out little hope for the company's long-term viability, and are predicting that sometime next year, the company is likely to file for bankruptcy and will dissolve without paying creditors, and leaving nothing for shareholders. **Which of the following statements is most accurate?**

   (a) Brenda's shares in the company are considered "worthless securities" and this entitles her to an "ordinary" loss deduction.

   (b) Brenda's shares in the company are considered "worthless securities" and this results in her recognition of a long-term capital loss.

   (c) Losing money is a risk of investing and assuming that the financial pundits are correct in their predictions about the company, Brenda is not likely to ever be entitled to any tax benefit if she continues holding onto her shares.

   (d) Losing money is a risk of investing and assuming that the financial pundits are correct in their predictions about the company, Brenda is likely to recognize a long-term capital loss if she continues holding onto her shares.

25.   A couple of years ago, Michael, a dentist, purchased a parcel of raw (vacant) land to hold for investment purposes. He paid $50,000 in cash for it and he has made no improvements to it (and it has remained vacant). Michael's investment strategy proved fruitful, as earlier this year, he sold the land to an unrelated individual for an agreed sales price of $200,000. They agreed that the buyer would pay Michael 10% of the sales price ($20,000) at the time of the sale (which was done), and 10% (or one-tenth) of the sales price each year for the next nine years. The buyer agreed to pay Michael interest, at a fair current market rate, each year on the then unpaid balance. This land was the only investment real estate that Michael owned. **Which of the following statements best describes Michael's recognition of gain resulting from the sale of the land?**

(a) $20,000 of gain will be recognized in the current year, and $20,000 of gain will be recognized in each of the next nine years.

(b)   No gain will be recognized in the current year. Michael will start to recognize gain only after he has received payments (exclusive of interest) totaling his $50,000 cost.

(c) $15,000 of gain will be recognized in the current year, and $15,000 of gain will be recognized in each of the next nine years.

(d)   Michael will recognize all of the gain in the current year, unless he elects to recognize the gain on the installment method over the years in which he receives payments of the sales price.

END OF EXAMINATION QUESTIONS

EXAM VI

FEDERAL INCOME TAX
MULTIPLE-CHOICE OBJECTIVE QUESTIONS
EXAM VI

Questions 1 through 3 are based on the following facts:

In July of last year, Skip, a high-school teacher, sold shares of XYZ Co. stock for $5,000. He says that he did not pay anything for them but, rather, received them as part of a deal for tutoring one of his students on weekends. He provided $4,000 worth of tutoring in early last year, and in April of last year, the student's parent, Paula, a stock market analyst, gave him in exchange 1) these shares of XYZ Co. stock worth $2,700 at the time (Paula originally paid $500 for them a few months earlier) and, 2) her expert stock/investment advice worth $1,300.

1. **Once the "deal" between Skip and Paula was complete, which answer best describes the income tax ramifications, vis-à-vis recognition of income, to both parties as a result of this deal?**

   (a) Neither Skip nor Paula has income from the deal, as it represents a tax-free barter transaction.

   (b) Skip and Paula each has $4,000 of gross income because this is a barter type transaction and both parties have derived $4,000 of financial benefit.

   (c) Skip and Paula each has $1,300 of gross income representing the value of "services" exchanged in this barter transaction.

   (d) Skip and Paula have $4,000 and $1,300 of income, respectively, as compensation from their services. In addition, Paula has a realized gain of $2,200 from the disposition of the stock.

   (e) Skip and Paula have $4,000 and $1,300 of income, respectively, as compensation from their services. Paula has no realized gain from the disposition of the stock because she is merely paying for the extra services.

2. **When Skip sold the shares XYZ Co. stock in July of last year, his realized gain was:**

   (a) $5,000.

   (b) $4,500.

   (c) $2,300.

   (d) $1,000.

   (e) None of the above responses is correct.

3.   **Does the "deal" between Skip and Paula give rise to any possible deductions for purposes of computing taxable income?**

   (a)   No.

   (b)   Yes. Skip has $1,300 of qualifying IRC § 212 expenses for the production of income.

   (c)   Yes. Paula has $4,000 of qualifying IRC § 213 medical care expenses.

   (d)   Yes. Both parties have some deduction: Skip for expenses for the production of income and Paula for childcare.

   (e)   Yes. Both parties have some deduction: Skip for expenses for the production of income and Paula for education expenses.

Questions 4 & 5 are based on the following facts:

Beatrice was the owner/insured of a $100,000 life insurance policy that named her son, Sam, as beneficiary. Sometime before Beatrice's death this year, Sam performed $4,000 worth of legal services for Beatrice for which she agreed to pay him. Instead of paying him in cash, she transferred this life insurance policy (i.e., ownership of the policy) to him which, at the time, was worth $10,000 (her basis in the policy was $5,000). In response to Sam's protests that she gave him too much ($6,000 too much), she told him to consider the extra amount a gift. Subsequent to the transfer of the policy to Sam, he paid one premium payment of $1,000 and shortly thereafter, Beatrice died. Sam recently collected the $100,000 benefit from the insurance company.

4. **Which of the following statements best describes the income tax consequences to Sam when Beatrice transferred the life insurance policy (ownership of the policy) to him?**

   (a) Sam had gross income of $10,000, the value of the life insurance policy at the time of the transfer. This was not a tax-free gift because Sam furnished consideration in the form of his services.

   (b) Sam had no recognition of gross income. The transfer of the policy culminated a transaction that was, in part, a sale and, in part, a gift. Because the consideration Sam was deemed to have paid was less than Beatrice's basis in the policy, the entire value of the policy Sam received constituted a tax-free gift pursuant to IRC § 102.

   (c) Sam had gross income of $4,000, the value of the services that he rendered to Beatrice. The additional value of the policy Sam received was a tax-free gift pursuant to IRC § 102.

   (d) Sam had no recognition of gross income because the value of the services Sam rendered was equal to the amount of consideration that he was deemed to have paid for the policy. The additional value of the policy he received was a tax-free gift pursuant to IRC § 102.

   (e) Sam had gross income of $6,000 representing the difference between the value of the policy and the consideration Sam was deemed to have paid for it.

5. **Must Sam recognize any income with respect to the $100,000 that he received from the insurance company as the policy beneficiary?**

   (a) Yes, he must recognize $4,000 of income – the value of the services performed for Wendy.

   (b) No, the entire $100,000 is properly excluded from income.

   (c) Yes, he must recognize $96,000 of income.

   (d) Yes, he must recognize $95,000 of income.

   (e) None of the above responses is correct.

Questions 6 through 9 are based on the following facts:

Maureen, a single parent, purchased a house in Atlanta ten years ago for $125,000 (paying all cash). Five years ago, when the house's value had increased to $300,000, Maureen took out a $150,000 recourse mortgage loan that was secured by the house. She used this money to purchase a new car and pay off debts unrelated to the house. Shortly thereafter, Maureen was transferred to her employer's Chicago office and moved there, allowing her single adult daughter, Denise, to continue living in the Atlanta home (Denise had been living with her mother since birth). Exactly one year ago, Maureen gave the house to Denise (transferring title to her name by deed). At the time, the house was worth $400,000 and the mortgage, to which Denise took the house subject to, was undiminished at $150,000.

6. **Which of the following statements best describes the income tax consequences to Maureen as a result of her gift to Denise?**

   (a) She is entitled to a deduction for the gift up to the amount indicated in IRC § 2503(b): $10,000 as indexed for inflation.

   (b) Has gross income of $150,000 representing the mortgage taken "subject to" by Denise.

   (c) Has a realized loss of $350,000 representing the difference between the house's fair market value of $400,000 and the $150,000 "consideration" received.

   (d) Has a realized gain of $25,000 representing the difference between the $150,000 "consideration" received and Maureen's $125,000 basis in the house.

   (e) She has no gain or loss realized from the transfer because it represents a tax-free gift to Denise.

7.　Assume for this question only, that today (exactly one year after receiving the house from her mother) Denise sold the house to an unrelated buyer for $450,000 (paying Denise $300,000 in cash and taking it subject to the still undiminished mortgage of $150,000). Also assume, for this question only, that Denise sold the house because she wants to buy a new house located closer to her job (of many years) in downtown Atlanta. **Does Denise have any recognized gain from the sale of this house?**

(a)　Yes. The full amount of her realized gain will be recognized in this situation.

(b)　Yes. She will have to recognize a gain only if, and to the extent, that her realized gain exceeds $250,000.

(c)　Yes. She will have to recognize a gain only if, and to the extent, that her realized gain exceeds $125,000.

(d)　No. Any realized gain is not recognized in this situation.

(e)　No, assuming that her new house cost at least $450,000 and that she purchases (and occupies) it within two years from the sale of her old home.

8.　**Would your answer to question 7, above, be different if Denise sold her house and moved to Phoenix because her doctor told her that to control her increasingly serious bouts with asthma, she had to move to a drier climate?**

(a)　Yes. In this revised scenario she would be entitled to exclude a greater amount of her realized gain.

(b)　Yes. In this revised scenario she would be entitled to exclude a smaller amount of her realized gain.

(c)　No. There would be no difference with respect to gain recognition in this revised scenario.

(d)　Possibly. There may be a difference with respect to gain recognition in this revised scenario depending, in the previous question, on the distances between her old/new homes and her job in Atlanta.

9. For this question only, assume that Maureen never mortgaged the Atlanta house (i.e., there were no loans on the property when she gave it to Denise). Also assume for this question only, that today (exactly one year after receiving the house from her mother) Denise sold the house to an unrelated buyer for $450,000 (paying Denise $450,000 in cash). Finally, for this question only, assume that she sold the house because she is moving to an apartment closer to her job in Atlanta. **Which of the following statements is correct?**

(a) Denise's basis, for purposes of determining gain or loss, is a carryover from that of her mothers. As a result of this, Denise can "tack" (add) on her mother's period of ownership, thereby qualifying for the $250,000 exclusion of gain provided in IRC § 121.

(b) Denise will have to recognize the full amount of her realized gain from the sale. She is not entitled to exclude any portion of the gain because she does not meet the ownership requirement of IRC § 121.

(c) Denise will be entitled to exclude up to $125,000 of any realized gain, but only if, within two years, she purchases (and occupies) a new home costing at least $450,000.

(d) Denise will be entitled to exclude up to $250,000 of any realized gain, but only if, within two years, she reinvests the profit from the sale of her old home in the purchase of a new home.

(e) None of the above statements is correct.

Questions 10 and 11 are based on the following facts:

In July of last year, Tina purchased a piece of fine crystal from her Uncle Jim for $5,000. At the time, this crystal had a true fair market value of $30,000. Jim, who purchased the crystal four years ago for only $4,000 (its fair market value at the time), was originally just going to give it to her, his favorite niece, for nothing. Tina, however, insisted on paying him and he reluctantly agreed. No gift tax resulted from this transfer from Jim to Tina. Jim became furious with her, however, when he found out that to get her hands on some quick cash, she sold the crystal less than a month later and received $28,000 for it.

10. **As to the transfer of the crystal from Jim to Tina in July of last year, which answer best describes the most likely income tax consequences to Tina and Jim?**

    (a)   Jim has a recognized loss of $25,000 because he is deemed to have sold the crystal to Tina. Because Tina cannot consider any portion of this transaction to be a gift, she has income of $25,000 (the difference between the value of the property and the amount that she paid for it).

    (b)   Jim has a realized loss of $25,000, but because this sale was to a related party, it is not recognized. Although Tina furnished consideration, the $25,000 gift element of this transaction is excluded from her gross income.

    (c)   Jim has no recognized gain or loss as a result of this transaction because the substance of the transfer was a gift to Tina. Similarly, Tina can exclude from her gross income the net benefit that she received.

    (d)   Jim has a recognized gain of $1,000 because he is deemed to have sold the crystal to Tina. Although Tina furnished consideration, the $25,000 gift element of this transaction is excluded from her gross income.

    (e)   Jim has a recognized gain of $1,000 because he is deemed to have sold the crystal to Tina. Because Tina cannot consider any portion of this transaction to be a gift, she has income of $25,000 (the difference between the value of the property and the amount that she paid for it).

11. **As a result of Tina's sale of the crystal, she:**

  (a) Has a realized gain of $23,000. This gain is recognized and qualifies as a long-term capital gain.

  (b) Has a realized gain of $24,000. This gain is recognized and qualifies as a long-term capital gain.

  (c) Has a realized gain of $23,000. This gain is recognized and qualifies as a short-term capital gain.

  (d) Has a realized gain of $24,000. This gain is recognized and qualifies as a short-term capital gain.

  (e) Has no realized or recognized gain because the crystal was a gift from Jim.

Questions 12 and 13 are based on the following facts:

Bill, a single individual, earned **$60,000** in wages last year. Other than the four capital gains and losses indicated below, he realized no additional income, nor incurred any deductions for last year. His capital gains and losses for last year were as follows:

Capital **Gains**	Capital **(Losses)**
Short-Term of $5,000	Short-Term of ($8,000)
Long-Term of $16,000	Long-Term of ($18,000)

12. **With respect to the foregoing, which of the following is the most accurate statement?**

  (a) Bill's adjusted gross income (AGI) for last year was $55,000.

  (b) Bill's adjusted gross income (AGI) for last year was 57,000, and there is a net short-term capital loss carryover to this year of $2,000.

  (c) Bill's adjusted gross income (AGI) for last year was 57,000, and there is a net long-term capital loss carryover to this year of $2,000.

  (d) Bill's adjusted gross income (AGI) for last year was $57,000, and there is a net capital loss carryover to this year of $3,000.

13. Continuing on from question 12, above, this year Bill again expects wages of $60,000. During the current year, he sold two automobiles used exclusively for pleasure. Bill sold automobile number <u>one</u> for $7,500 on April 1st. He received automobile number <u>one</u> as an inheritance from his Uncle Fred on March of this year (the day Fred died). Uncle Fred's adjusted basis in the automobile was $8,000 but it was worth only $4,000 on the date of his death. Automobile number <u>two</u> was sold for $3,000 on April 15th. Bill purchased automobile number <u>two</u> five years ago for $6,000. **Assuming that there are no other tax-related items for the current year, Bill's adjusted gross income for this year should be:**

(a) $57,000.

(b) $58,000.

(c) $60,500.

(d) $63,500.

(e) None of the above is correct.

14. Elsa is an employee of an advertising firm. Her job demands require her to travel extensively, by airplane, and her employer pays for all of her travel costs. Elsa is enrolled in a major airline's frequent flyer program, and she has accumulated a huge number of "frequent flyer miles" because of her business trips. Elsa's employer claims no rights to these frequent flyer miles, and Elsa, and all other employees, are free to use them as they wish (i.e., in whatever manner permitted by the frequent flyer program). **Which of the following statements is most accurate?**

(a) Elsa will have gross income when she redeems the frequent flyer miles for non-business related trips. The amount of income will equal the value of the ticket(s) received from the redemption(s).

(b) Elsa will have gross income as the frequent flyer miles are earned because her employer imposes no restrictions on their use.

(c) Elsa will have no gross income resulting in the accrual of frequent flyer miles or in their redemption because taxing such benefits would be in violation of the "Commerce Clause" of the Constitution.

(d) Elsa will have no gross income as the miles are earned, or when she redeems her miles for travel, travel-related in-kind benefits, or other non-cash benefits or services available to her under the frequent flyer plan.

15. Your client, Patrick, is recently divorced and he and his ex-spouse have a written spousal support agreement that is incorporated into their divorce decree (i.e., the court deciding the dissolution accepted their agreement). The agreement calls for Patrick to pay "alimony" to his former wife for a period of ten years, or until she remarries or dies, whichever occurs first. You notice that the alimony amounts vary dramatically with substantially larger amounts payable in the first few years, then declining to a much lower static amount thereafter. **Assuming the couple does not live together, what is the most likely income tax consequence to Patrick upon payment of the amounts stated in the support agreement?**

    (a)   The payments will be fully deductible as alimony because in their state, parties to a divorce are entitled to agree, with the court's acquiescence, on amounts for spousal support.

    (b)   The payments will not be deductible because it appears that he is trying to disguise as deductible alimony, nondeductible transfers of property that are incident to divorce pursuant to IRC § 1041.

    (c)   The payments will be deductible as alimony as long as the amounts in each of the years are considered "reasonable."

    (d)   The payments will effectively not be deductible in full because Patrick must recapture excess alimony pursuant to the provisions of IRC § 71(f).

    (e)   The payments will be deductible as alimony, but only up to the amount that the payments become static in later years.

16. Tami has her own very successful law firm (self-employed as an unincorporated sole proprietorship). On five occasions this year, she has rented a luxury "sky-box" at the FleetCenter (in Boston) for Celtic basketball games. In attendance with her at each game were various clients, and she wants to deduct the cost of the skybox rentals. **Which of the following statements is most accurate?**

    (a)   If the game followed or preceded bona fide business meetings, or if she actually conducted legitimate business during the games, she can deduct 100% of the cost of the tickets (their face amount) for non-luxury box seats.

    (b)   She can deduct 50% of the cost of the rentals assuming the games followed or preceded a bona fide business meeting, or if she actually conducted legitimate business during the games.

    (c)   She cannot deduct any of the costs because these expenditures are, pursuant to IRC § 274, considered unreasonable entertainment expenses.

    (d)   If the games followed or preceded a bona fide business meeting, or if she actually conducted legitimate business during the games, she can deduct 50% of the cost of tickets (their face amount) for non-luxury box seats.

17. Yolanda is a self-employed lawyer in San Diego, California and specializes in entertainment law. She owns a boat that she keeps docked in a local pleasure craft harbor. She uses the boat mostly on weekends and holidays taking existing and prospective clients out for boat trips (usually short, day-trips). She either conducts actual business on these trips or the trips immediately follow or precede a substantial business meeting in her office located within blocks of the harbor. She keeps meticulous records and indicates that she uses the boat 90% of the time for these trips with clients or prospective clients. The remaining 10% of the time, she uses the boat for matters totally unrelated to her business. **Which of the following answers best describe Yolanda's deductible expenditures with respect to the foregoing?**

(a) She will be entitled to deduct 90% of the costs of operating and maintaining the boat including dock rental charges, insurance, and the like. In addition she can take depreciation deductions with respect to 90% of the boat's costs.

(b) She will be entitled to deduct 45% (50% of 90%) of the costs of operating and maintaining the boat including dock rental charges, insurance, and the like. She will not, however, be entitled to any depreciation deductions with respect to the boat.

(c) She will not be entitled to deduct costs associated with this boat or the client trips, as the boat is an "entertainment facility."

(d) She will be entitled to deduct 50% of the costs for food, gas, hired help, and other direct costs associated with the actual client/prospective client trips. She will not, however, be entitled to deduct other operating and maintenance costs, (including dock rental charges, insurance, and the like), or depreciation deductions associated with the boat.

---

18.   Earlier this year, Greg, a plumber, loaned $5,000 to his good friend Tony. This was not a gift, but was a true loan evidenced by a promissory note. Tony indicated that he needed the money to pay some medical bills. Unbeknownst to Greg, Tony had a severe substance abuse problem, and the borrowed funds were quickly depleted on things other than medical bills. Tragically, Tony died within weeks of obtaining the loan from Greg. After Tony's death, it became apparent that no funds were available to repay Greg (or any of Tony's many other creditors). **Given that there is no chance of Greg being repaid any portion of the $5,000 he loaned to Tony, which answer best describes the federal income tax consequences to Greg.**

(a)   Greg is entitled to a $5,000 deduction.

(b)   This loss (a bad debt) is characterized by statute as a short-term capital loss to Greg, and the amount of this loss is limited to $3,000.

(c)   Greg is not entitled to any tax benefit (i.e., a deduction) because this is considered a "nonbusiness bad debt."

(d)   The financial loss Greg suffered is treated as a $5,000 short-term capital loss.

(e)   Greg is not entitled to any tax benefit (i.e., a deduction) because Greg had no "basis" in the debt.

19.   Adjusted Gross Income (AGI) is significant for many reasons. **For what reasons is AGI important?**

I.   The determination of the amounts or availability of deductions allowed in computing AGI itself.

II.   The determination of amounts or availability of exclusions from gross income.

III.   The determination of amounts or availability of deductions allowed from AGI to derive taxable income.

IV.   The determination of self-employment taxes for an unincorporated self-employed individual.

(a)   Items I, II, and III only.

(b)   Items II and III only.

(c)   Items I, II, III, and IV

(d)   Items I and III only.

(e)   None of the above responses is correct

20. Hal and Wanda, a married couple filing a joint return, have *Adjusted Gross Income* (AGI) of $40,000 in 2002. Hal turned 65 years old in September 2002 (Wanda is only 58) and they both have good eyesight. In 2002, they paid real property taxes of $3,900 on their home and $6,950 in prescription drugs (there was no reimbursement by insurance or otherwise for the medicine). **Based on the foregoing, should they *itemize* deductions or take the *standard deduction* for 2002?**

  (a) They can do either because the amount of their *itemized deductions* is equal to their *standard deduction*.

  (b) They should take the *standard deduction* because it is greater than their *itemized deductions*.

  (c) They should choose to take their *itemized deductions* because this amount exceeds their *standard deduction*.

  (d) They should do neither because their total *personal exemption deductions* exceed their *itemized deductions* as well as their *standard deduction*.

Questions 21 through 23 are based on the following facts:

Tammy's only child Chuck, age 12, lives with her (Tammy's husband died almost ten years ago and Tammy has not remarried). Chuck does some acting work in commercials and will earn $5,000 this year. Tammy provides literally all of Chuck's support. Tammy also provides the majority of the support for her unmarried nephew Ned, whose parents tragically died in an accident a few years ago. Ned turned age 20 this year, and he just completed his second year of college (he does not live with Tammy). Ned will earn $5,000 in the current year from a part-time job. Besides the rigors of full-time school, Ned has had a difficult year recuperating from a hit-and-run auto accident. Please assume, for this series of questions, that the inflation-adjusted deduction for a personal exemption is $5,000 or less (e.g., the personal exemption deduction for 2002 is $3,000). All parties are U.S. citizens.

21. **In addition to a deduction for her own personal exemption, Tammy will be entitled to claim:**

   (a) An additional personal exemption deduction for both Chuck and Ned. Chuck qualifies as Tammy's dependent and while his gross income is not less than the exemption amount, he is under the age of 19 at the end of the year. Similarly, Ned qualifies as Tammy's dependent and while his gross income is not less than the exemption amount, he is a full-time student under the age of 24 at the end of the year.

   (b) No additional personal exemption deductions. While Chuck and Ned are Tammy's dependents, she is not entitled to either individual's personal exemption deduction because they both earned too much money.

   (c) An additional personal exemption deduction for Chuck but not for Ned. Chuck qualifies as Tammy's dependent and while his gross income is not less than the exemption amount, he is under the age of 19 at the end of the year. While Ned qualifies as Tammy's dependent, she is not entitled to his personal exemption deduction because Ned is not Tammy's child.

   (d) An additional personal exemption deduction for Chuck but not for Ned. Chuck qualifies as Tammy's dependent and while his gross income is not less than the exemption amount, he is under the age of 19 at the end of the year. Ned does not satisfy the requirements of being Tammy's dependent and, therefore, she cannot claim a personal exemption deduction for him.

   (e) None of the above responses is correct.

22. **Which of the following statements most accurately describes Tammy's probable filing status for the current year?**

   (a)   She qualifies as "head of household" because she is unmarried and has a qualifying dependent in either Chuck or Ned.

   (b)   She qualifies as "head of household" because Chuck is her son.

   (c)   She qualifies as "head of household" only because Chuck qualifies as a dependent and she is entitled to a deduction for his personal exemption.

   (d)   She qualifies as a "surviving spouse" because she was married, and Chuck is her dependent son for whom she is entitled to a deduction for his personal exemption.

   (e)   She qualifies as an "unmarried individual" because of the answer to question 21, above.

23. During the current year, Tammy paid $2,000 in health insurance premiums ($1,000 each for her and Chuck, respectively). In addition, she paid $7,000 of Ned's doctor and hospital costs resulting from his auto accident (he has no insurance and these amounts will not be reimbursed or paid by any other means). **What is the extent of Tammy's qualified medical care expenses for purposes of IRC § 213?**

   (a) $2,000 representing the cost of the health insurance premiums for her and Chuck. The $7,000 paid for Ned's medical costs is not deductible by Tammy because she is not entitled to a deduction for his personal exemption.

   (b) $9,000 representing the total cost of the health insurance premiums plus Ned's medical costs. She is entitled to deduct the health insurance and medical costs for both Chuck and Ned because both individuals qualify as her dependents.

   (c) $1,000 representing the health insurance cost for her alone. The amounts paid for Chuck's health insurance and Ned's medical costs are not deductible because she is not entitled to a personal exemption deduction for either of them.

   (d)   Zero, because the health insurance is not a qualified medical expense and, while Ned's medical costs are qualifying medical care expenses, Tammy is not entitled to deduct them.

   (e)   None of the above responses is correct.

Questions 24 and 25 are based on the following facts:

Robert died in mid January of last year, and is survived by his spouse, Allison. Prior to Robert's death, the couple had consistently filed "joint returns." They had no children and now, at age 86, Allison lives alone (unmarried). Last year, Allison had substantial taxable income and expects the same for the current year.

24. **Which of the following statements most accurately describes Allison's "filing status" for <u>last year</u> for purposes of determining the rate schedule used in computing her tax liability?**

 (a) She can use the rate schedule in IRC § 1(a) for "Married individuals filing joint returns and surviving spouses" because she qualifies as a "surviving spouse" pursuant to IRC § 2(a).

 (b) She must use the rate schedule in IRC § 1(c) for "Unmarried individuals (other than surviving spouses and heads of households)" because marital status is determined as of the last day of the taxable year and Allison was not married at that time.

 (c) She can use the rate schedule in IRC § 1(a) for "Married individuals filing joint returns and surviving spouses" because her husband died in the current year and she had not remarried.

 (d) She must use the rate schedule in IRC § 1(d) for "Married individuals filing separate returns" because income in the year of a spouse's death must be reported separately by the respective spouse.

25. **Assuming Allison does not remarry, which of the following statements most accurately describes Allison's "filing status" for the <u>current year</u> for purposes of determining the rate schedule used in computing her tax liability?**

 (a) She can use the rate schedule in IRC § 1(a) for "Married individuals filing joint returns and surviving spouses" because she qualifies as a "surviving spouse" pursuant to IRC § 2(a).

 (b) She must use the rate schedule in IRC § 1(c) for "Unmarried individuals (other than surviving spouses and heads of households)."

 (c) She can use the rate schedule in IRC § 1(b) for "Heads of households" because although she does not qualify as a "surviving spouse" pursuant to IRC § 2(a), she does meet the requirements of IRC § 2(b).

 (d) She can choose between the respective rate schedules in IRC § 1(a) or 1(b) for "Unmarried individuals (other than surviving spouses and heads of households)" or "Married individuals filing joint returns and surviving spouses."

END OF EXAMINATION QUESTIONS

EXAM VII

FEDERAL INCOME TAX
MULTIPLE-CHOICE OBJECTIVE QUESTIONS
EXAM VII

Questions 1 through 6 are based on the following facts:

Note: This series of questions are year-specific (2002) and are intended to both highlight specific income tax issues and illustrate how the pieces fit together in computing taxable income. In a form uncharacteristic to this professor's objective exams, the correct analysis of some of the following questions requires substantially correct analyses of other questions. [Appendix B, contains relevant, year-specific information applicable to 2002.] This series of questions is easily adaptable to years different than 2002.

Daniel is 22 years old, single, with good eyesight, and a child of Mom. He is also a full-time college student and has gross income of $8,000 in 2002. For 2002, Daniel has no "above the line" deductions for purposes of computing adjusted gross income (AGI), nor does he have any qualifying "itemized" deductions. Mom unequivocally provides more than one-half of Daniel's support. Mom meets the requirements for claiming Daniel as her dependent for the year 2002.

1. **In computing Daniel's taxable income for 2002, to what extent can he deduct his personal exemption deduction of $3,000 (for 2002)?**

    (a) Daniel is entitled to take the full $3,000 deduction, but only if Mom chooses not to take his $3,000 deduction in computing her taxable income.

    (b) Daniel is not entitled to take any portion of the $3,000 deduction regardless of whether Mom chooses to take or not take his $3,000 deduction in computing her taxable income.

    (c) Daniel is entitled to take the full $3,000 deduction because while he is a "dependent" for purposes of IRC § 152, he does not meet the requirements of IRC § 151 allowing Mom to take his deduction in computing her taxable income.

    (d) Daniel is not entitled to take any portion of the $3,000 deduction because he has no "itemized" deductions.

2. Assume for this question only, that all of Daniel's $8,000 of gross income in 2002 is from investment sources (e.g., taxable interest and dividends received). Also assume that Mom will properly claim Daniel as her dependent for 2002 (and claim his personal exemption deduction in computing her taxable income). **For purposes of computing Daniel's taxable income for 2002, Daniel's "standard deduction" will be:**

    (a) $4,700.

    (b) $3,000.

    (c) $750.

    (d) Zero.

    (e) None of the above responses is correct.

3. Assume for this question only, that $2,000 of Daniel's $8,000 of gross income comes from wages ("earned" income), and $6,000 is derived from investment sources (e.g., taxable interest and dividends received). Also assume that Mom will properly claim Daniel as her dependent for 2002. **For purposes of computing Daniel's taxable income for 2002, Daniel's "standard deduction" will be:**

    (a)   Zero.
    (b) $750.
    (c) $2,000.
    (d) $4,700.
    (e)   None of the above responses is correct.

4. Assume for this question only, that all of Daniel's $8,000 of gross income in 2002, is from wages ("earned" income). Also assume that Mom will properly claim Daniel as her dependent for 2002. **For purposes of computing Daniel's taxable income for 2002, Daniel's "standard deduction" will be:**

    (a) $8,250.
    (b) $8,000.
    (c) $4,950.
    (d) $4,700.
    (e)   None of the above responses is correct.

5. Assume the same facts as in question 2, above (i.e., Daniel's $8,000 of gross income is derived solely from investment sources). **Daniel's "taxable income" for 2002 will be:**

    (a)   Zero.
    (b) $300.
    (c) $3,300.
    (d) $7,250.
    (e) $8,000.

6.   Assume for this question only, that Daniel provides all of his own support for 2002 (and Mom, therefore, is not entitled to claim Daniel as her dependent). Also assume, for this question only, that all of Daniel's $8,000 of gross income is from wages. **Daniel's "taxable income" for 2002 will be:**

(a)   Zero.

(b) $300.

(c) $3,300.

(d) $5,000.

(e)   None of the above responses is correct

Questions 7 through 9 are based on the following facts:

Note: This series of questions are year-specific (2002) and are intended to both highlight specific income tax issues and illustrate how the pieces fit together in computing taxable income. In a form uncharacteristic to this professor's objective exams, the correct analysis of some of the following questions requires substantially correct analyses of other questions. [Appendix B, contains relevant, year-specific information applicable to 2002.] This series of questions is easily adaptable to years different than 2002.

Susan and Wally, both age 70, are married, have good eyesight, and file a joint return for 2002. Neither Susan nor Wally receives Social Security benefits. Susan, however, has $10,000 in wages for 2002. In addition, the couple has, in 2002, $20,000 in interest earned on monies deposited in a regular savings account at their local bank. For 2002, the couple has no "above the line" deductions for purposes of computing adjusted gross income (AGI). The couple's cash contributions to qualified charities in 2002 are, in the aggregate, $8,000.

7.   **For purposes of computing the joint "taxable income" for Susan and Wally for 2002, their "standard deduction" will be:**

(a) $7,850.

(b) $8,750.

(c) $9,650.

(d) $10,150.

(e)   None of the above responses is correct.

8. For purposes of computing the joint "taxable income" for Susan and Wally for 2002, their total deduction for personal exemptions will be:

    (a) $3,000.

    (b) $6,000.

    (c) $7,850.

    (d) $12,000.

    (e) None of the above responses is correct.

9. Assuming that the introductory facts to this series of questions represent all possible tax related items for Susan and Wally for 2002, their joint "taxable income" will be:

    (a) $6,350.

    (b) $14,200.

    (c) $14,350.

    (d) $16,000.

    (e) None of the above responses is correct.

10. In 2002, Tammy earned $6,400 in "regular" bank interest and $600 in wages. She had no other income and no IRC § 62 "above the line" deductions or "itemized deductions." Tammy is 20 years old, single, and a full-time student at the University of Oregon. While she lives by herself in an apartment near school, her father unequivocally provides the majority of her support. Her father told Tammy that even if he is entitled to claim her as a dependent in 2002, he will not do so. **Based on this information, Tammy's taxable income for 2002 is:**

    (a) Zero.

    (b) $2,300.

    (c) $6,150.

    (d) $6,250.

    (e) None of the above responses is correct.,

Questions 11 through 25 are based on the following facts:

Note: This is a very comprehensive and difficult series of questions that contain numerous income tax components, all pertinent to the computation of "taxable income." These questions are year specific (2002) and are intended to both highlight specific income tax issues and illustrate how the pieces fit together in computing taxable income. In a form uncharacteristic to this professor's objective exams, the correct analysis of some of the following questions requires substantially correct analyses of other questions. [Appendix

B, contains relevant, year-specific information applicable to 2002.] This series of questions is easily adaptable to years different than 2002.

Tad, a single individual with no children, is 27, and is visually impaired to such a severe degree that he has virtually no eyesight. For the past few years, Tad had been employed by a local law firm, working as a paralegal. In August 2002, Tad left his job to attend an accredited Law School on a full-time basis. He earned $26,000 in wages prior to leaving the law firm. In 2002, he received a $20,000 scholarship covering a portion of his law school tuition for the 2002/2003 academic year (Fall and Spring semesters of his first year). The balance of his tuition for each semester of his first year is $2,000, and he paid for both semesters (i.e., the full $4,000) when he began school in the Fall. Tad paid $6,000, in 2002, for room and board while attending school.

Tad's other expenditures for 2002 are as follows:
- $3,000 in cash contributions to the American Heart Association.
- $ 600 in legitimate, unreimbursed business expenses for Tad's job while he was still employed earlier in the year.
- $1,000 in state income taxes.
- $1,000 in interest on federally sponsored student loans used for his undergraduate tuition.
- $2,000 in "alimony" (meeting all the requirements of § 71(b)) to his ex-wife Nan.
- $ 800 in state "intangibles" taxes (an annual ad-valorem tax on stocks owned).
- $1,600 in veterinary fees for his Seeing Eye dog.
- $ 400 in "over the counter" allergy medicines recommended by Tad's doctor.
- $ 800 in state and local sales taxes.

Even though Tad had been working, his mother, Marlo, has continually been providing most of Tad's support (he had been living with her until he started law school in the Fall of 2002). Notwithstanding the scholarship awarded to Tad, Marlo provided more than one-half of his support for 2002. Marlo doesn't know if she is entitled to claim the personal exemption deduction for Tad for 2002, but she has told Tad that he can take his own exemption deduction even if she is entitled to claim him.

In each of the following questions, please assume that the foregoing represents all of the tax-related items pertaining to Tad for 2002.

11. **Which of the following statements is most accurate in describing Tad's "gross income" for 2002?**

   (a)   The $26,000 of wages is fully included in gross income. The $20,000 scholarship is also fully included in Tad's gross income because law school is not considered education that is "below the graduate level" and, therefore, not excludable as qualified tuition reduction pursuant to IRC § 117(d)

   (b)   The $26,000 of wages is fully included in gross income. The $20,000 scholarship is also fully included in Tad's gross income because law school is considered "graduate" level education and, therefore, not excludable pursuant to IRC § 127.

   (c)   The $26,000 of wages is fully included in gross income. All but $5,250 of the $20,000 scholarship is also included in gross income. While law school is considered "graduate" level education, the 2001 Tax Act extended this IRC § 127 exclusion (maximum of $5,250) to include graduate level courses.

   (d)   The $26,000 of wages is fully included in gross income. One-half of the $20,000 scholarship is also included in Tad's gross income because one-half of the benefit does not relate to the 2002 tax year but, rather, relates to 2003.

   (e)   The $26,000 of wages is fully included in gross income. The $20,000 scholarship is fully excludable from Tad's gross income because "qualified scholarships" for purposes of exclusion under IRC § 117(a) make no distinction between graduate and non-graduate levels of education.

12. **Does the $4,000 Tad paid in tuition, in the Fall of 2002, give rise to an income tax deduction for him in 2002?**

   (a)   No, because Tad's law school education qualifies him to enter into a new trade or business.

   (b)   Yes. Tad is entitled to deduct $3,000 of the $4,000 paid for tuition assuming that his "adjusted gross income" (as defined in IRC § 222(b)(2)(C)) does not exceed a certain level.

   (c)   Yes. Tad is entitled to deduct $2,000 paid for tuition for the Fall 2002 semester assuming that his "adjusted gross income" (as defined in IRC § 222(b)(2)(C)) does not exceed a certain level. No portion of the $2,000 paid that relates to the Spring 2003 semester's tuition is deductible in 2002 because it was paid too far in advance.

   (d)   Yes. The $4,000 will qualify as an IRC § 162 business expense deduction but only if Tad does not use his law degree to enter into a new trade or business.

   (e)   Yes. Tad is entitled to deduct the full $4,000 paid for tuition assuming that his "adjusted gross income" (as defined in IRC § 222(b)(2)(C)) does not exceed a certain level.

13. **Most likely, does the $6,000 that Tad paid in room and board give rise to an income tax deduction for him in 2002?**

   (a)   No, because room and board are not considered "qualified tuition and related expenses."

   (b)   Yes, but only if the law school is located a sufficient distance from his former place of work or residence, so that he is considered traveling "away from home."

   (c)   No, and the $6,000 must be added to his gross income for income tax purposes.

   (d)   No, because room and board do not qualify as excludable as a "qualified scholarship" pursuant to IRC § 117(b).

14. **Does the tuition and room/board that Tad paid result in a potential income tax credit for him in 2002?**

    (a)   Yes, the $4,000 and $6,000 that Tad paid for law school tuition and room/board, respectively, represent qualifying expenses for purposes of determining the "Hope Scholarship Credit."

    (b)   Yes, the $4,000 that Tad paid in law school tuition is a qualifying expense for purposes of determining the "Hope Scholarship Credit."

    (c)   Yes. $2,000 of the $4,000 law school tuition that Tad paid may qualify for the "Lifetime Learning Credit."

    (d)   Yes, the full $4,000 of law school tuition that Tad paid in 2002 may qualify for the "Lifetime Learning Credit."

    (e)   None of the above responses is correct.

15. **Which of the following statements best describes the income tax consequences to Tad with respect to the $1,000 in interest that he paid on his undergraduate student loans?**

    (a)   Tad is entitled to deduct the interest in full because, pursuant to IRC § 163(a), all interest paid on indebtedness is deductible. Since this interest is "personal" in nature, it is deductible "below the line" (from adjusted gross income) as an itemized deduction in computing taxable income.

    (b)   Tad is not entitled to deduct any of this interest, as it is considered "personal interest."

    (c)   Tad may be entitled to deduct some or all of the $1,000 interest pursuant to IRC § 221 depending on whether, and to what extent, his "modified adjusted gross income" (as defined in IRC § 221(b)(2)(C)) exceeds certain statutory amounts. This deduction, to the extent that it qualifies under IRC § 221, is deductible "above the line" in computing adjusted gross income.

    (d)   Assuming that Tad has not been paying interest on the student loans for more than 60 months, he may be entitled to deduct some or all of the $1,000 interest pursuant to IRC § 221. The amount of his deduction, if any, depends on whether, and to what extent, his "modified adjusted gross income" (as defined in IRC § 221(b)(2)(C)) exceeds certain statutory amounts. This deduction, to the extent that it qualifies under IRC § 221, is deductible "above the line" in computing adjusted gross income.

    (e)   Tad may be entitled to deduct some or all of the $1,000 interest pursuant to IRC § 221 depending on whether, and to what extent, his "modified adjusted gross income" (as defined in IRC § 221(b)(2)(C)) exceeds certain statutory amounts. This deduction, to the extent that it qualifies under IRC § 221, is deductible "below the line" (from adjusted gross income) as an itemized deduction in computing taxable income.

16. **To what extent is Tad entitled to income tax deductions in 2002, for the amounts that he paid for state income taxes, state "intangibles" taxes, or state and local sales taxes?**

   (a)   The $1,000 in state income taxes is deductible. Tad is not entitled to a deduction for either the $800 intangibles taxes or the $800 sales taxes that he paid.

   (b)   Tad is entitled to deduct the full amount of all three taxes paid.

   (c)   Tad is not entitled to deduct any portion or any of these three taxes paid.

   (d)   The $1,000 in state income taxes and $800 in state intangibles taxes are both deductible. Tad is not entitled to a deduction for the $800 that he paid in state/local sales taxes

   (e)   The $1,000 in state income taxes and the $800 is state/local sales taxes are both deductible. Tad is not entitled to a deduction for the $800 that he paid in state intangibles taxes.

17. **Which of the following statements is most accurate in describing the deductibility in 2002 for the amounts that Tad paid for veterinary fees (for his Seeing Eye dog) and for his over-the-counter medicines?**

   (a)   The veterinary fees that Tad paid will be considered qualifying medical care expenses, but only if Tad was originally required to pay to acquire the Seeing Eye dog, and such expenditure was deductible as a medical care expense. The over-the-counter allergy medicines are not considered qualified medical care and, therefore, are not deductible.

   (b)   The veterinary fees that Tad paid are considered qualifying medical care expenses and are deductible to the extent that they, combined with any other qualifying medical care expenses, exceed 7.5% of his adjusted gross income (AGI). The over-the-counter allergy medicines are not considered qualified medical care and, therefore, are not deductible.

   (c)   The veterinary fees that Tad paid are not deductible as medical care expenses because they represent medical care expenses for his dog. Deductions are allowed only for expenses for medical care for the taxpayer, the taxpayer's spouse, or the taxpayer's dependent. The Seeing Eye dog does not qualify as Tad's dependent. Additionally, the over-the-counter allergy medicines are not considered qualified medical care and, therefore, are not deductible

   (d)   The veterinary fees that Tad paid are not deductible as medical care expenses because they represent medical care expenses for his dog. Deductions are allowed only for expenses for medical care for the taxpayer, the taxpayer's spouse, or the taxpayer's dependent. The Seeing Eye dog does not qualify as Tad's dependent. Because the over-the-counter allergy medicines were recommended by Tad's doctor, they do qualify as medical care expenses and are deductible to the extent that they, combined with any other qualifying medical care expenses, exceed 7.5% of Tad's adjusted gross income (AGI).

   (e)   The veterinary fees Tad paid are considered qualifying medical care expenses. So, too, are the costs of his over-the-counter allergy medicines because his doctor recommended them. Together, these expenses, combined with any other qualifying medical care expenses, are deductible to the extent that the total exceeds 7.5% of his adjusted gross income (AGI).

18. **Which of the following answers best describes the deductibility of Tad's $3,000 cash contributions that he made to the American Heart Association?**

   (a) Tad is entitled to a $3,000 charitable deduction which is an *above the line* deduction (a deduction from gross income to arrive at adjusted gross income (AGI).

   (b) Tad is not entitled to a charitable deduction because he is Marlo's dependent.

   (c) Tad is entitled to a $3,000 charitable deduction which is a *below the line* deduction, a component of his itemized deductions.

   (d) Tad is not entitled to a charitable deduction because the amount of the charitable contribution most likely exceeds the statutory limitation regarding such contributions.

19. **Does the $600 in expenses that Tad paid in connection with his paralegal job give rise to an income tax deduction for him in 2002?**

   (a) Yes. Tad is entitled to an *above the line* deduction (a deduction from gross income to arrive at adjusted gross income (AGI)) as an IRC § 162 trade/business expense.

   (b) No. Because Tad is attending a program of education (law school) that will qualify him to enter a new trade or business (the practice of law is a different trade or business from that of a paralegal), the $600 does not qualify as a deductible business expense.

   (c) Yes. Tad is entitled to a *below the line* deduction (a deduction from adjusted gross income (AGI) to arrive at taxable income) as an IRC § 162 trade/business expense. However, its actual deductibility, along with other "miscellaneous itemized deductions," is, in the aggregate, subject to a two percent (2%) of adjusted gross income (AGI) nondeductible floor.

   (d) Yes. Tad is entitled to a *below the line* deduction (a deduction from adjusted gross income (AGI) to arrive at taxable income) as an IRC § 162 trade/business expense. This is deductible in full in computing the total amount of Tad's "itemized deductions."

   (e) No. This expenditure does qualify as a business expense deduction and would be considered part of Tad's "itemized deductions." However, Tad is not entitled to benefit from itemized deductions because he is Marlo's dependent.

20. **Is Tad entitled to an income tax deduction in 2002, for the $2,000 in alimony payments that he made to his ex-wife Nan?**

    (a)   Yes, and the $2,000 is deductible as part of "itemized deductions" in computing Tad's taxable income.

    (b)   Yes, and the $2,000 is deductible from gross income in computing Tad's adjusted gross income (AGI).

    (c)   No, assuming that their divorce was more than six years ago.

    (d)   No, unless Tad receives notice that Nan is reporting the $2,000 alimony received as income.

21. **For purposes of computing Tad's taxable income for 2002, he will be entitled to a personal exemption deduction of:**

    (a)   Zero, because Tad is Marlo's dependent and, as such, she is the only person entitled to claim Tad's personal exemption deduction.

    (b) $2,000.

    (c) $3,000.

    (d) $6,000.

    (e) $3,000, but only if Marlo, who is entitled to take Tad's personal exemption deduction, makes an irrevocable election (with her tax return) that she is not the deduction.

22. **For purposes of computing Tad's taxable income for 2002, his "standard deduction" will be:**

    (a)   The greater of: 1) $750, or 2) the amount of Tad's "earned income" plus $250. This is a special standard deduction limitation applicable to persons who are *dependents* of another.

    (b) $4,700, but only because applying the special standard deduction limitation applicable in this case (because Tad is Marlo's dependent), results in an amount greater than the regular standard deduction for a single person.

    (c) $4,700.

    (d) $5,600

    (e) $5,850.

23. **Based upon the above information, and assuming that deductions are taken whenever possible (even if it means forgoing a possible tax credit), Tad's "adjusted gross income" (AGI) for 2002 is:**

   (a) $20,000

   (b) $23,000

   (c) $24,000

   (d) $26,000

   (e) None of the above responses is correct.

24. **Based upon the above information, and assuming that deductions are taken whenever possible (even if it means forgoing a possible tax credit), Tad's "taxable income" for 2002 is:**

   (a) $18,150

   (b) $17,000

   (c) $11,150

   (d) $10,000

   (e) None of the above responses is correct.

25. For this question only, assume that in 2002, Tad incurred costs for doctor visits. Further assume for this question that Tad's mother, Marlo, paid for these costs and that they were not reimbursed by insurance or otherwise. **Is Marlo entitled to a deduction with respect to these medical costs that she paid on Tad's behalf?**

   (a) Yes, because Tad is her dependent.

   (b) No, because Tad is not her dependent.

   (c) Yes, regardless of whether or not Tad is Marlo's dependent, because she paid for the medical costs.

   (d) No, because Marlo is not entitled to claim Tad's *personal exemption deduction* in computing her taxable income.

END OF EXAMINATION QUESTIONS

EXAM VIII

FEDERAL INCOME TAX
MULTIPLE-CHOICE OBJECTIVE QUESTIONS
EXAM VIII

1. Robert succumbed to cancer five years ago (at age 36) and was survived by his spouse, Tiffany (now age 40). Tiffany has not remarried and lives alone (she and Robert had no children). In the current year (2002) Tiffany expects to have "taxable income" of $100,000. **Assuming Tiffany does not remarry during 2002, her "regular" federal income tax liability for 2002 (ignoring any potential additional taxes and before any tax credits) will be approximately:**

    (a) $20,796.

    (b) $30,000.

    (c) $22,105.

    (d) $24,315.

    (e)   None of the above responses is correct.

2. The Economic Growth and Tax Relief Reconciliation Act of 2001 (the "2001 Tax Act"), which was signed into law in 2001, made numerous changes in tax law. **As to the income tax rate structure for individuals, the 2001 Tax Act:**

    (a)   Introduced a new 10% tax bracket starting in 2001, and "phases-in," over a period of years, reductions to all other existing tax rates.

    (b)   Introduced a new 10% bracket starting in 2001 that replaces, in whole, the 15% tax bracket (the lowest tax bracket prior to enactment of the 2001 Tax Act).

    (c)   Introduced a new 10% tax bracket starting in 2002, and "phases-in," over a period of years, reductions to all other existing tax rates.

    (d)   Retains the 15% tax rate bracket without reduction to the rate in future years, but does, for certain taxpayers, eventually "phase-in" a substantial widening of this bracket.

    (e)   More than one of the above responses is correct.

3.   The Economic Growth and Tax Relief Reconciliation Act of 2001 (the "2001 Tax Act"), which was signed into law in 2001, made numerous changes in tax law. **Which of the following responses best describes the effect of the "sunset provision" which is part of the 2001 Tax Act?**

(a)   Unless affirmatively changed by Congress and enacted into law, all changes made and provisions enacted by the 2001 Tax Act will disappear after December 31, 2010, and tax laws will revert to their status immediately prior to the enactment of the 2001 Tax Act.

(b)   All changes made and provisions enacted by the 2001 Tax Act will disappear after December 31, 2010, and tax laws will revert to their status immediately prior to the enactment of the 2001 Tax Act. This, however, will only occur if certain budget deficit thresholds are reached. Otherwise, the 2001 Tax Act provisions will automatically become permanent.

(c)   Unless affirmatively changed by Congress and enacted into law, the changes made by the 2001 Tax Act as they relate only to income tax rates, will disappear after December 31, 2010, and will revert to their status immediately prior to the enactment of the 2001 Tax Act. The "sunset clause" does not affect other changes made and provisions enacted by the 2001 Tax Act.

(d)   It is an example of Congress's bipartisan poetic expression that is rarely incorporated into law. It describes the beauty and soft tranquil glow of a late summer's day when the sun gently slips below the horizon, and all is well with the world.

4.   Irv and Lorraine are married, file a joint income tax return, and are both 68 years old. They are wonderful people, enjoy life and are fortunate to have substantial amounts of income (in excess of $500,000 per year). They have no deductible expenditures to speak of with the exception of charitable contributions of approximately $30,000 per year. They also have no dependents. **Which of the following statements best describes their "personal exemption" deduction(s)?**

(a)   They are entitled to a total of four (4) personal exemption deductions in computing taxable income because of their age.

(b)   They are entitled to a total of two (2) personal exemption deductions in computing their taxable income.

(c)   While they are seemingly entitled to a total of two (2) personal exemption deductions, the aggregate amount of such deductions for the foreseeable tax years will most likely be zero.

(d)   While they are seemingly entitled to a total of four (4) personal exemption deductions, the aggregate amount of such deductions for the foreseeable tax years will most likely be zero.

(e)   While seemingly they are entitled to a total of two (2) personal exemption deductions, the amounts of such deductions will most likely be zero for tax years up through, and including, the year 2005.

5.   As indicated in question 4, above, Irv and Lorraine have approximately $30,000 of qualified charitable contributions. **Which of the following statements best describes to what extent that they will be entitled to a deduction for such qualified charitable contributions?**

(a)   Charitable contributions are deductible, and if this is the couple's only deductible expenditure, they will have approximately $30,000 in *itemized deductions* that are allowed as a deduction in computing their *taxable income*.

(b)   Charitable contributions are deductible, and if this is the couple's only deductible expenditure, the couple's total *itemized deductions* will be substantially less than $30,000.

(c)   The couple, in this situation, is not entitled to any deduction vis-à-vis their charitable contributions.

(d)   Their charitable contributions will give rise to an *above the line* deduction in computing their adjusted gross income (AGI).

6. **Notwithstanding any potential limitations, if a taxpayer has a choice of a tax deduction or a tax credit, of equal amounts, which is usually more beneficial to the taxpayer for income tax purposes?**

    (a)   Neither is more beneficial as a tax deduction and a tax credit are both equally beneficial to a taxpayer.

    (b)   A tax credit is more beneficial than a tax deduction because the former represents a dollar-for-dollar reduction of tax liability.

    (c)   A tax deduction is more beneficial than a tax credit because the former reduces taxable income.

    (d)   A tax credit is more beneficial than a tax deduction because the former represents taxes that the taxpayer has already paid which, if the total exceeds the tax liability, will be refunded.

7. There are numerous "tax credits" available to qualifying individuals. Two such credits are the "earned income credit" and the "lifetime learning credit." **Which of the following statements is most accurate regarding these two credits?**

    (a)   The *earned income credit* and the *lifetime learning credit* are "refundable" and "nonrefundable" credits, respectively.

    (b)   The *earned income credit* and the *lifetime learning credit* are "nonrefundable" and "refundable" credits, respectively.

    (c)   Both the *earned income credit* and the *lifetime learning credit* are "refundable" credits.

    (d)   Both the *earned income credit* and the *lifetime learning credit* are "nonrefundable" credits.

8. Baxter is a single parent with one child, Celia age 5. Celia lives with Baxter. He works full-time and in order to work, he needs someone to look after Celia. On many days, Baxter's mother, Monica, takes care of Celia (at no charge). Other days, Baxter pays an unrelated individual to come to his home to look after Celia. Celia is Baxter's dependent (and he is entitled to claim her "personal exemption deduction" in computing his taxable income). **Most likely, is Baxter entitled to some tax benefit for the payments he makes for Celia's childcare?**

    (a)   No, assuming that Baxter's adjusted gross income (AGI) exceeds a certain amount.

    (b)   Yes, but only if Celia's health is such that "taking care of" or "looking after" her requires some degree of medical care.

    (c)   Yes, he will be entitled to a "childcare" credit regardless of the amount of his adjusted gross income (AGI).

    (d)   No. Childcare is a nondeductible personal expense pursuant IRC § 262.

9. Gerri, a single parent, has three young children living with her. Their respective ages are 10 months, 2 years, and 4 years. In order for Gerri to be able to work full-time, during working hours her children are cared for in a full-service state licensed day care facility. In the current year, Gerri estimates that her costs for the day care will be $4,000 per child. Gerri estimates that her adjusted gross income (AGI) for the current year will be $45,000. All three of Gerri's children are her dependents (and she is entitled to claim their *personal exemption deductions* in computing her taxable income). Please assume that "the current year" is 2002 or later. **Most likely, Gerri's childcare tax credit pursuant to IRC § 21 will be:**

    (a) $2,400.

    (b) $2,100.

    (c) $1,800.

    (d) $1,200.

    (e) None of the above responses is correct.

10. This year (assume the year 2002 or later) Sonia adopted a healthy two-year-old baby boy, Adam. She incurred, and paid, significant costs associated with this adoption including adoption fees, court costs and attorney fees. **Is Sonia entitled to an income tax credit with regard to this adoption?**

    (a) Yes, assuming that Sonia's income does not exceed a certain amount, she may be entitled to a tax credit for the adoption related costs that she paid up to $10,000 (indexed for inflation after 2002).

    (b) No, because the adoption tax credit expired at the end of 2001, except for adoptions of "special needs" individuals.

    (c) Yes, assuming that Sonia's income does not exceed a certain amount, she may be entitled to a tax credit for the adoption related costs that she paid up to $5,000.

    (d) No, because adoption costs do not give rise to a tax credit. However, if Sonia's employer paid or reimbursed her for her adoption related costs, she may be entitled to exclude some or all of these amounts from her gross income.

11. Justin, a single individual age 38, wants to set up a "traditional" Individual Retirement Account (IRA) because he read in a magazine that they can produce some nice income tax benefits. He is currently working in the production department of a major entertainment company and he is covered by the company's pension/retirement plan (the company makes contributions to this plan on his behalf and he can make voluntary contributions to the plan). Justin makes a fair amount of money from his job but he also makes substantial alimony payments to his ex-wife Ellen (the alimony payments qualify as deductions for Justin). **If Justin makes contributions to a "traditional" IRA, which of the following statements best describes Justin's current income tax benefits?**

(a) Because he is a participant in his company's pension/retirement plan, he is not entitled to any deduction for contributions made to a "traditional" IRA.

(b) He may be entitled to some deduction for contributions to a "traditional" IRA depending on his amount of adjusted gross income (AGI). In this regard, his alimony payments will be beneficial to him.

(c) He may be entitled to some deduction for contributions to a "traditional" IRA depending on his amount of adjusted gross income (AGI). His alimony payments are irrelevant for purposes of this question.

(d) He will be entitled to a deduction (within certain limits) for his contributions to a "traditional" IRA. The fact that he is a participant in another pension/retirement plan is no longer a relevant factor in determining the deductibility of such contributions.

12. Ellen, Justin's ex-wife in question 11, above, is also considering establishing an Individual Retirement Account (IRA) for her. She receives approximately $15,000 per year in alimony (includible in her gross income pursuant to IRC § 71) and has minimal earnings of $1,500 from a part-time job. She does have other sources of income such as rental income, interest and dividends. She is 42 years old and has no interest in any company retirement or pension plan. Assume for this question that the year is 2003, and that Ellen wants to make a contribution to a "traditional" IRA up to the maximum amount allowed. **Most likely, how much of a deduction will she be entitled to as a result of this contribution?**

(a) $3,000.

(b) $1,500.

(c) $3,000 or less depending on the amount of her adjusted gross income (AGI).

(d) Zero because Ellen is not a full-time employee.

13. Lucinda, a lawyer, purchased a single-family residence about four years ago. She has always held this property as an investment, renting it to individuals unrelated to her. This property has produced a net profit every year even after deducting the allowed amount of depreciation expense. Lucinda sold the property this year for a substantial gain. **Which of the following statements is most accurate?**

   (a)   Lucinda's entire recognized gain from this sale will be considered "ordinary income" because the house was investment residential real estate.

   (b)   Lucinda's entire recognized gain from this sale will be considered a "long-term capital gain" because this was investment residential real estate.

   (c)   Assuming Lucinda made no special elections regarding depreciation for this property, it is likely that a portion of her recognized gain will be treated as "ordinary income." The balance of the gain will qualify as a "long-term capital gain."

   (d)   Because this property was a single-family residence, Lucinda will likely be able to exclude (not recognize) some or all of the gain resulting from its sale. Any recognized portion will qualify as a "long-term capital gain."

14. Lucinda, in problem 13, above, practices law as an unincorporated sole proprietor (a.k.a., self-employed or an independent contractor). A few years ago, she purchased some furniture, and has been taking depreciation deductions with respect to such property. Lucinda recently sold this furniture and, much to her surprise, she sold it for more than she originally paid for it. **Which of the following statements is most accurate?**

   (a)   If she utilized an allowed "accelerated" method of depreciation regarding the property, then a portion of the total amount of depreciation deductions taken will be "recaptured" as "ordinary" income.

   (b)   She is not required to recapture any amount of her gain as "ordinary" income because she is operating her business as an unincorporated sole proprietorship.

   (c)   Notwithstanding any "deprecation recapture" provisions, all of her gain is ordinary income because the furniture is business property.

   (d)   The total amount of her depreciation deductions taken with respect to the furniture will be "recaptured" as "ordinary" income.

15. Colleen is a full-time law professor at an accredited law school. She teaches classes in Torts and Constitutional Law. She has an office at the law school (with unrestricted use thereof), but she finds it more convenient to do much of her class preparation and research work while at home. At home, she uses the family computer that is located in the family/TV room to do much of her online research and some of her work. To do her class preparations and most of her writing, she uses her laptop computer, most often in her (and her husband's) bedroom because she finds it to be a comfortable and generally quiet place to work. One of Professor Colleen's colleagues, who also conducts a lot of his work at home, says that he takes income tax deductions for a portion of his household operating expenses. He claims that these are business expenses for an "office" in his home. Professor Colleen rents the home in which she, and her family, are living, and wonders if she is entitled to deduct a portion of her rent, and other operating costs associated with the house, as a business expense because she performs so much of her job-related work there. **Most likely, will Professor Colleen be entitled to do so?**

(a) No, but only because she does not use a specific portion of the residence exclusively for business purposes.

(b) Possibly. Assuming that she carefully documents the time spent working on job-related matters, she may be entitled to business deductions relating to the operating costs of her residence.

(c) No, but only because her working at home is not for the convenience of her employer.

(d) Yes, assuming that she can adequately show that her working at home is for the convenience of her employer, notwithstanding that it may also be convenient for her too.

(e) No, the circumstances of her work habits at home, the nature of her work, and that working at home is for her convenience are enough to preclude business deductions for any portion of her rent or other operating costs of her home.

16. **In general, is the "alternative minimum tax" (AMT) a good thing for individual taxpayers?**

    (a) Yes, it is a special provision that, for some taxpayers, generates a smaller amount of income tax liability when compared with a regularly computed income tax liability.

    (b) No, it is a special provision that, for some taxpayers, generates a greater amount of income tax liability when compared with a regularly computed income tax liability.

    (c) Yes, but only if a "qualified" individual makes an affirmative election to this alternative method of tax computation.

    (d) No, but in rare situations, a "qualified" individual will elect this alternative method of computing tax because it can have a beneficial impact to certain "non-tax" matters.

17. Last year, Victor paid substantial hospital costs following a serious illness. These costs were not covered by insurance. Last year tax-wise, Victor had substantial "taxable income" resulting in an income tax liability. After discovering errors in their accounting software and reviewing all patient accounts, the hospital discovered that they had overcharged Victor. This year, Victor received a refund from the hospital in the amount overcharged. **Does this refund represent gross income to Victor this year?**

    (a) Yes, but only if, and to the extent by which, Victor benefited from a medical deduction last year. This would be the amount by which his qualifying medical care expenses exceeded 7.5% of his adjusted gross income (AGI).

    (b) Yes, but only if, and to the extent by which, Victor benefited from "itemizing" deductions last year. This would be the amount, if any, that his total allowed itemized deductions exceeded his standard deduction.

    (c) Yes, but only if, and to the extent by which, Victor benefited from a medical deduction last year. This would be the amount by which his qualifying medical care expenses exceeded 7.5% of his adjusted gross income (AGI), and then only if, and to the extent by which, his total allowed itemized deductions exceeded his standard deduction.

    (d) No, none of the refund represents income to Victor in the current year. Rather, he must go back and amend his income tax return for the prior year to reflect the corrected amount of qualifying medical expense.

    (e) It may represent income to Victor in the current year. He has a choice of either 1) reporting it as income in the current year to the extent that he benefited from the deduction in the prior year, or 2) amending his income tax return for the prior year to reflect the corrected amount of qualifying medical care expense.

18. Elaine has, for the past eight years, filed individual income tax returns in a timely manner (at least one month before the April 15th due date), and paid what she believed was the correct amount of tax in each of these years. Now a second year law student enrolled in a federal income tax course, Elaine learned, for the first time, about the education related "hope" and "lifetime learning" credits. She now realizes that she could have taken advantage of these credits in prior years to reduce her tax liabilities. **Can Elaine do anything to take advantage of these missed opportunities?**

   (a) No. Any tax benefits are available only for the appropriate years and she cannot receive the benefit of them in the current year.

   (b) Yes. Elaine can file amended income tax returns for prior years to claim the benefits and receive refunds resulting therefrom.

   (c) Yes. Elaine can claim these credits in her current year's income tax return as long as they were not claimed in income tax returns for prior years.

   (d) Yes. Elaine can file amended income tax returns (and claim any appropriate tax benefit) for any of her returns that were filed within the past three years.

   (e) Yes. Elaine can file amended income tax returns (and claim any appropriate tax benefit) for any years' returns where the due date for filing such returns was within the last three years.

19. Terrance's income tax return for last year was audited and the I.R.S. has assessed a deficiency (i.e., additional tax owed). Terrence does not agree with the I.R.S.'s position but has been unable to resolve this controversy with the I.R.S. **Assuming that he has exhausted all possible means of appealing the assessment with the I.R.S., which of the following courts are available to him for purposes of resolving the issue?**

   I. The U.S. Tax Court.
   II. The U.S. District Court for the jurisdiction in which Terrance resides.
   III. A U.S. District Court in a jurisdiction other than that in which Terrance resides.
   IV. The U.S. Court of Federal Claims.
   V. The U.S. Court of Appeals for the jurisdiction in which Terrance resides.

   (a) I, II & IV only.

   (b) I only.

   (c) I and IV only.

   (d) I and V only.

   (e) None of the above responses is correct.

20. **If Terrance, in question 19, above, wants to have his issue resolved in court, must he first pay the proposed I.R.S. assessment before bringing the action?**

   (a) Yes.

   (b) No.

   (c) Yes, but only if he wishes to, and can, bring the action in the U.S. Tax Court.

   (d) No, but only if he wishes to, and can, bring the action in the U.S. Tax Court.

21. **On March 3, 1791, the government of the United States first exercised its power to tax as a means of collecting revenue through the imposition of a tax on:**

   (a) Real estate.

   (b) Income.

   (c) Distilled spirits and stills.

   (d) Carriages.

22. **The federal income tax was first actually imposed upon individuals via the:**

   (a) 16th Amendment.

   (b) Article 1, § 8 of the Constitution.

   (c) Article 1, § 9 of the Constitution.

   (d) Revenue Act of 1913.

23. Congress has just passed a law whereby income taxes for the current year will be assessed according to income earned in prior years. Betty, a taxpayer, is upset by this new law and would like to challenge the retrospective manner through which taxes will be imposed. **Her best argument and the likely result would be:**

   (a) Betty can argue that this law violates her 5th Amendment Due Process rights, and she will most likely lose.

   (b) Betty can argue that this law violates her 5th Amendment Due Process rights, and she will most likely prevail.

   (c) Betty can argue that this law violates the 16th Amendment because taxes are limited to income earned in the current tax year, and she will most likely prevail.

   (d) Betty can argue that this law violates the 16th Amendment because Congress cannot modify the current tax structure, and she will most likely prevail.

24. Dave has earned income through various illicit sources and does not report it on his tax return. **Once caught, his best argument and the likely outcome in any pending litigation would be:**

    (a) Dave could argue that such disclosure would violate his 5th Amendment right against self-incrimination, and he will most likely prevail.

    (b) Dave could argue that such disclosure would violate his 5th Amendment right against self-incrimination, and he will most likely lose.

    (c) Dave could argue that such disclosure violates the 16th Amendment since income derived through such means is not included in tax calculation, and he will most likely prevail.

    (d) Dave could argue that such disclosure is not specifically required by state law and is therefore unnecessary. Dave will most likely prevail.

25. **Critics of a consumption based tax, in place of or augmenting the current income tax, argue that it:**

    (a) Lacks administrative simplicity.

    (b) Does not promote fairness since it is regressive.

    (c) Will cause unnecessary litigation.

    (d) Will encourage tax evasion.

END OF EXAMINATION QUESTIONS

**ANSWER KEY
EXAM I**

1.   **The best answer is (c).** Melinda will be required to recognize income because of her personal use of the company owned Ferrari. She has derived a net economic benefit that is not excludable from her gross income.

IRC § 61 defines gross income as "all income from whatever source derived." From your initial study of gross income's scope, you probably found it to be broadly defined, including the taxpayer's receipt of some net economic benefit or net accession to wealth. In class, you also discover that gross income is also not limited to the receipt of cash. [Reg. § 1.61-1(d) (compensation received in forms other than in cash).] Is Melinda receiving a net economic benefit from ABC vis-à-vis the use of the Ferrari? The answer is yes. She has been given the free use of the automobile, the value of which can easily be determined based on a fair rental or lease rate for the car. Barring any specific income exclusion provisions, Melinda has gross income.

But wait, isn't Melinda merely using her own automobile? Gross income does not go so far as to impute income to one's own use of assets. For example, when you live in your own house, you are <u>not</u> required to assign a fair rental value to such use and include it in your gross income for income tax purposes. In effect, isn't this the situation with Melinda? Technically the corporation (ABC) owns the vehicle, but Melinda *is* the corporation, owning 100% of it. Unfortunately for Melinda, the "technical" fact that the corporation is the owner of the automobile <u>cannot</u> be ignored. Melinda's wholly owned corporation *is* a person or entity that is separate and distinct from Melinda for income tax purposes. [*Dean v. Comm'r*, 187 F.2d 1019 (3rd Cir.1951).] For purposes of this question, ABC could just as well be any other corporation, one in which Melinda has no ownership interests. When an employer provides an employee with "in-kind" economic benefits, their value nonetheless represents income. While certain employer-provided "fringe benefits" are excludable from income, these excludable benefits do not include the full-time personal use of an automobile.

While not one of the answers to this question, Melinda's gross income could alternatively be viewed as income in the form of a dividend as she is the sole shareholder of ABC.

Answer (a) is incorrect because this does not represent an excludable fringe benefit to Melinda. Please see other questions in this book dealing with excludable fringe benefits. **Answer (b) is incorrect** because, as discussed above, Melinda's corporation is treated as a separate person or entity for income tax purposes. **Answer (d) is incorrect** because it is Melinda's current personal "use" of the car that is a net economic benefit to her and, therefore, represents gross income.

- **Additional references:** See DANIEL Q. POSIN, FEDERAL INCOME TAXATION OF INDIVIDUALS ¶¶ 1.02(2), 2.01 (5th ed. 2000).

2. **The best answer is (a).** IRC § 61 defines gross income as "all income from whatever source derived." From your initial study of gross income's scope, you probably found it to be broadly defined, including the taxpayer's receipt of some net economic benefit or net accession to wealth. In class, you also discover that gross income is also not limited to the receipt of cash. Tricia, the undisputed owner of the "treasure trove," has derived an economic benefit and the value of the property $6,000, represents income to her.

The Regulations specifically identify as income: "Treasure trove, to the extent of its value in United States currency, constitutes gross income for the taxable year in which it is reduced to undisputed possession." [Reg. 1.161-14(a)]

Answer (b) is incorrect because she has, as discussed above, income in the current year. **Answer (c) is incorrect** because gross income is more broadly defined than the definition given in this answer. **Answer (d) is incorrect** because, as indicated above, it was not until the current year that the coins were "reduced to undisputed possession."

- **Additional references:** *See* DANIEL Q. POSIN, FEDERAL INCOME TAXATION OF INDIVIDUALS ¶¶ 2.01, 3.13(3) (5th ed. 2000).

3. **The most likely correct answer is (c).** Interest received is included in income unless there is a specific provision granting an exclusion from income. Of the three sources of John's interest, only the interest from the Maine bond is excludable from gross income. IRC § 103(a) excludes, from income, interest from state and local bonds. Commonly, this is referred to as tax-free state or municipal (or "muni") bond interest. Interest from such bonds is not excluded from gross income, however, if the state or local bond is either not issued in registered form, is a "private activity" or "arbitrage" type of bond (John's Maine bond is none of these types).

EXCEPTIONS

Interest from obligations of the United States is generally fully includible in gross income. This is sometimes the source of confusion among students. While not the subject of this book, interest from U.S. obligations is generally excluded from income for state and local income tax purposes (for those states, counties or cities imposing an income tax). Also not at issue in this problem is IRC § 135 that provides for a very limited and narrow exclusion of certain interest received by certain individuals from Series EE U.S. Savings Bonds, the proceeds of which are used for certain education purposes.

The interest that John receives from his Swiss bank account is, most likely, also included in his gross income for U.S. income tax purposes. U.S. citizens and U.S. residents are taxed (for U.S. income tax purposes) on a "world-wide" basis. Simply put, this means that such individuals must include in gross income, unless otherwise excludable, all income regardless of its geographic source. Gross income includes "all income from whatever source derived." [IRC § 61(a).] There are a limited number of special situations for certain taxpayers, earning certain types of income in certain foreign countries. It is extremely unlikely that any such exception would apply to John given our facts.

Answers (a), (b), (d), and (e) are all incorrect because none reflects the correct combination of taxable interest.

- **Additional references:** *See* DANIEL Q. POSIN, FEDERAL INCOME TAXATION OF INDIVIDUALS ¶ 2.01 (5th ed. 2000).

4. **Answer (e) is the most accurate.** Paul will have to recognize all but $15,000 of the award amount (i.e., he must recognize $85,000 in gross income). Because this was not a "physical" tort, Paul can only exclude the $15,000 representing the amount of the award allocated to cover his actual medical costs.

Students universally dislike "none of the above" answers and are justified in doing so. They do provide, however, a powerful testing tool for professors and, in this case, none of the answers provided in (a) through (d) are correct. The "bottom line" correct numeric answer for this question is that Paul would have to recognize $85,000 of income or, to put it another way, he would be entitled to exclude from income $15,000 of the $100,000 received. This question involves the exclusion of "compensation for injuries or sickness" provided in IRC § 104. This section has a long, complex and capricious past vis-à-vis what is within its umbrella of exclusion. In its most basic form, an individual receiving damages, by award or settlement, for physical injuries or physical sickness can exclude such amounts from income. [IRC § 104(a)(2).] In its current form (reflecting changes made by the "Small Business Job Protection Act of 1996"), this section generally excludes amounts received (other than punitive damages) for <u>physical tort</u> awards and settlements. In the body of IRC § 104(a), the law indicates that "emotional distress shall not be treated as a physical injury or physical sickness." At this point, it would appear that Paul would have to include the entire $100,000 received because his cause of action was that of emotional distress. However, the section goes on to effectively say that the recipient can <u>exclude</u> the amount of damage award/settlement that is payment for his/her costs of actual medical care attributable to the emotional distress. In our question, $15,000 of Paul's settlement was to cover his hospital costs and, therefore, representing the only portion of the settlement that is excludable from income.

[handwritten margin note: emotional distress doesn't count unless there are physical manifestations]

Do not fall into the trap of trying to "bootstrap" this section's exclusion application to awards/settlements emanating from an emotional distress cause of action because the plaintiff's emotional distress manifests itself into an actual physical injury.

The difficulty of questions involving IRC § 104 can vary dramatically depending on how thoroughly one's professor covers the exclusion as to its history, policy foundations, and the like. This is a good area of tax law for in-depth class analysis, so take this into consideration when addressing questions involving the subject. Much of this Code section's history centered on the breadth of this exclusion with, at varying times, exclusions allowed for damages received from non physical tort or "tort type" causes of action, and punitive damages.

Answers (a), (b) and (c) are incorrect because each of these answers, in varying degrees, incorrectly brings within the scope of the IRC § 104(a)(2) exclusion, amounts received that arose from a "non-physical" injury/sickness. **Answer (d) is incorrect** because it fails to recognize the limited exclusion for the portion of Paul's emotional distress based settlement identified to repay him for his actual medical expenses.

- **Additional references:** See DANIEL Q. POSIN, FEDERAL INCOME TAXATION OF INDIVIDUALS ¶ 3.11(2) (5th ed. 2000).

5.   **The correct answer is (a).** The receipt of a scholarship is clearly a financial benefit that, but for some specific exclusion, would be included in a taxpayer's gross income under the broad definition thereof. IRC § 117 excludes, from income, "qualified scholarships." In general, amounts received as a scholarship, scholarship grant or fellowship grant are excluded from income to the extent that they are used for tuition and fees required for enrollment, or for fees, books, supplies, and equipment required for courses. [IRC §§ 117(a) and (b).] In this question, the $20,000 and $500 going towards tuition and books, respectively, fit squarely within this scholarship exclusion. However, the $5,000 designated for her housing costs and the $4,500 in cash, even if used for meals and living costs, do not fit within the scope of excludable scholarship amounts under IRC § 117. [Prop.Reg. § 1.117-6(c).] Therefore, the $9,500 sum of these latter two amounts is included in Amy's gross income (i.e., are taxable).

It should be noted that this general scholarship exclusion rule applies only to students who are "candidates for a degree." In addition, this exclusion is available only for students attending a qualified educational institution, which means a school that normally maintains a regular faculty, curriculum and regularly enrolled student body in attendance. [IRC §§ 117(b)(2)(A) and 170(b)(1)(A)(ii).]

Amy's enrollment at an accredited law school satisfies these requirements. While not pertinent to our facts, the growing trend of "distance learning" raises interesting questions as to what constitutes a "school" for scholarship exclusion purposes.

Students are often surprised that scholarship amounts for room and board, as well as cash as an "allowance" generally are not excludable from gross income. Not a semester goes by that this professor does not have a student who asks about a "friend's" scholarship experience in their undergraduate education in which this "friend" received room, board and an allowance without any of it being taxable. Upon further discussion, the "friend's" determination of non-taxability usually came by way of this person not receiving any official statement or form (such as a W-2 or 1099) from the school indicating that anything was taxable. Students are also often then surprised to learn that they are not relieved of their requirement to report (e.g., taxable scholarships) merely because the payor (e.g., the university or college) failed in their obligation to send any required forms to the taxpayer or the I.R.S. In other words, the duty to report taxable income is incumbent on the taxpayer.

Is it possible that any of this "scholarship" can be excluded pursuant to some other Code provision? In class, you may have discussed the statutory exclusion for gifts, bequests and devises of IRC § 102. If so, can we attempt to use this section to exclude some or all of Amy's scholarship benefits in this question? The answer, unfortunately for Amy, is no. The regulations at Reg. § 1.117-1(a) state that "[t]he exclusion from gross income of an amount which is a scholarship or fellowship grant is controlled solely by section 117." While not the subject of this question, it should be noted that there are other education-related benefits that may qualify for exclusion such as tuition reduction/remission and education assistance programs. [See IRC §§ 117(d) and 127, respectively.]

Answers (b) and (c) are incorrect because both answers incorrectly expand the scope of amounts excludable as a qualified scholarship under IRC § 117. Answers (b) and (c) fail to include, in income, the $5,000 of the scholarship designated for housing costs and answer (c) additionally fails to include the $4,500 cash allowance component of the scholarship in income. **Answer (d) is incorrect** because it incorrectly includes in income the $500 component of the scholarship used for required books, which is within the scope of the IRC § 117 exclusion. **Answer (e) is incorrect** because, as discussed above, the $4,500 cash allowance component of the scholarship is not excludable in this situation.

- **Additional references:** *See* DANIEL Q. POSIN, FEDERAL INCOME TAXATION OF INDIVIDUALS ¶ 3.09(2) (5th ed. 2000).

---

6.   **The most accurate statement is (c).** Westlaw's TWEN is a great online class tool (that is used extensively by this professor), and Amy is very fortunate to have received such a nice prize. IRC § 61 defines gross income as "all income from whatever source derived . . ." From your initial study of gross income's scope, you probably found it to be broadly defined, including a taxpayer's net accession to wealth or receipt of an economic benefit. In class, you also discover that gross income is not limited to the receipt of cash. Amy received a net accession to wealth, or a financial benefit, of $3,000 (the value of the laptop) and this amount is included in her gross income. IRC § 74 specifically addresses "prizes and awards" and its general rule, at § 74(a), states: Except as otherwise provided in this section or in section 117 (relating to qualified scholarships), gross income includes amounts received as prizes and awards."

Answer (a) is incorrect but is an answer that is commonly selected. It appears to be a possible correct answer after a casual reading of IRC § 74(b). This provision does exclude from gross income certain prizes and awards that are directly assigned to a qualified charitable organization. However, this "exclusion by assignment" provision is applicable only to prizes and awards "made primarily in recognition of religious, charitable, scientific, educational, artistic, literary, or civic achievement." [IRC § 74(b) (emphasis added).] Additionally, this provision requires that the "recipient was selected *without* any action on his part to enter the contest or proceeding." [IRC § 74(b)(1) (emphasis added).] Think of the "Nobel" prize as an example to which this provision could apply. Amy's prize resulted from a typical contest, not from a prize situation meeting the requirements of IRC § 74(b). Knowing something about charitable deductions (discussed elsewhere in this book) one might logically wonder about the actual significance of this exclusion by assignment provision. What if Amy does assign her computer over to a charitable organization – so she has gross income equal to $3,000 but is not she then entitled to a $3,000 deduction resulting in the same net effect of the IRC § 74(b) exclusion provision? Yes, Amy would most likely be entitled to a $3,000 charitable deduction, but no, the end result is probably not the same, nor as favorable, as the IRC § 74(b) provision. This is because, as discussed in other problems in this book, Amy's charitable deduction is a "below the line" itemized deduction (a deduction from adjusted gross income (AGI) to compute taxable income). Depending on the extent of her other itemized deductions compared with her "standard deduction" she may not, when all is said and done, realize the full benefit of the deduction. Other unfavorable consequences may include disqualification for numerous deductions and exclusions or reduction of various deductions, based on her higher AGI that reflects the inclusion of the prize. [See Appendix A for more information about how income and deductions fit together in computing taxable income and AGI.]

Congratulations if you win the lottery, the "Publisher's Clearing House Giveaway, money or prizes on a game show, and the like, but be aware that the money and prizes are taxable.

Answer (b) is incorrect because the measure of income for property received is the fair market value of the property, not the transferor's basis in the property. **Answer (d) is also incorrect** but does introduce another commonly misunderstood provision of IRC § 74. IRC § 74(c) provides for another possible exclusion to the recipient of certain awards. There is a separate exclusion from gross income but it is limited to certain "low value" property awards for employee achievement such as for length of employment, safety record, retirement, and the like. Amy's laptop from Westlaw does not fit within this category. **Answer (e) is also incorrect** because Amy's prize does not meet the requirements for an excludable qualified scholarship pursuant to IRC § 117. Please see other questions in the book addressing qualified scholarships for more information.

- **Additional references:** See DANIEL Q. POSIN, FEDERAL INCOME TAXATION OF INDIVIDUALS ¶ 3.09(1) (5th ed. 2000).

7.   **Answer (a) is correct.** With Wendy's death, Hank has suffered a terrible loss. He will, however, financially benefit as the beneficiary of the life insurance policy on Wendy's life. The $8,000 that Hank receives from the insurance company is income to him, as it does not represent receipt of the actual insurance proceeds. Rather, the money received represents interest on the proceeds left on deposit with the insurance company.

While accessions to wealth arise when one receives life insurance benefits, the statute confers favorable tax treatment for much of the benefits associated with life insurance. IRC § 101(a) declares the general rule that life insurance proceeds received by reason of the insured's death are excluded from gross income of the beneficiary. Had Hank simply received the $100,000 from the insurance company, it would have been fully excluded from income. In this question, however, Hank leaves the funds on deposit with the insurance company, earning interest thereon. The exclusion of life insurance proceeds pursuant to IRC § 101 extends only to the life insurance proceeds and <u>not</u> to any earnings therefrom. The $8,000 Hank expects to receive will be fully included in his gross income.

IRC § 101(c) specifically addresses our situation and confirms the interest to be taxable. This provision does make sense. This is no different in principle, to Hank depositing $100,000 in a bank account and earning interest thereon. Clearly, the interest in such a situation is includible in gross income. Similarly, when a donee receives a true gift of money and subsequently invests it, while the gift itself may be excluded from income (IRC § 102) the monies earned from its subsequent investment is not excluded.

Answers (b) and (c) are incorrect because the inclusion of interest earned on life insurance proceeds has no correlation to one's life expectancy or the planned duration of the investment. See other questions in this book that involve an "annuity type payout" of life insurance benefits. **Answer (d) is incorrect** for the reasons discussed above. There is no exclusion "magic" merely because this interest comes from a life insurance company.

- **Additional references:** See DANIEL Q. POSIN, FEDERAL INCOME TAXATION OF INDIVIDUALS ¶¶ 3.06, 3.07 (5th ed. 2000).

8.   **The best answer is (d).** IRC § 61 defines gross income as "all income from whatever source derived." From your initial study of gross income's scope, you probably found it to be broadly defined, including the taxpayer's receipt of some net economic benefit or net accession to wealth. In class, you also discover that gross income is also not limited to the receipt of cash. [Reg. § 1.61-1(d) (compensation received in forms other than in cash).] Brian receives an economic benefit each day when he eats lunch at the company dining facility. He is receiving "something" (a fine meal) for less than its true value and he is receiving this benefit by reason of his employment. Barring a specific exclusion provision, the benefit he is receiving (the fair value of the meals on the "outside" less what he is paying for them) represents income to him.

Fortunately for Brian, he might be entitled to relief. A host of employee fringe benefits are excluded pursuant to IRC § 132, and the benefit Brian is receiving in this problem invokes the "de minimis" fringe benefit. [IRC §§ 132(a)(4) and 132(e).] More specifically, there is a special provision within the *de minimis* fringe material in the statute that addresses "certain eating facilities." [IRC § 132(e)(2).] The statute addresses situations exactly like the one presented in our facts. Where an employer operates an eating facility on (or near) the employer's business premises and the employees pay less than the true fair value of the meals provided, if certain requirements are met, the employees can exclude, as a *de minimis* fringe benefit, the extra value of the meals received.

The primary requirement for this special category of excludable *de minimis fringe* benefits is that the amount the employees do pay for the meals at least covers the employer's "direct operating costs of such facility." [IRC § 132(e)(2)(B).] The regulations define these costs to be the employer's cost of food (which is likely at wholesale prices) and other direct costs of operating the facility such as the cost of labor (cooks, waiters, etc.). [Reg. § 1.132-7(b).] The statute also requires that the employer not discriminate in favor of "highly compensated employees" as to the availability among employees to such eating facility. [IRC § 132(e)(2).]

Brian's employer makes this dining facility available to all employees and assuming that the price the employees pay for their meals at least equals the employer's "direct operating costs" for the facility, the benefit Brian receives is excludable from gross income.

Law students might be familiar with this type of eating facility when working for some of the larger law firms. It is not uncommon for such firms to have an "attorneys' dining room" where otherwise expensive meals are available at a very reasonable cost to the employee. Most likely, the benefit received by employees (from the discounted meals) is excludable from gross income under these same provisions. It should be noted that an employer could discriminate and provide access to only certain employees (such as "attorneys") as long as it does not result in "per se" discrimination in favor of "highly compensated employees" (e.g., a "partners only" dining room would probably not qualify). [See Reg. § 1.132-8(d)(2).]

Answer (a) is incorrect because it fails to reflect the statutory requirement that the employees cover at least the direct operating costs of the eating facility. **Answer (b) is not the best answer** because the benefit that Brian receives might be excluded as a *de minimis* fringe benefit as discussed above. **Answer (c) is also not correct.** This special category of the *de minimis* fringe benefit contains no requirement that the employer deems it necessary to have the employees remain on the business premises. If such is the case, then another employee related exclusion provision, IRC § 119, might be applicable. However, this answer is not correct because this latter provision in IRC § 119 is not the only reason why Brian might be able to exclude the benefit he is receiving.

- **Additional references:** *See* DANIEL Q. POSIN, FEDERAL INCOME TAXATION OF INDIVIDUALS ¶ 2.02(1) (5th ed. 2000).

9. **The correct answer is (b).** IRC § 61 defines gross income as "all income from whatever source derived." From your initial study of gross income's scope, you probably found it to be broadly defined, including a taxpayer's net accession to wealth or receipt of an economic benefit. Modernly, no distinction is made, for gross income purposes, whether the wealth is derived from legal or illegal activities. Malcolm must include in gross income, amounts he earns from all three of the sources indicated.

Answers (a), (c) and (d) are incorrect because each answer fails to include in Malcolm's gross income amounts earned from all of the sources indicated.

- **Additional references:** *See* DANIEL Q. POSIN, FEDERAL INCOME TAXATION OF INDIVIDUALS ¶ 3.13(2) (5th ed. 2000).

10. **Answer (e) is correct.** Social Security benefits historically were fully excluded from gross income under the auspices of that all legislatively provided social benefit programs for the promotion of the general welfare were not taxable. Things changed in 1983 with the enactment of IRC § 86. This section, as modified over the years, makes Social Security benefits includible in gross income depending on the taxpayer's level of other types of income. If certain threshold limits are reached then up to 85% of the Social Security benefits received will be included in the taxpayer's gross income.

It should be noted that the depth of coverage given to IRC § 86 in the basic federal income tax course might vary considerably. This question covers only the basic concept of the taxability of Social Security benefits.

Answers (a) and (b) are incorrect because Social Security benefits are <u>not</u> taxed at <u>rates</u> up to 50% or 80% but, rather, these represent the portion of one's Social Security benefits that may be included in gross income depending on the level of the taxpayer's other income. **Answer (c) is incorrect** because the stated answer is opposite to that what has transpired over the past two decades. **Answer (d) is also incorrect.** While the historical perspective is generally correct, benefits are <u>not fully includible</u> in gross income. At most, 85% of Social Security benefits will be includible in a taxpayer's gross income.

11. **The best answer is (b).** United States Savings Bonds (Series EE) are issued in various "face amount" denominations (e.g. a $50 U.S. Savings Bond), but are purchased at a fraction of this face amount (usually at one-half of the face amount). These bonds *do* pay interest, but not in the normal form of a stated interest rate on money invested (as with a savings account at a bank). Rather, the interest accrues on the original discounted purchase price. Much to the disappointment of many a young person receiving a U.S. Savings Bond from his or her grandmother, the bond cannot be "cashed in" right away with the receipt of the face amount. One must wait many years until the bond "matures" to receive its face value. These years until the bond's maturity is the period when the interest accrues on the bond, bringing its value up from the original discounted purchase price to the face amount. This difference, therefore, represents interest, and it is taxable interest for U.S. income tax purposes.

Unless an individual affirmatively elects to report, as interest, the annual increases in such a bond's value, the recognition of interest is deferred until the bond matures (or is redeemed or otherwise disposed of sooner). [IRC § 454(a).] This deferred interest is all of the interest earned on the bond, which is measured by the difference between its face amount and its original discounted purchase price.

Answer (a) is incorrect. Interest from obligations of the United States is generally fully includible in gross income. This is sometimes the source of confusion among students. While not the subject of this book, interest from U.S. obligations is generally excluded from income for state and local income tax purposes (for those states, counties or cities imposing an income tax). Also not at issue in this problem is IRC § 135 that provides for a very limited and narrow exclusion of certain interest received by certain individuals from Series EE United States Savings Bonds, the proceeds of which are used for certain education purposes. **Answer (c) is also incorrect.** Taxpayers can affirmatively elect to recognize interest annually from U.S. Savings Bonds (Series EE), but the default recognition is at the bond's maturity. This answer switches the default and elective recognition of such interest. **Answer (d) is incorrect** because the annual recognition of such interest is an election, not a requirement. In addition, this answer does not reflect the default recognition of such interest at the bond's maturity.

12.   **Answer (c) is correct.** When a "devise" appears in the facts, the inclination is to look at IRC § 102, the section that excludes from income amounts received by gift, bequest, devise, and inheritance. However, the fact that property or money comes from a decedent by way of a will (or intestate succession) does not assure the application of IRC § 102 or exclusion status. If, as it appears to be the case here, the devise is in satisfaction of some contractual agreement between the decedent and the beneficiary, then we do not view the transfer as an excludable devise pursuant to IRC § 102 but, rather, a fulfillment of the contract between the parties.

In this case, Nathan is not, for tax purposes, receiving a devise but, rather, is being repaid the money previously loaned to Debra. While this is not an excludable devise, the repayment of a loan does not give rise to income to Nathan. Income, while broadly defined, does not include the repayment of monies loaned (we are ignoring any interest in this problem). Just as the debtor has no income when money is borrowed (there is no net accession to wealth to the debtor), there is no income to the creditor when the money is repaid (there is no net accession to wealth to the creditor). It is for this reason that Nathan has no income in this question.

Contrast the situation in our problem with one that would result in the recognition of income from a "devise." As an example, say that rather than Nathan loaning money to Debra, he performed services for her that were worth $10,000 and she promised to pay him for them and did prior to her death. This would, of course, result in compensation income to Nathan. An alternative situation that the promised $10,000 payment for Nathan's services came through Debra's will as a devise, would not change the character of the income to Nathan. In other words, there is no magical exclusion merely because property or cash is received from a decedent.

Answer (a) is incorrect. While Nathan has no gross income in this question, it is not because the $10,000 is an excludable devise pursuant to IRC § 102. **Answer (b) is also incorrect**. Although it does recognize that Nathan's receipt of the $10,000 is not excludable as a devise, this answer fails to correctly characterize the receipt of the money as a non-taxable event, the repayment of a loan. **Answer (d) is incorrect** because, as indicated above, Nathan has no net accession to wealth as a result of being repaid the money loaned to Debra.

- **Additional references:** *See* DANIEL Q. POSIN, FEDERAL INCOME TAXATION OF INDIVIDUALS ¶¶ 3.08(4) (5th ed. 2000).

13. **The best answer is (c).** The possible exclusion of the value of the lodging provided to Paulette and Dave is under the auspices of IRC § 119, exclusion of meals and lodging provided for the convenience of the employer. If there is a valid reason why it is important or necessary for the couple to be "on call" at the facility during off-hours, the value of their free lodging should be excluded from their income.

From your initial study of gross income's scope, you probably found it to be broadly defined, including the taxpayer's receipt of some net economic benefit or net accession to wealth. In class, you also discover that gross income is also not limited to the receipt of cash. [Reg. § 1.61-1(d) (compensation received in forms other than in cash).] Paulette and Dave are receiving an economic benefit as a result of the lodging provided, free of charge, by their employer, and the value of this benefit should be includible in their gross income. The fact that the couple owns 100% of their employer corporation does not, in and of itself, change this, as the corporation's separate identity must be respected for income tax purposes. [See *Dean v. Comm'r*, 187 F.2d 1019 (3rd Cir.1951).]

IRC § 119 provides that meals and lodging provided to an employee are excludable from the employee's income *if* they are provided for the *convenience of the employer*. In addition to being for the convenience of the employer, qualified lodging must be on the business premises of the employer and be a condition of the taxpayer's employment. [IRC § 119(a)(2).]

The determination of whether providing such a lodging benefit is for the convenience of the employer, one must look for substantial noncompensation factors or reasons. The most common situations in which IRC § 119 exclusions arise are those where it is necessary to have an employee on duty or on-call to handle business matters that might arise at any time, day or night. A typical example is that of an on-site manager of an apartment complex who may be required to handle tenant matters during off-hours (typically during overnight periods). Assuming it is important or commonplace for a sewage treatment plant to have an on-site manager at all times to handle situations that might arise, the couple's residency at the plant would appear to be for the convenience of the employer.

The bungalow is located on the business premises of The Corporation's sewage treatment facility (albeit as far away as possible from the open sewage pits as possible). The fact that The Corporation leases the underlying property does not undermine the application of IRC § 119 because this is still considered the employer's premises (The Corporation's leasehold interest is sufficient for this purpose).

With respect to the requirement that the couple lives on the premises as a condition of their employment, the fact that Paulette (as The Corporation's president) basically made this requirement of herself (and Dave) has a certain, excuse the pun, strange "odor" to it. When this "requirement" is made in situations where the employee is also the sole or majority shareholder, or in intra-family situations, the validity of the "requirement" is naturally suspect. A "requirement" solely for the purpose of meeting the "form" of the statutory requirement would clearly be a sham and would be ignored for these purposes. However, the relationship between the employer and employee does not preclude meeting a valid "requirement for employment" from existing. If the true nature of the required on-site lodging is legitimate, than the fact that a related party (or the same person) acting on behalf of the employer made this a requirement of employment, is legitimate. As long as there is a legitimate important business reason that Paulette (and/or Dave) resides at the facility, then their lodging should be excludable from their gross income.

Answer (a) is incorrect because, as indicated above, the fact that Paulette, acting as President of The Corporation, required herself and Dave to live at the facility will not, in and of itself, preclude the exclusion of lodging under IRC § 119. **Answer (b) is incorrect** because The Corporation is a separate and distinct person from Paulette and Dave, the individuals, notwithstanding their 100% ownership of The Corporation. The employees Paulette and Dave *did* receive a financial benefit from their employer and its value is includible in their gross income barring any exclusion. **Answer (d) is incorrect** because the fact that The Corporation has a leasehold interest in the land is sufficient to deem it to be The Corporation's business premises.

- **Additional references:** *See* DANIEL Q. POSIN, FEDERAL INCOME TAXATION OF INDIVIDUALS ¶ 2.02(2) (5th ed. 2000).

14. **The best answer is (b).** This question raises one of the classic doctrines in income tax law; "assignment of income." The "assignment of income" doctrine is, arguably, best known from the case *Lucas v. Earl.* [281 U.S. 111, 50 S.Ct. 241 (1930).] Income is income (for tax purposes) to the taxpayer who earns it. One cannot transfer the tax obligation to another person merely by "assigning" the income to such person. One cannot say, "I earned the income, but do not give it to me, give it to my son instead" (who happens to be in a much lower income tax bracket) and have it work that way for income tax purposes. As far as the contract regarding Patricia's salary, she cannot merely assign this income to her daughter, Denise. Patricia earned the income and she must include all of it in her gross income.

The fees received from her work with the school's outreach program present more of a problem. On the surface, there is little distinction from the situation regarding her salary payable to her daughter. Patricia earned this income and ostensibly, she cannot just assign it to another person. This is not to be confused with a concept of "disclaiming" (waiving, rejecting, etc.) income before it is earned. Such disclaimers may prevent recognition of income as long as they are made before the income is earned and there is no assignment of the disclaimed income (i.e., directing that it go to someone else). Relief for Patricia is found in I.R.S revenue rulings. In a factually similar situation, the I.R.S., while applying assignment of income rules and finding no escape, has held that, "the Internal Revenue Service has recognized that amounts that would otherwise be deemed income are not, in certain unique factual situations, subject to the broad rule of inclusion provided by section 61(a) of the Code." [Rev.Rul. 74-581, 1974-2 C.B. 25.] This revenue ruling held that a law professor receiving statutory fees for representing clients in the school's clinical program was not required to include them in gross income when his employment contract required that these amounts be remitted to the school. Similarly, Revenue Ruling 69-274 (1969-1 C.B. 36) held, in facts almost identical to ours, that the fees remitted to the employer as required by the employment contract were excludable from income. Therefore, it is very likely that Patricia will not have to include, in gross income, the fees that she receives and remits to the university pursuant to her employment contract.

Answer (a) is incorrect because, as discussed above, Patricia will most likely be able to exclude from income the outside fees received and remitted to her employer. **Answer (c) is incorrect** because even if the assignment is "anticipatory" (made before Patricia earned the income) such assignments are still ineffective for income tax purposes. Her assignment is not an unconditional waiver or disclaimer of her future earnings. **Answer (d) is also incorrect.** But for the Revenue Rulings discussed above, this would be a good answer.

15. **Answer (b) is correct.** We will conclude below that none of Tad's debt was discharged or forgiven and, therefore, Tad realizes no income.

Forgiving a debt, in whole or in part, generally results in the realization of gross income to the debtor. It makes sense that being relieved of a liability (a financial obligation) results in a net accession to wealth (i.e., income) to the debtor. This type of income is referred to as "income from discharge of indebtedness" and is specifically identified by the Code as constituting gross income. [IRC § 61(a)(12).] However, to realize income from discharge of indebtedness, one must first have a cognizable or liquidated "debt" that has been discharged or forgiven. In our question, what was the amount of debt Tad owed to Carl? Carl would assert that it was $15,000, yet Tad would assert that it was only $10,000. In our question the actual amount owed is in dispute. When there is a legitimate (good faith) disagreement as to what the actual amount of debt is, an agreement or settlement as to the debt amount is not considered a discharge or forgiveness of debt. It bears repeating that to have a discharge or forgiveness of debt (giving rise to income) one must first have a "debt" which is subsequently discharged/forgiven in whole or in part. This is what is sometimes referred to as the "contested or disputed liability doctrine." [See *Zarin v. Comm'r*, 916 F.2d 110 (3rd Cir.1990).]

In this problem, the liability was in dispute and the settled amount of $12,000 represents the cognizable or liquidated debt. Carl's compromise from $15,000 down to $12,000 does not represent income from discharge of indebtedness. Rather, pursuant to the contested/disputed liability doctrine, it is the process to determine the actual uncontested amount of the debt owed. Tad then fully pays the liquidated debt of $12,000. There is, therefore, no income to Tad from discharge of any debt. Although not the case in our question, if after the parties had settled on $12,000 as the amount owed and subsequently some or all of this amount was forgiven, then income from discharge of indebtedness would have resulted.

A word of caution about language used on exams. There are many instances where the common use of a term does not necessarily correspond to its official "tax" counterpart. Labels can be deceiving and do not be fooled by their use in lay terms on an exam. Problems involving what may appear to be income from discharge of indebtedness are fertile ground for tricky questions vis-à-vis terminology. The next to the last sentence in this question could have read, "Tad then paid Carl $12,000, *fully discharging the debt*." Our answer to this question would have remained unchanged. The lay use of the word "discharge" (to fully pay off a debt) would not correspond to the official "tax" counterpart where "discharge" of debt represents a forgiveness of debt.

Answers (a) and (c) are incorrect because as indicated above, there is no income from discharge of indebtedness resulting from a settlement of a contested liability. While not relevant for this question, answer (a) does bring up an important concept. Had there been, in this case, income realized from discharge of indebtedness, it is always important to ask if such realized income is recognized? There are provisions that may exclude this from gross income. For example, income from forgiven debt may be excluded from income pursuant to IRC § 102, if it can be shown that the forgiveness was gratuitous. Another example of a possible exclusion lies in IRC § 108, applying to insolvent or bankrupt debtors. **Answer (d) is incorrect** because while Tad does not have income from discharge of indebtedness in our question, he does not have income from any services performed. <u>Carl</u> has income from services performed, but this is not germane to the question.

- **Additional references:** See Daniel Q. Posin, Federal Income Taxation of Individuals ¶¶ 3.10(1), 3.10(2) (5th ed. 2000).

16. **Answer (c) is correct.** This question involves the exclusion of "compensation for injuries or sickness" provided in IRC § 104. This section has a long, complex and capricious past vis-à-vis what is within its umbrella of this exclusion. In its most basic form, an individual receiving damages, by award or settlement, for physical injuries or physical sickness can exclude such amounts from income. [IRC § 104(a)(2).] In its current form (reflecting changes made by the "Small Business Job Protection Act of 1996"), this section generally excludes amounts received (other than punitive damages) for <u>physical tort</u> awards and settlements. The entire amount of Dave's award, in this question, originates from his physical injury arising from the negligence cause of action and, therefore, is excluded from gross income.

The difficulty of questions involving IRC § 104 can vary dramatically depending on how thoroughly one's professor covers the exclusion as to its history, policy foundations, and the like. This is a good area of tax law for in-depth class analysis, so take this into consideration when addressing questions involving the subject. Much of this Code section's history centered on the breadth of this exclusion with, at varying times, exclusions allowed for damages received from non physical tort or "tort type" causes of action, and punitive damages.

The problem students usually have with this question is the reluctance to exclude the portions of Dave's award identified as replacement for "lost wages" and "emotional distress." As for the replacement of lost wages, one might logically argue (as did the I.R.S. for many years) that they should not be within the scope of IRC § 104's exclusion because wages, had he not been injured, would have been taxable. Historically, this was the subject of much tax litigation. However, the answer is now clear that these amounts do not represent taxable wages even if the award amount is measured by the amount of wages that could have been earned but for the injuries. [Rev.Rul. 85-97, 1985-2 C.B. 50.]

Regarding the "emotional distress" component of the award, there is often confusion because of the language in the body of IRC § 104(a) that states, "emotional distress shall not be treated as a physical injury or physical sickness." Remembering that "physical" injury/sickness is required for exclusion, it might appear that the portion of Dave's award identified for emotional distress is not excludable. However, because Dave's cause of action was the physical injury, and the emotional distress emanated therefrom, the amount is within the scope of the exclusion.

Answers (a), (b) and (d) are incorrect because they all, to some degree, do not represent the full scope of the IRC § 104(a)(2) exclusion as it applies to this question. Please see the discussion for the correct answer (c), immediately above, for more information. **Answer (e) is incorrect** because there is a correct answer in response (c).

It should be noted that this question, and others in this book that specifically identify component parts of a personal injury award, are a bit removed from "real world" circumstances. Lawyers specializing in the practice of personal injury law will acknowledge that many, if not most, personal injury awards and settlements do not separate damage awards/settlements with such specificity. Correct application of income tax rules is further frustrated by the additional "real world" fact that the underlying cause of action, or basis on which a tort related lawsuit damages are awarded, is not always clear or separable from other causes of action.

- **Additional references:** See DANIEL Q. POSIN, FEDERAL INCOME TAXATION OF INDIVIDUALS ¶¶ 3.11(1), 3.11(2) (5th ed. 2000).

17. **The correct answer is (b).** Annuities contracts come in many different varieties and the tax ramifications associated with payments thereunder can be complex. This question, however, is designed to address the basic or standard type of annuity contract (and the corresponding tax rules). The income tax ramifications of payments received pursuant to an annuity contract are contained in IRC § 72. One look at this section, that is well over a dozen pages long, gives some hint to the possible complexity of the subject. Be aware that your professor may cover the material in much greater depth than is addressed in this basic question.

The most basic example of an annuity contract is that you give money to someone (typically a life insurance company) and they promise to pay you a specific amount of money at set intervals for as long as you live. Without knowing anything more about the tax rules of annuity payments, logic tells us that you *should not* be taxed on the amount that you get back from them that is equal to the amount you gave them (i.e., you are merely getting your money back). Any "extra" amount you receive must be coming from earnings on your money (similar to interest on money deposited in a bank) and that *should* be taxable (represent gross income). Basically, this is how the most basic annuity taxation rules of IRC § 72 work.

The only real question is one of "timing." When does the *taxable portion* start? Do you get to first recoup the amount contributed, and only have gross income once you have received all of your contributed money back? The answer is no. IRC § 72 requires that an "exclusion ratio" be established based on certain criteria. In essence, a *portion* of each payment received from the annuity contract is excluded (recouping your original contribution) and a portion of each such payment is included in gross income (representing earnings on your money deposited). After applying this ratio to each payment received, once the taxpayer (the "annuitant") receives, in the aggregate, the amount of his or her original contribution, this prorated exclusion ends and the full amount of each subsequent payment is included in income.

Again, this is the most basic of income tax rules of what, in reality, are a very complex set of rules associated with annuities.

It should be noted that the rules applicable to annuities are different from "annuity like payments of life insurance benefits" under a life insurance contract (paid by reason of the death of the insured). That issue is addressed in another question in this book.

Answer (a) is incorrect but would be the preferred way for a taxpayer to treat annuity payments. Unfortunately, the statute does not allow this method of nonrecognition. **Answer (c) is incorrect** because annuity payments do not garner such favorable tax treatment under the statute. However, please see at least one other question in this book addressing annuity type payment of life insurance benefits that do receive this favorable tax treatment. **Answer (d) is incorrect** because the statute does not provide for such degree of nonrecognition. The fact that life insurance companies are often involved in annuity contracts should not be confused with exclusions provided to life insurance benefits received by reason of the death of the insured. [See IRC § 101.]

- **Additional references:** *See* DANIEL Q. POSIN, FEDERAL INCOME TAXATION OF INDIVIDUALS ¶ 3.07 (5th ed. 2000).

18. **Answer (d) is correct.** There is no doubt that Cheryl received a financial benefit from her short-term rental activities and, barring any specific exclusion provision, the $18,000 would be included in her gross income. Fortunately for Cheryl, there is such an exclusion provision and it proves very beneficial to Cheryl in this case. IRC § 280A(g) provides that a taxpayer renting out his or her home for less than fifteen (15) days during the year, excludes, from gross income, any rent received for such period. The dollar amount of this exclusion is unlimited. To be fair, this section also precludes any rental expense deductions for this period. Basically, if the rental period of one's house is short enough, we pretend, for tax purposes, that is was not rented out at all. A very nice result for Cheryl in our problem.

   Answers (a), (b), and (c) are incorrect because none of these answers properly reflects this short-term house rental exclusion from income. **Answer (e) is incorrect** because as long as Cheryl's home is rented for less than fifteen days, there is no statutory limit on the amount of rental income excludable.

   - **Additional references:** *See* DANIEL Q. POSIN, FEDERAL INCOME TAXATION OF INDIVIDUALS ¶ 6.02(11) (5th ed. 2000).

19. **The most likely answer is probably, maybe (d), but answer (a) might also be acceptable.** This is a very close call and subject to some debate. In any event, as discussed below, Sid should be able to fully exclude the value of his use of the luxury penthouse suite from his gross income.

   IRC § 61 defines gross income as "all income from whatever source derived." From your initial study of gross income's scope, you probably found it to be broadly defined, including the taxpayer's receipt of some net economic benefit or net accession to wealth. In class, you also discover that gross income is also not limited to the receipt of cash. [Reg. § 1.61-1(d) (compensation received in forms other than in cash).] Sid is clearly receiving an substantial economic benefit by being provided with the luxurious free lodging and, absent a specific exclusion provision, the value of this benefit represents income to Sid.

   The primary exclusion of the value of Sid's lodging comes by way of IRC § 119. IRC § 119 provides that meals and lodging provided to an employee are excludable from the employee's income *if* they are provided for the *convenience of the employer*. In addition to being for the convenience of the employer, qualified lodging must be on the business premises of the employer <u>and</u> be a condition of the taxpayer's employment. [IRC § 119(a)(2).]

The determination of whether providing such a lodging benefit is for the convenience of the employer, one must look for substantial noncompensation factors or reasons. The most common situations in which IRC § 119 exclusions arise are those where it is necessary to have an employee on duty or on-call to handle business matters that might arise at any time, day or night. A typical example is that of an on-site manager of a hotel or an apartment complex who may be required to handle guest/tenant matters during off-hours (typically during overnight periods). It is quite logical to come to the conclusion that Sid's "on-site" living is for the convenience of his employer. In addition, this "living on the premises" (the hotel) is a requirement for all of Tillie's hotel manager employees.

The problem in our facts is with the type of free lodging being provided to Sid, especially when compared to that provided to all of her other hotel managers. A careful review of the Code and Regulations for IRC § 119 does not reveal any sort of "reasonableness" test. It is for that reason why **answer (a)** might be an acceptable response. However, the totality of the facts (the type of accommodations provided to Sid and the that his employer is his mother who would do anything for her son) raises some suspicion. Specifically, the nexus between the "lodging provided for the <u>convenience of the employer</u>" and the degree of the benefit that is provided to Sid, appears to be a bit tenuous. The author would argue that a "reasonableness" standard is inherent in exclusion for lodging provided in IRC § 119. If this is the case, then the value of Tillie's typical hotel manager's lodging would be excluded by IRC § 119, but any excess would not be covered by this exclusion.

Continuing with the theme that not all of the value of Sid's lodging is excluded via IRC § 119, we must venture further to find tax relief for Sid. If you have studied the IRC § 102 exclusion for gifts, bequests and devises, that might be a logical place to look for a potential exclusion for this "extra" benefit that Sid receives. Under the general rule of § 102(a), gifts are excluded from the gross income of the donee/recipient. While no statutory definition of a gift exists, it is generally defined as a transfer without consideration that is made out of emotions of detached and disinterested generosity. [See *Comm'r v. Duberstein*, 363 U.S. 278, 80 S.Ct. 1190 (1960).] This sounds perfect for Sid as the facts clearly imply such that Tillie has such motives with respect to her son, Sid. However, we must address a major hurdle located at IRC § 102(c). This subsection provides, in general, that the possible exclusion from gross income of property acquired by gift, bequest or devise, does <u>not</u> apply to transfers between employers and employees. In other words, "gifts" to employees are not excludable from gross income under IRC § 102. As applied to most employees, this subsection is not merely a presumption. Rather, "gifts" to most employees are not excludable gifts at all.

The author, in the preceding paragraph, states that the IRC § 102(c) denial of ex-cludable gifts applies with respect to "most employees." For discussion purposes and totally divorced from the facts of our question, suppose a parent employs a child. Let's further suppose that the employer (parent) makes no gifts to any em-ployees but on the child's 25th birthday, the parent gives the child a new automo-bile. In the familial context, we have a parent making a gift to a child most likely out of emotions of detached and disinterested generosity, qualifying it for exclu-sion from income to the child pursuant to IRC § 102(a). However, we also factu-ally have an employer making a gift to an employee that, pursuant to the language in IRC § 102(c), cannot be considered an excludable gift to the employee. Does this preclude any gifts, in the traditional and excludable sense, when the donor and donee happen to have an employment relationship such as this? Proposed regulations answer this question as follows: "For purposes of section 102(c), *ex-traordinary* transfers to the natural objects of an employer's bounty will *not be considered transfers to, or for the benefit of, an employee if the employee can show that the transfer was not made in recognition of the employee's employment. Accordingly, section 102(c) shall not apply to amounts transferred between re-lated parties (e.g., father and son) if the purpose of the transfer can be substan-tially attributed to the familial relationship of the parties and not to the circum-stances of their employment.*" [Prop.Reg. § 1.102-1(f)(2) (emphasis added).] In the hypothetical presented in this paragraph, the parent's gift of the car to the child is, in all likelihood, an example of an excludable gift notwithstanding the employment relationship between the two.

Now back to the facts of the question presented. Sid is the "natural object" of his mother's "bounty" (using the somewhat odd vernacular of the regulations), and it appears that the excess benefit (the luxury penthouse three-bedroom suite) Tillie is providing Sid is extraordinary in nature. We can also logically infer from the facts that Tillie does not provide Sid with these luxurious accommodations in rec-ognition of Sid's employment, or in the context of their employment relationship, but rather, it is attributable to their familial relationship. Based upon this, Sid should be able to exclude as a gift, pursuant to IRC § 102, the "excess" benefit he receives vis-à-vis his luxury accommodations.

Answer (b) is incorrect. This answer is a diversion to the statutory fringe bene-fits excluded pursuant to IRC § 132. As discussed in other questions in this book, many of the fringe benefits excluded pursuant to that Code provision carry con-tain a "nondiscrimination" requirement (regarding highly compensated employ-ees) and if breached, the entire value of the benefit received is included in income. Sid's lodging benefit is not one of the IRC § 132 fringe benefits. **Answer (c) is also incorrect.** Assuming the "extra" benefit Sid receives is not excluded pursu-ant to IRC § 119, it is excludible as a gift under IRC § 102.

- **Additional references:** *See* DANIEL Q. POSIN, FEDERAL INCOME TAXATION OF INDIVIDUALS ¶¶ 2.02(2), 3.08(1), 3.08(2) (5th ed. 2000).

20. **The best answer is (a).** IRC § 61 defines gross income as "all income from whatever source derived." From your initial study of gross income's scope, you probably found it to be broadly defined, including the taxpayer's receipt of some net economic benefit or net accession to wealth. In class, you also discover that gross income is also not limited to the receipt of cash. [Reg. § 1.61-1(d) (compensation received in forms other than in cash).] Sid (through his family) received an economic benefit when Sid's wife and children were entitled to stay, free of charge, for the two nights in Beverly Hills. It is by reason of Sid's employment that his family received this benefit and, absent a specific exclusion provision, the value of this benefit represents income to Sid.

Fortunately for Sid, he is entitled to relief in this case. A host of employee fringe benefits are excluded pursuant to IRC § 132, and the benefit Sid (through his family) is receiving in this problem invokes the "no-additional-cost service" fringe benefit. [IRC §§ 132(a)(1) and 132(b).] Perhaps you have worked for an airline and were to fly for free (or at a reduced fair) when empty seats were available. Or, as in our example, you worked for a hotel chain and could stay in any of the chain's hotel for free (or for a reduced charge) when rooms were available. If so, did you include, in income, the value of the benefit received? Most likely the answer is <u>no</u>, and the most likely reason is that the benefit you received was an excludible *no-additional-cost service* fringe. Although restrictions and limits may apply, the *no-additional-cost service* fringe enables employers to allow employees receive free (or discounted) services that the employer provides to the public, without the value of such services being included in the employee's gross income.

There are two major requirements or limitations applicable to this fringe benefit. First, the service that the employee is receiving must be the type of service offered for sale to customers in the line of business in which the employee is working. [IRC § 132(b)(1).] This is the so-called "line of business" test. Ostensibly, this requirement exists to prevent conglomerates from providing across the board free or discounted services to all employees in all lines of the employer's business that are perceived to be unfair when compared to non-conglomerates. Sid (through his family) is receiving the free hotel nights (considered a service), and he is provided this benefit by working in the same line of business (the lodging industry). The "line of business" requirement is somewhat of a "non-issue" for a most "single line" business such as Tillie's.

The second major limitation is the employer cannot incur substantial additional cost in providing such service to the employee. [IRC § 132(b)(2).] If an employer looses revenue because of the service provided, this requirement is not met. The benefit provided in this question is free lodging "as long as there are vacancies." This condition placed on the fringe benefit in question assures that it will not be a substantial additional cost to Sid's employer. This situation is sometimes referred to as "excess capacity services." [See Reg. § 1.132-2(a)(2).] The fact that the employer incurs incidental costs, such as maid service, during an employee's stay, does not render the fringe benefit taxable, as these costs are not "substantial." [See Reg. § 1.132-2(a)(5)(ii).]

Does the fact that Sid's family is receiving this benefit without Sid's presence impact what appears to be a tax-free *no-additional-cost service* fringe benefit? Fortunately for Sid, his spouse and dependent children are part of an expanded definition of an employee for purposes of the *no-additional-cost service* fringe benefit (as well as the "qualified employee discount," another IRC § 132 fringe benefit). [IRC § 132(2).] Sid's spouse and dependent children can be the beneficiaries of this fringe benefit (even without the Sid's presence) and it does jeopardize its otherwise tax-free status.

While not an issue in this problem, it should be mentioned that the statute provides that an employer cannot provide some, but not all, of the fringe benefits enumerated in IRC § 132 to employees on a discriminatory basis (in favor of only highly compensated employees as defined by the statute). The *no-additional-cost service* is one such benefit that cannot be provided to employees in a discriminatory manner. [IRC § 132(j)(1).] This is not an issue in our question as the fringe benefit at issue is offered to all full-time employees and therefore, does not offend these discrimination rules. Limiting this benefit to just "full-time" employees is most likely not discriminatory for purpose of IRC § 132. [Reg. § 1.132-8(d)(2).] It should also be noted that if this fringe benefit were to discriminate in favor of highly compensated employees, the <u>entire</u> value of the free service received would be included in income (and not just any extra benefit that may be provided to such employees). [Reg. § 1.132-8(a)(2).]

It should also be noted that this is a fairly basic question regarding the *no-additional-cost service* fringe benefit. Your professor may cover the material in much greater depth and there are many ancillary issues regarding this and other IRC § 132 fringe benefits.

Answer (b) is incorrect because the *no-additional-cost service* fringe benefit, as well as all fringe benefits enumerated in IRC § 132, do not have as a requirement that the benefit be provided for the convenience of the employer. **Answer (c) is incorrect** because, as discussed above, this fringe benefit can be provided, without tax consequence, to the employee's spouse and dependent children. While not at issue in this question, this fringe benefit (as well as the "qualified employee discount") can also be provided to retired or disabled employees as well as a deceased employee's surviving spouse. [See IRC § 132(h) (and for an employee's "parents" in the case of airline travel as a *no-additional-cost service* fringe benefit).] **Answer (d) is incorrect** because this is an excludable fringe benefit without any showing of a business purpose for the service provided. **Answer (e) is incorrect** because, as discussed above, the benefit is provided across the board to all full-time employees on a non discriminatory basis.

- **Additional references:** *See* DANIEL Q. POSIN, FEDERAL INCOME TAXATION OF INDIVIDUALS ¶ 2.02(1) (5ᵗʰ ed. 2000).

21.   **The best answer is (c).** IRC § 61 defines gross income as "all income from whatever source derived." From your initial study of gross income's scope, you probably found it to be broadly defined, including the taxpayer's receipt of some net economic benefit or net accession to wealth. In class, you also discover that gross income is also not limited to the receipt of cash. [Reg. § 1.61-1(d) (compensation received in forms other than in cash).] Emmy, the employee in question, derived an economic benefit with her four-night free stay at the fully Tillie's fully booked New York hotel.

Once again, we turn to the fringe benefits of IRC § 132 in search of relief for this employee. At first glance, one might go to the *no-additional-cost service* fringe benefit discussed in question 20, above. In this case, however, the employer <u>did</u> incur substantial additional cost, in the form of lost revenue, by allowing the employee to "bump" a paying customer. [See Reg. § 1.132-2(a)(1)(ii) (foregone revenue is a substantial additional cost).]

Next, we might consider the "de minimis" fringe benefit in IRC §§ 132(a)(4) and 132(e). A *de minimis* fringe "means any property or service the value of which is (after taking into account the frequency with which similar fringes are provided by the employer to the employer's employees) so small as to make accounting for it unreasonable or administratively impracticable." [IRC § 132(e)(1).] Looking at examples of *de minimis* fringe benefits in the regulations, a four-night free stay at a luxury hotel hardly seems to qualify (this is not the proverbial doughnuts and coffee at the office). The regulations, in examples of what sort of benefits do <u>not</u> constitute *de minimis* fringes include "use of employer-owned facilities (such as an apartment, hunting lodge, boat, etc.) for a weekend." [Reg. § 1.132-6(e)(2).]

Emmy still has hope for some relief, and looking back to the regulations addressing the *no-additional-cost service* fringe, we are given some guidance. In discussing excess capacity as a potential indication of no cost incurred by an employer, the regulations state: "Employees who receive non-excess capacity services may, however, be eligible for a qualified employee discount of up to 20 percent of the value of the service provided. See § 1.132-3." [Reg. § 132-2(a)(2).] So off the *qualified employee discount* fringe benefit.

It is here that we fine at least *some* relief for Emmy. The *qualified employee discount* fringe benefit can be found in IRC §§ 132(a)(2) and 132(c). While students usually encounter this fringe benefit at some former job working in retail and being entitled to a 15%, 20%, etc. employee discount on merchandise purchased from the store. Although restrictions and limits may apply, the *qualified employee discount* allows employers to allow employees to buy their products or services at a discount, without that discount being included in the employee's gross income. Emmy's situation is a bit unusual as we are examining the *qualified employee discount* in relation to the 100% discount that she received. Nonetheless, it is a discount and

There are two major requirements or limitations applicable to this fringe benefit. First, the discount the employee is receiving must be with respect to products or services that are in the line of business in which the employee is working. [IRC § 132(c)(4).] This is the so-called "line of business" test. Ostensibly, this requirement exists to prevent conglomerates from providing across the board discounts to all employees in all lines of the employer's business that are perceived to be unfair when compared to non-conglomerates. We have, in question 20, above, already addressed this requirement with respect to Tillie's employees, and Emmy passes this test.

The second major limitation is the amount of the discount available. Basically, the *qualified employee discount* will be viewed as a tax-free fringe benefit as long as "it doesn't cost the employer too much money" in providing the benefit. The statutory maximum tax-free discount applicable to employer provided "services" is 20%. [IRC 132(c)(1)(B).] In the case of discounts for products (tangible personal property), the statute does not set a specific discount percentage amount but, rather, states that the discount cannot exceed the employer's "gross profit percentage." [IRC § 132(c)(1)(A).] The computation of a company's "gross profit percentage" is defined in IRC § 132(c)(2) and can be a bit cumbersome to compute. Fortunately, it should be fairly clear that Emmy's free hotel stay is classified as the receipt of a service, and, therefore, the statutory 20% maximum discount applies. The repercussion to Emmy is that she has received a discount well in excess of the statutory allowed maximum (recall, she received a 100% discount). The result is that Emmy can exclude the statutory maximum 20% discount applicable to services. In other words, Emmy can exclude, from income, 20% of the value of her four-night New York hotel stay. She must include in income, however, 80% (the excess discount) of the value of her lodging.

Note that the fact that one fails to qualify for a particular tax-free fringe benefit (such as the *no-additional-cost service* fringe in Emmy's case), does not preclude the application of another fringe benefit exclusion provision.

While not an issue in this problem, it should be mentioned that the statute provides that an employer cannot provide some, but not all, of the fringe benefits enumerated in IRC § 132 to employees on a discriminatory basis (in favor of only highly compensated employees as defined by the statute). The *qualified employee discount* is one such benefit that cannot be provided to employees in a discriminatory manner. [IRC § 132(j)(1).] This is not an issue in our question as the fringe benefit at issue is offered to all full-time employees and therefore, does not offend these discrimination rules. Limiting this benefit to just "full-time" employees is most likely not discriminatory for purpose of IRC § 132. [Reg. § 1.132-8(d)(2).] It should also be noted that if this fringe benefit were to discriminate in favor of highly compensated employees, the <u>entire</u> value of the free service received would be included in income (and not just any extra benefit that may be provided to such employees). [Reg. § 1.132-8(a)(2).]

- **Additional references:** *See* DANIEL Q. POSIN, FEDERAL INCOME TAXATION OF INDIVIDUALS ¶ 2.02(1) (5th ed. 2000).

22. **The best answer is (c).** Brandon will not have to recognize as income, any of the debt that was forgiven because of the degree of his insolvency.

This is a fairly difficult question and involves multiple steps to arrive at the correct answer. The two major questions that need to be answered are: 1) does Brandon, on a prima facie basis, have "income from discharge of indebtedness?" and 2) if so, is this income recognized or is there a statutory non-recognition (or exclusion) provision that is applicable?

Forgiving a debt, in whole or in part, generally results in the realization of gross income to the debtor. It makes sense that being relieved of a liability (a financial obligation) results in an economic benefit or net accession to wealth (i.e., income) to the debtor. This type of income is referred to as "income from discharge of indebtedness" and is specifically identified by the Code as constituting gross income. [IRC § 61(a)(12).] Brandon owed $50,000 to a sub-contractor, $25,000 of which was forgiven. <u>So far, Brandon appears to have $25,000 in income from discharge of indebtedness.</u> This $25,000 will be recognized in Brandon's gross income unless there is some specific Code provision allowing for its exclusion. In general, on any question (multiple choice or essay) where it appears that there is income to be recognized, do not just stop at that point. Go on to make sure that no exclusion or non-recognition provisions apply to the situation presented in the question.

In the area of "income from discharge of indebtedness," there are two major ex-
clusion/non-recognition provisions to think about. The exclusion from gross income to the recipients of gifts (made out of detached and disinterested generosity)
under IRC § 102, and the potential exclusion of income from discharge of indebtedness for taxpayers in dire financial straits pursuant to IRC § 108. The former
occurs where the facts give some indication that the debt was gratuitously forgiven, typically where there is a familial or close relationship between the debtor
and creditor. There is no indication from our facts that the sub-contractor gratuitously forgave the $25,000. Exclusion as a gift, therefore, is not relevant. The
latter exclusion, under IRC § 108, applying to certain debtors in poor financial
straits, looks promising for Brandon.

IRC § 108(a)(1) provides, in part, that some or all of otherwise includible income
from discharge of indebtedness is <u>excludable</u> from income for "<u>insolvent debtors</u>"
or where the debt is discharged in a <u>bankruptcy proceeding</u>. For debts discharged
or forgiven in a bankruptcy proceeding, there is full exclusion from gross income
for the amount discharged. When the debt is not discharged in formal bankruptcy
proceedings, the otherwise includible income from the forgiven debt may, nonetheless, be excluded from income (in whole or in part) if the debtor was "insolvent" at the time of the forgiveness. Insolvency is defined, in IRC § 108(d)(3), as
an individual who, immediately before the debt in question is discharged, has total
liabilities in excess of the total value of his or her assets. Unfortunately, many
people fit this definition of insolvency including law students with huge student
loan debt and little in the way of assets. Brandon's $25,000 of forgiven debt was
not discharged in bankruptcy. However, his $350,000 of liabilities before the dis-
charge exceeds his total assets valued at $320,000 and, therefore, Brandon was in-
solvent. For insolvent debtors, the exclusion from gross income may be limited,
as the excluded amount cannot exceed the amount by which the debtor was insolvent <u>immediately before the discharge</u>. Any amount forgiven that exceeds the
debtor's degree of insolvency is included in gross income. Brandon was insolvent
to the tune of $30,000 ($350,000 of debt less the $320,000 <u>value</u> of his assets) and
the debt forgiven was less, at $25,000. Therefore, Brandon has no income recog-
nition as a result of the debt discharged.

Answer (a) is incorrect because the cited provision is not applicable to our facts.
IRC § 108 is a very complex section and contains many special provisions. Depending on the depth in which your professor covers these provisions, you may or
may not encounter the cited provision at § 108(e)(5). Basically, that section provides exclusion relief for "solvent" debtors in certain "purchase-money" debt
situations. **Answer (b) is incorrect** because it reflects an improper determination
of Brandon's insolvency. To determine insolvency, the total <u>value</u> of assets is
used, not their adjusted basis. This answer incorrectly used Brandon's adjusted

basis in his assets to determine insolvency. **Answer (d) is incorrect** because measurement of income and possible exclusion thereof from discharge of debts is determined at the time the debt is discharged, not at the end of the tax year.

- **Additional references:** See DANIEL Q. POSIN, FEDERAL INCOME TAXATION OF INDIVIDUALS ¶ 3.10(1) (5th ed. 2000).

23.   **The answer to this very complex question is (e).** Students universally dislike "none of the above" answers, and are justified in doing so. They do provide, however, a powerful testing tool for professors and, in this case, none of the answers provided in (a) through (d) are correct. The "bottom line" correct numeric answer for this question is that the net operating loss carryover (NOL) will be eliminated, and the basis of his assets will be reduced by $15,000. This question is a somewhat unfair extension of the immediately preceding question 22. It requires delving deeper into the quagmire of the IRC § 108 provisions excluding otherwise includible income resulting from discharge of indebtedness. This professor, over the past few years, has not covered IRC § 108 in sufficient depth to answer this question. Your professor, however, may cover this section more thoroughly and, if such is the case, this question is pertinent. This question is also a bit unfair in that it requires, in part, a correct analysis of the previous question. This professor would not ask such a series of interrelated multiple-choice questions on an exam. Rather, this series of questions was derived from an exam essay question.

With the introduction out of the way, we know, from the previous question, that Brandon's $25,000 discharge of indebtedness is properly excludable form gross income because he was "insolvent" by more than the amount of the debt forgiven. The issue addressed in this question, is whether Brandon has to pay some later "price" for the exclusion. No, Brandon does not have to recognize the previously excluded income should, for example, he become solvent down the road. However, Brandon may, indeed, have to pay some price for this exclusion that can be extracted by other indirect means. IRC § 108(b) is the potential payback provision titled "reduction of tax attributes." The basic concept here is that if a taxpayer qualified for the benefit of excluding otherwise taxable income from discharge of indebtedness, he or she may have to reduce other "good tax things" to which they may be entitled – we have to open up the taxpayer's tax treasure chest and possibly take out some beneficial items. This provision requires Brandon to take the $25,000 that he is entitled to exclude (because of his insolvency) and reduce, by up to that amount, certain "tax attributes" or benefits. This provision is difficult enough without the added difficulty that some, if not most, of these "tax attributes" may not readily be understood. These "tax attributes," in the order of their reduction, are as follows:

- Net operating losses (NOL).
- General business credits pursuant to IRC § 38.
- Minimum tax credits available pursuant to IRC § 53(b).
- Capital losses for the current year and carryovers to the current year under IRC § 1212.
- Reduction of adjusted basis in the taxpayer's property.

Without presenting a treatise on the issue, we take Brandon's $25,000 and start eliminating or reducing, as the case may be, the above "tax attributes" in the order presented. Brandon's $5,000 net operating loss (NOL) is the first to go. The NOL is completely eliminated, using up $5,000 of his $25,000 excluded amount. We take the remaining $20,000 of benefit and go down the list. The facts indicate that he has no general business credits, or minimum tax credits or capital losses/carryovers. That takes us down to the reduction of the basis of his property. We can see that reducing Brandon's adjusted basis in his property by $20,000 will not be a beneficial thing for him. The mechanics of this adjusted basis reduction is not, however, that simple. The Code, in IRC § 108(b)(2)(D) directs us to IRC § 1017 for the mechanics of making this basis reduction. Unfortunately, IRC § 1017 is another daunting section. With some variations, the basic mechanism for basis reduction is to reduce the basis of the taxpayer's property with a <u>maximum</u> or <u>limit</u> on such reduction equal to the amount by which the taxpayer's total adjusted basis in property exceeds his or her total liabilities, both measured immediately after the discharge of debt. Huh? Let's use the facts in our problem to try to explain this. At this point, Brandon has $20,000 of excluded benefit for which he has not paid any price (recall he started with $25,000 of exclusion benefit, but $5,000 was used to eliminate his NOL). The total adjusted basis in Brandon's property is given as $340,000. Brandon's liabilities, immediately after the discharge, are $325,000 ($350,000 total liabilities less the $25,000 forgiven). Therefore, the maximum or limit for basis reduction for Brandon is $15,000 (the amount by which his $340,000 total adjusted basis in assets exceeds his $325,000 of debt).

This finally brings us to our correct answer. Brandon was able to exclude the entire $25,000 of forgiven debt because of the degree of his insolvency. His "payback" was the elimination of his $5,000 net operating loss (NOL) and a reduction in the total adjusted basis of his assets to the tune of $15,000. Note that in this question, Brandon did not have to fully "pay" for his exclusion through the reduction of tax attributes.

Answers (b), (c) and (d) are incorrect because, to varying degrees, they do not reflect the proper method of reducing Brandon's tax attributes for the exclusion benefit that he received. **Answer (a) is incorrect** because, unless a special election is made (and the facts indicate that this is not the case) the tax attributes listed must be reduced in the order they are presented above.

- **Additional references:** See DANIEL Q. POSIN, FEDERAL INCOME TAXATION OF INDIVIDUALS ¶¶ 3.10 (5th ed. 2000).

24. **Answer (b) is correct.** Normally, an individual does not have income when he or she repays a debt. Had Brandon paid his sub-contractor/creditor $25,000 in cash, Brandon would have no income realization – he has no net accession to wealth as gross income is commonly defined. However, Brandon paid off his debt with his services and that <u>does</u> create income for him. This is a concept upon which students sometimes stumble because it somehow does not seem fair to Brandon. In class, this professor utilizes a couple of methods or illustrations to help clarify the point. One such method is to recast, or view in a different light, the transaction in an equivalent manner. We could break down the transaction into something like this. Brandon performs $25,000 worth of services for the sub-contractor and the sub-contractor <u>pays</u> Brandon $25,000 <u>in cash</u>. At this point, it is clear Brandon would have income. Next, Brandon turns around and gives $25,000 to the sub-contractor to pay off his debt. The payment of the debt is not the taxable component but, rather, it is the performance of services that generates the income to Brandon. In substance, we have the same result as given in the facts: Brandon performed services and the debt he owed was paid.

Another example used by this professor in class is as follows: I arranged it with my University employer to give me loans or advances each month in an amount that equals my next month's salary. We agree that I will pay back these debts by performing teaching services. Should I not have any income with this plan? Does it seem unfair that I have income? I got paid, albeit in advance, for work performed. In effect, this is Brandon's situation in our question.

Answer (a) is not correct because while Brandon is paying a debt, he is also deriving a benefit from the services he performed. **Answer (c) is incorrect** because Brandon's repayment has nothing to do with discharge of indebtedness and the resulting potential exclusion based on insolvency. **Answer (d) is incorrect** because barter exchanges, involving services, is income to the party or parties rendering services. Brandon, in this question, rendered services for a benefit (the payment of his debt). **Answer (e) is incorrect** because we do have a correct response in (b).

- **Additional references:** See DANIEL Q. POSIN, FEDERAL INCOME TAXATION OF INDIVIDUALS ¶ 2.01 (5th ed. 2000).

25.   **The most accurate answer is (d).** Professor P will, for 2002, most likely be able to exclude up to $80,000 of income "earned" outside the U.S. pursuant to IRC §911. He will most likely qualify for this exclusion by meeting the "physical presence" test of IRC §911.

Most individuals traveling outside of the U.S. for extended periods of time on business are somewhat familiar with the issue raised in this question. It may not, however, receive a great deal of coverage in some federal income tax courses. The section is IRC § 911 and its first sentence (at IRC § 911(a)) can be music to the ears of U.S. citizens or residents living abroad: ". . . there shall be excluded from income . . ." But first, a brief explanation of the scope of the U.S. income tax system vis-à-vis foreign source income and U.S. persons residing outside of the U.S.

The geographic source of Professor P's income is, to start, irrelevant for U.S. income tax purposes. U.S. citizens and U.S. residents are taxed (for U.S. income tax purposes) on a "world-wide" basis. Simply put, this means that such individuals must include in gross income, unless otherwise excludable, all income regardless of its geographic source and regardless of where such person is living when the income is generated. Gross income includes "all income from whatever source derived." [IRC § 61(a).] The U.S. income tax system, unlike many other countries, is not situs or residence based. For example, another country may tax only income derived from sources within that country, and may have limited reach to tax their citizens residing outside their country of citizenship. One always hears the stories of famous individuals taking up residence in another country to avoid their home country's high tax rates. Simply put, this strategy generally does <u>not</u> work for U.S. citizens (and, U.S. "residents").

Professor P's income from whatever sources while he is living and traveling abroad *will* be, but for some specific exclusion, included in gross income for U.S. income tax purposes. This brings us to a possible exclusion in IRC § 911. This section allows "qualified" individuals to exclude, from gross income (for U.S. income tax purposes) up to $80,000 per year of "earned income." [IRC § 911(b)(2)(D)(i) (the exclusion amounts for years prior to 2002, were less to varying degrees).] "Earned income," for purposes of this section, generally means wages, salaries, payments for services, etc. (it does not include income such as interest, dividends, rentals, royalties and other "non-compensation" type income).

An individual "qualifies" for this exclusion if he or she meets either of two tests: commonly referred to as the "residence test" or the "physical presence" test. Simplified, the *residence test* is met when an individual is a bona fide *resident* of one or more foreign countries for an uninterrupted period including an entire tax year. [IRC § 911(d)(1)(A).] The *residence* test can be difficult to satisfy and represents more than just an individual's mere physical presence outside the U.S. for one year. Establishing one's "residence" in a foreign country usually requires affirmative steps on the part of the individual. An example of an individual meeting the *residence* test might be an attorney (U.S. citizen) working full-time (and for the foreseeable future – probably for years) in their firm's Tokyo office. While not really necessary to answer our question, it is extremely unlikely that Professor P would meet the *residence* test.

The *physical presence test* is usually the easier of the two qualifying tests to meet. To qualify, an individual must, in any period of twelve consecutive months, be physically present in one or more foreign countries during at least 330 full days. The requirement is not that the individual be "working" for 330 full days abroad during a twelve month period. Days abroad working, days vacationing, days playing, and days doing nothing all count towards the 330 day minimum. There is also no requirement that the days abroad be in any one country. Analyzing our facts, Professor P will, most likely, meet the *physical presence test* and could exclude up to $80,000 of his foreign source "earned" income. He will be outside of the U.S. for all of 2002, except for the two weeks visiting friends in California. For 2002, that leaves about 351 days that he will be physically present outside the U.S.

While not part of this question, IRC § 911 also provides for certain housing cost exclusions, and for meals and lodging furnished at certain foreign "camps" (e.g. isolated foreign work sites).

It should be noted that this question addresses only some of the U.S. income tax aspects of foreign activities. Many other U.S. income tax issues may be relevant when dealing with non-U.S. activities. In addition, foreign jurisdiction taxation may be applicable, as well as the matter of income tax treaties that the United States has entered into with many other countries.

Answer (a) is incorrect because of its incorrect interpretation of the *physical presence* test. All days outside of the U.S. count towards the 330-day requirement, including vacation/leisure days. **Answer (b) is incorrect** because it imposes no qualifying tests or limiting amounts for the exclusion of foreign source income. **Answer (c) is incorrect** because it does not correctly reflect that the taxpayer must meet either of the two tests discussed above to exclude his "earned income" (and then, only up to $80,000). It then incorrectly applies the IRC § 911 qualifications and exclusion limitations to "unearned" income (none of which is excluded pursuant to IRC § 911).

ANSWER KEY
EXAM II

FEDERAL INCOME TAX
MULTIPLE-CHOICE QUESTIONS
ANSWER KEY AND EXPLANATIONS
EXAM II

1.   **Answer (b) is correct.** Alfred's qualifying medical care "expenses" consist of $5,000 of the elevator's costs and $1,000 for the cost of its maintenance.

IRC § 213 allows for a deduction of certain qualified medical expenses. Once one makes the determination of what constitutes "qualified" medical care expenses, the subject of this question, the deduction is allowed as an "itemized deduction" only to the extent that the total qualifying expenses exceeds 7.5% of adjusted gross income (AGI). [See Appendix A for more information about how income and deductions fit together in computing taxable income.] Qualified medical care expenses include typical costs for doctors, dentists, hospital, health insurance, and the like. [See IRC § 213(d).]

Addressing first the easier issue of Alfred's over-the-counter medicines that were recommended by his doctor. While logically it would appear that such costs would qualify, the Code specifically allows deductions only for prescription drugs (and insulin in those areas where its sale is allowed without a prescription). [IRC § 213(b).] Therefore, <u>none</u> of the $200 Alfred paid for the medicine will qualify as medical care expenses, even though his physician recommended the medicine.

The cost of the elevator, and its maintenance, present other issues. The cost of a major and permanent improvement, such as an elevator, is not really an "expense" at all but, rather, is considered a "capital expenditure." Major improvement capital expenditures, are generally not deductible expenses but serve to increase the adjusted basis in the property being improved. [IRC §§ 263 and 1016.] However, if the capital expenditure is primarily health-related, as is the case for Alfred's elevator installation, a medical care expense is allowed but only to the extent that the cost of the improvement exceeds the increase in value to the underlying property resulting from the improvement. [See Reg. § 1.213-1(e)(iii).] For Alfred, the $20,000 cost of the elevator less the $15,000 resulting increase in the value of his home, or <u>$5,000</u> is the amount of qualifying medical care expense. The regulations go on to provide that 100% of the operating and maintenance costs associated with such an improvement are deductible regardless of the amount, if any, of the original expenditure for the medically related improvement that qualified as a medical care expense. This assumes, of course, that the medical condition, for which the expenditure was made, still exists. For Alfred, even though only a portion of the elevator installation costs qualified as a medical care expense, the entire $1,000 of maintenance costs qualifies.

Answer (a) is incorrect. This answer does accurately reflect the $5,000 qualifying medical care expense associated with the elevator's $20,000 installation cost (representing one-fourth of the total cost). However, it incorrectly prorates the maintenance costs, allowing only one-fourth of the total $1,000, or $250. **An-**

swers (c) and (d) are incorrect because both of these answers incorrectly include the entire $20,000 elevator installation costs as a qualifying medical care expense. Answer (e) is incorrect because a correct answer (b) is presented.

- **Additional references:** *See* DANIEL Q. POSIN, FEDERAL INCOME TAXATION OF INDIVIDUALS ¶ 7.01(7) (5th ed. 2000).

2.   **The best answer is (c).** The principal Code section permitting business deductions is IRC § 162. None of Tom's cost for airfare to/from Providence is deductible because the trip was not primarily for business. However, the costs associated with his stay in Providence for the one day that he did conduct substantial business, Friday, qualify as deductible business expenses (meals qualifying at 50% of their costs). A more comprehensive analysis follows.

The first sentence of IRC § 162 (which appears in subsection (a)) enumerates, for all intents and purposes, four basic requirements for a business deduction. A business deduction is allowed for all (read as one continuous phrase with four distinct requirements):

> ➢   Ordinary and necessary
> ➢   Expenses
> ➢   Paid or incurred during the taxable year
> ➢   In carrying on any trade or business.

These four requirements often represent, in federal income tax classes and in real life, separate and significant points of contention. Business deductions come in a million different flavors, but all qualifying deductions must meet those four criteria. The study, in tax classes, of business deductions can be long and comprehensive. At times, it may seem like many business deductions have their own set of rules, as if permitted by a separate Code section. There are many business deductions that almost take on a life of their own primarily because of explanations and interpretations from the Code subsections, regulations, court decisions, I.R.S. pronouncements, and the like.

IRC § 162(a)(2) specifically identifies that expenditures associated with "traveling away from home" constitute qualifying business expenses. While this subsection appears to add additional requirements to the four listed above for such traveling expenditures, a careful examination of the statutory language reveals no more than a reiteration of the four basic requirements, albeit in a different form. It is clear that Tom, in this question, did spend some of his time on business matters on his trip to Providence. The regulations promulgated for IRC § 162 are extensive and help clarify the issues relating to Tom as well as many other business expense issues that are not the subject of this question. For discussion purposes, Tom's potential qualifying business expenses are bifurcated into two parts:

his <u>transportation costs</u> to/from Providence, and his <u>costs incurred during his stay</u> in Providence. At the outset, however, before discussing these two components, it should be noted that this question addresses potential business travel "away from home" as distinguished from "local" business travel. Business travel "away from home" generally means traveling far enough and long enough away from one's home to require an overnight stay (i.e., it would not be reasonable to expect someone to travel long distances after a long business day's work). [See *United States v. Correll*, 389 US 299, 88 S.Ct. 445 (1967).] Business travel "away from home" opens the door to potential deductions for lodging, non-entertainment meals, incidentals, etc. Other questions in this book address the issue of where a taxpayer's "home" is located, and the issue of "local" travel for business (usually concerned only with deductions for transportation related expenses).

Tom's transportation costs to/from Providence (his airfare) qualifies as a business expense <u>if</u> the "trip is related primarily to [his] . . . trade or business." [Reg. § 1.162-2(b)(1).] In Tom's case, we need not delve any further into the regulations to determine, based on a common sense analysis of the facts, that his trip to Providence was primarily for pleasure and not for business purposes. Just in case we want to verify this result, the regulations, at § 1.162-2(b)(2), provide that this determination be made based on the facts and circumstances in each case. These regulations indicate that an important factor for making this determination is the number of days spent on business compared to the number of days spent for pleasure. Again, hopefully it is fairly apparent from the facts that Tom's trip to Providence was <u>not</u> made primarily for business purposes. Tom's transportation costs to/from Providence (his airfare) do <u>not qualify</u> as deductible business expenses. Note that for domestic travel, as is the case in this problem, deduction of transportation costs for traveling away from home is generally an "all or nothing" proposition. If the trip is primarily for business, 100% of the taxpayer's transportation related costs generally qualify as business expenses pursuant to IRC § 162. Alternatively, as is the case with Tom, <u>none</u> of the transportation costs qualify as business expenses if the trip is primarily for pleasure. It should be noted that the rules for "foreign" travel may differ and proration of transportation costs between deductible business and nondeductible personal expenses may be appropriate.

The Regulations do provide, however, that "expenses while at the destination which are properly allocable to the taxpayer's trade or business are deductible even though the traveling expenses to and from the destination are not deductible." [Reg. §1.162-2(b).] The twelve hours that Tom spent on Friday meeting with the firm's client was clearly spent conducting business. For this one day, Friday, Tom was traveling away from home in connection with the conduct of a trade or business. Therefore, his expenses relating to that one day qualify as § 162 business expenses. These include the cost of his lodging and incidentals for

Friday, as well as 50% of his meals for that day. The 50% deduction limitation for business meals comes not from IRC § 162 but, rather, is supplied by IRC § 274(n)(1). While not the subject of this question, the scope of this 50% limit covers more than unreimbursed employee business meals (as in this question). It is also applicable to most business meals and entertainment related business expenses that are otherwise allowed as deductions. Please see other questions in this book that relate to entertainment expenses.

It should be noted that an individual can incur qualifying § 162 expenses in the context of working as an employee (as Tom in our question) or in an individual's own business (someone who alternatively referred to as being self-employed, an independent contractor, or operating his or her business as an "unincorporated sole proprietorship"). The requirements for deductibility pursuant to § 162 are the same for an employee or a self-employed individual. However, "where" and "how" these deductions are taken does vary. Other questions in this book address these issues.

Answer (a) is incorrect. First, his transportation costs to/from Providence are not deductible because his trip was primarily for pleasure and not primarily for business. The second part of this answer, deducting costs for pleasure days to the extent of the airfare savings derived by staying longer, is a legitimately allowed technique, but requires that the transportation costs qualify as business expenses. **Answer (b) is incorrect** because, as stated, his transportation costs are not deductible. **Answer (d) is incorrect** because Friday, and Tom's expenses associated with that day, qualifies as a business day for Tom. **Answer (e) is incorrect** because the fact that his trip was primarily for pleasure does not preclude the deduction for expense incurred while conducting business during the trip.

- **Additional references:** *See* DANIEL Q. POSIN, FEDERAL INCOME TAXATION OF INDIVIDUALS ¶¶ 6.02(1)(a), 6.02(1)(b), 6.02(4) (5th ed. 2000).

3. **Answer (c) is correct.** Tom is not entitled to any interest deduction here. But wait, surely this is an ordinary and necessary business expense, and IRC § 162 allows deductions for such expenses. True, if this was not "interest," we could stop here and the deduction would be allowed pursuant to IRC § 162. However, we are dealing with interest expense and because of that, we must turn to the more specific IRC § 163, dealing with deductions for interest paid. If, for some reason, the interest Tom incurs in our question is disallowed as a deduction by IRC § 163, it will effectively trump any possible deduction pursuant to IRC § 162. And, unfortunately, IRC § 163 effectively disallows a deduction for the interest that Tom pays in this question. The assayer lies hiding in IRC § 163(h): "Disallowance of deduction for personal interest."

For casual readers of the Code, IRC § 163(a) provides a simple and broad sounding deduction for interest stating, in part: "There shall be allowed as a deduction all interest paid . . . within the taxable year on indebtedness." The Tax Reform Act of 1986 introduced subsection (h), located quite some written distance from the general allowance for interest deductions of subsection (a). IRC § 163(h) starts out deceptively, and unfavorably, simply by stating, in part: "In the case of a taxpayer other than a corporation, no deduction shall be allowed . . . for personal interest paid . . . during the taxable year." We will come to the conclusion for our question that Tom's interest will be classified as disallowed "personal" interest.

The definition of "personal" interest, which is not deductible, if found in IRC § 163(h)(2) and takes the form of a negative definition – personal interest is interest "other than" those listed in subparagraphs (A) through (F). The key, therefore, to finding interest that is deductible, is to fit within one of these specified categories of what does not constitute nondeductible personal interest. Among the categories of interest that are not personal interest is what might be the familiar category of "qualified residence interest" (typical interest paid on a home mortgage). [IRC § 163(h)(2)(D).] Somewhat less familiar, but logically not included as personal interest, is "interest properly allocable to a trade or business." [IRC § 163(h)(2)(A).] The interest that Tom pays in our question, would seem to fit within this category of non-personal interest, thus allowing for its deduction. However, careful reading of IRC § 163(h)(2)(A) reveals, in parentheses, that non-personal trade or business interest does not include what is effectively trade or business interest that is incurred by an employee. In other words, interest paid by an individual in an employment setting that looks, smells and tastes like "trade or business" is not "trade or business" interest, but, rather, by definition is nondeductible "personal" interest. This long, circuitous route leaves us with Tom's interest paid in this question being nondeductible personal interest. Students are often frustrated by this result that apparently, and unfortunately, defies logical explanation.

Note that had the facts of this question been different with Tom as a self-employed individual, the interest would have been deductible.

Answers (a) and (b) are incorrect because, as discussed above, qualifying under the general business deduction IRC § 162 is insufficient when dealing with interest expenses. The presence of interest requires one to analyze its deductibility under potentially more restrictive provisions of IRC § 163. In our case, the interest Tom pays is rendered nondeductible as discussed above. **Answer (d) is incorrect** but it points towards a category of interest that, pursuant to IRC § 163(h), is not personal interest and, therefore, is deductible by individuals. "Qualified residence interest" is not nondeductible personal residence interest. Exactly what constitutes qualified residence interest can be a somewhat complex question and is addressed in other questions in this book. The short answer here on why Tom's interest is not deductible qualified residence interest is because the loan on, which Tom is paying interest, is not secured by a qualified residence which is a requirement. [See IRC §§ 163(h)(3)(B)(i)(II) and (h)(3)(C)(i).]

- **Additional references:** *See* DANIEL Q. POSIN, FEDERAL INCOME TAXATION OF INDIVIDUALS ¶ 7.02(3) (5th ed. 2000).

4. **Answer (c) is correct.** IRC § 165(d) allows an individual to deduct gambling (or wagering) losses to the extent that such individual has wagering gains in the same year. However, an individual who is not engaged in the business of gambling cannot just offset gambling winnings with gambling losses. Such individuals, as all individuals, must include in gross income, total gross gambling winnings. They are entitled to claim gambling losses to the extent of these gross gambling winnings (but not more) as a separate deduction. This deduction is allowed *below the line* (a deduction from adjusted gross income to arrive at taxable income) as part of the group of deductions known collectively as *itemized deductions*. [Reg. § 1.165-10.] More specifically, this gambling loss deduction is part of a sub-group known as "miscellaneous itemized deductions." It should be noted that this deduction for gambling losses is <u>not</u> subject to the 2% of AGI nondeductible floor that is applicable to most other "miscellaneous itemized deductions."

Answer (a) is incorrect because in certain circumstances, as discussed above, gambling losses do give rise to a deduction. **Answer (b) is incorrect** because, as discussed above, when applicable gambling losses generate a separate deduction that does not serve to offset gambling winnings (the deduction is taken as part of *itemized deductions*). **Answer (d) is incorrect** because it does not reflect the conditional nature of the deduction (that it is allowed only to the extent of gambling winnings).

- **Additional references:** *See* DANIEL Q. POSIN, FEDERAL INCOME TAXATION OF INDIVIDUALS ¶ 7.01(5)(b) (5th ed. 2000).

5. **Answer (a) is the best response.** This is a relatively complex question involving the deductibility of interest. We will conclude that Tim should be entitled to deduct the interest paid with respect to the full amount of the loans involved.

Our primary statutory focus for this question is IRC § 163, dealing with the deductibility of interest paid. Summarizing the answer, "qualified residence interest" is deductible. To be classified as such, one must be paying interest on either "acquisition" or "home equity" indebtedness that is secured by a "qualified residence" (two residences may qualify). Both Tim's principal residence and his vacation cabin are considered "qualified residences." Tim's "acquisition indebtedness" is comprised of the original $200,000 loan on his principal residence, $80,000 of the $160,000 second mortgage on his principal residence that was used for the bedroom addition, and the $100,000 mortgage loan to purchase the vacation cabin. The other $80,000 of the $160,000 second mortgage on his principal residence that was used to purchase stocks and pay for the cruise qualifies as "home equity indebtedness." The total of his "acquisition" and "home equity" indebtedness does not exceed the statutory maximums of $1 million and $100,000, respectively. Therefore, all of the interest Tim pays with respect to all of these loans is deductible as "qualified residence interest." A more thorough analysis follows.

IRC § 163(a) provides a simple and broad sounding deduction for interest stating, in part: "There shall be allowed as a deduction all interest paid . . . within the taxable year on indebtedness." The Tax Reform Act of 1986 introduced subsection (h), located quite some written distance from the general allowance for interest deductions of subsection (a). IRC § 163(h) starts out deceptively, and unfavorably, simple by stating, in part: "In the case of a taxpayer other than a corporation, no deduction shall be allowed . . . for personal interest paid . . . during the taxable year." The definition of "personal" interest, which is not deductible, is found in IRC § 163(h)(2) and takes the form of a negative definition – personal interest is interest "other than" those listed in subparagraphs (A) through (F). The key, therefore, to finding interest that is deductible, is to fit it within one of these specified categories of what does not constitute nondeductible personal interest. One such category of interest that is not considered personal interest is "qualified residence interest." [IRC § 163(h)(2)(D).]

Qualified residence interest is addressed in IRC §§ 163(h)(3) and (h)(4). To obtain deductible qualified residence interest status, a taxpayer must have two things:
  ➤ A "qualified residence"
  ➤ The property type of indebtedness associated with such qualified residence.

A qualified residence includes the taxpayer's principal residence and one other residence (e.g., a vacation home) that meets certain requirements. [IRC § 163(h)(4)(A).] A principal residence can include the typical house (as our couple's in this question), a condominium, townhouse, co-op, etc. A principal residence can consist of a boat, trailer, motor home, or similar vehicle if, generally, they contain sleeping, eating and bathroom facilities. While the determination of one's principal residence is usually not at issue for most people (as it is not an issue here regarding Tim's *principal residence*), there are (i.e., your professor can discuss) situations that present more of a challenge. The "one other residence" as a qualified residence for purposes of deductible qualified residence can present its own host of issues, some involving rather complex statutory rules involving very convoluted definitions. For our facts, however, the classification of Tim's vacation cabin is fairly simple. Because he uses the cabin solely for personal purposes and it is not rented out during the year, it qualifies as a *qualified residence*. [IRC § 163(h)(4)(A)(iii).] While not at issue here, if the "one other residence" is rented out, the statute directs you to the somewhat bizarre definition rules in IRC § 280A(d)(1).

There are two proper types of indebtedness recognized by the statute in this area: "acquisition indebtedness" and "home equity indebtedness." It is important to recognize that the statute requires that either of these two types of loans must be **secured** by the applicable qualified residence in order to qualify. [IRC § 163(h)(3)(A).] All of Tim's loans in this question are secured by the appropriate *qualified residence* (the original and second mortgage loans secured by his principal residence and the vacation mortgage loan secured by his vacation cabin).

Acquisition indebtedness is defined in IRC § 163(h)(3)(B), and is fairly straightforward for most taxpayers. Acquisition loans are money borrowed to **acquire, construct, or substantially improve** a qualified residence. Tim's first mortgage loan, still at $200,000, was used to purchase his qualified principal residence and, therefore, is properly classified as *acquisition indebtedness*. His second mortgage of $160,000 presents a bit of a challenge as $80,000 of it was used for a room addition to his house, and the remaining $80,000 was used for things unrelated to the house (to purchase stocks and pay for a cruise). For debt classification purposes, we split this loan into component parts with the $80,000 of this loan used to "substantially improve" his qualified residence also qualifying as *acquisition indebtedness*. The remaining $80,000 portion of this loan is not acquisition indebtedness but, rather, is discussed below under *home equity indebtedness*. Tim's $100,000 loan to purchase the *qualified residence* vacation cabin is also *acquisition indebtedness*. So far, the interest Tim pays with respect to his $200,000 original house loan, $80,000 of his second mortgage on his house, and the $100,000 loan appears to be deductible under IRC § 163 as qualified residence interest. In the aggregate, Tim has $380,000 of *acquisition indebtedness* ($200,000 + $80,000 + $100,000).

One last issue to consider regarding deduction of interest on *acquisition indebtedness* is that there is a $1 million cap on the amount of loans qualifying as *acquisition indebtedness*. [IRC § 163(h)(3)(B)(ii).] This means that for acquisition loans, only the interest on the first $1 million of such loans is deductible here. This $1 million cap is on the amount of loans and not a much larger $1 million cap on deductible interest. It should also be noted that this $1 million acquisition indebtedness cap is in the aggregate – $1 million total for all acquisition loans for the principal and one other qualifying residence (not a $1 million cap for each ac-quisition loan or a separate $1million acquisition loan cap for each of two possi-ble qualifying residences). As indicated, Tim's total *acquisition indebtedness* is $380,000, well below $1 million cap.

While not at issue in this question, it should be noted that loans used to replace existing "acquisition indebtedness" (e.g., a straight refinancing), takes on the character of the loan being replaced and itself becomes acquisition indebtedness.

Home equity indebtedness is also an issue in this question. Home equity indebt-edness is defined in IRC § 163(h)(3)(C) and, typically, is money borrowed against an existing qualified residence (secured by the qualified residence) that is used for purposes *other than* substantial improvements to the qualified residence. Adver-tisements for "tapping the equity" in one's house to buy a new car or boat, go on a vacation, pay off credit card debts, student loans or consolidate all those existing bills, strike at the center of what "home equity indebtedness" is all about. Bor-rowing money, using your house, for such things as buying a car can generate de-ductible interest, while interest paid on a regular car loan from a bank, credit un-ion or automotive financing companies will generally be nondeductible "per-sonal" interest. This is, in part, what Tim has done with respect to the $160,000 second mortgage loan he took out on his principal residence. We have already said $80,000 of this loan qualifies as *acquisition indebtedness*, but what about the deductibility of interest Tim pays with respect to the remaining $80,000 of this loan that was used to purchase stocks and pay for a cruise? A statutory require-ment of "home equity indebtedness" (in addition that it must be secured by the qualifying residence) is that such loan cannot exceed the "equity" in the qualified residence. "Equity" is the one figure of which most homeowners are constantly aware. Equity is the difference between the value of the home and the amount of outstanding loans with respect to the home. Say, for example, that you own a home worth $350,000, and that you have an outstanding first mortgage (acquisi-tion debt) of $150,000. Your "equity" in the home is $200,000. This is the amount or value of your home that you really own – how much you would expect to "pocket in cash" upon selling (after the debt is paid off). In our problem, Tim has no problem with this equity limitation for *home equity indebtedness*.

Another important statutory limit looms large with respect to home equity debt in that there is an aggregate $100,000 of debt that can qualify as home equity in-debtedness. As with the acquisition indebtedness cap, this is a single cap for all of the home equity loans. Interest on any loan or portion of loan in excess of this cap generally becomes nondeductible "personal" interest. As for Tim, while his second mortgage loan was $160,000, we are only concerned with the $80,000 portion of the borrowed funds that were not used to improve his home. Since this

$80,000 is less than the cap for *home equity indebtedness* Tim *can* deduct the interest paid on this $80,000 portion of the second mortgage.

In summary, the total amount of Tim's borrowing results in *acquisition indebtedness* of $380,000 and *home equity indebtedness* of $80,000, and the interest he pays on all of this borrowed money is deductible as *qualified residence interest*.

A word of **caution** about language used on exams. There are many instances where the common use of a term does not necessarily correspond to its official "tax" counterpart. Labels can be deceiving, and do not be fooled by their use in lay terms on an exam. The "home equity loan" label is a classic case in point. A home equity loan, a second mortgage, the cash portion of a cash-out refinance, a home equity based line of credit are all typically referred to, in the real world, as home equity loans. Be careful here because, as we saw above in Tim's case, the fact that money is borrowed using the equity in a qualified residence as security does not necessarily render the loan as *home equity indebtedness*. If the borrowed funds are used to substantially improve the qualified residence, the loan, or applicable part thereof, is characterized as the more favorable (higher loan cap) *acquisition indebtedness*. Do not be fooled by language used to describe the facts of a loan. Tim's loan was, for loan description purposes, a home equity loan (he "tapped into the equity" of his house). However an incorrect classification of the entire loan as *home equity indebtedness* for tax purposes would have invoked the $100,000 loan cap. As mentioned, the $80,000 of this loan used for the room addition is considered *acquisition indebtedness* (and is subject to the much higher $1million loan cap).

It should be noted that there are special rules applicable to loans incurred before October 14, 1987. [IRC § 163(h)(3)(D).]

Answer (b) is incorrect and represents the "tricky" answer. It falls into the trap of characterizing all of Tim's $160,000 "home equity loan" (the common use label) as *acquisition indebtedness* for tax purpose (and then subjects it to the $100,000 cap for such indebtedness). As discussed above, $80,000 of this "home equity loan" is classified, for tax purposes, as *acquisition indebtedness* because it was used to substantially improve Tim's *qualified* principal residence. **Answer (c) is incorrect** because it incorrectly classifies, for tax purpose, the entire $160,000 second mortgage loan and the $100,000 borrowed to purchase the vacation cabin as *home equity indebtedness* (and subjecting it to the $100,000 loan cap). **Answer (d) is also incorrect** because it incorrectly classifies the vacation cabin purchase loan as *home equity indebtedness*.

- **Additional references:** *See* DANIEL Q. POSIN, FEDERAL INCOME TAXATION OF INDIVIDUALS ¶ 7.01(3) (5th ed. 2000).

6.   **Answer (d) is correct.** We will conclude, below, that Tim will be entitled to deduct, in the current year, only a portion of the "points" that he paid. Specifically, he can deduct, in full, one percent of $80,000 of his home equity loan in the current year. The points paid with respect to the remaining amounts of monies borrowed will be deducted on a pro-rata basis over the respective lives of the loans.

This question is a logical extension of question 5, above, and while it is a bit unfair, as it requires a substantially correct analysis of the previous question, it does provide a more in-depth analysis of interest deductions. The "real-world" issue of deductibility of "points" paid with respect to obtaining home financing is a big issue and often misunderstood. One cannot hear a commercial or read an advertisement regarding home loans and not be exposed to the issue of "points." It is not uncommon to see a lender's loan rates listed at various different levels with corresponding variations in the number of *points* charged.

"Points" appear in the form of a number such as 1 point, 1.5 points, 2 points, etc., with the number corresponding to a "percentage" (e.g., 1 point = 1%). Although for first time borrowers the concept seems strange, this percentage number represents an amount of money that the <u>borrower</u> has to pay to the lender in order to borrow the money – the applicable point percentage of the amount borrowed! For illustration purposes (facts unrelated to our problem), let us assume that you are purchasing your first home for $250,000, paying $25,000 in cash and obtaining a typical 30-year mortgage loan for the balance of the purchase price ($200,000). Let us further assume that the lender's interest rate is 6.5% plus "1.5 points." Of course, you will be making monthly payments on the money borrowed, but to just borrow the money, you would have to pay the lender 1.5% of $200,000, or $1,500. This is in addition to other fees that might be associated with the loan (e.g., title fees, appraisal fees, document charges, escrow fees, etc.).

What are points? They represent "interest" that is being "prepaid" to the lender when the loan is obtained. One only need venture to various Web sites to see a variety of lender's "loan packages," with differing loan rates related, inversely, to different "point" charges. The deductibility of points associated with a variety of personal-use home loans, involves two issues:

   1)   Are the points associated with loans for which the regular interest will be deductible as *qualified residence interest*, and if so,
   2)   When is the taxpayer entitled to deduct them.

Because points represent interest, albeit prepaid, it is necessary to first determine if they are deductible <u>at all</u>. For discussion purposes, we will not duplicate the exhaustive requirements for IRC § 163(h)(3) *qualified residence interest* (e.g., qualified residence(s), loans secured by the residence, loan limits for acquisition and home equity indebtedness, etc.). But, making this determination, about the underlying loan upon which points are being paid, is critical. If points are paid with respect to any loan, or any portion of a loan, that will not give rise to *qualified residence interest*, they will <u>not</u> be deductible. Rather, these points (or portion thereof) will be considered nondeductible *personal interest*.

As far as Tim is concerned, we determined, in problem 5, above, that all of his loans generate *qualified residence interest*. The $160,000 second mortgage loan that he obtained on his principal residence was split into two components: $80,000 of *acquisition indebtedness* (for the home improvement) and $80,000 of *home equity indebtedness* (for the investments and cruise vacation). The $100,000 loan used to purchase the vacation cabin qualified as *acquisition indebtedness*. The aggregate amount of Tim's loans in either category of qualified indebtedness did not exceed the statutory limits.

At this juncture, we know that the "one point" that he paid with respect to both of these loans in the current year, <u>will be</u> deductible. While the question does not require us to actually compute the amount of money he was required to pay in points, the amount is easily determined. $1,600 in points for the $160,000 second mortgage (1% of $160,000) and $800 for the cabin loan (1% of $80,000). The **major issue** now, is **when are these amounts deductible?**

A simple reading of IRC §163 might infer that the entire amount paid for points is deductible in the current year – deductible in the year paid. Tim, as well as most borrowers, would like for this to be the result (for Tim it means a possible $2,400 interest deduction in addition to whatever regular monthly interest he will pay on these loans). However, deductions for prepayments of otherwise deductible expenses are usually not allowed for expenses that are properly attributable to future tax years. Points, by their nature, represent prepayment of a small amount of interest that would otherwise be payable over the entire life of the loan (typically 30 years). Indeed, IRC §461(g)(1) generally disallows the deduction of prepaid interest, and requires the taxpayer to deduct the prepaid amount in a ratable fashion over the life of the loan.

In true law school form, there is an "exception" to this rule forbidding deductions of prepaid interest. IRC § 461(g)(2) allows for the current deduction, in the year paid, for points paid with respect to loans (otherwise qualifying as discussed above) that are used to "acquire" or "improve" one's "principal residence." Points paid for monies borrowed for those two purposes <u>are deductible now</u>, when paid. Points paid for other monies borrowed <u>are deductible ratably over the life of the loan</u>.

Applying these rules to Tim's loans obtained in the current year, we have a few problems. The $100,000 loan obtained to acquire the cabin (while considered *acquisition indebtedness*) was <u>not</u> used to acquire Tim's <u>principal residence</u>. Therefore, the one point associated with that loan ($800) is <u>not</u> deductible in full in the current year, but must be deducted ratably over the life of the loan (e.g., 1/30th each year for a thirty year loan). As for the second mortgage obtained on his principal residence, $80,000 of it <u>was</u> used to improve his principal residence and the other $80,000 was used for unrelated matters. This requires us to bifurcate the loan for point deductibility purposes. One point associated with the $80,000 used to improve his home (or $800) is deductible in full in the current year pursuant to IRC § 461(g)(2). The one point paid for the remaining $80,000 of this second mortgage (also $800) is not deductible now, but is deductible ratably over the life of the loan.

While this issue of point deductibility may appear confusing at first (and it is to many borrowers as well as misinformed lenders), the rules are fairly straightforward. Students sometimes run into problems when attempts are made to coordinate the current deductibility of points with the deductibility of different classifications of *qualified residence interest*.

While not at issue in this problem, points paid with respect to "refinancing" an existing loan (e.g. declining interest rates prompt a homeowner, to replace an existing home loan with a new, lower rate loan) are <u>not</u> deductible in the year paid. They do not meet the requirements of IRC §461(g)(2). [See Rev.Rul. 87-22, 1987-1 C.B. 146, (refinanced loans are not actually used to purchase or improve a principal residence but, rather, are at best, replacing such loans).]

Answer (a) is incorrect because while all of Tim's loans will generate *qualified residence interest*, not all of the loans were used to purchase or improve his principal residence. **Answer (b) is also incorrect.** While it is correct with respect to the $80,000 portion of the $160,000 second mortgage that Tim used for improving his principal residence, it incorrectly includes within the IRC §461(g)(2) provision, the points paid on his vacation cabin. The cabin is not his principal residence. **Answer (c) is incorrect** because it too does not properly identify the loans for which points can be deducted currently. **Answer (e) is incorrect** because a correct answer (d) is presented.

- **Additional references:** *See* DANIEL Q. POSIN, FEDERAL INCOME TAXATION OF INDIVIDUALS ¶ 7.01(3) (5th ed. 2000).

7.   **The best answer is (b).** The primary focus for this question is IRC § 162, deductions for business expenses. Ben's $500 seminar course fee and the $50 in transportation costs to/from the seminar qualify as deductible business expenses pursu-

ant to IRC § 162. His costs for lodging and meals do not qualify as deductible business expenses because he is not considered to be *traveling away from home*. A more comprehensive (and sorry, but long) analysis follows.

The first sentence of IRC § 162 (which appears in subsection (a)) enumerates, for all intents and purposes, four basic requirements for a business deduction. A business deduction is allowed for all (read as one continuous phrase with four distinct requirements):

➤ Ordinary and necessary
➤ Expenses
➤ Paid or incurred during the taxable year
➤ In carrying on any trade or business.

These four requirements often represent, in federal income tax classes and in real life, separate and significant points of contention. Business deductions come in a million different flavors, but all qualifying deductions must meet those four criteria. The study, in tax classes, of business deductions can be long and comprehensive. At times, it may seem like many business deductions have their own set of rules, as if permitted by a separate Code section. There are many business deductions that almost take on a life of their own primarily because of explanations and interpretations from the Code subsections, regulations, court decisions, I.R.S. pronouncements, and the like.

In Ben's case, we are dealing with two or three sub-sets or specific types of IRC § 162 business expenses: business related education expenses and transportation expenses (with discussion of traveling away from home expenses for lodging and meals).

The "basic taxation for lawyers" seminar

The first issue, and partial foundation for our answer, is that of business related education: Ben's "basic taxation for lawyers" seminar. Of the four IRC § 162 requirements above, we have potential issues with whether the seminar was *ordinary and necessary*, and if it is with respect to Ben's *carrying on a trade or business*. While specific regulations under IRC § 162 provide guidance in the area of business related education expenses, let us first try to analyze the facts in Ben's case using the basic IRC § 162 requirements. We then will turn to the regulations. The object here is not to create additional work nor extend the length of this analysis but, rather, it provides us with a good opportunity to work through the IRC § 162 requirements and then see how the regulations address the issue.

The seminar is necessary for Ben. "Necessary," for the purpose of IRC § 162, is not necessary in the sense that it is absolutely critical that Ben takes this course.

Rather, "necessary" has been interpreted to be a taxpayer-*subjective* test of whether the taxpayer thought the expense was "appropriate or helpful." There is very little second-guessing here. Ben thought that this course would be appropriate or helpful and, therefore, it is necessary. The "ordinary" aspect of an IRC § 162 is an *objective* test – generally whether such an expenditure is common, accepted, customary, or usual in the taxpayer's line of business. Arguably, a lawyer taking a state bar sponsored course sounds fairly ordinary without much more information. Heck, if the state bar approves the course for attendance by lawyers, it almost has the "ordinary" seal of approval. Looking a bit deeper, it seems logical that a lawyer practicing in most areas of law, especially personal injury law (see IRC § 104 for example) would want to know something about tax law. Most likely, this is sufficient analysis to determine the seminar expenditure was *ordinary and necessary*. Whether attending the seminar relates to *carrying on* Ben's business, is effectively tied, in our facts, to whether the expense is *ordinary*. Ben is already a practicing lawyer (i.e., he is in a trade or business) and the seminar, learning something about income taxes, is in relation to that business. Most situations involving this issue involve questions of whether the expenditure is associated with the taxpayer entering a new or different business. A taxpayer can be engaged in business in various ways including as an employee (Ben in our case) or as self-employed (a.k.a., independent contractor, or unincorporated sole proprietor), Ben appears to easily meet the in *carrying on a trade or business* requirement of IRC § 162. As of this point, Ben's $500 course fees appear to qualify as IRC § 162 business expense. Now for further analysis of this issue referencing the regulations.

The regulations provide substantial guidance on business education issues. [Reg. § 1.162-5.] This is an example of where one type of business expense seems to take on a life of its own, and have its own set of rules and requirements. However, the regulation is merely providing interpretations or explanations of the basic IRC § 162 requirements as they pertain to business-related education expenses. In an interpretation of the general IRC § 162 requirements, the regulations provide that generally, education will qualify as a business expense, "if the education –

> 1) Maintains or improves skills required by the individual in his employment or other trade or business, or
> 2) Meets the express requirements of the individual's employer, or the requirement of applicable law or regulations, imposed as a condition to the retention by the individual of an established employment relationship, status, or rate of compensation."
> [See Reg. § 1.162-5(a).]

A lawyer must maintain (and hopefully improve) one's skills in the practice of law. For Ben, the basic tax seminar appears to easily meet this requirement. The seminar may even meet the second test listed above, depending on his state's bar requirements for continuing legal education. If they impose continuing legal education requirements to maintain one's license to practice law (e.g., so many hours of continuing legal education per year), Ben's state bar sponsored tax seminar would certainly qualify. The regulations go on to state instances where education will not qualify as an IRC § 162 business expense, and they include:

> "[E]ducation which is required of him in order to meet the minimum educational requirements for qualification in his employment or other trade or business" [Reg. § 1.162-5(b)(2).], and
> "[E]ducation which is part of a program of study being pursued by him which will lead to qualifying him in a new trade or business." [Reg. § 1.162-5(b)(3).]

Examples of the former might be education related to obtaining a teaching credential, so that one can become an elementary school teacher, law school education required to become a lawyer, etc. Examples of the latter tend to overlap the former and can include an engineer wanting to change jobs and embarking on a field of study to become a veterinarian. Ben's tax seminar clearly does not fit within these examples of nondeductible education expenses.

We conclude that Ben's $500 seminar fee qualifies as an IRC § 162 business expense. Now on to his other expenditures related to the seminar experience.

<u>Transportation costs related to business</u>

Looking at transportation costs, we are faced with the same basic IRC § 162 requirements listed above. As with business education, particular rules have evolved regarding deductible business transportation. Distilled to its most basic form for this question, if the tax seminar Ben attended qualifies as a business expense, the cost of getting to and from it also qualify. This is no different than, for example, Ben driving to a client's office. At one point, the I.R.S. made distinctions whether business transportation initiated from home versus the office, but this is no longer relevant for transportation to what is considered a non-regular place of business. [Please see other problems in this book that address such issues (in conjunction with nondeductible "commuting" transportation.] The facts indicate that Ben incurred $50 in transportation costs to/from the seminar. This $50, therefore qualifies as a § 162 expense. All that is left to discuss is Ben's costs for the lodging and meals, which brings up the issue of *traveling away from home*.

<u>Is Ben "traveling away from home" on business?</u>

IRC § 162(a)(2) specifically identifies that expenditures associated with "traveling away from home" constitute qualifying business expenses. While this subsection appears to add additional requirements to the four listed above for such traveling expenditures, a careful examination of the statutory language reveals no more than a reiteration of the four basic requirements, albeit in a different form. At the outset, an important issue needs to be addressed. *Traveling away from home* on business is a bit special and should be distinguished with what is commonly referred to as *local transportation*. Traveling away from home is where you leave your office in Seattle to see a client in Chicago for a two-day business meeting. Local transportation is where you leave your office in Beverly Hills to see a client ten miles away in Santa Monica. Distinguishing between the two can make a huge difference for tax purposes (business deductions). Business travel *away from home* generally means traveling far enough and long enough away from one's home to require an overnight stay (i.e., it would not be reasonable to expect someone to travel long distances after a long business day's work). [See *United States v. Correll*, 389 US 299, 88 S.Ct. 445 (1967).] Business travel *away from home* opens the tax doors to potential deductions (in addition to transportation costs) for lodging, non-entertainment meals, incidentals, etc. while traveling away from home on business. Whereas, local transportation for business purposes gives rise to deductions generally limited to transportation costs and parking charges at the business destination. For local transportation situations, meals are not deductible at all, and neither is lodging (client meals and entertainment is a different issue and may give rise to some deductions).

Therefore, the key to deductions for his lodging and meals rests with the determination of whether Ben, traveling 30 miles each way to the seminar lasting six hours a day, is considered *traveling away from home*. Is it unreasonable for Ben to return 30 miles after spending six hours on business matters (the seminar)? The likely answer is no. Both the distance to the seminar and the time spent on business at that location, is too short to conclude that he is *traveling away from home*. Therefore, he is not entitled to a business deduction for the cost of his meals nor his lodging. A similar example is an everyday commute to work. Once you get there, you cannot deduct your meals (unless they relate to business/entertainment) nor can you deduct lodging near work merely because you do not feel like driving home on a particular evening.

A potential twist that is not given as a possible answer to this question

There is a possible argument that Ben should be entitled to a little greater deductible amount than indicated in the correct answer to this problem (but rest assured, it is also not contained in any other answer provided). An I.R.S. Private Letter Ruling addressed the situation of a taxpayer traveling away from home primarily on business, but spent some pleasure (non-business) days while on the trip. These pleasure days happened to coincide with the taxpayer's "Saturday night stay-over" which substantially reduced his or her airfare. This private letter ruling said, basically, that some of the otherwise nondeductible costs for the non-business days, *could* qualify for a business deduction to the extent such costs did not exceed the airfare saved by the Saturday night stay-over. The theory being that had the taxpayer left immediately after the business concluded, the airfare would have been much higher (and also deductible) – so to the extent that the airfare would have been deductible (and the savings resulting form the Saturday night stay-over) represent business deductions for costs that are really not business related. [See Priv.Ltr.Rul. 9237014 (06/10/1992).] It is sort of a "fairness" principle. So why is this possibly relevant to Ben in our case? Had he gone back home after the first seminar day and returned for the next day, his transportation costs (most likely double the $50) would have been deductible as *local business transportation*. Utilizing the logic of the aforementioned I.R.S. Private Letter Ruling, one could make a case that at least $50, of his nondeductible lodging or meals (at 50% pursuant to IRC § 274(n), should be deductible.

Lastly, it should be noted that an individual can incur qualifying IRC § 162 expenses in the context of working as an employee (as Ben in our question) or in an individual's own business (someone who alternatively referred to as being self-employed, an independent contractor, or operating his or her business as an "unincorporated sole proprietorship"). The requirements for deductibility pursuant to IRC § 162 are the same for an employee or a self-employed individual. However, "where" and "how" these deductions are taken does vary. Other questions in this book address these issues.

Answer (a) is incorrect because the $100 in lodging is not a deductible business expense, as Ben was most likely not *traveling away from home*. **Similarly, Answer (c) is incorrect** because neither the lodging nor meals (at 50%) are deductible business expenses because Ben is most likely not *traveling away from home*. **Answer (d) is incorrect** because it fails to recognize that the $50 in transportation costs is a deductible business expense. **Answer (e) is incorrect** because it incorrectly presumes that the tax seminar (and all related costs) was not unrelated to Ben's current trade or business.

- **Additional references:** *See* DANIEL Q. POSIN, FEDERAL INCOME TAXATION OF INDIVIDUALS ¶¶ 6.02(1), 6.02(2)(b), 6.02(4) (5th ed. 2000).

8.   **The best answer is (b).** This question raises the issue of "depreciation" deductions. The *concept* of depreciation is not too difficult. Its real-world application, however, with all of the analytical twists and turns, can be daunting. The study of depreciation varies considerably among law school tax courses: from a casual mention of the topic to a full-blown, in-depth analysis of the various depreciation

methods (past and present), class lives, conventions, elective provisions, etc. For this book, the author has chosen to cover the issue of depreciation in its most basic form, and forego analysis of the many in-depth, analytical rules. This choice was made primarily to leave room for the host of other tax issues that require discussion. The author does acknowledge that this level of coverage may be disappointing for those students whose professor more fully covers the issue of depreciation in class.

Generally, the costs of major permanent improvements to existing business property or the purchase of business property having a useful life of more than one year are not fully deductible in that year. [IRC § 263.] These types of expenditures are commonly referred to as "capital expenditures." This result is also consistent with the requirements of the general business deduction section, IRC § 162. For expenditures to be fully deductible now (when incurred) IRC § 162 requires that the expenditure be (read as one continuous phrase with four distinct requirements):
  ➤ Ordinary and necessary
  ➤ Expense
  ➤ Paid or incurred during the taxable year
  ➤ In carrying on any trade or business.

Capital expenditures, as are Abigail's costs for the warehouse and manufacturing equipment, do not represent *expenses* and, therefore, do not qualify as business deductions pursuant to IRC § 162. *Capital expenditures* and *expenses* are mutually exclusive.

IRC § 167 provides, however, that the cost of most business (or investment) *capital expenditures* can be deducted over time (or expensed) through the concept of depreciation deductions. Do not be confused with the word "depreciation." For income tax purposes, property need not decline in value in order to claim deductions for depreciation. Rather, for income tax purposes, depreciation is the methodical deduction, over time, of a capitalized cost. Since Abigail's business expenditures for the warehouse and equipment are *capital expenditures*, their costs will be expensed over time in the form of depreciation deductions.

Well beyond the scope of the author's coverage of depreciation in this book, are the numerous methods of depreciation, depreciation elections and various periods of depreciation for different types of business assets. Be aware that while these extensive and complex rules are not discussed in this book, your professor may cover this issue in much greater detail.

Answer (a) is incorrect because the manufacturing equipment Abigail purchased for her business most assuredly represents capital expenditures. **Answer (c) is in-**

correct because the fact that Abigail's business is operated as an unincorporated sole proprietorship does not allow her to "expense" these expenditures. The concepts of capitalization and depreciation apply to business regardless of their form. **Answer (d) is incorrect** because while Abigail's expenditures are not deductible in full in the current year, they do not represent "start-up" costs pursuant to IRC § 195.

- **Additional references:** *See* DANIEL Q. POSIN, FEDERAL INCOME TAXATION OF INDIVIDUALS ¶¶ 6.02(1), 6.02(2), 6.02(12) (5th ed. 2000).

9. **The most accurate answer is (c).** The general starting place for determining one's basis (adjusted basis hereinafter, AB) is one's cost. [IRC §§ 1011 and 1012.] Abigail paid $1million for the manufacturing building and that is our starting point for her AB. IRC § 1016 requires that certain adjustments be made to the basis of property. While not relevant in our facts, the AB of property is *increased* for such things as major improvements to the property. This section also provides that in general, a property's AB shall be *decreased* by (among other things) the amount of depreciation deductions *allowable* under the law. [IRC § 1016(a)(2).] This means that one's AB in property must be decreased by depreciation deductions that were allowed to the taxpayer regardless of whether the taxpayer actually claimed the deductions.

In our case, therefore, Abigail's AB in the manufacturing building will be the $1 million cost less depreciation *allowable* (even if she chose not to deduct any).

It should be noted that if a taxpayer does not claim the allowed depreciation deductions, the *allowable* depreciation that serves to reduce AB is computed using a particular method of depreciation (among many that might be available if the taxpayer actually claims depreciation deductions). While not at issue in our case, it also should be noted that the reduction of one's AB by depreciation allowed may be limited in certain circumstances when the depreciation allowed would not have resulted in a reduction of taxable income (e.g., the taxpayer had no taxable income before considering any allowed depreciation deductions).

Answer (a) is incorrect. While this is her initial cost basis in the property, as discussed above, it must be reduced by the depreciation that she was allowed to claim as deductions. **Answer (b) is not the most accurate answer** although it could be considered correct. As indicated above, one's AB in property is reduced by the amount of depreciation deductions *allowable*. AB reduction does not require, as implied by this answer, that the taxpayer actually claims the allowed depreciation deductions. **Answer (d) is incorrect** because while it is true that the land portion of property is generally not a depreciable asset, the cost of the building component is a depreciable asset. The AB of the land and building combined (the property) will be the total aggregate cost less the depreciation allowable (which is the amount related to the building component of the property).

- **Additional references:** *See* DANIEL Q. POSIN, FEDERAL INCOME TAXATION OF INDIVIDUALS ¶¶ 4.03(2), 6.02(12) (5th ed. 2000).

10. **Answer (d) is correct.** The principal Code section permitting business deductions is IRC § 162. The first sentence of that section (contained in subsection (a)) enumerates, for all intents and purposes, the basic requirements for a business deduction. A deduction is allowed for all "ordinary and necessary" "expenses" "paid or incurred during the taxable year" "in carrying on any trade or business." The compartmentalized quotation marks signify what are commonly considered the four basic requirements for a business deduction. These four requirements often represent, in federal income tax classes and in real life, separate and significant points of contention. Business deductions come in a million different flavors, but all qualifying deductions must meet those four criteria. The study, in tax classes, of business deductions can be long and comprehensive. At times, it may seem like many business deductions have their own set of rules, as if permitted by a separate Code section. There are many business deductions that almost take on a life of their own primarily because of explanations and interpretations from the Code subsections, regulations, court decisions, I.R.S. pronouncements, and the like.

Deductions for transportation costs, the subject of this question, is one such business deduction that appears to have its own set of rules. Wendy, in our problem, drives her car to and from work, between work locations, etc. Some, but not all, of this driving is considered for business purposes (giving rise to deductions for the costs associated therewith). Currently, the general rules for what constitute business and nonbusiness transportation can be distilled into a few basic components.

- Driving to and from one's home and a "regular" (not temporary) place of work are <u>nondeductible</u> commuting miles.
- Driving between two or more "regular" places of work (including different jobs) <u>are</u> deductible business miles.
- Driving to and from a "regular" place of work and a "temporary" or "non-regular" place of work (e.g., a client's office) <u>are</u> deductible business miles.
- Driving to and from one's home and a "temporary" or "non-regular" place of work (e.g., a client's office) <u>are</u> deductible business miles.

A visual depiction of the deductible/nondeductible driving map, as applied to the facts in our question, is as follows:

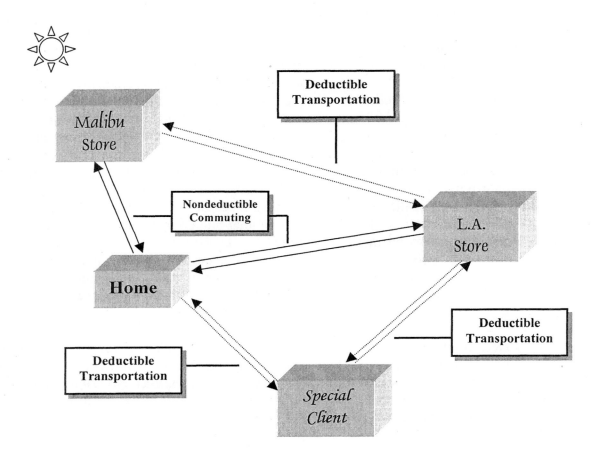

Wendy's driving percentages that qualify for business miles is 40%, the sum of the 25% store-to-store component and the 15% customer-to-home or office component.

This mileage rubric can easily be adapted to various occupations. A physician may have multiple "regular places of work" such as his or her office, and hospitals at which he or she regularly sees patients. A lawyer may have an office and regularly make appearances at particular courthouse venues. Historically, the business mileage rules discussed above were different and not always as clear. Additionally, these are merely the "general" rules that apply to the most common business mileage situations. Your professor may cover material far beyond the current and most basic rules.

Answer (a) is incorrect because while the 15% portion of Wendy's miles do constitute business miles, this answer fails to include the additional 25% qualifying portion. **Answer (b) is similarly incorrect**, failing to include the total qualifying business portions of Wendy's miles driven. **Answer (c) is incorrect** because this answer reflects what was a historical distinction made by the I.R.S. for travel between a temporary place of work, and one's regular place of work versus one's home. **Answer (e) is incorrect** because a correct response (d) is presented.

- **Additional references:** *See* DANIEL Q. POSIN, FEDERAL INCOME TAXATION OF INDIVIDUALS ¶ 6.02(1) (5ᵗʰ ed. 2000).

11. **Answer (a) is the best response.** Okay, so maybe a pet clothing boutique sounds a bit goofy (no offense to pet owners), but it is sometimes difficult to come up with a fact pattern that encourages thoughtful discussion (this question was originally part of an exam essay question).

The principal Code section permitting business deductions is IRC § 162. Most likely, none of Wendy's cost for airfare to/from Seattle is deductible because based on the facts, the trip was not primarily for business. However, if the "pet clothing" sales business is considered the same business as her current business (or a logical expansion or extension thereof), then some of her costs while in Seattle will qualify as deductible business expenses. A more comprehensive analysis follows.

The first sentence of IRC § 162 (which appears in subsection (a)) enumerates, for all intents and purposes, four basic requirements for a business deduction. A business deduction is allowed for all (read as one continuous phrase with four distinct requirements):
  - Ordinary and necessary
  - Expenses
  - Paid or incurred during the taxable year
  - In carrying on any trade or business.

These four requirements often represent, in federal income tax classes and in real life, separate and significant points of contention. Business deductions come in a million different flavors, but all qualifying deductions must meet those four criteria. The study, in tax classes, of business deductions can be long and comprehensive. At times, it may seem like many business deductions have their own set of rules, as if permitted by a separate Code section. There are many business deductions that almost take on a life of their own primarily because of explanations and interpretations from the Code subsections, regulations, court decisions, I.R.S.

pronouncements, and the like. In *Wendy's* case, the point of contention is the last of the four IRC § 162 requirements listed above.

Is Wendy Carrying on with Her Existing Business While in Seattle?

The issue distilled is whether or not the retail sale of pet clothing could be considered the same business, an expansion of, or a logical extension of, as that in which she is currently involved. In other words, for there to be *any possible* business deductions arising from her Seattle trip, she has to be carrying on her existing trade or business. IRC § 162 deductions do not encompass expenses associated with starting up (or investigating) a new and different trade or business. As indicated, this question was originally part of an exam essay question and was designed to elicit insightful discussions. There is probably no *correct* answer to this particular element as extrapolation from examples in the regulations and from court decisions could point in either direction. If the two businesses are the same trade or business, then we can continue, but if they are considered two different trades or businesses, the discussion ends (with respect to IRC § 162 at least). Because some of the answers to this question contain "assuming that the two are the same" type of language, we will continue with our analysis of her Seattle trip vis-à-vis IRC § 162 business deductions.

Wendy's Trip to Seattle and IRC § 162 Business Expense Deductions

IRC § 162(a)(2) specifically identifies that expenditures associated with "traveling away from home" constitute qualifying business expenses. While this subsection appears to add additional requirements to the four listed above for such traveling expenditures, a careful examination of the statutory language reveals no more than a reiteration of the four basic requirements, albeit in a different form. If we are to assume that the "carrying on a trade or business" requirement of IRC § 162 is met, Wendy did spend some of her time in Seattle on business matters (searching out possible store locations, making business contacts, and talking with suppliers). The regulations promulgated for IRC § 162 are extensive and help to clarify the issues relating to Wendy as well as many other business expense issues that are not the subject of this question. For discussion purposes, Wendy's potential qualifying business expenses are bifurcated into two parts: her transportation costs to and from Los Angeles to Seattle, and her costs incurred during hers stay in Seattle. At the outset, however, before discussing these two components, it should be noted that this question deals with potential business travel "away from home" as distinguished from "local" business travel. Business travel "away from home" generally means traveling far enough and long enough away from one's home to require an overnight stay. [See *United States v. Correll*, 389 US 299, 88 S.Ct. 445 (1967).] Business travel "away from home" opens the door to potential deductions for lodging, non-entertainment meals, incidentals, etc. Other questions in this book address the issue of where a taxpayer's "home" is located and the issue of "local" travel for business (usually concerned only about deductions for transportation related expenses).

Wendy's transportation costs to/from Seattle (her airfare) qualifies as a business expense if the "trip is related primarily to [her] . . . trade or business." [Reg. § 1.162-2(b)(1).] The regulations, at Reg. § 1.162-2(b)(2), provide some guidance in making this determination. The regulation indicates that this determination is to be made based on the facts and circumstances in each case. The regulation also indicates that an important factor for making this determination is the number of days spent on business compared to the number of days spent for pleasure. Basing a decision on the totality of our facts, we would most likely conclude that Wendy's Seattle trip was not made primarily for business purposes. Wendy's round-trip airfare from Los Angeles to Seattle does not qualify as a deductible business expense. Note that for domestic travel, as is the case in this problem, deduction of transportation costs for traveling away from home is an "all or nothing" proposition. If the trip is primarily for business, 100% of the taxpayer's transportation related costs generally qualify as business expenses pursuant to IRC § 162. Alternatively, as is the case with Wendy, none of the transportation costs qualify as business expenses if the trip is primarily for pleasure. It should be noted that the rules for "foreign" travel may differ and proration of transportation costs between deductible business and nondeductible personal expenses may be appropriate.

The Regulations do provide, however, that "expenses while at the destination which are properly allocable to the taxpayer's trade or business are deductible even though the traveling expenses to and from the destination are not deductible." The days that Wendy spent on business activities while in Seattle, should be considered as traveling away from home in connection with the conduct of a trade or business. Her expenses related to those days would qualify as IRC § 162 business expenses. While not necessary to answer this question, these expenses could include the cost of lodging and incidentals for full business-related days as well as 50% of her meals for days that she spent conducting business. The 50% deduction limitation for business meals comes not from IRC § 162 but, rather, is supplied by IRC § 274(n)(1). This 50% limitation is applicable to most business meals and entertainment-related business expenses that are otherwise allowed as deductions. Please see other questions in this book relating to entertainment expenses.

It should be noted that an individual can incur qualifying IRC § 162 expenses in the context of working as an employee, or, like in Wendy's case, in an individual's own business (someone who alternatively referred to as being self-employed, an independent contractor, or operating his or her business as an "unincorporated sole proprietorship"). The requirements for deductibility pursuant to IRC § 162 are the same for an employee or a self-employed individual. However, "where" and "how" these deductions are taken does vary. Other questions in this book address these issues.

While not specifically addressed in this question, our facts do raise another important tax issue (i.e., an issue that would be discussed if these facts were presented in essay question form). IRC § 195 addresses "start-up expenditures." Basically, these are expenditures that would qualify as IRC § 162 business expenses *but for the fact* that the taxpayer is not carrying on an existing trade or business. In essay form, our facts would elicit this issue because Wendy's contemplated pet clothing business is, arguably, a new and different business for her. In such a case, as discussed above, her business related expenses (site investigation, supplier meetings, etc.) would not qualify as IRC § 162 expenses. If Wendy decided to enter this new business, these expenditures would, however, qualify as IRC § 195 start-up expenditures. IRC § 195 does not allow an immediate deduction by the taxpayer for these expenditures, but provides the taxpayer with an election to "amortize" (or deduct ratably) these expenditures over a period of time (a minimum period of 60 months). [IRC § 195(b).]

Answer (b) is incorrect because it incorrectly states that none of Wendy's costs while in Seattle qualify as IRC § 162 business expenses even if she is considered to be involved in the same trade or business. **Answer (c) is incorrect** because the transportation costs for domestic business travel is not prorated. Rather, it is fully deductible if the trip was primarily for business purposes or, not deductible at all if the trip was primarily for pleasure. **Answer (d) is incorrect** because her airfare is most likely not a deductible business expense. **Answer (e) is incorrect** because her transportation costs are most likely nondeductible, and at most, only some of her costs while in Seattle qualify as deductible business expenses.

- **Additional references:** *See* DANIEL Q. POSIN, FEDERAL INCOME TAXATION OF INDIVIDUALS ¶¶ 6.02(1), 6.02(4), 6.02(6) (5th ed. 2000).

12. **The correct answer is (b).** As with question 11, above, our analysis begins with deductions for business expenses under IRC § 162. An individual can incur qualifying § 162 expenses in the context of working as an employee, or, as a self-employed individual (a.k.a., independent contractor or unincorporated sole proprietor). The four basic requirements for qualified business expense deductions are the same for an employee or a self-employed individual. In general, IRC § 162 allows for business deductions that are (read as one continuous phrase with four distinct requirements):
   - ➢ Ordinary and necessary
   - ➢ Expenses

> ➢ Paid or incurred during the taxable year
> ➢ In carrying on any trade or business.

Arguably, some of Hank's expenses while in Seattle would satisfy these requirements. However, to spare the reader from what would be a long, and in the end, an irrelevant discussion, another Code section bears mentioning. While short and somewhat obscure, IRC § 274(m)(2) provides us with the ultimate answer that Hank's expenditures do <u>not</u> give rise to deductible expenses by stating: "No deduction shall be allowed under this chapter for expenses for travel as a form of education."

Answer (a) is incorrect because this deduction preclusion provision applies to both employees and self-employed individuals. **Answers (c) and (d) are both incorrect** because, as discussed above, none of Hank's costs associated with this trip are deductible.

- **Additional references:** *See* DANIEL Q. POSIN, FEDERAL INCOME TAXATION OF INDIVIDUALS ¶ 6.02(2)(b)(i) (5th ed. 2000).

13. **Answer (b) is correct.** The weight-loss program fees paid by Chad and Donna will qualify as medical care expenses pursuant to IRC § 213.

IRC § 213 allows for a deduction of certain qualified medical expenses. Once one makes the determination of what constitutes "qualified" medical care expenses, the subject of this question, the deduction is allowed as an "itemized deduction" only to the extent that the total qualifying expenses exceeds 7.5% of Adjusted Gross Income (AGI). [See Appendix A for more information about how income and deductions fit together in computing taxable income.] Qualified medical care expenses include typical costs for doctors, dentists, hospital, health insurance, and the like. [See IRC § 213(d).] The I.R.S. has not, until recently, been particularly lenient when it comes to weight-loss programs qualify as deductible medical care expenses. Revenue Ruling 2002-19 presents facts that are essentially identical to those in our question, and the I.R.S. concludes that our answer (b) is correct. [Rev.Rul. 2002-19, 2002-16 I.R.B. 778.]

Historically, Donna's weight-loss program fees were more likely to qualify as medical care expenses than those for Chad. Losing weight to improve a taxpayer's general health is not considered a disease, giving rise to deductible medical health care expenses, and historically, it was not apparent that the I.R.S. considered obesity as a disease. However, in the above-cited Revenue Ruling, the I.R.S. does recognize obesity to be a "disease in its own right." Costs for losing weight to treat a disease, for Chad's obesity and directed by Donna's physician for her hypertension, are qualified medical care expenses.

However, the costs of the program's diet food items do not qualify as medical care expenses as they are substitutes for the food that Chad and Donna would "normally consume to satisfy their nutritional requirements." [Rev.Rul. 2002-19, 2002-16 I.R.B 778.]

Answer (a) is incorrect but, until the recent Revenue Ruling discussed above, would have most likely been the correct answer. **Answer (c) is incorrect** because it incorrectly includes the diet foods as qualifying medical care expenses. **Answer (d) is incorrect** because it fails to recognize that Chad's weight-loss program/meeting fees qualify as medical care expenses. In addition, it incorrectly includes Donna's food costs as qualifying medical care expenses. **Answer (e) is incorrect** because a correct answer (b) is presented.

- **Additional references:** *See* DANIEL Q. POSIN, FEDERAL INCOME TAXATION OF INDIVIDUALS ¶ 7.01 (5th ed. 2000).

14. **The best answer is (c).** Shirin is facing the problem that many new (and not so new) professionals face: a huge outlay of funds for new clothes. Unfortunately, these costs are rarely deductible as business expenses. While those having to wear such attire may subjectively view this type of clothing as a *uniform*, objectively it is not the type of *uniform* for which business deductions are allowed.

In general, IRC § 162 allows for business deductions that are (read as one continuous phrase with four distinct requirements):
  ➢ Ordinary and necessary
  ➢ Expenses
  ➢ Paid or incurred during the taxable year
  ➢ In carrying on any trade or business.

Shirin may argue that her expenditures for her newly acquired business wardrobe meets these requirements, but the I.R.S. sees it otherwise. Their position is that *uniforms* qualify as deductible business expenses only if "(1) the uniforms are specifically required as a condition of employment and (2) are not of a type adaptable to general or continued usage to the extent that they take the place of ordinary clothing." [Rev.Rul. 70-474, 1970-2 C.B. 34.] Work required safety clothes, helmets, work gloves, special boots, and the like, are examples of deductible items, as are uniforms worn by police, athletes, airline pilots, and the like (assuming the individual has to pay for them and is not reimbursed for their cost).

Unfortunately, Shirin's business attire does not fit the I.R.S.'s interpretation of deductible work clothes. While most likely not applicable to Shirin, there have been rare instances, and under somewhat extraordinary circumstances, where certain clothing has been allowed as a business deduction notwithstanding that it could have been worn in public. [See *Betsy Lusk Yeomans*, 30 T.C 757 (1958), (fashion coordinator for high-end shoe manufacturer allowed to deduct costs of latest fashions that she was required to wear on the job that were not suitable for her private and personal use).] Another interesting case involved "America's favorite family – the "Nelsons." The Adventures of Ozzie and Harriet, a television series that aired long before most of today's students were born, had a little known "income tax" issue associated with the program. Ozzie deducted the costs of his and his family's everyday clothing used on the series claiming that the test for deductibility should be applied on the basis of whether the clothing was actually worn in public. In this rare instance, the Tax Court agreed (as to the parent's clothes only, as they could not show that the their two sons, David and the "irrepressible little Ricky," did not wear their "TV" clothes while off the set). [*Oswald Nelson v. Comm'r*, ¶66224 P-H T.C. (1966).]

Answer (a) is incorrect because even if this were a factor, her clothes would most likely not qualify for business deductions as discussed above. **Answer (b) is also incorrect**. While not likely in Shirin's case, there have been a few extraordinary instances where deductions have been allowed in such situations. **Answer (d) is incorrect** because the fact that Shirin's employer requires her to wear such attire does not render it deductible as discussed above. **Answer (e) is incorrect** because these could not be considered qualifying "start-up" costs pursuant to IRC § 195, as they would not otherwise qualify, as discussed above, as deductible business expenses.

- **Additional references:** *See* DANIEL Q. POSIN, FEDERAL INCOME TAXATION OF INDIVIDUALS ¶ 6.02 (5th ed. 2000).

15. **Response (c) is the best answer.** This question is a bit unfair because the correct answer requires a substantially correct analysis of the previous question, 14. This professor would not ask both of these questions in an objective exam. Rather, these two questions were derived from an exam essay question. Unfortunately for Shirin, and most other individuals facing high costs of clothes maintenance (i.e., the costs of dry-cleaning), these costs do not qualify as deductible business expenses.

Maintenance costs for clothes, the purchase of which gave rise to a business deduction, are also deductible. For Shirin to deduct her clothes maintenance costs, this would mean that the cost of her business clothes would have had to qualify as deductible business expenses. As discussed above, unfortunately, her clothes are most likely not considered deductible *uniforms* because of the I.R.S.'s position on the issue. Recall that *uniforms* qualify as deductible business expenses only if "(1) the uniforms are specifically required as a condition of employment and (2) are not of a type adaptable to general or continued usage to the extent that they take the place of ordinary clothing." [Rev.Rul. 70-474, 1970-2 C.B. 34.]

Answer (a) is incorrect because even the time she is wearing her clothes on business, the maintenance of them is not considered a deductible business expense. **Answer (b) is incorrect** because her clothes did not qualify as a deductible business expense as discussed in the analysis to question 14, above. **Answer (d) is incorrect** because in cases where the cost of clothing does give rise to legitimate business deductions, the cost of their maintenance also generally qualifies as a business expense.

- **Additional references:** *See* DANIEL Q. POSIN, FEDERAL INCOME TAXATION OF INDIVIDUALS ¶ 6.02(1) (5th ed. 2000).

16. **Statement (b) is the most accurate.** The principal Code section permitting business deductions is IRC § 162. The first sentence of that section (contained in subsection (a)) enumerates, for all intents and purposes, the basic requirements for a business deduction. A deduction is allowed for all "ordinary and necessary" "expenses" "paid or incurred during the taxable year" "in carrying on any trade or business." The compartmentalized quotation marks signify what are commonly considered as the four basic requirements for a business deduction. These four requirements often represent, in federal income tax classes and in real life, separate and significant points of contention. Business deductions come in a million different flavors, but all qualifying deductions must meet those four criteria. The study, in tax classes, of business deductions can be long and comprehensive. At times, it may seem like many business deductions have their own set of rules, as if permitted by a separate Code section. There are many business deductions that almost take on a life of their own primarily because of explanations and interpretations from the Code subsections, regulations, court decisions, I.R.S. pronouncements, and the like.

The $2,000 Janet paid in rental costs for the construction equipment fits squarely within the requirements for business deductions under IRC § 162. The $160 in sales tax that was charged on the rental is also deductible as part of the rental cost pursuant to IRC § 162. Thus, Janet is entitled to deduct the full $2,160 associated with this equipment rental as a business expense.

For the deductibility of the $2,400 Janet paid in sales tax on her personal-use car, we need to turn to IRC § 164. This section lists various taxes that are deductible including: state, local and foreign real property taxes and income taxes, and state and local personal property taxes. State and local sales taxes are not listed as deductible taxes in IRC § 164 and, therefore, are not deductible *pursuant to this section*. This means that the $2,400 in sales tax that Janet paid on the purchase of her personal-use automobile is not deductible.

The deductibility of sales tax is sometimes bothersome for students especially in situations such as in this question. IRC § 164 appears to control deductions for taxes paid. Indeed, as mentioned above, *sales tax* is not among the list of deductible taxes. Sales tax, in and of itself, is not deductible under IRC § 164. This is why Janet is not entitled to deduct the sales tax on her car, nor can she or other taxpayers deduct sales tax paid on personal-use items such as food, clothing, electronics, etc. However, just because the deduction for sales tax is not allowed by IRC § 164, does not mean that it is not deductible under some other Code provision. In Janet's case, the *sales tax* paid on the equipment rental is also a qualified business deduction pursuant to IRC § 162. The sales tax she paid on her car, however, is not deductible under some other Code provision. In other words, IRC § 164 does not limit or preclude a deduction under other Code provisions because it does not qualify as deductible under IRC § 164. While not relevant for this question, the application of IRC § 164 can be distinguished from that of IRC § 163 dealing with deductions for interest paid. If a taxpayer pays interest, it must pass through the limitations and requirements imposed by IRC § 163 to be deductible at all – IRC § 163 acts as a clearinghouse for deductibility for all interest paid. A good example of this, again not related to this question, is interest incurred by an employee in a business context. It would appear that such interest would be deductible under IRC § 162 as a business expense without any other restrictions (as is the case with Janet's sales tax on the equipment rental). However, because interest is involved, IRC § 163 must be addressed and, as indicated in other problems in this book, such "business" interest is actually nondeductible personal interest, notwithstanding that it would qualify as a deductible expense under IRC § 162. Again, IRC § 164, identifying deductible taxes paid, is a section that precludes qualification for deductibility under another Code provision.

While not part of this question, it should be noted that Janet's qualifying business expenses of $2,160 is deductible, along with other IRC § 162 business expenses, "above the line" (to get to adjusted gross income (AGI)) in the computation of her taxable income. [Please see Appendix A for more information about how income and deductions fit together in the computation of taxable income and AGI.]

Answer (a) is incorrect because it fails to recognize that the sales tax Janet paid with respect to the equipment rental does not require IRC § 164 to be deductible but, rather, is deductible as a business expense under IRC § 162. **Answer (c) is incorrect** because sales tax is not deductible pursuant to IRC § 164 regardless of who imposes them. **Answer (d) is incorrect** because it fails to recognize the deductibility of the equipment rental, and related sales tax, as qualified business expenses under IRC § 162.

- **Additional references:** *See* DANIEL Q. POSIN, FEDERAL INCOME TAXATION OF INDIVIDUALS ¶ 6.02(1) (5th ed. 2000).

17. **The best answer is (d).** The answer to this question is, ultimately, fairly simple, but it does raise tax issues that are somewhat complex. This question invokes possible business expense deductions, under IRC § 162, *for traveling away from home*. The issue of qualifying for deductions associated with business travel away from home is the subject of other questions in this book and the details of such need not really be discussed in connection with this question. Suffice it to say such deductions require that the taxpayer conduct some form of business while traveling away from one's home. *Where* one's home is located is more of an issue in this problem. In a nutshell, the I.R.S. takes the position that one's "home" (for purposes of traveling away therefrom) is the taxpayer's principal place of work – one's so-called "tax home." Most individuals, if asked where "home" is, would probably respond that it is where they "live" (maintain a house, where their family resides, where they "hang their hat," etc.) Some courts agree, and use that as the definition of one's "home" (for purposes of traveling away therefrom). Now for most people, these two definitions result in a home location within the same general area, and home location therefore does not become an issue when they are traveling away from home on business. However, when the two possible locations are some distance apart (as in our facts), the location of one's "home" may be an issue.

Having said all that, <u>where</u> Rachael's "home" is located will not result in divergent income tax consequences based on the given facts. Utilizing the I.R.S.'s definition, Rachael's "home" (or tax home) would, with all probability, be in San Francisco. To be sure, when she travels to Los Angeles she is "traveling away from home" but the problem is, she is <u>not</u> traveling away from home for *business purposes* (she is visiting her family and her *home*-home). No business or other deduction is allowed for such non-business travel. If we say her "home" is Los Angeles, then her transportation costs to and from work are also <u>not</u> deductible business expenses, nor are the costs for her lodging and food. Rather, the transportation is nondeductible personal commuting and her other expenditures are nondeductible personal expenses. [See Rev.Rul. 56-25, 1956-1 C.B 152 (superceded with respect to an unrelated issue); Reg. § 1.162-2(e).] Granted, Rachael has one heck of a long commute, but she chooses to live where she wants to live, and the government does not subsidize such decisions through the tax Code by way of deductions.

Note that the situation would be *very* different if, for example, her employer had her working three days a week in their San Francisco offices and two days a week in their offices in Los Angeles. Then "traveling away from home" for business purposes and *where* Rachael's home is located would take on great significance.

Answers (a), (b), and (c) are all incorrect because regardless of which location is deemed to be Rachael's home, her traveling expenses are not business related and, therefore, are not deductible.

- **Additional references:** *See* DANIEL Q. POSIN, FEDERAL INCOME TAXATION OF INDIVIDUALS ¶ 6.02(1) (5th ed. 2000).

18.   **The most accurate statement is (c).** The path to reach the conclusion in this question is somewhat long. Takuma's activities appear to be business related, and would seem to be deductible if we were to apply the requirements for business deductions of IRC § 162 (that the expenditures be *ordinary and necessary expenses paid in connection with carrying on a trade or business*). [IRC § 162(a).] Because of the "entertainment" like nature of these business activities, the more restrictive provisions of IRC § 274 are applicable. As more thoroughly discussed below, Takuma will be entitled to deduct 50% of the ticket and food costs because these activities are considered "directly related to" the active conduct of his business. A more thorough analysis follows.

As indicated, when business activities have an entertainment, amusement, recreation, or fun sort of "flavor" to them, we have to go beyond the normal business deduction requirements of IRC § 162, and look to IRC § 274. [Please see other questions in this book addressing the general business deduction requirements of IRC § 162.] IRC § 274 is a limiting section, enacted to curtail what were considered abuses to entertainment related business deductions. Right off the bat, IRC § 274 generally limits the deduction of any qualifying entertainment expenses (including non-entertainment business meals) to 50% of the qualifying expense. [IRC § 274(n).] Before one even gets to this 50% deduction provision, the expenses have to qualify as deductible entertainment expenses.

IRC § 274 allows a deduction (at 50%) for entertainment *activities* that are considered either 1) directly related to the active conduct of a trade or business, or 2) associated with the active conduct of a trade or business. These two alternative qualifications are commonly known as the "directly related" and "associated with" tests. Satisfying the *directly related* test generally requires that during the entertainment activities, the taxpayer is discussing real, substantive business with a client/customer (or prospective client/customer) ostensibly aimed at obtaining immediate revenue. [Reg. § 1.274-2(c)(3).] Satisfying the *associated with* test is often less difficult. To qualify, no business need be conducted during the entertainment activity itself, but only needs to directly precede or follow a bona fide and substantial business meeting with the client/customer (or prospective client/customer). [Reg. § 1.274-2(d).]

Takuma's business/entertainment activities appear to meet the requirements of the *directly related to* test in that he did discuss actual business with potential client Christina. Before the end of the game, Christina became more of an *actual* client than merely a potential one, even discussing issues pertinent to her estate. Before we can conclude that Takuma is in the clear, we must address a regulation that is on point. The regulations, at Reg. § 1.274-2(c)(7), discuss the *directly related to* test and state: "Expenditures for entertainment, even if connected with the taxpayer's trade or business, will be considered *not directly related to* the active conduct of the taxpayer's trade or business, *if the entertainment occurred under circumstances where there was little or no possibility of engaging in the active conduct of a trade or business.*" The regulations go on to say: "The following circumstances will *generally* be considered circumstances where there was little or no possibility of engaging in the active conduct of a trade or business: . . . (ii) The distractions were substantial, such as – (a) A meeting or discussion at night clubs, theaters, and **sporting events** . . ." Finally, on this matter, the regulations state: "An expenditure for entertainment in any such case is considered not to be directly related to the active conduct of the taxpayer's trade or business *unless the taxpayer clearly establishes to the contrary.*" [Reg. § 1.274-2(c)(7) (emphasis added).]

Pursuant to the regulations, Takuma's business/entertainment activities at the baseball game presumptively do not meet the *directly related to* test because of the inherent distractions at such an event. As indicated, these regulations are only presumptive in nature and it appears likely that Takuma could clearly establish that he did actively conduct business at the baseball game, notwithstanding his surroundings. And no, the author does **not** mean to imply by this question that a Colorado Rockies baseball game is less than an "action packed" event (well maybe not to the same degree as a Dodger game).

In conclusion, Takuma is entitled to deduct (at 50%) the costs of the tickets and food for the baseball game. While not at issue in this question, because Takuma is self-employed, he would be entitled to this deduction (and his other normal IRC § 162 business expenses) *above the line* in computing his adjusted gross income (AGI). [Please see Appendix A for more information about how income and deductions fit together in computing taxable income and AGI.]

It should be noted that this question assumes that the Rockies tickets were not purchased for more than face value (e.g. from a scalper or ticket broker). If such were the case, the deduction (at 50%) would be limited to the face value of the ticket (50% thereof). [IRC § 274(l)(1)(A).]

Answer (a) is incorrect because, as discussed above, the preclusion of legitimate business activities in such environments is only a presumption. The facts indicate that Takuma most likely can overcome this presumption. Answer (b) is incorrect because, as discussed above, Takuma most likely meets the *directly related* test. This answer describes the alternative *associated with* test that, indeed, Takuma would fail based on these facts. Answer (d) is incorrect because this would *not* qualify under the *associated with* test. A business meeting the following week would not be considered a business meeting "immediately preceding or following" the entertainment activity. [Please see other questions in this book that address other aspects of entertainment related business expenses.]

- **Additional references:** *See* DANIEL Q. POSIN, FEDERAL INCOME TAXATION OF INDIVIDUALS ¶¶ 6.02(1), 6.02(5), 6.02(7) (5th ed. 2000).

19. **Statement (b) is the most accurate.** This question is exactly the same as question 18, above, except that our taxpayer, Takuma, is engaged in his business as an employee rather than being self-employed (a.k.a., independent contractor or unincorporated sole proprietor). This is an important question because it points out the *requirements* for IRC § 162 business deductions and the related (more restrictive) IRC § 274 business entertainment expense deductions are **exactly the same regardless of in what capacity one conducts his or her business, whether it is as an employee (as in this question) or as a self-employed person (as in the previous question).**

We concluded above (in the previous question), and conclude here as well, that Takuma will be entitled to deduct 50% of the ticket and food costs because these activities are considered "directly related to" the active conduct of his business. The expenditures in question are IRC § 162 business expenses and meet the more restrictive requirements of IRC § 274 for entertainment related business expenses. [Please see the analysis of question 18, above, for a more thorough discussion.]

The key issue to this question is *where and how* Takuma is entitled to this deduction (for purposes of computing taxable income. In very broad terms, there are two camps of deductions for purposes of computing taxable income. There are deductions that are subtracted from *gross income* to arrive at an intermediary point called *adjusted gross income* (AGI). These are commonly referred to as "above the line" deductions, with AGI representing "the line." The other camp of deductions consists of those that are subtracted from AGI to arrive at *taxable income*. These are commonly referred to as "below the line" deductions. The components making up this camp of *below the line* deductions can include something called the "standard deduction" or, in the alternative, a group of deductions called "itemized deductions." In addition, one or more personal exemption deductions may be included in *below the line* deductions. [For more information about how this all fits together, please see IRC § 62, Appendix A, and other questions in this book.]

When, in question 18, above, Takuma incurred these deductible expenses in the context of his self-employed business, such deductions are taken *above the line* in computing AGI. [IRC § 62.] Acknowledging that the thought of looking at actual federal tax forms may seem repulsive, the federal individual income tax return form 1040, Schedule C (or C-EZ), presents a very good visual representation of IRC § 162 (and IRC § 274) business related deductions for a self-employed individual (independent contractor or unincorporated sole proprietor).

For most employees, however, IRC § 162 business expenses (including the more restrictive IRC § 274 business entertainment expenses) are not deductible *above the line* in computing AGI. Rather, they are part deductible *below* (deductions from AGI to compute taxable income). These IRC § 162 and IRC § 274 "employee" business related expenses are part of a large group of deductions referred to as "itemized deductions." This "itemized deduction" grouping is comprised of various types of deductions such as certain medical care expenses (IRC § 213), certain interest and tax expenses (IRC §§ 163 and 164), charitable contributions (IRC § 170), and others. One sub-group of itemized deductions is a specific category referred to as "miscellaneous itemized deductions." Generally, unreimbursed employee IRC §§ 162 and 274 business related expenses (and IRC § 212 expenses unrelated to rentals or royalties) comprise this special "miscellaneous itemized deduction" sub-group. The significance of this sub-group of deductions is that, pursuant to IRC § 67, they are deductible, in the aggregate, only to the extent that they exceed 2% of the individual's AGI. Back to the federal income tax forms, Form 1040, Schedule A is a good visual representation of the entire "itemized deduction" group and it depicts the "miscellaneous itemized deduction" sub-group complete with the 2% of AGI floor calculation. [See Appendix A for more information about how income and deductions fit together in computing taxable income and AGI.]

Below the line deductions that are limited in their deductibility, as is the case here, *are less valuable* than generally unrestricted *above the line* deductions. This, therefore, yields our correct answer (b). Please be aware that this is often a very difficult concept to grasp and this issue is not the subject of discussion in all basic federal income tax courses. [Please see other questions in this book and Appendix A for more information about how income and deductions fit together in computing taxable income.]

Answer (a) is incorrect because the requirements for qualification under IRC §§ 162 and 274 are <u>not</u> more restrictive or different for an employee versus a self-employed individual. **Answer (c) is incorrect** because the 50% factor applies equally to *entertainment* related business expenses for employees and self-employed individuals. **Answer (d) is incorrect** because both the baseball game tickets and the meals are, pursuant to IRC § 274, deductible only at 50% of the qualifying expenses. **Answer (e) is incorrect** because it is not true that entertainment related business expenses are not qualified deductions for employees. As mentioned above, IRC §§ 162 and 274 make <u>no</u> distinction between employees or self-employed individuals for purposes of qualification.

- **Additional references:** *See* DANIEL Q. POSIN, FEDERAL INCOME TAXATION OF INDIVIDUALS ¶¶ 6.02(1), 6.02(5), 6.02(7) (5th ed. 2000).

20.   **The most accurate answer is (a).** Ostensibly, our analysis of this question begins with IRC § 162: deductions business related expenses. We will see that Monet's trip to France <u>is</u> considered primarily for business purposes. However, because of statutory provisions applicable to certain foreign travel, her transportation costs will have to be allocated based upon the respective time spent on business and pleasure. A more thorough analysis follows.

As indicated, the starting point for our analysis is IRC § 162. The first sentence of IRC § 162 (which appears in subsection (a)) enumerates, for all intents and purposes, four basic requirements for a business deduction. A business deduction is allowed for all (read as one continuous phrase with four distinct requirements):
  ➢ Ordinary and necessary
  ➢ Expenses
  ➢ Paid or incurred during the taxable year
  ➢ In carrying on any trade or business.

These four requirements often represent, in federal income tax classes and in real life, separate and significant points of contention. Business deductions come in a million different flavors, but all qualifying deductions must meet those four criteria. The study, in tax classes, of business deductions can be long and comprehensive. At times, it may seem like many business deductions have their own set of rules, as if permitted by a separate Code section. There are many business deductions that almost take on a life of their own primarily because of explanations and interpretations from the Code subsections, regulations, court decisions, I.R.S. pronouncements, and the like.

IRC § 162(a)(2) specifically identifies that expenditures associated with "traveling away from home" constitute qualifying business expenses. While this subsection appears to add additional requirements to the four listed above for such traveling expenditures, a careful examination of the statutory language reveals no more than a reiteration of the four basic requirements, albeit in a different form.

It is clear that Monet plans to spend the majority of her trip to France on business matters. Had this question involved domestic, as opposed to foreign travel, our answer would be relatively simple. The regulations promulgated for IRC § 162 are extensive and specifically address business transportation costs in general. For purposes of IRC § 162 qualification, transportation costs are deductible, in full, if the "trip is related primarily to [her] . . . trade or business." [Reg. 1.162-2(b)(1).] At this point, in Monet's case, we need probably not delve any further into the regulations to determine that her trip to France is primarily for business purposes. Just in case we want to verify this result, the regulations, at Reg. § 1.162-2(b)(2), provide that this determination be made based on the facts and circumstances in each case. These regulations indicate that an important factor for making this determination is the number of days spent on business compared to the number of days spent for pleasure. Again, hopefully it is fairly apparent from the facts that Monet's trip to France is primarily for business purposes.

Thus far, we have only addressed the requirements of IRC § 162 which, if this were the extent of the law applicable to Monet's trip, would result in a deduction of 100% of her transportation costs. And that is how it works for domestic travel – deduction of transportation costs for traveling away from home is an "all or nothing" proposition. If the trip is primarily for business, then 100% of the taxpayer's transportation related costs generally qualify as business expenses pursuant to IRC § 162. Alternatively, none of the transportation costs qualify as business expenses if the trip is primarily for pleasure. Monet's is not a domestic trip but, rather, involves foreign travel, and foreign business travel triggers the application of additional statutory provisions.

IRC § 274(c) addresses *foreign business travel* and its rules for deductibility of transportation costs may diverge from those for domestic travel discussed above. The general rule for deductibility of foreign travel is the same as that for domestic travel if:
  ➤ The foreign travel does not exceed one week, **or**
  ➤ The pleasure portion of the foreign travel is not more than 25% of the total foreign travel time. [IRC § 274(c)(2).]

If the foreign travel does *not* meet these criteria, then the statute requires that the foreign transportation costs be prorated based on business and non-business days, with only the business portion deductible. [IRC § 274(c)(1).] In Monet's case, her trip is expected to last more than one week, and her one-third pleasure travel portion of the trip exceeds 25%. Therefore, for deduction purposes she must prorate her transportation costs – two-thirds (her business portion of the trip) of such costs being deductible and the balance nondeductible.

Please note that this is a rather simplified question involving foreign business travel. The regulations contain many <u>very</u> specific rules regarding numerous aspects of foreign travel that your professor may choose to address.

Answer (b) is incorrect. This would be the correct answer if Monet's trip involved domestic travel only. As indicated above, and in other problems in this book, that if a domestic trip is made primarily for business purposes, then 100% of the round-trip transportation costs are qualified business deductions pursuant to IRC § 162 notwithstanding that the taxpayer enjoys some pleasure days while on the trip. **Answers (c) and (d) are also incorrect.** While both answers introduce the IRC § 274(c) restrictions for foreign travel, they both incorrectly conclude that none of Monet's transportation costs are deductible.

- **Additional references:** *See* DANIEL Q. POSIN, FEDERAL INCOME TAXATION OF INDIVIDUALS ¶ 6.02(4) (5th ed. 2000).

21. **The most accurate statement is (a).** Pursuant to changes made by the *"Job Creation and Worker Assistance Act of 2002,"* Jeremy is entitled to deduct $250 in computing his adjusted gross income (AGI). The remaining $750 is considered a "miscellaneous itemized deduction" which is deductible only to the extent that the aggregate of such category of deductions exceeds 2% of his AGI.

Jeremy's expenditures for supplies and computer software qualify as deductible IRC § 162 trade or business expenses. The first sentence of IRC § 162 (contained in subsection (a)) enumerates, for all intents and purposes, the basic requirements for a business deduction. A deduction is allowed for all "ordinary and necessary" "expenses" "paid or incurred during the taxable year" "in carrying on any trade or business." The compartmentalized quotation marks signify what are commonly considered the four basic requirements for a business deduction. These four requirements often represent, in tax classes and in real life, separate and significant points of contention. Business deductions come in a million different flavors, but all qualifying deductions meet those four criteria. The study, in tax classes, of business deductions can be long and comprehensive. Without too much strain, it appears that Jeremy's $1,000 in expenditures meet all of the IRC § 162 requirements.

The key issues in this question are where and how, in computing Jeremy's taxable income, this $1,000 is deductible. An individual can incur qualifying IRC § 162 expenses in the context of working as an employee or in an individual's own business (someone who alternatively referred to as being self-employed, an independent contractor, or operating his or her business as an "unincorporated sole proprietorship"). The requirements for deductibility pursuant to IRC § 162 are the same for an employee or a self-employed individual. However, "where" and "how" these deductions are taken does vary. A self-employed individual is usually entitled to deduct IRC § 162 business expenses in computing adjusted gross income (AGI). [IRC § 62.] This is commonly referred to as an "above the line" (AGI representing "the line") deduction. Acknowledging that the thought of looking at actual federal tax forms may sound repulsive, the federal individual income tax return form 1040, Schedule C (or C-EZ), presents a very good visual representation of IRC § 162 business deductions for a self-employed individual (independent contractor or unincorporated sole proprietor). For most employees, however, IRC § 162 business expenses are not deductible "above the line" in computing AGI. Rather, they are part of a large group of deductions referred to as "itemized deductions." This "itemized deduction" grouping is comprised of various types of deductions such as certain medical care expenses (IRC § 213), certain interest and tax expenses (IRC §§ 163 and 164), charitable contributions (IRC § 170), and others. The entire group of "itemized deductions" are commonly referred to as "below the line" deductions as they are deductible, if at all, after AGI ("the line") to arrive at "taxable income." [See Appendix A for visual framework of the taxable income computation.] One sub-group of itemized deductions is a specific category referred to as "miscellaneous itemized deductions." Generally, unreimbursed employee IRC § 162 business expenses (and IRC § 212 expenses unrelated to rentals or royalties) comprise this special "miscellaneous itemized deduction" sub-group. The significance of this sub-group of deductions is that, pursuant to IRC § 67, they are deductible, in the aggregate, only to the extent that they exceed 2% of the individual's AGI. Back to the federal income tax forms, Form 1040, Schedule A is a good visual representation of the entire "itemized deduction" group and it depicts the "miscellaneous itemized deduction" sub-group complete with the 2% of AGI floor calculation.

At this point, it appears that we have selected the wrong "correct" answer. All of Jeremy's $1,000 of IRC § 162 business expenses were incurred as an employee and would seem to be deductible as part of the "miscellaneous itemized deduction" group of deductions only to the extent that the total of all such deductions exceed 2% of Jeremy's AGI. As of this writing, this would be the correct answer in years other than **2002 and 2003**. As part of the "*Job Creation and Worker Assistance Act of 2002*," a provision was enacted that specifically applies in Jeremy's situation. This provision (adding IRC § 62(a)(2)(D)) allows a full-time elementary or secondary school teacher (grades K-12) to deduct "above the line" (to compute AGI), up to $250 spent on books, supplies (with some restrictions for certain items for health and physical education courses), computer related items, etc., that are for use in the classroom. Jeremy's expenditures for classroom supplies and computer software qualify. Therefore, $250 of the $1,000 he spent is deductible "above the line" in computing his AGI. The remaining $750 falls into the special category of "miscellaneous itemized deductions" that are, in the aggregate, subject to the 2% of AGI floor deduction restriction.

Note that this relatively small, albeit beneficial, provision of IRC § 62(a)(2)(D) is applicable for only two years: **2002 and 2003**. While you may not cover this limited-life provision in your federal income tax course, it serves as a good example of how quickly tax laws can change and how fleeting certain provisions may be.

Answer (b) is incorrect. Qualifying IRC § 162 business expenses for most employees are not deductible "above the line" in computing AGI. The limited IRC § 62(a)(2)(D) provision for certain school teacher expenditures is an exception, but it is limited to $250 in each of the years 2002 and 2003. **Answer (c) is incorrect** because the fact that Jeremy is an employee does not preclude deductions for qualified IRC § 162 business expenses. **Answer (d) is incorrect.** But for this new and limited provision of IRC § 62(a)(2)(D), this answer would be correct. Absent changes in the law subsequent to this writing, this answer will be the correct answer for years starting in 2004.

22. **The correct answer is (d).** First, this is a year-specific question (2003) but is easily adaptable to other tax years. Second, this is a difficult and a somewhat tricky question. Additionally, this material is not covered in all federal income tax classes sufficiently to answer this question. With that said, Teresa may be entitled to deduct some of the interest she expects to pay in 2003 on her law school loans, but this depends on the amount of her "modified" adjusted gross income for 2003.

IRC § 163 is the primary section at issue for deductions related to interest paid. For casual readers of the Code, IRC § 163(a) provides a simple and broad sounding deduction for interest stating, in part: "There shall be allowed as a deduction all interest paid . . . within the taxable year on indebtedness." Under this general definition, the interest Teresa pays on her law school loans would give rise to a deduction. However, the Tax Reform Act of 1986 added subsection (h) to IRC § 163 located quite some written distance from the general allowance for interest deductions of subsection (a). IRC § 163(h) starts out deceptively, and unfavorably, simple by stating, in part: "In the case of a taxpayer other than a corporation, no deduction shall be allowed . . . for personal interest paid . . . during the taxable year."

The definition of *personal interest*, which is not deductible, if found in IRC § 163(h)(2) and takes the form of a negative definition – *personal interest* is interest "other than" those listed in subparagraphs (A) through (F). The key, therefore, to finding interest that is deductible, is to fit within one of these specified categories of what does not constitute nondeductible personal interest. Among the categories of interest that are not personal interest is what might be the familiar category of "qualified residence interest" (typical interest paid on a home mortgage). [IRC § 163(h)(2)(D).] Somewhat less familiar, but logically not included as personal interest, is "interest properly allocable to a trade or business." [IRC § 163(h)(2)(A).] As seen in other questions in this book, "business" interest, rather oddly, does not include business interest incurred by an employee. Also listed among the categories of interest that is <u>not</u> considered personal interest is, "any interest allowable as a deduction under section 221 (relating to interest on educational loans)." [§ 163(h)(2)(F).] We will, below, conclude that the interest Teresa pays on her student loans in 2003 *may* qualify as deductible education loan interest pursuant to IRC § 221.

IRC § 221, a relatively new section effective in 1998, allows for a limited deduction for certain interest paid on certain educational loans. This deduction, if allowed, is a valuable "above the line" deduction – a deduction from gross income in computing adjusted gross income (AGI). To qualify as an educational loan for this section, the loan proceeds generally must be used for tuition, fees, books, room/board or related expenses while attending a college, university or vocational school. This includes graduate, post graduate studies, professional degree programs, etc. So far, Teresa's loan qualifies. Qualified educational loans do <u>not</u> include money borrowed from certain "related parties." [IRC § 221(d)(1).] Teresa's loans were from traditional law school loan sources (not from "related" individuals) and her loans are considered qualified education loans used for qualified higher education expenses.

The interest Teresa pays on this qualified higher education loan is subject to two important limitations. First, the amount of interest deductible under IRC § 221 is limited, by statute, to $2,500 per year (in the aggregate for all such loans). While this question does not ask for a specific numeric answer, Teresa's expected $2,800 of interest exceeds this limit and, therefore, her deduction for interest would, at this point, be limited to $2,500. If allowed, as discussed below, this deduction is taken "above the line" in computing Teresa's adjusted gross income (AGI) (i.e., it is an amount that is subtracted from *gross income* to compute AGI). [Please see Appendix A for more information about how income and deductions fit together to compute AGI and taxable income.]

The second important limitation kicks in if the taxpayer's adjusted gross income (AGI), as modified by IRC § 221(b)(2)(C), exceeds certain levels. If it does, the otherwise allowed IRC § 221 interest deduction is reduced or "phased-out" utilizing a formula contained in the statute. Pursuant to IRC § 221(b)(2)(B), the level of "modified adjusted gross income" at which this deduction starts to "phase-out" (be reduced) is $50,000 for single individuals or $100,00 for married individuals filing a joint return. The deduction for student loan interest is totally eliminated for single individuals with "modified adjusted gross income" of $65,000 or more, and at $130,000 or more for married individuals filing a joint return. The statute uses the term "modified adjusted gross income" because true adjusted gross income will reflect any deduction allowed by this IRC § 221 (see above). Modified adjusted gross income is basically *adjusted gross income* computed before you compute any possible deduction under this IRC § 221 (and other sections not applicable to this problem). [IRC § 221(b)(2)(C).]

As for Teresa, we do not know her marital status or what her "modified adjusted gross income" will be for 2003. We do know that she expects to have "gross income" of $105,000 for 2003, but gross income is not the measuring rod for reductions of possible deductions under IRC § 221. We do not know the extent of Teresa's other possible *above the line* deductions for 2003 will be subtracted from gross income to arrive at her *adjusted gross income* (and basically, her "modified adjusted gross income"). At this point, it might help to discuss, using illustrations or examples, why answers (a), (b) and (c) are not the best answers

Answer (a) is not the best answer. It cannot be said for sure that Teresa will not be entitled to any deduction for her student loan interest. Let us assume for the moment that Teresa is married (filing a joint return with her spouse). Even if she has no other *above the line* deductions, her modified adjusted gross income would be $105,000, allowing at least some deduction of her student loan interest under IRC § 221. In the alternative, let us assume for the moment that she is single. It is possible that she could have enough other *above the line* deductions that when subtracted from her $105,000 of gross income, her "modified adjusted gross income" would be within the range of $50,000 to $65,000, thus allowing for some deduction.

Answer (b) is also not the best answer. It cannot be said for sure that Teresa will be entitled to a $2,500 deduction for her student loan interest. Let us assume for the moment that Teresa is single and further that she has no other *above the line* deductions for 2003. Her resulting "modified adjusted gross income" at $105,000 would be well in excess of the $65,000 maximum limit and she would be entitled to <u>no</u> deduction for her student loan interest under IRC § 221. Similarly, let us assume for the moment that Teresa is married (and files a joint return with her spouse) and she has no other *above the line* deductions. Again, her "modified adjusted gross income" would be $105,000, which would be in excess of $100,000, the beginning of the range where the IRC § 221 deduction would be reduced.

Answer (c) is also not the best answer. It is true that if Teresa is married (and files a joint return with her spouse) she will be entitled to at least a partial deduction of her student loan interest in 2003. However, it is not true that "only if she is married" will she possibly be entitled to a deduction for her student loan interest. As indicated in the discussion of the incorrect answer (a) above, she could be *single* and have substantial *above the line* deductions to reduce her "modified adjusted gross income" to levels between $50,000 and $65,000 thereby allowing some deduction for her student loan interest.

23.   **Answer (d) is correct.** Bill and Wilma will be entitled to claim a total of five personal exemption deductions, one each for Bill, Wilma and their three children.

First and foremost, students should be aware that this question is date or year sensitive. As indicated in the preface of this book, many tax related provisions change for each tax year. Sometimes it is necessary to ask questions for a specific year as opposed to in the abstract. This is one such situation and it involves de-ductions for personal exemptions. Every living person has, in his or her figurative pocket, a "coupon" good for a personal exemption deduction for each tax year. There is no real "coupon" involved, but it helps to think of the personal exemption deduction as such. The amount of this exemption deduction is listed in IRC § 151 of the Code as $2,000. However, this amount has been adjusted (increased) each year since 1990 to reflect the general level of inflation. The personal exemption deduction amount at the time of this writing is $3,000 for the year 2002. [Please see Appendix B for other inflation adjusted tax items for the year 2002.] The key to this problem is determining who gets to use these $3,000 personal exemption deduction "coupons" for 2002. Does each person get to use his or her own "coupon" and get a $3,000 deduction (for 2002), or does somebody else get to claim that person's "coupon" and take the deduction?

Those students having come into a law school income tax course knowing little about income tax, probably know something about this issue. Parents claiming their children as dependents and getting an extra deduction for them is precisely the issue that we are faced with in this question. Right out of the box, Bill and Wilma filing one return together (a joint return) are entitled to two personal exemption deductions, one for Bill and one for Wilma. Bill and Wilma each get to use their own personal exemption "coupon." The bigger issue here is whether Bill and Wilma get to take their kids' "coupons" and get more personal exemption deductions (on Bill and Wilma's joint income tax return for purposes of computing their taxable income), or do the kids get to use their own "coupons" for a personal exemption deduction (on their respective income tax returns for purposes of computing their respective taxable income). To determine if Bill and Wilma are entitled to get their kids' personal exemption "coupons" (claim them as dependents and get to deduct their $3,000, for 2002, personal exemption deductions) involves a two-step (with many sub-steps) analysis, which in simplified form, is as follows:

Step One: Is this person (e.g. a kid) your "**Dependent**" pursuant to IRC § 152? (All requirements must be met).

> ➤ Person must be a U.S. citizen, resident or national, or a resident of Canada, Mexico for any part of the tax year.
> ➤ Person must be either related to you, or be a member of your household for the entire year. [See IRC §§ 152(a)(1)-(a)(8) for definitions of "relatives," and IRC § 152(a)(9) for other qualifying individuals.]
> ➤ You must have provided more than one-half this person's total support for the year.

Step Two: If this person is your **Dependent** (from Step One, above), are you allowed to take a **deduction** (personal exemption deduction) for this dependent? [IRC § 151(c).]

> ➤ Your Dependent must not file a joint return with a spouse for the year.
> ➤ Your Dependent must either:
>> ▪ Have "gross income" less than the "exemption amount" for that year, or
>> ▪ Be your child (or step-child) who is under the age of 19 at the end of the year, **or**
>> ▪ Be your child (or step child) who is under the age of 24 at the end of the year and is a full-time student for some part of each of five months during the year.

If **both** of these two steps are satisfied with respect to someone for whom you are trying to get their exemption deduction "coupon," then that person is your dependent and you are entitled to deduct their personal exemption deduction amount (e.g., $3,000 for 2002).

Wilma and Bill satisfy step one, above, with respect to all three of their children. Jeremy, Heidi and Marsha are all U.S. citizens, they are "related" to Wilma and Bill as defined in the Code (children are considered related pursuant to IRC § 152(a)(1)), and the facts indicate that our couple provides more than one-half of each child's total support for the year). Note that there is no requirement that any "related" person (listed in IRC §§ 152(a)(1)-(a)(8)) lives with anyone in particular to attain dependent status.

Step two of the dependent exemption deduction analysis will be discussed separately with respect to each of Bill and Wilma's three children. **Jeremy** is unmarried, but does he have "gross income" less than the "exemption amount" for the year in question? And what does this mean? The measuring gross income level of "the exemption amount" is the amount of the personal exemption deduction –

$3,000 in our case for the year 2002. Jeremy's gross income of $3,200 is <u>not</u> less than the $3,000 exemption amount (for 2002). We do not, however, stop at this point as the operative word in this part of the step two is "either." Going onto to the next "either" requirement, Jeremy <u>is</u> Bill and Wilma's child and is less than 19 years old (as of the end of the year). We can stop here with respect to **Jeremy** – Bill and Wilma are entitled to get Jeremy's personal exemption deduction "coupon."

Heidi is also unmarried. Heidi's gross income of $8,200 is clearly not less than the $3,000 exemption amount (for 2002). Going to the next step, she is Bill and Wilma's child but she is not <u>less than</u> age 19 (as of the end of the year). Heidi does, however, qualify under the last option – she is less than 24 years of age (as of the end of the year) and is a full-time student at UCLA. Therefore, with respect to **Heidi**, Bill and Wilma are entitled to get her personal exemption deduction "coupon."

Marsha is also not married. Marsha's $2,950 of gross income for the year <u>is</u> less than the $3,000 exemption amount. Therefore, we need not go any further as with respect to **Marsha**, Bill and Wilma are entitled to get her personal exemption deduction "coupon."

In conclusion, Bill and Wilma are entitled to a $3,000 (for 2002) deduction for each of them, as well as a $3,000 deduction for each of their dependent children, for a total of **five**. Note the total deduction of $15,000 ($3,000 x 5) is substantial. While not the subject of this problem, there are provisions in the Code and the 2001 Tax Act that may affect this total personal exemption deduction depending on the extent of Bill and Wilma's income. This latter concept of "phasing-out" personal exemption deductions is complex and is addressed in another question in this book.

As indicated, this question is date sensitive, applicable to the 2002 tax year. This question can easily be modified to accommodate years subsequent to 2002 by incorporating the applicable inflation adjusted personal exemption deduction amount for any particular year.

Answer (a) is incorrect because it fails to recognize any of the three children as dependents for whom the couple is entitled personal exemption deductions. **Answers (b) and (c) are incorrect** because both answers do not recognize that Bill and Wilma are entitled to the personal exemption deduction for <u>all</u> of their three children.

24.   **The best answer is (e).** IRC § 163 is the primary section at issue for deductions related to interest paid. For casual readers of the Code, IRC § 163(a) provides a

simple and broad sounding deduction for interest stating, in part: "There shall be allowed as a deduction all interest paid . . . within the taxable year on indebtedness." Under this general definition, the "margin" loan interest that Ida paid would give rise to a deduction. However, the Tax Reform Act of 1986 added subsection (h) to IRC § 163, located quite some written distance from the general allowance for interest deductions of subsection (a). IRC § 163(h) starts out deceptively, and unfavorably, simply by stating, in part: "In the case of a taxpayer other than a corporation, no deduction shall be allowed . . . for personal interest paid . . . during the taxable year."

The definition of *personal interest*, which is not deductible, is found in IRC § 163(h)(2) and takes the form of a negative definition – *personal interest* is interest "other than" those listed in subparagraphs (A) through (F). The key, therefore, to finding interest that is deductible, is to fit within one of these specified categories of what does not constitute nondeductible personal interest. Among the categories of interest that are not personal interest is what might be the familiar category of "qualified residence interest" (typical interest paid on a home mortgage). [IRC § 163(h)(2)(D).] Somewhat less familiar, but logically not included as personal interest, is "interest properly allocable to a trade or business." [IRC § 163(h)(2)(A).] As seen in other questions in this book, "business" interest, rather oddly, does not include business interest incurred by an employee. Also listed among the categories of interest that are not considered personal interest is, "any investment interest (within the meaning of subsection (d))." [§ 163 (h)(2)(B).] We will, below, conclude that Ida's "margin" loan interest represents "investment interest" that, pursuant to IRC §163(d), is deductible only to the extent that she has "net investment income" in the year. Any excess nondeductible interest is carried over to future years and deductible to the extent of "net investment income."

Basically, *Investment interest*, is interest paid on monies used for investment purposes. Interest paid on "margin" loans to purchase stocks for investment purposes is a classic example of *investment interest*. IRC § 163(d) allows for an individual to deduct such interest, but only to the extent of the individual's "net investment income" for the year. [IRC § 163(d)(1).] While the definition of *net investment income* can, at times, be rather complex, it generally means the aggregate amount of net income that the individual earns from his or her investments (gross income from all investment activities less investment-related expenses other than *investment interest*). In effect, this provision limiting deductions for *investment interest*, prevents such interest from being used to reduce an individuals other, non-investment, income (e.g., wages or net business earnings).

Ida's situation is somewhat simple in that her investment activities are comprised of her stock ownership and monies invested in savings accounts. Her *net invest-*

ment income for last year consists of the $500 dividend income (from her stocks) and the $300 in interest from her savings accounts. In her simplified case, she has *net investment income* of $800 ($500 plus $300). Therefore, of the $3,000 that Ida paid last year in *investment interest*, she could only deduct (last year) $800, the amount of her *net investment income*. Notice that this brings her net profit from her investment activities (for tax purposes) to zero. While not applicable in this fact pattern, *net investment income* can include certain gains from sales of investment property. [See IRC § 163(d)(4)(B).]

What happens to Ida's *investment interest* that she was not entitled to deduct last year because of this *net investment income* limitation? It is not lost but, rather, is carried forward to succeeding taxable years, and deducted to the extent of the applicable year's *net investment income*. [IRC § 163(d)(2).] For Ida, the $2,200 of *investment interest* that she could not deduct last year ($3,000 less the $800 of deductible interest), is carried forward to this year and as many succeeding years as necessary to deduct the interest to the extent of *net investment income*.

Please note that the area of *investment interest* can be very complex, and your professor may cover this material in much greater depth than is presented in this problem.

Answer (a) is incorrect because the Ida's interest is not nondeductible "personal interest." **Answer (b) is incorrect** because, as discussed above, the deduction for investment interest is limited. **Answer (c) is incorrect** because it does not properly reflect her total "net investment income" for the year. **Answer (d) is incorrect** because it fails to recognize the carryover aspect of nondeductible investment interest.

- **Additional references:** *See* DANIEL Q. POSIN, FEDERAL INCOME TAXATION OF INDIVIDUALS ¶ 7.01(3) (5th ed. 2000).

25. **The best answer is (c).** It is great that Bonnie remembers some of the material from her tax class, and that she is thinking creatively about tax issues. Unfortunately, her plan most likely falls within what are known as the "hobby loss" rules of IRC § 183. This section addresses the deductibility of expenses for activities "not engaged in for profit."

For now, let's assume that Bonnie's contemplated plan will be considered an activity not engaged in for profit. If such is the case, IRC § 183 generally limits the allowable deductions associated with this activity to the amount of income generated from this activity (with some exceptions not applicable here). In other words, the best you can do, tax wise, is to "break-even."

To be considered in an activity engaged in for profit, making a profit must be the **primary** motive for engaging in the activity. Profit as a secondary or incidental motive is not enough. Making a profit from an activity such as that contemplated by Bonnie is essentially not even on the map. Activities that are too centered around someone's hobby, where fun and personal pleasure are paramount, almost always run afoul with these rules. The statute does provide a "presumptive" test. It is presumed to be engaged in for profit (and thereby allowing deductions for all business expenses) if the activity shows a profit for any three or more out of five consecutive years (or two out of seven years for horse breeding, racing, or showing). [IRC § 183(d).] This is merely a presumptive test, and taxpayers legitimately engaged in a trade or business for profit can be considered a "for profit" business despite failing this test.

Answer (a) is incorrect because "looking" like a business will not, by itself, constitute a "for profit" business activity. **Answer (b) is also incorrect.** The fact that some personal pleasure is derived from an otherwise "for profit" business activity does subject the business to the hobby loss rules of IRC § 183. However, making a profit must be the primary motive for engaging in the activity. **Answer (d) is also incorrect.** The criteria for determining "for profit" business activity enumerated in the statute at IRC § 183(d) is only a presumptive test.

- **Additional references:** *See* DANIEL Q. POSIN, FEDERAL INCOME TAXATION OF INDIVIDUALS ¶¶ 4.04(3), 6.02(9) (5th ed. 2000).

ANSWER KEY
EXAM III

1.   **Answer (b) is correct.** This question involves the exclusion of "compensation for injuries or sickness" provided in IRC § 104. This section has a long, complex and capricious past vis-à-vis what is within its umbrella of exclusion. In its most basic form, an individual receiving damages, by award or settlement, for physical injuries or physical sickness can exclude such amounts from income. [IRC § 104(a)(2).] In its current form (reflecting changes made by the "Small Business Job Protection Act of 1996"), this section generally excludes amounts received (other than punitive damages) for physical tort awards and settlements. The entire amount of Ann's award, in this question, originates from her physical injury arising from the negligence cause of action and, therefore, is excluded from gross income.

The difficulty of questions involving IRC § 104 can vary dramatically depending on how thoroughly one's professor covers the exclusion as to its history, policy foundations, and the like. This is a good area of tax law for in-depth class analysis, so take this into consideration when addressing questions involving the subject. Much of this Code section's history centered on the breadth of this exclusion with, at varying times, exclusions allowed for damages received from non physical tort or "tort type" causes of action, and punitive damages.

The problem students usually have with this question is the reluctance to exclude the portions of Ann's award identified as replacement for "lost wages" and "emotional distress." As for the replacement of lost wages, one might logically argue (as did the I.R.S. for many years) that they should not be within the scope of IRC § 104's exclusion because wages, had she not been injured, would have been taxable. Historically, this was the subject of much tax litigation. However, the answer is now clear that these amounts do not represent taxable wages even the award amount is measured by the amount of wages that could have been earned but for the injuries. [Rev.Rul. 85-97, 1985-2 C.B. 50.]

Regarding the "emotional distress" component of the award, there is often confusion because of language in the body of IRC § 104(a) that states, "emotional distress shall not be treated as a physical injury or physical sickness." Remembering that "physical" injury/sickness is required for exclusion, it might appear that the portion of Ann's award identified for emotional distress is not excludable. However, because Ann's cause of action was the physical injury, and the emotional distress emanated therefrom, the amount is within the scope of the exclusion.

Answers (a), (c) and (d) are incorrect because they all, to some degree, do not represent the full scope of the IRC § 104(a)(2) exclusion as it applies to this question. Please see the discussion for the correct answer (b), immediately above, for more information. **Answer (e) is incorrect** because the exclusion provided in

IRC § 104(a)(2), as has been discussed, is designed specifically for compensatory damages resulting from a physical injury/sickness.

- **Additional references:** *See* DANIEL Q. POSIN, FEDERAL INCOME TAXATION OF INDIVIDUALS ¶¶ 3.11(1), 3.11(2) (5th ed. 2000).

2. **Answer (d) is the most accurate.** With one narrow exception (see discussion of incorrect answer (b) below, punitive damages are <u>not</u> within the scope of excludable awards for physical injury/sickness as provided in IRC § 104(a)(2). While historically, exclusion of punitive damages has varied, current law is very clear on the matter. A plain reading of the statute (at IRC § 104(a)(2)) reveals, in a parenthetical phrase, that punitive damages are not within the scope of the exclusion. Therefore, in this question, the punitive damage award Ann receives is included, in full, in gross income.

As indicated above, the difficulty of questions involving IRC § 104 can vary dramatically depending on how thoroughly one's professor covers the exclusion as to its history, policy foundations, and the like. This is a good area of tax law for in-depth class analysis, so take this into consideration when addressing questions involving the subject. Much of this Code section's history centered on the breadth of this exclusion with, at varying times, exclusions allowed for damages received from non-physical tort or "tort type" causes of action, and punitive damages.

Answer (a) is incorrect but is a commonly selected answer because it corresponds to what could have been a correct answer had this question asked about the historical application of IRC § 104. One iteration of this Code section (at one time) arguably allowed for the exclusion of punitive damages arising from an underlying physical tort or tort type cause of action. However, this is no longer the case and such a distinction is irrelevant for exclusion purposes.

Answer (b) is incorrect because there is no such qualified exception to the rule of punitive damage inclusion applicable to our fact pattern. However, there is, in IRC § 104(c), a narrow exception where one can exclude punitive damages received. Specifically, punitive damages are excluded from gross income if they were awarded based on a "wrongful death" action <u>and</u> under applicable state law, which was in effect on September 13, 1995, punitive damages are the only type of damages that can be awarded in such an action. The facts in our question do not fit within this very limited exception. **Answer (c) is incorrect** because no such correlation for inclusion or exclusion exists.

- **Additional references:** *See* DANIEL Q. POSIN, FEDERAL INCOME TAXATION OF INDIVIDUALS ¶¶ 3.11(1), 3.11(2) (5th ed. 2000).

3.   **Answer (a) is correct.** As in questions 1 and 2, above, this question involves the exclusion of "compensation for injuries or sickness" provided in IRC § 104. Also, as previously indicated, this section has a long, complex and capricious past vis-à-vis what is within its umbrella of exclusion. As discussed above, in its current form (reflecting changes made by the "*Small Business Job Protection Act of 1996*"), this section generally excludes amounts received (other than punitive damages) for <u>physical tort</u> awards and settlements. In the body of IRC § 104(a), the law specifies that "emotional distress shall not be treated as a physical injury or physical sickness." This Code section goes on to effectively say that not withstanding that emotional distress is not a physical tort, amounts received from an award/settlement arising therefrom are excludable to the extent that it represents payment for his/her costs of actual medical care attributable to the emotion distress. In our question, because Bob's claim is based on the tort of emotional distress, his settlement would not be excludable except for the amount designated as payment for his actual medical costs.

As indicated in another question in this book, do not fall into the trap of trying to "bootstrap" within this section's exclusion, awards/settlements emanating from an emotional distress cause of action because the plaintiff's emotional distress manifests itself into an actual physical injury. **Answer (d) is incorrect** for this reason.

It bears repeating that the difficulty of questions involving IRC § 104 can vary dramatically depending on how thoroughly one's professor covers the exclusion as to its history, policy foundations, and the like. This is a good area of tax law for in-depth class analysis, so take this into consideration when addressing questions involving the subject. Much of this Code section's history centered on the breadth of this exclusion with, at varying times, exclusions allowed for damages received from non physical tort or "tort type" causes of action, and punitive damages.

Answer (b) is incorrect but is the source of some confusion because of the historical application of IRC § 104. Under old law, the basic starting point for exclusion under this section was whether the award/settlement arose from a "tort or tort type" cause of action. Using this as a benchmark for qualification under the current statute, however, is far too broad. Confusing to students is that, as of this writing, the regulations do not reflect the current state of the law. For example, Reg. § 1.104-1(c) states, in part: "Section 104(a)(2) excludes from gross income the amount of any damages received (whether by suite or agreement) on account of personal injuries or sickness. The term 'damages received (whether by suit or agreement)' means an amount received . . . through prosecution of a legal suit or action based upon tort or tort type rights . . ." Utilizing the language in this regulation, it would appear that Bob's settlement would be excludable because "emotional distress" is clearly a tort. However, this regulation does not reflect changes made to the statute in 1996 that narrowed the exclusion to "physical" injury/sickness and the specific designation that emotional distress is not physical in nature. One can correctly speculate that under prior law, the determination of whether a specific award was received under a tort or tort type cause of action was the source of much debate and litigation.

Answer (c) is incorrect because it fails to recognize the limited exclusion for payments of medical costs for otherwise includible emotional distress based claims.

- **Additional references:** *See* DANIEL Q. POSIN, FEDERAL INCOME TAXATION OF INDIVIDUALS ¶¶ 3.11(1), 3.11(2) (5th ed. 2000).

4.   **Answer (c) is the most accurate.** As in questions 1, 2 and 3, above, this question involves the exclusion of "compensation for injuries or sickness" provided in IRC § 104. Without duplicating the entire analysis of those questions, the key item in this question 4, is that Ann's defamation action is <u>not</u> a physical injury/sickness and, therefore, not excludable from gross income. To be sure, defamation <u>is</u> a tort. However under the current law narrowing the exclusion under IRC § 104 does not qualify.

Answers (a), (b) and (d) are incorrect because Ann's defamation cause of action from which the settlement arose, was not a "physical" injury/sickness. As mentioned in the analysis of the answers to the previous questions in this series, the law in this area has changed dramatically over the years, generally narrowing the scope of the IRC § 104 exclusion. Your professor may discuss, in some depth, the historical progression of this section. There was a time when non-physical torts, such as defamation, gave rise to excludable damage awards. At one time there was, arguably, a distinction as to whether the harm was to one's personal reputation (excludable), or to their business/professional reputation (potentially non-excludable). However, with the narrowing of the statute to physical injury/sickness, most of these contentious issues have evaporated.

- **Additional references:** *See* DANIEL Q. POSIN, FEDERAL INCOME TAXATION OF INDIVIDUALS ¶¶ 3.11(1), 3.11(2) (5th ed. 2000).

5.   **The best answer is (e).** This question is a good example of how, in a progressing fact pattern, the subject matter can quickly change to a completely different tax issue. In class, and in the Code, the subject of exclusion for amounts received for injuries is miles away (no pun intended) the subject of moving expense deductions covered here. We conclude below, that the couple will be entitled to deduct their moving costs assuming Bob works an aggregate of thirty-nine weeks in

Awayville during the twelve-month period immediately following their move there last November.

The Code, in IRC § 217, provides for deductions for certain moving costs if specific requirements are met. IRC § 217 can yield a nice little (sometimes *big*) deduction for many taxpayers. The policy for allowing this deduction is to encourage mobility in the work force – to encourage people to move to where the jobs are located. There is, as you suspect, a "work" requirement to this deduction. In fact, there are two requirements or tests to qualify for deducting moving expenses under IRC § 217:

> ➤ The "distance" test, **and**
> ➤ The "work" or "time" test.

Note that both tests/requirements must be met to qualify for the moving expense deduction under IRC § 217. In our case, we have both Ann and Bob moving from Centerville to Awayville. For married couples filing a joint return, only **one spouse** need meet the two tests in order for the couple to deduct qualifying moving costs. But note, this does not mean that one spouse can pass only the first test and the other spouse can pass only the second test. One spouse must meet both of the requirements.

The Distance Test

The magic qualifying distance is **50 miles or more**, but how this is computed is a bit convoluted and depends on the relationship of three location variables: 1) the taxpayer's old home, 2) the taxpayer's old place of work (if any), and 3) the taxpayer's new place of work. The actual statutory distance test is stated as follows: "[T]he taxpayer's new principal place of work [must be] at least 50 miles farther from his former residence than was his former principal place of work, or if he had no former principal place of work, [it must be] at least 50 miles from his former residence." [IRC § 217(c)(1).] Not the most clear definition, but in effect what it says is take the distance from your **old home** to your **new work** and subtract from that the distance from your **old home** and your **old work** (if any). If the result is **50 miles or more**, the requirement is satisfied.

In our question, both spouses' new jobs in Awayville are about 55 miles from their old home in Centerville. As for Ann, the initial facts for this series of questions indicate that her old job in Nearbyville was 10 miles from their Centerville home. Ann fails the distance test, as the difference between the two is only 45 miles, and not the minimum 50 miles required by statute. If our couple has any hopes of deducting their moving costs it is up to Bob. Again, his new job in Awayville is 55 miles from their old home in Centerville. The key question now is whether or not Bob is considered to have an "old place of work." If we must count his old job in Otherville (30 miles from their old home), Bob too would clearly fail the test. But do we count this old job? His old job ended at least five years ago and he has not worked since then (until his new job after the move to Awayville). Bob's break in service has been so substantial that he is not considered to have an old job for purposes of calculating the distance test. With no "old job" to consider in the calculation for Bob, his new job, 55 miles from his old house, is a distance of 50 miles or more and he therefore passes the distance test.

The Work or Time Test
As the impetus for the moving expense deduction of IRC § 217 is to encourage mobility in the work force, it makes sense that the deduction requirements include a work or employment component. For employees, IRC § 217 requires that the taxpayer work full-time for at least 39 weeks during the first 12-month period immediately following the move. [IRC § 217(c)(2)(A).] For self-employed individuals, the test is more demanding. [See IRC § 217(c)(2)(B).] There is no requirement that the new employment be in any particular line of business, that it be a continuous period of employment for 39 weeks, or that it be the same job for the requisite 39-week period. While not applicable for Bob in our question, the statute provides that failure to meet this "work/time test" will be ignored for certain reasons such as disability, transfer to a new job location by the employer, and certain involuntary terminations from employment.

Bob is the only spouse that we need to address, as Ann did not pass the distance test discussed above. The facts indicate that within weeks of the move, Bob found employment. He has continued full-time employment since then and assuming he continues to work full-time, he will pass the "work/time test." For determining the number of full-time weeks employed, it is irrelevant that he quit his first job in Awayville as he immediately started work in a new job.

Assuming Bob continues to work full-time, he will have passed both the "distance" and "work/time" tests, thereby entitling the couple to deduct their moving costs pursuant to IRC § 217.

Although not necessary to answer this question, the IRC § 217 moving expense deduction is an *above the line* deduction (subtracted from gross income in computing adjusted gross income (AGI)). [Please see Appendix A for more information about how income and deductions fit together in computing taxable income and AGI.]

Answer (a) is incorrect because IRC § 217 provides for such a deduction for qualified moves. **Answer (b) is incorrect** because, as discussed above, Bob's break in service from his old job was so substantial that for purposes of the "distance test," Bob is not considered to have had an old job. **Answer (c) is incorrect** because the fact that Bob changed jobs is irrelevant in determining whether he meets the "work/time test." **Answer (d) is incorrect** because, as discussed above, Ann does not meet the "distance test."

- **Additional references:** *See* DANIEL Q. POSIN, FEDERAL INCOME TAXATION OF INDIVIDUALS ¶ 6.02(8) (5ᵗʰ ed. 2000).

6.   **The best answer is (a).** IRC § 213 allows for a deduction of certain qualified medical care expenses. Once one makes the determination of what constitutes "qualified" medical care expenses, the subject of this question, the deduction is allowed as an "itemized deduction" only to the extent that the total qualifying expenses exceeds 7.5% of Adjusted Gross Income (AGI). [See Appendix A for more information about how income and deductions fit together in computing taxable income.] Qualified medical care expenses include typical costs for doctors, dentists, hospital, health insurance, and the like. See IRC § 213(d).

Ann and Bob made substantial modifications to their new home that were related to Ann's medical condition: installation of ramps, railings, widening doorways for wheelchair access, etc. In addition, they purchased an expensive motorized wheelchair for Ann. Do these expenditures qualify as medical care *expenses*? These costs are not really "expenses" at all but, rather, are considered "capital expenditures." Capital expenditures (permanent improvements and most asset purchases) are generally not deductible expenses but serve to either increase the adjusted basis in the property being improved or create a basis in the property acquired, as the case may be. [IRC §§ 263 and 1016.] However, if capital expenditures are primarily health-related, which would be the case for the house modifications and the wheelchair in our facts, they are not precluded from qualifying as medical care expenses.

The regulations, at Reg. § 1.213-1(e)(iii) indicate that costs for such medically related *capital expenditures* as Seeing Eye dogs, artificial teeth and limbs, wheelchairs, and the like represent *qualifying medical care expenses*. [Reg. § 1.213-1(e)(iii).] The cost of Ann's wheelchair most likely fully qualifies as a medical care expense. For health-related capital improvements to property, the normal rule is that a medical care expense is allowed but only to the extent that the cost of the improvement exceeds the increase in value to the underlying property resulting from the improvement. [See Reg. § 1.213-1(e)(iii).] Certain improvements, by their nature, add minimal or no value to the underlying property and, therefore, qualify in full as a medical care expenses. The home modifications made by the taxpayers in our problem most likely qualify in full a medical care expenses. [See Rev.Rul. 87-106, 1987-2 C.B. 67 (I.R.S. holding that accommodating expenditures such as those in our problem generally do not increase the fair market value of a personal residence, and, therefore, fully qualify as a medical care expense).]

In summary, all of the costs of the home modifications and Ann's wheelchair most likely qualify for medical care expenses notwithstanding that they are capital expenditures.

Answer (b) is most likely incorrect. This answer presents a correct analysis of the rules but gets off track in applying the facts of our case. The house modifications will most likely <u>not</u> increase the value of their house and, therefore, will not preclude their costs from qualifying as medical care expenses. **Answer (c) is incorrect** because it fails to recognize that in the medical area, capital expenditures and medical care expenses are <u>not</u> mutually exclusive. **Answer (d) is incorrect** because with medical related items such as those involved in our case, a physician need not specifically prescribe them.

- **Additional references:** *See* DANIEL Q. POSIN, FEDERAL INCOME TAXATION OF INDIVIDUALS ¶ 7.01(7) (5th ed. 2000).

7. **Answer (a) is correct.** Larry is not entitled to any interest deduction here because the interest that he pays to his grandmother, Glenda, is considered nondeductible personal interest pursuant to IRC § 163(h).

IRC § 163 is the primary section at issue for deductions related to interest paid. For casual readers of the Code, IRC § 163(a) provides a simple and broad sounding deduction for interest stating, in part: "There shall be allowed as a deduction all interest paid . . . within the taxable year on indebtedness." Under this general definition, the interest Larry paid to Glenda would give rise to a deduction. However, the Tax Reform Act of 1986 added subsection (h) to § 163, located quite some written distance from the general allowance for interest deductions of subsection (a). IRC § 163(h) starts out deceptively, and unfavorably, simply by stating, in part: "In the case of a taxpayer other than a corporation, no deduction shall be allowed . . . for personal interest paid . . . during the taxable year."

The definition of *personal interest*, which is not deductible, if found in IRC § 163(h)(2) and takes the form of a negative definition – *personal interest* is interest "other than" those listed in subparagraphs (A) through (F). The key, therefore, to finding interest that <u>is</u> deductible, is to fit within one of these specified categories of what does <u>not</u> constitute nondeductible personal interest. Among the categories of interest that are <u>not</u> personal interest is what might be the familiar category of "qualified residence interest" (typical interest paid on a home mortgage). [IRC § 163(h)(2)(D).] Somewhat less familiar, but logically not included as personal interest, is "interest properly allocable to a trade or business." [IRC § 163(h)(2)(A).] As seen in other questions in this book, "business" interest, rather oddly, does not include business interest incurred by an employee. Unfortunately for Larry, there is no category listed that would remove the nondeductible *per-*

sonal interest taint from the interest he pays to his grandmother. Therefore, the interest is not deductible.

Answer (b) is incorrect because the interest Larry pays to his grandmother is not "investment interest." Investment interest is a special category of potentially deductible interest associated with the purchase, maintenance, etc. of investment property such as a rental house, stocks, etc. [IRC § 163(d).] At least one question in this book deals with the issue of investment interest. **Answer (c) is also incorrect.** While IRC § 221 does allow, in certain circumstances, deduction for interest on loans used for education, this section is not applicable here. Not to get into too much detail here, the loan between Glenda and Larry is not the type of loan that qualifies for the IRC § 221 deduction of interest because Larry borrowed the money from a "related party," his grandmother. [See IRC § 221(d)(1) and question 8, below.] **Answer (d) is incorrect** because there is no such broad restriction regarding deductible interest. **Answer (e) is incorrect** because, as discussed above, the interest Larry pays to his grandmother is nondeductible personal interest.

- **Additional references:** *See* DANIEL Q. POSIN, FEDERAL INCOME TAXATION OF INDIVIDUALS ¶¶ 7.01(3) (5th ed. 2000).

8. **The correct answer is (c).** This is a somewhat tricky question, and this professor would not present such a question on an exam immediately following the preceding, very similar question. This question is an example of how critical the facts can be for a correct analysis of a question – one slight change to the facts can make a dramatic change to the outcome, as it does here.

As indicated in the analysis for question 7, above, IRC § 163 is the primary section dealing with the deductibility of interest. We saw that Larry's interest payments to grandmother, Glenda did not result in a deduction because the interest was classified as nondeductible personal interest pursuant to IRC § 163(h). We, once again, need to turn to IRC § 163(h) to see if the interest paid on the loan from his aunt Ann, in this question, yields a different result.

The definition of *personal interest*, which is not deductible, if found in IRC § 163(h)(2) and takes the form of a negative definition – *personal interest* is interest "other than" those listed in subparagraphs (A) through (F). The key, therefore, to finding interest that is deductible, is to fit within one of these specified categories of what does not constitute nondeductible personal interest. Listed among the categories of interest that are not considered personal interest is, "any interest allowable as a deduction under section 221 (relating to interest on educational loans)." [IRC § 163(h)(2)(F).] We will, below, conclude that the interest Larry paid to his aunt Ann may qualify as deductible education loan interest pursuant to IRC § 221.

IRC § 221, a relatively new section effective in 1998, allows for a limited deduction for certain interest paid on certain educational loans. This deduction, if allowed, is a valuable "above the line" deduction – a deduction from gross income in computing adjusted gross income (AGI). To qualify as an educational loan for this section, the loan proceeds generally must be used for tuition, fees, books, room/board or related expenses while attending a college, university or vocational school. This includes graduate, post graduate studies, professional degree programs, etc. So far, Larry's loan qualifies. Qualified educational loans do not, however, include money borrowed from "related parties." [IRC § 221(d)(1).] In a familial situation, such as Larry's in this question, the definition of whom is considered related, is very specific and includes only, "brothers and sisters (whether by the whole or half blood), spouse, ancestors, and lineal descendants." [IRC § 267(b)(4) (definition as directed to by IRC § 221(d)(1).] Larry's aunt, Ann is not a related individual pursuant to this definition (an aunt is the lineal descendant [daughter] of an ancestor [grandparent], or the sibling [sister] of an ancestor [parent]). Therefore, Larry's loan from his aunt Ann is a qualified education loan used for qualified higher education expenses.

The interest Larry pays on this qualified higher education loan is subject to two important limitations. First, the amount of interest deductible under IRC § 221 is limited, by statute, to $2,500 per year (in the aggregate for all such loans). Larry's $1,100 in interest is well under this maximum deduction. The second limitation kicks in, if the taxpayer's adjusted gross income (AGI), as modified by IRC § 221(b)(2)(C), exceeds certain levels. If it does, the otherwise allowed IRC § 221 interest deduction is reduced or "phased-out" utilizing a formula contained in the statute. We now have our answer to this question that Larry is entitled to a deduction of this interest paid assuming that his income is not sufficient to invoke the phase-out provisions reducing or eliminating the deduction. It is beyond the scope of this question to discuss, in detail, the mechanics of this phase-out provision. At least one question in this book addresses IRC § 221 in more detail, and utilizes numbers.

Answer (a) is incorrect because, as discussed above, the interest Larry paid to his aunt, Ann is not "personal interest" but, rather, qualifies as deductible education loan interest under IRC § 221. **Answer (b) is incorrect** because the interest Larry pays to his grandmother is not "investment interest." Investment interest is a special category of potentially deductible interest associated with the purchase, maintenance, etc. of investment property such as a rental house, stocks, etc. [IRC § 163(d).] At least one question in this book deals with the issue of investment interest. **Answer (d) is incorrect** because there is not such broad restriction regarding deductible interest. **Answer (e) is incorrect** because, as discussed above, the interest Larry pays to his grandmother is nondeductible personal interest.

9. **Answer (c) is correct.** This is a very straightforward question. Gross income is defined in IRC § 61 as income from whatever source derived. You know from your initial study of the subject that this definition is broadly defined. We do not have to go too broad to find that the interest received is included in the recipient's gross income. Interest is specifically identified as an example of gross income at IRC § 61(a)(4). Therefore, the interest Larry pays Glenda is included in her gross income.

    Answer (a) is incorrect because Larry's payment of interest, pursuant to a promissory note, cannot be considered a gift. There is no magical provision that strips away all income tax consequences with respect to familial transactions. **Answer (b) is incorrect** because the inclusion in income by one party is not determined by the availability of a deduction to the payor. For example, you pay to have someone wash your personal car. The payment is not deductible by you, but does represent gross income to the payee. The author can think of only one situation that is discussed in this book where the two are tied together, but in a somewhat opposite way. If alimony received is income to the recipient ex-spouse, the payor is entitled to a deduction – if the payments do not represent taxable alimony to the recipient ex-spouse, they are not deductible by the payor. **Answer (d) is also incorrect.** The fact that a taxpayer does not have sufficient taxable income to generate a tax is irrelevant for purposes of determining what is or is not included in gross income.

10. **Answer (a) is most accurate.** While at first, this discharge of Larry's debt looks like a classic case of "income from discharge of indebtedness, the gratuitous nature of the debt forgiveness results in a gift, excluded from his gross income under IRC § 102. To properly analyze this question, there are two major questions that need to be answered: 1) Does Larry, on a prima facie basis, have "income from discharge of indebtedness?" and 2) if so, is this income recognized or is there a statutory non-recognition (or exclusion) provision that is applicable?

    Forgiving a debt, in whole or in part, generally results in the realization of gross income to the debtor. It makes sense that being relieved of a liability (a financial obligation) results in a net accession to wealth (i.e., income) to the debtor. This type of income is referred to as income from discharge of indebtedness and is specifically identified by the Code as constituting gross income. [IRC § 61(a)(12).] Larry owed $15,000 to his grandmother, Glenda, of which $5,000 was forgiven. So far, Larry appears to have $5,000 in income from discharge of indebtedness. This $5,000 will be recognized in Larry's gross income unless there is some specific Code provision allowing for its exclusion. In general, on any question (multiple choice or essay) where it appears that there is income to be recognized, do not just stop at that point. Go on to make sure that no exclusion or non-recognition provisions apply to the situation presented in the question.

In the area of "income from discharge of indebtedness," there are two major exclusion/non-recognition provisions to think about. The exclusion from gross income to the recipients of gifts (made out of detached and disinterested generosity) under IRC § 102, and the potential exclusion of income from discharge of indebtedness for taxpayers in dire financial straits pursuant to IRC § 108. The former occurs where the facts give some indication that the debt was gratuitously forgiven, typically where there is a familial or close relationship between the debtor and creditor. This, most likely, is applicable to Larry's situation in this question. This situation is replete with facts indicating that Glenda acted out of detached and disinterested generosity, the general definition of a gift for purposes of exclusion under IRC § 102. Larry was her "favorite grandchild," "without hesitation" she forgave $5,000 of the loan, she even told him to "take as long as he needed to pay her back." all of which point to a gratuitous motive for the discharge. Larry, therefore, can exclude, as a gift under § 102, the $5,000 debt forgiven.

Answer (b) is incorrect because this answer fails to recognize that the income from discharge of indebtedness is subject to exclusion, in Larry's case as a gift. **Answer (c) is also incorrect.** This answer could possibly be correct, but for the way in which the answer is worded. While it is possible that Larry could exclude, from income, the $5,000 discharged because of insolvency, it is not the *only* possibility for exclusion (i.e., the answer ignores the [more likely] possibility that the exclusion can result from the discharge of debt representing a gift). For more information about exclusion of income from discharge of indebtedness by reason of insolvency, please see other questions in this book. **Answer (d) is incorrect** because it too fails to recognize that income from indebtedness is subject to possible exclusion.

- **Additional references:** *See* DANIEL Q. POSIN, FEDERAL INCOME TAXATION OF INDIVIDUALS ¶¶ 3.08(1), 3.08(2), 3.10(1) (5th ed. 2000).

11.   **This is a close call, but (d) is the most accurate statement.** To start, the payment of one's debt by one's employer is usually treated as compensation received, albeit indirectly. From your initial exploration of the scope of gross income, you probably learned that income need not be in the form of cash. Specifically regarding compensation, it can take the form of property, services received or, as here, an indirect financial benefit represented by the employer's payment of an employee's obligation. Initially, therefore, it appears that Larry has $10,000 in compensation income from his employer's payment of Larry's debt. In substance, it is as if Larry's employer gave Larry a $10,000 cash bonus that Larry

then used to pay off the debt. The "compensation" element might be easier to see in this recast state.

The next logical question to ask is whether any provision in the Code would apply to exclude, from income, the $10,000 that Larry effectively received. If you have studied the IRC § 102 exclusion for gifts, bequests and devises, that might be a logical place to look for a potential exclusion. Under the general rule of § 102(a), gifts are excluded from the gross income of the donee/recipient. While no statutory definition of a gift exists, it is generally defined as a transfer without consideration that is made out of emotions of detached and disinterested generosity. [See *Comm'r v. Duberstein*, 363 U.S. 278, 80 S.Ct. 1190 (1960).] Ultimately, our analysis will find that the $10,000 Larry indirectly received is excludable by this section as a gift. However, we first have to address a major hurdle located at IRC § 102(c). This subsection provides, in general, that the possible exclusion from gross income of property acquired by gift, bequest or devise, does not apply to transfers between employers and employees. In other words, "gifts" to employees are not excludable from gross income under IRC § 102. As applied to most employees, this subsection is not merely a presumption. Rather, "gifts" to most employees are not excludable gifts at all.

The author, in the preceding paragraph, states that the IRC § 102(c) denial of excludable gifts applies with respect to "most employees." For discussion purposes and totally divorced from the facts of our question, suppose a parent employs a child. Let us further suppose that the employer (parent) makes no gifts to any employees but on the child's 25th birthday, the parent gives the child a new automobile. In the familial context, we have a parent making a gift to a child most likely out of emotions of detached and disinterested generosity, qualifying it for exclusion from income to the child pursuant to IRC § 102(a). However, we also factually have an employer making a gift to an employee that, pursuant to the language in IRC § 102(c), cannot be considered an excludable gift to the employee. Does this preclude any gifts, in the traditional and excludable sense, when the donor and donee happen to have an employment relationship such as this? Proposed regulations answer this question as follows: "For purposes of section 102(c), *extraordinary* transfers to the natural objects of an employer's bounty will *not be considered transfers to, or for the benefit of, an employee if the employee can show that the transfer was not made in recognition of the employee's employment. Accordingly, section 102(c) shall not apply to amounts transferred between related parties (e.g., father and son) if the purpose of the transfer can be substantially attributed to the familial relationship of the parties and not to the circumstances of their employment.*" [Prop.Reg. § 1.102-1(f)(2) (emphasis added).] In the hypothetical presented in this paragraph, the parent's gift of the car to the child is, in all likelihood, an example of an excludable gift notwithstanding the employment relationship between the two.

Now back to the facts of the question presented. Larry is the "natural object" of his father's "bounty" (using the somewhat odd vernacular of the regulations), and it appears that this transfer (although indirect) is extraordinary in nature. We can also logically infer from the facts that Larry's father did not make this payment on his behalf in recognition of Larry's employment or in the context of their employment relationship, but rather, it was attributable to their familial relationship. Based upon this, Larry can exclude the $10,000 benefit that he received as a gift pursuant to IRC § 102.

Answer (a) is incorrect because Larry's debt was not "discharged" in the tax sense (no debt was forgiven by the creditor but, rather, the debt was fully repaid, albeit not by Larry. **Answer (b) is also incorrect**. This answer would be correct but for the gift exclusion provision that the author believes is applicable to these facts. **Answer (c) is incorrect** because like incorrect answer (a), it incorrectly concludes that there is a discharge of indebtedness issue in these facts.

12.   **Answer (a) is correct.** The "alimony" payments that Wanda receives will <u>not</u> be income to her nor give rise to a deduction for Harold. The "alimony" payments do not qualify as alimony pursuant to IRC §§ 71 and 215.

"Alimony" is income to the payee spouse (or ex-spouse) and a corresponding deduction to the payor spouse. [IRC §§ 71(a) and 215(a), respectively.] However, there are many instances where the common use of a term does not necessarily correspond to its official "tax" counterpart. Labels can be deceiving and do not be fooled by their use in lay terms on an exam. "Alimony" (spousal support, separate maintenance payments, etc.) for tax purposes, is defined in IRC § 71(b)(1) with five basic requirements, all of which must be met:

    1)   The payment must be in cash. [IRC § 71(b)(1).]
    2)   The payment must be received by (or on behalf of) the payee pursuant to a divorce or separation instrument. [IRC § 71(b)(1)(A).]
    3)   The divorce or separation instrument does not designate such payment as "non alimony." [IRC § 71(b)(1)(B).]
    4)   In most situations (a "legal divorce" or "legal separation"), the payee and payor cannot be living together when the payment is made. [IRC § 71(b)(1)(C).]
    5)   There is no obligation for payments to continue beyond the death of the payee spouse. [IRC § 71(b)(1)(D).]

Payments for "child support" often accompany alimony payments and it is important to distinguish between the two. Unlike alimony, child support is neither income to the recipient spouse nor a deduction to the payor spouse. [IRC § 71(c).] Therefore, it may be helpful to include as a sixth requirement of alimony that: 6) such payment is not "child support."

Each of these six requirements may be, alone or in combination, the source of an exam question. Therefore, it is a good idea to run every alimony or child support question through the gauntlet. Be aware that each of these six requirements has numerous sub issues and nuances that are fertile testing grounds.

This question falls squarely on the above listed item number three. This "requirement" effectively gives parties to a divorce the opportunity to "opt-out" of the normal tax treatment of alimony. In this instance, Harold and Wanda agreed, albeit in a tone that makes it sound a bit devious or smelling of "unclean hands," to affirmatively treat their payments not as alimony with the result that it is neither income to Wanda nor a deduction to Harold. Their motive is irrelevant and, in fact, the nature of this requirement is designed to allow flexibility among parties with respect to the income tax implications.

As indicated, it is always a good idea to run any alimony or child support question through the gauntlet to make sure that no other issue is involved or gives rise to a better answer. In this question the other requirements are met as follows:
  ➢ The payment was in cash.
  ➢ The payment was received pursuant to their divorce decree that qualifies as a written divorce or separation instrument. [§ 71(b)(2)(A).]
  ➢ Wanda and Harold are not living together when the payment is made.
  ➢ Their decree calls for Harold to make payments to Wanda for her life or until she remarries. This satisfies the requirement that payments do not extend beyond the life of the payee.
  ➢ There is no indication that any part of this payment relates to support for their child, Charles.

Answers (b) and (d) are incorrect because this answer is opposite to what the above-described provision allows. As indicated above, the statutory definition of alimony allows the parties to opt-out of alimony treatment for income tax purposes even though the payments would otherwise qualify as alimony. This provision (IRC § 71(b)(1)(B)) does not allow parties to affirmatively define what constitutes alimony when the requirements thereof are not met. The "above the line" and "below the line" distinction in answers b and d, respectively, is irrelevant for this question. For future reference, however, if these payments were qualifying alimony with income to Wanda, Harold would be entitled to an "above the line" deduction. [See Appendix A for more information about how income and deductions fit together in the computation of taxable income.]

Answer (c) is incorrect but is, nonetheless, a favorite choice among students. It makes sense that when the parties opt-out of alimony status as permitted by statute, as Wanda and Harold have done in our question, there should be no deduction allowed to the payor (Harold in our question). The IRC § 215 allowance for a deduction for alimony paid is directly linked to the above-described definition of alimony in IRC § 71 – no deduction for alimony is allowed unless it corresponds to income recognition to the recipient. This explains the requirement, on the individual tax return form 1040, that the payor spouse taking a deduction for alimony must provide the social security number of the payee spouse (for purposes of matching the income on the payee spouse's income tax return).

The difficulty students have with this answer is with respect to the recipient spouse Wanda. Often the first steps in a semester's trek through income tax starts with the concept of "gross income." Usually after a few cases trying to decipher just how broad the scope of gross income is, one sees that gross income is very broad indeed. Notwithstanding any statutory definition of alimony, Wanda, the recipient in our question, appears to have such a net accession to wealth and, therefore, gross income. However, the recipient of nondeductible alimony is not required to payments in gross income, as the two sections (IRC §§ 71 and 215) are effectively mutually dependent.

- **Additional references:** *See* DANIEL Q. POSIN, FEDERAL INCOME TAXATION OF INDIVIDUALS ¶¶ (5th ed. 2000).

13.   **Answer (d) is correct.** Harold is <u>not</u> entitled to a deduction for any of his payments because they do not meet the statutory requirements for alimony.

This is a difficult and somewhat tricky question that combines a couple of the alimony related issues. This is a good example of why, when you have an alimony or child support question, it is important to go through all of the IRC § 71(b) requirements of alimony, and consider the issues associated with child support in IRC § 71(c).

As indicated in the analysis for question 12, above, alimony is income to the recipient and a corresponding deduction to the payor. Remember that IRC § 215, the section allowing a deduction for alimony to the payor, is linked to the definition, and inclusion in income to the payee, as defined in IRC § 71. Therefore, any analysis of a possible deduction for alimony requires an analysis of the qualification of payments as alimony pursuant to IRC § 71. In addition, child support is neither income to the recipient nor a deduction to the payor. In this question we are concerned with the possible deduction to Harold, the payor.

Usually what first catches the student's eye in this question is the $2,000 component of the $20,000 annual payment that is labeled as "alimony" in the couple's divorce decree. Warning: do not be fooled by the "alimony" label attached to this payment, as we know that for tax purposes, things can often be different from what they may appear to be. Logically, this $2,000 component appears not to be alimony but, rather, represents child support. This $2,000 does, indeed, represent child support and is not deductible by Harold. While the decree in our question does not specifically mention child support, IRC § 71(c)(2) directs us to find the $2,000 per year to be child support. This is because the payments to Wanda labeled as "alimony" will be reduced by $2,000 when their child, Charles, reaches a certain age, dies or marries, whichever occurs first.

This leaves us, so far, with $2,000 as nondeductible child support and the $18,000 balance as possibly deductible alimony. Again, running this $18,000 balance through the requirements of alimony (see question 12, above) is critical to determine the deductibility to Harold. In order, we go through the IRC § 71 definitional components of alimony:
  ➢ The payment here is in cash.
  ➢ The payment was received pursuant to their divorce decree that qualifies as a written divorce or separation instrument. [IRC § 71(b)(2)(A).]
  ➢ Wanda and Harold are not living together when the payment is made.
  ➢ **In this question**, their decree calls for Harold to make payments to Wanda for **ten years or until she remarries**. It is this alimony requirement that presents us with problems in this question.

Wanda and Harold's divorce decree does <u>not</u>, in and of itself, satisfy the requirement that payments may not extend beyond the life of the payee spouse. This is because Wanda could die, having not remarried, before the ten-year period has expired – payments then continuing beyond her death. This would mean that the $18,000 would not meet the requirement of alimony and, therefore, would not be deductible by Harold. Thus, we are left with no deductions for Harold (none for the $2,000 child support and none for the $18,000 qualifying as alimony).

Students should be aware that the "no liability for payment beyond the death of the payee spouse" requirement may be satisfied by local law in situations such as those in our question. If local law terminates the payor's obligation upon death of the payee spouse, then this requirement is satisfied. However, careful reading of the general facts for our question indicates that "[f]or these questions you are to assume that applicable state law has no provision regarding cessation of support obligations upon the death of a spouse receiving support payments." This fact negates any application of state law to "save" the payment as alimony in this question.

Answer (a) is not correct because the mere labeling of the payments as "alimony" does not, as discussed above, make it alimony for tax purposes. As discussed, $2,000 is not alimony but, rather, represents child support, and the remaining $18,000 does not meet the definition of alimony for tax purposes.

Answer (b) is not correct. As far as incorrect answers are concerned, students most often select (b). The provision regarding Charles correctly classifies $2,000 of the total $20,000 annual payment as nondeductible child support. However, students often miss the fact regarding the cessation (or non-cessation in this question) of spousal support payments at the death of the payee spouse. Note, however, that this answer could be correct if the facts to this question were slightly different. If the facts indicated that the local law governing Wanda and Harold's divorce decree automatically terminates spousal support payments at the death of the payee spouse if the decree is silent as to that point, then $18,000 of the annual payments would qualify as alimony and would be deductible by Harold. Your professor may also incorporate into this issue, a specific state, and the laws of which regarding cessation of support payments may be discussed. For example, the author sometimes uses a California divorce decree, and in class we discuss that California law provides for the automatic cessation of support payments at the death of the payee spouse unless the decree indicates otherwise.

Answer (c) is not correct because it has no real basis for validity other than possible confusion between the deductibility and non-deductibility of alimony and child support payments.

- **Additional references:** *See* DANIEL Q. POSIN, FEDERAL INCOME TAXATION OF INDIVIDUALS ¶ 6.02(14) (5th ed. 2000).

14. **Answer (a) is the most accurate.** In this question, Harold will be entitled to deduct one-half of the house insurance and gardening expenses as "alimony" paid on behalf of Wanda.

Again, as in the question above, the determination of deductible alimony to the payor under IRC § 215 rests on whether the payment qualifies as alimony pursuant to IRC § 71. As indicated in the analysis of question 12, above, for tax purposes, "alimony" is defined in IRC § 71(b)(1) with five basic requirements, all of which must be met:

1) The payment must be in cash. [IRC § 71(b)(1).]
2) The payment must be received by (or on behalf of) the payee pursuant to a divorce or separation instrument. [IRC § 71(b)(1)(A).]

3)   The divorce or separation instrument does not designate such payment as "non alimony." [IRC § 71(b)(1)(B).]

4)   In most situations (a "legal divorce" or "legal separation"), the payee and payor cannot be living together when the payment is made. [IRC § 71(b)(1)(C).]

5)   There is no obligation for payments to continue beyond the death of the payee spouse. [IRC § 71(b)(1)(D).]

The second alimony requirement listed above is important for this question. Specifically, the parenthetical "on behalf of" language intimates that payments made to someone other than the former spouse that, nonetheless, benefit the former spouse, may satisfy this alimony requirement. The regulations indicated that such "indirect" or "on behalf of" payments can, indeed, qualify as alimony. [See Temp.Reg. § 1.71-1T(b) Q & A-6.] The facts of our question indicate that Harold is required to pay the insurance and gardening expenses for the house in which Wanda is living. At first glance, these payments by Harold appear to fit within this qualifying indirect form of payment. However, this regulation goes on to state: "Any payments to maintain property owned by the payor spouse and used by the payee spouse (including mortgage payments, real estate taxes and insurance premiums) are not payments on behalf of a spouse even if those payments are made pursuant to the terms of the divorce or separation instrument." [See Temp.Reg. § 1.71-1T(b) Q & A-6.] If our facts were to indicate that Wanda is the sole owner of the house in which she is residing, then 100% of Harold's payments for insurance and gardening would comply with this qualifying indirect form of payment. Alternatively, if our facts were to indicate that Harold is the sole owner of the house in which Wanda is residing, then none of Harold's payments for insurance or gardening would qualify. However, our facts indicate that Wanda and Harold each own 50% of the house in which Wanda is residing. Therefore, we must bifurcate the application of this rule. The insurance and gardening payments made by Harold with respect to the 50% of the house that Wanda owns would comply with this qualifying indirect form of payment. The insurance and gardening payments made by Harold with respect to the 50% of the house that he owns would <u>not</u> comply with this qualifying indirect form of payment.

So far, we have determined that 50% of Harold's payments for insurance and gardening expenses for the house in which Wanda lives satisfy the second of our alimony requirements regarding payment pursuant to a divorce or separation instrument. As indicated in the analysis of the previous two questions, it is always a good idea to run any alimony or child support question through the gauntlet of the alimony requirements to make sure that no other issue is involved or gives rise to a better answer. In this question the other requirements are met as follows:

➢ These payments will be in cash.

> ➤ Wanda and Harold will not be living together when the payments are made.
> ➤ In this question, their decree calls for Harold to make these payments on Wanda's behalf for as long as Wanda remains living in the house, marries or dies, whichever is sooner. This satisfies the requirement that the payments do not extend beyond the life of the payee.
> ➤ Lastly, there is no indication that any part of these payments relates to support for their child, Charles.

Since all of the alimony requirements appear to be met with respect to 50% of the payments Harold will be making in this question for insurance and gardening expenses, he will be entitled to a corresponding deduction pursuant to IRC § 215.

Answers (b) and (c) are incorrect based on the discussion above. **Answer (d) is incorrect** because there is no logical reason to distinguish between insurance and gardening expenses for purposes of maintenance costs qualifying for the indirect form of alimony payments.

• **Additional references:** *See* DANIEL Q. POSIN, FEDERAL INCOME TAXATION OF INDIVIDUALS ¶ 6.02 (5th ed. 2000).

15.   **The correct answer is (c).** This is a good example of a question that, to a student studying income tax, may appear to exist purely as an academic exercise. While it does contain aspects that present an academic challenge, this question reflects a surprisingly common "real world" tax situation. Wanda will have to recognize $145,000 of gain from the sale of the XYZ shares. This gain is characterized as "long-term capital gain."

In every fact pattern in which something is sold, the author likes to go through the following analysis:

    1)   Does the sale result in a <u>realized</u> gain or loss and if so, what is the <u>amount</u>?
    2)   If we have a <u>realized</u> gain or loss, is it <u>recognized</u> (i.e. reportable for income tax purposes)?
    3)   If the gain or loss is recognized, is it accorded "capital" gain or loss treatment?

Because this question involves a multi-step analysis and because the author recognizes the value of your time, both **abbreviated/short** and **comprehensive/long** analyses are provided below.

The abbreviated/short version of the analysis for this question is that Wanda's realized gain is the difference between the $150,000 sales price and her basis in the shares of $5,000, or $145,000. Her basis in the shares is a $5,000 carryover basis from Harold rather than the $50,000 that she paid for them because her purchase from Harold was from her former spouse and it was "incident to divorce (occurring within one year of their divorce). [See IRC § 1041.] This gain is recognized and is characterized as a long-term capital gain. This is because the shares represent capital assets and Wanda's holding period, with the tacking of Harold's and the couple's holding period, was more than one year. [See IRC §§ 1221, 1222 and 1223(2).]

The following comprehensive/long (very long) analysis presents a step-by-step discussion of the answer to this question that can be applied to other gain/loss questions.

The first step is determining whether Wanda has a realized gain or loss on the sale of the stock. For this, we need two basic components: her sales price ("amount realized" or, hereinafter, AR) and her basis in the shares ("adjusted basis or, hereinafter, AB). The difference between the two represents a realized gain or loss. [IRC § 1001(a).] Each of these two components, AR and AB, can present a variety of complex tax issues for exam and real-world tax purposes. The AR side is straightforward in our question, and is her $150,000 sales price. Other questions in this book present more complex issues involving a taxpayer's AR. The AB component is a bit more difficult to derive in this question.

The general starting place for determining one's AB in property is one's cost. [IRC §§ 1011 and 1012.] "Adjustments" to one's basis, while not at issue in this question, can result from many reasons including capital improvements (increasing basis), and depreciation expenses (reducing basis). [IRC § 1016.] Applying the general cost basis rule in our question, Wanda's AB would appear to be $50,000, the amount that she paid Harold for the shares. There are, however, statutory exceptions where one's cost is not the general starting point in determining one's AB. Some of these exceptions, such as property received as a gift or devise, are the subject of other questions in this book. A major exception that is relevant to our question, is the special basis rule when we have transfers between spouses or transfers between former spouses that are considered "incident to divorce." IRC § 1041(b) provides, in a nutshell, that when spouses transfer property to each other, or when former spouses transfer property to each other and such transfer is "incident to their divorce," the transferee spouse (or former spouse) takes a carryover basis. This section does not distinguish as to the type of inter vivos transfer involved – it covers gifts, sales, exchanges, etc.

In our question, we have <u>two</u> transfers potentially subject to this special AB rule: 1) the awarding of the shares to Harold at the time of their divorce in June of last year, and 2) Harold's sale of the shares to Wanda in April of this year. The focus in our question will be on the latter transaction (although the divorce transfer to Harold will be addressed). As to Wanda, the consequences of coming within the scope of IRC § 1041 will make a dramatic difference in her AB in the shares. If we find that Wanda's purchase of the shares from Harold is within the confines of IRC § 1041, she will have an AB in the shares of only $5,000 (carried over from Harold's original purchase price). Alternatively, if this purchase does not fit within the confines of IRC § 1041, Wanda's AB in the shares will be her $50,000 cost of the shares. The difference in AB will, of course, impact the amount of gain she realizes from her subsequent sale of the shares.

At this point, we are at the critical juncture of whether or not Harold's sale of the shares to Wanda in April of this year is within the parameters of IRC § 1041 – was this a transfer between spouses or former spouses that is "incident to divorce?" Clearly, it was not a transfer between spouses as they were divorced at the time (they divorced in June of last year). It was a transfer between former spouses, but was it considered "incident to divorce" as required by the statute? A transfer "incident to divorce" has a statutory definition as being either 1) <u>any</u> transfer within one year of the divorce, or 2) a transfer "relating to the cessation of the marriage." (See IRC § 1041(c). Temporary regulations define transfers that are considered "relating to the cessation of the marriage" as a transfer provided for by a "divorce or separation instrument" (see questions in this book relating to alimony) and is transferred, pursuant to this instrument, within six years of the divorce. [Temp.Reg. § 1.1041-1T(b) Q & A-7.] [Please see other questions in this book relating to divorce issues for more information.]

The facts indicate that Harold's sale of the shares to Wanda occurred in April of this year and that they divorced in June of last year. This April "sale" was within one year of their divorce and, therefore, is deemed to be a transfer that is "incident to divorce." With this sale being deemed a transfer incident to divorce, Wanda's AB in the shares is not her $50,000 purchase price but, rather, a $5,000 carryover basis from that of Harold. Until now, we have not addressed Harold's AB in the shares. However, it is not too difficult to see that his AB was also governed by IRC § 1041. The transfer of the shares to him was clearly "incident to divorce" (he received them not only within one year of the divorce, but also pursuant to the decree and within six years of the divorce). Harold's AB, therefore, is a carryover from the couple's original $5,000 purchase price. This hardly seems fair to Wanda, but it is the law and provides students with a great illustration of why it is important to the tax ramifications of one's legal advice (i.e., a malpractice claim may await Wanda's attorney if he or she did not apprise Wanda of this result).

Note that the sale of these shares between Harold and Wanda is deemed "incident to divorce" notwithstanding the fact that it was not pursuant to any agreement relating to their divorce. This is often an elusive point with students. IRC § 1041(c) dictates a non-rebuttable presumption that any transfer within one year of divorce is deemed incident to divorce. To extend this classification to transfers made more than one year after divorce, the transfer must be pursuant to their divorce or separation instrument (e.g., divorce decree). [See Temp.Reg. 1.1041-1T(b) Q & A-7.]

A corollary provision of IRC § 1041 is that the transferor recognizes no gain or loss from a transfer "incident to divorce." While not at issue in our question, Harold's sale to Wanda resulted in a realized gain to him of $45,000 ($50,000 AR less $5,000 AB), this gain is not recognized (i.e., not reported for income tax purposes).

Now back to the income tax consequences to Wanda of her sale of the shares in May for $150,000. We can now answer the question in the first step of our gain/loss analysis: the amount of Wanda's realized gain. Wanda has a realized gain of $145,000 representing her AR (sales price) of $150,000 less her AB (as determined above) of only $5,000.

The next step in our analysis of gain/loss situations is to determine the extent to which any realized gain is recognized. Recognition of gain basically means that it is reported as income for income tax purposes. IRC § 1001(c) provides that unless otherwise provided for in the Code, all realized gains and losses are recognized. The above-discussed provision of IRC § 1041 is one such "otherwise provided for" non-recognition provisions (and is the reason why Harold's realized gain is a recognized gain). Another frequently addressed non-recognition provision is the IRC § 121 exclusion of gain from the sale of a principal residence (see other questions in this book addressing this issue). For realized losses, there are many "non-recognition" provisions that are discussed elsewhere in this book. Unfortunately for Wanda, there are no exclusion or non-recognition provisions applicable in these facts and her $145,000 realized gain will be recognized. Do not fall into the trap that some students do in this question, reasoning that because Wanda's subsequent sale of the shares in May of this year was within one year of her divorce that the non-recognition provisions of IRC § 1041 apply to that sale. IRC § 1041 applies only to transfers between spouses and former spouses. Wanda's sale of the shares in May was to someone other than Harold, her former spouse. Had her sale in May been back to Harold, then, indeed, the non-recognition and carryover basis provisions of IRC § 1041 would be applicable. Always be careful with questions involving transfers between spouses and former spouses.

The last part of the analysis is to determine whether Wanda's $145,000 of recognized gain is accorded special "capital gain" treatment. Historically, gains from the sale of certain types of assets have been accorded preferential tax treatment. While it is far beyond the scope of analysis for this question, modernly, "long-term" capital gains ("net capital gains" to be more specific), while included in a taxpayer's gross and taxable incomes, may be taxed at favorable (i.e., lower) tax rates. A capital gain analysis requires that we first determine that we are dealing with a "capital asset," after which the gain is characterized as having either long-term or short-term status.

IRC § 1221(a) defines a capital asset in a negative fashion, but for purposes of this analysis, it includes, by process of elimination, assets held for investment and personal-use purposes. There is little question that Wanda's XYZ Co. shares qualify as a capital asset. Long-term status is reserved for those assets held for more than one year (short-term status for assets held one year or less). [See IRC § 1222.] On the surface, Wanda purchased the shares from Harold in April and sold them one month later in May. At first brush, Wanda's capital gain from the sale of the shares appears to be a short-term capital gain. Determining the holding period, for short and long term gain/loss classification, is controlled by IRC § 1223. At IRC § 1223(2), we have the so-called "tacking" rule, which essentially applies to situations where the taxpayer's AB is a carryover AB. Where this is the case, as it is in our question because Harold's sale to Wanda was a transfer incident to divorce, the transferee (Wanda) can add to her holding period, that of the transferor (Harold). Tacking on Harold's holding period from their divorce in June of the prior year, Wanda, at the time of her sale, still has a holding period that is shy of one year. We apply IRC § 1223(2) again because Harold received the shares incident to divorce and, therefore, has the $5,000 carryover AB dating back to "many years ago" when the couple first purchased the stock. Adding all of this time together, it becomes clear that Wanda is deemed to have held the shares for more than one year, thus resulting in a long-term capital gain.

Other situations where this tacking rule often applies is with respect to inter vivos gifts where a transferee's AB is usually the same as the transferor's AB. The language of the statute more specifically makes this rule applicable where the transferee's AB is determined "in whole or in part" with reference to the transferor's AB. This language allows for tacking of the holding period to apply to gift situations where a gift tax results, and the transferee's AB is increased pursuant to IRC § 1015(d) because of the gift tax. Be careful with gifts, however, where the "special loss rule" (discussed elsewhere in this book) applies or where the transaction in which the taxpayer received the property was in part a sale and in part a gift (also discussed elsewhere in this book). In those gift related situations, the tacking rule may or may not apply depending on whether the transferee's AB was or was not essentially a carryover AB.

Answer (b) is incorrect. While it indicates the correct $145,000 or recognized gain, it fails to utilize the tacking rules for Wanda's holding period as discussed above. **Answer (a) is incorrect.** However, it is probably the incorrect answer that is selected most often. In our question, Wanda's purchase of the stock from Harold is deemed "incident to divorce" notwithstanding the fact that it was not pursuant to any agreement relating to their divorce. This is often an elusive point with students. IRC § 1041(c) dictates a non-rebuttable presumption that any transfer within one year of divorce is deemed incident to divorce. It is bothersome to many that a transaction such as this, which clearly had nothing to do with their divorce, is, nonetheless, a transaction that is deemed incident to their divorce. On essay questions similar to this fact pattern, it is not unusual for a student to logically, but underlinedincorrectly respond: "While Harold's sale to Wanda occurred within one year of their divorce, it did not relate to their divorce (i.e., it was not pursuant to their divorce decree) and, therefore, is not incident to the divorce." It is true, however, that extending this IRC § 1041 classification to transfers made more than one year after divorce, the transfer must be pursuant to their divorce or separation instrument (e.g., divorce decree). [See Temp.Reg. § 1.1041-1T(b) Q & A-7.]

Answer (d) is also incorrect. However, it too is a commonly selected incorrect answer. As warned above, do not fall into the trap that because Wanda's subsequent sale of the shares in May of this year was within one year of her divorce, the non-recognition provisions of IRC § 1041 apply to that sale. IRC § 1041 applies only to transfers between spouses and former spouses. Wanda's sale of the shares in May was to someone other than Harold, her former spouse. Had her sale in May been back to Harold, then, indeed, the non-recognition and carryover basis provisions of IRC § 1041 would be applicable (and Harold would have a $5,000 carryover AB with a "tacked" long-term holding period).

- **Additional references:** *See* DANIEL Q. POSIN, FEDERAL INCOME TAXATION OF INDIVIDUALS ¶¶ 4.02(2), 4.03 (5th ed. 2000).

16. **The correct answer is (c).** Each year, Americans give billions of dollars to charities. Fostering charitable giving has long been an important component of government policy. A deduction, for income tax purposes, for contributions made to charitable organizations has had a long-time presence in our country's tax structure. IRC § 170(a) facilitates deductions for contributions of cash and property to qualified charities. One need not be a student in income tax to surmise that the American Red Cross qualifies as charitable organization. Indeed, the American Red Cross is a qualified charitable organization as generally defined in IRC § 170(c) and Philip's cash gifts thereto will be tax deductible (subject to limits discussed below). Contrary to what is a common public belief, contributions made

to an individual (unless to an individual acting as an agent for a qualified organization) do not give rise to charitable deductions. Therefore, Philip's cash gifts to the homeless individuals are not tax deductible.

The total amount of an individual's charitable deductions in any one year is limited or capped at a ceiling that varies depending on the nature of contribution (cash or property) and the charitable recipients. This deduction ceiling or limit for cash gifts made to most charitable organizations (commonly referred to as "public charities") is 50% of the taxpayer's "contribution base." [IRC § 170(b)(1)(A).] Philip's cash contributions to the American Red Cross (representing all of his qualified charitable contributions in the year for this question) are deductible up to 50% of his contribution base. While not necessary to answer this question, an individual's "contribution base" is basically the individuals adjusted gross income (AGI) calculated before deducting any "net operating loss" (NOL) carryback (most individuals do not have a NOL carryback, so their AGI is their "contribution base"). [See IRC § 170(b)(1)(F).]

While also not a part of this question, it should be noted that charitable contributions made in any year that, in the aggregate, exceed the deduction ceiling, are carried forward for up to the next five tax years (and deductible subject to the applicable year's limits).

Answers (a) and (b) are incorrect because those answers incorrectly include as deductible charitable contributions, Philip's cash gifts made to homeless individuals. **Answer (d) is incorrect** because it applies the wrong deduction limit or ceiling. Other questions in this book discuss the application of a lower 30% of "contribution base" ceiling for other charitable contribution situations.

- **Additional references:** *See* DANIEL Q. POSIN, FEDERAL INCOME TAXATION OF INDIVIDUALS ¶ 7.01(8) (5th ed. 2000).

17.   **The correct answer is (a).** Unfortunately for Philip, and contrary to popular belief, no charitable deduction arises from the contribution of one's services. [Reg. § 1.170A-1(g).] Philip's contributed services, like that of a lawyer providing pro bono services, is commendable, meritorious and a very rewarding public service. The rewards for such service do not, however, include tax deductions.

Philip <u>is</u> entitled to a charitable deduction, however, for costs that he incurs in connection with the charitable work he performs. [Reg. § 1.170A-1(g).] His driving costs related to the charitable services that he performs for Habitat for Humanity is a deductible expense. Generally, an individual can deduct (subject to charitable contribution ceilings) either the actual operating costs of his or her vehicle for the charitable related miles, or a statutory rate per charitable mile driven (14¢ per mile as of this writing).

Answers (b) and (d) are incorrect because Philip is not entitled to a deduction for the value of his services rendered. Answer (d) is further incorrect because a taxpayer is entitled to deduct charitable related transportation notwithstanding from where the trips originate. **Answer (c) is incorrect** because it does not reflect the deductible charitable miles. **Answer (e) in incorrect** because, as mentioned, a taxpayer is entitled to deduct charitable related transportation notwithstanding from where the trips originate.

- **Additional references:** *See* DANIEL Q. POSIN, FEDERAL INCOME TAXATION OF INDIVIDUALS ¶ 7.01(8) (5th ed. 2000).

18. **Answer (c) is the best response.** IRC § 170(a) facilitates deductions for contributions of cash and property to qualified charities. As indicated in the answer to question 16, above, the American Red Cross is a qualified charitable organization. The <u>value</u> of the property donated is usually the measurement for the charitable deduction. [Reg. § 1.170A-1(c).] Most students have heard, on radio commercials, the tax benefits of donating a car, boat or other property to charity: *"and you may be entitled to a tax deduction equal to the full fair market value of your car, often more than you would receive on a trade-in. Consult your tax advisor for more information."* <u>You</u> are the "tax advisor" here and yes, the fair market value of Philip's car qualifies as a charitable contribution. The appreciated fair market value of the GM stock Philip donated also qualifies as a charitable contribution. This too is advertised by charities as being beneficial because the taxpayer is usually entitled to deduct the appreciated fair market value of the property without any recognition of gain (which would be the case if the stock had been sold and the cash proceeds donated to the charity). A deduction equal to the fair market value of appreciated property is generally limited to property that would have produced a long-term capital gain if it had been sold (as is the case with Philip's GM stock in this question).

As with cash contributions in question 16, above, the deduction for charitable donations of property is limited by a ceiling, based on a percentage of the taxpayer's "contribution base" (usually the taxpayer's AGI). [IRC § 170(b)(1).] While this question does not specifically refer to this limit, generally the deduction for contributions of non-appreciated property (e.g. Philip's car) is limited (in the aggregate combined with all additional such contributions and contributions of cash) to 50% of the taxpayer's "contribution base" (AGI for most individuals). Deduction for contributions of most appreciated property (e.g., Philip's GM stock) is limited (in the aggregate combined with all additional such contributions and contributions of cash) to 30% of the taxpayer's "contribution base" (AGI for most individuals). [IRC § 170(b)(1)(C).] Be aware that your professor may cover this material in much greater depth, with more detailed attention to contribution limits and other issues including special elections that may be made with respect to donations of appreciated property.

As for the $500 that Philip paid for the tickets to the special American Red Cross Cirque du Soleil event, one might logically think that he would be entitled to a charitable contribution deduction of $500, the amount paid. However, when the donor receives something in return, the charitable deduction is normally limited to the amount contributed less the value of what is received. [Reg. § 1.170A-1(h).] In this case, Philip received the Cirque du Soleil tickets, worth $100 in return for his $500 contribution. Therefore, his charitable deduction is the $400 difference. This is a logical conclusion. Otherwise, an individual could generate deductible charitable contributions for non-charitable expenditures.

Again, your professor may cover the charitable deduction area in much greater detail. Not mentioned in this, or other problems in this book, are different deduction ceilings for donations to "non-public" charities (e.g., many "private foundations"), charitable contributions of business related property, requirements for receipts for deductions of certain amounts of cash or property contributions, etc.

Answer (a) is incorrect because it indicates the wrong charitable deduction assessment for the GM shares donated and overstates the charitable deduction for the Cirque du Soleil event donation. **Answer (b) is incorrect** because it indicates the wrong charitable deduction assessment for the GM shares donated. **Answer (d) is incorrect** because it indicates an incorrect deduction for Philip's car, using its original cost as opposed to the correct fair market value figure. **Answer (e) is incorrect** because a correct answer (c) is presented.

- **Additional references:** *See* DANIEL Q. POSIN, FEDERAL INCOME TAXATION OF NDIVIDUALS ¶ 7.01(8) (5th ed. 2000).

19. **The correct answer is (d).** IRC § 170(a) facilitates deductions for contributions of cash and property to qualified charities. The facts indicate that the "university" in this question is a qualified charitable organization. However, as discussed below, Philip's "contribution" to the university will not give rise to a charitable deduction because in substance, it is the payment of his daughter's tuition. Samantha will not have gross income resulting from this most likely because it constitutes a gift, albeit an indirect one, from her father.

As for Philip's "contribution" to the university, the analysis is similar to that in question 18, above. When a donor receives something in return for the contribution to charity, the deduction is normally limited to the amount contributed less the value of what is received. [Reg. § 1.170A-1(h).] In this case, Philip received the benefit of Samantha's tuition being covered in exchange for his contribution of an equivalent amount. Therefore, he is not entitled to any net charitable deduction. This is a logical conclusion. Otherwise, an individual could generate deductible charitable contributions for non-charitable expenditures. Specifically on point is Revenue Ruling 83-104. [Rev.Rul. 83-104, 1983-2 C.B. 46]. It states that, "the presence of one or more of the following factors creates a presumption that the payment is not a charitable contribution: the existence of a contract under which a taxpayer agrees to make a "contribution" and which contains provisions ensuring the admission of the taxpayer's child; a plan allowing taxpayers either to pay tuition or to make "contributions" in exchange for schooling; the earmarking of a contribution for the direct benefit of a particular individual; or the otherwise-unexplained denial of admission or readmission to a school of children of taxpayers who are financially able, but who do not contribute." Clearly, Philip's "contribution" fits squarely within the borders of this revenue ruling.

As for Samantha, she received a financial or economic benefit that will be income unless an exclusion provision applies. While it is debatable whether the "scholarship" could be considered a qualified scholarship and excludable pursuant to IRC § 117, it is more likely an indirect gift to her from Philip. IRC § 102 excludes, from gross income, amounts received as a gift. While other questions in this book address the issue of gifts in more detail, suffice it to say that Philip's motives for benefiting his daughter were almost assuredly of the requisite "detached and disinterested generosity" variety.

Answer (a) is incorrect because, as discussed above, Philip will not be entitled to a charitable deduction for his "contribution" to the university. Samantha's exclusion of the scholarship pursuant to IRC § 117 is also debatable. **Answer (b) is incorrect** because Samantha will be able to exclude the benefit that she received – most likely it will be considered a gift from her father. **Answer (c) is incorrect** because Philip will not be entitled to a charitable deduction for his "contribution" to the university.

20.   **The best response is (c).** Both the cash and the value of the car that Kathy received will be included in her gross income. They do not represent excludable gifts because of Kathy's employment relationship with XYZ.

From your initial study of gross income's scope, you probably found it to be broadly defined, including the taxpayer's receipt of an economic benefit or a net accession to wealth. Gross income is also not limited to the receipt of cash. [See Reg. § 1.61-2(d) (compensation paid in forms other than in cash).] Kathy clearly received a net financial benefit upon receiving both the cash and automobile. Barring any specific income exclusion provision that might be applicable in this situation, Kathy would include, in her gross income the $5,000 cash received plus the $25,000 value of the property received. [Reg. § 1.61-2(d).] While this result reflects the correct answer to this question, we should further explore this issue to better understand the subject and to rule out other possible answers to this question. It will also aid in reviewing issues arising in other questions in this book.

One specific income exclusion provision that is potentially relevant here is IRC § 102. This section's general rule provides for a very beneficial exclusion from income of amounts received as gifts, bequests, devises, and inheritances. [IRC § 102(a).] While not defined in statutes, a gift, for purposes of this exclusion, is a transfer made for insufficient consideration with the donor acting from "detached and disinterested generosity." [See *Comm'r v. Duberstein*, 363 U.S. 278, 80 S.Ct. 1190 (1960).] It could be argued that XYZ, Kathy's employer, had such motives in giving the cash and automobile to Kathy and, therefore, Kathy could exclude them from gross income. Unfortunately for Kathy, the general exclusion rule of IRC § 102(a) is nullified by subsection IRC § 102(c). This subsection provides, in general, that the possible exclusion from gross income of property acquired by gift (or bequest, devise or inheritance) does <u>not</u> apply to transfers between employers and employees. In other words, "gifts" to employees are not excludable from gross income under IRC § 102. This subsection is not merely a presumption. Thus, "gifts" to employees are not excludable by this section notwithstanding that an employer can demonstrate that the gift was made out of "detached and disinterested generosity." Therefore, despite the likelihood that XYZ's motives for making the gift were genuinely gratuitous, the $5,000 cash and $25,000 value of the automobile both represent income to Kathy in the form of compensation.

The proposed regulations provide for a limited exception to this IRC § 102(c) exclusion denial for gifts to employees. Proposed Regulation § 1.102-1(f)(2) states that "[f]or purposes of section 102(c), extraordinary transfers to the natural objects of an employer's bounty will not be considered transfers to, or for the benefit of, an employee if the employee can show that the transfer was not made in recognition of the employee's employment. Accordingly, section 102(c) shall not apply to amounts transferred between related parties (e.g., father and son) if the purpose of the transfer can be substantially attributed to the familial relationship of the parties and not to the circumstances of their employment."

Answer (a) is not the best response. As indicated above, IRC § 102(c) generally precludes excludable gifts from employers to employees notwithstanding the employer's motives for making the gift. **Answer (b) is incorrect** because there is no relevant distinction applicable in these facts, for gift or compensation purposes, between transfers of money and transfers of property. With some exceptions, not applicable here, both represent income to the recipient employee. **Answer (d) is incorrect.** This answer hints of statutory exclusions relevant to employee "fringe benefits." However, no such fringe benefit provisions are applicable to the facts in this question.

21.   **Answer (b) is correct.** Kathy must include $2,000 of the $4,000 discount that she received with respect to the life insurance policy. This is because the discount that she received exceeds the maximum amount allowed by statute.

IRC § 61 defines gross income as "all income from whatever source derived." From your initial study of gross income's scope, you probably found it to be broadly defined, including the taxpayer's receipt of some net economic benefit or net accession to wealth. In class, you also discover that gross income is also not limited to the receipt of cash. [Reg. § 1.61-1(d) (compensation received in forms other than in cash).] Kathy received an economic benefit when she purchased the life insurance policy from her employer in the form of the discount that she received. It is by reason of her employment that she received the $4,000 discount and, barring a specific exclusion provision, this amount represents income to her.

Fortunately for Kathy, she is entitled to *some* relief. A host of employee fringe benefits are excluded pursuant to IRC § 132, and the benefit Kathy is receiving in this problem invokes the "qualified employee discount" fringe benefit. [IRC §§ 132(a)(2) and 132(c).] Anyone who has ever worked in retail is probably familiar with this fringe benefit. Did you include, in income, the 15% or 20% employee discount that you received on merchandise purchased while working at that department store? Most likely the answer is <u>no</u>, and the most likely reason is that the benefit that you received was an excludable *qualified employee discount*. Although restrictions and limits may apply, the *qualified employee discount* allows employers to allow employees to buy their products or services at a discount, without that discount being included in the employee's gross income.

There are two major requirements or limitations applicable to this fringe benefit. First, the discount the employee is receiving must be with respect to products or services that are in the line of business in which the employee is working. [IRC § 132(c)(4).] This is the so-called "line of business" test. Ostensibly, this requirement exists to prevent conglomerates from providing across the board discounts to all employees in all lines of the employer's business that are perceived to be unfair when compared to non-conglomerates. Kathy is receiving a discount in XYZ's insurance line of business. The facts indicate that Kathy, as an officer of XYZ, performs a substantial amount of work in all areas of XYZ's operations. Kathy *does* satisfy this line of business test. The fact that she works in more than one of the company's line of business does not preclude her from the *qualified employee discount* fringe benefit. [Reg. § 1.132-4(a)(1)(iii).] Examples of an employee not satisfying this requirement would be a desk clerk working in the company's hotel line of business receiving a discount on insurance purchased from the company, or that same employee receiving discounts in XYZ's consumer electronics products.

The second major limitation is the amount of the discount available. Basically, the *qualified employee discount* will be viewed as a tax-free fringe benefit as long as "it does not cost the employer too much money" in providing the benefit. The statutory maximum tax-free discount applicable to employer provided "services" is 20%. [IRC 132(c)(1)(B).] In the case of discounts for products (tangible personal property), the statute does not set a specific discount percentage amount but, rather, states that the discount cannot exceed the employer's "gross profit percentage." [IRC § 132(c)(1)(A).] The computation of a company's "gross profit percentage" is defined in IRC § 132(c)(2). The facts for this question indicate that XYZ's "gross profit percentage" in their insurance line of business is 40%. At first glance, it looks as if Kathy's 40% discount she received on the purchase of the life insurance policy does not exceed the maximum discount allowed. Unfortunately, "life insurance" is considered a "service" and not a "product" (tangible personal property). The repercussion to Kathy is that she has received a discount in excess of the statutory allowed maximum. The result is that Kathy can exclude the statutory maximum 20% discount applicable to services. The value of the discount that she received in excess of this will be includible in her gross income. Putting numbers to this, the policy normally sells for $10,000 and she received a 40% discount or $4,000. Her maximum exclusion is only 20% of the $10,000 cost of the policy or $2,000. Therefore, the amount includible in Kathy's gross income is the $4,000 discount she received, less the $2,000 allowed maximum, or $2,000 ($4,000 - $2,000).

There is one last issue to consider in this question. The statute provides that an employer cannot provide some, but not all, of the fringe benefits enumerated in IRC § 132 to employees on a discriminatory basis (in favor of only highly compensated employees as defined by the statute). The *qualified employee discount* is one such benefit that cannot be provided to employees in a discriminatory manner. [IRC § 132(j)(1).] While Kathy is a "highly compensated employee," this insurance discount is offered to all full-time employees and therefore, does not offend these discrimination rules. Limiting this benefit to just "full-time" employees is most likely not discriminatory for purpose of IRC § 132. [Reg. § 1.132-8(d)(2).] The fact that in the current year only Kathy and one other officer took advantage of the insurance discount does not render it discriminatory, as it was available to all full-time employees. It should be noted that if the discount benefit did discriminate in favor of highly compensated employees, the entire discount received by a highly compensated employee would be included in income (and not just the extra benefit provided to such employees). [Reg. § 1.132-8(a)(2).]

It should also be noted that this is a fairly basic question regarding the *qualified employee discount* fringe benefit. Your professor may cover the material in much greater depth and there are many ancillary issues regarding this and other IRC § 132 fringe benefits.

Answer (a) is incorrect because the maximum excludable employee discount available is 20% (because life insurance is considered a service). **Answer (c) is incorrect** because Kathy need not include the entire amount of the discount that she received. **Answer (d) is also incorrect.** $6,000 represents the amount Kathy *paid* for the policy. With the *qualified employee discount* we are focusing on the benefit that she receives vis-à-vis her discount.

- **Additional references:** *See* DANIEL Q. POSIN, FEDERAL INCOME TAXATION OF INDIVIDUALS ¶ 2.02(1) (5ᵗʰ ed. 2000).

22.   **Answer (a) is correct.** XYZ's payment of Kathy's dues and periodical costs represent tax-free "working condition" fringe benefits.

IRC § 61 defines gross income as "all income from whatever source derived." From your initial study of gross income's scope, you probably found it to be broadly defined, including the taxpayer's receipt of some net economic benefit or net accession to wealth. In class, you also discover that gross income is also not limited to the receipt of cash. [Reg. § 1.61-1(d) (compensation received in forms other than in cash).] It is clear that Kathy is receiving some economic benefit from her XYZ's payment of her association dues and the cost of the periodicals. This will represent income to Kathy unless it is specifically excluded by some provision.

A host of employee fringe benefits are excluded pursuant to IRC § 132, and the benefit Kathy is receiving in this problem is excludable as a "working condition" fringe benefit. [IRC §§ 132(a)(3) and 132(d).] Basically, an excludable *working condition fringe* is any property or service provided to an employee which would, had the employee had to pay for such items, have given rise to a business deduction by such employee. In other words, if an employee were to make an expenditure for something that would be considered a qualified business expense, then having the employer pay for it instead will <u>not</u> be considered income to the employee (i.e., a *working condition fringe* benefit). The exclusion of an employer provided benefit as a *working condition fringe*, rests on whether the item paid for by the employer would have given rise to a qualified business deduction to the employee under IRC § 162 (had the employee paid for the item).

In general, IRC § 162 allows for business deductions that are (read as one continuous phrase with four distinct requirements):

> ➢ Ordinary and necessary
> ➢ Expenses
> ➢ Paid or incurred during the taxable year
> ➢ In carrying on any trade or business.

Had Kathy paid for her association dues and business related periodicals, there is little doubt that they would have been considered qualified business expenses. Therefore, XYZ's payment of these items result in an excludable *working condition fringe* benefit to Kathy and she need not recognize any income because of this.

Unlike some of the other excludable fringe benefits of IRC § 132, an employer can provide a *working condition fringe* benefit to employees on a discriminatory basis (in favor of highly compensated employees). Therefore, the fact that XYZ's policy of providing these benefits only to "highly compensated employees" (such as Kathy) does not preclude the exclusion.

While not necessary to answer this question, one may ask why the *working condition fringe* benefit is really necessary. If the employer paid benefit were to be included in an employee's income, would not the employee then be entitled to a corresponding IRC § 162 business deduction, thus resulting in no net difference than if the amount was excluded form income in the first place? Those students familiar with "how" and "where" an employee's business expenses are deductible, may see the benefit of the *working condition fringe* exclusion. Far beyond the scope of this question, most employees' IRC § 162 business expenses are deductible in the less favored *below the line* location (deductions from adjusted gross income (AGI) to compute taxable income). These IRC § 162 "employee" business related expenses are part of large group of deductions referred to as "itemized deductions." This "itemized deduction" grouping is comprised of various types of deductions such as certain medical care expenses (IRC § 213), certain interest and tax expenses (IRC §§ 163 and 164), charitable contributions (IRC § 170), and others. One sub-group of itemized deductions is a specific category referred to as "miscellaneous itemized deductions." Generally, unreimbursed employee IRC § 162 business related expenses (along with other specific deductions) comprise this special "miscellaneous itemized deduction" sub-group. The significance of this sub-group of deductions is that, pursuant to IRC § 67, they are deductible, in the aggregate, only to the extent that they exceed 2% of the individual's AGI. In addition, the total *itemized deductions* must exceed something called the *standard deduction* in order to be of any benefit for income tax purposes. Thus, having an employer provided *working condition fringe* benefit excluded from income can be much more valuable than the alternative of having the benefit included in income with a corresponding employee business expense deduction. [See Appendix A for more information about how income and deductions fit together in computing taxable income.]

Answer (b) is incorrect because an employer can discriminate in favor of certain classes of employees for purposes of the *working condition fringe* benefit. **Answer (c) is incorrect** because the benefit provided to Kathy in this question is not a "qualified employee discount." **Answer (d) is incorrect** because Kathy's professional business related periodicals qualify as legitimate business expenses for her.

- **Additional references:** *See* DANIEL Q. POSIN, FEDERAL INCOME TAXATION OF INDIVIDUALS ¶ 2.01(2) (5th ed. 2000).

23.   **The best answer is (b).** This question raises some of the most classic doctrines in income tax law. We have two parts to this question and both involve issues of "to whom does the income/gain belong." Or more appropriately, who <u>must</u> recognize the income derived. The first part of the problem is the issue of the April rents, and the second part is the sale of the property in May. Both issues involve essentially the same tax concepts.

The analysis starts with the "assignment of income" doctrine that arguably is best known from the case *Lucas v. Earl*. [281 U.S. 111, 50 S.Ct. 241 (1930).] Income is income (for tax purposes) to the taxpayer who earns it. One cannot transfer the tax obligation to another person merely by "assigning" the income to such person. One cannot say, "I earned the income, but do not give it to me, give it to my son instead" (who happens to be in a much lower income tax bracket) and have it work that way for income tax purposes.

Similarly, income from property is the income of the owner of the property and cannot be "detached" and given to someone else. For tax purposes, it will not work if one says, "the interest that is earned on my money deposited with your bank, I do not want it given to me. Rather, give the interest to my son" (who happens to be in a much lower income tax bracket. Of course, this can be done, but the owner of the account will have to recognize the interest earned on the money. This is the so-called "fruit and tree" doctrine. The fruit (income) that the tree (the underlying property) bears belongs to the owner of the tree (the property). If one wishes another person to recognize income earned from the property the underlying property must be transferred to such person. The fruit just cannot be "picked" or separated from the tree and given to another, without first giving the tree.

Corollary to this fruit and tree concept is that one cannot avoid recognition of income from property that is already earned but has not yet been received. One cannot transfer a tree to another with fruit already "ripened" and have the picked fruit be considered belonging to the new owner. This is sometimes referred to as the doctrine of "ripeness" – once the fruit is ripe, it belongs to the owner of the tree notwithstanding that the tree is transferred to another before the fruit is picked.

Back from the garden to address the April rental income from the apartment building. Martha, owner at the beginning of the April rent period, transferred the apartment building to her son, Steve midway through the month. Back to our garden analogy, the rental income earned up through the middle of April represents "ripened" fruit for Martha. While the rental income was not actually received until after she transferred the property (the tree), she cannot effectively assign the rental income earned up to the time of transfer. In other words, half of the April rents belong to, and must be recognized by, Martha (it is her fruit!). From the period that Steve owned the property in mid April, the rental income earned belongs to him. Therefore, the April rents should be recognized one-half by Martha and one-half by Steve.

As for the sale of the property, we have the same concept of "ripeness" to consider. Had Martha, before transferring the property to Steve, arranged the sale of the property to Peter and, for all intents and purposes, contracted to sell the property to Peter, the income (gain in this case) has "ripened." Transferring the property at this point would not result in the transfer (or assignment) of the gain to Steve. However, we have no facts in the problem indicating what, if anything, Martha did vis-à-vis the sale to Peter, while she still owned the property. If Martha was not involved with the sale prior to her transfer of the property to Steve, then whatever income Steve derives from the property (including gain from its sale) correctly belongs to him (and will be recognized by him). The only answer that correctly reflects this (and the issue of the April rents) is (b).

Answer (a) is incorrect because the April rental income is not all recognizable by Steve as discussed above. The latter part of this answer may be true depending on the degree of Martha's involvement regarding the sale prior to her transferring the property to Steve. **Answer (c) is incorrect** because the gain from the sale is not necessarily Martha's to recognize. There is no assignment of income when the fruit has not yet ripened. **Answer (d) is incorrect** because Martha does not recognize all of the April rents. The rental income earned after the transfer of the property to Steve belongs to Steve, not Martha.

- **Additional references:** *See* DANIEL Q. POSIN, FEDERAL INCOME TAXATION OF INDIVIDUALS ¶¶ 5.01, 5.02 (5th ed. 2000).

24.   **The best answer is (c).** IRC § 164 is a key section for addressing deductions for taxes paid. This section allows a deduction for, among other taxes, "state and local real property taxes" that have been "paid." While the real property tax in our problem is clearly the type of tax deductible pursuant to IRC § 164, there is some question as to Peter's "payment of it. On January 1st of this year, Martha paid the $12,000 in property taxes for the full year. What happens when this property is sold to Peter during the year vis-à-vis property taxes? In most real-life instances, the buyer reimburses the seller (as part of the sales transaction) a proportionate amount of the property taxes that were paid by the seller. This apportioned amount represents the period for which the seller paid taxes for the property that is now owned by the buyer. In our simplified calendar year property tax scenario, Peter's purchase of the property on May 1st is four months into the twelve-month assessment period, or 4/12ths (one-third). Peter's share of the assessment year for which property taxes have already been paid is the other 8/12ths (two-thirds). Again, in real-world transactions of this sort, Peter would reimburse the seller 8/12ths (two-thirds) of the taxes paid or $8,000 of the $12,000 taxes paid in our facts.

The above method of apportionment is generally *required* for purposes of determining *who* gets to deduct *what* amount of property tax in sale situations such as ours. [IRC § 164(d).] Pursuant to this provision, the purchaser Peter, is entitled to an apportioned $8,000 deduction of the total $12,000 property taxes paid (and the seller is entitled to a deduction for the remaining $4,000 of property taxes). The Regulations indicate that this method of apportionment "shall apply whether or not the seller and the purchaser apportion such tax." [Reg. § 1.164-6(b)(1)(i).] Therefore, Peter's property tax deduction is approximately $8,000 regardless of whether or not he made the reimbursement to Steve (or Martha).

Please note that the answer indicates "approximate" values as the method of apportionment that is required under the Code (and as is the case in real-world transactions) is based upon actual *days* of ownership as opposed to whole months as used in our problem.

Answer (a) is incorrect. While Peter was not the owner of the property when the taxes were paid on January 1st, the statute requires apportionment of the deduction for property taxes nonetheless. **Answer (b) is incorrect** because as mentioned above, apportionment of the deduction of property taxes pursuant to IRC § 164(d) does not require that the buyer and seller actually apportion such taxes between themselves for purposes of reimbursement. **Answer (d) is incorrect** because property taxes *are* deductible taxes pursuant to IRC § 164 (and possibly under other sections as well). **Answer (e) is incorrect** because the apportionment rule discussed above does not require actual apportionment and reimbursement of property taxes between buyer and seller.

- **Additional references:** *See* DANIEL Q. POSIN, FEDERAL INCOME TAXATION OF INDIVIDUALS ¶ 7.01(4) (5th ed. 2000).

25. **The most accurate statement is (a).** This is not so much a question of *what* is deductible by Peter, but, rather, *where* Peter is entitled to deductions relating to his rental property for purposes of computing "taxable income." The "*what is* deductible portion" of this problem is easy. IRC § 164 is one section that allows for the deduction of real property taxes. There is little doubt that next year, Peter will be entitled to deduct the property taxes he will pay with respect to the apartment building. As discussed below, Peter will be entitled to this deduction "above the line" in computing his adjusted gross income (AGI).

As far as deductions are concerned, there are two major camps of deductions for purposes of computing taxable income. There are deductions that are subtracted from *gross income* to arrive at our intermediary AGI. These are commonly referred to as "above the line" deductions, with AGI representing "the line." The other camp of deductions is comprised of those that are subtracted from AGI to arrive at *taxable income*. These are commonly referred to as "below the line" deductions. The components making up this camp of *below the line* deductions can include something called the "standard deduction" or, in the alternative, a group of deductions called "itemized deductions." In addition, one or more personal exemption deductions may be included in *below the line* deductions. [For more information about how this all fits together, please see IRC § 62; Appendix A; other questions in this book.]

IRC § 62 is a "signpost" section identifying those deductions (allowed by other Code sections) that are deductible "above the line" in computing adjusted gross income AGI. We find, at IRC § 62(a)(4) the answer to our question. "Deductions attributable to rents and royalties," such as the property taxes that Peter will pay with respect to his apartment building, are deductible "above the line" in computing AGI. While not necessary to answer this question, Peter's other deductible expenses associated with his apartment building (e.g., maintenance, repairs, insurance, and the like as well as possible interest and depreciation deductions) are also deductible above the line pursuant to IRC § 62(a)(4). Although well beyond the scope of this question, it should be noted that various limitations and restrictions might be applicable to deductions related to certain types of rental activities.

Answer (b) is incorrect because these property taxes are related to Peter's investment/rental activities. Had these been real property taxes paid with respect to Peter's personal residence, then this answer would be correct. **Answer (c) is incorrect** because payment of property taxes in this situation *does* give rise to deductions. There is also no provision applicable here that would provide for the property taxes paid to be added to the basis of the property. **Answer (d) is incorrect** because an "exclusion" represents an item that is otherwise included in gross income, but is not because of some "exclusion" or nonrecognition provision. Property taxes paid represent deductions, and not exclusions from income.

- **Additional references:** *See* DANIEL Q. POSIN, FEDERAL INCOME TAXATION OF INDIVIDUALS ¶¶ 6.01, 6.02(3), 7.01(4) (5th ed. 2000).

ANSWER KEY
EXAM IV

1.   **Answer (e) is the correct answer.** Situations involving the exchange, between two parties, of services and/or property, usually result in some confusion among students at first. The bottom-line answer with respect to Cassandra is that she rendered $4,000 worth of services and was compensated for them, albeit not in cash form but, by receiving other "stuff" (the baseball card) worth $4,000. Cassandra has $4,000 of income as a result. To eliminate other possible answers presented, she is also deemed to have "paid" $4,000 for the baseball card and, therefore has a basis in the card of $4,000. The correct answer, by process of elimination, is the awful "none of the above."

What is bothersome for students in such exchange transactions, is the lack of cash being received for services rendered or property transferred. Somehow the re-sulting income tax consequences seem to be incorrect or unfair. A more thorough discussion of the transaction from Cassandra's perspective follows. Please see question 2 (immediately following this question), for the analysis of the facts from Roger's perspective.

The transaction from Cassandra's perspective

Early on in classroom discussion of gross income, we discover that gross income need not be in the form of cash. A lawyer, for example, who performs legal work for a client and is paid in cash has gross income. A lawyer who performs legal work for a client and receives property as payment has gross income equal to the fair market value of the property received. A lawyer who performs legal work for a client and receives a combination of cash and property as payment has gross income equal to the cash plus the fair market value of the property received. A lawyer who performs legal work for a client and receives the client's services as payment (in exchange) has income equal to the value of the services. A lawyer who performs legal work for a client and receives cash, property and the client's services as payment has gross income equal to the cash, the fair market value of the property, and the fair market value of the services. [See Reg. § 1.61-1(d) (compensation received in forms other than in cash).] When an individual per-forms services and receives "something" in exchange, that "something" (or the value thereof) represents gross income. The form of that "something" is generally irrelevant. In our question, Cassandra rendered $4,000 worth of services and re-ceived $4,000 worth of stuff in return: $4,000 worth of property in the baseball card.

In class, this professor likes to recast, or view in a different light, exchange or barter transactions in an essentially equivalent manner involving the transfer of cash back and forth between the parties. We could break down the transaction between Cassandra and Roger into something like this. Cassandra performs $4,000 worth of services for Roger and Roger pays Cassandra $4,000 in cash. At this point, it is clear Cassandra would have income. Next, Cassandra buys a rare baseball card worth $4,000 from Roger, <u>paying</u> him $4,000 <u>in cash</u>. The economic substance of viewing the transaction in this manner (with cash going back and forth) is the same as that given in our facts, but it sometimes helps to identify the separate components involved.

Because Cassandra is deemed to have "paid" Roger $4,000 for the baseball, that represents her basis (or adjusted basis (AB)) pursuant to the general "cost" basis rules of IRC §§ 1011 and 1012.

[For more information about barter/exchange transactions, see Reg. § 1.61-1(d); Rev.Rul. 79-24, 1979-1 C.B. 60.]

Answer (a) is incorrect because, as discussed above, the "barter transactions" in our facts does result in income tax ramifications to Cassandra. **Answer (b) is also incorrect**. It correctly identifies Cassandra's gross income of $4,000, but provides for a bogus business deduction for purchasing the baseball card. **Answer (c) is incorrect** because Cassandra does have immediate income tax consequences in the recognition of $4,000 of income for her services rendered. **Answer (d) is also incorrect.** It, too, correctly identifies the $4,000 of gross income to Cassandra, but incorrectly states her basis in the baseball card received in exchange.

- **Additional references:** *See* DANIEL Q. POSIN, FEDERAL INCOME TAXATION OF INDIVIDUALS ¶ 2.01 (5th ed. 2000).

2. **The best answer is (e).** As mentioned in the analysis to the companion question 1, above, situations involving the exchange, between two parties, of services and/or property, usually result in some confusion among students at first. Roger did two things: Roger paid for $4,000 of tax advice, albeit not in the form of cash, but in the form of property (the baseball card) which gives rise to a deductible IRC § 162 business expense. Roger also disposed of his baseball card worth $4,000 and received consideration for it, albeit not in the form of cash, but by receiving other stuff (services from Cassandra) worth $4,000. Roger's receipt of $4,000 consideration for the baseball card less his cost basis ("adjusted basis" hereinafter AB) of $2,500, results in a realized gain of $1,500.

What is bothersome for students in such exchange transactions, is the lack of cash being received for services rendered or property transferred. Somehow the resulting income tax consequences seem to be incorrect or unfair. A more thorough discussion of the transaction from Roger's perspective follows. Please see question 1 (immediately preceding this question), for the analysis of the facts from <u>Cassandra's</u> perspective

The transaction from Roger's perspective

Let us view these tax results to Paula utilizing our "recast" cash version of this barter transaction (from the analysis of question 1, above). We break down the transaction between Cassandra and Roger as follows: Cassandra performs $4,000 worth of services for Roger and Roger pays Cassandra $4,000 in cash. Next, Cassandra buys a rare baseball card worth $4,000 from Roger, paying him $4,000 in cash. The economic substance of viewing the transaction in this manner (with cash going back and forth) is the same as that given in our facts, but it sometimes helps identify the separate components involved.

Roger effectively paid $4,000 for tax advice related solely to his unincorporated sole proprietor computer consulting business. In general, IRC § 162 allows for business deductions that are (read as one continuous phrase with four distinct requirements):
  ➤ Ordinary and necessary
  ➤ Expenses
  ➤ Paid or incurred during the taxable year
  ➤ In carrying on any trade or business.

We need not dig too deep here to see that Roger's "expenditure" for tax advice qualifies as a business expense deduction. The fact that he "paid" for this business related expense in a form other than cash is irrelevant.

The other part of the transaction from Roger's perspective was the disposition of his baseball card. A sale or disposition of property results in the realization of a gain or loss to transferor measured by the difference between the "amount realized" (AR) and the transferor's AB. [IRC § 1001(a).] The AR side of this sale or disposition equation is obscured just a bit. One's AR from a sale or disposition of property is usually received in the form of cash. However, AR is broader than that, and basically includes the value of any "stuff" received in exchange for property whether it be other property or services (money's worth). Here Roger received $4,000 worth of "stuff" (Cassandra's services) as consideration. Roger's AB is straightforward in this question, and is his $2,500 original cost of the baseball card. [See IRC §§ 1011 and 1012.] In effect, Roger sold the baseball card and received $4,000 consideration (in the form of Cassandra's services), resulting in a realized gain of $1,500 ($4,000 AR less his AB of $2,500).

In the aggregate, therefore, Roger has a $4,000 IRC § 162 business expense deduction, and a $1,500 realized gain from the sale of his baseball card.

[For more information about barter/exchange transactions, see Reg. § 1.61-1(d); Rev.Rul. 79-24, 1979-1 C.B. 60.]

Answer (a) is incorrect but is sometimes chosen as the answer under the misconception that anytime there is a barter transaction, both parties have equal amounts of income. While this may be true if the barter transaction is a straight "services for services" exchange, our facts present a different situation that requires a careful analysis of each component part. **Answer (b) is also incorrect**. While Roger has no income from the performance of services, he does have income in the form of gain from the disposition of the baseball card. In addition the indicated amount of his deduction is incorrect. **Answer (c) is incorrect** because while it does indicate the correct amount of gain realized, the amount for his business deduction is wrong. **Answer (d) is incorrect** but it is commonly selected as the correct answer. The problem with this answer lies in the classification of Roger's $4,000 deduction. There is some overlap in IRC §§ 162 and 212. IRC § 212 does allow a deduction for tax advice type fees. [IRC § 212(3).] However IRC § 212 expenses, by their definition, are not expenses associated with one's trade or business. Rather, IRC § 212 provides deductions for investment-related activities and nonbusiness tax related fees (advice, tax return preparation, tax audit assistance, etc.). In Roger's case, this tax advice was related solely to his consulting business and, therefore, is properly classified as IRC § 162 trade or business related expense. [Please see other questions in this book that address IRC § 212 in greater detail.]

- **Additional references:** *See* DANIEL Q. POSIN, FEDERAL INCOME TAXATION OF INDIVIDUALS ¶¶ 4.01, 4.03, 6.01, 6.02(1) (5th ed. 2000).

3.   **Answer (a) is correct.** IRC § 102 is a wonderful section for recipients of gifts, bequests and devises. While Tom did realize a net accession to wealth (he was better off financially by reason of the devise to him), the full $35,000 value of the shares received is excluded from gross income by IRC § 102. This exclusion section is usually fairly straightforward, as it is here, but one need be on the watch for potential problem areas, usually revolving around what exactly constitutes a "gift" or "bequest/devise." Specifically in the bequest/devise area, while not at issue in this question, are situations where the "bequest/devise" may not be such but, rather, some contractual benefit received pursuant to a will.

Answer (b) is incorrect because the exclusion in IRC § 102 applies to testamentary bequests/devises as well as inter vivos gifts. **Answer (c) is incorrect** because there is no blanket "tax-free" provision for transfers between family members. **Answer (d) is incorrect** because the exclusion of IRC § 102 is not dependent on any subsequent transaction by the donee, beneficiary/devisee.

- **Additional references:** *See* DANIEL Q. POSIN, FEDERAL INCOME TAXATION OF INDIVIDUALS ¶¶ 3.08(1), 3.08(2) (5th ed. 2000).

Watch out for k-val & benefits received pursuant to a will!!

4.   **Answer (a) is correct.** When Tom sells the shares of stock, he realizes a gain or a loss measured by the difference between the sales price (or in tax terms: the amount realized or AR) and his adjusted basis (AB) in the shares. [IRC § 1001(a).] The AR portion of the equation in this problem is simply the $40,000 sales price for the shares. The key component to this question is the determination of Tom's AB in the shares.

While a taxpayer's cost is normally the starting point for determination of one's AB in property (IRC §§ 1011 and 1012), when property is received as a bequest/devise, as is the case here, there really is no "cost" to the taxpayer. The seemingly logical result of a zero AB is neither desirable nor, thankfully, appropriate. IRC § 1014(a)(1) provides the general rule that the AB of property acquired from a decedent shall be the property's fair market value at the date of the decedent's death. The shares Tom received were worth $35,000 at his grandmother's death and, therefore, represents Tom's AB in the shares.

When Tom sells the property for $40,000, his realized gain is the difference between the $40,000 and his basis of $35,000 or $5,000.

Note, that the fair market value basis rule of IRC § 1014(a)(1) is commonly referred to as the "step-up" in basis for property received from a decedent. This is because we like to think, or at least hope, that property has appreciated in the hands of the decedent and the testamentary beneficiary gets as his/her basis a new "higher" or "stepped-up" basis. For appreciated property, this Code provision is a great tax savings device that effectively makes, for income tax purposes, any gains from unrealized appreciation in the decedent's hands evaporate. Unfortunately, when property has depreciated in the decedent's hands, the testamentary beneficiary effectively gets a "stepped-down" basis.

Answer (b) is incorrect because to have a ($10,000) realized loss as result of Tom's sale, his basis would have had to be $50,000. Students sometimes select this answer because they mistakenly use the general inter vivos gift "carryover" basis rule of IRC § 1015(a). **Answer (c) is similarly incorrect**. This answer, again, has the student in the incorrect arena of determination of a transferee's basis in an inter vivos gift environment. Specifically, the potential application of the "special loss rule" of IRC § 1015(a) and the regulations addressing subsequent sales by the donee at a price between that of the donor's basis and the lower fair market value at the time of the inter vivos gift. [Reg. § 1.1015-1(a)(2).] **Answer (d) is incorrect** because it does not really address Tom's subsequent sale of the shares. It is true that he has no income pursuant to IRC § 102 from the receipt of these shares from his grandmother's devise to him, but that exclusion has no application to gains derived from a subsequent sale of such property.

New Law Caution. The Economic Growth and Tax Relief Reconciliation Act of 2001 ("2001 Tax Act"), signed into law in 2001, made numerous changes throughout the Internal Revenue Code. The 2001 Tax Act is rather complex with many of its provisions phasing-in and phasing-out over a period of many years. As of this writing, the above described basis rules of IRC § 1014 are repealed with respect to decedents dying after December 31. 2009. [IRC § 1014(f).] The change, with limited exceptions, is basically to a "carryover" basis rule, similar to that applicable to inter vivos gifts in IRC § 1015. [See IRC § 1022 (effective for years after 2009).] This change was enacted to coincide with the 2001 Tax Act's abolishment of the federal estate tax effective for years after 2009. Whether these changes will come to pass without change in the intervening years is unknown as of this writing. However, as discussed in the preface to this book, the 2001 Tax Act, as enacted, contains a rather unique "sunset clause" that could, unless amended, make the above described 2010 changes evaporate in 2011, leaving us with the current IRC § 1014 rules.

- **Additional references:** *See* DANIEL Q. POSIN, FEDERAL INCOME TAXATION OF INDIVIDUALS ¶¶ 4.01, 4.03 (5th ed. 2000).

5. **Answer (e) is correct.** This question, unfortunately, requires, in part, a correct analysis of the previous question. This professor would not ask such a series of interrelated multiple-choice questions on an exam. Rather, this series of questions was derived from an exam essay question. With that said, we know, from the previous question, that Tom's realized gain was $5,000. The only available answer with the correct amount of realized gain is (b) and, therefore, it must be eliminated if that answer is correct. Response (b) is almost correct in that the realized gain was $5,000. The gain is recognized pursuant to IRC § 1001(c), as all gains are recognized unless there is some specific non-recognition or exclusion section. No such non-recognition or exclusion section exists with respect to our facts. Further, the gain is a "capital" gain as the shares of stock, as investments, represent capital assets. [IRC § 1221(a).] However, we will conclude that Tom's $5,000 capital gain is a long-term capital gain.

Because Tom's capital gain is long-term (and why it is long-term), it renders answer (b) incorrect (and by default, (e) is the correct answer). Determining the holding period, for short and long term gain/loss classification, is controlled by IRC § 1223. While long-term status is generally reserved for assets held for more than one year (IRC § 1222), property received from a decedent effectively gets automatic long-term status in most situations pursuant to IRC § 1223(11). This is not the so called "tacking" of holding period pursuant to IRC § 1223(2) which effectively applies to situations where there is a "carryover" basis such as with most inter vivos gifts. Even if tacking were to apply here, which it does not, adding

Gloria's holding period to that of Tom's would still result in a "short-term" period of one year or less.

Note, that as the law now stands, receipt of appreciated property from a decedent can have very beneficial effects: a "stepped-up" basis to the beneficiary and automatic long-term holding period for capital gain purposes.

Answer (b) is incorrect because Tom's capital gain is a long-term gain because of IRC § 1223(11), as discussed above. **Answers (a), (c) and (d) are incorrect** prima facially because the amount of recognized gain (or lack thereof) indicated is not the correct amount. Additionally, answers (c) and (d) again incorrectly apply the holding period rules of § 1223(2) to this fact pattern.

- **Additional references:** *See* DANIEL Q. POSIN, FEDERAL INCOME TAXATION OF INDIVIDUALS ¶¶ 4.01, 4.03, 4.05(1) (5th ed. 2000).

6. **The correct answer is (a).** This is a fairly straight application of the gain exclusion provisions of IRC § 121. Effective for sales of a taxpayer's principal residence after May 6, 1997, IRC § 121 provides for the exclusion of up to $250,000 of gain ($500,000 in the case of certain married individuals) if certain conditions are met. There are two basic requirements for this exclusion, commonly referred to as the "ownership" and "use" tests. The taxpayer must have owned the house for at least two years (looking back five years from the date of sale), and must have used it as his or her principal residence for two years (looking back five years from the date of sale). [IRC § 121(a).] Brad clearly meets both the ownership and use tests having owned and used the house as his principal residence for at least two years within the last five years (he has owned the house and has lived there for four years in this question). Therefore, he will be entitled to exclude the gain from the sale of his house up to a maximum of $250,000. Should he have gain in excess of $250,000, it will be recognized, as there are no other non-recognition or exclusion provisions applicable here.

While not at issue in this problem, it should be noted that generally, the exclusion provisions of IRC § 121 cannot be used more than once in a two-year period. [IRC § 121(b)(3).] It is a logical assumption from the facts presented that this limitation would not apply to Brad in this question.

It should also be noted that the statute does not require that the requisite two-year "use" and "ownership" period be co-extensive. While again, this is not an issue in this question, it is a common misunderstanding (read as "good testing area") that the two "two-year" qualifying periods must be at the same time. It is also a common misunderstanding (again, read as "good testing area") that the "five-year look back period" for purposes of determining two-year ownership and use somehow requires that the taxpayer either owned or used the house for at least five years. This is not correct, and again, while this is not at issue in this question, it might be helpful for your analysis of other IRC § 121 related questions.

Answers (b) and (e) are incorrect because there are simply no such provisions in the Code. **Answer (c) is incorrect** because while the exclusion limit of IRC § 121 increases to $500,000 in the case of certain married individuals, Brad and Gail are not, in this question, married. Gail is not entitled to any exclusion on her own because she is not an owner of the property.

Answer (d) is incorrect but is the source of much confusion among students and the general public. Prior to the $250,000/$500,000 exclusion of IRC § 121, the primary provision affecting gain recognition from the sale of a principal residence was IRC § 1034. This latter section, which was repealed and replaced by current IRC § 121 in 1997, also provided for gain exclusion, but its mechanism for doing so was very different. Basically, this old section provided that if you purchased (and occupied) a new principal residence within a two year period of selling your old principal residence (either before or, as was more common, after the sale), then gain was recognized only to the extent, if any, that the purchase price of the new house was less than the sales price of the old house. In other words, if a taxpayer always "moved-up" to a more expensive house, gain was not recognized. However, this old IRC § 1034 provision was merely a "deferral" mechanism because any gain not recognized pursuant to this provision, served to reduce the adjusted basis of the new house (to be potentially recognized upon a subsequent sale). As indicated, this old § 1034 is no longer valid law (but if your professor covers this material in greater depth, be aware that prior deferrals of gain under that law may still be reflected in a taxpayer's adjusted basis for their home). Current IRC § 121 does not require that the taxpayer purchase a new house, and any gain excluded pursuant to the section is a real exclusion (not merely a deferral of recognition) with no effect on the adjusted basis of any subsequent house purchase.

Not to add additional superfluous information, there was an "old" IRC § 121 that was also repealed with enactment of current IRC § 121 in 1997. The old section was a "once in a lifetime" exclusion of a certain dollar amount of gain from the sale of a principal residence for taxpayers fifty-five years of age or older. This old IRC § 121 was in addition to old IRC § 1034, and their combination was a logistics mess (and a difficult area for instruction) when compared to the relatively straightforward rules of current IRC § 121. The current IRC § 121 has no age limit, can be used over and over again to exclude gain (generally just not more than once every two years), and has larger exclusion limitations. Again, while this old IRC § 121 is no longer valid law, it is the source of some confusion among taxpayers.

- **Additional references:** *See* DANIEL Q. POSIN, FEDERAL INCOME TAXATION OF INDIVIDUALS ¶¶ 4.01, 4.03, 4.04(5) (5th ed. 2000).

7.   **The correct answer is (e).** The maximum gain from the sale of a principal residence doubles from $250,000 to $500,000 for certain married individuals. A husband and wife filing a joint return are entitled to this larger exclusion if <u>both</u> spouses meet the two-year "use" test, and <u>either</u> spouse meets the two-year "ownership" test. [IRC § 121(b)(2).] Note that only one spouse need meet the ownership test and in our question, Brad qualifies. Gail's lack of ownership interest in the property does not preclude them from this larger exclusion limitation. As indicated, both spouses must meet the "use" test for this larger exclusion and here, both Brad and Gail have used this house as their principal residence for at least two years (looking back five years). There is no statutory requirement that their two years of use must be while they were married (or co-extensive for that matter). Students sometimes suspect that because our couple was married for only six months prior to the sale, it negatively affects the application of this larger exclusion for married couples. However, the requirement is only that they be married at the time of the sale and that they file a joint return. [IRC § 121(b)(2).]

Answer (a) is incorrect because as mentioned above, for married individuals filing a joint return, there is no requirement that both spouses own the property for the requisite two-year period. **Answers (b) and (d) are incorrect** because they both reflect the mistaken belief that their qualifying two-year "use" period had to be when they were married. **Answer (c) is incorrect** because they do qualify for a larger exclusion than in the previous question.

- **Additional references:** *See* DANIEL Q. POSIN, FEDERAL INCOME TAXATION OF INDIVIDUALS ¶¶ 4.01, 4.03, 4.04(5) (5th ed. 2000).

8.   **The correct answer is (b).** Richard has suffered a terrible loss with the death of his wife, Sonia. However, he has received an immediate net accession to wealth upon receipt of the $100,000 life insurance proceeds. Given the broad and inclusive nature of gross income, this $100,000 will be income unless there is a specific "exclusion" provision in the law. Fortunately, for Richard, there is in IRC § 101. This section's general rule is that life insurance proceeds received by reason of the insured's death are excluded from gross income of the beneficiary. This question is a straightforward life insurance question and the entire $100,000 Richard receives is excludable from income pursuant to the general rule of IRC § 101(a).

It should be noted that this general exclusion for life insurance proceeds has no dollar limitations. Ten million dollars of life insurance proceeds are as excludable as one thousand dollars of proceeds.

Answer (a) is incorrect because the receipt of life insurance proceeds by reason of the insured's death is not treated as a sale or other disposition transaction with gain or loss realized. Rather, as discussed above, the proceeds are simply excluded in full under the general rule of IRC § 101(a). **Answer (c) is incorrect** because while there is an accession to wealth, IRC § 101(a) specifically provides for its exclusion under the facts in this question. **Answer (d) is incorrect** because it is simply not true and has no foundation in income tax laws.

- **Additional references:** *See* DANIEL Q. POSIN, FEDERAL INCOME TAXATION OF INDIVIDUALS ¶¶ 3.06, 3.07 (5th ed. 2000).

9. **The correct answer is (c).** From the analysis to question 8, above, we know that life insurance proceeds receive favorable income tax treatment pursuant to IRC § 101. In general, the proceeds are excludable from gross income. Instead of receiving the $100,000 death benefit right now, that we know from the previous question would be tax-free, Richard has selected an annual lifetime payout option. Assuming that he remains alive for exactly forty years, Richard will have received a total of $400,000 from the life insurance company ($10,000/year multiplied by 40 years). Where does all of this money come from, and how can the insurance company afford to pay so much more? The insurance company continues to invest the retained portion of the $100,000 it does not have to currently pay out and Richard benefits, in part, from these subsequent earnings. In effect, Richard is investing with the insurance company, the $100,000 owed to him. We need know very little about income tax rules to logically conclude that Richard will be able to exclude from income a total of $100,000 under IRC § 101(a) as this amount represents the actual death benefit proceeds. The excess he receives ($300,000 if he lives exactly forty years) is not excludable but, rather, represents taxable earnings on his invested money. The issue is in what manner do we reflect the exclusion when life insurance proceeds are paid out over time as they are here?

IRC § 104(d) and the regulations (at Reg. § 1.101-4), prescribe a "pro rata" method. Again, logic prevails, and even the most math sensitive student should have little difficulty reaching the correct conclusion here. We already have the numbers necessary and can compute the prorated exclusion in at least two different, and equally correct, ways. In our question, $100,000 is the total amount to be excluded. Dividing the $100,000 by 40 (the given life expectancy for Richard) equals $2,500, and this is the portion of each $10,000 annual payment that is excludable (the other $7,500 of each annual payment is income).

$$\frac{\text{Lump Sum Death Benefit}}{\text{Life Expectancy}} = \text{Amount Excluded}$$

The numbers in our problem:

$$\frac{\$100,000}{40 \text{ Years}} = \begin{array}{l}\$2,500 \text{ Excluded} \\ \text{per Year}\end{array}$$

An alternative approach is taking $100,000 (the total excludable benefit) and dividing it by $400,000 (the total we calculated Richard will receive over 40 years). This quotient is ¼ or 25%. One-fourth (or 25%) of each $10,000 payment ($2,500) is excludable and the balance is income.

$$\frac{\text{Excludable Death Benefit}}{\text{Total Expected Return}} = \text{\% of Each Payment Excluded}$$

The numbers in our problem:

$$\frac{\$100,000}{\$400,000} = \begin{array}{l}25\% \text{ or } ¼ \text{ of} \\ \text{Each Payment Excluded}\end{array}$$

Answer (a), (b) and (d) are incorrect because they do not correspond to the method of prorating payments prescribed by the Code and regulations.

- **Additional references:** *See* DANIEL Q. POSIN, FEDERAL INCOME TAXATION OF INDIVIDUALS ¶¶ 3.06, 3.07 (5th ed. 2000).

10. **The correct answer is (c).** In question 9, above, we calculated Richard's prorated excluded amount of each payment based on his given forty-year life expectancy. In that question we calculated that his $10,000 annual payment was split into non-taxable and taxable components of $2,500 and $7,500, respectively. That conclusion sounds fine for the payments to be received over the forty-year life expectancy. After forty years of payments, Richard will have excluded the full $100,000 of death benefits. Logic might dictate that when Richard receives his forty-first payment, it would be fully taxable having already excluded, over the past forty years, the full $100,000 original death benefit – everything from this point on would appear to be taxable "gravy." Fortunately, and somewhat surprisingly, this logic is wrong. Richard continues to use the same excludable/includible portions as originally calculated regardless if he "outlives" his life expectancy. [See Reg. § 1.101-4(c).]

Please note that in this series of questions we are concerned with life insurance. Specifically in this question 10 and question 9 above, we have an "annuity type" payout of life insurance benefits. The rules for true annuity contracts (where typically a living individual, the annuitant, gives money to a life insurance company and the company pays the annuitant a specified periodic dollar amount for his/her life) are different. Please see other questions in this book that address the income tax consequences of annuities.

Answer (a) is incorrect, although it is a logical choice. As indicated above, the exclusion/inclusion portions of each payment, as originally calculated, continue regardless of how long the recipient lives. **Answer (b) is incorrect** and, if anything, is the opposite of what one might logically expect. **Answer (d) is incorrect** but is a commonly selected answer. Please be careful when reading the "call of a question." Unlike question 9 that asks for the excluded portion, this question 10 asks for the portion of the payment included in Richard's gross income. Unfortunately some students, who know how this bifurcated exclusion/inclusion rule works, answer this question incorrectly because of the call of the question. **Answer (e) is incorrect** because of the application of the partial exclusion "consideration" rule discussed above.

- **Additional references:** *See* DANIEL Q. POSIN, FEDERAL INCOME TAXATION OF INDIVIDUALS ¶¶ 3.06, 3.07 (5th ed. 2000).

11. **The most accurate answer is (b).** This is a difficult question that requires us to explore many diverse income tax issues. We will conclude that Richard will only be able to exclude, from income, $33,000 of the $100,000 insurance proceeds received. The excludable portion represents the sum of the $30,000 consideration that he paid for the policy, plus the $3,000 in premiums paid subsequent to his receipt of the policy.

From the preceding questions in this series, we are well versed in the general rule of IRC § 101(a) excluding from income, the proceeds of life insurance paid by reason of the insured's death. This question introduces an important issue in the life insurance area. When there has been a transfer, for valuable consideration, of a life insurance policy during the insured's life, the aforementioned general rule of full exclusion may not be applicable to benefits received by reason of the insured's death. We are about to start a trek down a long and tortured road that requires careful attention to statutory road signs. Be aware, that this intricate material makes for very fertile testing grounds.

IRC § 101(a)(2) contains this exception the general exclusion rule of life insurance benefits. When a life insurance policy has been transferred for consideration, as it was in the facts of our question, the exclusion for benefits proceeds received at the insured's death is <u>limited</u> to the consideration paid by the transferee plus any additional premiums paid by the transferee subsequent to the transfer. In our problem, transferee Richard paid $30,000 in consideration for the policy plus $3,000 in policy premiums subsequent to the transfer. Applying this "consideration" limitation of IRC § 101(a)(2) to these facts, Richard's exclusion is limited to only $33,000 ($30,000 plus $3,000) of the $100,000 received. The $67,000 of remaining proceeds would not be excluded pursuant to this rule. This ends up being the correct answer (b) in this question. We should, however, further explore this issue to better understand the subject and to rule out other possible answers to this question. It will also aid in reviewing issues that arise in questions unrelated to life insurance.

The "consideration" exception (IRC § 101(a)(2)) to the general full exclusion rule (IRC § 101(a)) has, in classic law school form, exceptions thereto. One such "exception to the exception" is at issue in this question, and it requires the application of Code sections seemingly unrelated to the insurance provisions at issue. Specifically, § 101(a)(2)(a) effectively provides that you can forget the aforementioned "consideration" limitation and qualify for full exclusion of life insurance proceeds even if the policy was transferred for consideration <u>if</u>, the basis of the policy in the hands of the transferee is "determined in whole or in part by reference" to the basis of the policy in the hands of the transferor. In other words, even though there has been a transfer of a policy for consideration, if the transferee's basis is essentially a carryover basis from the transferor, the "consideration" limitation evaporates, and proceeds from the policy are fully excluded.

The issues of basis (or adjusted basis) in property is more thoroughly discussed in other questions in this book, typically in those involving sales, gains, losses, etc. Generally, one's basis in property is determined by the taxpayer's cost of the property. [IRC §§ 1011 and 1012.] Applying this general rule in our fact pattern, Richard's basis in the life insurance policy purchased from Sonia is his $30,000 cost. There are a few instances, however, when the consideration paid does not necessarily represent one's resulting basis. These situations are critical to the analysis of this question. One such situation is when we have transfers between spouses or former spouses that are considered "incident to divorce." IRC § 1041(b) provides, in a nutshell, that when spouses transfer property to each other, or when former spouses transfer property to each other and it is "incident to their divorce," the transferee spouse (or former spouse) takes a carryover basis. This section does not distinguish as to the type of inter vivos transfer involved – it covers gifts, sales, exchanges, etc.

Let us step back for a second and see where we are at this point. If we find that Sonia's sale of the insurance policy to Richard is within the confines of IRC §

1041, Richard will have a carryover basis in the policy. This, in turn, will place him squarely within the exception of IRC § 101(a)(2)(A) which, in turn, overrides the "consideration" limitation, which ultimately would result in exclusion of the full $100,000 insurance proceeds received. Alternatively, if his purchase does not fit within the confines of IRC § 1041, Richard has a "cost" basis rather than a carryover basis. In turn, he would not qualify under the exception in IRC § 101(a)(2)(A), which ultimately would result in his exclusion of the life insurance proceeds being limited to $33,000.

After having read the preceding paragraph a few times to get our bearings, we are ready to continue with our analysis. We are at the critical juncture of whether or not Sonia's transfer of the insurance policy to Richard in May 2001 is within the parameters of IRC § 1041 – was this a transfer between spouses of former spouses that is "incident to divorce?" Clearly, it was not a transfer between spouses as they were divorced at the time (they divorced in January 2000). It was a transfer between former spouses, but was it considered "incident to divorce" as required by the statute? A transfer "incident to divorce" has a statutory definition as being either 1) any transfer within one year of the divorce, or 2) a transfer "relating to the cessation of the marriage." [See IRC § 1041(c).] Temporary regulations define transfers that are considered "relating to the cessation of the marriage" as a transfer provided for by a "divorce or separation instrument" and is transferred, pursuant to this instrument, within six years of the divorce. [Temp.Reg. §1.1041-1T(b); Please see other questions in this book relating to divorce issues for more information.] We now see that Richard's purchase of the policy from Sonia was not a transfer "incident to divorce." Richard's purchase of the policy from Sonia was not within one year of their divorce. Alternatively, even though the transfer occurred within six years of their divorce, it was not called for by their divorce decree (this is indicated in the facts) and, therefore, is not related to the cessation of the marriage. This means that the transfer between Sonia and Richard does not fall within the parameters of IRC § 1041 which, in turn, means Richard does not have a carryover basis in the policy. As previously indicated, Richard, consequently, does not fit within the IRC § 101(a)(2)(A) exception to the limited exclusion "consideration" rule. Richard, therefore, can only exclude $33,000 of the $100,000 insurance proceeds received (the $30,000 consideration that he paid plus the $3,000 in premiums subsequent to his purchase).

Answer (a) is incorrect but is close to being correct. It is true that Richard's purchase of the policy from Sonia was not incident to divorce and, therefore, he is stuck with the limited exclusion under the "consideration" rule. Richard paid consideration of $30,000, which is excludable, but he is also entitled to exclude the $3,000 that he paid in insurance premiums subsequent to his purchase. **Answer (d) is incorrect** because as indicated above, not just any transfer within six years of divorce is considered "relating to the cessation of the marriage." If the transfer occurs more than one year after the divorce, the divorce or separation instrument must have called for such a transfer. Here, the facts indicate that Richard's purchase of the policy was not pursuant to any oral or written agreement relating to the divorce. Since the transfer was not, by definition, incident to divorce, IRC § 1041(b) does not apply, so the exception in IRC § 101(a)(2)(A) does not apply and Richard cannot exclude the full amount of the proceeds. **Answer (c) is incorrect** because it has no relationship to the law and the facts of the question.

- **Additional references:** *See* DANIEL Q. POSIN, FEDERAL INCOME TAXATION OF INDIVIDUALS ¶¶ 3.06, 3.07, 4.02(2), 6.02(14)(b) (5th ed. 2000).

12. **Answer (e) is the most accurate.** This is very similar to question 11, above. On an actual class exam, the author would not include a question so similar and in such proximity to the question immediately preceding it. It is presented here, however, as a good review and to illustrate the marked difference in the answer resulting from a slight change in the facts.

So as not to torture the reader, the lengthy analysis for the preceding question, while relevant, will not be repeated here in full. We will pick up near the end of the analysis from the previous question dealing with the determination of Richard's basis in the insurance policy. Recall that Richard's goal of full exclusion rests on whether or not his basis in the policy was essentially a carryover basis from Sonia. As discussed above, this requires that his May 2001 purchase of the policy be considered a "transfer incident to divorce." Recall that in question 11, we found this not to be the case because the transfer was neither within one year of the divorce, nor pursuant to their "divorce or separation instrument" and occurring within six years. In the revised facts of this question, however, the May 2001 transfer was within one year of their January 2001 divorce and, therefore, is deemed "incident to divorce." The significance of this makes a dramatic difference in the tax consequences to Richard. With the transfer incident to divorce, he has a carryover basis in the policy, he meets the exception in IRC § 101(a)(2)(A) to the limited exclusion "consideration" rule, and the general full exclusion rule of IRC § 101(a) applies.

Note that the sale of the life insurance policy between Sonia and Richard is deemed "incident to divorce" notwithstanding the fact that it was not pursuant to any agreement relating to their divorce. This is often an elusive point with students. IRC § 1041(c) dictates a non-rebuttable presumption that any transfer within one year of divorce is deemed incident to divorce. To extend this classification to transfers made more than one year after divorce, the transfer must be pursuant to their divorce or separation instrument (e.g., a divorce decree). [See Temp.Reg. § 1.1041-1T(b) Q & A-7.]

Answers (a) and (b) are not correct because as discussed above, Richard is not relegated to a limited exclusion based on the consideration that he paid. **Answers (c) and (d) are also incorrect.** They both have the correct numeric answer that the full proceeds are excludable from Richard's gross income, but they state incorrect reason for this exclusion.

- **Additional references:** *See* DANIEL Q. POSIN, FEDERAL INCOME TAXATION OF INDIVIDUALS ¶¶ 3.06, 3.07, 4.02(2), 6.02(14)(b) (5th ed. 2000).

13.   **The correct answer is (c).** This is a relatively simple problem. Determining Roxanne's realized gain or loss in this question requires us to identify two basic components: her sales price ("amount realized" or, hereinafter, AR) and her basis in the jewelry ("adjusted basis or, hereinafter, AB). The difference between the two represents a <u>realized</u> gain or loss. [IRC § 1001(a).] Each of these two components, AR and AB, can present a variety of complex tax issues for exam and real-world tax purposes. The AR side is straightforward in our question, and is her $42,000 sales price. Other questions in this book present more complex issues involving a taxpayer's AR.

The AB component is the more challenging component of this question, but is not as complex as AB issues presented in other questions in this book. While a taxpayer's cost is normally the starting point for determination of one's basis in property (IRC §§ 1011 and 1012), when property is received as a gift, as is the case here, there really is no "cost" to the taxpayer. The seemingly logical result of a zero basis is neither desirable nor, thankfully, appropriate. IRC § 1015 provides us with the rules for determining a donee's AB in property received as a gift. The general rule for most gifts is that the donee takes the donor's AB in the property, or what is commonly referred to as a "carryover" AB. In Roxanne's case, this would be her aunt Martha's original $20,000 cost of the jewelry. There are no other facts presented in this problem that require any further adjustments to Roxanne's carryover AB (e.g., gift tax paid adjustment, special loss rule, etc.).

The calculation of Roxanne's gain is now a simple matter. Her AR of $42,000 less her $20,000 AB results in <u>a realized gain of $22,000</u>. While not the subject of this question, issues of gain <u>recognition</u> and <u>characterization</u> (i.e., capital gain materials), are related testable material. For information purposes, Roxanne's $22,000 gain would be recognized and characterized as a "long-term capital gain." [Please see other questions presented in this book where recognition and characterization issues are addressed.]

Answer (a) is incorrect because it is a misrepresentation of a certain situation involving the "special loss rule" when determining the AB of property received as a gift. The special loss rule can apply when the fair market value of the gift (at the time of the gift) is less than the donor's AB in the property. Our facts do not implicate the *special loss rule*. **Answer (b) is incorrect** because this answer reflects the mistaken belief that Roxanne's AB is equal to the fair market value at the time of the gift. This answer would have been correct had Roxanne received the jewelry from Martha at Martha's death by devise, bequest or inheritance as the rules for determining the transferee's AB in such situations are quite different. Please see other problems in this book addressing the issue of the AB of property received from a decedent. **Answer (d) is incorrect** because it fails to reflect the AB rules for gifts as discussed above.

- **Additional references:** *See* DANIEL Q. POSIN, FEDERAL INCOME TAXATION OF INDIVIDUALS ¶ 4.03 (5th ed. 2000).

14. **Answer (c) is correct.** Situations involving the exchange, between two parties, of services and/or property, usually result in some initial confusion among students. Although it is a bit obscured in this problem, Roxanne really did two things in this transaction: sold the jewelry worth $42,000 to Carl in exchange for $42,000 of consideration, and she effectively paid Carl $2,000 for his dental services. With respect to the former, the consideration Roxanne received from the jewelry transfer was not in the form of cash but, rather, she received $42,000 worth of stuff (the payoff of her $40,000 loan to Carl, plus Carl's services worth $2,000). Roxanne's receipt of $42,000 consideration for the jewelry less his basis ("adjusted basis" hereinafter AB) in the jewelry of $20,000 (carryover gift AB from her aunt), results in a realized <u>gain</u> to Roxanne of <u>$22,000</u>.

What is bothersome for students in such exchange transactions, is the lack of cash being received for services rendered or property transferred. Somehow the resulting income tax consequences seem to be incorrect or unfair. A more thorough discussion of the transaction from <u>Roxanne's</u> perspective follows. [Please see question 15, immediately following this question, for the analysis of the facts and income tax consequences from Carl's perspective.]

<u>The transaction from Roxanne's perspective</u>

In class, this professor likes to recast, or view in a different light, exchange or barter transactions in an essentially equivalent manner involving the transfer of cash back and forth between the parties. We could break down the transaction between Roxanne and Carl into something like this. Roxanne *sells* the jewelry to Carl for $42,000 <u>in cash</u>. Roxanne then takes $40,000 of this <u>cash</u> and gives it back to *Carl,* fully paying off her $40,000 debt to him. Roxanne then takes the $2,000 of <u>cash</u> that she has left after paying off the debt, and <u>pays</u> Carl $2,000 for the dental work he performs for her. The economic substance of viewing the transaction in this manner (with cash going back and forth) is the same as given in our facts, but it sometimes helps identify the separate components involved. Either way we look at it, in the end Roxanne has no cash, no longer has the jewelry, her debt has been repaid, and she has received dental services.

Now let us look at Roxanne's disposition of the jewelry. A sale or disposition of property results in the realization of a gain or loss to transferor measured by the difference between the "amount realized" (AR) and the transferor's AB. [IRC § 1001(a).] The "AR" side of this sale or disposition equation is easy if viewed in light of our "recast" facts. Roxanne sold the jewelry for $42,000 and that is her AR. One's AR need not be comprised of cash as AR is much broader than that. AR basically includes the value of any "stuff" received in exchange for property whether it be other property or services (money's worth). Viewed through the tangled actual facts of the problem Roxanne received $42,000 worth of "stuff." She received the benefit of her $40,000 debt to Carl being fully paid off (she no longer has this obligation) plus she received $2,000 worth of Carl's dental services, for a total of $42,000. Turning to Roxanne's AB in the jewelry, her AB is $20,000 which is a carryover AB from her aunt Martha, from whom she received the gift (see question 13, above for a more thorough discussion of AB in property received as a gift).

At this point, Roxanne's gain calculation is simple: her AR of $42,000 less her $20,000 AB results in a realized gain of <u>$22,000</u>.

A word of caution about language used in this question and on exams in general. There are many instances where the common use of a term does not necessarily correspond to its official "tax" counterpart. Labels can be deceiving and do not be fooled by their use in lay terms on an exam. Problems involving what may appear to be income from discharge of indebtedness are fertile ground for tricky questions vis-à-vis terminology. For example, in this question, after receiving the jewelry from Roxanne, "Carl *discharged the debt.*" The lay use of the word *discharge* in our question (to fully pay off a debt) does not correspond to the official "tax" counterpart where "discharge" of debt represents a forgiveness of debt (and prima fascia realization of income).

While not required to answer this question, there is one more tax-related item that is pertinent if we are to consider *all* of the income tax implications of the facts. We indicated that Roxanne effectively *paid* Carl for $2,000 worth of dental services. Discussed in more detail in other questions in this book, this $2,000 would be a qualifying medical care expense for Roxanne for deduction purposes under IRC § 213.

[For more information about barter/exchange transactions, see Reg. § 1.61-1(d); Rev.Rul. 79-24, 1979-1 C.B. 60.]

Answers (a) and (b) are incorrect because for both there was no *discharge of indebtedness,* from an income tax perspective, involved in this problem. Please see the "caution about language" discussion above. **Answer (d) is also incorrect.** While it correctly notes that Roxanne realizes no income from discharge of indebtedness, it incorrectly classifies the $2,000 services she received as some general form of income instead being part of her AR from the disposition of the jewelry.

- **Additional references:** *See* DANIEL Q. POSIN, FEDERAL INCOME TAXATION OF INDIVIDUALS ¶ 4.03 (5th ed. 2000).

15. **The correct answer is (a).** As mentioned in the analysis to the companion question 14, above, Situations involving the exchange, between two parties, of services and/or property, usually result in some confusion among students at first. Although it is a bit obscured in this problem, Carl really did just one thing, that results in the realization of income, for purposes of this question: he rendered services worth $2,000 to Roxanne in exchange for $2,000 of consideration. Separately, from a tax perspective, Roxanne repaid the debt that she owed to Carl.

What is bothersome for students in such exchange transactions, is the lack of cash being received for services rendered or property transferred. Somehow, the resulting income tax consequences seem to be incorrect or unfair. A more thorough discussion of the transaction from Carl's perspective follows. [Please see question 14, immediately preceding this question, for the analysis of the facts and income tax consequences from Roxanne's perspective.]

The transaction from Carl's perspective

Recall how we recast this barter transaction in the analysis of question 14, above, in an essentially equivalent manner involving the transfer of cash back and forth between the parties. We broke down the transaction between Roxanne and Carl into something like this. Carl *buys* the jewelry from Roxanne $42,000 in cash. Roxanne then takes $40,000 of this cash and gives it back to *Carl,* with Carl accepting this money as payment, in full, for the $40,000 Roxanne owed to him (on a personal loan unrelated to his business). Carl then performs $2,000 worth of dental work for Roxanne and she *pays* him $2,000 in cash for the work (this was all the money that she had left after paying off the debt). The economic substance of viewing the transaction in this manner (with cash going back and forth) is the same as given in our facts, but it sometimes helps identify the separate components involved. Either way we look at it, in the end Carl had the debt Roxanne owed to him fully repaid, and Carl received *payment* for his $2,000 worth of dental services.

With respect to Roxanne's repayment of the $40,000 she owed Carl, this does not give rise to any income to Carl. You probably learned early on in your discovery of *gross income* that borrowing money is income to the debtor (as there is no net accession to wealth, or net economic benefit) and similarly, there is no income to the creditor when the amount is repaid. Wh break down the transaction into its component pieces, this is what is happening when Carl accepts the jewelry, in part, as payment for Roxanne's debt.

As for Carl's dental services rendered to Roxanne, early on in classroom discussion of gross income, we discover that gross income need not be in the form of cash. A lawyer, for example, who performs legal work for a client and is paid in cash, has gross income. A lawyer who performs legal work for a client and receives property as payment has gross income equal to the fair market value of the property received. A lawyer who performs legal work for a client and receives a combination of cash and property as payment has gross income equal to the cash plus the fair market value of the property received. A lawyer who performs legal work for a client and receives the client's services as payment (in exchange) has income equal to the value of the services. A lawyer who performs legal work for a client and receives cash, property and the client's services as payment has gross income equal to the cash, the fair market value of the property, and the fair market value of the services. [See Reg. § 1.61-1(d) (compensation received in forms other than in cash).] When an individual performs services and receives "**something**" in exchange, that "something" (or the value thereof) represents gross income. The form of that "something" is generally irrelevant. In our question, Carl rendered $2,000 worth of services and received $2,000 worth of stuff in return: the value of the jewelry in excess of the amount going to pay off the debt.

In summary, Carl has $2,000 of gross income in the form of compensation for his services.

Answer (b) is incorrect because Carl does not have income merely when a debt owed to him is repaid. See the discussion above for more information. **Answers (c) and (d) are incorrect** because they both fail to reflect Carl's income from his services to Roxanne. **Answer (e) is incorrect** because the debt owed to him has been fully repaid.

- **Additional references:** *See* DANIEL Q. POSIN, FEDERAL INCOME TAXATION OF INDIVIDUALS ¶ 2.01 (5th ed. 2000).

16. **The best answer is (c).** We know that the "gross income" net is large, including just about every economic benefit a taxpayer might receive (with, of course, numerous holes for escape through specific statutory exclusions). Just in case there is any question about the inclusion of federal or state unemployment benefits, IRC § 85 specifically provides for their inclusion in gross income. Donald's benefits are, therefore, included in his gross income.

    Answer (a) is incorrect. Modernly, unemployment benefits are included in the recipient's gross income. However, this was not always the case as at one time, unemployment benefits were excluded under the belief that general governmental welfare benefits should not be taxed. **Answer (b) is incorrect** because unemployment compensation does not qualify for exclusion under IRC § 101 as compensation for injuries or sickness. This is distinguished from government *disability* benefits, which may be excludable from gross income. **Answer (d) is incorrect** because there is no such fringe benefit, or other employer/employee related exclusion, applicable to government paid unemployment benefits.

17. **Answer (b) is correct.** As with other questions presented in this book, every time a fact pattern presents a sale of property, the author likes to go through the following analysis:

    1) Does the sale result in a <u>realized</u> gain or loss and if so, what is the <u>amount</u>?
    2) If we have a <u>realized</u> gain or loss, is it <u>recognized</u> (i.e. reportable for income tax purposes)?
    3) If the gain or loss is recognized, is it accorded "capital" gain or loss treatment?

    Donald does realize a $40,000 loss on the sale of his house, the difference between the $360,000 sales price and his basis in the house of $400,000. His basis in the house is his original $400,000 purchase. This $40,000 loss, however, is not recognized pursuant to IRC § 165(c) as Donald used the house for personal purposes (living there as opposed to using it for business or investment purposes). Since Donald's loss is not recognized, its characterization as a "capital loss" is neither relevant nor appropriate. A more comprehensive analysis of this answer follows.

    The first step is determining whether Donald has <u>realized</u> a gain or loss on the sale of the house. For this, we need two basic components: his sales price ("amount realized" or, hereinafter, AR) and his basis in the shares ("adjusted basis or, hereinafter, AB). The difference between the two represents a <u>realized</u> gain or loss. [IRC § 1001(a).] Each of these two components, AR and AB, can present a variety of complex tax issues for exam and real-world tax purposes. The AR side is straightforward in our question, and is his $360,000 sales price. Other questions in this book present more complex issues involving a taxpayer's AR.

The AB component in this problem is also fairly straightforward. The general starting place for determining one's AB is one's cost. [IRC §§ 1011 and 1012.] Our starting, and ending, point is what Donald paid for the house five years ago. The $400,000 Donald originally paid for the property represents his AB. Computing Donald's gain or loss realized from the sale of the house is not a simple matter. His AR (selling price) of $360,000 less his AB of $400,000 results in a realized loss of $40,000.

Now to the second step of our gain/loss analysis: whether Donald's $40,000 loss recognized. IRC § 1001(c) provides that, unless otherwise indicated in the Code, all realized gains and losses are recognized. This would cement the recognition of Donald's loss, if it were not for an "otherwise indicated" Code section, namely IRC § 165. At first glance, the "general rule" in IRC § 165(a) looks to be in Tom's favor allowing a deduction for "any loss sustained during the taxable year . . ." Reading further at IRC § 165(c) we come across an ominous sounding subsection: "Limitation on losses of individuals." In class, this professor refers to this as the "section 165(c) hoop," complete with graphic depictions on the board. Figuratively, the goal is to jump from the "realized" loss side, through the hoop to the land of "recognized" losses. This hoop, however, is more akin to a semi-permeable membrane than an unobstructed open space. We see, in IRC §§ 165(c)(1)-(c)(3), that business losses, investment losses and personal-use "casualty" losses, break on through to the recognized loss side. By default, however, losses from personal-use assets (other than casualty losses) do not make it through this "section 165(c) hoop" and go unrecognized. This explains why, for example, when you sell your personal-use car for a loss (which is almost always the case), the loss is realized but not recognized – i.e., you get no tax benefit from such a loss.

This, then, brings us to Donald's realized loss. While the facts indicate that he had hoped his house would have been a better *investment*, the fact that he used the house as his residence negates any investment intentions. These facts represent a very common misconception about personal residences vis-à-vis their "investment" status for loss recognition. Donald's use of the house as his personal residence relegates it to a personal-use asset, notwithstanding the magnitude or conviction of his accompanying investment intentions. Donald is left, therefore, with a $40,000 realized loss that is <u>not</u> recognized. And, unfortunately for Donald, this is where the answer ends.

Donald's house is a capital asset as defined in IRC § 1221 (capital assets are generally, by definitional default, investment or personal-use assets). This has, however, no relevance to the answer, but it is a correct statement. There is often some confusion with respect to this as Donald's house meets the definition of a capital asset. [IRC § 1221 (capital assets are generally, by definitional default, investment or personal-use assets).] If Donald's house is a capital asset, which it is, then why isn't the loss on the sale thereof a capital loss? The answer to this can be found in the definition of capital losses in IRC §§ 1222(2) or 1222(4). Capital losses are losses from the sale or exchange of a capital asset "if and to the extent that such loss is taken into account in computing taxable income." We hit the IRC § 165(c) barrier with respect to personal-use assets and losses resulting from their sale or exchange are <u>not</u> taken into account in computing taxable income. In class, this professor stresses to students the importance of going "step-by-step" through the above discussed three prong analysis whenever an asset is sold (or exchanged). Students often run into trouble when losses are at issue, and they leapfrog over the "recognition" step two.

Students are often bothered by the lack of symmetry in that gains from the sale of personal-use assets <u>are</u> recognized (must be included in income unless a specific exclusion provision is applicable), but losses from the sale of such assets are not recognized (no tax benefit for these losses). Unfortunately, income tax laws are not always fair.

Answer (a) is incorrect. As discussed above, this is a common misunderstanding dealing with losses from the sale of personal-use assets. As discussed above, Donald's house is, indeed, a capital asset. However, because his realized loss is precluded form recognition by IRC § 165(c), no capital loss results. Capital losses can result only from losses that pass our second step of recognition. Characterization of the loss as either a long-term or short-term capital loss is neither relevant nor appropriate because the loss must first be recognized, which it is not in this case. **Answer (c) is incorrect** because it reflects an incorrect recognition of Donald's loss from the sale of his house. While not particularly relevant, this answer is also incorrect for stating that the house is not a capital asset. **Answer (d) is also incorrect.** While the answer correctly states that Donald's $40,000 loss is not recognized, there is no such provision allowing him to increase the basis in any new house by the amount of unrecognized loss from the sale of this house. Donald's unrecognized loss is just "gone" with no tax benefits (present, past or future) resulting therefrom. **Answer (e) is incorrect** because a correct answer (b) is presented.

- **Additional references:** *See* DANIEL Q. POSIN, FEDERAL INCOME TAXATION OF INDIVIDUALS ¶¶ 4.03, 4.04(1), 4.04(2) (5th ed. 2000).

18. **Answer (d) is correct.** There are two major parts to this question: 1) *which* of Donald's expenditures give rise to deductions, and 2) *where or how* any such deductions are allowed for purposes of computing his taxable income. As to which of Donald's expenditures give rise to deductions, IRC § 164 is the key section for addressing the taxes paid, and IRC § 212 is our primary focus for the CPA fees paid. We will conclude that Donald is entitled to deduct, as part of his "itemized deductions," the $1,000 paid to his CPA to the extent that the aggregate of it and any other "miscellaneous" itemized deductions exceed 2% of his adjusted gross income (AGI), and the $750 in State income taxes. However the $2,000 that he paid in Federal taxes will not give rise to a deduction for income tax purposes.

As indicated, IRC § 164 is the delimiting section for deducting taxes paid. State income taxes are among those listed as deductible (IRC § 164(a)(3)), so the $750 in state income taxes paid is deductible. However, <u>no</u> deduction is allowed for *federal income taxes* paid. Federal income tax is not among those listed as deductible in IRC § 164, and, just to be sure, IRC § 275 specifically denies any deduction of federal income taxes. The $2,000 Donald paid in federal income taxes are, therefore, not deductible.

The $1,000 in CPA fees paid by Donald for assistance with his federal and state income tax audits also qualifies as a deductible expense pursuant to IRC § 212. IRC § 212 allows for deductions for ordinary and necessary expenses paid in connection with, "1) the production or collection of income; 2) the management, conservation, or maintenance of property held for the production of income; or 3) *the determination, collection or refund of any tax.*" [IRC § 212 (emphasis added).] The $1,000 Donald paid qualifies under the last (the third) category listed in IRC § 212. Other common examples qualifying here include tax preparation fees (including annual personal tax preparation software) and amounts paid for personal tax advice.

Now that we have identified that the $750 and $1,000 Donald paid in state income taxes and CPA fees, respectively, are deductible, the next issue is where and how they are deducted in computing taxable income. This is necessary to distinguish answers (c), (d) and possibly (e).

In very broad terms, there are two camps of deductions for purposes of computing taxable income. There are deductions that are subtracted from *gross income* to arrive at an intermediary point called *adjusted gross income* (AGI). These are commonly referred to as "above the line" deductions, with AGI representing "the line." The other camp of deductions is comprised of those that are subtracted from AGI to arrive at *taxable income*. These are commonly referred to as "below the line" deductions. The components making up this camp of *below the line* deductions can include something called the "standard deduction" or, in the alternative, a group of deductions called "itemized deductions." In addition, one or more personal exemption deductions may be included in *below the line* deductions. [For more information about how this all fits together, please see IRC § 62, Appendix A, and other questions in this book.]

Donald's deductible state income tax and CPA fees are part of the group of deductions known collectively as "itemized deductions." This *itemized deduction* grouping is comprised of various types of deductions including certain medical care expenses (IRC § 213), certain interest and tax expenses (IRC §§ 163 and 164), charitable contributions (IRC § 170), and others. Donald's $750 in state income taxes, allowed by IRC § 164 as discussed above, fits clearly within this *itemized deduction* group. One sub-group of *itemized deductions* is a specific category referred to as "miscellaneous itemized deductions." This sub-group of *miscellaneous itemized deductions* contains IRC § 212 expenses (other than those related to rentals or royalties which is not the case here). While not at issue in this question, this sub-group of *miscellaneous itemized deductions* also contains unreimbursed employee IRC § 162 business expenses. The significance of this sub-group of deductions is that, pursuant to IRC § 67, they are deductible (includible with the rest of the regular *itemized deductions*), only to the extent that they (in the aggregate) exceed 2% of the individual's AGI. Donald's CPA fees, as IRC § 212 expenses, fit into this category of *miscellaneous itemized deductions* and this completes the answer to this question.

While law students, for the most part, are not enamored with the thought of looking at actual income tax forms, they can, as in this case, present a very good visual depiction of how income and deductions fit together. "Schedule A" of the basic individual tax Form 1040 is a very good visual representation of the entire "itemized deduction" group and it even shows the "miscellaneous itemized deduction" sub-group complete with the 2% of AGI floor calculation.

The diagram, below, depicts the major components in computing taxable income as well as an expanded depiction of the most common "itemized deductions."

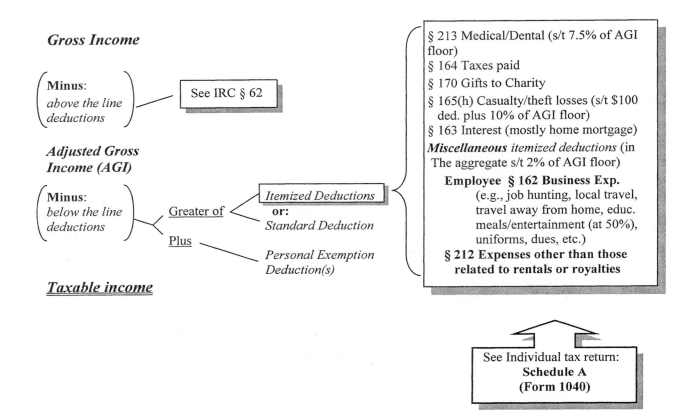

While not part of this question, it should be noted that for certain high-income individuals, the aforementioned group of *itemized deductions* is subject to possible reductions as income exceeds certain amounts. [IRC §68.] At least one question in this book addresses this issue.

Answer (a) is incorrect because, as discussed above, the state income taxes and the CPA fees do give rise to possible deductions. **Answer (b) is incorrect** because while it properly identifies the state income tax as a deductible expense, it fails to recognize the CPA fees as also giving rise to a deduction. **Answer (c) is incorrect** because while it properly identifies Donald's deductible expenditures, it fails to recognize the special characterization of the CPA fees as a *miscellaneous itemized deduction* and the 2% of AGI floor applicable to this sub-group of itemized deductions. **Answer (e) is incorrect** because the $2,000 federal income tax Donald paid does not give rise to a deduction for federal income tax purpose.

- **Additional references:** *See* DANIEL Q. POSIN, FEDERAL INCOME TAXATION OF INDIVIDUALS ¶¶ 7.01(1), 7.01(2), 7.02 (5th ed. 2000).

19. **The best answer is (b).** The Parking provided to Mark by his employer is excludable from his gross income up to $185 per month (for 2002) as a "qualified transportation" fringe benefit. Please note that this question is *year-specific* (for 2002), but can easily be adapted to other years, or be asked in a more generic non-year-specific form.

It is clear that Mark's free parking at work results in his receipt of a financial benefit or net accession to wealth that will be included in gross income unless it is specifically excluded by some provision. A host of employee fringe benefits are excluded pursuant to IRC § 132, and employer provided parking is among them. One such excludable fringe benefit is "Qualified parking" (a sub-part of the "qualified transportation" fringe benefits). [IRC § 132(f).] *Qualified Parking* includes employer provided parking provided to an employee on or near the employer's business premises, as is provided to Mark in our question. [IRC § 132(f)(5)(C).] There is, however, a statutory dollar limit to the amount of this qualified parking fringe benefit; which is listed in IRC § 132(f)(2)(B) as $175 per month (of parking benefit received). As with many dollar amounts listed in the statute, the monthly dollar limit of excludable parking value is "indexed" for inflation. [IRC § 132(f)(6).] The maximum value of parking provided by an employer that can be excluded under this provision for *2002* is $185. The monthly value of parking provided in excess of this amount (or the appropriate amount for the year in question) represents income.

Unlike some of the other excludable fringe benefits of IRC § 132, an employer can provide the qualified parking fringe benefit (part of the qualified transportation fringe benefit) to employees on a discriminatory basis (in favor of highly compensated employees). Therefore, the parking provided to Mark by his employer is excludable up to $185 per month (for 2002) regardless of whether this benefit is offered to other employees.

Students familiar with other IRC § 132 fringe benefits may question whether employer provided parking (at the work location) may be considered an excludable "working condition fringe" – an expense, had the employee paid for it would have given rise to a IRC § 162 business deduction. This, however, is generally not the case as parking at one's place of work (as an employee or a self-employed individual) is considered part of nondeductible personal "commuting" expenses. It is interesting to note that at one time (prior to 1993) the "qualified transportation" category of excludable fringe benefits did not exist, but employer provided parking was included in a special category of excludable "working condition" fringes.

Answer (a) is incorrect because it fails to recognize the existence of the qualified parking/transportation fringe benefit under IRC § 132. **Answers (c) and (d) are incorrect** because the qualified parking/transportation fringe benefit can be offered on a discriminatory basis (in favor of highly compensated employees). **Answer (e) is incorrect** because a correct answer (b) is presented.

- **Additional references:** *See* DANIEL Q. POSIN, FEDERAL INCOME TAXATION OF INDIVIDUALS ¶ 2.02 (5th ed. 2000).

20. **Answer (c) is correct.** This question, except for one critical date in the facts, is identical to another question appearing elsewhere in this book. The answer, however, is quite different with Tom's realized gain equal to $2,000.

Determining Tom's realized gain or loss in this question requires us to identify two basic components: his sales price ("amount realized" or, hereinafter, AR) and his basis in the watch ("adjusted basis or, hereinafter, AB). The difference between the two represents realized gain or loss. [IRC § 1001(a).] Each of these two components, AR and AB, can present a variety of complex tax issues for exam and real-world tax purposes. The AR side is straightforward in our question, and is his $23,000 sales price. Other questions in this book present more complex issues involving a taxpayer's AR. The AB component is the more challenging component of this question.

While a taxpayer's cost is normally the starting point for determination of one's basis in property (IRC §§ 1011 and 1012), when property is received as a gift, as is the case here, there really is no "cost" to the taxpayer. The seemingly logical result of a zero basis is neither desirable nor, thankfully, appropriate. IRC § 1015 provides us with the rules for determining a donee's AB in property received as a gift. The general rule for most gifts is that the donee takes the donor's AB in the property, or what is commonly referred to as a "carryover" AB. In Tom's case, this would be Tom's Aunt's original $18,000 cost. This is Tom's starting point in determining his AB.

We say "starting point" because there was a gift tax paid in connection with the 1975 gift to Tom. Discussion of gift taxes is beyond the scope of this book, and most basic federal income tax courses. Suffice it to say that a gift tax is based on the value of the property transferred and the tax is an obligation of the donor/transferor. It is a given, in our facts, that Tom's Aunt incurred and paid a $7,000 gift tax on the 1975 gift to Tom. While the study of gift taxes is beyond our scope, their effect on a donee/transferee's AB is not. IRC § 1015(d) provides for a "gift tax paid adjustment" to AB (an increase to AB). The method of calculating this positive, and favorable, adjustment varies depending on when the gift was made, with the critical date (of the gift) being December 31, 1976. The gift to Tom was in <u>1975</u> and the "gift tax paid adjustment" rules for pre-1977 gifts are contained in § 1015(d)(1). Basically, the donee/transferee is entitled to add to his or her AB, the gift tax paid on the transfer with a limit that the result cannot exceed the fair market value of the property at the time of the gift. Adding the $7,000 gift tax to Tom's carryover AB of $18,000 equals $25,000. However, this is more than the $21,000 value at the time of the gift in 1975, so <u>Tom's AB is limited to $21,000</u>. The gift tax paid adjustment to AB for gifts made after December 31, 1976, is the subject of at least one question presented elsewhere in this book.

The calculation of Tom's gain is now a simple matter. His AR of $23,000 less his $21,000 AB results in <u>a realized gain of $2,000</u>. While not the subject of this question, issues of gain <u>recognition</u> and <u>characterization</u> (i.e., capital gain materials) are related testable material. For information purposes, Tom's $2,000 gain would be recognized and characterized as a "long-term capital gain." Please see other questions presented in this book addressing the recognition and characterization of gains and losses.

Answer (a) is incorrect. This answer utilizes the correct pre-1977 "gift tax paid adjustment" to the degree that the $7,000 gift tax is added to Tom's carryover AB. However it fails to limit the resulting AB to the $21,000 fair market value at the time of the gift. Incorrectly ignoring this AB limitation, Tom's AB would have been $25,000 ($18,000 carryover AB plus $7,000 gift tax paid adjustment). Incorrectly using this as Tom's basis results in a ($2,000) loss when subsequently sold for $23,000. **Answer (b) is incorrect** because it utilizes the "gift tax paid adjustment" rules for post-1976 gifts found in IRC § 1015(d)(6). An analysis of these rules is presented elsewhere in this book. **Answer (c) is incorrect** because it fails to reflect any "gift tax paid adjustment," rendering Tom's AB in the watch as a straight "carryover" of $18,000. **Answer (d) is incorrect** because a correct response (c) is presented.

- **Additional references:** *See* DANIEL Q. POSIN, FEDERAL INCOME TAXATION OF INDIVIDUALS ¶¶ 4.01, 4.03 (5th ed. 2000).

21. **Answer (a) is the most likely result.** From all indications, Taylor dearly loved her grandfather, Grant, and his death is a sad loss for Taylor. One hates to think of income taxes at moments like these, but we must for purposes of this analysis. Taylor, with the receipt of the XYZ shares has realized a financial benefit or net accession to wealth, the general measuring rod inclusion in the broadly defined definition of gross income. There is, however, a specific exclusion section in IRC § 102 that is most likely applicable here. This section's general rule provides for a very beneficial exclusion from income of amounts received as gifts, bequests, devises, and inheritances. [IRC § 102(a).] Grant's devise of the XYZ shares to

Taylor in his will seems to fit within this exclusion and, is the most likely result in this question.

An excludable devise/bequest is similar to excludable inter vivos gifts in that the primary motivation by the transferor is donative in nature. The language of Grant's devise raises the possibility (at least for exam discussion purposes) that perhaps the devise was made as payment for services that Taylor had rendered to her grandfather. The fact that property or money comes from a decedent by way of a will does not assure exclusion status. For example, if the facts were such that Taylor performed services with a determinable value for Grant, an unrelated individual, and Grant promised to pay her for them and did so prior to his death, this would result in compensation income to Taylor. The alternative situation, that the promised payment for her services came through Grant's will as a devise, does not change the character of the income to Taylor. In other words, there is no magical exclusion merely because property or cash is received from a decedent. Having said that, statements of devises given as a "thank you" or "in appreciation of" or like sentiments, do not characterize the devise as payment for services. Rather, as it most likely is the case in our question, such statements are more general statements of affection and appreciation, and absent more concrete evidence of a contractual situation, the devise is excludable pursuant to IRC § 102.

Answers (b), (c), and (d) are all incorrect because to some degree all of these answers incorrectly classify the excludable devise to Taylor as income.

- **Additional references:** *See* DANIEL Q. POSIN, FEDERAL INCOME TAXATION OF INDIVIDUALS ¶¶ 3.08(1), 3.08(4) (5th ed. 2000).

22.   **The correct answer is (c).** While a taxpayer's cost is normally the starting point for determination of one's basis in property (IRC §§ 1011 and 1012), when property is received as a bequest/devise, as is the case here, there really is no "cost" to the taxpayer. The seemingly logical result of a zero basis is neither desirable nor, thankfully, appropriate. IRC § 1014(a)(1) provides the *general* rule that the basis of property acquired from a decedent shall be the property's fair market value at the date of the decedent's death. Note that is *general* fair market value basis rule of IRC § 1014(a)(1) is commonly referred to as the "step-up" in basis for property received from a decedent. This is because we would like to think, or at least hope, that property has appreciated in the hands of the decedent and the testamentary beneficiary gets, as his or her basis, a new "higher" or "stepped-up" basis. For appreciated property, the general rule of this Code provision is a great tax savings device that effectively makes, for income tax purposes, the unrealized appreciation and gain in the decedent's hands evaporate. Utilizing this *general* rule of § 1014(a)(1) it would appear that Taylor's basis in the XYZ shares received as

a devise from her grandfather, Grant, would be their $50,000 fair market value at Grant's death.

Unfortunately, Taylor innocently falls into a special provision designed to prevent a manipulation of basis among taxpayers in certain situations. For discussion purposes, let us assume that Taylor did not transfer the stock to her grandfather with the hope that he would use it for his benefit. Rather, let us assume that she knew Grant would not live that long and that he would most likely devise, back to her, anything that she gave to him before his death. Looking at her meager $15,000 cost basis in the XYZ shares, she comes up with a rather morbid plan: give the shares to her dying grandfather and when she gets them back at his death (by devise or other similar means), voila, she has a "new and improved" "stepped-up" basis of $50,000. To prevent this sort of basis manipulation (yes, people actually do such things) IRC § 1014(e) was enacted. Basically, this provision says that if appreciated property was acquired by the decedent by gift within one year of his or her death, *and* the property (at the decedent's death) goes back to the donor who made the gift (or the donor's spouse), then the beneficiary is treated as receiving an inter vivos gift. The general basis rules for gifts result in a "carry-over" basis. The result is that the original donor, trying to get a stepped-up basis, ends up having the same basis with which he or she started.

anti-abuse exception

Now back to our situation. While Taylor's gift to her grandfather hardly smells of such a devious plot to get a stepped-up basis in the shares, the gift to Grant was within one year of his death, and she did get the shares back at his death (by intestate succession). This special provision in IRC § 1014(e) is applied notwithstanding the motives behind Taylor's transfer to Grant or the fact that Taylor received the shares back through intestate succession. This provision does apply to Taylor, and her basis in the XYZ shares received from Grant is $15,000 (her original cost).

Answer (a) is incorrect because, as discussed above, the general fair market value basis rule for property received from a decedent, does not apply to this set of facts. **Answer (b) is also incorrect.** When Taylor made a gift of the shares to her grandfather, he took, as his basis, the carryover $15,000 basis from Taylor (pursuant to the general gift rules of IRC § 1015). Grant's basis in the shares was not $40,000, the fair market value at the time of the gift. Since Taylor takes Grant's basis on his death (because of the application of IRC § 1014(e) to these facts), her basis is $15,000. **Answer (d) is incorrect** because a correct response (c) is presented.

- **Additional references:** *See* DANIEL Q. POSIN, FEDERAL INCOME TAXATION OF INDIVIDUALS ¶ 4.03(2)(e) (5th ed. 2000).

New Law Caution. The Economic Growth and Tax Relief Reconciliation Act of 2001 ("2001 Tax Act"), signed into law in 2001, made numerous changes throughout the Internal Revenue Code. The 2001 Tax Act is rather complex with many of its provisions phasing-in and phasing-out over a period of many years. As of this writing, the above described basis rules of IRC § 1014 are repealed with respect to decedents dying after December 31, 2009. [IRC § 1014(f).] The change, with limited exceptions, is basically to a "carryover" basis rule, similar to that applicable to inter vivos gifts in IRC § 1015. [See IRC § 1022 (effective for years after 2009).] The limited exceptions provide step-up basis for a certain dollar amount given to certain individuals. This change was enacted to coincide with the 2001 Tax Act's abolishment of the federal estate tax effective for years after 2009. IRC § 1022 (effective for years after 2009) contains a provision similar to current IRC § 1014(e) with an extended gift window. Whether these changes will come to pass without change in the intervening years is unknown as of this writing. However, as discussed in the preface to this book, the 2001 Tax Act, as enacted, contains a rather unique "sunset clause" that could, unless amended, make the above described 2010 changes evaporate in 2011, leaving us with the current IRC § 1014 rules (including § 1014(e)).

23.   **The correct answer is (c).** IRC § 61 defines gross income as "all income from whatever source derived." From your initial study of gross income's scope, you probably found it to be broadly defined, including the taxpayer's receipt of some net economic benefit or net accession to wealth. In class, you also discover that gross income is also not limited to the receipt of cash. Is Jonathan receiving net economic benefit from his Nevada corporation by its purchase of assets used by Jonathan for personal purposes and its payment of his personal expenses? The answer is yes.

For assets purchased by the corporation that Jonathan uses for personal purposes, he has income equal to the fair value of such use. For example, if his corporation purchases a house and he lives in it without paying rent to the corporation, he will have income equal to the fair rental value of the house. Similarly, if his corporation pays for his personal expenses, he will have income equal to the amount that his corporation paid on his behalf.

The confusion that surrounds this area is based on the belief that the corporation and the sole shareholder (and employee in this case) are really the same person. The concept of gross income for tax purposes does not go so far as to impute income to one's own use of assets. For example, when you live in your own house, you are not required to assign a fair rental value to such use and include it in your gross income for income tax purposes. In effect that is what many people believe to be the case in situations such as Jonathan's. Sure, technically the corporation may own the assets and pay the bills, but since Jonathan owns 100% of the corporation, isn't it merely Jonathan paying for such things? Unfortunately for Jonathan, the "technical" fact that the corporation and Jonathan (the individual) are two distinct entities, is a distinction that is not ignored for income tax purposes. Jonathan's wholly owned Nevada corporation *is* a person or entity that is separate and distinct from Jonathan for income tax purposes. [See *Dean v. Comm'r*, 187 F.2d 1019 (3rd Cir.1951).] For purposes of this question, Jonathan's corporation could just as well be any other corporation, one in which Jonathan has no ownership interests. When an employer provides an employee with "in-kind" economic benefits, their value nonetheless represents income. [Reg. § 1.61-1(d).] While certain employer-provided "fringe benefits" are excludable from income, these excludable benefits do not include the non-work related personal items in this question.

Answer (a) is incorrect because Jonathan will also have income associated with the personal-use of assets purchased (and owned) by the corporation. **Answer (b) is incorrect** for the reasons discussed above. **Answer (d) is incorrect** because the state of incorporation and domicile of its owner is irrelevant to the income tax consequences discussed here.

- **Additional references:** *See* DANIEL Q. POSIN, FEDERAL INCOME TAXATION OF INDIVIDUALS ¶¶ 2.01, 2.04(3) (5th ed. 2000).

24. **The correct answer is (e).** The author apologizes for another of the dreaded "none of the above" answers. The Economic Growth and Tax Relief Reconciliation Act of 2001 (the "2001 Tax Act"), which was signed into law in 2001, made numerous changes in tax law. Added by the 2001 Tax Act are IRC §§ 132(a)(7) and 132(m), providing for a new excludable fringe benefit for employer provided retirement planning services. But for some exclusion section, Marshall's receipt of this economic benefit would constitute gross income. [IRC § 61(a)(1).] IRC § 132 provides a host of excludable fringe benefits (many of which are explored elsewhere in this book). As indicated, the 2001 Tax Act added an excludable fringe benefit specifically covering the retirement related services that Marshall received in this question.

This new excludable fringe benefit is defined in IRC § 132(m) and generally covers "any retirement planning advice or information provided to an employee and his spouse by an employer maintaining a qualified employer plan." [IRC § 132(m)(1).] Suffice it to say that the 401(k) plan in which Marshall is a participant, is a "qualified employer plan." The House Report explaining this new provision of the law states, in part, that; "[t]he exclusion is not limited to information regarding the qualified plan, and, thus, for example, applies to advice and information regarding retirement income planning for an individual and his or her spouse and how the employer's plan fits into the individual's overall retirement income plan. On the other hand, the exclusion does not apply to services that may be related to retirement planning, such as tax preparation, accounting, legal or brokerage services." [H.R. CONF. REP. 107-84.]

Similar to some, but not all, of the other fringe benefit exclusions listed in IRC § 132, this new provision is subject to certain nondiscrimination rules (the availability cannot favor "highly compensated" employees). [IRC § 132(m)(2).] The retirement planning services provided by Marshall's employer is available on a nondiscriminatory basis and, therefore, the value of Marshall's retirement planning services that he received is excludable from gross income.

Answer (a) is not the best answer. Prior to enactment of this new excludable fringe benefit, there was some thought that the employer provided retirement planning services might be excludable as a "de minimis" fringe benefit. Basically, excludable de minimis fringe benefits are property transfers and services provided to employees that are so small as to make accounting for them unreasonable or administratively impracticable." [IRC § 132(e).] The aforementioned House Report refers to this possibility. Indeed, services of relatively minor value could qualify as a de minimis fringe. However, services received that are of substantial value, as the $800 value of services that Marshall received in our question, would likely not qualify as a de minimis fringe benefit.

Answer (b) is close but, is also not the best answer. The retirement planning services that Marshall received might also be excludable under another Code provision: IRC § 127 educational assistance programs. Basically, if certain requirements are met, up to $5,250 of employer provided educational assistance can be excluded from an employee's gross income each year. The specific rules of this section are far beyond the scope of this problem and although the services provided to Marshall in this problem are not typical of those covered by this section, the exclusion under § 127 would, nonetheless, most likely be excludable. The aforementioned House Report also refers to the possible application of IRC § 127 to employer provided retirement planning advice. The reason why this answer (b) is not the best answer lies in the language of this answer: IRC § 127 is not the only statutory provision excluding the benefit Marshall received. In fact, the new IRC § 132 fringe discussed above is more directly on point regarding the source of Marshall's exclusion.

Answer (c) is also not correct. The "working condition fringe" benefit is explained in IRC § 132(d). This excluded fringe benefit is basically any benefit paid for by the employer, that had the employee paid for it, would have given rise to a IRC § 162 business deduction. A typical example of a working condition fringe is a law firm (employer) paying an associate lawyer's (employee) state bar association dues. This benefit would be excludable from the associate lawyer's gross income because such employee would have been entitled to a business deduction had he or she paid such association dues. While business deductions are the source of other questions in this book, had Marshall paid for the retirement planning services himself, it probably would not have given rise to a business deduction. Again, beyond the scope of this question, such a payment by Marshall probably would have given rise to an IRC § 212 investment related expense deduction. However, the working condition fringe exclusion does cover "would have been deductible expenses" pursuant to IRC § 212.

Answer (d) is not correct because, as discussed above, we have at least one exclusion section applicable to the retirement planning services that Marshall received.

25. **Answer (d) is correct.** Interest on debt obligations of the U.S. is, despite some common belief to the contrary, generally included in gross income for federal income tax purposes. U.S. Savings Bonds (Series EE) are U.S. obligations and the interest earned on them is also included in gross income, barring any specific exclusion thereof. There is a limited and rather narrow statutory exclusion provision regarding U.S. EE Savings Bond interest where the bond proceeds are used for certain education purposes. This is IRC § 135 and may apply to Ara depending on various factors discussed below.

The method and timing of reporting such interest for tax purposes is a bit different from typical interest bearing instruments. United States Savings Bonds (Series EE) are issued in various "face amount" denominations (e.g. a $50 U.S. Savings Bond) but are purchased at a fraction of this face amount (usually at one-half the face amount). These bonds *do* pay interest, but not in the normal form of a stated interest rate on money invested (as with a savings account at a bank). Rather, the interest accrues on the original discounted purchase price. Much to the disappointment of many a young person receiving a U.S. Savings Bond from his or her grandmother, the bond cannot be "cashed in" right away with the receipt of the face amount. One must wait many years until the bond "matures" to receive its face value. These years until the bond's maturity is the period when the interest accrues on the bond, bringing its value up from the original discounted purchase price to the face amount. This difference, therefore, represents interest, and it is taxable interest for U.S. income tax purposes.

Unless an individual affirmatively elects to report, as interest, the annual increases in such a bond's value, the recognition of interest is deferred until the bond matures (or is redeemed or otherwise disposed of sooner). [IRC § 454(a).] This deferred interest is all of the interest earned on the bond, which is measured by the difference between its face amount and its original discounted purchase price. One can "cash in" or redeem U.S. Savings Bonds prior to their maturity, as is the case with Ara in our problem. Of course, something less than the face value of the bond is received, but the difference between the amount received and the original discounted purchase price still represents taxable interest (at the time of redemption unless an election is made to report the annual accrued interest).

IRC § 135 provides that if the proceeds from "qualified U.S. Savings Bonds" are used for "qualified higher education expenses" then the interest component of the proceeds will be excluded from the taxpayer's gross income as long as the taxpayer's income does not exceed certain levels. The term "qualified U.S. savings bonds means U.S. Series EE Savings Bonds issued after 1989, to an individual 24 years of age or older. [IRC § 135(c)(1).] The bonds that Ara redeemed meet this definition (and Ara purchased them when he was 26 years old).

IRC § 135 next requires that the proceeds of a qualifying bond be used for "qualified higher education expenses." Qualified higher education expenses means "tuition and fees for the enrollment or attendance of" the taxpayer, the taxpayer's spouse, or any dependent of the taxpayer (whose *personal exemption deduction* can be claimed by the taxpayer pursuant to IRC § 151) at an "eligible educational institution." *Eligible educational institutions* include most colleges, universities, community (junior) colleges, and vocational and nursing schools. [IRC § 135(c)(3).] Ara's vocational school tuition should qualify. It should be noted that the exclusion under IRC § 135 is based upon the full proceeds from the Bonds redeemed being used for qualifying expenses, and not merely the "interest" component of the bond proceeds. The statute allows for a potential pro-rata exclusion based upon the percentage of the bonds used for qualified purposes. [IRC § 135(b)(1).] While not applicable here, it should be noted that courses involving sports, games or hobbies do not qualify unless as part of a degree program. [IRC § 135(c)(2)(B).]

Unfortunately, the use of this IRC § 135 exclusion is limited for individuals whose adjusted gross income (AGI), as modified, exceeds a certain threshold amount. [IRC § 135(b)(2).] The level of AGI (as modified) at which this "phase-out" of the exclusion begins varies depending on one's filing status and changes every year (the thresholds are indexed for inflation). Our question does not involve dollar amounts, but for information purposes, the threshold level at which this phase-out begins is, for 2002, $57,600 for most single individuals, and $86,400 for most married individuals filing a joint return. The mechanism for the actual reduction of the exclusion is a bit complex, but the IRC § 135 exclusion is completely eliminated, for 2002, for taxpayer's with AGI (as modified) reaches $72,600 or $116,400 for single and joint filers, respectively.

Therefore, Ara may be entitled to exclude the otherwise taxable U.S. Savings Bond interest if he uses the entire proceeds from their redemption for his vocational school tuition, and his income is below the phase-out threshold applicable to him.

It should be noted that there are many other education-related benefits provided by the Code and there are numerous rules relating to their interaction that may affect anticipated benefits.

Answer (a) is incorrect because it fails to recognize the potential exclusion of this interest pursuant to IRC § 135. **Answer (b) is incorrect** because interest from obligations of the U.S. is generally taxable. **Answer (c) is incorrect** because full exclusion under IRC § 135 requires use of the full <u>proceeds</u> from the bond redemption for qualifying educational costs, not just the interest component of the bond proceeds. **Answer (e) is incorrect** because the IRC § 135 exclusion provision is not that restrictive.

ANSWER KEY
EXAM V

1.   **The correct answer is (c).** Pursuant to IRC § 1011(a), the adjusted basis in property (hereinafter AB) is the "cost basis" of the property adjusted for certain items. The cost basis is, in most instances, simply the cost of the property. [IRC § 1012.] In the present case, the $400,000 Tom and Edna originally paid for the property four years ago represents their cost basis, the starting point for determining their AB, of the property. Adjustments increasing the basis of their property resulted from the major additions and improvements they made to the property. Similar to the purchase of their house, their AB in the house is increased by the $110,000 cost of such additions/improvements. [IRC § 1016(a); Reg. § 1.1016-2(a).] The resulting AB is, therefore, $510,000 ($400,000 plus $110,000).

The AB of property is important for many reasons including, as is ultimately the case in this series of questions, determining the amount of gain or (loss) resulting from a subsequent sale of the property. Because gain or (loss) is generally computed by subtracting the AB from the sales price (or amount realized, AR), the greater the AB, the lower the potential taxable gain (or greater the potential deductible loss) results. For "real-world" purposes, it is important, therefore, to keep track of improvements made to one's house and other property. This professor always suggests to students to keep a receipt box or drawer where one can toss receipts for home, or other property, related expenditures. The new patio cover, the landscaping project, the new kitchen fixtures, and the like are examples of expenditures that may increase one's AB in property. It is surprising how much of those weekend visits to the home improvement store can effect the AB in one's house or other property. While not pertinent to this question, issues can arise as to what constitutes an improvement versus expenditures for normal maintenance and repairs that do not increase the AB in property.

Answer (a) is incorrect because it does not reflect the addition to the AB of the house resulting from the improvements. **Answer (b) is incorrect** because the increase to the house's AB is the cost of the improvements and not the increase in value because of the improvements (either more or less, as is the case here, than their cost). While not at issue in this question, there is one situation, where the cost of improvements is medically related, where the value added by the improvement is a factor. Please see other questions in this book dealing with that medical related issue. **Answer (d) is incorrect** because a correct answer (c) is presented.

- **Additional references:** *See* DANIEL Q. POSIN, FEDERAL INCOME TAXATION OF INDIVIDUALS ¶ 4.03(2) (5th ed. 2000).

2.   **Answer (c) is the best response.** The couple's borrowing of the $110,000 does not, in and of itself, represent a taxable event. No income is realized from borrowing money, as there is no net accession to wealth (a general prerequisite for

income realization). [See *Comm'r v. Glenshaw Glass Co.*, 348 U.S. 426, 75 S.Ct. 473 (1955).] If borrowed funds are not repaid and the debt is discharged in whole or in part, then there is a net accession to wealth and, with some exceptions, income is recognized. This latter point, however, is not an issue in this question.

As for the deduction of interest paid on this $110,000 loan, we must turn to IRC § 163 dealing with deductions for interest paid. As discussed below, the interest the couple pays with respect to this loan is deductible "qualified residence" interest, with this entire loan deemed to be "acquisition indebtedness." A more thorough explanation follows.

IRC § 163(a) provides a simple and broad sounding deduction for interest stating, in part: "There shall be allowed as a deduction all interest paid . . . within the taxable year on indebtedness." The Tax Reform Act of 1986 introduced subsection (h), located quite some written distance from the general allowance for interest deductions of subsection (a). IRC § 163(h) starts out deceptively, and unfavorably, simple by stating, in part: "In the case of a taxpayer other than a corporation, no deduction shall be allowed . . . for personal interest paid . . . during the taxable year." The definition of "personal" interest, which is not deductible, if found in IRC § 163(h)(2) and takes the form of a negative definition – personal interest is interest "other than" those listed in subparagraphs (A) through (F). The key, therefore, to finding interest that <u>is</u> deductible, is to fit within one of these specified categories of what does <u>not</u> constitute nondeductible personal interest. One such category of interest that is <u>not</u> considered personal interest is "qualified residence interest." [IRC § 163(h)(2)(D).]

Qualified residence interest is addressed in IRC §§ 163(h)(3) and (h)(4). To obtain deductible qualified residence interest status, a taxpayer must have two things:
> ➤ A "qualified residence"
> ➤ The property type of indebtedness associated with such qualified residence.

A <u>qualified residence</u> includes the taxpayer's principal residence and one other residence (e.g., a vacation home) that meets certain requirements. [IRC § 163(h)(4)(A).] A principal residence can include the typical house (as our couple's in this question), a condominium, townhouse, co-op, etc. A principal residence can consist of a boat, trailer, motor home, or similar vehicle if, generally, they contain sleeping, eating and bathroom facilities. While the determination of one's principal residence is usually not at issue for most people, there are (i.e., your professor can discuss) situations that present more of a challenge. The "one other residence" as a qualified residence for purposes of deductible qualified residence can present its own host of issues, some involving rather complex statutory rules. Some of these issues are presented in other questions in this book.

There are two proper types of indebtedness recognized by the statute in this area: "acquisition indebtedness" and "home equity indebtedness." It is important to recognize that the statute requires that either of these two types of loans must be secured by the applicable qualified residence in order to qualify. [IRC § 163(h)(3)(A).] The couple's loan, in our question, is secured by a qualified residence (their house).

Acquisition indebtedness is defined in IRC § 163(h)(3)(B), and is fairly straightforward for most taxpayers. Acquisition loans are money borrowed to **acquire, construct, or substantially improve** a qualified residence. Our couple's loan in this question was used to "substantially improve" their qualified residence (their house) and, therefore, constitutes acquisition indebtedness. While not at issue in this question, it should be noted that loans used to replace existing "acquisition indebtedness" (e.g., a straight refinancing), takes on the character of the loan being replaced and itself becomes acquisition indebtedness.

At this point, we are close to concluding the analysis of our facts. So far, the interest on Tom and Edna's $110,000 loan appears to be deductible under § 163 as qualified residence interest (their house as a qualified residence and the loan secured thereby qualifying as acquisition indebtedness). There is one last issue to consider that is not particularly relevant to the majority of taxpayers, but is of concern to certain taxpayers and certain housing markets in the country including this professor's Malibu, California law school location. There is a $1 million cap on the amount of loans qualifying as acquisition indebtedness. [IRC § 163(h)(3)(B)(ii).] This means that for acquisition loans, only the interest on the first $1 million of such loans is deductible here. This $1 million cap is on the amount of loans and not a much larger $1 million cap on deductible interest. It should also be noted that this $1 million acquisition indebtedness cap is in the aggregate – $1 million total for all acquisition loans for the principal and one other qualifying residence (not a $1 million cap for each acquisition loan or a separate $1 million acquisition loan cap for each of two possible qualifying residences). Tom and Edna have no problem with this acquisition debt limit in our facts as the $110,000, given as their only loan, is well below $1 million. All of the interest our couple pays, therefore, is deductible qualified residence interest.

Home equity indebtedness is not at issue in this question, but is addressed here to better understand the subject, and to clear up any confusion that might exist regarding Tom and Edna's loan in this question. Home equity indebtedness is defined in IRC § 163(h)(3)(C) and, typically, is money borrowed against an existing qualified residence (secured by the qualified residence) that is used for purposes other than substantial improvements to the qualified residence. Advertisements for "tapping the equity" in one's house to buy a new car or boat, go on a vacation, pay off credit card debts, student loans or consolidate all those existing bills, strike at the center of what "home equity indebtedness" is all about. Borrowing money, using your house, for such things as buying a car can generate deductible interest while interest paid on a regular car loan from a bank, credit union or automotive financing companies will generally be nondeductible "personal" interest. A "real-world" note of caution, however, is that home equity debt puts one's residence at risk if one defaults on payments on a loan used, for example, to buy a car.

A statutory requirement of "home equity indebtedness" (in addition that it must be secured by the qualifying residence) is that such loan amount cannot exceed the "equity" in the qualified residence. "Equity" is the one figure of which most homeowners are constantly aware. Equity is the difference between the value of the home and the amount of outstanding loans with respect to the home. Say, for example, you own a home worth $350,000, and you have an outstanding first mortgage (acquisition debt) of $150,000. Your "equity" in the home is $200,000. This is the amount or value of your home that you really own – how much you would expect to "pocket in cash" upon selling (after the debt is paid off). Another important statutory limit looms large with respect to home equity debt in that there is an <u>aggregate</u> $100,000 of debt that can qualify as home equity indebtedness. As with the acquisition indebtedness cap, this is a single cap for all of the home equity loans. Interest on any loan or portion of a loan in excess of this cap generally becomes nondeductible "personal" interest.

A home equity loan, a second mortgage, the cash portion of a cash-out refinance, a home equity based line of credit typically characterize home equity indebtedness. Be careful here because, as we saw above in our couple's case, the fact that money is borrowed using the equity in a qualified residence as security does not necessarily render the loan as "home equity indebtedness." If the borrowed funds are used to substantially improve the qualified residence, the loan is characterized as the more favorable (higher loan cap) acquisition indebtedness. Do not be fooled by language used to describe the facts of a loan. Tom and Edna's loan was, for loan description purposes, a home equity loan. However such classification for tax purposes would have invoked the $100,000 loan cap. As mentioned, for tax purposes their loan is considered acquisition indebtedness (and is subject to the much higher $1 million loan cap).

One final note about the loan caps for acquisition and home equity indebtedness. While not at issue in this question, these two limitation amounts can effectively be combined for the purchase, construction or improvement of a qualified residence. For example, suppose an individual purchases a $2 million home (principal residence), paying $500,000 in cash and borrowing the $1,500,000 balance with a loan secured by the house. The $1 million and $100,000 acquisition and home equity loan caps can be combined and the individual would be entitled to deduct (as qualified residence interest) the interest paid on $1,100,000 of loans (this assumes the individual has no other loans on another qualified residence).

It should be noted that there are special rules applicable to loans incurred before October 14, 1987. [IRC § 163(h)(3)(D).]

Answers (a) and (d) are incorrect because the initial statement in these answers, that the $110,000 borrowed represents income, is incorrect. **Answer (b) is incorrect** because it incorrectly characterized the couple's loan as "home equity indebtedness" thereby imposing the $100,000 applicable to such debt. **Answer (e) is incorrect** because a correct answer (c) is presented.

- **Additional references:** *See* DANIEL Q. POSIN, FEDERAL INCOME TAXATION OF INDIVIDUALS ¶ 7.01(3) (5th ed. 2000).

3.   **Answer (e) is correct.** Students universally dislike "none of the above" answers and are justified in doing so. They do provide, however, a powerful testing tool for professors and, in this case, none of the answers provided in (a) through (d) are correct. This question is a bit unfair, as its analysis requires a correct answer to question 1, above. This professor would not ask such a series of interrelated multiple-choice questions on an exam. Rather, this series of questions was derived from an exam essay question. The "bottom line" correct numeric answer for this question is that Tom realizes a $130,000 loss from the sale of the house, but this loss is <u>not</u> recognized (i.e., the loss results in no income tax benefit to Tom).

This is a good example of a question that, to a student studying income tax, may appear to exist purely as an academic exercise. While it does contain aspects that present an academic challenge, this question reflects a surprisingly common "real world" tax situation. In every fact pattern in which something is sold, the author likes to go through the following analysis:

1)   Does the sale result in a <u>realized</u> gain or loss and if so, what is the <u>amount</u>?

2)   If we have a <u>realized</u> gain or loss, is it <u>recognized</u> (i.e. reportable for income tax purposes)?

3)   If the gain or loss is recognized, is it accorded "capital" gain or loss treatment?

Because this question involves a multi-step analysis and because the author recognizes the value of your time, both **abbreviated/short** and **comprehensive/long** analyses are provided below.

The abbreviated/short version of the analysis for this question is that Tom's realized loss is the difference between the $380,000 sales price and his basis in the houses of $510,000, or $130,000. His basis in the house is a $510,000 carryover basis from his and Edna's basis (the $400,000 purchase price increased by the $110,000 of additions/improvements) because he received the house (his and Edna's share) "incident to their divorce." [See IRC § 1041.] Tom's loss is not recognized pursuant to IRC § 165(c) as the house was used for personal purposes. Since Tom's loss is not recognized, its characterization as a "capital loss" is neither relevant nor appropriate.

The following comprehensive/long (very long) analysis presents a step-by-step discussion of the answer to this question that can be applied to other gain/loss questions.

The first step is determining whether Tom has a realized gain or loss on the sale of the house. For this, we need two basic components: his sales price ("amount realized" or, hereinafter, AR) and his basis in the shares ("adjusted basis or, hereinafter, AB). The difference between the two represents a realized gain or loss. [IRC § 1001(a).] Each of these two components, AR and AB, can present a variety of complex tax issues for exam and real-world tax purposes. The AR side is straightforward in our question, and is his $380,000 sales price. Other questions in this book present more complex issues involving a taxpayer's AR.

The AB component is slightly more difficult to derive in this question. The general starting place for determining one's AB is one's cost. [IRC §§ 1011 and 1012.] Our starting point is what Tom and Edna paid for the house four years ago. The $400,000 Tom and Edna originally paid for the property represents their cost basis. As previously discussed, adjustments increasing the basis of their property resulted from the major additions and improvements they made to the property. Similar to the purchase of their house, their AB in the house is increased by the $110,000 cost of such additions/improvements. [IRC § 1016(a); Reg. § 1.1016-2(a).] The resulting AB is, therefore, $510,000 ($400,000 plus $110,000). In this question, Tom ends up owning 100% of the house when Edna's interest is transferred to him two years ago pursuant to their divorce decree. While the question does not state the form of title in which Tom and Edna held the house nor the respective interests Tom and Edna had in the house while married, such information is not particularly relevant, as discussed below. We do know that Tom was awarded the entire house by the divorce decree, and it is relevant that Tom received Edna's interest in the manner in which he did (pursuant to the divorce decree).

IRC § 1041 provides, in part, special rules for determining the AB in property that is transferred between former spouses. If such transfer between former spouses is considered a transfer "incident to divorce," then the transferee ex-spouse takes a carryover AB from the transferor ex-spouse. [IRC § 1041(b).] This section does not distinguish as to the type of inter vivos transfer involved – it covers gifts, sales, exchanges, etc. In our question, we have only one transfer potentially subject to this special AB rule: the awarding of the house to Tom at the time of their divorce two years ago. Specifically, the issue is whether Tom's receipt of the house (whatever Edna's interest was in the house) is "incident to divorce" resulting in a carryover AB of $510,000. A transfer "incident to divorce" has a statutory definition as being either 1) any transfer within one year of the divorce, or 2) a transfer "relating to the cessation of the marriage." [See IRC § 1041(c).] Temporary regulations define transfers that are considered "relating to the cessation of the marriage" as a transfer provided for by a "divorce or separation instrument" (see questions in this book relating to alimony) and is transferred, pursuant to this instrument, within six years of the divorce. [Temp.Reg. § 1.1041-1T(b) Q & A-7.] It is fairly easy to see that Tom's AB in the house is governed by IRC § 1041. The transfer of the house to him was clearly "incident to divorce" (he received all of the house not only within one year of the divorce, but also pursuant to the decree and within six years of the divorce). Tom's AB in the house, therefore, is a carryover from the couple's AB of $510,000. [Please see other questions in this book addressing other aspects of IRC § 1041 and more complex issues relating thereto.]

Having determined Tom's AB to be $510,000, it is easy to compute his realized gain or loss: AR (selling price) of $380,000 less his AB of $510,000 resulting in a realized loss of $130,000.

Now to the second step of our gain/loss analysis: whether Tom's $130,000 loss is recognized. IRC § 1001(c) provides that, unless otherwise indicated in the Code, all realized gains and losses are recognized. This would cement the recognition of Tom's loss if it were not for an "otherwise indicated" Code section, namely IRC § 165. At first glance, the "general rule" in IRC § 165(a) looks to be in Tom's favor allowing a deduction for "any loss sustained during the taxable year . . ." Reading further at § 165(c) we come across an ominous sounding subsection: "Limitation on losses of individuals." In class, this professor refers to this as the "section 165(c) hoop," complete with graphic depictions on the board. Figuratively, the goal is to jump from the "realized" loss side, through the hoop to the land of "recognized" losses. This hoop, however, is more akin to a semi-permeable membrane than an unobstructed open space. We see, in IRC §§ 165(c)(1)-

(c)(3), that business losses, investment losses and personal-use "casualty" losses, break on through to the recognized loss side. By default, however, losses from personal-use assets (other than casualty losses) do not make it through this "section 165(c) hoop" and go unrecognized. This explains why, for example, when you sell your personal-use car for a loss (which is almost always the case), the loss is realized but not recognized – i.e., you get no tax benefit from such a loss.

This, then, brings us to poor Tom. Oh, the facts sound good: "[t]hey bought the house strictly for investment purposes" fully intending to either sell it or rent it after they made their additions/improvements. And that Tom, after the divorce, was still hoping that the house would "prove to be a good investment." These facts represent a very common misconception about personal residences vis-à-vis their "investment" status for loss recognition. Tom's (and the couple's) use of the house as their personal residence relegates it to a personal-use asset, notwithstanding the magnitude or conviction of their investment intentions. We are left, therefore, with a realized loss from the sale of a personal-use asset that, by definition, is not a recognized loss. And, unfortunately for Tom, this is where the answer ends.

Students are often bothered by the lack of symmetry in that gains from the sale of personal-use assets are recognized (must be included in income unless a specific exclusion provision is applicable) but losses from the sale of such assets are not recognized (no tax benefit for these losses). Unfortunately, income tax laws are not always fair.

Answer (a) is incorrect because Tom's $130,000 loss is not recognized. Characterization of the loss as either a long-term or short-term capital loss is neither relevant nor appropriate. There is often some confusion with respect to this as Tom's house meets the definition of a capital asset. [IRC § 1221 (capital assets are generally, by definitional default, investment or personal-use assets).] If Tom's house is a capital asset, which it is, then why isn't the loss on the sale thereof a capital loss? The answer to this can be found in the definition of capital losses in IRC §§ 1222(2) or 1222(4). Capital losses are losses from the sale or exchange of a capital asset "if and to the extent that such loss is taken into account in computing taxable income." We hit the IRC § 165(c) barrier with respect to personal-use assets and losses resulting from their sale or exchange are not taken into account when computing taxable income. In class, this professor stresses to students the importance of going "step-by-step" through the above discussed three prong analysis whenever an asset is sold (or exchanged). Students often run into trouble when losses are at issue and they leapfrog over the "recognition" step two.

Answer (b) is incorrect because it utilizes an incorrect AB (the fair market value of the property at the time of their divorce) in determining Tom's gain or loss.

Answer (c) is incorrect because Tom does realize a loss on the sale of the house. **Answer (d) is incorrect** because Tom's loss is <u>not</u> recognized.

- **Additional references:** *See* DANIEL Q. POSIN, FEDERAL INCOME TAXATION OF INDIVIDUALS ¶ 4.02(2), 4.03, 4.04(1), 4.04(2) (5th ed. 2000).

4. **Answer (d) is correct.** Compensation need not be paid in cash to be considered income. When an employee receives property, it will be, barring any exclusion, included in the employee's gross income measured by the value of the property received. [Reg. § 1.61-1(d) (compensation received in forms other than in cash).] On the surface the employees in this question (other than Todd at this point) each have <u>income of $20,000</u>, the value of the commemorative plate received. This, we will see, ends up being the correct answer. For tax purposes, this is equivalent to each employee receiving a cash bonus of $20,000, and then having them turn around and buying this plate for $20,000 (this analogy will be useful for later questions). **This eliminates response (a) as a correct answer** as compensation need not be in the form of cash.

The next logical question to ask is whether any provision in the Code would apply to exclude, from income, the plate received. Foraging through the "fringe benefit" exclusions of IRC § 132, one might try to apply the exclusion for "de minimis" benefits. However, that exclusion requires that the value of the property (or service) received by the employee be "so small as to make accounting for it unreasonable or administratively impracticable." Commemorative plates worth $20,000 each hardly qualify. **This eliminates response (c) as a correct answer.**

If you have studied the IRC § 102 exclusion for gifts, bequests and devises, that might be the next logical place to look for a potential exclusion for the receipt of the commemorative plates. Unfortunately, The Tax Reform Act of 1986 essentially eliminated that possibility here by enacting IRC § 102(c). This subsection provides, in general, that the possible exclusion from gross income of property acquired by gift, bequest or devise, does <u>not</u> apply to transfers between employers and employees. In other words, "gifts" to employees are not excludable from gross income under IRC § 102. This subsection is not merely a presumption. Thus, "gifts" to employees are not excludable by this section even if the employer can show that the gift was made out of "detached and disinterested generosity," the general standard for defining a gift for this section. **This eliminates response (b) as a correct answer.**

As mentioned above, the <u>value</u> of property received by an employee represents compensation income. Each employee (not considering Todd at this point) therefore has income of $20,000. **Response (e) is incorrect** because while the reason for inclusion in income is correct, it is incorrect as to the amount of income includible in gross income.

- **Additional references:** *See* DANIEL Q. POSIN, FEDERAL INCOME TAXATION OF INDIVIDUALS ¶ 2.01 (5th ed. 2000).

5. **Answer (a) is correct.** Borrowing from the analysis of the answer to question 4, above, we came to the conclusion that each employee has compensation income of $20,000 resulting from the receipt of the commemorative plate. How then, you might ask, could the answer to this question possibly be any different? In our problem, the answer <u>is</u> the same, and Todd also has $20,000 of income in the form of compensation. But this question does bring up an important issue that requires discussion, if only to rule out other possible answers.

For discussion purposes and totally divorced from the facts of our question, suppose a parent employs a child. Let us further suppose that the employer (parent) makes no gifts to any employees but on the child's 25th birthday, the parent gives the child a new automobile. In the familial context, we have a parent making a gift to a child most likely out of emotions of detached and disinterested generosity, qualifying it for exclusion from income to the child pursuant to IRC § 102(a). However, we also factually have an employer making a gift to an employee that, pursuant to the language in IRC § 102(c), cannot be considered an excludable gift to the employee. Does this preclude any gifts, in the traditional and excludable sense, when the donor and donee happen to have an employment relationship such as this? The proposed regulations answer this question as follows: "For purposes of section 102(c), *extraordinary* transfers to the natural objects of an employer's bounty will *not be considered transfers to, or for the benefit of, an employee if the employee can show that the transfer was not made in recognition of the employee's employment. Accordingly, section 102(c) shall not apply to amounts transferred between related parties (e.g., father and son) if the purpose of the transfer can be substantially attributed to the familial relationship of the parties and not to the circumstances of their employment.*" [Prop.Reg. § 1.102-1(f)(2) (emphasis added).] In the hypothetical presented in this paragraph, the parent's gift of the car to the child is, in all likelihood, an example of an excludable gift notwithstanding the employment relationship between the two.

Now back to the facts of the question presented. While Todd is the "natural object" of his mother's "bounty"(using the somewhat odd vernacular of the regulations), it would be an unreasonable application of this regulation exception to the facts given. The transfer was not "extraordinary" when compared to every other employee – the "gift" to Todd was identical to the "gift" made to every employee. Similarly, the fact that everyone received the same "gift" would make it extremely unlikely that Todd would be able to show that the gift was attributable to the familial relationship with his mother and not in the employment context. One must examine this familial gift in relation to the employment gifts. Because they are identical, then Todd's gift would fall within the "non-exclusion" provisions of IRC § 102(c).

Answer (b) is incorrect because income to Todd is measured by the $20,000 value of the property received, and not the employer's cost. **Answer (c) is incorrect** based on the above discussion. **Answer (d) is incorrect**. While he is treated like other employees, he, and the other employees, each have $20,000 of gross income from the "gift."

- **Additional references:** *See* DANIEL Q. POSIN, FEDERAL INCOME TAXATION OF INDIVIDUALS ¶¶ 2.01, 3.08 (5th ed. 2000).

6.   **The correct answer is (b).** This is a basic gain calculation with a slight twist. When Marcia sells the commemorative plate, she realizes a gain or loss measured by the difference between the sales price (or in tax terms: the amount realized or AR) and her adjusted basis (AB) in the property. [IRC § 1001(a).] The amount realized (AR) portion of the equation in this problem is simply the $23,000 sales price for the plate. The key component to this question is the determination of Marcia's adjusted basis in the property. We will conclude, below, that $20,000 will be her adjusted basis in the commemorative plate, thus resulting in a realized gain of $3,000.

A taxpayer's cost is normally the starting point for determining one's basis in property. [IRC §§ 1011 and 1012.] Here, while it is a bit obscured, Marcia paid $20,000 for the commemorative plate. From the analysis of the correct answer to question 4, above, we know that Marcia had $20,000 in income, in the form of compensation, upon receipt of the plate (income equal to the value of the property received). At this point, it might be helpful to recast, or view in a different light, the transaction of receiving the plate. In effect, we could view this as equivalent to Marcia receiving a cash bonus of $20,000, and then turning around and purchasing the commemorative plate for $20,000. The end result is the same, Marcia with the plate, but breaking the transaction down this way may make it easier to see the component parts. As we said, she had compensation of $20,000 and we can also see that she paid $20,000 for the commemorative plate (her resulting AB in the property). This concept in determining Marcia's basis in property received as compensation is sometimes referred to as her "tax cost" and is described, albeit in a somewhat cryptic fashion, in the regulations at Reg. § 1.61-2(d)(2)(i).

The gain calculation is now easy to accomplish. The $23,000 sales price (AR) less her $20,000 basis (AB) results in a realized gain of $3,000.

Answers (a) and (c) are incorrect because Marcia's adjusted basis (AB) as stated in both of these answers is incorrect, resulting in an incorrect gain calculation. **Answer (d) is incorrect** because Marcia's subsequent sale of the commemorative plate is a separate transaction from the receipt of the plate (which, is also incorrectly stated in this answer).

- **Additional references:** *See* DANIEL Q. POSIN, FEDERAL INCOME TAXATION OF INDIVIDUALS ¶¶ 4.01, 4.03 (5th ed. 2000).

7. **Answer (c) is correct.** Gains that are "realized," as was Marcia's gain from her sale of the plate, are also "recognized" (or reported as income for tax purposes) unless there is some specific non-recognition or exclusion Code provision. [IRC § 1001(c).] No such non-recognition or exclusion section exists with respect to our facts. Further, the gain is a "capital" gain as Marcia held the commemorative plate for investment purposes (rendering it a capital asset). [IRC § 1221(a).] Lastly, Marcia's capital gain from the sale of the plate is a "short-term" capital gain because she did not hold the property for more than one year. [See IRC § 1222.] She received it (in effect purchased it) in January of this year and sold it in March of the same year.

Answer (a) is incorrect because, as discussed in question 6, above, her sale of the commemorative plate did result in a gain. **Answers (b) and (d) are not correct** because she did not hold the property for the requisite length of time. **Answer (e) is incorrect** because there is no "non-recognition" or gain exclusion Code provision applicable to the facts presented in this question.

- **Additional references:** *See* DANIEL Q. POSIN, FEDERAL INCOME TAXATION OF INDIVIDUALS ¶¶ 4.01, 4.02, 4.03, 4.05, 4.06 (5th ed. 2000).

8. **The answer that is most likely correct is (d).** This is a difficult question and the author recognizes that there may be some disagreement as to the "most likely" answer. Todd's sale of his plate for $14,000, results in a "realized" loss to him of $6,000. As discussed in the analysis of question 6, above, this is derived from the difference between the selling price (AR) and his basis (AB). Unlike Marcia, however, Todd's sale resulted in a loss. It is with the "recognition" of this loss (something that Todd would like to do as it would have the same effect as a deduction) where issues arise.

As previously mentioned, IRC § 1001(c) provides that, unless otherwise indicated in the Code, all realized gains and losses are recognized. This would cement the recognition of Todd's loss if it were not for an "otherwise indicated" Code section, namely IRC § 165. At first glance, the "general rule" in IRC § 165(a) looks to be in Todd's favor allowing a deduction for "any loss sustained during the taxable year . . ." Reading further at IRC § 165(c) we come across an ominous sounding subsection: "Limitation on losses of individuals." In class, this professor refers to this as the "section 165(c) hoop," complete with graphic depictions on the board. Figuratively, the goal is to jump from the "realized" loss side, through the hoop to the land of "recognized" losses. This hoop, however, is more akin to a semi-permeable membrane than an unobstructed open space. We see, in IRC § 165(c)(1)-(c)(3), that business losses, investment losses and personal-use "casualty" losses, break on through to the recognized loss side. By default, however, losses from personal-use assets (other than casualty losses) do not make it through this "section 165(c) hoop" and go unrecognized. This explains why, for example, when you sell your personal-use car for a loss (which is almost always the case), the loss is realized but not recognized – i.e., you get no tax benefit from such a loss.

This, then, brings us to poor Todd. The facts of this question indicated that once he received his commemorative plate, he rather foolishly used it for everyday dinnerware, not the sort of behavior one associates with holding property for investment purposes. In an attempt to solidify his use as personal, the facts also indicated that he did not treat the plate as an investment. We are left, therefore, with a realized loss from the sale of a personal-use asset which, by definition, is not a recognized loss.

While the author believes (d) is the most likely result, a possible argument can be made that personal-use of an asset and holding an asset for investment purposes are not mutually exclusive. Perhaps Todd could consider the commemorative plate an investment asset notwithstanding his use of it as everyday dinnerware. This is, however, a weak argument. It is basically the same argument used when an individual sells a principal residence for a loss and attempts to recognize the loss claiming that the house was purchased primarily with investment intentions. Use of the house as a personal residence, however, trumps any investment intention, and the law is clear that a loss realized from the sale thereof is not recognized. Another example the author uses in class to illustrate this issue is where someone, usually a spouse, attempts to justify to someone else, usually the other spouse, the purchase of an expensive automobile (e.g., a Porsche) as a good "investment" even though it will be used for everyday personal driving. Later, if the car is sold for a loss, it too will not be recognized (no deduction for the loss) despite claims that it was purchased as an investment. **Answer (b) is not the most likely answer** but, as discussed above, is a close second.

Students are often bothered by the lack of symmetry in that gains from the sale of personal-use assets <u>are</u> recognized (must be included in income unless a specific exclusion provision applies) but losses from the sale of such assets are not recognized (no tax benefit for these losses). Unfortunately, income tax laws are not always fair.

Answers (a) and (c) are incorrect because Todd does not have a realized gain from the sale of the commemorative plate. **Answer (e) is incorrect** because Todd does have a realized loss from the sale of the property. This answer (e), however, is a fairly popular selection, perhaps being confused with the sale of property that had been received as a gift that, in certain fact patterns, result in no gain or loss realization.

- **Additional references:** *See* DANIEL Q. POSIN, FEDERAL INCOME TAXATION OF INDIVIDUALS ¶¶ 4.04(1), 4.04(2) (5th ed. 2000).

9.   **Answer (d) is the best answer.** To properly determine whether Mark realizes a gain on the transfer of the property to Brian, we need to know two things: Mark's adjusted basis (AB) in the property, and the amount of the loan on the property.

A gift of property generally does not result in realization of gain or loss to a donor. However, under certain circumstances (i.e., if a donor receives "consideration"), a gift may in fact constitute a "part sale/part gift" with a resulting realization of gain. In a part sale/part gift situation, gain is realized to the extent the consideration received (amount realized" or hereinafter AR) by the donor exceeds the donor's basis ("adjusted basis" or hereinafter AB) in the property. [Reg. § 1.1001-1(e).] This is consistent with the general principals of IRC § 1001(a) – the difference between the AR and AB represents <u>realized</u> gain or loss. When Mark makes the gift to Brian, Mark does not have an AR in the traditional sense such as in a sale of property. However, Mark is deemed to have received consideration (an AR) for income tax purposes. Pursuant to *Crane v. Commissioner* (331 U.S. 1, 67 S.Ct. 1047 (1947)), a liability associated with transferred property is considered an amount realized even when a transferee merely takes property subject to a mortgage. It is irrelevant, here, whether or not Mark was personally liable for the loan (i.e., for this fact pattern, it does not matter whether Mark's loan was "recourse" or "nonrecourse"). Additionally, when the transferee of property takes it "subject to" the loan (or "assumes" it for that matter) the AR includes the full amount of the loan regardless of the property's fair market value (even if the property is worth less than the amount of mortgage). [See *Comm'r v. Tufts* 461 U.S. 300, 103 S.Ct. 1826 (1983).] Therefore, while this appears to be just a gift, it is, in reality, a part sale/part gift situation with Mark deemed to have received consideration (AR) equal to the amount of the loan taken "subject to" by Brian.

To determine if Mark has a realized gain from this transfer to Brian, we do need to know his AB in the property transferred. As mentioned above, if the loan amount (the consideration received by Mark or his AR) exceeds his AB in the property, a realized gain will result. Therefore, the items that we need to make this determination are only items I and III: Mark's adjusted basis in the property and the amount of the loan, respectively.

Answers (a) and (b) are incorrect because both answers include, to different degrees, components that are not necessary for purposes of determining Mark's realized gain, if any. **Answer (c) is incorrect** because it does not contain one of the critical components (the amount of the loan being taken "subject to" by Brian) for purposes of determining Mark's realized gain, if any. **Answer (e) is incorrect** because the correct answer (d) presented.

- **Additional references:** *See* DANIEL Q. POSIN, FEDERAL INCOME TAXATION OF INDIVIDUALS ¶¶ 4.03(1), 4.03(2) (5th ed. 2000).

10.   **Answer (e) is correct.** This question, unfortunately, requires, in part, a correct analysis of the previous question. This professor would not ask such a combination of interrelated multiple-choice questions on an actual exam. This question is presented here, however, to reinforce understanding of the subject. Brian has no income as a result of receiving the property from his brother Mark. Brian's adjusted basis (AB) in the property is equal to the greater of Mark's AB in the property at the time of the gift, or the amount of the loan to which Brian took the property "subject to."

As discussed in the analysis of question 9, above, the "gift" to Brian was actually a part sale/part gift situation. The transfer was in part a sale because Brian was deemed to provide consideration, as discussed below, in the form of taking the property subject to the mortgage. The transfer was also, in part, a gift because the consideration paid (the amount of the loan) was given in the facts to be less than the value of the property. As for the true "gift" element of this transaction, Brian does <u>not</u> have to include it (or any amount) in his gross income. While it is true that "gross income" is broadly defined, gifts made out of detached and disinterested generosity are generally excludable from gross income under IRC § 102 (general exclusion for gifts, bequests, devises and inheritances). Mark's gift to Brian (of the portion considered to be a gift) would most likely be excluded from Brian's gross income.

As for Brian's resulting basis in the real property, because this was a "part sale/part gift" transaction, there are two basis (or adjusted basis hereinafter AB) rules that logically could apply: those for a gift and those for a sale (or purchase with respect to Brian). In such part sale/part gift situations, the resulting transferee's AB is the <u>greater</u> of: (1) the amount paid by the donee, or (2) the donor's AB at the time of the gift. [Reg. 1.1015-4(a) (the greater of these two is also increased for any gift tax paid adjustment – this is not present here).] While in this question, Brian did not pay any monies to Mark to acquire the house, the afore-mentioned *Crane* case also stands for the proposition that a mortgage loan taken "subject to" by a transferee is deemed consideration paid. [See *Crane v. Comm'r* (331 U.S. 1, 67 S.Ct. 1047 (1947).] The amount of the loan to which Brian took the property "subject to," therefore, represents the amount paid for purposes of determining AB. Therefore, Brian's AB is equal to the greater of his brother Mark's AB in the property at the time of the gift, or the amount of the loan to which he took the property "subject to."

Answers (a) and (b) are incorrect because the only part of this transaction which could be considered income to Brian, represents an excludable gift. **Answers (c) and (d) are not the best answers.** While both answers correctly reflect the exclusion from Brian's gross income of the gift, they do not adequately reflect the correct method for determining Brian's basis in the property received. Had this question provided numbers for Mark's AB in the property and the amount of the loan to which Brian took the property "subject to," one of these answers, depending on the numbers, would be correct.

- **Additional references:** *See* DANIEL Q. POSIN, FEDERAL INCOME TAXATION OF INDIVIDUALS ¶¶ 4.03(1), 4.03(2) (5th ed. 2000).

11. **Answer (a) is correct.** We have some encouraging words for poor Dan. Your broken heart will eventually heal and forget about the ring and the car – there are more important things in life. Okay, the author will stick to income tax issues. We do have some potentially good income tax news for Dan. His losses, from both the theft and the "unusual" automobile mishap, will qualify as "casualty losses" resulting in a possible deduction for Dan.

IRC § 165 is the primary section at issue in this question. Individuals suffering a "casualty loss" may be entitled to some deduction even if the property involved is of a personal-use nature (as is the case with Dan's property losses). [IRC § 165(h).] A *casualty loss* for personal-use property (property not used in a business or investment activity) is one that occurs from "fire, storm, shipwreck, or other casualty, or from theft." [IRC § 165(c)(3).] The loss must have resulted from some sudden, unexpected, or unusual cause. The theft of Dan's ring, as well as the loss of his car, represent classic examples of casualty losses (although not under conditions as unique as Dan's situation).

The measurement of the loss for *casualty loss* purposes is prescribed by the regulations. For thefts of personal-use property, the loss is the lesser of: 1) the property's basis (adjusted basis or AB) of the property immediately before the theft, or 2) the fair market value of the property immediately before the theft. [Reg. §§ 1.165-7(b) and 1.165-8(c).] Either amount is reduced by any compensation from insurance or otherwise. For Dan, although the ring was worth $25,000 at the time of the theft, the amount of his *casualty loss* will be his lower AB of <u>$20,000</u> (his original cost). He received no compensation from insurance or other sources.

Similarly for other casualties involving personal-use property, the loss is also the lesser of: 1) the property's AB immediately before the casualty, or 2) the property's fair market value immediately before the casualty. [Reg. § 1.165-7(b).] For property that is totally destroyed, such as in Dan's car, either amount must be reduced by any salvage value, insurance proceeds or other amounts received on account of the loss. Dan's car was a total loss having no salvage value and he received no compensation for this loss from insurance or other sources. Comparing his $30,000 AB in the car with its $25,000 fair market value at the time of the incident, the amount of his *casualty loss* will be the lower <u>$25,000</u> (its fair market value).

Exactly what amount of these losses Dan will be entitled to deduct, is not part of this question. Please see question 12, below, for more information.

Answer (b) is incorrect because the values given in this answer incorrectly reflect taking the "greater" of the property's AB or its fair market value for determining the amount of *casualty losses*. **Answer (c) is incorrect** because the loss of Dan's automobile is also considered a *casualty loss*. **Answer (d) is incorrect** because the value of the loss for the ring is incorrectly determined using its fair market value at the time of the theft instead of its lower AB. **Answer (e) is incorrect** because both the ring theft and the car loss represent legitimate *casualty losses*.

- **Additional references:** *See* DANIEL Q. POSIN, FEDERAL INCOME TAXATION OF INDIVIDUALS ¶¶ 7.01(5) (5th ed. 2000).

12. **The correct answer is (e).** This is where the news is not very good for Dan. Once the amount of one's *casualty loss* is determined (see question 11, above) the actual deduction for individuals is limited in two ways. First, for **each** casualty, $100 is not deductible. [IRC 165(h)(1).] This concept is similar to that of car insurance where you may have a $100 or $500 "deductible," the amount that you have to pay before the insurance kicks in. This Code provision is basically a $100 "deductible" plan with the government – no potential benefit (tax deduction) for the first $100 of loss <u>per casualty</u>.

The second, and more detrimental limit is that once you take off the first $100 per casualty, the remaining aggregate amount of *casualty loss* is deductible only to the extent that it <u>exceeds 10%</u> of the taxpayer's adjusted gross income (AGI). [IRC § 165(h)(2)(A).] AGI is discussed elsewhere in this book, but basically it is an intermediate point in the computation of taxable income. Gross income less certain deductions (listed in IRC § 62 and known as *above the line deductions*) take you to AGI. Other deductions (known as *below the line deductions*) are then subtracted to arrive at *taxable income*. While not required for this problem, the amount calculated as a deductible *casualty loss* is included as part of a group of *below the line* deductions known collectively as *itemized deductions*. This group of deductions is taken (if larger than the taxpayer's *standard deduction*) from adjusted gross income (AGI) in computing taxable income. [See Appendix A for more information about how various items of income and deductions fit together in the computation of taxable income and AGI.] This 10% of AGI floor was introduced into tax law in the early 1980's and is a substantial hurdle for the actual deduction of casualty losses.

While not required for this problem, let us use Dan's *casualty losses* to illustrate the operation of these limitations. Recall from question 11, above, that Dan's *casualty losses* were $20,000 for the ring and $25,000 for the automobile. Let us assume, for illustration purposes that Dan's AGI is a lofty $300,000. His actual *casualty loss* deduction would be $14,800 calculated as follows:

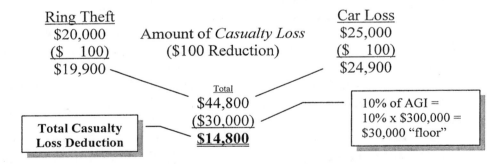

Answer (a) is incorrect because it fails to reflect the second of the two limitations for *casualty loss* deductions: the nondeductible 10% of *AGI* floor. **Answer (b) is incorrect** because it fails to reflect that the $100 reduction of *casualty losses* is on a "per casualty" basis. In addition, this answer fails to reflect the second of the two limitations for *casualty loss* deductions: the nondeductible 10% of *AGI* floor. **Answer (c) is incorrect** because it utilizes the wrong percentage for the nondeductible floor limitation. While not pertinent to this question, deductions for "medical care expenses" are subject to a 7.5% of AGI floor. [IRC § 213(a).] **Answer (d) is incorrect** because it fails to apply the $100 reduction on a "per casualty" basis as required by statute.

• **Additional references:** *See* DANIEL Q. POSIN, FEDERAL INCOME TAXATION OF INDIVIDUALS ¶¶ 7.01(5) (5th ed. 2000).

13. **The correct answer is (b).** The loss of Dan's business-use car (as is the case in this question) is still characterized as a *casualty loss*. [IRC § 165.] However, the rules for the amount of the *casualty loss,* and its deductibility differ from those previously discussed regarding personal-use assets.

The measurement of the loss for *casualty loss* purposes is generally the same as those used for personal-use casualties: the lesser of: 1) the AB of the property immediately before the casualty, or 2) the fair market value of the property immediately before the casualty. [Reg. § 1.165-7(b).] However, when a business-use asset is totally destroyed, the property's AB is the measurement of the *casualty loss* (notwithstanding its fair market value at the time). [Reg. § 1.165-7(b)(1).] Because Tom's business-use automobile (in this question) was a total loss, the amount of his *casualty loss* is the car's AB at the time of the loss, which is our answer (b).

Unlike the *casualty loss* deduction for individuals regarding personal-use property, *casualty losses* of business-use property is not subject to the $100 "per casualty" nondeductible amount. Nor are such business *casualty losses* subject to the 10% of AGI nondeductible floor that applies to personal-use casualty losses.

Answer (a) is incorrect because the personal-use loss Dan suffered with respect to his car is also a *casualty loss*, as discussed in problem 11, above. There is no change in this regard because the loss in this problem stems from a business-use asset. **Answer (c) is also incorrect.** This answer states the general rule for determining the amount of *casualty loss* for business-use assets. However, as indicated above, the regulations provide that a "total loss" of a business-use asset results in the amount of *casualty loss* equal to the property's AB, regardless of its value. **Answer (d) is also incorrect.** While this answer properly reflects that business-use *casualty losses* are not subject to the 10% of AGI nondeductible floor, it is incorrect in applying the $100 per casualty nondeductible amount to business-use *casualty losses*. **Answer (e) is incorrect** because the amount of Dan's *casualty loss* changes, as does the amount of the actual deduction for the *casualty loss*.

- **Additional references:** *See* DANIEL Q. POSIN, FEDERAL INCOME TAXATION OF INDIVIDUALS ¶ 7.01(5) (5th ed. 2000).

14. **The correct answer is (b).** Determining Thelma's realized gain or loss in this question requires us to identify two basic components: her sales price ("amount realized" or, hereinafter, AR) and her basis in the stock ("adjusted basis or, hereinafter, AB). The difference between the two represents a <u>realized</u> gain or loss. [IRC § 1001(a).] Each of these two components, AR and AB, can present a variety of complex tax issues for exam and real-world tax purposes. The AR side is

straightforward in our question, and is her $6,000 sales price of the stock. Other questions in this book present more complex issues involving a taxpayer's AR. The AB component is the more challenging in this question. We will conclude, after a lengthy discussion below (mostly eliminating the possible application of some rather complex basis rules), that Thelma's AB in the stock is $5,000, resulting in a realized gain to her of $1,000.

While a taxpayer's cost is normally the starting point for determination of one's basis in property (IRC §§ 1011 and 1012), when property is received as a gift, as is the case here, there really is no "cost" to the taxpayer. The seemingly logical result of a zero basis is neither desirable nor, thankfully, appropriate. IRC § 1015 provides us with the rules for determining a donee's AB in property received as a gift. The general rule for most gifts is that the donee takes the donor's AB in the property, or what is commonly referred to as a "carryover" AB. In Thelma's case, this would be her father, Frank's original $5,000 cost. A careful reading of IRC § 1015(a), juxtaposed with our facts, requires us to exam the possible application of something called the "special loss rule." If at the time of the gift, the fair market value of the property is less than the donor's AB, then "for purposes of determining a loss" the donee takes the lower fair market value as his or her AB (and not the carryover AB from the donor). Indeed, the $4,000 value of the shares at the time of their gift to Thelma was less than Frank's AB. However, do not fall into the "let us make a quick tax rule" trap of concluding that Thelma's AB in the stock is this lower $4,000. As quoted, the statute effectively says that we apply this rule *if* the donee later sells for a *loss*. For example, if the facts were changed and Thelma later sold the stock for $1,500, the "special loss rule" would apply and her AB would properly be $4,000. However, in our facts, the stocks rebound in value and she sells them for $6,000, a gain no matter how we look at it. Therefore, the "special loss rule" is <u>not</u> applicable and the starting point for Thelma's AB is the general carryover basis rule for gifts: $5,000 (a carryover of Frank's AB of the same amount).

We say that $5,000 is the "starting point" for determining Thelma's AB. This is because there was a gift tax paid in connection with this gift, last year, to Thelma. A discussion of gift taxes is beyond the scope of this book, and most basic federal income tax courses. Suffice it to say that a gift tax is based on the value of the property transferred and is an obligation of the donor/transferor. It is a given, in our facts, that Frank incurred and paid a $2,000 gift tax on this gift to Thelma. While the study of gift taxes is beyond our scope, their effect on a donee/transferee's AB is not. IRC § 1015(d) provides for a "gift tax paid adjustment" to AB (an increase to AB). The method of calculating this positive, and favorable, adjustment varies depending on when the gift was made, with the critical date (of the gift) being December 31, 1976. The gift tax paid adjustment to AB for gifts made before 1977, is the subject of at least one question presented elsewhere in this book. In this question, the gift to Thelma was made "last year," and the "gift tax paid adjustment" rules for post-1976 gifts are applicable. This rule appears in IRC § 1015(d)(6), and unfortunately for students, the gift tax paid adjustment calculation for post-1976 gifts is a more difficult arithmetic affair than that for gifts made before 1977. The calculation is a prorated type of computation and is an example of what this professor's students refer to as the dreaded algebra infused "Code ratio." [Please see Appendix C for examples of "Code math."] Recognizing that any type of formula may strike fear in the hearts of some law students, rest assured that the calculations are not really that bad.

The gift tax paid adjustment, or the amount by which Thelma can increase her $5,000 carryover AB from her father, will be represented by the variable "X" in the following formula:

$$\frac{X}{\text{Gift Tax Paid}} = \frac{\text{``Net Appreciation'' of Property in Donor's Hands at Time of Gift}}{\text{Value of Gift at Time of Gift}}$$

The term "net appreciation" as used in the numerator on the right-hand side of this equation is simply how much the property has appreciated in value from the time the donor acquired the property until he or she made the gift. Alternatively stated, the "net appreciation" is any *positive* difference between the value of the gift at the time of the gift, and the donor's AB in the property. The above formula adjusted to reflect this definition is:

$$\frac{X}{\text{Gift Tax Paid}} = \frac{(\text{Value of Gift at Time of Gift} - \text{Donor's AB in Gift})}{\text{Value of Gift at Time of Gift}}$$

Utilizing the numbers from our facts, the formula is:

$$\frac{X}{\$2,000} = \frac{(\$4,000 - \$5,000)}{\$4,000} \qquad \text{or:} \qquad \frac{X}{\$2,000} = \frac{\$0}{\$4,000}$$

In our facts, there was <u>no</u> *net appreciation* in Frank's hands. We do not calculate for a negative gift tax paid adjustment. Solving for "X" is very simple in our situation as the zero divided by a number is zero, which means **X** equals **zero**. In other words, we have no gift tax paid adjustment in our case (because there was no net appreciation of the stock in Frank's hands at the time of the gift). After all of that, (sorry, but the author hopes that going though the complete analysis will assist in understanding the material) we end up with Thelma's AB being $5,000 (the same carryover AB with no gift tax paid adjustment)

The calculation of Thelma's gain is now a simple matter. Her AR of $6,000 less her $5,000 AB results in a realized gain of $1,000. While not the subject of this question, issues of gain recognition and characterization (i.e., capital gain materials) are related testable material. For information purposes, Thelma's $1,000 gain would be recognized and characterized as a "long-term capital gain." [Please see other questions presented in this book where recognition and characterization issues are addressed.]

Answer (a) is incorrect because it incorrectly uses $4,000, the fair market value at the time of the gift, as Thelma's AB in the stock. **Answer (c) is incorrect** because it incorrectly reflects an AB to Thelma of $7,000 (most likely from an incorrect application of the gift tax paid adjustment attempting to utilize the pre-1977 rules of adding the $2,000 gift tax paid to the $5,000 carryover AB). **Answer (d) is incorrect** because the result in this answer occurs when the donee sells property at a price between that of the donor's AB and a lower fair market value of the property at the time of the gift. This does not represent the facts in our case.

- **Additional references:** *See* DANIEL Q. POSIN, FEDERAL INCOME TAXATION OF INDIVIDUALS ¶¶ 4.01, 4.03 (5th ed. 2000).

15. **The correct answer is (a).** This question may have little relevance to those students having no contact with states having "community property" laws. For those students concerned with community property, this question represents a very important "real-world" tax issue. This question centers on one's basis (or "adjusted basis" hereinafter AB) in property. A taxpayer, if given the choice between having a higher or lower AB for property with no additional costs involved, would, for income tax purposes, usually select the higher AB. The higher the AB, the lower the potentially taxable gain (or greater loss) results from a subsequent sale. There are two general rules regarding AB that come into play for this question. The first is that a taxpayer's basis in property is usually determined by its cost. [IRC §§ 1011 and 1012.] The second general rule applicable here is the determination of a taxpayer's AB in property acquired from a decedent. IRC § 1014(a)(1) provides that the basis of property acquired from a decedent shall be the property's fair market value at the date of the decedent's death (commonly referred to as a "step-up" in basis for appreciated property). Let us analyze this question and apply these rules utilizing the facts in our question, illustrated with some numbers.

Assume that our Wife and Husband purchased the vacant lot many years ago for $200,000. Let us further assume that the lot has appreciated in value to $800,000 and one spouse, the Wife, dies. We will analyze these facts in the alternative scenarios that the property was titled in "joint tenancy" and "community property."

Joint Tenancy Analysis

Joint tenants each have an undivided one-half ownership interest in property while both co-tenants are alive. Joint tenancy carries with it, the right of survivorship, where, by operation of law, at the death of one co-tenant, his or her one-half interest vests in (goes to) the surviving co-tenant. At Wife's death, her one-half interest in the property would go to Husband, resulting in Husband's 100% ownership of the property. But what is Husband's AB? He already owned one-half of the property prior to his wife's death, and to this one half, we apply our "cost" AB rule – Husband's one-half of the original $200,000 purchase price is $100,000. Husband's AB in the one-half that he already owned prior to Wife's death is $100,000.

As for the one-half interest in the property owned by Wife that Husband receives by operation of law at Wife's death (as the surviving joint tenant), we apply the rules of IRC § 1014(a)(1) – Husband's AB in this one-half interest received from decedent Wife is one-half of the property's $800,000 fair market date of death value, or $400,000. Husband's resulting AB is $500,000 comprised of $100,000 representing the AB for the one-half of the property that he originally owned and $400,000 representing the AB for the one-half of the property that he received from decedent Wife at her death. We see that Husband received a so-called "stepped up" basis in one-half of the property (the share coming from Wife at her death). This result is illustrated in the following diagram:

Joint Tenancy Analysis

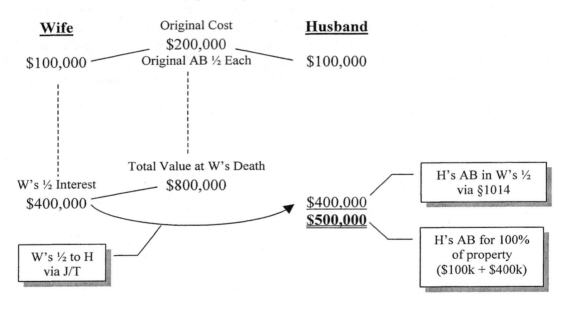

Community Property Analysis

Similar to joint tenancy, a husband and wife each has an undivided one-half interest in community property. Regular community property, as is the case here, does not have the automatic "transfer at death" mechanism of joint tenancy. A spouse is free to devise her or his one-half community property interest to anyone. Absent a devise, the deceased spouse's interest goes by state intestacy laws. To make this illustration consistent with that of joint tenancy, where the surviving spouse ends up owning 100% of the property, we will assume that Wife's will devises her one-half community property interest to Husband. In this scenario, Husband again owns 100% of the property after Wife's death, but what is his AB in this property. Applying the basic rule of IRC § 1014(a)(1) Husband's AB in the one-half interest he received from decedent Wife equals one-half of the property's $800,000 fair market date of death value, or $400,000. And the AB in the one-half interest Husband already owned? This is where a special and magical rule, at IRC § 1014(b)(6), comes into play. For AB determination purposes, this rule says that we treat the <u>Husband's</u> one-half interest in the community property (that he already owns) as if it too was received from his wife at her death. This then translates into application of the general date of death valuation as AB rule for property received from a decedent. Husband's AB in <u>his</u> one-half of the property also gets "stepped-up" to the fair market value of that one-half at Wife's death – $400,000 in our illustration. Husband's resulting AB is $800,000 or a so-called "double step-up" in basis for community property. This result is illustrated in the following diagram:

Community Property Analysis

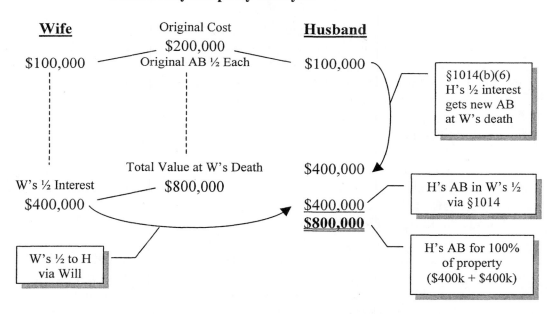

Surviving Husband has an AB of $500,000 if they held the property as joint tenants. Alternatively, surviving Husband has an AB of $800,000 if they held it as community property. Clearly, the latter result is better for Husband in this set of facts.

For appreciated property, this special community property provision can be a great tax savings devise that effectively makes, for income tax purposes, all unrealized appreciation and gain in the decedent's hands evaporate.

Answer (b) is incorrect because IRC § 1041 has no application with respect to the facts in this problem. **Answer (c) is incorrect** because IRC § 1014(b)(6), while not applicable to spousal joint tenancies, would produce a more favorable result to the surviving spouse vis-à-vis the surviving spouse's resulting AB in the appreciated property. **Answer (d) is incorrect** because "community property" does, indeed, produce a more favorable result to the surviving spouse in this appreciating property value situation vis-à-vis the surviving spouse's resulting AB in the property.

New Law Caution. The Economic Growth and Tax Relief Reconciliation Act of 2001 ("2001 Tax Act"), signed into law in 2001, made numerous changes throughout the Internal Revenue Code. The 2001 Tax Act is rather complex with many of its provisions phasing-in and phasing-out over a period of many years. As of this writing, the above described basis rules of IRC § 1014 are repealed with respect to decedents dying after December 31, 2009. [IRC § 1014(f).] The change, with limited exceptions, is basically to a "carryover" basis rule, similar to that applicable to inter vivos gifts in IRC § 1015. [See IRC § 1022 (effective for years after 2009).] This change was enacted to coincide with the 2001 Tax Act's abolishment of the federal estate tax effective for years after 2009. Whether these changes will come to pass without change in the intervening years is unknown as of this writing. However, as discussed in the preface to this book, the 2001 Tax Act, as enacted, contains a rather unique "sunset clause" that could, unless amended, make the above described 2010 changes evaporate in 2011, leaving us with the current IRC § 1014 rules.

16. **The correct answer is (c).** This question is very similar to question 15, immediately preceding this question. This professor would not ask two closely related questions such as these on an exam. It is presented here, however, to reinforce understanding of the subject.

In this question, we are faced with an asset that is continually declining in value rather than an asset, as in question 15, which has enjoyed appreciation. The focus of this problem is also the surviving spouse's basis (or "adjusted basis" herein after AB) in the property with the higher the AB, the better for income tax purposes. The decedent spouse's one-half interest in property held in joint tenancy that passes, by operation of law, to the surviving co-tenant spouse, receives a new basis in the hands of such surviving spouse that is equal to one-half of the property's fair market value at the decedent's death. This is the general rule of IRC § 1014(a)(1). While with appreciated property, this is referred to as a "stepped-up" basis in that one-half interest, for the property that has depreciated in value, the result is a "stepped-down" basis. As for the one-half interest in joint tenancy property that the surviving spouse already owned as when his or her spouse died, the AB remains as a higher cost basis. The fact that the one-half share coming from the deceased spouse receives a "stepped-down" basis, is not favorable.

However, it is only one-half of the property that gets this "stepped-down" basis treatment, the other one-half interest retaining its higher cost AB.

If the couple holds the property as community property, with the first spouse to die devising his or her one-half interest in the property to the surviving spouse, we have a different and less favorable result. The one-half interest devised to the surviving spouse, from the deceased spouse, receives a new AB equal to one-half the value of the property at the date of the decedent's death. This is pursuant to the general rule of IRC § 1014(a)(1), and is the same "stepped-down" result in this one-half interest that we saw in the preceding paragraph regarding property held in joint tenancy. Unfortunately for the surviving spouse, the one-half interest in the property that he or she already owned is also "stepped-down" pursuant to IRC § 1014(b)(6). This is the same provision that worked so well in the previous problem dealing with appreciated property, giving the surviving spouse a so-called "double step-up" in AB (both halves of community property receiving a new fair market value AB). It works the same way, and not so well, when dealing with depreciated property. This is sometimes referred to as the "double step-down" basis for depreciated property.

Answer (c), therefore is correct because at least with joint tenancy, only one-half of the property receives a "stepped down" AB for the recipient spouse. A more comprehensive analysis of this question utilizing the facts in our question illustrated with some numbers might be helpful. This illustration is very similar to that utilized in the analysis of question 15, but with the respective numbers representing the couple's original cost and fair market value at Wife's death reversed.

> *Assume that our Wife and Husband purchased the vacant lot many years ago for $800,000. Let us further assume that the lot has depreciated in value to $200,000 and one spouse, the Wife, dies. We will analyze these facts in the alternative scenarios that the property was titled in "joint tenancy" and "community property."*

Joint Tenancy Analysis

Joint tenants each have an undivided one-half ownership interest in property while both co-tenants are alive. Joint tenancy carries with it, the right of survivorship, where, by operation of law, at the death of one co-tenant, his or her one-half interest vests in (goes to) the surviving co-tenant. At Wife's death, her one-half interest in the property would go to Husband, resulting in Husband's 100% ownership of the property. But what is Husband's AB? He already owned one-half of the property prior to his wife's death, and to this one half, we apply our "cost" AB rule – Husband's one-half of the original $800,000 purchase price is $400,000.

Husband's AB in the one-half that he already owned prior to Wife's death is $400,000.

As for the one-half interest in the property owned by Wife that Husband receives by operation of law at Wife's death (as the surviving joint tenant), we apply the rules of IRC § 1014(a)(1) – Husband's AB in this one-half interest received from decedent Wife is one-half of the property's $200,000 fair market date of death value, or $100,000. Husband's resulting AB is $500,000 comprised of $400,000 representing the AB for the one-half of the property that he originally owned and $100,000 representing the AB for the one-half of the property that he received from decedent Wife at her death. We see that Husband received a so-called "stepped down" basis in one-half of the property (the share coming from Wife at her death). This result is illustrated in the following diagram:

Joint Tenancy Analysis

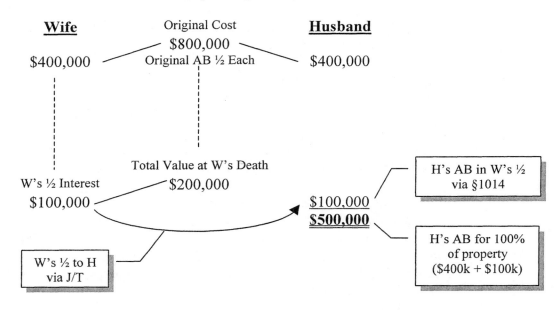

Community Property Analysis

Similar to joint tenancy, a husband and wife each has an undivided one-half interest in community property. Regular community property, as is the case here, does not have the automatic "transfer at death" mechanism of joint tenancy. A spouse is free to devise her or his one-half community property interest to anyone. Absent a devise, the deceased spouse's interest goes by state intestacy laws. To make this illustration consistent with that of joint tenancy, where the surviving spouse ends up owning 100% of the property, we will assume that Wife's will devises her one-half community property interest to Husband. In this scenario, Husband again owns 100% of the property after Wife's death, but what is his AB in this property. Applying the basic rule of IRC § 1014(a)(1) Husband's AB in the one-half interest that he received from decedent Wife equals one-half of the property's $200,000 fair market date of death value, or $100,000. And the AB in the one-half interest Husband already owned? This is where a special rule, at IRC § 1014(b)(6), comes into play. For AB determination purposes, this rule says that we treat the <u>Husband's</u> one-half interest in the community property (that he already owns) as if it too was received from his wife at her death. This then translates into application of the general date of death valuation as AB rule for property received from a decedent. Husband's AB in <u>his</u> one-half of the property also gets "stepped-down" to the fair market value of that one-half at Wife's death – $100,000 in our illustration. Husband's resulting AB is <u>$200,000</u> or a so-called "double step-down" in basis for community property that has declined in value. This result is illustrated in the following diagram:

Community Property Analysis

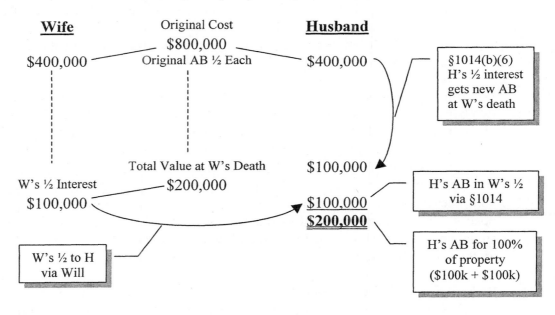

Surviving Husband has an AB of <u>$500,000</u> if they held the property as joint tenants. Alternatively, surviving Husband has an AB of <u>$200,000</u> if they held it as community property. Clearly, the latter result is worse for Husband in this set of facts.

For appreciated property, this special community property provision can be a great tax savings device that effectively makes, for income tax purposes, all unrealized appreciation and gain in the decedent's hands evaporate. However, for property that has declined in value, the special community property rule can produce unfavorable results.

Answer (a) is incorrect because in this question, there is no step-up in basis for property that has declined in value. As discussed above, IRC §§ 1014(b)(6) and 1014(a) work in concert to produce a "double step-down" in basis for community property that has declined in value. **Answer (b) is incorrect** because IRC § 1041 has no application with respect to the facts in this problem. **Answer (d) is incorrect** because "joint tenancy" does, indeed, produce a more favorable result to the surviving spouse in this <u>declining</u> property value situation vis-à-vis the surviving spouse's resulting AB in the property.

17.   **The correct answer is (b).** In every fact pattern in which something is sold, the author likes to go through the following analysis:

     1)   Does the sale result in a <u>realized</u> gain or loss and if so, what is the <u>amount</u>?

     2)   If we have a <u>realized</u> gain or loss, is it <u>recognized</u> (i.e. reportable for income tax purposes)?

     3)   If the gain or loss is recognized, is it accorded "capital" gain or loss treatment?

Determining Sean's realized gain or loss in this question requires us to identify two basic components: his sales price ("amount realized" or, hereinafter, AR) and his basis in the land ("adjusted basis or, hereinafter, AB). The difference between the two represents <u>realized</u> gain or loss. [IRC § 1001(a).] Each of these two components, AR and AB, can present a variety of complex tax issues for exam and real-world tax purposes. Although this question lacks numbers, conceptually both the AB and AR components are fairly straightforward in our question. Sean's AB is his original cost of the raw land. The land in question declined in value, and since Sean sold it for its then lower fair market value, he <u>realized</u> a <u>loss</u> on the sale of the land.

It should be noted that, while not at issue in this question, adjustments to a taxpayer's basis in an asset can result from many reasons including capital improvements (increasing basis), and depreciation expenses (reducing basis). [IRC § 1016.] In this question there are no indications that improvements have been made to the land. It should be noted that raw land is generally not "depreciable."

The next step in our analysis of gain/loss situations is to determine the extent to which any this <u>realized</u> loss is <u>recognized</u>. Recognition of loss basically means that it is reflected, as a deduction, in computing taxable income. IRC § 1001(c) provides that unless otherwise provided for in the Code, all realized gains and losses are recognized. Unfortunately, this is such an "otherwise provided for" non-recognition provision applicable to Sean's loss in this situation. IRC § 267 disallows deductions for losses resulting from sales between certain related individuals. In other words, a loss realized from the sale to certain related individuals will not be recognized. Sean's mother, Marta, is considered a "related" individual for purposes of this section (IRC § 267(c)(4) defines related individuals as siblings, stepsiblings, spouses, ancestors and lineal descendants). Therefore, Sean's realized loss is <u>not recognized</u>. In other words, Sean gets no income tax benefit from this loss.

Note that we need not proceed to the third step in our analysis of gain/loss situations (determining capital gain/loss treatment), because Sean's loss is not recognized. Basically, we stop at step two, as we only go to the third step in the analysis for gains/losses that are recognized (which is not the case here with Sean's loss). Students sometimes jump straight to the capital gain/loss step three without first making the critical determination of gain/loss recognition. For example, Sean's land would be considered a capital asset and would have given rise to a capital loss had his loss been recognizable. Sean does <u>not</u> have a capital loss from this sale even though the land was a capital asset in Sean's hands because the loss never gets past the "recognition" stage. Had Sean sold the land to an individual "unrelated" to him, the loss would have been recognized and we would have continued to the capital loss, step three, of our analysis.

Answer (a) is incorrect. While it is true that gifts do not result in recognized losses, sales to related parties do not necessarily result in a gift. A sale of an asset for its full fair market value, as was Sean's sale to his mother Marta, does not result in a gift. The fact that Sean was financially strapped and that Marta felt sorry for Sean, is irrelevant in this case. **Answer (c) is incorrect** because notwithstanding other non-recognition provisions (such as our related party disallowance) realized losses from the sale of investment property are generally recognized. **Answer (d) is incorrect** because it, like answer (a), incorporates "gift" concepts that are inapplicable to the facts of this question.

- **Additional references:** *See* DANIEL Q. POSIN, FEDERAL INCOME TAXATION OF INDIVIDUALS ¶¶ 4.01, 4.03, 4.05(6) (5th ed. 2000).

18. **Answer (a) is correct.** This question is very similar to question 17 immediately above. However, the results are very different. Although it may be tedious for the reader, a step-by-step complete analysis is appropriate for this question. As previously indicated, in every fact pattern in which something is sold, the author likes to go through the following analysis:

1) Does the sale result in a <u>realized</u> gain or loss and if so, what is the <u>amount</u>?

2) If we have a <u>realized</u> gain or loss, is it <u>recognized</u> (i.e. reportable for income tax purposes)?

3) If the gain or loss is recognized, is it accorded "capital" gain or loss treatment?

We will conclude that Sean's loss <u>is</u> recognized and it will qualify as a capital loss.

Determining Sean's realized gain or loss in this question requires us to identify two basic components: his sales price ("amount realized" or, hereinafter, AR) and his basis in the land ("adjusted basis or, hereinafter, AB). The difference between the two represents a <u>realized</u> gain or loss. [IRC § 1001(a).] Although this question also lacks numbers, conceptually both the AB and AR components are fairly straightforward in this question. Sean's AB is his original cost of this parcel of raw land. The land in question declined substantially in value, and since Sean sold it to his brother-in-law Bob for its then lower fair market value, Sean <u>realized</u> a <u>loss</u> on the sale of the land.

It should be noted that, while not at issue in this question, adjustments to a taxpayer's basis in an asset can result from many reasons including capital improvements (increasing basis), and depreciation expenses (reducing basis). [IRC § 1016.] In this question there are no indications that improvements have been made to land. It should be noted that raw land is generally, not "depreciable."

The next step in our analysis of gain/loss situations is to determine the extent to which any of this <u>realized</u> loss is <u>recognized</u>. Recognition of loss basically means that it is reflected, as a deduction, in computing taxable income. IRC § 1001(c) provides that unless otherwise provided for in the Code, all realized gains and losses are recognized. In question 17, immediately preceding this question, we addressed IRC § 267, which disallows deductions for losses resulting from sales between certain related individuals. Sean's mother Marta was a "related" individual for purposes of this disallowance section. Is brother-in-law Bob considered "related" for purposes of IRC § 267? IRC § 267(c)(4) defines a "related" individual as a sibling, a stepsibling, a spouse, an ancestor (e.g., parent, grandparent, etc.), and a lineal descendant (e.g., child, grandchild, etc.). An "in-law," such as Bob, is <u>not</u>, for purposes of this section, considered related. Therefore, IRC § 267 does not, in this question, block Sean's recognition of his realized loss resulting from his sale to Bob. So far, so good.

Continuing with the second step in the analysis of gains/losses, whether a realized loss is recognized, we need to address another issue. Anytime we are addressing the recognition of a loss sustained by an individual, as we are here, we must also address IRC § 165. At first glance, the "general rule" in IRC § 165(a) looks great, allowing a deduction for "any loss sustained during the taxable year . . ." Reading further at IRC § 165(c) we come across an ominous sounding subsection: "Limitation on losses of individuals." In class, this professor refers to this as the "section 165(c) hoop," complete with graphic depictions on the board. Figuratively, the goal is to jump from the "realized" loss side, through the hoop to the land of "recognized" losses. This hoop, however, is more akin to a semi-permeable membrane than an unobstructed open space. We see, in IRC § 165(c)(1)-(3), that business losses, investment losses and personal-use "casualty" losses, break on through to the recognized loss side. By default, however, losses from personal-use assets (other than casualty losses) do not make it through this "section 165(c) hoop" and go unrecognized. This explains why, for example, when you sell your personal-use car for a loss (which is almost always the case), the loss is realized but not recognized – i.e., you get no tax benefit from such a loss. Turning to Sean in our problem, the facts indicate that he purchased and held the real estate for investment purposes and that there is no indication that he used it for personal or pleasure purposes. Even though it proved to be a poor investment for Sean, it was an investment nonetheless. Sean's realized loss, therefore, passes through this recognition hoop of IRC § 165(c) and is recognized.

Barring further potential nonrecognition provisions, of which there are none applicable to Sean in our facts, we proceed to the third step in our gain/loss analysis: is Sean's recognized loss on the sale of the land to Bob a "capital loss?" A capital loss analysis requires first determining that we are dealing with a "capital asset" after which the gain is characterized as having either long-term or short-term status. IRC § 1221(a) defines a capital asset in a negative fashion, but for purposes of this analysis, it includes, by process of elimination, assets held for investment and personal-use purposes. As indicated, Sean held the raw land for investment purposes. Therefore, Sean's realized, and recognized loss, is properly characterized as a <u>capital loss</u>. At this point, the analysis would normally continue to determine whether the capital loss is characterized as long-term or short-term, with long-term status reserved for those assets held for more than one year. However, we are not given the length of Sean's holding period for the land in this problem and, therefore, can go no further in our analysis.

Answer (b) is incorrect because the IRC § 267 disallowance of losses on sales between related parties does not apply in this situation, as Bob is not, for purposes of this section, considered a related party. **Answer (c) is incorrect**. It is correct to the extent that it reflects Sean has a recognized loss. However, this answer fails to reflect the proper characterization of the land as a capital asset. **Answer (d) is incorrect** because it does not properly reflect the above discussed nonrecognition rules of IRC § 165(c).

- **Additional references:** *See* DANIEL Q. POSIN, FEDERAL INCOME TAXATION OF INDIVIDUALS ¶¶ 4.01, 4.03, 4.05(6) (5th ed. 2000).

19. **The correct answer is (b).** This is a fairly complex question, and it requires a somewhat lengthy step-by-step analysis. This is another example of a question that, to a student studying income tax, may appear to exist purely as an academic exercise. While it does contain aspects that present an academic challenge, this question reflects a surprisingly common "real world" tax situation. We will conclude that Winnie and Herb each has a <u>realized</u> gain of $100,000 from the sale of their respective interests in the home. However, pursuant to IRC § 121, they will both be able to fully exclude their gains from recognition as income.

In every fact pattern in which something is sold, the author likes to go through the following analysis:

1) Does the sale result in a <u>realized</u> gain or loss and if so, what is the <u>amount</u>?

2) If we have a <u>realized</u> gain or loss, is it <u>recognized</u> (i.e. reportable for income tax purposes)?

3) If the gain or loss is recognized, is it accorded "capital" gain or loss treatment?

Because this question involves a multi-step analysis and because the author recognizes the value of your time, both **abbreviated/short** and **comprehensive/long** analyses are provided below.

The <u>abbreviated/short</u> version of the analysis for this question begins with the understanding that at the time of the house sale, we have two separate and unmarried individuals, Winnie and Herb, each selling an undivided one-half interest in the house. Both Winnie and Herb each *realize* a $100,000 gain from the sale. This gain is the difference between the $250,000 sales price for each of their one-half shares ($500,000 combined sales price) less their respective bases of $150,000. Winnie's basis is her "cost" for the one-half interest (one-half of her original $300,000 cost for the entire house). Herb's basis in his one-half interest in the house is a "carryover" basis from Winnie's cost basis for the one-half interest because Herb received his one half interest in the house as a transfer "incident to their divorce."

Neither Winnie nor Herb will have to *recognize* their respective gains. Analyzing each of them, and their respective realized gains, *independently* (they are no longer married), they both can exclude (not recognize) their realized gain pursuant to IRC § 121, the exclusion of gain from the sale of a personal residence.

The following comprehensive/long (very long) analysis presents a step-by-step discussion of the answer to this question that can be applied to other gain/loss questions.

The first step in our analysis process is determining whether Winnie and Herb have *realized* gains or losses from the sale of their respective one-half interests in the house. It is important to understand that at the time of the house sale, we have two separate and unmarried individuals, Winnie and Herb, each selling an undivided one-half interest in the house. Essentially, we have two separate sales to analyze.

To determine the *realized* gain or loss from the sale of the interests in the house, we need two basic components: the sales price ("amount realized" or, hereinafter, AR) and the basis in the property interest ("adjusted basis or, hereinafter, AB). The difference between the two represents realized gain or loss. [IRC § 1001(a).] Each of these two components, AR and AB, can present a variety of complex tax issues for exam and real-world tax purposes. The AR side for both Winnie and Herb is straightforward in our question, and is $250,000 for each of them (the combined selling price of the house was $500,000.

The general starting place for determining one's AB in property is one's cost. [IRC §§ 1011 and 1012.] "Adjustments" to one's basis, while not at issue in this question, can result from many reasons including capital improvements (increasing basis), and depreciation expenses (reducing basis). [IRC § 1016.] Applying the general cost basis rule in our question, Winnie's AB is her "cost" for the one-half interest (one-half of her original $300,000 cost for the entire house) or $150,000. The determination of Herb's AB is a bit more involved but not too complex. There is no indication that Herb paid anything for his one-half interest in the house. Rather, he received his one-half ownership interest pursuant to his and Winnie's divorce decree. The AB of property transferred between spouses, or former spouses that are "incident to divorce," is controlled by IRC § 1041(b). In a nutshell, it provides that when spouses transfer property to each other, or when former spouses transfer property to each other and it is "incident to their divorce," the transferee spouse (or former spouse) takes a carryover basis. This section does not distinguish as to the type of inter vivos transfer involved – it covers gifts, sales, exchanges, etc. The term "incident to divorce" means any transfer within one year of the divorce or generally within six years of the divorce such transfer is called for by the divorce instrument (e.g., divorce decree). This is not a significant issue in our case and when Herb receives the one-half interest in the house, he takes as his AB the AB that Winnie had in that one-half interest. We have already determined that Winnie's AB in the property is her cost and, therefore, Herb, like Winnie, has a $150,000 AB in his one-half interest in the house.

The determination of *realized* gains or losses to Winnie and Herb is now an easy task:

Winnie		Herb
$250,000	Amount realized (AR)	$250,000
($150,000)	Adjusted basis (AB)	($150,000)
$100,000	***Realized* Gain**	**$100,000**

The next step in our analysis of gain/loss situations is to determine the extent to which any <u>realized</u> gain is <u>recognized</u>. Recognition of gain basically means that it is reported as income for income tax purposes. IRC § 1001(c) provides that unless otherwise provided for in the Code, all realized gains and losses are recognized. One such "unless otherwise provided" nonrecognition section is IRC § 121, relating to gains from the sale of a taxpayer's principal residence. Effective for sales of a taxpayer's principal residence after May 6, 1997, IRC § 121 provides for the exclusion of up to $250,000 of realized gain ($500,000 in the case of certain married individuals) if certain conditions are met. There are two basic requirements for this exclusion, commonly referred to as the "ownership" and "use" tests. The taxpayer must have owned the house for at least two years (looking back five years from the date of sale), <u>and</u> must have used it as his/her principal residence for two years (looking back five years from the date of sale). [IRC § 121(a).] Because Winnie and Herb are two separate individuals, with two separate realized gains, the section requirements must be analyzed separately with respect to Winnie and Herb.

<u>Winnie: *Recognition* of Gain and Application of IRC § 121</u>

As to Winnie's one-half interest in the house, she easily meets the two-year "ownership" test, having owned at least a one-half interest for five years. Winnie also easily meets the two-year "use" test as she has been using the house as her principal residence for five years. Winnie meets the requirements of IRC § 121, and she can exclude up to $250,000 of realized gain (remember, she is single at this point). Her realized gain of $100,000 does not exceed this maximum so all of her gain is excluded from gross income (or <u>not</u> *recognized*). Because none of her gain is *recognized*, there is no need to continue to the third step in our analysis, the characterization of recognized gains.

<u>Herb: *Recognition* of Gain and Application of IRC § 121</u>

It was exactly one year ago that the couple divorced, and Herb received his one-half interest in the house (pursuant to their divorce decree). In real terms, Herb has owned his one-half interest for only one year, which is less than the requisite two-year period. Herb, however, is in luck because of the "special rule" at IRC § 121(d)(3)(A) that states: "In the case of an individual holding property transferred to such individual in a transaction described in section 1041(a), the period such individual owns such property shall include the period the transferor owned the property." Herb *did* receive his one-half interest from Winnie incident to their divorce (a transaction to which IRC § 1041 applies). This special rule allows Herb to "tack," or add, Winnie's period of ownership (prior to Herb receiving his interest) onto his ownership period resulting in Herb owning his one-half interest for five years. Thus, Herb does meet the two-year ownership test.

The two-year "use" test presents a similar problem. Herb did use the house as his principal residence for one year (the year he was married to Winnie). Recall that he then moved out of the house at the couple's divorce and did not live in the house for the subsequent year. In real terms, Herb has used the house as his principal residence for only one year. Again, Herb is in luck. Another "special rule" at IRC § 121(d)(3)(B) states: "Solely for purposes of this section, an individual shall be treated as using the property as such individual's principal residence during any period of ownership which such individual's spouse or former spouse is granted use of the property under a divorce decree or separation instrument." This provision allows Herb to "tack," or add, on to his one-year use period, the one year that Winnie has used the house as her principal residence subsequent to their divorce. Fortunately for Herb, this adds up to a total of two years of use, thus meeting the two-year "use" test. Note that the tacking of use is not the same as that for ownership. Tacking of "use" is tacking the other spouse's period of use forward from the divorce. Tacking of "ownership" is tacking the other spouse's ownership back from the divorce.

With the help of these two special rules, Herb meets the requirements of IRC § 121, and he can exclude up to $250,000 of realized gain (remember, he is single at this point). His realized gain of $100,000 does not exceed this maximum, so all of his gain is excluded from gross income (or _not_ *recognized*). Because none of his gain is *recognized*, there is no need to continue to the third step in our analysis, the characterization of recognized gains.

While not at issue in this problem, it should be noted that generally, the exclusion provisions of IRC § 121 cannot be used more than once in a two-year period. [IRC § 121(b)(3).] It is a logical assumption from the facts presented that this limitation would not apply to Herb in this question.

It should also be noted that the statute does not require that the requisite two-year "use" and "ownership" period be co-extensive. While again, this is not an issue in this question, it is a common misunderstanding (read as "good testing area") that the two "two-year" qualifying periods must be at the same time. It is also a common misunderstanding (again, read as "good testing area") that the "five-year look back period" for purposes of determining two-year ownership and use somehow requires that the taxpayer either owned or used the house for at least five years. This is not correct and again, while this is not at issue in this question, it might be helpful for your analysis of other IRC § 121 related questions.

Answer (a) is incorrect but it does raise an interesting issue. As discussed in other questions in this book, the IRC § 121 exclusion provisions might apply on a prorated basis if one's sale of their principal residence was for reasons of health, job change, or for "unforeseen circumstances." In our problem, Herb met the two qualifying tests of IRC § 121 because of the special "tacking" rules. However, had he not met both tests for the full two-year period, would he be entitled to a prorated exclusion based on the theory that his divorce (and subsequent sale) is an "unforeseen circumstance?" As of this writing, the Treasury has not issued regulations as to what constitutes "unforeseen circumstances," and the I.R.S. has indicated that taxpayers may not rely on their own definition of what constitutes "unforeseen circumstances." **Answer (c) is incorrect** because the nonrecognition provisions of IRC § 1041 apply only to transfers between spouses or former spouses if incident to divorce. Gains from sales to "outside" parties, such as is the case here, are not covered by IRC § 1041. **Answer (d) is incorrect** because it fails to recognize that Winnie and Herb are two separate, unmarried individuals, who have two separate *realized* gains. Please see other questions in this book that address the application of IRC § 121 to married individuals. **Answer (e) is also incorrect**. This answer does not correctly apply the "tacking" rules to the sale of Herb's one-half interest in the house.

- **Additional references:** *See* DANIEL Q. POSIN, FEDERAL INCOME TAXATION OF INDIVIDUALS ¶¶ 4.01, 4.02, 4.04(5), 6.02(14)(b) (5th ed. 2000).

20.   **The correct answer is (b).** This question, except for one critical date in the facts, is identical to another question appearing elsewhere in this book. The answer, however, is quite different with Tom realizing a $4,000 gain from the sale of the watch.

Determining Tom's realized gain or loss in this question requires us to identify two basic components: his sales price ("amount realized" or, hereinafter, AR) and his basis in the watch ("adjusted basis or, hereinafter, AB). The difference between the two represents realized gain or loss. [IRC § 1001(a).] Each of these two components, AR and AB, can present a variety of complex tax issues for exam and real-world tax purposes. The AR side is straightforward in our question, and is his $23,000 sales price. Other questions in this book present more complex issues involving a taxpayer's AR. The AB component is the more challenging in this question.

While a taxpayer's cost is normally the starting point for determination of one's basis in property (IRC §§ 1011 and 1012), when property is received as a gift, as is the case here, there really is no "cost" to the taxpayer. The seemingly logical result of a zero basis is neither desirable nor, thankfully, appropriate. IRC § 1015 provides us with the rules for determining a donee's AB in property received as a gift. The general rule for most gifts is that the donee takes the donor's AB in the property, or what is commonly referred to as a "carryover" AB. In Tom's case, this would be Tom's Aunt's original $18,000 cost. This is Tom's starting point in determining his AB.

We say "starting point" because there was a gift tax paid in connection with the 1990 gift to Tom. Discussion of gift taxes is beyond the scope of this book, and most basic federal income tax courses. Suffice it to say that a gift tax is based on the value of the property transferred and is an obligation of the donor/transferor. It is a given, in our facts, that Tom's Aunt incurred and paid a $7,000 gift tax on the 1990 gift to Tom. While the study of gift taxes is beyond our scope, their effect on a donee/transferee's AB is not. IRC § 1015(d) provides for a "gift tax paid adjustment" to AB (an increase to AB). The method of calculating this positive, and favorable, adjustment varies depending on when the gift was made, with the critical date (of the gift) being December 31, 1976. The gift tax paid adjustment to AB for gifts made before 1977, is the subject of at least one question presented elsewhere in this book. In this question, the gift to Tom was in 1990 and the "gift tax paid adjustment" rules for post-1976 gifts are contained in IRC § 1015(d)(6). Unfortunately for students, the gift tax paid adjustment calculation for post-1976 gifts is a more difficult arithmetic affair than that for gifts made before 1977. The calculation is a prorated type of computation and is an example of what this professor's students refer to as the dreaded algebra infused "Code ratio" [See Appendix C for explanation of "Code" math.] Recognizing that any type of formula may strike fear in the hearts of some law students, rest assured that the calculations are not really that bad.

The gift tax paid adjustment, or the amount by which Tom can increase his $18,000 carryover AB from his aunt, will be represented by the variable "X" in the following formula:

$$\frac{X}{\text{Gift Tax Paid}} = \frac{\text{"Net Appreciation" of Property in Donor's Hands at Time of Gift}}{\text{Value of Gift at Time of Gift}}$$

The term "net appreciation" as used in the numerator on the right-hand side of this equation is simply how much the property has appreciated in value from the time the donor acquired the property until he or she made the gift. Alternatively stated, the "net appreciation" is the difference between the value of the gift at the time of the gift, and the donor's AB in the property. The above formula adjusted to reflect this definition is:

$$\frac{X}{\text{Gift Tax Paid}} = \frac{(\text{Value of Gift at Time of Gift} - \text{Donor's AB in Gift})}{\text{Value of Gift at Time of Gift}}$$

Utilizing the numbers from our facts, the formula is:

$$\frac{X}{\$7,000} = \frac{(\$21,000 - \$18,000)}{\$21,000} \qquad \text{or:} \qquad \frac{X}{\$7,000} = \frac{\$3,000}{\$21,000}$$

Our task now is to try to remember high-school algebra and solve for the variable "X." There are a variety of ways to solve for X. One such way is to first simplify the right-hand side of the equation, if possible, then isolate X on the left-hand side of the equation by multiplying both sides by the denominator on the left-hand side of the equation – then multiply and divide the numbers on the right-hand side of the equation as necessary to find the numeric value. Another method is to "cross multiply," then isolate X and solve for its numeric value. Or, as is the case with our facts, you may be able to just "eye-ball" the answer. The value for "X" in our problem is $1,000. Tom's "gift tax paid adjustment," the amount he is entitled to add to his carryover AB is $1,000 (the solved value of "X"). Tom's resulting AB is, therefore, $19,000 (the $18,000 carryover AB plus the $1,000 gift tax paid adjustment).

The calculation of Tom's gain is now a simple matter. His AR of $23,000 less his $19,000 AB results in a realized gain of $4,000. While not the subject of this question, issues of gain <u>recognition</u> and <u>characterization</u> (i.e., capital gain materials) are related testable material. For information purposes, Tom's $4,000 gain would be recognized and characterized as a "long-term capital gain." Please see other questions presented in this book that address issues of gain and loss recognition and characterization.

Answer (a) is incorrect. This answer utilizes an incorrect interpretation of what is the pre-1977 "gift tax paid adjustment" rule that is covered in at least one question elsewhere in this book. **Answer (c) is incorrect** because it utilizes the pre-1977 "gift tax the "gift tax paid adjustment" rule, albeit in a correct manner. The gift to Tom in this question utilizes the gift tax paid adjustment for post-1976 gifts pursuant to IRC § 1015(d)(6). **Answer (d) is incorrect** because it fails to reflect any "gift tax paid adjustment," rendering Tom's AB in the watch as a straight "carryover" of $18,000. **Answer (e) is incorrect** because a correct response (b) is presented.

- **Additional references:** *See* DANIEL Q. POSIN, FEDERAL INCOME TAXATION OF INDIVIDUALS ¶¶ 4.01, 4.03 (5th ed. 2000).

21. **The correct answer is (e).** Alicia falls within the so-called "wash sale" rules that prevent the recognition of the loss she sustained from her December sale of the XYZ shares. There is no question that Alicia "realized" a loss from the sale of her shares in December measured by her $10,000 cost of the shares less the $4,000 selling price (a realized loss of $6,000). IRC § 1001(c) states that unless otherwise provided for in the Code, all realized gains and losses are recognized. Unfortunately, there is such an "otherwise provided for" non-recognition provision applicable to Alicia's loss realized from the December sale of her shares.

IRC § 1091, in an attempt to prevent manipulation of losses by taxpayers, provides, in its most basic form, that if you sell shares of stock for a loss and within thirty days you purchase the same stock, you do <u>not</u> get to recognize the loss from the sale. This is referred to as a "wash sale." In effect, you are treated as if you never disposed of the shares in the fist place. In Alicia's case, while she had no manipulative intent (trying to benefit from a loss before the end of the year and then reestablish her position in the stock a short time later), she did repurchase the same number of XYZ shares within thirty days of selling them for a loss. This law makes no motivational distinctions and, unfortunately for Alicia, prevents the recognition of her December loss.

Answer (a) is incorrect because there is no such mechanism in the statute to provide for such a result. **Answer (b) is incorrect** because Alicia's sale and repurchase precludes the recognition of the December loss. **Answer (c) is incorrect** because the wash sale rules contain no such "safe harbor" for transactions straddling different tax years. Rather, the prohibited purchase period is a straight "thirty days" (either before or, as is the more common situation as presented in our facts, after the loss sale). **Answer (d) is incorrect** because "intent" is irrelevant in application of the IRC § 1091 wash sale rules.

- **Additional references:** *See* DANIEL Q. POSIN, FEDERAL INCOME TAXATION OF INDIVIDUALS ¶ 4.05(5) (5th ed. 2000).

22.   **The correct answer is (c).** This question is a companion to the immediately preceding question 21. It would be a bit unfair to ask both this and the preceding question on an exam as the answer for this question is somewhat dependent on arriving at the correct answer to question 21, above. However, it is presented to further explore the area of "wash sales."

Looking at the situation logically, before going into any specific statutory rules, it would seem unfair to disallow the recognition of a loss because of the *wash sale* provisions and then not have it affect (in a positive way) the basis of the replacement shares. In our question, Alicia originally paid $10,000 for her 500 shares of XYZ stock. After selling them, she repurchased 500 shares of XYZ stock for only $3,500. In computing her gain when she sells this second block of shares (for $15,000), is it fair that she must use as her basis the $3,500 cost of these shares (resulting in a huge gain) when she was not allowed to recognize the $6,000 loss from her December sale of the shares (because of the wash sale rules)? This doesn't "smell" right and indeed, the statute provides otherwise.

Normally, a taxpayer's basis in property is its costs. [IRC §§ 1011 and 1012.] When a loss is not allowed because of the wash sale rules, the statute provides a rather cryptic definition of the basis in the new shares purchased. The statute states that "the basis of the stock . . . so sold [they are referring to the stock that was sold resulting in the wash sale] . . ., increased or decreased, as the case may be, by the difference, if any, between the price at which the property was acquired [meaning the new, replacement shares] and the price at which such substantially identical stock . . . [was] sold . . ." [IRC § 1091(d).] Okay, how about this instead? Take the basis or her first block of XYZ shares ($10,000) and decrease it by $500 (the difference between the $4,000 sales price of her old shares and the $3,500 repurchase price), resulting in a basis of $9,500. Another interpretation: Take the cost of her new shares $3,500 and add her $6,000 loss that was not allowed to be recognized because of the wash sale rules, to get her basis in the new shares of $9,500.

Confusing to say the least, but after careful thought, the result *does* make sense.

Answer (a) is incorrect because it does not reflect the special basis rules applicable to wash sales. **Answers (b) and (d) are incorrect** because they do not reflect an accurate interpretation of the basis rules applicable to wash sales. **Answer (e) is incorrect** because the correct answer (c) is presented.

- **Additional references:** *See* DANIEL Q. POSIN, FEDERAL INCOME TAXATION OF INDIVIDUALS ¶ 4.05(5) (5ᵗʰ ed. 2000).

23. **Answer (a) is the most accurate.** A gift of property generally does not result in realization of a gain or loss to a donor. However, under certain circumstances (i.e., if a donor receives "consideration"), a gift may in fact constitute a "part sale/part gift" with a resulting realization of gain. In a part sale/part gift situation, a gain is realized (by the donor/transferor) to the extent the consideration received (amount realized or hereinafter AR) by the donor exceeds the donor's basis (adjusted basis or hereinafter AB) in the property. [Reg. § 1.1001-1(e).] This is consistent with the general principals of IRC § 1001(a) – the difference between the AR and AB represents a _realized_ gain or loss. When Derrick made the gift of the stock to Gail, he did not receive consideration in the traditional sense. However, Derrick did receive consideration, albeit indirectly, by Gail paying the gift tax on the transfer. While an in-depth discussion of gift taxes is far beyond the scope of this book, suffice it to say that any gift tax resulting from a gift is the obligation of the *donor*. Gail's payment of Derrick's obligation *is* consideration to Derrick. Relief of Derrick's obligation (the gift tax) represents a net financial benefit or accession to wealth to him. This concept is similar to that where an employer pays an obligation owed by one of its employees. If the employer seeks no repayment by the employee, the employee is deemed to have received consideration (extra compensation). [See *Old Colony Trust Co. v. Comm'r*, 279 U.S. 716, 49 S.Ct. 499 (1929); Reg. § 1.61-14.]

Therefore, while this appears to be just a gift, it is, in reality, a part sale/part gift situation with Derrick deemed to have received consideration (AR) equal to the amount of the gift tax paid by Gail. If the gift tax paid by Gail exceeds Derrick's AB in the shares, then Derrick has a realized and recognized gain resulting from the transfer. [See *Diedrich v. Comm'r*, 457 U.S. 191, 102 S.Ct. 2414 (1982) (donee's payment of donor's gift tax was deemed "consideration" for purposes of determining gain to the donor).]

Answer (b) is incorrect because the gift tax paid by Gail is not income but, as discussed above, represents the AR component of a potential sales-like transfer. Derrick's income, if any, will be in the form of a gain measured by the amount of consideration that he received (AR) that is in excess of his AB. **Answer (c) is incorrect** right out of the box because the payment of gift taxes does not give rise to a deduction for federal income tax purposes. **Answer (d) is incorrect** because the fact that Gail is deemed to have paid consideration does not preclude the gift element of the transfer (the value of the shares in excess of what she is deemed to have paid for them) from exclusion under IRC § 102.

- **Additional references:** *See* DANIEL Q. POSIN, FEDERAL INCOME TAXATION OF INDIVIDUALS ¶ 4.03(2)(a)(iii)(B) (5th ed. 2000).

24. **The most accurate statement is (d).** Normally, recognition of a loss relating to investments requires results from some triggering event such as a sale. When a security (stock, bond, etc.) becomes *totally worthless*, it gives rise to a capital loss for most individuals. [IRC §§ 165(a) and (g)(1).] For this result to occur, the stock must be totally worthless. The regulations, at Reg. § 1.165-4(a) state: "No deduction shall be allowed under section 165(a) solely on account of a decline in the value of stock owned by the taxpayer . . . A mere shrinkage in the value of the stock owned by the taxpayer, even though extensive, does not give rise to a deduction under section 165(a) if the stock has any recognizable value . . ."

The fact that Brenda's stock currently has <u>some</u> market value, albeit minimal, it is <u>not</u> totally worthless. Therefore **answers (a) and (b) cannot be correct.** However, if, down the road, the company does, in fact, "go under" leaving nothing for the common shareholders, then Brenda's shares *will* become *worthless*, resulting in a recognized capital loss. Because she would have held these shares for more than one year, the characterization of this capital loss would be *long-term*. [IRC § 1222.]

Answer (c) is incorrect because recognized losses from investment assets, whether caused by sale or worthlessness, gives rise to tax benefits in the form of recognized losses (usually "capital" in nature).

While not at issue in this problem, Brenda could force a current recognition of the loss in her shares by selling them. Please see other problems in this book addressing the realization, recognition and characterization of losses resulting from sales of assets.

- **Additional references:** *See* DANIEL Q. POSIN, FEDERAL INCOME TAXATION OF INDIVIDUALS ¶ 7.07(6)(b) (5th ed. 2000).

25. **The correct answer is (c).** This question raises the issue of "installment sales," and the principal Code section involved is IRC § 453. The first steps of the analysis, however, is more basic: determining the amount of Michael's *realized* gain or loss, and then determining whether any such gain or loss is *recognized*. The installment sales issue addresses the *timing* of gain recognition.

Determination of Michael's *realized* gain of loss is a simple exercise in this question. Other questions in this book address more challenging aspects of gain or loss realization. Michael's *realized* gain is $150,000, the difference between the $200,000 selling price and his basis (adjusted basis or AB) or $50,000. [IRC § 1001(a).] His AB in the land is simply its cost in this situation as no improvements had been made thereto and the land is not depreciable. [See IRC §§ 1011 and 1012 (for cost basis); IRC § 1016 (for adjustments to basis).] Michael's gain from the sale of the land is also *recognized*. Pursuant to IRC § 1001(c), all gains and losses are recognized unless otherwise provided for in the Code. There are no "nonrecognition" or "exclusion" provisions applicable in Michael's situation. The key issue here is *when* Michael recognizes this gain (i.e., reports it on his income tax return as income).

With some restrictions, when a "nondealer" sells property for a gain and at least one payment is to be received after the close of the current tax year (in which the sale took place), the recognized gain is reported (for income tax purposes) as payments are received. This is commonly referred to as the installment method of reporting gain. [IRC § 453.] Michael is not a "dealer" of property (this was his only piece of investment real estate) and his sales price is to be paid to him over ten years (first payment at sale and nine additional payments at one per year).

The mechanism for calculating the amount of gain to be reported with each payment is logical, and not nearly as bad as it sounds from reading IRC § 453. In Michael's somewhat simple situation, we know that his total gain is $150,000 and that he is receiving 10% (one-tenth) of the $200,000 sales price in each of ten years (starting with the sale date). While not exactly the method prescribed in the Code, it is logical (and correct in this situation) to conclude that Michael will report 10% (one-tenth) of the $150,000 or $15,000 with each payment of $20,000 that he receives. The Code method is a bit more complex but necessary for some situations other than our simple gain situation.

The mechanism for computing installment gain that is found in the Code establishes a "gross profit ratio" that is applied to each payment received. The *gross profit ratio* is the amount of gross profit from the sale ($150,000 for Michael) divided by the total "contract price" ($200,000 for Michael). Michael's *gross profit ratio* is 150,000/200,000 or 75%. This, then, is applied to each payment received (exclusive of any interest). 75% of the $20,000 that Michael receives as his first payment at the time of the sale, results in $15,000 of gain to be reported. Assuming Michael receives each additional $20,000 in coming years as planned, the same 75% ratio is applied to each payment (resulting in $15,000 of gain reported with each payment). While not applicable to our question, the "contract price," used in determining the *gross profit ratio*, may be different from the sales price.

The "contract price" is generally the selling price, reduced by debt on the property that the buyer either assumes or takes subject to.

For "nondealers" the installment method cannot be used for sales of publicly traded stocks or other securities. There are also limitations on its use with respect to certain depreciable assets and sales between related parties. Assuming none of these situations apply (which they do not in our question), the installment method of reporting gain for "nondealers" is <u>automatic</u>, and to not use it (i.e., report all of the recognized gain at the time of sale) an individual must affirmatively "elect" to "opt-out." [IRC § 453(d).]

While not at issue in this problem, Michael will also have to report, as income, the interest received each year with respect to his installment sale of the land. Also not at issue in this problem is the characterization of Michael's *recognized* gain. Each reported installment portion of his gain will be a long-term capital gain (sale of a capital asset, the investment land, that he held for more than one year.

Answer (a) is incorrect because $20,000 represents 10% of the sales price and not the amount of Michael's recognized gain. **Answer (b) is incorrect** because the statute does not allow one to first recover one's basis before any gain is reported as income. **Answer (d) is incorrect** because, as discussed above, the installment method is the default method for Michael's reporting of gain. He would have to elect not to use the installment method.

- **Additional references:** *See* DANIEL Q. POSIN, FEDERAL INCOME TAXATION OF INDIVIDUALS ¶ 8.03 (5th ed. 2000).

ANSWER KEY
EXAM VI

1.   **Answer (d) is correct.** Situations involving the exchange, between two parties, of services and/or property, usually result in some confusion among students at first. The bottom-line answer with respect to Skip is that he rendered $4,000 worth of services, and was compensated for them, albeit not in cash form, but by receiving other "stuff" (services and property) worth $4,000. Skip has $4,000 of income as a result. Paula did two things: rendered services and disposed of XYZ Co. shares. She rendered $1,300 worth of services and was compensated from them, albeit not in cash form, but by receiving other stuff (services from Skip) worth $1,300. Paula also disposed of XYZ Co. shares worth $2,700 and received consideration for them, albeit not in the form of cash, but by receiving other stuff (services from Skip) worth $2,700. Paula's receipt of $2,700 consideration for the shares less her cost basis ("adjusted basis" hereinafter AB) of $500, results in a realized gain of $2,200.

What is bothersome for students in such exchange transactions, is the lack of cash being received for services rendered or property transferred. Somehow, the resulting income tax consequences seem to be incorrect or unfair. To more thoroughly discuss the answer to this question, the tax implications viewed from both Skip's and Paula's perspective will be discussed.

The transaction from Skip's perspective

Early on, in classroom discussion of gross income, we discover that gross income need not be in the form of cash. A lawyer, for example, who performs legal work for a client and is paid in cash, has gross income. A lawyer who performs legal work for a client and receives property as payment has gross income equal to the fair market value of the property received. A lawyer who performs legal work for a client and receives a combination of cash and property as payment has gross income equal to the cash plus the fair market value of the property received. A lawyer who performs legal work for a client and receives the client's services as payment (in exchange) has income equal to the value of the services. A lawyer who performs legal work for a client and receives cash, property and the client's services as payment has gross income equal to the cash, the fair market value of the property, and the fair market value of the services. [See Reg. § 1.61-1(d) (compensation received in forms other than in cash).] When an individual performs services and receives "something" in exchange, that "something" (or the value thereof) represents gross income. The form of that "something" is generally irrelevant. In our question, Skip rendered $4,000 worth of services, and received $4,000 worth of stuff in return: $2,700 worth of property and $1,300 worth of Paula's services. Skip has gross income of $4,000.

In class, this professor likes to recast, or view in a different light, exchange or barter transactions in an essentially equivalent manner involving the transfer of cash back and forth between the parties. We could break down the transaction between Skip and Paula into something like this. Skip performs $4,000 worth of services for Paula and Paula pays Skip $4,000 in cash. At this point, it is clear Skip would have income. Next, Paula performs $1,300 worth of services for Skip, and Skip pays Paula $1,300 in cash. Finally, Skip buys shares XYZ Co, stock worth $2,700 from Paula paying her $2,700 in cash. We will discuss the tax impact to Paula below, but in economic substance, viewing the transaction this way (with cash going back and forth) is the same as that given in our facts.

The transaction from Paula's perspective

Paula performed services worth $1,300 and was paid for these services, albeit not in the form of cash. We know, from our discussion above regarding Skip, that she has gross income regardless of the form of payment. So, for part of this transaction she received $1,300 worth of stuff (Skip's services) for her services, which, results in gross income of $1,300. The other part of the transaction from Paula's perspective was the disposition of the XYZ Co. shares. A sale or disposition of property results in the realization of a gain or loss to transferor measured by the difference between the "amount realized" (AR) and the transferor's AB. [IRC § 1001(a).] The AR side of this sale or disposition equation is obscured just a bit. One's AR from a sale or disposition of property is usually received in the form of cash. However, AR is broader than that and basically includes the value of any "stuff" received in exchange for property whether it be other property or services (money's worth). Here, Paula received $2,700 worth of "stuff" (Skip's services) as consideration. Paula's AB is straightforward in this question, and is her $500 original cost of the shares. [See IRC §§ 1011 and 1012.] In effect, Paula sold these shares and received $2,700 consideration (in the form of Skip's services), resulting in a realized gain of $2,200 ($2,700 AR less her AB of $500). In the aggregate, therefore, Paula has $1,300 gross income resulting from her services rendered, and a $2,200 realized gain from the disposition of her XYZ Co. shares.

Let us view these tax results to Paula utilizing our "recast" cash version of this transaction. Skip performs $4,000 worth of services for Paula and Paula pays Skip $4,000 in cash. Next, Paula performs $1,300 worth of services for Skip and Skip pays Paula $1,300 in cash. Finally, Skip buys shares XYZ Co, stock worth $2,700 from Paula paying her $2,700 in cash. It is now easy to see that Paula has $1,300 of gross income for her services rendered. It is also easy to identify the stock "sale or disposition" transaction with a $2,700 sales price resulting in $2,200 of realized gain to Paula ($2,700 AR less her AB of $500).

[For more information about barter/exchange transactions, see Reg. § 1.61-1(d); Rev.Rul. 79-24, 1979-1 C.B. 60.]

Answer (a) is incorrect because "barter" transactions such as the one in our question, are not tax-free transactions. **Answer (b) is incorrect** as to Paula's income tax consequences. The exchange from Paula's perspective is actually two transactions: rendering (and being paid for) services, and the sale of her stock. This answer fails to property identify the income tax consequences resulting from the stock sale component of the transaction. As to Skip, this answer is correct. **Answer (c) is incorrect** because it does not reflect the entire scope of the facts presented in the question. **Answer (e) is incorrect**. This answer would have been correct if Paula had paid for the extra $2,700 worth of Skip's services in cash. However, she paid for these extra services with property and, as discussed above, this represents a "sale or disposition" of the property, resulting in a gain.

- **Additional references:** *See* DANIEL Q. POSIN, FEDERAL INCOME TAXATION OF INDIVIDUALS ¶¶ 3.13(3), 4.01, 4.03 (5th ed. 2000).

2. **Answer (c) is correct.** This question, unfortunately, requires, in part, a correct analysis of the previous question. This professor would not ask such a series of interrelated multiple-choice questions on an exam. Rather, this series of questions was derived from an exam essay question.

This question presents a basic gain calculation with a slight twist. When Skip sells the XYZ Co. shares, he realizes a gain or loss measured by the difference between the sales price (or in tax terms: the amount realized or AR) and his adjusted basis (hereinafter AB) in the property. [IRC § 1001(a).] The AR portion of the equation in this problem is simply the $5,000 sales price for the XYZ Co. shares. The key component to this question is the determination of Skip's AB in the shares. We will conclude, below, that $2,700 will be his AB in the shares, thus resulting in a realized gain of $2,300 (AR of $5,000 less an AB of $2,700).

A taxpayer's cost is normally the starting point for determining one's basis in property. [IRC §§ 1011 and 1012.] Here, while it is a bit obscured, Skip paid $2,700 for the XYZ Co. shares in his exchange transaction with Paula. From the analysis of the correct answer to question 1, above, we know that Skip had, in part $2,700 of gross income, in the form of compensation, resulting from receiving the shares in the exchange (he also received an additional $1,300 of gross income, receiving Paula's services in exchange). At this point, it might be helpful to look at how we viewed the transaction in an alternate, but equivalent, form with cash going back and forth between the parties. Recall the "recast" transaction: Skip performs $4,000 worth of services for Paula and Paula pays Skip $4,000 in cash. Next, Paula performs $1,300 worth of services for Skip and Skip pays Paula $1,300 in cash. Finally, Skip buys shares XYZ Co, stock worth $2,700 from Paula paying her $2,700 in cash. Viewing the transaction from this revised vantage point, we see that Skip, in effect, paid $2,700 for the shares and that this represents his AB in the shares. This concept in determining Skip's AB in property received in payment for services rendered is sometimes referred to as "tax cost" and is described, albeit in a somewhat cryptic fashion, in the regulations at Reg. § 1.61-2(d)(2)(i).

Skip's gain calculation is now easy to accomplish. The $5,000 sales price (AR) less his $2,700 AB results in a realized gain of $2,300.

Answers (a) (b) and (d) are incorrect because none of these answers reflects a valid calculation of Skip's realized gain resulting from his sale of the XYZ Co. shares. **Answer (e) is incorrect** because a correct answer (d) is presented.

- **Additional references:** *See* DANIEL Q. POSIN, FEDERAL INCOME TAXATION OF INDIVIDUALS ¶¶ 4.01, 4.02, 4.03 (5th ed. 2000).

3. **The correct answer is (b).** To answer this question, it is helpful to "recast" this exchange transaction as illustrated in the analysis of the answers to questions 1 and 2, above. Skip performs $4,000 worth of services for Paula, and Paula <u>pays</u> Skip $4,000 <u>in cash</u>. Next, Paula performs $1,300 worth of services for Skip, and Skip <u>pays</u> Paula $1,300 <u>in cash</u>. Finally, Skip buys shares XYZ Co, stock worth $2,700 from Paula <u>paying</u> her $2,700 <u>in cash</u>. We can now more easily identify "payments" that may give rise to possible deductions.

Skip effectively paid $1,300 to Paula for expert stock/investment advice. Pursuant to IRC § 212 this expenditure most likely qualifies for a deduction. IRC § 212 allows for deductions for ordinary and necessary expenses paid in connection with 1) the production or collection of income, 2) the management, conservation, or maintenance of property held for the production of income, or 3) the determination, collection or refund of any tax. Other than the type of expenditure listed in item (3), these are commonly referred to as "investment related" expenses. They are very similar to IRC § 162 business expenses with the exception that the ordinary and necessary expenses deductible under IRC § 212 are associated with investment activities rather than a trade or business deductible pursuant to IRC § 162. Financial planning advice, including stock/investment advice generally fits within the parameters of an IRC § 212 deductible expense. It should be noted that commissions paid on the purchase and sale of investment products, such as stocks, are not deductible but, rather, are added to its costs (increasing AB) and subtracted from its sales price (AR), respectively.

While not pertinent to the answer for this question, "where," in computing taxable income, these IRC § 212 expenses are taken, is a related issue. Qualifying IRC § 212 deductions relating to a taxpayer's "rental and royalty" investment activities are deductible from gross income to compute adjusted gross income (also known as "above the line" deduction in computing AGI). [See IRC § 62.] All other qualifying IRC § 212 expenses are deductible as part of "itemized deductions" that may be utilized in computing taxable income (also known as "below the line" deductions possibly subtracted form AGI to compute taxable income). Additionally, IRC § 67 imposes a 2% of adjusted gross income nondeductible "floor" for "miscellaneous itemized deductions" (which includes IRC § 212 expenses other than those related to rentals and royalties). [See Appendix A for more information about how income and deductions fit together in computing AGI and taxable income.]

Answer (a) is incorrect because, as explained above, the $1,300 Skip effectively paid Paula for the stock/investment advise qualifies as an IRC § 212 deductible expense. Similar to the concept that a taxpayer in an exchange transaction can have gross income without the receipt of cash, deductible expenses do not necessarily require the payment of cash. **Answer (c) is incorrect** because although Paula effectively "paid" Skip $4,000 for "tutoring," such an expenditure is generally not considered a qualifying medical care expense for purposes of deductions pursuant to IRC § 213. **Answer (d) is incorrect** although it does correctly identify the deductibility of Skip's IRC § 212 expense "for the production of income." The $4,000 that Paula effectively "paid" Skip does not give rise to any deduction for "child care." **Answer (e) is similarly incorrect** because no type of deductible "education expense" results from Paula's effective $4,000 payment to Skip.

- **Additional references:** *See* DANIEL Q. POSIN, FEDERAL INCOME TAXATION OF INDIVIDUALS ¶ 6.02(3) (5th ed. 2000).

4. **The most accurate statement is (c).** Sam rendered services worth $4,000 and received consideration (albeit not in the form of cash) and, therefore, has $4,000 of income. The balance of the benefit that he receives is an excludable gift.

There is no doubt that Sam received economic benefit in this problem. You are also aware from your study of gross income, that the receipt of economic benefit, or a net accession to wealth, generally defines the scope of *gross income* pursuant to IRC § 61. Sam received $10,000 of economic benefit represented by the value of the life insurance policy received and, prima facially, has gross income. To completely analyze this question, it helps to identify the composition of this benefit that he received.

Early on in classroom discussion of gross income, we discover that gross income need not be in the form of cash. A lawyer, for example, who performs legal work for a client and is paid in cash, has gross income. A lawyer who performs legal work for a client and receives property as payment has gross income equal to the fair market value of the property received. A lawyer who performs legal work for a client and receives a combination of cash and property as payment has gross income equal to the cash plus the fair market value of the property received. A lawyer who performs legal work for a client and receives the client's services as payment (in exchange) has income equal to the value of the services. A lawyer who performs legal work for a client and receives cash, property and the client's services as payment has gross income equal to the cash, the fair market value of the property, and the fair market value of the services. [See Reg. § 1.61-1(d) (compensation received in forms other than in cash).] When an individual performs services and receives "something" in exchange, that "something" (or the value thereof) represents gross income. The form of that "something" is generally irrelevant. In our question, Sam rendered $4,000 worth of services and received property, the insurance policy, in return. Granted, the $10,000 value of the insurance policy received is greater than the $4,000 worth of services Sam rendered, but there is no question that Sam was paid for his services. Therefore, he has $4,000 of gross income as compensation for his services. The extra $6,000 of value that he received is addressed in the following paragraph.

The remaining $6,000 of financial benefit Sam received also constitutes gross income (an economic benefit or net accession to wealth), unless we can identify a Code provision specifically excluding it. One specific income exclusion provision that is very relevant here is IRC § 102. This section's general rule provides for a very beneficial exclusion from income of amounts received as gifts, bequests, devises, and inheritances. [IRC § 102(a).] While not defined in statutes, a gift, for purposes of this exclusion, is a transfer made for insufficient consideration with the donor acting from "detached and disinterested generosity." [See *Comm'r v. Duberstein*, 363 U.S. 278, 80 S.Ct. 1190 (1960).] It does not take too much analysis of the facts to conclude that the extra $6,000 worth of property Sam received was a gift from Beatrice, excludable by IRC § 102. The mother/son relationship between the parties and the Beatrice's statements referring to the extra amount as a "gift" are sufficient to make this conclusion. One might argue that the entire $10,000 (value of property) given to Sam should constitute an excludable gift. However, this would require that Sam's rendering of his services was gratuitous in nature and the facts do not indicate this to be the case (the familial relationship alone is not sufficient).

Answer (a) is incorrect because it does not reflect the excluded gift portion of the transaction. **Answer (b) is incorrect** because while this was a part sale/part gift transaction, it has no bearing on the amount of income that Sam is required to recognize. See question 5, below for implications of the part sale/part gift nature of this transaction. **Answer (d) is also incorrect.** The statement about his value of services rendered equaling the consideration that he is deemed to have paid for the policy is correct (and relevant in problem 5, below). However, it does not preclude his recognition of this as income. See problem 5, below, for more information. **Answer (e) is incorrect** because the $6,000 difference represents the excluded gift portion.

- **Additional references:** *See* DANIEL Q. POSIN, FEDERAL INCOME TAXATION OF INDIVIDUALS ¶¶ 2.01, 3.08(2) (5th ed. 2000).

5.   **The correct answer is (b).** The entire $100,000 received by Sam is excludable from his gross income pursuant to IRC §101.

This is a very difficult question, the answer to which will take us through many diverse income tax issues. Sam suffered a horrible loss with the death of his mother, Beatrice. Financially, however, Sam's receipt of the $100,000 life insurance proceeds represents a benefit to him that will, absent a specific exclusion provision, result in the recognition of gross income (gross income being broadly defined). IRC § 101 is a good starting place for Sam as its general rule provides that life insurance proceeds received by reason of the insured's death are excluded from gross income of the beneficiary. [IRC § 101(a).] Unfortunately, to properly analyze the income tax implications to Sam in this question, we must travel a rather bumpy road requiring careful attention to numerous statutory road signs. Needless to say, this type of multi-step analysis makes for very good testing material.

The first detour encountered is the potential that the above-mentioned general exclusion rule for life insurance proceeds (IRC § 101(a)) may not apply to those received by Sam. When there has been a transfer, for valuable consideration, of a life insurance policy during the insured's life, the aforementioned general rule of full exclusion <u>may</u> not be applicable to benefits received by reason of the insured's death. [IRC § 101(a)(2).] Sam, through his services, effectively "paid," at least in part, for the life insurance policy. In other words, Sam furnished some consideration in exchange for the policy. True, the consideration Sam furnished, $4,000, was not as much as the value of the policy that he received, $10,000, but he provided consideration nonetheless. To help clarify this, the transaction involving the transfer of the policy could be recast or viewed in an equivalent, but alternative, manner eliminating the "exchange" element, substituting it with the transfer of cash between the parties. Sam performs services for Beatrice worth $4,000. Beatrice pays Sam, in cash, the $4,000. Sam then turns around and buys, for $4,000, Beatrice's life insurance policy. Clearly, he purchased the policy for less than its $10,000 fair market value, and this bargain purchase gives rise to the that gift Sam is deemed to have received (please see the analysis for question 4, above, for more information).

As indicated, IRC § 101(a)(2) contains this "consideration" exception to general exclusion rule of life insurance benefits. When a life insurance policy has been transferred for consideration, as it was in the facts of our question, the exclusion for benefits proceeds received at the insured's death is <u>limited</u> to the consideration paid by the transferee plus any additional premiums paid by the transferee subsequent to the transfer. In our problem, transferee Sam "paid" $4,000 in consideration for the policy plus $1,000 in policy premiums subsequent to the transfer. Applying this "consideration" limitation of IRC § 101(a)(2) to these facts, Sam's exclusion would be limited to only <u>$5,000</u> ($4,000 plus $1,000) of the $100,000 received. The $95,000 of remaining proceeds would not be excluded pursuant to this rule.

This "consideration" exception (in IRC § 101(a)(2)) to the general full exclusion rule of IRC § 101(a) has, in classic law school form, exceptions thereto. One such "exception to the exception" is at issue in this question, and it requires the application of Code sections seemingly unrelated to the insurance provisions at issue. Specifically, IRC § 101(a)(2)(a) effectively provides that you can forget the aforementioned "consideration" limitation and qualify for full exclusion of life insurance proceeds even if the policy was transferred for consideration if, the basis of the policy in the hands of the transferee is "determined in whole or in part by reference" to the basis of the policy in the hands of the transferor. In other words, even though there has been a transfer of a policy for consideration, <u>if</u> the transferee's basis is essentially a carryover basis from the transferor, the "consideration" limitation evaporates, and proceeds from the policy are fully excluded. To determine if Sam qualifies for this "exception to the exception," we must determine Sam's basis in the policy and how such basis was derived. The stakes, for Sam are dramatic: a "carryover" basis resulting in full exclusion of the $100,000 life insurance proceeds received, while a non-carryover basis results in an exclusion of only $5,000 of the $100,000 received, the balance included in his gross income.

Beatrice's transfer of the policy to Sam was, in part, a "gift" and, in part, a "sale." In such part gift/part sale situations we have two possible rules to consider in determining Sam's (the transferee's) basis (or "adjusted basis" hereinafter AB). A donee's AB in property received as a gift is generally the AB of the donor/transferor – a so-called "carryover" AB. [IRC § 1015.] The AB in property purchased, however, is generally determined by the transferee's "cost." [IRC §§ 1011 and 1012.] In part gift/part sale situations the resulting transferee's basis is the <u>greater</u> of: (1) the amount paid by the donee, or (2) the donor's basis at the time of the gift. [Reg. 1.1015-4(a), (the greater of these two is also increased for any gift tax paid adjustment – this is not present here).] Sam's AB is the greater of the $4,000 consideration he was deemed to have paid for the policy, or Beatrice's AB in the policy of $5,000 (as indicated in this question's facts). Since Beatrice's $5,000 AB exceeds the $4,000 Sam "paid," Sam's AB in the policy is $5,000, a "carryover" AB.

Now that we have determined Sam's AB in the life insurance policy to be a carryover AB, this places him squarely within the exception of IRC § 101(a)(2)(A). This, in turn, overrides the "consideration" limitation, which ultimately results in Sam's exclusion of the full $100,000 insurance proceeds received.

Had the facts to this question been altered slightly so that, for example, Beatrice's AB in the policy was only $3,000 rather than the $5,000 in our question, the results to Sam would have been quite different. In this revised hypothetical, Sam's $4,000 consideration "paid" for the policy would have been greater than Beatrice's AB, resulting in Sam having a "cost" AB in the policy rather than a "carryover" AB. In turn, he would not qualify under the exception in IRC § 101(a)(2)(A), which ultimately would result in his exclusion of the life insurance proceeds being limited to only $5,000 ($4,000 consideration paid for the policy plus the $1,000 he paid in premiums subsequent to the transfer).

Answer (a) is incorrect. Sam does have gross income of $4,000, but this is not as a result of receiving the policy proceeds at Beatrice's death. Rather, Sam has $4,000 of gross income when Beatrice transferred the policy to him as "payment" for his services. This answer (a) corresponds to the correct answer for question 4, above. **Answers (c) and (d) are incorrect** because both answers fail to reflect that Sam meets the requirements of IRC § 101(a)(2)(A) and is therefore entitled to fully exclude the $100,000 insurance proceeds received. Answer (d) would be the correct answer had Sam's AB in the policy transferred from Beatrice not been a "carryover" AB. For more information see the revised fact hypothetical discussed in the analysis of the correct answer (b), above. **Answer (e) is incorrect** because the correct response (b) is presented.

- **Additional references:** *See* DANIEL Q. POSIN, FEDERAL INCOME TAXATION OF INDIVIDUALS ¶ 3.07 (5th ed. 2000).

6. **Answer (d) best describes the income tax consequences to Maureen.** This is a complex problem (as is this entire series of questions) and involves multiple steps to arrive at the correct answer. Determining Maureen's "adjusted basis" (AB) of the property is the first important component of this question. Pursuant to IRC § 1011(a), the AB of the property is the "cost basis" of the property adjusted for certain items. The cost basis is simply the cost of the property. [IRC § 1012).] In the present case, the $125,000 Maureen paid for the property ten years ago represents her cost basis of the property.

Maureen's borrowing of the $150,000 on the equity of the property five years ago, in and of itself, is of no income tax consequence. No income is realized from borrowing of monies, as there is no net accession to wealth (a general prerequisite for income realization) [See *Comm'r v. Glenshaw Glass Co.*, 348 U.S. 426, 75 S.Ct. 473 (1955).] The act of borrowing also has no direct affect on AB. The basis of property may be affected, however, if funds are actually used to make substantial improvements to such property. [IRC § 1016(a); Reg. § 1.1016-2(a).] Here the entire proceeds of the loan were used for matters unrelated to the house, so the loan has no impact on Maureen's AB in the house (it remains at $125,000). While not pertinent to this question, your professor can easily take a problem such as this and ask about numerous other items including the deductibility of interest on this loan, the basis of the car purchased with some of the loan proceeds, etc.

A gift of property generally does not result in realization of gain or loss to a donor. However, under certain circumstances (i.e., if a donor receives "consideration"), a gift may in fact constitute a "part sale/part gift" with a resulting realization of gain. In a part sale/part gift situation, gain is realized to the extent the "amount realized" (AR) by the donor exceeds the donor's AB in the property. [Reg. § 1.1001-1(e).] This is consistent with the general principals of IRC § 1001. In the present case, while Maureen does not have any amount realized in the traditional sense (money or other property received, § 1001(b)), an amount is nonetheless realized. Pursuant to *Crane v. Commissioner* (331 U.S. 1, 67 S.Ct. 1047 (1947)), a liability associated with transferred property is considered an amount realized even when a transferee merely takes property subject to a mortgage. Therefore, Maureen's AR equals the $150,000 mortgage to which the property was taken subject to by her daughter, Denise. Again, while not part of this question, always be on the lookout for situations where the loan involved is greater than the fair market value of the property at the time of the transfer. In that case (which is not the case in our question), the fair market value is generally irrelevant and "AR" is the full amount of the mortgage. [See *Comm'r v. Tufts* 461 U.S. 300, 103 S.Ct. 1826 (1983).]

Since the $150,000 amount realized by Maureen exceeds her AB of $125,000, a $25,000 gain is realized as a result of this "gift" to Denise. While not part of this question, pursuant to IRC § 1001(c), this gain is also recognized barring application of any nonrecognition provisions of the Code. Again, your professor could easily extend this question to encompass the IRC § 121 nonrecognition provisions for the sale of a principal residence.

Answer (a) is incorrect because no such income tax deduction exists for non-charitable gifts. There is, however, a "gift tax" provision that is often the source of confusion in this area. Gift taxes are a completely separate set of tax rules that, in general, may create a tax liability to the "donor" for the privilege of transferring wealth. The gift tax is usually not the subject of in-depth discussion in the basic federal income tax course but, rather, is often a separate law school course that also covers estate taxes and, perhaps, other subjects such as income taxation of estates and trusts, estate planning, and the like. With that said, there is a gift tax provision at IRC § 2503(b) that may exclude from taxable gifts for gift tax purposes, up to $10,000 (as indexed for inflation) per year, per donee. In other words, an individual can usually give $10,000 worth of assets (the number indexed for inflation) to a person (or any number of persons) in a year without such gift(s) counting as taxable gifts possibly subject to gift taxation. There is, however, no corresponding income tax deduction to the donor. While not part of this question, the value of gifts received by a donee ($250,000 to Denise representing the difference between the house's value and the consideration that she was deemed to have paid) is generally excludable from gross income pursuant to IRC § 102.

Answer (b) is incorrect because the $150,000 consideration deemed paid by Denise (see discussion for correct answer (d), above, is the "amount realized" component of a gain calculation, and not, income in and of itself. **Answer (c) is incorrect** because the numbers do not correspond to how a gain or loss is calculated. As indicated in the discussion for the correct response, above, a gain or loss is the difference between the amount realized by the transferor and the transferor's adjusted basis. The $400,000 in this question was the fair market value of the house at the time of the gift, but not Maureen's adjusted basis in it. **Answer (e) is incorrect** because while it is true that a portion of this transaction is a gift to Denise, and such portion most likely would be "tax-free" to Denise pursuant to IRC § 102, there still was consideration deemed paid by Denise. Because that consideration paid exceeded Maureen's adjusted basis in the property, the result is a gain realized by Maureen as discussed above.

- **Additional references:** *See* DANIEL Q. POSIN, FEDERAL INCOME TAXATION OF INDIVIDUALS ¶¶ 4.01, 4.03 (5th ed. 2000).

7.   **Answer (a) is correct.** This too is a difficult question involving multiple steps but caution, this easily could have been an even more difficult question. It should be noted that this series of questions was originally part of an even more "involved" essay question on one of the author's tax exams. Denise's sale does result in a realized gain and we will conclude that the entire amount of such gain will be <u>recognized</u>.

While this question does not require the actual calculation of such gain, it might be helpful to utilize the actual numbers provided and discuss the answer in this context. As with her mother, the first component of calculating Denise's gain from the house sale is to determine its adjusted basis (AB). As discussed with respect to question 6, above, the "gift" to Denise was actually a part sale/part gift situation. In such situations, the resulting transferee's basis is the <u>greater</u> of: 1) the amount paid by the donee, or 2) the donor's basis at the time of the gift. [Reg. § 1.1015-4(a) (the greater of these two is also increased for any gift tax paid adjustment – this is not present here).] While in this question, Denise did not pay any monies to Maureen to acquire the house, the aforementioned *Crane* case also stands for the proposition that a mortgage loan taken "subject to" by a transferee is deemed consideration paid. Denise took the property subject to the $150,000 loan and, therefore, this is deemed the amount paid for purpose of determining Denise's AB. Since the $150,000 exceeds Maureen's basis in the house of $125,000 (see above), Denise's AB in the house is $150,000.

Denise's subsequent sale of the property results in the realization of gain. As previously discussed in the correct answer to question 6, above, the amount of this gain is the "amount realized" (AR) from its sale (the sales price) less the "adjusted basis" (AB) in the property. [IRC § 1001(a).] Here, Denise sold the property for $450,000 and this is her AR for purposes of determining her gain. [See *Crane v. Comm'r* (331 U.S. 1, 67 S.Ct. 1047 (1947) (the mortgage being taken "subject to" by the buyer is included in the determination of the transferor's AR).] This results in a realized gain to Denise of $300,000 (AR of $450,000 less AB of $150,000). Again, the calculation of Denise's actual gain is not required for this particular question, but might be helpful in understanding the answer to this question or similar questions that you might face on an exam.

Now to the key part of this question: the recognition of this realized gain. Realized gains are recognized (reported as income) unless there is a particular Code provision providing for its exclusion or non-recognition. [IRC § 1001(c).] IRC § 121, "exclusion of gain from sale of principal residence," is one such non-recognition provision. Effective for sales of a taxpayer's principal residence after May 6, 1997, IRC § 121 provides for the exclusion of up to $250,000 of gain ($500,000 in the case of certain married individuals), if certain conditions are met. There are two basic requirements for this exclusion, commonly referred to as the "ownership" and "use" tests. The taxpayer must have owned the house for at least two years (looking back five years from the date of the sale), and must have used it as his/her principal residence for two years (looking back five years from the date of the sale). [IRC § 121(a).] This IRC § 121 exclusion provision is fertile grounds for examination questions both in multiple choice and essay forms. In this particular question, however, the determination of whether Denise can utilize this exclusion is fairly straightforward. She clearly meets the two-year "use" test having lived in this house since its purchase by her mother ten years earlier. However, she has owned the house for only one year, thus failing to meet the two-year ownership requirement. Because she has not met both of these requirements, Denise is not entitled to exclude any portion of the gain pursuant to IRC § 121. There is no other gain exclusion section that is applicable here.

Note that the statute does not require that the requisite two-year "use" and "ownership" period be co-extensive. While this is not an issue in this question, it is a common misunderstanding (read as "good testing area") that the two "two-year" qualifying periods must be at the same time. It is also a common misunderstanding (again, read as "good testing area") that the "five-year look back period" for purposes of determining two-year ownership and use somehow requires that the taxpayer either owned or used the house for at least five years. This is not correct and again, while this is not at issue in this question, it might be helpful for your analysis of other IRC § 121 related questions.

Answer (b) is incorrect because Denise is not entitled to the $250,000 exclusion provided in IRC § 121 as she fails the aforementioned two-year "ownership" requirement. **Answer (c) is also incorrect,** but is probably the most commonly selected incorrect answer. There is, in IRC § 121(c), a partial or "prorated" exclusion if the taxpayer fails to meet both of the two-year tests. However, this partial exclusion is applicable only when the house sale is "by reason of a change in place of employment, health, or, to the extent provided in regulations, unforeseen circumstances." [IRC § 121(c)(2)(B).] Denise did not sell her house due to a job change or for health reasons, and there is no indication of anything that might constitute "unforeseen circumstances" in this question. As of this writing, the Treasury has not issued regulations as to what constitutes "unforeseen circumstances," and the I.R.S. has indicated that taxpayers may not rely on their own definition of what constitutes "unforeseen circumstances." While not applicable to this question, there was, for sales of homes prior to August 5, 1999, a limited application of a partial exclusion under IRC § 121 notwithstanding a lack of job, health or other reason for such sale.

Answer (d) is incorrect because there is no blanket non-recognition provision applicable to "this situation." **Answer (e) is incorrect**, but it is also the source of much confusion among students and the general public. Prior to the $250,000/$500,000 exclusion of IRC § 121, the primary provision affecting gain recognition from the sale of a principal residence was IRC § 1034. This latter section, which was repealed and replaced by current IRC § 121 in 1997, also provided for gain exclusion, but its mechanism for doing so was very different. Basically, this old section provided that if you purchased (and occupied) a new principal residence within a two year period of selling your old principal residence (either before or, as was more common, after the sale), then gain was recognized only to the extent, if any, that the purchase price of the new house was less than the sales price of the old house. In other words, if a taxpayer always "moved-up" to a more expensive house, gain was not recognized. However, this old IRC § 1034 provision was merely a "deferral" mechanism because any gain not recognized pursuant to this provision, served to reduce the adjusted basis of the new house (to be potentially recognized upon a subsequent sale). As indicated, this old IRC § 1034 is no longer valid law (but if your professor covers this material in greater depth, be aware that prior deferrals of gain under that law may still be reflected in a taxpayer's adjusted basis for their home). Current IRC § 121 does not require that the taxpayer purchase a new house, and any gain excluded pursuant to the section is a real exclusion (not merely a deferral of recognition) with no effect on the adjusted basis of any subsequent house purchase.

Not trying to add additional confusion to the matter, there was an "old" IRC § 121 that was also repealed with enactment of current IRC § 121 in 1997. The old section was a "once in a lifetime" exclusion of a certain dollar amount of gain from the sale of a principal residence for taxpayers fifty-five years of age and older. This old IRC § 121 was in addition to old IRC § 1034 and their combination was a logistics mess (and tough area for instruction) when compared to the relatively straightforward rules of the current IRC § 121. The current IRC § 121 has no age limit, can be used over and over again to exclude gain (generally, just not more than once every two years), and has larger exclusion limitations. Again, while this old IRC § 121 is no longer valid law, it is the source of some confusion among taxpayers.

- **Additional references:** *See* DANIEL Q. POSIN, FEDERAL INCOME TAXATION OF INDIVIDUALS ¶¶ 4.01, 4.03, 4.04(5) (5th ed. 2000).

8. **Answer (a) is correct.** This question brings up the aforementioned partial or prorated non-recognition benefits of IRC § 121. Recall that the correct answer in question 7, Denise's realized gain was fully recognized. In that question she met the two-year "use" test for exclusion, but failed the two-year "ownership" requirement, resulting in no exclusion pursuant to IRC § 121. As indicated in the analysis of question 7 (discussing the then incorrect answer (c)), IRC § 121(c) does contain a "partial" or "prorated" exclusion for certain taxpayers failing to meet both of the two-year tests. This partial exclusion is applicable when the house sale is "by reason of a change in place of employment, health, or, to the extent provided in regulations, unforeseen circumstances." [IRC § 121(c)(2)(B).] In this question, Denise did sell her house because of health reasons and would be entitled to a partial exclusion. Therefore, answer (a) is correct.

While this question does not require that we compute Denise's maximum exclusion, it might be helpful to go through the numbers to illustrate how this partial exclusion works. To simplify the Code here, you look to see for what period of time the taxpayer actually met both the "ownership" and "use" requirements. In our case, while Denise's use easily exceeded the two-year period, her ownership was only for one year – so both requirements were met for only one year. (If you prefer, you can do this by taking whichever period, ownership or use, is less). To get the partial or prorated exclusion, you take that portion of the two-year period for which she did meet the requirements (here one of the two years or ½) and multiply that by the maximum available exclusion ($250,000 for a single person). So the actual maximum exclusion available to Denise in our problem is ½ of $250,000 or <u>$125,000</u>.

Answers (b) and (c) are incorrect because mathematically, they do not make sense. **Answer (d)** is incorrect because in the previous question there was no significance of her house location vis-à-vis her Atlanta job.

- **Additional references:** *See* DANIEL Q. POSIN, FEDERAL INCOME TAXATION OF INDIVIDUALS ¶¶ 4.01, 4.03, 4.04(5) (5th ed. 2000).

9.   **The correct answer is (b).** The questions in this series are somewhat tied together and, unfortunately, if you get off track with one, it may have a ripple effect causing errors in other questions. With this question, the answer is basically the same as in question 6 above but is, in reality, a bit more straightforward than that question. The difference in these facts is that the gift of the house from Maureen to Denise is a true gift as opposed to the part sale/part gift scenario in question 6. For purposes of this question, the only difference to Denise would be that her adjusted basis (AB) in the house is a gift "carryover" basis of $125,000. [IRC § 1015.] Again, this question does not really require that we determine Denise's AB. While Denise's AB in the house is different in this question, the balance of the analysis to question 6, above, is relevant. Looking at Denise's ownership and use for IRC § 121 gain exclusion qualification, we once again see that Denise falls short on the ownership requirement. Additionally, in this question she is not entitled to any portion or prorated exclusion, as she is not selling her house for any of the requisite reasons identified in IRC § 121(c). Therefore, she is not entitled to exclude any portion of the gain realized on the sale of her house.

While this question does not require that we compute the gain, for reference purposes, she would have a gain of $325,000 ($450,000 sales price (AR) less her AB of $125,000).

Answer (a) is incorrect, but it is the most commonly selected incorrect answer. Students are often confused about "tacking" (adding) on the holding period of another individual. The confusion seems to arise because there are instances, for purposes of IRC § 121 that we do tack on periods of ownership and use of another in certain instances. In addition, in some tax issues other than IRC § 121, we do "tack" (add) on the holding period of the transferor when the transferee's basis in the property is determined with reference to the basis of the transferor. Unfortunately, these two situations do not overlap here. IRC § 121(d) contains special rules for the application of that section's exclusion of gain from the sale of a principal residence. Specifically, "tacking" ownership and use periods is allowed in certain situations involving deceased and former spouses. [IRC §§ 121(d)(2) and (d)(3).] There is no general "tacking" provision for purposes of IRC §121, when property is received as a gift or other situations where there is a carryover basis. While Denise cannot tack or add on Maureen's holding period to determine her ownership for purposes of IRC § 121, she could, for example, tack on her mother's holding period for capital gain classification purposes. [IRC § 1223(2).] This latter issue, however, has no relevance for qualification under IRC § 121 exclusion of gain from the sale of a principal residence.

Answers (c) and (d) are incorrect because, as discussed in the answers to question 7, above, current law for the potential exclusion of gain from the sale of a principal residence no longer has, a requirement, that the taxpayer purchase a replacement residence. **Answer (e) is incorrect** because there is a correct answer: (b).

- **Additional references:** *See* DANIEL Q. POSIN, FEDERAL INCOME TAXATION OF INDIVIDUALS ¶¶ 4.01, 4.03, 4.04(5) (5th ed. 2000).

10. **The best answer is (d).** As discussed in more detail below, this is a "part sale/part gift" type of transaction. Jim's transfer of the fine crystal to Tina for consideration of $5,000 exceeds his $4,000 basis in the property, resulting in a realized (and recognized) gain to him of $1,000. As to Tina, the value of the property that she received in excess of what she paid for it represents a "gift" that is excludable from gross income pursuant to IRC § 102. A more thorough explanation follows.

The sale of property usually results in the realization of a gain or loss by the transferor. A gift of property, however, generally does not result in the realization of a gain or loss to a donor. Under certain circumstances (i.e., if a donor receives "consideration"), a "part sale/part gift" type transaction results. The transfer of the fine crystal from Jim to his niece Tina represents a *part sale/part gift* transaction. The sale component exists because Jim received consideration from Tina (the $5,000 in cash). A gift component also exists because the $30,000 value of the property far exceeded the amount Tina paid for it.

Income Tax Ramifications of the *Part Sale/Part Gift* Transaction to Jim (the transferor)

In *part sale/part gift* situations, the transferor (seller/donor) realizes *gain* to the extent the consideration received ("amount realized" or hereinafter AR) by the donor exceeds the donor's basis ("adjusted basis" or hereinafter AB) in the property. [Reg. § 1.1001-1(e).] This is consistent with the general principals of IRC § 1001(a) – the difference between the AR and AB represents a realized gain or loss. Jim received consideration of $5,000 (in the form of cash) from the transfer to Tina and this represents his AR. Jim's AB in the fine crystal is a straightforward proposition here and is his $4,000 cost. [IRC §§ 1011 and 1012.] Since Jim's $5,000 AR from the transfer exceeds his AB of $4,000, Jim realizes a gain of $1,000. Pursuant to IRC § 1001(c), this gain is also recognized barring application of any nonrecognition provisions of the Code. There are no such provisions applicable to these facts so Jim must *recognize* this $1,000 gain.

While not part of this question, Jim's $1,000 recognized gain would be classified as a long-term capital gain (the crystal qualifying as a capital asset and Jim held the property for more than one year before "selling" it).

Also not germane to this question but it bears mentioning, is that had Jim received consideration from Tina that was less than his AB (e.g. she paid him only $3,000) the regulations provide that no loss is recognized in such a part sale/part gift scenario. [Reg. § 1.1001-1(e).] This makes sense because pure gifts (where no consideration is received) would then result in realized losses to the donor.

Income Tax Ramifications to Tina Resulting from Jim's Transfer to Her
As indicated above, despite the fact that Tina *did* furnish some consideration to Jim, she received property of a value far in excess of what she paid. Logically, this is the "gift" component of the *part sale/part gift* type of transaction. IRC § 102 provides an exclusion from income to the recipient of gifts, bequests, devises, and inheritances. While no statutory definition of a gift exists, it is generally defined as a transfer without consideration that is made out of emotions of detached and disinterested generosity. [See *Comm'r v. Duberstein*, 363 U.S. 278, 80 S.Ct. 1190 (1960).] The facts are abundant to indicate that Jim's motivations were gratuitous. Jim "was originally just going to give it to her, his *favorite* niece," but she insisted on paying him something and he "reluctantly agreed." Therefore, the gift portion of this transaction ($25,000, the difference between the property's value and what Tina paid for it) is excludable from Tina's gross income as a gift pursuant to IRC § 102. .

Answer (a) is incorrect because the part sale/part gift rules preclude recognition of losses by the donor/seller. In addition, this answer is incorrect because the net $25,000 benefit that Tina received is excludable as a gift. **Answer (b) is also incorrect** but it is a commonly selected answer. Basically most of this answer is true except for the statement that a loss results and the reason for its nonrecognition. Because this is a *part sale/part gift* transaction, the gift element effectively precludes recognition of any loss. He really does not have a loss because of the huge gift component. [See Reg. § 1.11001-1(e).] Students sometimes confuse gift type sales such as this with losses between certain related parties that are not recognized pursuant to IRC § 267. Actually, a careful reading of IRC 267(c)(4) defining who constitutes a "related" party, will reveal that Tina is not related to

Jim for purpose of § 267. **Answer (c) is incorrect** because, as discussed above, Jim does realize (and recognize) a gain due to the amount of consideration received exceeding his AB in the property. **Answer (e) is also incorrect.** This answer properly reflects the tax ramifications to Jim, but fails to reflect that there is still a gift element to the transaction and it is excludable by Tina.

- **Additional references:** *See* DANIEL Q. POSIN, FEDERAL INCOME TAXATION OF INDIVIDUALS ¶¶ 4.01, 4.03 (5th ed. 2000).

11.   **The correct answer is (c).** This is a somewhat complex question that takes us through many steps and, unfortunately, is based upon a substantially correct analysis of the previous question 10. This professor would not ask such a combination of interrelated multiple-choice questions on an exam. Rather, these questions were developed from an exam essay question.

In every fact pattern in which something is sold, the author likes to go through the following three-step analysis:

1)   Does the sale result in a <u>realized</u> gain or loss and if so, what is the <u>amount</u>?

2)   If we have a <u>realized</u> gain or loss, is it <u>recognized</u> (i.e. reportable for income tax purposes)?

3)   If the gain or loss is recognized, is it accorded "capital" gain or loss treatment?

Because this question involves a multi-step analysis and because the author recognizes the value of your time, both an **abbreviated/short** and **comprehensive/long** analyses are provided below.

The <u>abbreviated/short</u> version of the analysis for this question is that Tina's realized gain is the difference between the $28,000 sales price and her basis in the fine crystal of $5,000, or <u>$23,000</u>. Her basis in the crystal is $5,000 because it exceeds what would have been a carryover basis from Jim of $4,000. This gain is <u>recognized</u> and is characterized as a <u>short-term capital gain</u>. This is because the crystal represents a capital asset and her holding period, was only a month. Because her basis was not a carryover basis from Jim, she is unable to "tack" Jim's four-year holding period onto hers. [See IRC §§ 1221, 1222 and 1223(2).]

The following <u>comprehensive/long</u> analysis presents a step-by-step discussion of the answer to this question that can be applied to other gain/loss questions.

The first step is determining whether Tina has a <u>realized</u> a gain or loss on the sale of the fine crystal. For this, we need two basic components: her sales price ("amount realized" or, hereinafter, AR) and her basis in the crystal ("adjusted basis or, hereinafter, AB). The difference between the two represents <u>realized</u> gain or loss. [IRC § 1001(a).] Each of these two components, AR and AB, can present a variety of complex tax issues for exam and real-world tax purposes. The AR side is straightforward in our question, and is her $28,000 sales price (much to the chagrin of Jim). Other questions in this book present more complex issues involving a taxpayer's AR. In this question, the AB component is a bit more difficult to derive.

The general starting place for determining one's AB in property is one's cost. [IRC §§ 1011 and 1012.] "Adjustments" to one's basis, while not at issue in this question, can result from many reasons including capital improvements (increasing basis), and depreciation expenses (reducing basis). Applying the general cost basis rule in our question, Tina's AB would appear to be $5,000, the amount that she paid Jim for the crystal. In fact, that will be her AB, but we need to consider other issues before arriving at that answer. Recall that the initial transfer of the crystal from Jim to Tina was considered a *part sale/part gift* type of transaction. Also recall that to Jim, we had to look at the amount of consideration that he received, and if it exceeded his AB, gain resulted. In fact, that is what did happen: Jim received consideration of $5,000 from Tina and his AB in the crystal was $4,000 (his original cost). We must look to these same *part sale/part gift* rules to determine Tina's AB in such a transaction. The two possible measurements for Tina's AB are either what she paid for it (her cost basis), because this was in part a sale/purchase, or Jim's carryover AB (pursuant to the general IRC § 1015 AB rules for gifts) because this was in part a gift. The regulations provide guidance in such *part sale/part gift* situations. The transferee's basis is the <u>greater</u> of: (1) the amount paid by the donee, or (2) the donor's basis at the time of the gift. [Reg. § 1.1015-4(a) (the greater of these two is also increased for any gift tax paid adjustment – this is not present here).] Since the $5,000 Tina paid Jim exceeds Jim's AB in the crystal, Tina's AB in the crystal is $5,000.

We can now answer the question in the first step of our gain/loss analysis: the amount of Tina's <u>realized</u> gain. Tina has a <u>realized</u> gain of <u>$23,000</u>, her AR (sales price) of $28,000 less her AB (as determined above) of $5,000.

The next step in our analysis of gain/loss situations is to determine the extent to which any <u>realized</u> gain is <u>recognized</u>. Recognition of gain basically means that it is reported as income for income tax purposes. IRC § 1001(c) provides that unless otherwise provided for in the Code, all realized gains and losses are recognized. While not at issue in this question, always be on the lookout for various nonrecognition provisions such as with sales between spouses and certain former spouses (IRC § 1041), gain from the sale of a principal residence (IRC § 121), and other nonrecognition provisions discussed elsewhere in this book. Unfortunately for Tina, there are no exclusion or non-recognition provisions applicable in these facts and her $23,000 realized gain will be <u>recognized</u>.

The last part of the analysis is to determine whether Tina's $23,000 of recognized gain is accorded special "capital gain" treatment. Historically, gains from the sale of certain types of assets have been accorded preferential tax treatment. While it is far beyond the scope of analysis for this question, modernly, "long-term" capital gains ("net capital gains" to be more specific), while included in a taxpayer's gross and taxable incomes, may be taxed at favorable (i.e., lower) tax rates. A capital gain analysis requires first determining that we are dealing with a "capital asset" after which the gain is characterized as having either long-term or short-term status.

IRC § 1221(a) defines a capital asset in a negative fashion, but for purposes of this analysis, it includes, by process of elimination, assets held for investment and personal-use purposes. There is little question that Tina's fine crystal qualifies as a capital asset. Long-term status is reserved for those assets held for <u>more than one year</u> (short-term status for assets held one year or less). [See IRC § 1222.] Tina purchased the crystal only one month prior to selling it and, at first brush, this appears to be the end of our analysis with Tina's gain characterized as a *short-term capital gain*. This is the correct answer, but one other issue needs to be addressed. Determining the holding period, for short and long term gain/loss classification, is controlled by IRC § 1223. At IRC § 1223(2) we have the so-called "tacking" rule, which essentially applies to situations where the taxpayer's AB is a carryover AB. Where this is the case, the transferee can add to his or her holding period, that of the transferor. This brings us to how we determined Tina's AB above. Recall that we determined her basis to be the greater amount that she paid (the $5,000) rather than Jim's AB of $4,000. Because Tina's AB was <u>not</u> a carryover AB, Tina is <u>not</u> entitled to "tack" or add on Jim's many-year holding period to hers. Therefore, Tina's holding period is measured by her actual holding period of a month (short-term status). Note, that had the facts been different here with the consideration Tina paid being less than Jim's AB, she would have had a long-term holding period via tacking.

In summary, Tina has a *realized* <u>$23,000 gain</u> from the sale of the crystal and it is a *recognized short term-capital gain*.

The issues of recognition, capital gain/loss treatment and holding periods (including "tacking" and other special rules) are addressed in other questions in this book. Needless to say, all of this material is *super fertile* ground for exam questions.

Answer (a) is incorrect because it wrongly classifies Tina's gain as a long-term capital gain. **Answer (b) is incorrect** because it states the wrong amount of Tina's gain and incorrectly classifies it as a long-term capital gain. Note, however, that had the facts been different with Tina's consideration being *less* than Jim's AB, this answer would most likely be the correct answer. **Answer (d) is incorrect** because it states the wrong amount of Tina's gain. **Answer (e) is incorrect** because this sale by Tina is separate from the initial transfer to her by Jim. Any nonrecognition because of the § 102 gift provisions does not carry over to this subsequent sale by Tina.

- **Additional references:** *See* DANIEL Q. POSIN, FEDERAL INCOME TAXATION OF INDIVIDUALS ¶¶ 4.03(1), 4.03(2)(c), 4.06 (5th ed. 2000).

12. **The most accurate statement is (c).** This question is designed to illustrate the coordination of capital gains and losses and how they are reflected in determining a taxpayer's "adjusted gross income" (hereinafter AGI). The facts present the results of four transactions that yielded capital gains and losses to Bill last year. Presentation of the gains and losses in this problem as long-term and short-term capital gains and losses presupposes that such gains and losses have been properly realized and recognized, as well as properly classified as to their long and short term capital gain and loss status. Questions presented elsewhere in this book address these realization, recognition, and classification issues. Bill's AGI for last year was $57,000 representing gross income of $60,000 less $3,000 of deductible losses. In addition, he has a $2,000 long-term capital loss carryover to the current year.

Once capital gains and losses have been classified as to their long or short term holding status, as is the case here, IRC § 1222 effectively requires that we combine and net such gains and losses in a particular manner. Simplifying the statutory rules, we split the gains and losses up based on holding period – separating them into two groups or columns: short-term gains/losses and long-term gains/losses. Bill's capital gains and losses for last year would be grouped as follows:

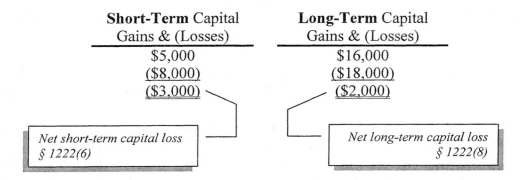

	Short-Term Capital Gains & (Losses)	**Long-Term** Capital Gains & (Losses)
	$5,000	$16,000
	($8,000)	($18,000)
	($3,000)	($2,000)

Net short-term capital loss § 1222(6)

Net long-term capital loss § 1222(8)

Note that the correct groupings of capital gains and losses presented above are different from the somewhat misleading (i.e., tricky) way in which the gains and losses are presented in the question facts. Also note from the above groupings that gains and losses are then combined and netted within their respective short-term and long-term columns.

Bill has $3,000 and $2,000 of short-term and long-term capital losses, respectively, for a total of $5,000 of losses. Can Bill deduct these $5,000 of losses in computing his AGI for the year involved? IRC § 1211(b) provides the answer. An individual is allowed to first use capital losses to offset capital gains, which is what we did by netting Bill's gains and losses above. Our facts yielded losses in both the short-term and long-term columns, but had there been a loss in one column and a gain in the other, we would net the two (i.e., using losses to offset gains). For an individual, once capital losses have been used to offset capital gains (accomplished by netting gains and losses), any remaining capital loss can be deducted up to a $3,000 limit. [IRC § 1211(b).] In Bill's case, he has capital losses (after netting with capital gains) totaling $5,000. Bill's deduction for capital losses last year is therefore limited to $3,000. Deductions for losses are allowed "above the line" in computing AGI. [IRC § 62.] We now have the answer to part of our question: Bill's AGI for last year was $57,000 ($60,000 of salary income less $3,000 of capital losses).

Last year, Bill had capital losses of $5,000 in the aggregate, but was allowed a deduction of only $3,000, leaving a total of $2,000 of capital losses unused (not deducted). Fortunately, individuals are entitled to carryover unused capital losses to future years (to offset future gains and/or be deducted subject to the same $3,000 per year limitation). Capital loss carryovers maintain their same status (as short or long term) for purposes of future year groupings and netting. Recall that last year, we determined Bill had net short-term capital losses of $3,000 and net long-term capital losses of $2,000. Recall that Bill was limited in his deduction of net capital losses to $3,000 resulting in $2,000 of losses to be carried over to this year. The question, at this point, is from where (short-term or long-term) does the $3,000 of losses used last year come? A corollary question is: what is the status (short-term or long-term) of the $2,000 in capital loss carried over to this year? This answer lies deeply concealed within IRC § 1212(b). The "quick and dirty" answer (that works in almost every instance) is that the "short-term" losses are the first to be used. In Bill's case, the $3,000 of capital losses allowed as a deduction last year came first, and entirely in Bill's case, from the shot-term side. The status of the $2,000 capital loss carryover to this year is, by default, long-term. This can be illustrated as follows:

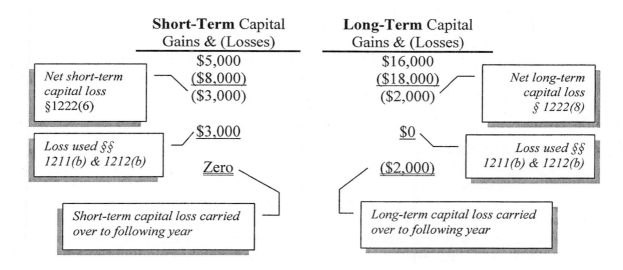

Note that our "quick and dirty" rule of IRC § 1212(b), that short-term capital losses get used first, is not something that you will find spelled out in the statute. Be aware that your professor may properly analyze the statutory provisions (which, in almost every case, will yield the same result as our simplified rule).

One might wonder why so much is made out of properly classifying capital gains and losses as short-term and long-term, and why there is so much attention paid, as in this question, to the proper utilization and carryover of capital losses. Historically, gains from the sale of certain types of assets (capital assets) that has been accorded preferential tax treatment. While it is far beyond the scope of the analysis for this question, modernly, "long-term" capital gains ("net capital gains" to be more specific), while included in a taxpayer's gross and taxable incomes, may be taxed at favorable (i.e., lower) tax rates. Proper classification of losses and gains (including capital loss carryovers) is critical in determining the extent of favorably taxed long-term capital gains.

Answer (a) is incorrect because it fails to recognize the $3,000 limitation for the deduction, in any one year, of excess capital losses. **Answer (b) is incorrect** because it incorrectly used long-term capital losses first to make up the $3,000 of deductible capital losses. **Answer (d) is not the best answer.** Technically, this answer could be considered a correct answer but it is not the <u>best</u> answer because it does not distinguish the status of the capital loss carryover as either short-term, long-term, or some combination thereof.

- **Additional references:** *See* DANIEL Q. POSIN, FEDERAL INCOME TAXATION OF INDIVIDUALS ¶¶ 4.01, 4.02, 4.03, 4.05, 4.06 (5th ed. 2000).

13.   **Answer (e) is correct.** This is a multi-step question that combines many diverse income tax issues, requires careful attention to math (albeit only addition and subtraction), is a bit unfair because it requires, in part, a correct analysis of the previous question (12), and to top it all off, the correct answer is the hated "none of the above." While the author apologizes for such a question, and, in advance, for the lengthy analysis to follow, it is a good problem to work through a host of income tax issues.

The abbreviated analysis is that of Bill's two car sales in this year, only the first (the car inherited from Fred) results in a recognized gain or loss. He recognizes a $3,500 gain, which is considered a *long-term capital gain*. The second car sale resulted in a realized loss of $3,000 but such loss is <u>not</u> recognized (and therefore is not classified as a capital loss). Next we take the $3,500 long-term capital gain and combine it with any capital loss carryovers from prior years (keeping short-terms and long-terms separate as is normally the case with multiple capital gains/losses). This long-term capital gain netted with the $2,000 long-term capital loss carried over from the prior year (see analysis for question 12) results in a net $1,500 long-term capital gain for the current year. As there are no additional capital gains or losses involved Bill simply adds this $1,500 capital gain to his given $60,000 of wages resulting in an adjusted gross income (AGI) of $61,500. Phew! Now for the more complete analysis that is long, but hopefully, helpful for a better understanding of this and other questions.

The <u>first</u> issue to be addressed is the realization, recognition and characterization of gains or losses resulting from the sale of the two automobiles. The <u>second</u> issue is that if we determine that the car sales result in recognized capital gains or losses, how do the current year's capital gain(s) or loss(es) fit together with the long-term capital loss carryover from the prior year? And <u>third</u>, how are the capital gain(s) or loss(es) reflected in computing Bill's adjusted gross income (AGI)?

<u>Realization, Recognition and Characterization of Gain or Loss from the Car Sales</u>

In every fact pattern in which something is sold, the author likes to go through the following analysis:

1)   Does the sale result in a <u>realized</u> gain or loss and if so, what is the <u>amount</u>?
2)   If we have a <u>realized</u> gain or loss, is it <u>recognized</u> (i.e. reportable for income tax purposes)?
3)   If the gain or loss is recognized, is it accorded "capital" gain or loss treatment?

Determining Bill's realized gains or losses in this question requires us to identify two basic components: The sales price of the cars ("amount realized" or, hereinafter, AR) and his basis in the cars ("adjusted basis or, hereinafter, AB). The difference between the two represents <u>realized</u> gain or loss. [IRC § 1001(a).] Let us examine the AB and AR components of each of Bill's two sales separately.

The AR for the first automobile that he sold is simple: The $7,500 sales price. As for Bill's AB in the car, a taxpayer's cost is normally the starting point for its determination. [IRC §§ 1011 and 1012.] When property is received as a bequest/devise/inheritance, as is the case here, there really is no "cost" to the taxpayer. The seemingly logical result of a zero basis is neither desirable nor, thankfully, appropriate. IRC § 1014(a)(1) provides the general rule that the basis of property acquired from a decedent shall be the property's fair market value at the date of the decedent's death. The automobile that Bill received from his uncle Fred was worth $4,000 at Fred's death and, therefore, this represents Bill's basis in the car. Note that Fred's AB (his original cost of $8,000) is irrelevant. While the fair market value basis rule of IRC § 1014(a)(1) is often referred to as the "step-up in basis" rule for receipt of appreciated property, the statutory provision also works as a "step-down" rule for depreciated property such as Fred's car. Subtracting Bills $4,000 AB from his $7,500 AR, results in a realized <u>gain of $3,500</u>.

AR	$7,500
minus: **AB**	($4,000)
Realized gain/(loss)	$3,500

Bill's AR and AB for the second car that he sold are more straightforward. The AR is his $3,000 sales price and his AB is his original cost of $6,000. This sale results in a realized <u>loss of $3,000</u>.

AR		$3,000
minus: **AB**		($6,000)
Realized gain/(loss)		($3,000)

The next step in our analysis of gain/loss situations is to determine the extent to which these <u>realized</u> gains and losses are <u>recognized</u>. Recognition basically means that the gains and losses will be reflected or counted in the computing of taxable income. Gains or losses that are <u>not</u> recognized, are, for all intents and purposes, ignored for income tax purpose. IRC § 1001(c) provides that unless otherwise provided for in the Code, all realized gains and losses are recognized. Bill's $3,500 gain from the first car sale <u>is</u> recognized as no "non-recognition" provision of the Code applicable to these facts.

The recognition of the $3,000 loss from the second car sale presents a bit of a problem for Bill. Unfortunately, there is an "otherwise indicated" Code section, namely IRC § 165, that affects Bill's recognition of his realized loss. At first glance, the "general rule" in IRC § 165(a) looks to be in Bill's favor allowing a deduction for "any loss sustained during the taxable year . . ." Reading further at IRC § 165(c) we come across an ominous sounding subsection: "Limitation on losses of individuals." In class, this professor refers to this as the "section 165(c) hoop," complete with graphic depictions on the board. Figuratively, the goal is to jump from the "realized" loss side, through the hoop to the land of "recognized" losses. This hoop, however, is more akin to a semi-permeable membrane than an unobstructed open space. We see, in IRC §§ 165(c)(1)-(c)(3), that business losses, investment losses and personal-use "casualty" losses, break on through to the recognized loss side. By default, however, losses from personal-use assets (other than casualty losses) do not make it through this "section 165(c) hoop" and go unrecognized. Bill realized a loss on the sale of this automobile but, unfortunately, he is <u>unable</u> to *recognize* this loss – i.e., Bill gets no tax benefit from such a loss and, for the sale of this automobile, the analysis stops here.

The third step in our analysis of gain/loss situations is whether Bill's gain is accorded special "capital gain" treatment. Note we are no longer concerned with his unrecognized loss on the second car sale (we go no further in the analysis once we have determined a gain or loss is <u>not</u> recognized). A capital gain analysis requires first determining that we are dealing with a "capital asset" after which the gain is characterized as being either long-term or short-term status. IRC § 1221(a) defines a capital asset in a negative fashion but for purposes of this analysis, it includes, by process of elimination, assets held for investment and personal-use purposes. Bill's car at issue at this point was used as a personal-use automobile. Therefore, Bill's $3,500 realized and recognized gain is properly characterized as a <u>capital gain</u>. Long-term status is reserved for those assets held for <u>more than one year</u> (short-term status for assets held one year or less). See § 1222. Bill sold the car that he inherited from Fred, about one month after receiving it. At first brush, Bill's capital gain from the sale of the car appears to be a short-term capital gain. Determining the holding period, for short and long term gain/loss classification, is controlled by IRC § 1223. While long-term status is generally reserved for assets held for more than one year, property received from a decedent effectively gets *automatic* long-term status in most situations pursuant to IRC § 1223(11). Bill's $3,500 gain is, therefore, a *long-term capital gain*.

<u>How Capital Gains/Losses are Combined, Including Carryovers from Prior Years</u>

As indicated in the analysis for question 12, above, capital gains and losses are separated according to their holding period – separating them into two groups or columns: short-term gains/losses and long-term gains/losses. Recall that in question 12, above, Bill had four capital gain or loss transactions and they were separated into these two groups. For reference purposes, Bill's capital gain/loss activity for the <u>prior year</u> is reproduced as follows:

Bill's Capital Gains and Losses for the <u>Prior Year</u>

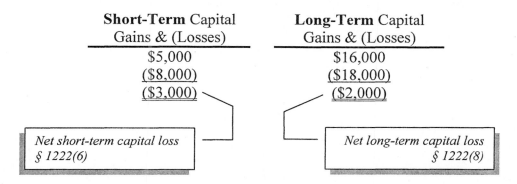

Without going through a complete explanation of the limits imposed on deductions of net capital losses (see analysis for question 12, above), Bill was able to use (or deduct) a total of $3,000 of these losses last year, all coming from the *short-term* side. Again, for reference purposes, a visual depiction of how this works is reproduced as follows:

Bill's Utilization of Capital Losses in the <u>Prior Year</u>

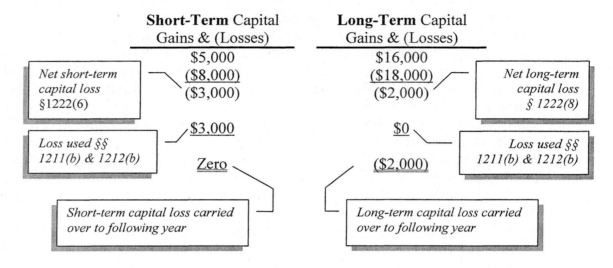

	Short-Term Capital Gains & (Losses)	**Long-Term** Capital Gains & (Losses)	

Net short-term capital loss §1222(6) — $5,000 / ($8,000) / ($3,000)

$16,000 / ($18,000) / ($2,000) — *Net long-term capital loss § 1222(8)*

Loss used §§ 1211(b) & 1212(b) — $3,000

$0 — *Loss used §§ 1211(b) & 1212(b)*

Zero

($2,000)

Short-term capital loss carried over to following year

Long-term capital loss carried over to following year

As we can see, last year, Bill was limited in the amount of capital loss he could deduct and was left with $2,000 *long-term capital loss* to be carried over to this, the current, year. From our analysis above, we know that in this year Bill has a $3,500 *long-term capital gain* from the first car sale. The mechanics of what we do now are relatively simple. We just go through the grouping and netting process again for the current year, making sure we properly reflect the carryover from the prior year. The grouping appears as follows:

Bill's Capital Gain/Loss Analysis for the Current Year

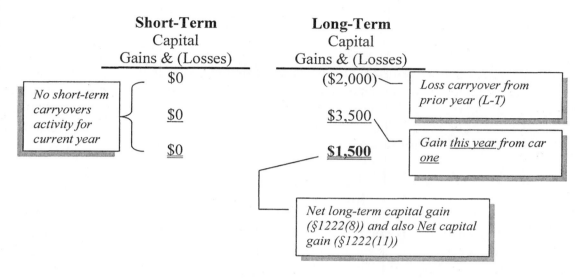

At this point, Bill has a net long-term capital gain (or net capital gain as defined in IRC § 1222(11)). The last part of this long analysis is how this gain is reflected in Bill's adjusted gross income (AGI).

Bill's Adjusted Gross Income (AGI) Reflecting Capital Gain

This is the easiest part. All gains (unless excluded) are reflected in a taxpayer's gross income. They may be offset by losses (as we saw in problem 12, above with Bill's capital losses offsetting his capital gains in the prior year), but the net amount of gain is included in gross income. For the current year, the facts indicate that Bill's wages are $60,000, and these, of course are part of his gross income. His $1,500 *net capital gain* is also included in gross income bringing the total to **$61,500**. As the facts state that there are no other tax-related items for the current year, and thus no deductions to arrive at adjusted gross income (these would be IRC § 62 so-called *above the line deductions*), Bill's adjusted gross income (AGI) is **$61,500**.

At this point, students often wonder why bother with the characterization of capital gains as long-term or short-term and the accompanying netting process. All gains, whether short-term, long-term, or "ordinary" gains are, under current law, included in gross income regardless of their character. The answer is that *long-term gains* (more specifically, net-net long-term capital gains [net capital gains]) historically have been accorded special tax treatment. The details of this favorable treatment are far beyond the scope of analysis for this question, but modernly, these *long-term capital gains* (while included gross and taxable income) are treated special when it comes time to actually compute the taxpayer's tax liability. The special treatment is that these *long-term capital gains* (net capital gains) may be taxed at lower tax rates than those applied to the taxpayer's other taxable income.

Answers (a), (b), (c), and (d) are all incorrect because they represent incorrect calculations to varying degrees including incorrect analysis of the preceding question 12, incorrect determination of the long-term capital loss carryover from the prior year, incorrect recognition of the loss from the sale of car <u>two</u>, and various combinations thereof.

- **Additional references:** *See* DANIEL Q. POSIN, FEDERAL INCOME TAXATION OF INDIVIDUALS ¶¶ 4.01, 4.02, 4.03, 4.05, 4.06 (5th ed. 2000).

14. **The correct answer is (d).** IRC § 61 defines gross income as "all income from whatever source derived." From your initial study of gross income's scope, you probably found it to be broadly defined, including the taxpayer's receipt of some net economic benefit or net accession to wealth. In class, you also discover that gross income is also not limited to the receipt of cash nor, in the case of employee compensation, need it be received directly by the taxpayer. Frequent flyer miles, and "points" earned under similar travel-related programs, do represent a benefit. Theoretically, if one's employer allows an employee to use benefits that accrued while working for personal purposes, income would result. Historically, however, the I.R.S. has not pursued this issue, as the administrative and technical issues are daunting at best.

In Announcement 2002-18, the I.R.S. has indicated that they "will not assert that any taxpayer has understated his federal tax liability by reason of the receipt or personal use of frequent flyer miles or other in-kind promotional benefits attributable to the taxpayer's business or official travel." [IRS Ann. 2002-10, I.R.B. 621.] However, it should be noted that this announcement goes on to say that, "[t]he relief provided by this announcement does not apply to travel or other promotional benefits that are converted to cash, to compensation that is paid in the form of travel or other promotional benefits, or in other circumstances where these benefits are used for tax avoidance purposes."

Elsa will clearly have no income merely by the accrual of her frequent flyer miles. She will also have no income on redemption of the frequent flyer miles for travel, or other non-cash benefits available to her under the plan.

Answers (a) and (b) are incorrect. As discussed above, the accumulation of miles or redemption for benefits do not give rise to income. **Answer (c) is incorrect** because the Commerce Clause of the Constitution is not applicable.

15. **The answer that is most likely correct is (d).** This question involves a rather complex issue relating to alimony that is known as "front-loading." The gist of this area is that if the "alimony" payments seem to be disproportionately high in the first few years immediately following a divorce, it does not "smell" right – the assumption being that the parties are attempting to change the tax character of certain transfers. Qualifying alimony (pursuant to IRC § 71) is deductible by the paying ex-spouse. [IRC § 215.] However, transfers of property (or payment for property or property rights) between former spouses, that is deemed "incident to divorce," does <u>not</u> give rise to deductions to the transferee ex-spouse. [IRC § 1041.] The "smell" of the "alimony" agreement in our fact pattern indicates that Patrick may be trying to draw into the deductible alimony category, nondeductible "incident to divorce" transfers of property or money.

IRC § 71(f) contains a complex set of rules that, in certain "front loaded" alimony situations, require the payor ex-spouse to recapture a portion of the "alimony" paid. Recapture, in this case, essentially means to bring back into the payor's income a portion of the alimony deducted (i.e., effectively reducing the net amount of alimony deducted). This professor does not usually cover the mechanics of these front-loading rules in the basic federal income tax course, and exact knowledge of how they work is not required to answer this question. Be aware, however, that your professor may cover this issue in greater depth and, accordingly, have exam questions requiring more intimate knowledge of these provisions.

Answer (a) is not likely to be correct because the disproportionately higher levels of "alimony" payable pursuant to the divorce agreement will, most likely, invoke the alimony recapture rules of IRC § 71(f). **Answer (b) is not correct.** While this answer correctly identifies the presumed motive for deduction on the part of Patrick, the result, that the alimony payments will not be deducted, is incorrect. Application of the alimony recapture rules still renders a portion of the otherwise qualifying alimony payments deductible. **Answer (c) is incorrect** because the application of the alimony recapture rules are not based on whether the payments are reasonable or unreasonable. Rather, they are applied based upon a defined, and complex, set of mathematical relationships of the amounts paid in particular years. **Similarly, answer (e) is incorrect** because the mathematical application of the alimony recapture rules does not yield this result (a static, net alimony deduction amount).

- **Additional references:** *See* DANIEL Q. POSIN, FEDERAL INCOME TAXATION OF INDIVIDUALS ¶ 6.02(14) (5th ed. 2000).

16. **The best answer is (d).** The path to reach the conclusion in this question is somewhat long. Tami's activities appear to be business related, and would seem to be deductible if we were to apply the requirements for business deductions of IRC § 162, that the expenditures be *ordinary and necessary expenses paid in connection with carrying on a trade or business*. [IRC § 162(a).] Because of the "entertainment" like nature of these business activities, the more restrictive provisions of IRC § 274 are applicable. As more thoroughly discussed below, Tami will be entitled to deduct 50% of the ticket (at their face amount) for non-luxury box seats. Her activities will be considered "associated with" the active conduct of her business. A more thorough analysis follows.

As indicated, when business activities have an entertainment, amusement, recreation, or fun sort of "flavor" to them, we have to look beyond the normal business deduction requirements of IRC § 162, and look to IRC § 274. [Please see other questions in this book addressing the general business deduction requirements of IRC § 162.] IRC § 274 is a limiting section enacted to curtail what were considered abuses to entertainment related business deductions. Right off the bat, IRC § 274 generally limits the deduction of any qualifying entertainment expenses (including non-entertainment business meals) to 50% of the qualifying expense. Before one even gets to this 50% deduction provision, the expenses have to qualify as deductible entertainment expenses.

IRC § 274 allows a deduction (at 50%) for entertainment *activities* that are considered either 1) directly related to the active conduct of a trade or business, or 2) associated with the active conduct of a trade or business. These two alternative qualifications are commonly known as the "directly related" and "associated with" tests. Satisfying the *directly related* test generally means that during the entertainment activities, the taxpayer is discussing real, substantive business with a client/customer (or prospective client/customer) ostensibly aimed at obtaining immediate revenue. [Reg. § 1.274-2(c)(3).] Satisfying the *associated with* test is often less difficult. To qualify, no business need be conducted during the entertainment activity itself, but only needs to directly precede or follow a bona fide and substantial business meeting with the client/customer (or prospective client/customer).

The facts that are indicated in answer (d) point toward the satisfaction of either of the two qualifying tests. It should be noted that Tami may have a more difficult time meeting the *directly related to* test because of the nature of the entertainment. The regulations, at § 1.274-2(c)(7), discuss the *directly related to* test and state: "Expenditures for entertainment, even if connected with the taxpayer's trade or business, will be considered *not directly related to* the active conduct of the taxpayer's trade or business, *if the entertainment occurred under circumstances where there was little or no possibility of engaging in the active conduct of a trade or business.*" The regulations go on to say: "The following circumstances will *generally* be considered circumstances where there was little or no possibility of engaging in the active conduct of a trade or business: . . . (ii) The distractions were substantial, such as – (a) A meeting or discussion at night clubs, theaters, and *sporting events* . . ." Finally, on this matter, the regulations state: "An expenditure for entertainment in any such case is considered not to be directly related to the active conduct of the taxpayer's trade or business *unless the taxpayer clearly establishes to the contrary.*" [Reg. § 1.274-2(c)(7).]

One last issue remains. "Skyboxes" are specifically addressed in IRC § 274(l)(2) and the statute states" "in the case of a skybox or other private luxury box leased for *more than 1 event*, the amount allowable as a deduction . . . shall not exceed the sum of the face value of non-luxury box seats for the seats . . ." The price for non-luxury box seats is normally considered to be the highest value of non-luxury box seats generally held for sale to the public on an event-by-event basis. Tami's skybox rental on five occasions places her within this special limitation limiting the qualifying entertainment/business cost to non-luxury box seats. Not to be forgotten, this amount is then subject to the 50% general limitation of IRC § 274.

While not at issue in this question, because Tami is self-employed, she would be entitled to this deduction (and her other normal § 162 business expenses) *above the line* in computing her adjusted gross income (AGI). [Please see Appendix A for more information about how income and deductions fit together in computing taxable income.]

Answer (a) is incorrect because it fails to recognize the general 50% limitation to entertainment/business costs imposed by IRC § 274. **Answer (b) is incorrect** because it fails to recognize the special limitations imposed on "skybox" rentals. **Answer (c) is incorrect** because the statute *does* allow for some deduction, if otherwise qualified, associated with skybox rentals.

- **Additional references:** *See* DANIEL Q. POSIN, FEDERAL INCOME TAXATION OF INDIVIDUALS ¶ 6.02(5) (5th ed. 2000).

17.   **The best answer is (d).** The path to reach the conclusion in this question is somewhat long. Yolanda's activities appear to be business related, and might be deductible, if we were to apply the requirements for business deductions of IRC § 162 (that the expenditures be *ordinary and necessary expenses paid in connection with carrying on a trade or business*). [IRC § 162(a).] Because of the "entertainment" like nature of these business activities, the more restrictive provisions of IRC § 274 are applicable. As more thoroughly discussed below, her boat is considered an "entertainment facility" and generally, deductions are not permitted

with respect to an *entertainment facility* (her boat). She will be entitled to deduct 50% of the direct costs associated with the actual entertainment activities (food, gas, hired help, etc.), assuming they are not extravagant, because these activities were either "directly related" to or "associated with" the active conduct of her business. A more thorough analysis follows.

As indicated, when business activities have an entertainment, amusement, recreation, or fun sort of "flavor" to them, we have to go beyond the normal business deduction requirements of IRC § 162, and look to IRC § 274. [Please see other questions in this book addressing the general business deduction requirements of IRC § 162.] IRC § 274 is a limiting section enacted to curtail what were considered abuses to entertainment related business deductions. Right off the bat, IRC § 274 generally limits the deduction of any qualifying entertainment expenses (including non-entertainment business meals) to 50% of the qualifying expense. Before one even gets to this 50% deduction provision, the expenses have to qualify as deductible entertainment expenses. IRC § 274(a)(1)(B) denies any deduction for expenses paid for an *entertainment facility* used in conjunction with an entertainment activity (see below). *Entertainment facilities* include such things as boats, swimming pools, beach cottages, ski lodges, tennis courts, hunting lodges, and *bowling alleys* (honest, it is in the regulations). [Reg. § 1.274-2(e)(2) (defining entertainment facilities for pre 1979 partial deduction allowed therefore).] Yolanda's "big ticket" costs associated with her boat, the maintenance, boat slip rental, insurance, and other related expenditures including "depreciation," are <u>not</u> deductible because her boat constitutes an *entertainment facility*. While not part of this problem, it should be noted that included in the definition of nondeductible entertainment facilities are dues to social, athletic, or sporting clubs. [IRC §§ 274(a)(2)(A) and (a)(3).]

The fact that Yolanda's boat is a nondeductible entertainment facility does not preclude deduction for qualifying "entertainment activities" associated with the use of her boat. [See I.R.S. Pub. 463, "Travel, Entertainment, Gift, and Car Expenses (for 2001 returns).] IRC § 274 allows a deduction (at 50%) for entertainment activities that are considered either 1) directly related to the active conduct of a trade or business, or 2) associated with the active conduct of a trade or business. These two alternative qualifications are commonly known as the "directly related" and "associated with" tests. Satisfying the *directly related* test generally means that during the entertainment activities, the taxpayer is discussing real, substantive business with a client/customer (or prospective client/customer) ostensibly aimed at obtaining immediate revenue. [Reg. § 1.274-2(c)(3).] Satisfying the *associated with* test is often less difficult. To qualify, no business need be conducted during the entertainment activity itself, but only needs to directly precede or follow a bona fide and substantial business meeting with the client/customer (or prospective client/customer). [Reg. § 1.274-2(d).] Yolanda's business activities related to her boat appear to qualify, with some of her business meetings during the boat trips considered as meeting the *directly related* test, and her other meetings directly preceding or following a substantial business meeting in her office as meeting the *associated with* test. It is assumed that Yolanda's meticulous record keeping will meet the substantiation requirements of IRC § 274(d).

In conclusion, Yolanda is entitled to deduct (at 50%) the actual costs (food, gas, hired help, etc.) associated with her client boat trips. She cannot, however, deduct any portion of the boat's other operating, maintenance, dock rental, insurance, etc. costs or depreciation.

While not part of this question, it should be noted that Yolanda's allowed deductions for her entertainment expenses are deductible, along with her normal IRC § 162 business expenses, "above the line" (to get to adjusted gross income (AGI)) in the computation of her taxable income. [Please see Appendix A for more information about how income and deductions fit together in the computation of taxable income and AGI.]

Answer (a) is incorrect because the characterization of her boat as an *entertainment facility* precludes this broad of a deduction. In addition, this answer does not reflect the overall 50% deduction limitation for qualifying entertainment activity expenses. **Answer (b) is incorrect** and, while not as broad as answer (a), is still too inclusive as to what is properly allowed as a deduction. **Answer (c) is incorrect** because it fails to recognize that one can have deductible entertainment activity expenses associated with a nondeductible entertainment facility.

- **Additional references:** *See* DANIEL Q. POSIN, FEDERAL INCOME TAXATION OF INDIVIDUALS ¶¶ 6.02(1), 6.02(5), 6.02(7) (5th ed. 2000).

18. **Answer (d) is correct.** Generally, when a *nonbusiness* bad debt becomes *totally* worthless, the loss is treated as a "short-term capital loss" loss (regardless of how long the debt had been outstanding before becoming worthless). [IRC § 166(d)(1); Reg. § 1.166-5.] Greg's loan to Tony was a nonbusiness bad debt, as the loan was not made in connection with Greg's business. [IRC § 166(d)(2).] Greg, therefore, has a $5,000 short-term capital loss resulting from this bad debt. This $5,000 short-term capital loss will be combined with any of Greg's other capital gains and losses. Capital gains and losses are combined and reflected in income utilizing a particular set of rules, which is the subject of other questions in this book.

It should be noted that the rules differ for "business" bad debts. [See, generally, IRC § 166.]

Answer (a) is not the best answer because it fails to characterize the loss (and potential deduction) as a short-term capital loss. **Answer (b) is also incorrect.** While it correctly classifies the bad debt as a short-term capital loss, the loss itself is not limited to $3,000. Other questions in this book explain that the total deduction for net capital losses in any one tax year may be limited to $3,000, but this is not equivalent to what is stated in this answer (b). **Answer (c) is incorrect** because a totally worthless nonbusiness bad debt *does* give rise to the recognition of a short-term capital loss. **Answer (e) is also incorrect.** While it is true that no benefit (loss or deduction) results if the creditor has no "basis" in the bad debt, Greg did have a $5,000 basis in the debt (his basis in the promissory note). This answer does bring up a common misconception about some bad debts. For example, say you perform some services for your neighbor in return for your neighbor's promise to pay you a specified amount (the value of your services). Should your neighbor fail to pay and this debt becomes totally worthless, you are not entitled to any benefit based upon the value of your services rendered. This is because you have no basis in the debt. Had you recognized *income* upon performing the services (say under the "accrual" method of accounting), *then* you would be entitled to a benefit from the worthless debt.

- **Additional references:** *See* DANIEL Q. POSIN, FEDERAL INCOME TAXATION OF INDIVIDUALS ¶ 7.01(6)(a) (5th ed. 2000).

19. **The correct answer is (a).** The concept of "adjusted gross income" (hereinafter AGI) is a bit amorphous, especially in one's initial study of income tax. The full comprehension of its significance sometimes does not come until very near the end of a full semester of studying tax. The long trek in the study of income, exclusions and deductions is to reach a computational goal of "taxable income" upon which tax rates are applied to get one's tax liability (before tax credits). In a nutshell, AGI is an intermediate point in this computation of taxable income.

In your study of the broad reach of gross income, you probably discuss specific statutory exclusions therefrom (such as those for gifts, bequests, etc., life insurance proceeds, and the like). In your study of *deductions*, you may cover many deductions including those for interest, business, medical, moving, etc. expenses. As far as deductions are concerned, there are two major camps of deductions for purposes of computing taxable income. There are deductions that are subtracted from *gross income* to arrive at our intermediary AGI. These are commonly referred to as "above the line" deductions, with AGI representing "the line." The other camp of deductions is comprised of those that are subtracted from AGI to arrive at *taxable income*. These are commonly referred to as "below the line" deductions. The components making up this camp of *below the line* deductions can include something called the "standard deduction" or, in the alternative, a group of deductions called "itemized deductions." In addition, one or more personal exemption deductions may be included in *below the line* deductions. [For more information about how this all fits together, please see IRC § 62, Appendix A, and other questions in this book.]

Why AGI is so important is the substance of this question. Some of the exclusions from gross income and deductions (both to AGI and from AGI) are based or dependent on the level of the taxpayer's AGI (in one form or another). Examples of some of these deductions and exclusions are mentioned below.

Common Examples of *Below the Line* Deductions that are Dependent or Based on AGI

- ➢ Medical care expenses deductible only to the extent that they exceed 7.5% of AGI. [IRC § 217.]
- ➢ Casualty losses deductible (after some adjustment) only to the extent that they exceed 10% of AGI. [IRC § 165(h).]
- ➢ Charitable contributions subject to a ceiling or cap in deductions based on varying percentages of AGI. [IRC § 170.]
- ➢ "Miscellaneous itemized deductions" deductible only to the extent that they exceed 2% of AGI. [IRC § 67.]
- ➢ "Itemized" deductions as a group subject to "phase-out" for Taxpayer's with AGI exceeding certain limits. [IRC § 68.]
- ➢ Personal exemption deduction phased-out for taxpayers with AGI exceeding certain limits. [IRC § 151(d)(3).]

Common Examples of *Above the Line* Deductions that are Dependent or Based on AGI

- ➢ Interest on student loans phased-out for taxpayers with AGI (modified) exceeding certain limits. [IRC § 221.]
- ➢ Deduction for certain higher education costs disallowed for taxpayers with AGI (modified) exceeding certain limits. [IRC § 222.]
- ➢ Certain retirement savings accounts phased-out for taxpayers with AGI (modified) exceeding certain limits. [IRC § 219.]

Common Examples of Exclusions From Income that are Dependent or Based on AGI

- ➢ Social Security benefits received not subject to exclusion from income (in varying degrees) for taxpayers with AGI (modified) exceeding certain limits. [IRC § 86.]
- ➢ Interest from U.S. Savings Bonds used for higher education not subject to exclusion from income (in varying degrees) for taxpayers with AGI (modified) exceeding certain limits. [IRC § 135.]

> ➢ Employer paid adoption assistance costs not subject to exclusion from income for taxpayers with AGI (modified) exceeding certain limits. [IRC § 137.]

As indicated by the deductions and exclusions listed above, AGI can be a very important factor, and can make a dramatic difference, in computing one's net income that is subject to tax (taxable income).

The one item presented in the question that is not dependent on AGI is the determination of a self-employed individual's "self-employment" tax. Beyond the scope of many federal income tax courses is the subject of self-employment tax. Basically, it is the *social security* and *Medicare* taxes that a self-employed individual has to pay on his or her net income (from such self-employed business). This tax is calculated and reported on, and payable with, an individual's regular income tax return, but it is not an income tax and the basis for its calculation is not impacted by AGI. For information purposes, the basis for calculating this tax is the individual's net income from his or her self-employed business activities (i.e., income from business as a self-employed person, independent contractor, or unincorporated sole proprietorship, less deductible business expenses associated therewith).

Answers (b), (c), and (d) are incorrect because they all contain an incorrect combination of items listed that are dependent or based on AGI. **Answer (e) is incorrect** because a correct answer (a) is present.

- **Additional references:** *See* DANIEL Q. POSIN, FEDERAL INCOME TAXATION OF INDIVIDUALS ¶ 6.01 (5th ed. 2000).

20.   **The correct answer is (b).** While this is a year-specific question (2002) it is easily adaptable to other tax years. As computed below, for 2002 the couple's *standard deduction* is $8,750 while their *itemized deductions* total only $7,850. It is, therefore, to their advantage to take the *standard deduction* in computing their taxable income.

In very broad terms, there are two camps of deductions for purposes of computing taxable income. There are deductions that are subtracted from *gross income* to arrive at an intermediary point called *adjusted gross income* (AGI). These are commonly referred to as "above the line" deductions, with AGI representing "the line." The other camp of deductions is comprised of those that are subtracted from AGI to arrive at *taxable income*. These are commonly referred to as "below the line" deductions. The components making up this camp of *below the line* deductions can include something called the "standard deduction" or, in the alternative, a group of deductions called "itemized deductions." In addition, one or more personal exemption deductions may be included in *below the line* deductions. [Please see Appendix A for more information about how income and deductions fit together in computing AGI and taxable income.]

In this question, we are concerned with two components of *below the line* deductions: the *standard deduction* and *itemized deductions*. Taxpayers have a choice: deduct either 1) the *standard deduction* amount, **or** 2) the total of *itemized deductions* (after applying all necessary limits and restrictions). In calculating "taxable income," a taxpayer takes, as a deduction, the greater of these two. The two deductions will be discussed separately. We are not concerned, in this problem, with *above the line* deductions as the couple's AGI is already given: $40,000.

The Couple's *Standard Deduction*
Many years ago, the concept of the "standard deduction" was introduced into tax law as a means of reducing an individual's record-keeping needs. As indicated, the *standard deduction* may be taken in place of a group of deductions known collectively as "itemized deductions."

IRC § 63(c) is the focal point for the *standard deduction*. The amount of this *standard deduction* can vary greatly from taxpayer to taxpayer depending on various factors including marital or filing status, age, degree of visual imparity, and whether the taxpayer is a "dependent" of another. In addition, *standard deduction* amounts are subject to change each tax year (and for the most part, do change each year) based on adjustments for "inflation" (i.e., the standard deduction amounts are *indexed* for inflation). The various *standard deduction* amounts listed in the statute (throughout IRC § 63) are not the actual amounts for the current year but, rather, are pre-inflation adjusted "base" amounts (that are well below the actual current amounts). [Appendix B contains the various *standard deduction* amounts for the year 2002 (the most current at the time of this printing).]

For 2002, the "regular" *standard deduction* for a married couple filing a joint return is $7,850 (corresponding to the statutory amount of $5,000 that is unadjusted for inflation). Note that this is **one** deduction for the joint return of both spouses, and not a deduction per spouse.

The *standard deduction* is **increased** for certain individuals based on age or visual imparity. [IRC § 63(b)(3).] For 2002, taxpayers age 65 and older (as of the end of the taxable year) are entitled to an extra $900 per qualifying individual when married and filing a joint return. This $900 for 2002 corresponds to the unadjusted for inflation amount of $600 listed in IRC § 63(f)(1). [See Appendix B for the 2002 *standard deduction* "extra amounts" for other classifications of individuals.] In our problem, Hal (but not Wanda) is the requisite age and they are entitled to "one" of these extra $900 standard deduction amounts. The couple's regular *standard deduction* of **$7,850** is **increased** by **$900**, resulting in a total *standard deduction* amount of **$8,750** for 2002.

[Please see other questions in this book that address the issue of visual imparity vis-à-vis the *standard deduction* amount as well as different or limited *standard deduction* amounts in other instances.]

Of interesting historical note, taxpayers age 65 or older (as well as a taxpayers with severely impaired vision) were entitled to an "extra" *personal exemption* deduction (discussed elsewhere in this book) rather than an increase in the *standard deduction*. However, in the 1980's this was changed and such factors as age and eyesight no longer give rise to extra personal exemption deductions but, as discussed above, now impact the determination of one's *standard deduction*.

The Couple's *Itemized Deductions*
Hal and Wanda have two expenditures that give rise to possible *itemized deductions*: real property taxes and medical care expenses.

IRC § 164 is a key section for addressing deductions for taxes paid. This section allows a deduction for, among other taxes, "state and local real property taxes" that have been "paid. [IRC § 164(a)(1).] The $3,900 Hal and Wanda paid in property taxes on their home are clearly deductible.

The $6,950 the couple spent on unreimbursed prescription drugs is the subject of IRC § 213. IRC § 213 allows for a deduction of certain qualified medical care expenses. Once one makes the determination of what constitutes "qualified" medical care expenses, the subject of this question, the deduction is allowed only to the extent that the total qualifying expenses exceeds 7.5% of the taxpayer's AGI. Qualified medical care expenses include typical costs for doctors, dentists, hospital, health insurance, and the like. [See IRC § 213(d).] In addition, qualified medical care expenses include costs for prescription drugs (and insulin in those areas where its sale is allowed without a prescription). [IRC § 213(b).] All of the couple's medicine costs were for prescription drugs and therefore, the $6,950 they spent qualifies as medical care expenses. To determine their actual medical expense deduction, we need to apply the 7.5% of AGI nondeductible "floor." The 7.5% nondeductible portion equals $3,000 (7.5% x $40,000 AGI). Their medical expense deduction is $6,950 less $3,000, or $3,950.

The total of the couple's *itemized deductions* equals the $3,900 in property taxes, plus the $3,950 medical expense deduction, or a total of **$7,850**.

Comparing this *itemized deduction* total of $7,850 to their $8,750 *standard deduction*, it is obvious that it is to their benefit to use the **standard deduction of $8,750**.

Answer (a) is incorrect because the two deductions are <u>not</u> equal (after factoring in the extra *standard deduction* amount allowed because of Hal's age). **Answer (c) is incorrect** because as indicated above, the *standard deduction* is the larger of the two. **Answer (d) is incorrect** because the deduction for *personal exemptions* is separate and is in <u>addition</u> to the greater of the *standard deduction* or total *itemized deductions*.

- **Additional references:** *See* DANIEL Q. POSIN, FEDERAL INCOME TAXATION OF INDIVIDUALS ¶¶ 6.01, 7.01(4), 7.01(7), 7.03 (5th ed. 2000).

21. **The best answer is (c).** This question involves deductions for personal exemptions. Every living person has, in his or her figurative pocket, a "coupon" good for a personal exemption deduction for each tax year. There is no real "coupon" involved, but it helps to think of the personal exemption deduction as such. The amount of this exemption deduction is listed in IRC § 151 of the Code as $2,000. However, this amount has been adjusted (increased) each year since 1990 to reflect the general level of inflation. The personal exemption deduction amount at the time of this writing is $3,000 for the year 2002. [Please see Appendix B for other inflation adjusted tax items for the year 2002.] This question does not indicate a particular year, but it does have you assume that the inflation adjusted personal exemption deduction for the year involved is less than $5,000. The key to this problem is determining who gets to use these personal exemption deduction "coupons" for the particular year. Does each person get to use his or her own "coupon" and get a personal exemption deduction (e.g. a $3,000 deduction for 2002), or does somebody else get to take another person's "coupon" and get the deduction? We conclude below that Tammy is entitled to take an additional personal exemption deduction for Chuck, but she is not entitled to Ned's personal exemption deduction.

Those students having come into a law school income tax course knowing little about income tax, probably know something about this issue. A parent claiming his or her children as dependents and getting an extra deduction for them is precisely the issue we are faced with in this question. Tammy, in our problem, is entitled to a personal exemption deduction for herself. The issue here is whether Tammy gets to take Chuck and Ned's "coupons" and thus get more personal exemption deductions (on her income tax return for purposes of computing her taxable income). Alternatively, do Chuck and Ned get to use their own "coupons" for a personal exemption deduction (on their respective income tax returns for purposes of computing their respective taxable income)? To determine if Tammy is entitled to get Chuck and Ned's personal exemption "coupons" (claim them as dependents and get to deduct their personal exemption deductions) involves a two-step (with many sub-steps) analysis, which in simplified form, is as follows:

> **Step One**: Is this person (e.g. a kid) your "**Dependent**" pursuant to IRC § 152? (All requirements must be met).
> - ➢ Person must be a U.S. citizen, resident or national, or a resident of Canada, Mexico for any part of the tax year.
> - ➢ Person must be either related to you, or be a member of your household for the entire year. [See IRC §§ 152(a)(1)-(a)(8) for definitions of "relatives," and IRC § 152(a)(9) for other qualifying individuals.]
> - ➢ You must have provided more than one-half this person's total support for the year.

> **Step Two**: If this person is your **Dependent** (from Step One, above), are you allowed to take a **deduction** (personal exemption deduction) for this dependent? [IRC § 151(c).]
> - ➢ Your Dependent must not file a joint return with a spouse for the year.
> - ➢ Your Dependent must either:
>   - ▪ Have "gross income" less than the "exemption amount" for that year, or
>   - ▪ Be your child (or step-child) who is under the age of 19 at the end of the year, **or**
>   - ▪ Be your child (or step child) who is under the age of 24 at the end of the year and is a full-time student for some part of each of five months during the year.

If **both** of these two steps are satisfied with respect to someone for whom you are trying to get their exemption deduction "coupon," then that person is your dependent and you are entitled to deduct their personal exemption deduction amount (e.g., $3,000 for 2002).

Tammy satisfies step one, above, with respect to both Chuck and Ned. Chuck and Ned are both U.S. citizens. Both Chuck and Ned are considered "related to" Tammy. Chuck is Tammy's child and considered "related" to Tammy pursuant to IRC § 152(a)(1)). Nephew Ned is also Tammy's relative pursuant to IRC § 152(a)(6) (Ned is, as stated in the Code, "a son or daughter of a brother or sister of the taxpayer"). The facts indicate that the support requirement is met with respect to both Chuck and Ned. Tammy provides "literally all" and "the majority of" Chuck's and Ned's support, respectively. Note, that there is no requirement that any "related" person (listed in IRC §§ 152(a)(1)-(a)(8)) <u>lives</u> with anyone in particular to attain dependent status.

Step two of the dependent exemption deduction analysis will be discussed separately with respect to Chuck and Ned. **Chuck** is unmarried, but does he have "gross income" less than the "exemption amount" for the year in question? And what does this mean? The measuring gross income level of "the exemption amount" is the amount of the personal exemption deduction (e.g., $3,000 for 2002). Jeremy's gross income of $5,000 is <u>not</u> less than the exemption amount that, for our question, is given as less than $5,000. We do not, however, stop at this point, as the operative word in this part of step two is "either." Going onto to the next "either" requirement, Chuck <u>is</u> Tammy's child and is less than 19 years old (as of the end of the year). We can stop here with respect to **Chuck** – Tammy is entitled to get Chuck's personal exemption deduction "coupon."

Ned is also not married. Ned's gross income, also $5,000 is <u>not</u> less than the exemption amount (given as less than $5,000 in our problem). Going on to either of the two next steps, Tammy is stopped in her tracks at the outset since Ned is <u>not</u> her child. Therefore, with respect to **Ned**, Tammy is <u>not</u> entitled to take Ned's personal exemption deduction "coupon."

In conclusion, Tammy is entitled to take a personal exemption deduction (e.g., $3,000 in 2002) for herself. She is also entitled to a personal exemption deduction for her son, Chuck. Although Ned is Tammy's dependent, she is not entitled to take his personal exemption deduction because based on his level of gross income, he would have to be Tammy's <u>child</u> which, he is not. It should be noted that while not the subject of this problem, there are provisions in the Code and the 2001 Tax Act that may effect this total personal exemption deduction depending on the extent of Tammy's income. This latter concept of "phasing-out" personal exemption deductions is complex and may be addressed by your professor.

Answer (a) is incorrect because Ned's age is irrelevant if he has gross income equal to or more than the exemption amount (which he has in our question) because he is not Tammy's child. This answer would have been correct if Ned was Tammy's child instead of her nephew. **Answer (b) is incorrect** because Tammy's child Chuck need not earn less than the exemption amount as long as he is Tammy's dependent and is either less than 19 years old or less than 24 years old and a full-time student for some part of each of five months during the year. **Answer (d) is incorrect** but is close to being correct. The statement in this answer that "Ned does not satisfy the requirements of being Tammy's dependent" is incorrect. Ned does qualify as Tammy's dependent (meeting the relationship and support tests). She just is not entitled to take his personal exemption deduction as discussed above. **Answer (e) is incorrect** because we do have a correct response in answer (c).

22.   **The best answer to this very tricky question is (b).** The author admits that this is an awful question. However, it serves to point out how carefully one must read the sometimes seemingly undecipherable language of the Code. This question also serves as an example of miniscule Code details at, or near, their worst. It also is a bit unfair to ask in conjunction with other question in this series, as the correct answer is substantially dependent on a correct analysis of other questions in this series. This professor would not ask such a series of interrelated multiple-choice questions on an exam. Rather, this series of questions were derived from an exam essay question. We will conclude that Tammy qualifies as a "head of household" because Chuck is her son, and she meets the statutory requirements of this filing status.

As you have most likely discussed in class, the tax rate schedules used to compute tax liability vary depending on one's *filing status*. IRC § 1 contains these rate schedules. Be aware, that the rate schedules appearing in IRC § 1 are "indexed for inflation," so the actual rate schedules for any particular year will vary. [Please see Appendix B for inflation-adjusted information for the 2002 tax year.] As you also have probably discussed, the rate schedules for individuals appear in order, in IRC §§ 1(a)-1(d), from the most favorable rates (the least amount of tax for any given amount of taxable income) to the least favorable rates. The primary issue for Tammy in this question is **whether she can qualify to file using the "heads of household" rates** in IRC § 1(b). This rate schedule is not quite as favorable as that for "married individuals filing a joint return", but it is better than the rate schedule for "unmarried individuals" (generally known as "single").

A *head of household* is defined in IRC §2 (b), and here is where the rules get tricky (and, you might say, picky too). The statutory definition of a *head of household* is a bit more inclusive than is necessary to address the facts in this question, so it is wise to carefully read all of the provisions in IRC § 2(b) for other situations that might arise.

Generally, we start with a *head of household* being an "unmarried individual" (although there is a notable exception for certain "separated" spouses), and Tammy meets this criteria. Next, to qualify for *head of household* status, the taxpayer (Tammy) must pay more than ½ of the costs of keeping up a home that was the primary home for more than ½ of the year for the taxpayer (Tammy) and at least one of the following:

➤ A **single** child or step-child (or any one of their descendents who is single),

> ➢ A **married** child or step-child (or any one of their descendents who is married), <u>but</u> only if such person is a dependent of the taxpayer (and the taxpayer is entitled to claim the dependent's *personal exemption deduction* pursuant to IRC § 151), or
> ➢ Any other "relative" (as defined in IRC §§ 152(a)(1)–(a)(8)) if such person is a dependent of the taxpayer (and the taxpayer is entitled to claim the dependent's *personal exemption deduction* pursuant to IRC § 151).

As for Tammy, she qualifies as *head of household* because her son, Chuck, lives with her for more than ½ of the year (he lives with her for the full year) in a home that Tammy is presumably paying all of the costs of maintaining. Note that because Chuck is unmarried, he need not be Tammy's dependent (although from problem 21, above, we concluded that he was) for purposes of qualifying her for *head of household* status. This is the reason why **answer (c) is incorrect**.

Answer (a) is incorrect because, as indicated above, Chuck need not, in this case, be Tammy's dependent in order for Tammy to qualify for *head of household* status. It is also incorrect because Ned is not living with Tammy (as required by statute) nor is Ned an individual for whom she can claim his *personal exemption deduction* pursuant to IRC § 151 (see discussion in problem 21, above). Note that there are special *head of household* qualifying rules with respect to utilizing one's dependent parent who is not required to live with the taxpayer. [See IRC § 2(b)(1)(B).] **Answer (d) is incorrect** because Tammy does not meet the requirements to qualify as a *surviving spouse* pursuant to IRC § 2(a). **Answer (e) is incorrect** because, as indicated above, Tammy qualifies for the more favorable *head of household* status even though she is an unmarried individual.

23. **Answer (b) is correct.** IRC § 213 allows for a deduction of certain qualified medical care expenses. Once one makes the determination of what constitutes "qualified" medical care expenses, the subject of this question, the deduction is allowed as an "itemized deduction" only to the extent that the total qualifying expenses exceeds 7.5% of adjusted gross income (AGI). [See Appendix A for more information about how income and deductions fit together to compute taxable income and AGI.] Qualified medical care expenses include typical costs for doctors, dentists, hospital, health insurance, and the like. [See IRC § 213(d).] The section specifically provides that qualifying medical care expenses are those paid by the taxpayer for the taxpayer, his or her spouse, or <u>a dependent (as defined in IRC § 152)</u>.

The $1,000 of health insurance premiums Tammy paid for herself clearly qualifies as medical care expenses. We have determined that Chuck is Tammy's dependent, so the $1,000 health insurance premiums Tammy paid for him are also qualifying expenses. And the $7,000 doctor and hospital costs Tammy paid for

Ned? The expenditures are surely the type qualifying for medical care expenses, but is Ned Tammy's "dependent as defined in IRC § 152? The answer is yes, as we have already established that Ned qualifies as Tammy's dependent because he is related to her and she provides more than one-half of his support. Therefore, the doctor and hospital costs Tammy paid for Ned are qualifying medical care expenses for her. But wait! In question 21, above, did we not say that Tammy could claim only Chuck, but not Ned, as a dependent for purposes of Tammy taking his personal exemption deduction? Yes, we did. However, recall that there are two steps in determining whether a taxpayer is entitled to take the personal exemption deduction of another. The first step is to determine whether, pursuant to IRC § 152, the person (e.g., Chuck or Ned) is a dependent of the taxpayer (e.g., Tammy). The second step is to determine whether, pursuant to IRC § 151, the taxpayer is entitled to claim the personal exemption deduction for such dependent. Recall that both Chuck and Ned are, pursuant to IRC § 152, dependents of Tammy, but only Chuck met the requirements of IRC § 151 allowing Tammy to take his personal exemption deduction. What does all this mean for purposes of this question? The statute allowing the deduction for medical care expenses paid for a dependent (IRC § 213) requires only that such person be a dependent pursuant IRC § 152, not that in addition, the taxpayer can claim such dependent's personal exemption deduction pursuant to IRC § 151.

In summary, Tammy's expenditures for all of the items listed for her, Chuck and Ned qualify as medical care expenses for purposes of IRC § 213.

Answer (a) is incorrect, but is a favorite choice. This answer incorrectly places the tougher requirement on a taxpayer deducting qualifying medical care expenses paid for another that not only must the other person qualify as a dependent of the taxpayer, but also that the taxpayer is entitled to claim the personal exemption deduction for such dependent. **Answer (c) is incorrect** because it fails to recognize that a taxpayer can deduct qualifying medical care expenses paid for certain other individuals. **Answer (d) is incorrect** because it fails to recognize that health insurance premiums represent qualifying medical care expenses. **Answer (e) is incorrect** because a correct response (b) is presented.

- **Additional references:** *See* DANIEL Q. POSIN, FEDERAL INCOME TAXATION OF INDIVIDUALS ¶ 7.01(7) (5th ed. 2000).

24. **The best answer is (c).** Sadly, Allison lost her spouse last year. For income tax purposes a joint return generally may be filed in the year a spouse dies. [IRC § 6013; Reg. 1.6013-3.] There are special rules regarding the allocation of income between the spouses' joint return and an income tax return for the decedent in the year of death (i.e., determining income and deductions that are included in the joint return). However, Allison's substantial amount of income for last year will

definitely benefit from the advantageous "married filing joint returns" income tax rates.

Answer (a) is incorrect but is an answer that is often selected. As is more thoroughly discussed in question 25, immediately following this question, "labels" for income tax purposes do not necessarily agree with those that we use in everyday language. To everyone, except the I.R.S., Allison was a "surviving spouse" once Robert passed away. For income tax purposes, however the term "surviving spouse" has a very particular meaning, defined in IRC § 2(a). Allison is <u>not</u> a "surviving spouse" for income tax purposes, as is more thoroughly discussed in question 25, below. **Answer (b) is incorrect** because as discussed above, in the year of her husband's death, Allison may still use the married filing joint rates. The statement in this answer about one's marital status being determined as of the last day of the taxable year is, however, generally true. **Answer (d) is incorrect** because there is no rule requiring Allison to use this rate schedule.

25.   **Answer (b) is correct.** Sadly, Allison lost her spouse last year and, unfortunately for tax purposes, this year she is *single* and will use the "unmarried" rate schedule for computing her tax liability. IRC § 1 sets out the tax computation rate schedules and as you have most likely studied, the rate schedules vary depending on one's *filing status*. Filing status is determined as of the end of the tax year and, as indicated in the facts, Allison is single.

A word of caution about language used on exams. There are many instances where the common use of a term does not necessarily correspond to its official "tax" counterpart. Labels can be deceiving and do not be fooled by their use in lay terms on an exam. In everyday language we would refer to Allison as a "surviving spouse." Looking at IRC § 1(a) we see a favorable tax rate schedule (compared to that for unmarried individuals) for certain married individuals and *surviving spouses*. The term *surviving spouse*, however, has a very specific and much narrower definition for federal income tax purposes (and the ability to use the more favorable rate schedule). IRC § 2(a) gives the *tax label* of *surviving spouse* for only the two years after the year in which the taxpayer's spouse died <u>and</u> only if:
- ➤ Such surviving spouse maintains as his or her home a household which constitutes for the taxable year the principal place of abode (as a member of such household) of a dependent
- ➤ Who (within the meaning of IRC § 152) is a son, stepson, daughter, or stepdaughter of the surviving spouse, and
- ➤ With respect to whom the surviving spouse is entitled to a deduction for the taxable year under IRC § 151.

Distilled, a *surviving spouse* for income tax purposes is an unmarried surviving spouse (for the two years subsequent to his or her spouse's death) who has dependent children living in his or her home. The facts state that Allison has no children. Even though to the entire non-tax world, Allison is a surviving spouse, she is not so considered for federal income tax purposes. Therefore, she is unable to use the more favorable married/surviving spouse rate schedule but, rather, must use the single/unmarried (non heads of households) rate schedule.

Answer (a) is incorrect because, as discussed above, Allison is <u>not</u> considered a surviving spouse for federal income tax purposes. **Answer (d) is incorrect** for the same reason that she does not qualify for surviving spouse status for income tax purposes.

Answer (c) is also incorrect. The tax rate schedule for *heads of households* is "in between" those for married/surviving spouses and unmarried/single (less favorable than the former but more favorable than the latter). Heads of households have a particular meaning for federal income tax purposes and Allison does not meet the requirements. [See IRC § 2(b).]

ANSWER KEY
EXAM VII

1. **Answer (b) is correct.** Daniel is Mom's dependent and, as discussed below, Mom meets the requirements for taking Daniel's personal exemption deduction ($3,000 for 2002) in computing her taxable income. Because Mom is *allowed* to take this deduction, Daniel cannot take it for himself. [IRC § 151(d)(2).] Contrary to a commonly held opinion (and common practice), there is no choice in the matter. Mom, if she is entitled to the deduction (see below) cannot say, "Daniel, I've decided not to take your personal exemption deduction this year –go ahead, you take it for yourself." A more thorough explanation follows.

    Every living person has, in his or her figurative pocket, a "coupon" good for a personal exemption deduction for each tax year. There is no real "coupon" involved, but it helps to think of the personal exemption deduction as such. The amount of this exemption deduction is listed in IRC § 151 of the Code as $2,000. However, this amount has been adjusted (increased) each year since 1990 to reflect the general level of inflation. The personal exemption deduction amount at the time of this writing is $3,000 for the year 2002. [Please see Appendix B for other inflation adjusted tax items for the year 2002.] The key to this problem is determining who gets to use these personal exemption deduction "coupons" for the particular year. Does each person get to use his or her own "coupon" and get a personal exemption deduction (e.g. a $3,000 deduction for 2002), or does somebody else get to take another person's "coupon" get the deduction?

    Those students having come into a law school income tax course knowing little about income tax, probably know something about this issue. A parent claiming his or her children as dependents and getting an extra deduction for them is precisely the issue that we are faced with in this question. Mom, in our problem, is entitled to a personal exemption deduction for herself. A critical issue here is whether Mom gets to take Daniel's "coupon" and thus get his personal exemption deduction (on her income tax return for purposes of computing her taxable income). Alternatively, and the call of this question, does Daniel get to use his own "coupon" for a personal exemption deduction (for purposes of computing his taxable income). To determine if Mom is entitled to get Daniel's personal exemption "coupon" (claim him as dependents and get to deduct his personal exemption deductions) involves a two-step (with many sub-steps) analysis, which in simplified form, is as follows:

    > **Step One**: Is this person (e.g. a kid) your "**Dependent**" pursuant to IRC § 152? (All requirements must be met).
    > > ➤ Person must be a U.S. citizen, resident or national, or a resident of Canada, Mexico for any part of the tax year.
    > > ➤ Person must be either related to you, or be a member of your household for the entire year. [See IRC §§ 152(a)(1)-(a)(8) for

definitions of "relatives," and IRC § 152(a)(9) for other qualifying individuals.]

➤ You must have provided more than one-half this person's total support for the year.

Step Two: If this person is your **Dependent** (from Step One, above), are you allowed to take a **deduction** (personal exemption deduction) for this dependent? [IRC § 151(c).]

➤ Your Dependent must not file a joint return with a spouse for the year.

➤ Your Dependent must either:

- Have "gross income" less than the "exemption amount" for that year, or
- Be your child (or step-child) who is under the age of 19 at the end of the year, **or**
- Be your child (or step child) who is under the age of 24 at the end of the year and is a full-time student for some part of each of five months during the year.

If **both** of these two steps are satisfied with respect to someone for whom you are trying to get their exemption deduction "coupon," then that person is your dependent and you are entitled to deduct their personal exemption deduction amount (e.g., $3,000 for 2002). If this is the case than the person being claimed as a dependent (e.g., Daniel) is not entitled to take the deduction. [IRC § 151(d)(2).]

Mom satisfies step one, above, with respect to Daniel. Daniel is a U.S. citizen and as Mom's child, he is considered "related" to Mom. [IRC § 152(a)(1)).] The facts indicate that the support requirement is also met: "Mom unequivocally provides more than one-half of Daniel's support." Note that there is no requirement that any "related" person (listed in IRC §§ 152(a)(1)-(a)(8)) <u>lives</u> with anyone in particular to attain dependent status.

On to step two of the dependent exemption deduction analysis, Daniel is unmarried, but does he have "gross income" less than the "exemption amount" for the year in question? And what does this mean? The measuring gross income level of "the exemption amount" is the amount of the personal exemption deduction (e.g., $3,000 for 2002). Daniel's gross income of $8,000 is clearly not less than the $3,000 exemption for 2002. We do not, however, stop at this point as the operative word in this part of the step two is "either." Going onto to the next "either" requirement, Daniel <u>is</u> Mom's child, but he is not <u>less than</u> age 19 (as of the end of the year). Daniel does, however, qualify under the last option – he is less than 24 years of age (as of the end of the year) and is a full-time college student.

Therefore, with respect to Daniel, Mom is entitled to get his personal exemption deduction "coupon."

As indicated above, IRC § 151(d)(2) indicates that if Daniel's personal exemption deduction is *allowable* to another individual (Mom in our case), Daniel is not entitled to take the personal exemption deduction himself for the purpose of computing his taxable income. There is only *one* personal exemption deduction per person and Mom, in our case, is entitled to take it. But can't Mom choose <u>not</u> to take the deduction and let Daniel take it for himself? The answer is no, because of the statutory use of the word *allowable*. If Mom *can* take Daniel's personal exemption deduction, then only she can take it and Daniel cannot.

As indicated, this question is date sensitive, applicable to the 2002 tax year. This question can easily be modified to accommodate years subsequent to 2002 by incorporating the applicable inflation adjusted personal exemption deduction amount for any particular year.

Answers (a) and (c) are incorrect because, as discussed above, Mom meets all of the requirements for claiming Daniel's personal exemption deduction. **Answer (d) is incorrect** because the personal exemption deduction is separate and distinct from "itemized deductions." The two deductions are not interrelated. [See Appendix A for more information on how income and deductions fit together for purposes of computing taxable income and AGI.]

2.   **Answer (c) is correct.** Many years ago, the concept of the "standard deduction" was introduced into tax law as a means of reducing an individual's record-keeping needs. The *standard deduction* may be taken in place of a group of deductions known collectively as "itemized deductions." Probably the most commonly known components of this latter group of *itemized deductions* include charitable contributions, deductible interest and taxes and qualifying medical deductions. Taxpayers have a choice: deduct either 1) the total of itemized deductions (after applying all necessary limits and restrictions as discussed elsewhere in this book), **or** 2) the *standard deduction* amount. In calculating "taxable income," a taxpayer takes as a deduction the <u>greater</u> of these two. [Please see Appendix A for more information about *where* these deductions fit within the framework of calculating taxable income.]

IRC § 63(c) is the focal point for the *standard deduction*. The amount of this *standard deduction* can vary greatly from taxpayer to taxpayer depending on various factors including marital or filing status, age, degree of visual imparity, and whether the taxpayer is a "dependent" of another. In addition, *standard deduction* amounts are subject to change each tax year (and for the most part, do change each year) based on adjustments for "inflation" (i.e., the standard deduction amounts are *indexed* for inflation). The various *standard deduction* amounts listed in the statute (throughout IRC § 63) are <u>not</u> the actual amounts for the current year but, rather, are pre-inflation adjusted "base" amounts (that are well below the actual current amounts). [Appendix B contains the various *standard deduction* amounts for the year 2002 (the most current at the time of this printing).]

For 2002, the "regular" *standard deduction* for a single individual is $4,700 (corresponding to the statutory amount of $3,000 that is unadjusted for inflation). Daniel may not, however, be entitled to this amount because of a special limitation provision in IRC § 63(c)(5). As indicated in our facts, and as discussed in problem 1, above, Daniel can properly be claimed as Mom's dependent, and Mom is also entitled to claim Daniel's personal exemption deduction in computing her taxable income pursuant to IRC § 151. This provision in IRC § 63(c)(5) may limit the standard deduction for an individual in Daniel's situation – an individual who can be claimed as a dependent (and whose personal exemption deduction can be used) by someone else. For **2002**, the limit imposed by this provision for Daniel's *standard deduction* is:

The greater of:
>> 1) $750, or
>> 2) Daniel's "earned" income + $250.

> Please note that the $750 amount above is for 2002, and corresponds to the statutory amount of $500 (that is unadjusted for inflation).

"Earned income" for this special limitation, basically means wages, salaries and other compensation like income. It does not include more passive income such as interest and dividends. In *this* question, Daniel has no *earned income,* so applying this special provision to Daniel, his *standard deduction* is <u>$750</u>.

Note, that the above special limitation calculation <u>cannot</u> yield a *standard deduction* that is greater than that which would otherwise apply to the individual (without such applying this special provision). [IRC § 63(c)(5).] This is not the case for Daniel in this question.

Answer (a) is incorrect because while $4,700 represents the basic 2002 *standard deduction* for single individuals, it does not apply to Daniel. Rather, as discussed above, the special limitation provision of IRC § 63(c)(5) is applicable to him. **Answer (b) is incorrect.** $3,000 represents the basic *standard deduction* for single individuals as listed in the statute. This statutory amount is unadjusted for inflation and has risen, for 2002, to $4,700. However, as indicated above, Daniel is not entitled to this amount because of IRC § 63(c)(5). **Answer (d) is incorrect** because at a minimum, Daniel is entitled to some amount of *standard deduction*

($750 in his case). **Answer (e) is incorrect** because the correct answer (c) is presented.

3.   **The correct answer is (e).** For this question, we will conclude that Daniel's "standard deduction" for 2002 is $2,250.

Many years ago, the concept of the "standard deduction" was introduced into tax law as a means of reducing an individual's record-keeping needs. The *standard deduction* may be taken in place of a group of deductions known collectively as "itemized deductions." Probably the most commonly known components of this latter group of *itemized deductions* include charitable contributions, deductible interest and taxes, and qualifying medical deductions. Taxpayers have a choice: deduct either 1) the total of itemized deductions*s* (after applying all necessary limits and restrictions as discussed elsewhere in this book), **or** 2) the *standard deduction* amount. In calculating "taxable income," a taxpayer takes as a deduction the <u>greater</u> of these two. [Please see Appendix A for more information about *where* these deductions fit within the framework of calculating taxable income.]

IRC § 63(c) is the focal point for the *standard deduction*. The amount of this *standard deduction* can vary greatly from taxpayer to taxpayer depending on various factors including marital or filing status, age, degree of visual imparity, and whether the taxpayer is a "dependent" of another. In addition, *standard deduction* amounts are subject to change each tax year (and for the most part, do change each year) based on adjustments for "inflation" (i.e., the standard deduction amounts are *indexed* for inflation). The various *standard deduction* amounts listed in the statute (throughout IRC § 63) are <u>not</u> the actual amounts for the current year but, rather, are pre-inflation adjusted "base" amounts (that are well below the actual current amounts). [Appendix B, contains the various *standard deduction* amounts for the year 2002 (the most current at the time of this printing).]

For 2002, the "regular" *standard deduction* for a single individual is $4,700 (corresponding to the statutory amount of $3,000 that is unadjusted for inflation). Daniel may not, however, be entitled to this amount because of a special limitation provision in IRC § 63(c)(5). As indicated in our facts, and as discussed in problem 1, above, Daniel can properly be claimed as Mom's dependent, and Mom is also entitled to claim Daniel's personal exemption deduction in computing her taxable income pursuant to IRC § 151. This provision in IRC § 63(c)(5) may limit the standard deduction for an individual in Daniel's situation – an individual who can be claimed as a dependent (and whose personal exemption deduction can be used) by someone else. For **2002,** the limit imposed by this provision for Daniel's *standard deduction* is:
     The greater of:
          1) $750, or

2) Daniel's "earned" income + $250.

Please note that the $750 amount above is for 2002, and corresponds to the statutory amount of $500 (that is unadjusted for inflation).

"Earned income" for this special limitation, basically means wages, salaries and other compensation like income. It does not include more passive income such as interest and dividends. In *this* question, Daniel has *earned income* of $2,000. Applying the above special provision, Daniel's *standard deduction* is the greater of $750, or $2,250 ($2,000 + $250). Daniel's *standard deduction*, in *this* question is, therefore <u>$2,250</u>.

Note that the above special limitation calculation <u>cannot</u> yield a *standard deduction* that is greater than that which would otherwise apply to the individual (without such applying this special provision). [IRC § 63(c)(5).] This is not the case for Daniel in this question.

Answer (a) is incorrect because Daniel, as discussed above, is entitled to some amount of *standard deduction*. **Answer (b) is incorrect** because Daniel had a sufficient amount of "earned income" that, when applying the special limitation provision, yields an amount greater than $750. **Answer (c) is incorrect** because it fails to add the $250 to his "earned income" of $2,000 in arriving at the correct *standard deduction* amount. **Answer (d) is incorrect** because in Daniel's situation, he is not entitled to the full *standard deduction* of $4,700 (for 2002) for single individuals.

4. **The correct answer is (d).** For this question, we will conclude that Daniel is entitled to the full "standard deduction" amount for single individuals: $4,700 for 2002.

Many years ago, the concept of the "standard deduction" was introduced into tax law as a means of reducing an individual's record-keeping needs. The *standard deduction* may be taken in place of a group of deductions known collectively as "itemized deductions." Probably the most commonly known components of this latter group of *itemized deductions* include charitable contributions, deductible interest and taxes, and qualifying medical deductions. Taxpayers have a choice: deduct either 1) the total of itemized deductions*s* (after applying all necessary limits and restrictions as discussed elsewhere in this book), **or** 2) the *standard deduction* amount. In calculating "taxable income," a taxpayer takes as a deduction the <u>greater</u> of these two. [Please see Appendix A for more information about *where* these deductions fit within the framework of calculating taxable income.]

IRC § 63(c) is the focal point for the *standard deduction*. The amount of this *standard deduction* can vary greatly from taxpayer to taxpayer depending on various factors including marital or filing status, age, degree of visual imparity, and whether the taxpayer is a "dependent" of another. In addition, *standard deduction* amounts are subject to change each tax year (and for the most part, do change each year) based on adjustments for "inflation" (i.e., the standard deduction amounts are *indexed* for inflation). The various *standard deduction* amounts listed in the statute (throughout IRC § 63) are <u>not</u> the actual amounts for the current year but, rather, are pre-inflation adjusted "base" amounts (that are well below the actual current amounts). [Appendix B, contains the various *standard deduction* amounts for the year 2002 (the most current at the time of this printing).]

For 2002, the "regular" *standard deduction* for a single individual is $4,700 (corresponding to the statutory amount of $3,000 that is unadjusted for inflation). Daniel may not, however, be entitled to this amount because of a special limitation provision in IRC § 63(c)(5). As indicated in our facts, and as discussed in problem 1, above, Daniel can properly be claimed as Mom's dependent, and Mom is also entitled to claim Daniel's personal exemption deduction in computing her taxable income pursuant to IRC § 151. This provision in IRC § 63(c)(5) may limit the standard deduction for an individual in Daniel's situation – an individual who can be claimed as a dependent (and whose personal exemption deduction can be used) by someone else. For **2002**, the limit imposed by this provision for Daniel's *standard deduction* is:

> **The greater of**:
> > 1) $750, or
> > 2) Daniel's "earned" income + $250.

> Please note that the $750 amount above is for 2002, and corresponds to the statutory amount of $500 (that is unadjusted for inflation).

"Earned income" for this special limitation, basically means wages, salaries and other compensation like income. It does not include more passive income such as interest and dividends. In *this* question, Daniel has *earned income* of $8,000. Applying the above special provision, Daniel's *standard deduction* is the greater of $750, or $8,250 ($8,000 + $250). It would <u>appear</u>, therefore, that Daniel's *standard deduction*, in *this* question is $8,250. This special limitation calculation <u>cannot</u> yield a *standard deduction* that is greater than that which would otherwise apply to the individual (without such applying this special provision). [IRC § 63(c)(5).] The regular *standard deduction* for a single individual (for 2002) is <u>$4,700</u> and this, therefore, is the proper amount that can be claimed by Daniel.

Answer (a) is incorrect because it fails to recognize that the standard deduction computed under the special "limitation" provision cannot exceed the regular *stan-*

dard deduction for such individual (without application of the special limitation provision). **Answer (b) is also incorrect.** This answer fails to add the $250 to Daniel's earned income for purposes of the special limitation provision in IRC § 63(c)(5). In any event, the amount still cannot exceed what would be his regular *standard deduction* of $4,700 (for 2002). **Answer (c) is incorrect** because it is the wrong number (and exceeds the regular *standard deduction*) in Daniel's case. **Answer (e) is incorrect** because the correct answer (d) is presented.

5.   **The correct answer is (d).** This question is designed to illustrate how the various components of income and deductions fit together to compute taxable income. This computation requires information about Daniel's income and deductions. A visual computational framework for taxable income is as follows:

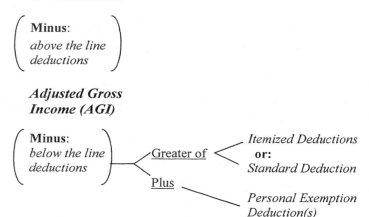

Gross Income

$\left(\begin{array}{l}\textbf{Minus:}\\ \textit{above the line}\\ \textit{deductions}\end{array}\right)$

Adjusted Gross Income (AGI)

$\left(\begin{array}{l}\textbf{Minus:}\\ \textit{below the line}\\ \textit{deductions}\end{array}\right)$ Greater of $<$ *Itemized Deductions* or: *Standard Deduction*

Plus — *Personal Exemption Deduction(s)*

<u>*Taxable income*</u>

In class, this professor also explains the computation of *taxable income* in a **six-step** approach as follows:

Step 1: Determine what is included in the taxpayer's <u>*Gross Income*</u>
      (This reflects all income and exclusions therefrom.)

Step 2: Determine the taxpayer's <u>*Adjusted Gross Income (AGI)*</u>
      (This requires subtracting from *Gross income* any deductions that are allowed *above the line* pursuant to IRC § 62 – see Appendix A for more information.)

Step 3: Determine the total amount of the taxpayer's <u>*Itemized Deductions*</u>

(This requires applying any applicable limitations, floors, or restrictions for certain types of these deductions – see Appendix A for more information.)

Step 4: Determine the amount of the taxpayer's _Standard Deduction_
(This is year-specific and varies by filing status, age, degree of visual impairment, and limitations for certain dependents.)

Step 5: Determine the amount of the taxpayer's _Personal Exemption Deduction(s)_
(This is a year-specific amount per person, and the number of such deductions a taxpayer may claim can vary based on issues of dependency.)

Step 6: Compute _Taxable Income_ by subtracting from _AGI_ (amount in **Step 2**):
  1) Either _itemized deductions_ (amount in **Step 3**), or the _standard deduction_ (amount in **Step 4**), whichever is the **greater** of the two, **and**
  2) The _personal exemption deduction(s)_ (amount in **Step 5**)

Daniel's gross income for 2002 consists solely of the $8,000 in interest that he receives (facts from question 2, above). The general facts of this series of questions indicate that Daniel has no _above the line_ deductions for 2002. In addition, the general facts indicate that he has no qualifying "itemized deductions" for 2002. From question 2, above, we saw that Daniel's _standard deduction_ for 2002 was limited to only $750. Finally, based on the general facts, as analyzed in question 1, above, Daniel is not entitled to take his $3,000 personal exemption for 2002 (Mom qualifies to claim the deduction in computing her taxable income).

Applying this **six-step** computation approach to Daniel, we have the following:

   Step 1: _Gross income_ = $8,000
   Step 2: _Adjusted gross income (AGI)_ = $8,000
   Step 3: _Itemized deductions_ = $0
   Step 4: _Standard deduction_ = $750
   Step 5: _Personal exemption deduction_ = $0
   Step 6: _Taxable income_ = $8,000
                                ($ 750) [the greater of $0 or $750]
                                ($ 0)
                                $7,250

A visual depiction of Daniel's *taxable income* computation for 2002 is as follows:

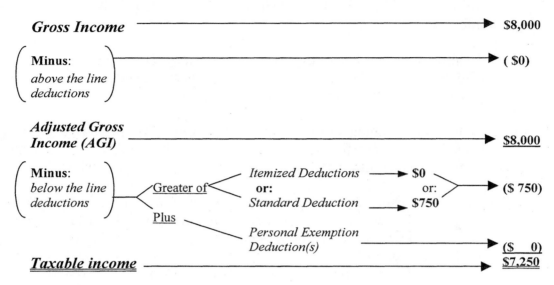

Answer (a) is incorrect because Daniel does, as indicated above, have taxable income. **Answer (b) is incorrect** because this answer reflects a regular $4,700 *standard deduction* and a $3,000 *personal exemption deduction,* both of which are not available to Daniel in this question. **Answer (c) is incorrect** because this answer reflects a regular $4,700 *standard deduction* that is not available to Daniel in this question. **Answer (e) is incorrect** because it does not reflect the $750 *standard deduction* to which Daniel is entitled.

- **Additional references:** *See* DANIEL Q. POSIN, FEDERAL INCOME TAXATION OF INDIVIDUALS ¶ 6.01 (5th ed. 2000).

6. **The correct answer is (b).** In this question, the facts indicate that Daniel provides all of his own support for 2002. Because of this change, Daniel is <u>no longer</u> Mom's *dependent*, as he had been in the other questions in this series. This fact has an impact on two deductions that are important in computing his *taxable income*: the *standard deduction* and the *personal exemption deduction*.

As for the *standard deduction*, because Daniel is not Mom's dependent he is not restricted to the special limitation calculation discussed in questions 2 through 4, above. Rather, he is entitled to the regular *standard deduction* for single individuals of <u>$4,700</u> (for 2002).

Similarly, Daniel's non-dependent status allows him to claim his own $3,000 *personal exemption deduction* for 2002. In the other questions in this series, only Mom was entitled to claim Daniel's *personal exemption deduction*.

Applying this **six-step** computation approach, Daniel's *taxable income* for 2002 is $300, computed as follows:

> **Step 1**: *Gross income* = $8,000
> **Step 2**: *Adjusted gross income (AGI)* = $8,000
> **Step 3**: *Itemized deductions* = $0
> **Step 4**: *Standard deduction* = $4,700
> **Step 5**: *Personal exemption deduction* = $3,000
> **Step 6**: *Taxable income* = $8,000
>   ($4,700) [the greater of $0 or $4,700]
>   ($3,000)
> $ 300

A visual depiction of the *taxable income* calculation is as follows:

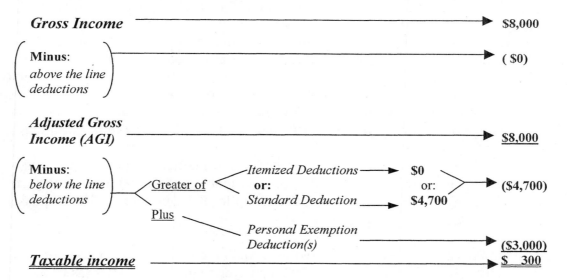

Answer (a) is incorrect based on the calculations above. **Answer (c) is incorrect** because this answer does not properly reflect the $3,000 *personal exemption deduction* to which Daniel is entitled. **Answer (d) is incorrect** because this answer does not properly reflect the $4,700 *standard deduction* to which Daniel is entitled. **Answer (e) is incorrect** because a correct answer (b) is presented.

- **Additional references:** *See* DANIEL Q. POSIN, FEDERAL INCOME TAXATION OF INDIVIDUALS ¶ 6.01 (5th ed. 2000).

7.   **The correct response is (c).** Many years ago, the concept of the "standard deduction" was introduced into tax law as a means of reducing an individual's record-keeping needs. The *standard deduction* may be taken in place of a group of deductions known collectively as "itemized deductions." Probably the most commonly known components of this latter group of *itemized deductions* include charitable contributions, deductible interest and taxes, and qualifying medical deductions. Taxpayers have a choice: deduct either 1) the total of itemized deductions (after applying all necessary limits and restrictions as discussed elsewhere in this book), **or** 2) the *standard deduction* amount. In calculating "taxable income," a taxpayer takes as a deduction the greater of these two. [Please see Appendix A for more information about *where* these deductions fit within the framework of calculating taxable income.]

IRC § 63(c) is the focal point for the *standard deduction*. The amount of this *standard deduction* can vary greatly from taxpayer to taxpayer depending on various factors including marital or filing status, age, degree of visual imparity, and whether the taxpayer is a "dependent" of another. In addition, *standard deduction* amounts are subject to change each tax year (and for the most part, do change each year) based on adjustments for "inflation" (i.e., the standard deduction amounts are *indexed* for inflation). The various *standard deduction* amounts listed in the statute (throughout IRC § 63) are not the actual amounts for the current year but, rather, are pre-inflation adjusted "base" amounts (that are well below the actual current amounts). [Appendix B contains the various *standard deduction* amounts for the year 2002 (the most current at the time of this printing).]

For 2002, the "regular" *standard deduction* for a married couple filing a joint return is $7,850 (corresponding to the statutory amount of $5,000 that is unadjusted for inflation). Note that this is **one** deduction for the joint return of both spouses, and not a deduction per spouse.

The *standard deduction* is **increased** for certain individuals based on age or visual imparity. [IRC § 63(b)(3).] For 2002, taxpayer's age 65 and older (as of the end of the taxable year) are entitled to an extra $900 per qualifying individual when married and filing a joint return. This $900 for 2002 corresponds to the unadjusted for inflation amount of $600 listed in IRC § 63(f)(1). [See Appendix B for the 2002 *standard deduction* "extra amounts" for other classifications of individuals.] Both Susan and Wally are the requisite age and their regular *standard deduction* of **$7,850** is **increased** by **$1,800** ($900 **each** for the two of them). Therefore, their *standard deduction* for 2002 is $9,650 ($7,850 + $900 + $900).

[Please see other questions in this book that address the issue of visual imparity vis-à-vis the *standard deduction* amount as well different or limited *standard deduction* amounts in other instances.]

Of interesting historical note, taxpayers age 65 or older (as well as taxpayers with severely impaired vision) were entitled to an "extra" *personal exemption* deduction (discussed elsewhere in this book) rather than an increase in the *standard deduction*. However, in the 1980's this was changed and such factors as age and eyesight no longer give rise to extra personal exemption deductions but, as discussed above, now impact the determination of one's *standard deduction*.

Answer (a) is incorrect because it fails to reflect the increase in the couple's *standard deduction* based on their respective ages. **Answer (b) is incorrect** because it fails to reflect that our couple is entitled to <u>two</u> of the extra $900 amounts (for 2002) because they are both ages 65 or older. **Answer (d) is incorrect** because it utilizes an incorrect number for the "extra" *standard deduction*. While not at issue in this problem, the "extra" *standard deduction* amount for a single individual (or head of household) in 2002 is $1,150. This answer incorrectly adds two of these amounts to the couple's regular *standard deduction*. **Answer (e) is incorrect** because a correct answer (c) is presented.

8.   **Answer (b) is correct.** This is a fairly straightforward question regarding the deduction for personal exemptions allowed by IRC § 151. Every living person has, in his or her figurative pocket, a "coupon" good for a personal exemption deduction for each tax year. There is no real "coupon" involved, but it helps to think of the personal exemption deduction as such. The amount of this exemption deduction is listed in IRC § 151 of the Code as $2,000. However, this amount has been adjusted (increased) each year since 1990, to reflect the general level of inflation. The personal exemption deduction amount at the time of this writing is $3,000 for the year 2002. [Please see Appendix B for other inflation adjusted tax items for the year 2002.] At the outset, Susan and Wally filing one return together (a joint return) are entitled to <u>two (2)</u> personal exemption deductions, one for Susan and one for Wally – they each get to use their own personal exemption "coupon." There is no indication that they have any dependents so the issue of whether they can claim someone else's personal exemption "coupon" and get the deduction is irrelevant. Therefore, their total deduction for personal exemptions in 2002 is <u>$6,000</u>.

While not at issue in this question, personal exemption deductions are subject to being "phased-out" (reduced or eliminated) in instances where a taxpayer's adjusted gross income (AGI) exceeds certain thresholds. These *threshold* amounts vary depending on "filing status" but are much higher than our couple's level of income (e.g., the starting point for 2002 for married individuals filing a joint return is AGI of $206,000). [See IRC § 151(d)(3) and other questions in this book that address this issue.]

Answer (a) is incorrect because Susan and Wally are <u>each</u> entitled to a personal exemption deduction of $3,000 (for 2002). **Answer (c) is incorrect** because this number represents the 2002 basic "standard deduction" for married individuals filing a joint return. The *standard deduction* is a deduction that is totally separate from the deductions at issue in this problem. Please see question 7, above, for a discussion of the couple's *standard deduction* for 2002. **Answer (d) is also incorrect.** Historically, taxpayers age 65 and older (as well as a taxpayers with severely impaired vision) were entitled to an "extra" *personal exemption* deduction. However, in the 1980's this was changed and such factors of age and eyesight no longer give rise to extra personal exemption deductions but, as discussed elsewhere in this book, now impact the determination of one's *standard deduction*. **Answer (d) is incorrect** because a correct answer (b) is presented.

9.   **Answer (c) is correct.** This question is designed to illustrate how the various components of income and deductions fit together to compute taxable income. This computation requires information about Susan and Wally's income and deductions. The computational framework for taxable income is as follows:

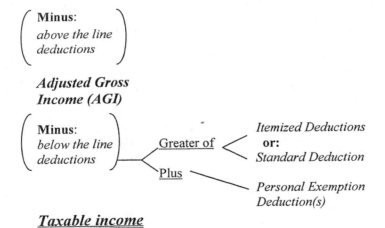

Gross Income

Minus:
above the line deductions

Adjusted Gross Income (AGI)

Minus:
below the line deductions   Greater of   *Itemized Deductions*
                                                   or:
                                                 Standard Deduction

                                 Plus   *Personal Exemption Deduction(s)*

<u>*Taxable income*</u>

In class, this professor also explains the computation of *taxable income* in a **six-step** approach as follows:

<u>Step 1</u>: Determine what is included in the taxpayer's <u>*Gross Income*</u>
            (This reflects all income and exclusions therefrom.)

Step 2: Determine the taxpayer's *Adjusted Gross Income (AGI)*
(This requires subtracting from *Gross income* any deductions that are allowed *above the line* pursuant to IRC § 62 – see Appendix A for more information.)

Step 3: Determine the total amount of the taxpayer's *Itemized Deductions*
(This requires applying any applicable limitations, floors, or restrictions for certain types of these deductions – see Appendix A for more information.)

Step 4: Determine the amount of the taxpayer's *Standard Deduction*
(This is year-specific and varies by filing status, age, degree of visual impairment, and limitations for certain dependents.)

Step 5: Determine the amount of the taxpayer's *Personal Exemption Deduction(s)*
(This is a year-specific amount per person, and the number of such deductions a taxpayer may claim can vary based on issues of dependency.)

Step 6: Compute *Taxable Income* by subtracting from *AGI* (amount in **Step 2**):
1) Either *itemized deductions* (amount in **Step 3**), or the *standard deduction* (amount in **Step 4**), whichever is the **greater** of the two, **and**
2) The *personal exemption deduction(s)* (amount in **Step 5**)

The couple's gross income for 2002 includes Susan's $10,000 in wages as well as their $20,000 in interest. [IRC §§ 61(a)(1) and (a)(4).] Pursuant to the facts, they have no other items of gross income.

As far as deductions are concerned, the general facts of this series of questions indicate that for 2002, our couple has no *above the line* deductions for purposes of computing adjusted gross income (AGI). The general facts do indicate that the couple has $8,000 of cash contributions to qualified charities in 2002. Pursuant to IRC § 173, this gives rise to a deduction. Charitable deductions are part of a group of *below the line* deductions known collectively as "itemized deductions." This group of deductions also includes such items as qualifying medical care expenses, and certain interest and taxes paid, among others. Some of these itemized deductions are subject to certain restrictions and limitations. The total amount of charitable contributions deductible in any one year is subject to certain limits or caps depending on the type of contribution and the charitable recipient. For most cash contributions, the deduction cannot exceed 50% of the taxpayer's AGI. Our couple's $8,000 of charitable contributions does not exceed 50% of their $30,000 AGI (see AGI calculation below).

There are two other deductions that need to be addressed before we have all of the components necessary to compute Susan and Wally's taxable income: their *standard deduction* and their *personal exemption deduction(s)*. As discussed in question 7, above, our couple is entitled to a $9,650 *standard deduction* for 2002. Recall that because they both are 65 years of age or older, their basic married *standard deduction* of $7,850 (for 2002) was increased by $1,800 (an extra $900 for each of them). Their personal exemption deductions total $6,000 for 2002 ($3,000 for each of them).

Applying this **six-step** computation approach, our couple's *taxable income* for 2002 is $14,350, computed as follows:

> **Step 1**: *Gross income* = $30,000
> **Step 2**: *Adjusted gross income (AGI)* = $30,000
> **Step 3**: *Itemized deductions* = $8,000
> **Step 4**: *Standard deduction* = $9,650
> **Step 5**: *Personal exemption deduction* = $6,000
> **Step 6**: *Taxable income* = $30,000
>   ($ 9,650) [the greater of $8,000 or $9,650]
>   ($ 6,000)
> $14,350

A visual depiction of the *taxable income* calculation is as follows:

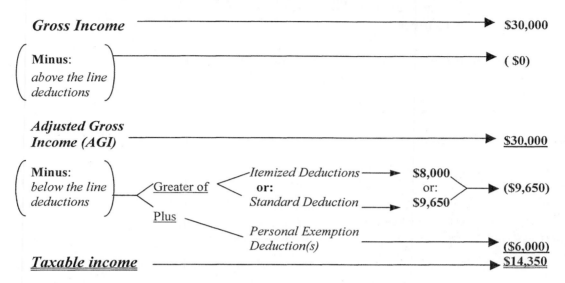

Answer (a) is incorrect because this answer reflects the incorrect deduction for both the couple's *itemized deductions* and their *standard deduction* (in addition to their *personal exemption deductions*). **Answer (b) is also incorrect.** This answer reflects a comparison of their $8,000 of *itemized deductions* to their regular *standard deduction* of $7,850 (not including the extra amounts because of their ages). The extra $900 deduction for each of them, because of their age, must be added to the regular *standard deduction* before this comparison is made. This answer mistakenly takes the $8,000 *itemized deductions* (greater than the regular *standard deduction*) and then adds the $1,800 extra ($900 for each spouse) to the $8,000 for a total of $9,800. This is a somewhat common calculation error. **Answer (d) is incorrect** because the answer reflects the selection of their $8,000 in *itemized deductions* as opposed to the greater *standard deduction* (in their case) of $9,650. **Answer (e) is incorrect** because a correct answer (c) is presented.

- **Additional references:** *See* DANIEL Q. POSIN, FEDERAL INCOME TAXATION OF INDIVIDUALS ¶ 6.01 (5th ed. 2000).

10. **The correct answer is (c).** *This question is year-specific (2002) and is intended to both highlight specific income tax issues and illustrate how the pieces fit together in computing taxable income. The question itself is not complex, as far as "taxable income" questions go, but it does involve multiple steps necessitating a lengthy analysis. [Appendix B, contains relevant, year-specific information applicable to 2002.] This question is easily adaptable to years different than 2002.*

Tammy's taxable income is **$6,150**. This computation requires information about Tammy's income and deductions. A visual computational framework for taxable income is as follows:

Gross Income

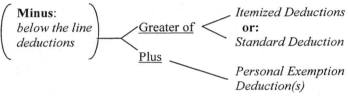

Adjusted Gross Income (AGI)

Taxable income

In class, this professor also explains the computation of *taxable income* in a **six-step** approach as follows:

Step 1: Determine what is included in the taxpayer's *Gross Income*
(This reflects all income and exclusions therefrom.)

Step 2: Determine the taxpayer's *Adjusted Gross Income (AGI)*
(This requires subtracting from *Gross income* any deductions that are allowed *above the line* pursuant to IRC § 62 – see Appendix A for more information.)

Step 3: Determine the total amount of the taxpayer's *Itemized Deductions*
(This requires applying any applicable limitations, floors, or restrictions for certain types of these deductions – see Appendix A for more information.)

Step 4: Determine the amount of the taxpayer's *Standard Deduction*
(This is year-specific and varies by filing status, age, degree of visual impairment, and limitations for certain dependents.)

Step 5: Determine the amount of the taxpayer's *Personal Exemption Deduction(s)*
(This is a year-specific amount per person, and the number of such deductions a taxpayer may claim can vary based on issues of dependency.)

Step 6: Compute *Taxable Income* by subtracting from *AGI* (amount in **Step 2**):
1) Either *itemized deductions* (amount in **Step 3**), or the *standard deduction* (amount in **Step 4**), whichever is the **greater** of the two, **and**
2) The *personal exemption deduction(s)* (amount in **Step 5**)

For Tammy, Steps 1, 2 and 3 are rather simple. Tammy's gross income consists of her $6,400 in interest and $600 in wages for a total gross income (Step 1) of $7,000. The facts indicate that Tammy has no *above the line deductions* so her adjusted gross income (Step 2) remains the same at $7,000. The facts also indicate that she has no "itemized deductions" so the amount for Step 3 is $0. Steps 4 and 5 require some discussion and will be separately addressed below, after which, everything will be put together to compute Tammy's "taxable income" (Step 6).

Step 4, Tammy's *Standard Deduction*

Many years ago, the concept of the "standard deduction" was introduced into tax law as a means of reducing an individual's record-keeping needs. The *standard deduction* may be taken in place of a group of deductions known collectively as "itemized deductions." Probably the most commonly known components of this latter group of *itemized deductions* include charitable contributions, deductible interest and taxes and qualifying medical deductions. Taxpayers have a choice: deduct either 1) the total of itemized deductions (after applying all necessary limits and restrictions as discussed elsewhere in this book), **or** 2) the *standard deduction* amount. In calculating "taxable income," a taxpayer takes as a deduction the greater of these two. [Please see Appendix A for more information about *where* these deductions fit within the framework of calculating taxable income.]

IRC § 63(c) is the focal point for the *standard deduction*. The amount of this *standard deduction* can vary greatly from taxpayer to taxpayer depending on various factors including marital or filing status, age, degree of visual imparity, and whether the taxpayer is a "dependent" of another. In addition, *standard deduction* amounts are subject to change each tax year (and for the most part, do change each year) based on adjustments for "inflation" (i.e., the standard deduction amounts are *indexed* for inflation). The various *standard deduction* amounts listed in the statute (throughout IRC § 63) are not the actual amounts for the current year but, rather, are pre-inflation adjusted "base" amounts (that are well below the actual current amounts). [Appendix B contains the various *standard deduction* amounts for the year 2002 (the most current at the time of this printing).]

For 2002, the "regular" *standard deduction* for a single individual is $4,700 (corresponding to the statutory amount of $3,000 that is unadjusted for inflation). Tammy may not, however, be entitled to this amount because of a special limitation provision in IRC § 63(c)(5). As we will see later in this problem, in the discussion of Step 5 (Tammy's *personal exemption deduction*) Tammy can properly be claimed as her Father's dependent, and her Father is also entitled to claim Tammy's personal exemption deduction in computing his taxable income. This provision in IRC § 63(c)(5) may limit the standard deduction for an individual in Tammy's situation – an individual who can be claimed as a dependent (and whose personal exemption deduction can be used) by someone else. For **2002,** the limit imposed by this provision for Tammy's *standard deduction* is:

> **The greater of**:
> 1) $750, or
> 2) Tammy's "earned" income + $250.

> Please note that the $750 amount above is for 2002, and corresponds to the statutory amount of $500 (that is unadjusted for inflation).

"Earned income" for this special limitation, basically means wages, salaries and other compensation like income. It does not include more passive income such as interest and dividends. In *this* question, Tammy has *earned income* of only $600. Applying the above special provision, Tammy's *standard deduction* is the greater of $750, or $850 ($600 + $250). Tammy's *standard deduction*, in *this* question is, therefore $600.

Note that the above special limitation calculation <u>cannot</u> yield a *standard deduction* that is greater than that which would otherwise apply to the individual (without such applying this special provision). [IRC § 63(c)(5).] This is not the case for Tammy in this question.

Step 5, Tammy's *Personal Exemption Deduction*
Every living person has, in his or her figurative pocket, a "coupon" good for a personal exemption deduction for each tax year. There is no real "coupon" involved, but it helps to think of the personal exemption deduction as such. The amount of this exemption deduction is listed in IRC § 151 of the Code as $2,000. However, this amount has been adjusted (increased) each year since 1990 to reflect the general level of inflation. The personal exemption deduction amount at the time of this writing is $3,000 for the year 2002. [Please see Appendix B for other inflation adjusted tax items for the year 2002.] The key to this problem is determining who gets to use these personal exemption deduction "coupons" for the particular year. Does each person get to use his or her own "coupon" and get a personal exemption deduction (e.g. a $3,000 deduction for 2002), or is somebody else entitled to take another person's "coupon" get the deduction?

Those students having come into a law school income tax course knowing little about income tax probably know something about this issue. A parent claiming his or her children as dependents and getting an extra deduction for them is precisely the issue we are faced with in this question. Tammy's Father, in our problem, is entitled to a personal exemption deduction for himself. The critical issue here is whether Tammy's Father gets to take Tammy's "coupon" and thus get her personal exemption deduction (on his income tax return for purposes of computing his taxable income). Alternatively, and what is necessary for us to compute Tammy's taxable income, does Tammy get to use her own "coupon" for a personal exemption deduction (for purposes of computing her taxable income). To determine if Tammy's Father is entitled to get Tammy's personal exemption "coupon" (claim her as dependent and get to deduct her personal exemption deduction) involves a two-step (with many sub-steps) analysis, which in simplified form, is as follows:

> **Step One**: Is this person (e.g. a kid) your "**Dependent**" pursuant to IRC § 152? (All requirements must be met).
>   ➤ Person must be a U.S. citizen, resident or national, or a resident of Canada, Mexico for any part of the tax year.
>   ➤ Person must be either related to you, or be a member of your household for the entire year. [See IRC §§ 152(a)(1)-(a)(8) for definitions of "relatives," and IRC § 152(a)(9) for other qualifying individuals.]
>   ➤ You must have provided more than one-half this person's total support for the year.

> **Step Two**: If this person is your **Dependent** (from Step One, above), are you allowed to take a **deduction** (personal exemption deduction) for this dependent? [IRC § 151(c).]
>   ➤ Your Dependent must not file a joint return with a spouse for the year.
>   ➤ Your Dependent must either:
>   ▪ Have "gross income" less than the "exemption amount" for that year, or
>   ▪ Be your child (or step-child) who is under the age of 19 at the end of the year, **or**
>   ▪ Be your child (or step child) who is under the age of 24 at the end of the year and is a full-time student for some part of each of five months during the year.

If **both** of these two steps are satisfied with respect to someone for whom you are trying to get their exemption deduction "coupon," then that person is your dependent, and you are entitled to deduct their personal exemption deduction amount (e.g., $3,000 for 2002). If this is the case than the person being claimed as a dependent (e.g., Tammy) is not entitled to take the deduction. [IRC § 151(d)(2).]

Tammy's Father satisfies step one, above, with respect to Tammy. Tammy is a U.S. citizen and as a child, she is considered "related" to her Father. [IRC § 152(a)(1).] The facts indicate that the support requirement is also met: "Father unequivocally providing the majority of her support." Note that there is no requirement that any "related" person (listed in IRC §§ 152(a)(1)-(a)(8)) lives with anyone in particular to attain dependent status.

On to step two of the dependent exemption deduction analysis, Tammy is unmarried, but does she have "gross income" less than the "exemption amount" for the year in question? And what does this mean? The measuring gross income level of "the exemption amount" is the amount of the personal exemption deduction (e.g., $3,000 for 2002). Tammy's gross income of $7,000 is clearly not less than the $3,000 exemption for 2002. We do not, however, stop at this point as the operative word in this part of step two is "either." Going onto to the next "either" requirement, Tammy is her Father's child but she is not less than age 19 (as of the end of the year). Tammy does, however, qualify under the last option – she is less than 24 years of age (as of the end of the year) and is a full-time college student. Therefore, with respect to Tammy, her Father is entitled to claim her personal exemption deduction "coupon."

As indicated above, IRC § 151(d)(2) indicates that if Tammy's personal exemption deduction is *allowable* to another individual (Father in our case), Tammy is not entitled to take the personal exemption deduction herself for purposes of computing her taxable income. There is only *one* personal exemption deduction per person, and Father, in our case, is entitled to take it. But can't he choose not to take the deduction and let Tammy take it for himself? The answer is no, because of the statutory use of the word *allowable*. If Father *can* take Tammy's personal exemption deduction, then only he can take it and Tammy cannot.

This means that for Step 5 in our taxable income calculation for Tammy, her *personal exemption* deduction is $0. This is also the reason why, in determining Tammy's *standard deduction* in Step 4, above, that Tammy was not entitled to the normal *standard deduction* for a single individual.

Putting it All Together – Tammy's *Taxable Income*

Applying this **six-step** computation approach to Tammy, we have the following:

Step 1: *Gross income* = $7,000
Step 2: *Adjusted gross income (AGI)* = $7,000
Step 3: *Itemized deductions* = $0
Step 4: *Standard deduction* = $850
Step 5: *Personal exemption deduction* = $0
Step 6: *Taxable income* = $7,000
                                ($ 850) [the greater of $0 or $750]
                                ($ 0)
                                $6,150

A visual depiction of Tammy's *taxable income* computation for 2002 is as follows:

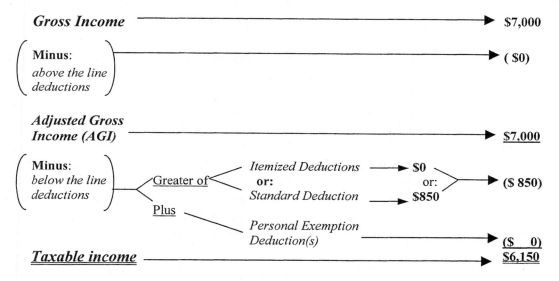

Answer (a) is incorrect. This answer incorrectly reflects a full $4,700 *standard deduction* as well as a *personal exemption deduction* of $3,000. **Answer (b) is incorrect.** This answer incorrectly reflects a full $4,700 *standard deduction* in computing Tiffany's *taxable income*. **Answer (d) is also incorrect.** This answer incorrectly reflects a *standard deduction* of $750 instead of the correct amount of $850. **Answer (e) is incorrect** because a correct response (c) is presented.

- **Additional references:** *See* DANIEL Q. POSIN, FEDERAL INCOME TAXATION OF INDIVIDUALS ¶ 6.01 (5th ed. 2000).

11.   **Answer (e) is correct.** This first question in this complex "taxable income" series of questions is fairly straightforward and not too difficult. Early in your class discussion of "gross income" for income tax purposes, you learned that its scope is very broad. Not only does IRC § 61 proclaim that gross income includes "all

income from whatever source derived," its definition encompasses net economic benefits or net accessions to wealth experienced by an individual. Generally, to exclude from gross income any such benefit received, a specific statutory provision must apply.

Tad clearly has to include in his gross income for 2002, the $26,000 in wages that he received. There is no statutory provision excluding such wages from gross income. The other cognizable economic benefit Tad receives is the $20,000 scholarship. Ostensibly, this would also be included in his gross income. However, IRC § 117 provides that "qualified scholarships" (or fellowships) are excluded from gross income.

Generally, a *qualified scholarship* is one that is used to pay for a student's tuition and fees required for enrollment, fees, books, supplies, and equipment required for courses. [IRC §§ 117(a) and 117(b).] While not at issue in this question, any scholarship monies for room and board are not excludable *qualified scholarships*. In addition this general scholarship exclusion rule applies only to students who are candidates for a degree, and who are students attending a qualified educational organization, the latter defined as a school that normally maintains a regular faculty, curriculum and regularly enrolled student body in attendance. [IRC §§ 117(b)(2)(A) and 170(b)(1)(A)(ii).] While not pertinent to our facts, the growing trend of "distance learning" raises interesting questions as to what constitutes a "school" for scholarship exclusion purposes. Tad's $20,000 scholarship is solely for his tuition and his enrollment at an accredited law school satisfies the other requirements for exclusion. IRC § 117 makes no distinction between graduate and undergraduate levels of education for exclusion purposes.

Tad's *gross income* for 2002 is $26,000, representing his wages for the year. The $20,000 law school scholarship is fully excludable from gross income pursuant to IRC § 117.

Answer (a) is incorrect because there is no such restriction for exclusion of qualified scholarships under IRC § 117. While not pertinent to our facts, the exclusion of certain tuition reduction programs for employees of educational institutions is usually not applicable to graduate study. **Answer (b) is also incorrect.** Tad is entitled to a full exclusion of his scholarship pursuant to IRC § 117. Another Code provision, IRC § 127, provides for a different, and more limited, exclusion for "employer-provided" educational assistance. Tad's scholarship is not an employer-provided educational benefit. Even if Tad's employer was providing educational assistance for his law school study, this answer is incorrect because the 2001 Tax Act extended the application of the IRC § 127 exclusion for employer-provided educational assistance to graduate level study starting in 2002. **Answer (c) is also incorrect.** This answer correctly outlines the exclusion provided in IRC § 127 for employer-provided educational assistance. However, Tad's scholarship is not an employer-provided educational benefit. Rather, Tad's scholarship is a fully excludable qualified scholarship pursuant IRC § 117. **Answer (d) is incorrect** because the scholarship exclusion provisions of IRC § 117 are not so limited in its application.

- **Additional references:** *See* DANIEL Q. POSIN, FEDERAL INCOME TAXATION OF INDIVIDUALS ¶¶ 2.01, 3.09(2) (5th ed. 2000).

12. **The correct answer is (b).** This is a difficult question and is particularly year-sensitive. As we will discuss below, this question is also a bit unfair to ask at this point in this series of questions because its answer is contingent on the answer to question 21, below.

The "Economic Growth and Tax Relief Reconciliation Act of 2001" (the 2001 Tax Act) was signed into law in June 2001, and made numerous and major changes to tax laws including many in the "income tax" area. The 2001 Tax Act added IRC § 222, a deduction for "qualified tuition and related expenses." This new IRC § 222 is the focus of this question. Pursuant to the 2001 Tax Act, and as of the time of this writing, this new section is effective for only four years; 2002 through 2005. Starting in 2002 a deduction is allowed, with certain restrictions and limitations, for "qualified tuition and related expenses." This deduction, if allowed, is taken *above the line* in determining a taxpayer's adjusted gross income (AGI). [IRC § 62(a)(18).] This will play a critical role in the proper determination of Tad's other deductions and taxable income (presented in other questions in this series).

The term "qualified tuition and related expenses" generally means costs for tuition, fees, books, room/board or related expenses while attending a college, university or vocational school. This includes graduate, post graduate studies, professional degree programs, etc. The $4,000 that Tad pays for his law school tuition appears to be such a qualifying expense. For years 2002 and 2003, the maximum deduction for amounts paid for qualifying education expenses is **$3,000** (the amount increases to $4,000 in years 2004 and 2005). At this point in our analysis, Tad's possible deduction under new IRC § 222 for 2002 would be limited to $3,000. The maximum deduction for 2004 and 2005 is different.

There is another limitation regarding this deduction that is rather complex in its application. As with some other income tax deductions (and exclusions from income), this deduction is allowed only if the taxpayer "doesn't make too much" during the year. More specific, for 2002 and 2003, if a single individual's adjusted gross income (AGI) is more than $65,000, the deduction is disallowed. [IRC § 222(b)(2)(A).] This limit is double or $130,000 (for 2002 and 2003) for married individuals filing a joint return. The AGI levels applicable to 2004 and 2005 are stepped at two levels (as is the maximum amount of deduction). The problem with this determination (one that we will eventually make when computing Tad's actual *AGI* and *taxable income*) is that how does one figure out one's AGI for purposes of this deduction when this deduction itself is allowed in computing AGI. The basic answer is that AGI is first determined without regard to this section (as if the deduction did not exist) and then the AGI limitations are examined. [IRC § 222(b)(2)(C).] In Tad's case, this will be examined in later questions in this series when *AGI* and *taxable income* are computed.

So far, we still have a $3,000 potential IRC § 222 deduction in 2002 for Tad's tuition costs. There are, however, a few more issues to address before we conclude that answer (b) is correct. IRC § 222(c)(3) provides that an individual is not entitled to this deduction if he or she is a "dependent" of another (and this other person can claim his or her personal exemption deduction). Later, in question 21, we will make the determination that while Tad is Marlo's dependent, Marlo is <u>not</u> entitled to claim Tad's *personal exemption deduction*. Rather confusing at this point, but suffice it to say that IRC § 222(c)(3) will not preclude Tad from a deduction under this section.

Another issue that we must address is the "timing" of Tad's $4,000 tuition payment. The facts indicate that his tuition obligation (after his scholarship) is $2,000 for each of the Fall and Spring semesters of his first year at law school (Fall 2002 and Spring 2003). As indicated, he paid the entire amount for both semesters ($4,000) when he began law school in the Fall of 2002. Technically, Tad is "prepaying" his 2003 Spring semester tuition in 2002. IRC § 222 generally requires the year of payment to match-up with the year of enrollment. [IRC § 222(c)(3)(A).] However, the statute allows the prepayment of tuition and related expenses for an "academic term" beginning during the first three months of the next year. Tad's Spring semester in 2003, will begin during the first three months (most likely within three weeks or less) of 2003. Therefore, this will not preclude Tad's IRC § 222 deduction for both semester's tuition payment in Fall 2002 (limited, of course, to the aforementioned $3,000 maximum).

The exact amount of Tad's deduction pursuant to IRC § 222, if any, will be determined in later questions that involve computation of his *AGI* and *taxable income*. But at this point, we can say that Tad would be entitled to a $3,000 deduction assuming that his *AGI* does not exceed a certain level. **This is our answer (b).**

Lastly, it should be mentioned that Tad's tuition costs might qualify for some type of educational tax credit (to be discussed in question 14, below). The statute precludes a "double benefit," and should Tad be entitled to and choose to take his education related expenditures as a tax credit, no deduction is allowed under IRC § 222. [IRC § 222(c)(2)(A).] Other restrictions may apply in situations different from those presented in our question set.

Answer (a) is incorrect because the new IRC § 222 deduction contains no "business" requirement. Granted, Tad's tuition costs would not give rise to a business deduction (pursuant to IRC § 162) because this education would qualify him for a new trade or business. **Answer (c) is incorrect** because, as addressed above, the statute allows for limited prepayments of qualified tuition and related expenses. **Answer (d) is incorrect** because for IRC § 162 business expense purposes, it is irrelevant whether Tad plans to use his law degree to enter a new trade or business. Under the regulations for that section, a deduction would be denied because it will *qualify* him to enter a new trade or business. **Answer (e) is incorrect** because it fails to reflect the $3,000 maximum deduction limitation for 2002.

13.   **Answer (a) is correct.** For analysis purposes, this question is a continuation of question 12, above. The simple answer here is that room and board (lodging and food) costs do not give rise to any income tax deduction for Tad. The new IRC § 222 deduction for certain qualified higher education expenses discussed in question 12, is not applicable to room and board as they are not considered "qualified tuition and related expenses." [IRC 222(d)(1) (referring to the definition in IRC § 25A(f).]

Lodging and meals (at 50%) are deductible if they qualify under IRC § 162 as business expenses while "traveling away from home." None of Tad's costs for his legal education qualify as deductible business expenses (pursuant to IRC § 162), because this education will qualify him for a new trade or business. [Reg. § 1.162-5(b)(3).]

Answer (b) is incorrect because this answer presupposes that Tad's education costs would qualify as deductible business expenses under IRC § 162. As discussed above, they do not. **Answers (c) and (d) are incorrect** because Tad is not *receiving* the $6,000, or a benefit of that value. While not the facts in our problem, had Tad *received a scholarship* to cover his room and board, that amount would be included in his gross income because scholarships for such items are generally not excludable from income. IRC § 117(b)(2) defining qualified scholarships for exclusion purposes.

14.   **The best answer is (d).** An income tax credit is a very valuable tax benefit as it represents a dollar-for-dollar reduction of a taxpayer's computed tax liability. There are two major tax credits with respect to "higher" education: the "Hope Scholarship Credit" and the "Lifetime Learning Credit." IRC § 25A is the primary Code section dealing with both of these credits. We will conclude, below,

that the $4,000 Tad paid in law school tuition (in 2002) will be qualified expenses for purposes of determining the *Lifetime Learning Credit*.

As indicated, IRC § 25A contains provisions for both the *Hope Scholarship* and the *Lifetime Learning* credits. The former (*Hope Scholarship Credit*) is not applicable in our case, as that credit is generally available for certain qualifying higher education costs associated with only the first two years of undergraduate (post-secondary) education. [IRC § 25A(b)(2).] Our focus is on the *Lifetime Learning Credit* and the statutory provisions in IRC § 25A(c).

Basically, the *Lifetime Learning Credit* equals 20% of up to $5,000 of "qualified tuition and related expenses." Tuition, fees and books (but not room or board) to attend most post-secondary institutions (colleges, universities, vocational schools, etc.) are considered "qualified tuition and related expenses." This credit, unlike the *Hope Scholarship Credit*, is available for undergraduate and graduate studies. Mathematically, the maximum credit available for 2002 is $1,000 (20% of $5,000). It should be noted that starting in 2003, the maximum qualified expenses increases from $5,000 to $10,000.

For Tad, the $4,000 paid for law school tuition represents his "qualified tuition and related expenses" for the purposes of the *Lifetime Learning Credit*. While $2,000 of this amount represents tuition for the <u>spring 2003</u> semester, such pre-payments are allowed (for credit purposes) as long as the semester, for which the tuition is paid, begins within three months of the following year. This does not present a problem in the present case. While the answer to this problem does not require the computation of Tad's *Lifetime Learning Credit*, his "potential" credit would be $800 (20% of $4,000). This is his "potential" credit because this credit, like many other credits, deductions and exclusions, is "phased-out" for taxpayer's with income levels above a certain amount. For illustration purposes, for 2002 the phase-out of this credit begins and ends at $41,000 and $51,000 of adjusted gross income (AGI as modified), respectively (for married individuals filing a joint return, the 2002 "phase-out" range is $82,000 through $102,000). We do not know, at this point, whether Tad's potential *Lifetime Learning Credit* will be reduced because we have yet to compute his AGI.

Lastly, it should be mentioned that Tad's tuition costs might qualify for a deduction pursuant to new IRC § 222, discussed in problem 12, above. The statute precludes a "double benefit," and should Tad be entitled to and choose to take the *Lifetime Learning Credit*, he cannot take the deduction for the same expenses pursuant to IRC § 222. Other restrictions may apply in situations different from those presented in our question set.

[For more information about the *Hope Scholarship Credit* and the *Lifetime Learning Credit*, see I.R.S. Pub. 970, "Tax Benefits for Higher Education" (for 2001 returns).]

Answers (a) and (b) are incorrect because Tad's expenses associated with Tad's graduate studies do not qualify for the *Hope Scholarship Credit*. That credit is generally available only for the first two years of post-secondary education. In addition, costs for room/board are not qualifying expenses for the *Hope Scholarship Credit* (as indicated in answer (a)). **Answer (c) is incorrect** because, as discussed above, the entire $4,000 tuition that Tad paid in 2002 qualifies notwithstanding that $2,000 of this amount represents tuition for the spring 2003 semester. **Answer (e) is incorrect** because a correct response (d) is presented.

- **Additional references:** *See* DANIEL Q. POSIN, FEDERAL INCOME TAXATION OF INDIVIDUALS ¶ 10.07 (5th ed. 2000).

15. **The best answer is (c).** This is also a difficult question. While in this question we need not determine Tad's actual deduction for his student loan interest, we will be doing so in other questions in this series, where it will be necessary to compute *adjusted gross income (AGI)* and *taxable income*. As discussed below, Tad might be entitled to deduct, some or all, of the $1,000 interest paid pursuant to IRC § 221.

The analysis starts with IRC § 163. This is the primary section at issue for deductions related to interest paid. For casual readers of the Code, IRC § 163(a) provides a simple and broad sounding deduction for interest stating, in part: "There shall be allowed as a deduction all interest paid . . . within the taxable year on indebtedness." Under this general definition, the interest that Tad pays on his law school loans would give rise to a deduction. However, the Tax Reform Act of 1986 added subsection (h) to § 163, located quite some written distance from the general allowance for interest deductions of subsection (a). IRC § 163(h) starts out deceptively, and unfavorably, simple by stating, in part: "In the case of a taxpayer other than a corporation, no deduction shall be allowed . . . for personal interest paid . . . during the taxable year."

The definition of *personal interest*, which is not deductible, if found in IRC § 163(h)(2) and takes the form of a negative definition – *personal interest* is interest "other than" those listed in subparagraphs (A) through (F). The key, therefore, to finding interest that is deductible, is to fit within one of these specified categories of what does not constitute nondeductible personal interest. Among the categories of interest that are not personal interest is what might be the familiar category of "qualified residence interest" (typical interest paid on a home mortgage). [IRC § 163(h)(2)(D).] Somewhat less familiar, but logically not included as personal interest, is "interest properly allocable to a trade or business." [IRC § 163(h)(2)(A).] As seen in other questions in this book, "business" interest, rather oddly, does not include business interest incurred by an employee. Also listed among the categories of interest that is not considered personal interest is, "any interest allowable as a deduction under IRC § 221 (relating to interest on educational loans)." [IRC § 163(h)(2)(F).] We will, below, conclude that the interest Tad pays on his student loans in 2003, *may* qualify as deductible education loan interest pursuant to IRC § 221.

IRC § 221, a relatively new section effective in 1998, allows for a limited deduction for certain interest paid on certain educational loans. This deduction, if allowed, is a valuable "above the line" deduction – a deduction from gross income in computing adjusted gross income (AGI). To qualify as an educational loan for this section, the loan proceeds generally must be used for tuition, fees, books, room/board or related expenses while attending a college, university or vocational school. This includes undergraduate, graduate, post graduate studies, professional degree programs, etc. So far, Tad's loan qualifies. Qualified educational loans do not include money borrowed from certain "related parties." [IRC § 221(d)(1).] Tad's loans were from federally sponsored loan sources (not from "related" individuals), and his loans are considered qualified educational loans used for qualified higher education expenses.

The interest Tad pays on this qualified higher education loan is subject to two important limitations. First, the amount of interest deductible under IRC § 221 is limited, by statute, to $2,500 per year (in the aggregate for all such loans). Tad's $1,000 of interest does not exceed this limit. If allowed, as discussed below, this deduction is taken "above the line" in computing Tad's *adjusted gross income (AGI)* (i.e., it is an amount that is subtracted from *gross income* to compute AGI). [Please see Appendix A for more information about how income and deductions fit together to compute AGI and taxable income.]

The second important limitation kicks in if the taxpayer's *adjusted gross income (AGI)*, as modified by IRC § 221(b)(2)(C), exceeds certain levels. If it does, the otherwise allowed IRC § 221 interest deduction is reduced or "phased-out" utilizing a formula contained in the statute. Pursuant to IRC § 221(b)(2)(B), the level of "modified adjusted gross income" at which this deduction starts to "phase-out" (be reduced) is $50,000 for single individuals or $100,00 for married individuals filing a joint return. The deduction for student loan interest is totally eliminated for single individuals with "modified adjusted gross income" of $65,000 or more, and at $130,000 or more for married individuals filing a joint return. The statute uses the term "modified adjusted gross income" because true adjusted gross income will reflect any deduction allowed by this IRC § 221 (see above). Modified adjusted gross income is basically *adjusted gross income* computed before you compute any possible deduction under this IRC § 221 (and other sections). [IRC § 221(b)(2)(C).]

The exact amount of Tad's deduction pursuant to IRC § 221, if any, will be determined in later questions that involve computation of his *AGI* and *taxable income*. But at this point, we can say that Tad will be entitled to deduct some or all of his $1,000 interest paid depending on the amount of his *AGI* (as modified). **This, essentially, is our answer (c).**

Answer (a) is incorrect because *personal interest* is not deductible at all pursuant to IRC § 163(h). **Answer (b) is incorrect** because the interest Tad pays on his student loans might (and will as is discussed in later questions) be deductible student loan interest pursuant to IRC § 221. **Answer (d) is also incorrect.** Before 2002, the deductibility of student loan interest under IRC § 221 was generally limited to interest paid only during the first 60 months of loan payments. This provision was repealed, effective for 2002, by the 2001 Tax Act. **Answer (e) is incorrect** because, as discussed above, deductions allowed for student loan interest pursuant to IRC § 221 are deductible *above the line* in computing *adjusted gross income (AGI)*.

16.   **Answer (d) is correct.** For most individuals, IRC § 164 is the delimiting section for deducting taxes paid. State income taxes are among those listed as deductible (IRC § 164(a)(3)), so Tad's $1,000 of state income taxes are deductible. The statute also allows deductions for state and local personal property taxes. [IRC § 164(a)(2).] Tad's $800 of state intangibles tax fits into this category. An intangibles tax, in its most common form (which, is not that common, as very few states, or subdivisions thereof, assess such a tax), is an annual tax based on the value (ad-valorem) of securities (stocks, bonds, etc.) owned by the taxpayer. Securities are considered "intangible" personal property, and the annual ad-valorem tax thereon, as well as ad-valorem taxes on other personal property. are very similar to state and local real property taxes (also deductible under IRC § 164). The difference between "personal" property taxes and "real" property taxes is the character of the underlying property subject to tax: personal (including intangible) property and real property, respectively.

Prior to the enactment of the *1986 Tax Reform Act*, taxpayers were also entitled to deduct state and local sales taxes under IRC § 164. Now, however, state and local sales taxes are not listed as a deductible tax in IRC § 164 and, therefore, are generally not deductible.

While not necessary to answer our question, it should be noted that deductible taxes, pursuant to IRC § 164, are part of the large group of "itemized deductions" that might come into play in computing taxable income. See problem 24, below, for the composition of Tad's itemized deductions in this series of questions, and their relevance in computing Tad's taxable income. It should also be noted that generally, deductions for taxes paid pursuant to IRC § 164 are not subject to any nondeductible "floor" such as those for qualifying medical care expenses and "miscellaneous itemized" deductions.

Answers (a), (b), (c), and (e) are incorrect because they do not reflect the correct combination of deductible taxes.

- **Additional references:** *See* DANIEL Q. POSIN, FEDERAL INCOME TAXATION OF INDIVIDUALS ¶ 7.01(4) (5th ed. 2000).

17. **The correct answer is (b).** IRC § 213 allows for a deduction of certain qualified medical care expenses. Once one makes the determination of what constitutes "qualified" medical care expenses, the subject of this question, the deduction is allowed as an "itemized deduction" only to the extent that the total qualifying expenses exceeds 7.5% of Adjusted Gross Income (AGI). Qualified medical care expenses include typical costs for doctors, dentists, hospital, health insurance, and the like. [See IRC § 213(d).]

Addressing first the easier issue of Tad's over-the-counter allergy medicines that were recommended by his doctor. While logically it would appear that such costs would qualify, the Code specifically allows deductions only for prescription drugs (and insulin in those areas where its sale is allowed without a prescription). [IRC § 213(b).] Therefore, none of the $400 that Tad paid for the allergy medicine will qualify as medical care expenses even though his physician recommended the medicine.

The $1,600 in veterinary fees that Tad paid with respect to his Seeing Eye dog presents other issues. IRC § 213 allows a deduction for medical care expenditures made for the taxpayer, his or her spouse, or *dependents*. Non-humans, however, do not qualify as dependents and Tad's vet bills for his Seeing Eye dog are not deductible by *this* means. However, the vet bills are deductible by Tad for other reasons. While not really necessary for the answer to this question, it is helpful to address the tax ramifications (deductibility) of the cost, if any, that Tad had to pay to acquire the Seeing Eye dog. For the sake of discussion, let us say that Tad had to purchase the Seeing Eye dog. This purchase would not really constitute an "expense," but, rather, would be considered a "capital expenditure." *Capital expenditures* and *expenses* are usually mutually exclusive items, with IRC § 213 medical deductions limited to qualified medical care *expense*. However, if the capital expenditure primarily health-related, which would be the case in our assumed hypothetical of Tad purchasing the Seeing Eye dog, it is not precluded from qualifying as a medical care expense. The regulations, at Reg. § 1.213-

1(e)(iii), indicate that costs for such medically related *capital expenditures* as Seeing Eye dogs, artificial teeth and limbs, wheelchairs, and the like represent *qualifying medical care expenses*. [Reg. § 1.213-1(e)(iii).] The regulations go on to provide that 100% of the operating and maintenance costs associated with such capital expenditures are deductible regardless of the amount, if any, of the original expenditure for the medically related expenditure that qualified as a medical related expense. Therefore, notwithstanding how much, if anything, Tad paid for the Seeing Eye dog, the entire $1,600 in veterinary fees (considered maintenance expenses for the dog) qualifies as a medically related expense.

As indicated above, the aggregate of Tad's qualifying medical expenses, $1,600 in this case, is deductible, as an itemized ("below the line") deduction to the extent that they exceed 7.5% of his adjusted gross income (AGI). See question 24 below, for this computation in conjunction with computing his taxable income for the year.

Answer (a) is incorrect. While this answer correctly states the non-deductibility of his over-the-counter allergy medicines, it is not correct regarding the vet fees. As indicated above, the deduction of the maintenance costs for the Seeing Eye dog is not predicated upon either Tad paying for the dog or whether or not, if he did pay for it, the cost was deductible. **Answer (c) is also incorrect.** Again, this answer correctly states the non-deductibility of his over-the-counter allergy medicines. However, it is incorrect regarding the vet fees. True, Tad is not entitled to deduct them because the dog is his dependent but, rather, as explained above they represent qualifying medical care expenses for *Tad*. **Answer (d) is incorrect** on both counts: the non-deductibility of the vet fees and the deductibility of the over-the-counter allergy medicines. **Answer (e) is incorrect** because it incorrectly includes, as qualifying medical care expenses, the costs for his over-the-counter allergy medicines.

- **Additional references:** *See* DANIEL Q. POSIN, FEDERAL INCOME TAXATION OF INDIVIDUALS ¶ 7.01(7) (5th ed. 2000).

18. **The correct answer is (c).** Each year, Americans give billions of dollars to charities. Fostering charitable giving has long been an important component of government policy. A deduction, for income tax purposes, for contributions made to charitable organizations has had a long-time presence in our country's tax structure. IRC § 170(a) facilitates deductions for contributions of cash and property to qualified charities. One need not be a student in income tax to surmise that the American Heart Association qualifies as a charitable organization. Indeed, the American Heart Association is a qualified charitable organization as generally defined in IRC § 170(c), and Tad's cash gifts thereto will be tax deductible (subject to limits discussed below).

The total amount of an individual's charitable deductions in any one year is limited or capped at a ceiling that varies depending on the nature of the contribution (cash or property) and the charitable recipients. This deduction ceiling or limit for cash gifts made to most charitable organizations (commonly referred to as "public charities") is 50% of the taxpayer's "contribution base." [IRC § 170(b)(1)(A).] Tad's cash contributions to the American Red Cross (representing all of his qualified charitable contributions in the year for this question) are deductible up to 50% of his contribution base. This, we will see in later questions, does not pose as a limitation to Tad's charitable deductions. While not necessary to answer this question, an individual's "contribution base" is basically the individuals adjusted gross income (AGI) calculated before deducting any "net operating loss" (NOL) carryback (most individuals do not have a NOL carryback so their AGI is their "contribution base"). [See IRC § 170(b)(1)(F).]

While also not a part of this question, it should be noted that charitable contributions made in any year that, in the aggregate, exceed the deduction ceiling, are carried forward for up to the next five tax years (and deductible subject to the applicable year's limits).

What is pertinent for this question, is where, in computing taxable income, charitable contributions are deductible. In very broad terms, and very important for this series of questions, there are two camps of deductions for purposes of computing taxable income. There are deductions that are subtracted from *gross income* to arrive at an intermediary point called *adjusted gross income* (AGI). These are commonly referred to as "above the line" deductions, with AGI representing "the line." The other camp of deductions is comprised of those that are subtracted from AGI to arrive at *taxable income*. These are commonly referred to as "below the line" deductions. The components making up this camp of *below the line* deductions can include something called the "standard deduction" or, in the alternative, a group of deductions called "itemized deductions." In addition, one or more personal exemption deductions may be included in *below the line* deductions. [Please see Appendix A for more information about how income and deductions fit together in computing taxable income and AGI.]

Deductions for charitable contributions fit into the *itemized deduction* camp which are, as a group, part of the *below the line* deductions – possible deductions subtracted from adjusted gross income (AGI) in computing taxable income. [Please see Appendix A, and other questions in this series (especially questions 23 and 24).]

Answer (a) is incorrect. While this answer correctly recognized that Tad's $3,000 cash contribution to the American Heart Association gives rise to a charitable contribution deduction, it is incorrect regarding "where" the deduction is taken. **Answer (b) is incorrect** because charitable deductions (and other *itemized deductions*) are not predicated upon one's status as a dependent of another. **Answer (d) is incorrect** because, as indicated above, the charitable deduction limit is essentially 50% of the taxpayer's AGI. The $3,000 contributed is not close to approaching this limit. Please see questions 23 and 24 for a more complete picture of Tad's AGI and taxable income).

- **Additional references:** *See* DANIEL Q. POSIN, FEDERAL INCOME TAXATION OF INDIVIDUALS ¶ 7.01(8) (5th ed. 2000).

19. **Answer (c) is the most accurate.** It is virtually a given that Tad's "legitimate, unreimbursed business expenses" qualify as deductible IRC § 162 trade or business expenses. The first sentence of IRC § 162 (contained in subsection (a)) enumerates, for all intents and purposes, the basic requirements for a business deduction. A deduction is allowed for all "ordinary and necessary" "expenses" "paid or incurred during the taxable year" "in carrying on any trade or business." The compartmentalized quotation marks signify what are commonly considered the four basic requirements for a business deduction. These four requirements often represent, in tax classes and in real life, separate and significant points of contention. Business deductions come in a million different flavors, but all qualifying deductions meet those four criteria. The study, in tax classes, of business deductions can be long and comprehensive. Presumptively, Tad's $600 expenditures relating to his paralegal job meet all of the IRC § 162 requirements.

The key issue in this question (and the comprehensive taxable income question later in this series) is where and how, in computing Tad's taxable income, this $600 is deductible. An individual can incur qualifying IRC § 162 expenses in the context of working as an employee or in an individual's own business (someone who alternatively referred to as being self-employed, an independent contractor, or operating his or her business as an "unincorporated sole proprietorship"). The requirements for deductibility pursuant to IRC § 162 are the same for an employee or a self-employed individual. However, "where" and "how" these deductions are taken does vary. A self-employed individual is usually entitled to deduct IRC § 162 business expenses in computing adjusted gross income (AGI). [IRC § 62.] This is commonly referred to as an "above the line" (AGI representing "the line") deduction. Acknowledging that the thought of looking at actual federal tax forms may sound repulsive, the federal individual income tax return form 1040, Schedule C (or C-EZ), presents a very good visual representation of IRC § 162 business deductions for a self-employed individual (independent contractor or unincorporated sole proprietor). For most *employees*, however, IRC § 162 business expenses are not deductible "above the line" in computing AGI. Rather, they are part of a large group of deductions referred to as "itemized deductions." This "itemized deduction" grouping is comprised of various types of deductions such as certain medical care expenses (IRC § 213), certain interest and tax expenses (IRC §§ 163 and 164), charitable contributions (IRC § 170), and others. The entire group of "itemized deductions" are commonly referred to as "below the line" deductions as they are deductible, if at all, <u>after</u> AGI ("the line") to arrive at "taxable income." One sub-group of itemized deductions is a specific category referred to as "miscellaneous itemized deductions." Generally, unreimbursed employee IRC § 162 business expenses (and IRC § 212 expenses unrelated to rentals or royalties) comprise this special "miscellaneous itemized deduction" sub-group. The significance of this sub-group of deductions is that, pursuant to IRC § 67, they are deductible, in the aggregate, only to the extent that they exceed 2% of the individual's AGI. Back to the federal income tax forms, Form 1040, Schedule A is a good visual representation of the entire "itemized deduction" group and it depicts the "miscellaneous itemized deduction" sub-group complete with the 2% of AGI floor calculation. [See question 24, below, and Appendix A for how income and deductions fit together in computing taxable income and AGI.]

Tad's $600 of qualified IRC § 162 business expenses are deductible, but are part of the sub-group of "miscellaneous itemized deductions" that, in the aggregate, are subject to a 2% of AGI nondeductible floor. Please see question 24, below, for a complete picture of how this deduction factors into the computation of Tad's taxable income for 2002.

Answer (a) is incorrect because for most individuals, *above the line* deductions of IRC § 162 business expenses are reserved for the self-employed (a.k.a., independent contractor, unincorporated sole proprietor). **Answer (b) is incorrect** because the business expenses in question relate to Tad's trade/business while employed as a paralegal. They have nothing to do with his law school education. **Answer (d) is also incorrect.** This answer correctly identifies the deduction as a qualified business expense and that it is deductible *below the line* in computing Tad's taxable income. However, this incorrectly states that it is deductible as part of itemized deductions *without* the implication of the 2% of AGI nondeductible floor applicable to "miscellaneous itemized deductions" (of which this is a part). **Answer (e) is incorrect** because while Tad is Marlo's dependent (see question 22, below), this does not preclude Tad from utilizing itemized deductions.

- **Additional references:** *See* DANIEL Q. POSIN, FEDERAL INCOME TAXATION OF INDIVIDUALS ¶¶ 6.01, 6.02(1), 7.02 (5th ed. 2000).

20. **The correct answer is (b).** This is a relatively easy question because, in effect, the correct answer is given in the facts to the problem. Most of the questions addressing "alimony" in this book are concerned about its inclusion in the income of

the recipient. "Qualification" as alimony for this purpose requires that the payments in question meet certain requirements prescribed by IRC § 71. There is no need to delve into those requirements, as the facts indicated that Tad's alimony payment to his ex-wife Nan meet all such requirements. Please see other problems in this book that address specific IRC § 71 requirements for alimony. In this problem, we focus on Tad, the *payor*.

Qualifying alimony (pursuant to IRC § 71) is income to the recipient and a corresponding deduction to the payor pursuant to IRC § 215. The deduction to the payor section, IRC § 215, is linked to the definition, and inclusion in income to the payee, as defined in IRC § 71. Therefore, any analysis of a possible deduction for alimony turns on whether the payments constitute alimony income, pursuant to IRC § 71, to the recipient, which gives us our answer to this question. It is given that the alimony Tad pays to Nan meets all of the requirements of IRC § 71 and, therefore, is automatically a deduction to Tad pursuant to IRC § 215.

How this $2,000 alimony deduction for Tad fits into the scheme of deductions is critical.

In very broad terms, and very important for this series of questions, there are two camps of deductions for purposes of computing taxable income. There are deductions that are subtracted from *gross income* to arrive at an intermediary point called *adjusted gross income* (AGI). These are commonly referred to as "above the line" deductions, with AGI representing "the line." The other camp of deductions is comprised of those that are subtracted from AGI to arrive at *taxable income*. These are commonly referred to as "below the line" deductions. The components making up this camp of *below the line* deductions can include something called the "standard deduction" or, in the alternative, a group of deductions called "itemized deductions." In addition, one or more personal exemption deductions may be included in *below the line* deductions. [Please see Appendix A for more information about how income and deductions fit together in computing taxable income and AGI.]

IRC § 62 is a "signpost" section, identifying what deductions, allowed by various Code sections, are deducted *above the line* in determining AGI. A quick glance at IRC § 62 finds that deductible "alimony" paid, is one of the *above the line deduction* – subtracted from gross income to get to AGI. This will play a critical role in the proper determination of Tad's other deductions and taxable income (presented in other questions in this series).

Answer (a) is incorrect because the deduction alimony paid is not an *itemized deduction*. Rather, as discussed above, it is deductible *above the line* in computing AGI. **Answer (c) is incorrect** because there is no time limit for the duration of alimony deductions other than the life of the payee ex-spouse. **Answer (d) is**

incorrect because this is not a requirement for deductibility by the payor ex-spouse. However, the payor, on his or her income tax return, is required to furnish the payee's Social Security number.

- **Additional references:** *See* DANIEL Q. POSIN, FEDERAL INCOME TAXATION OF INDIVIDUALS ¶ 6.02(14) (5ᵗʰ ed. 2000).

21.   **The correct answer is (c).** This sounds strange, but Tad is Marlo's *dependent*. However, the requirements entitling Marlo to take Tad's personal exemption deduction are not, as discussed below, met. Because this deduction is not available to another (namely Marlo), Tad will be entitled to take his own personal exemption deduction (which is $3,000 for 2002). *If* the requirements were met allowing Marlo to take Tad's personal deduction, then only Marlo would be entitled to take it. [IRC § 151(d)(2).] Contrary to a commonly help opinion (and common practice), there is no choice in the matter. Marlo, if she were entitled to the deduction (which she is not in our case – see below) cannot say, "Tad, I've decided not to take your personal exemption deduction this year – go ahead, you take it for yourself." A more thorough explanation follows.

Every living person has, in his or her figurative pocket, a "coupon" good for a personal exemption deduction for each tax year. There is no real "coupon" involved, but it helps to think of the personal exemption deduction as such. The amount of this exemption deduction is listed in IRC § 151 of the Code as $2,000. However, this amount has been adjusted (increased) each year since 1990 to reflect the general level of inflation. The personal exemption deduction amount at the time of this writing is $3,000 for the year 2002. [Please see Appendix B for other inflation adjusted tax items for the year 2002.] The key to this problem is determining who gets to use these personal exemption deduction "coupons" for the particular year. Does each person get to use his or her own "coupon" and get a personal exemption deduction (e.g. a $3,000 deduction for 2002), or does somebody else get to take another person's "coupon" get the deduction?

Those students having come into a law school income tax course knowing little about income tax, probably know something about this issue. A parent claiming his or her children as dependents and getting an extra deduction for them is precisely the issue we are faced with in this question. Marlo, in our problem, is entitled to a personal exemption deduction for herself. A critical issue here is whether she gets to take Tad's "coupon" and thus get his personal exemption deduction (on her income tax return for purposes of computing her taxable income). Alternatively, and the call of this question, does Tad get to use his own "coupon" for a personal exemption deduction (for purposes of computing his taxable income). To determine if Marlo is entitled to take Tad's personal exemption "coupon" (claim him as a dependent and get to deduct his personal exemption deductions) involves a two-step (with many sub-steps) analysis, which in simplified form, is as follows:

> **Step One**: Is this person (e.g. a kid) your "**Dependent**" pursuant to IRC § 152? (All requirements must be met).
> > ➤ Person must be a U.S. citizen, resident or national, or a resident of Canada, Mexico for any part of the tax year.
> > ➤ Person must be either related to you, or be a member of your household for the entire year. [See IRC §§ 152(a)(1)-(a)(8) for definitions of "relatives," and IRC § 152(a)(9) for other qualifying individuals.]
> > ➤ You must have provided more than one-half this person's total support for the year.

> **Step Two**: If this person is your **Dependent** (from Step One, above), are you allowed to take a **deduction** (personal exemption deduction) for this dependent? [IRC § 151(c).]
> > ➤ Your Dependent must not file a joint return with a spouse for the year.
> > ➤ Your Dependent must either:
> > > ▪ Have "gross income" less than the "exemption amount" for that year, or
> > > ▪ Be your child (or step-child) who is under the age of 19 at the end of the year, **or**
> > > ▪ Be your child (or step child) who is under the age of 24 at the end of the year and is a full-time student for some part of each of five months during the year.

If **both** of these two steps are satisfied with respect to someone for whom you are trying to get their exemption deduction "coupon," then that person is your dependent and you are entitled to deduct their personal exemption deduction amount (e.g., $3,000 for 2002). If this is the case than the person being claimed as a dependent (e.g., Tad) is not entitled to take the deduction. [IRC § 151(d)(2).]

Marlo satisfies step one, above, with respect to Tad. Tad is a U.S. citizen and as Marlo's child, he is considered "related" to Mom. [IRC § 152(a)(1)).] The facts indicate that "[n]otwithstanding the scholarship awarded to Tad, Marlo provided more than one-half of his support for 2002." Tad's scholarship does not count in determining the amount of support provided to him and the relative share that Marlo provides (i.e., she, as the facts indicate, furnishes more than on-half of his support – not counting the scholarship). The reason why Tad's scholarship is not factored into the support equation is because of a special provision (good testing nuance) at IRC § 152(d). In general, it provides that scholarships are not counted as support if received by a son, stepson, daughter or stepdaughter of the taxpayer. If Marlo were Tad's aunt instead of his mother, then the scholarship *would* figure into the support test. Another testing nuance upon a nuance – the *scholarship*, for purposes of this support issue, need not be a "qualified scholarship" excludable by the recipient under IRC § 117 (Tad's scholarship happens to be excludable from his gross income – see question 11, above). Note that there is no requirement that any "related" person (listed in IRC §§ 152(a)(1)-(a)(8)) <u>lives</u> with anyone in particular to attain dependent status. So at this point, we conclude that Tad <u>is</u>, pursuant to IRC § 152, Marlo's dependent. Tad being a *dependent* of Marlo does <u>not</u> automatically mean that Marlo is now entitled to take Tad's personal exemption deduction. For that determination, we need to go on to the second step of the analysis.

On to step two of the dependent exemption deduction analysis, Tad is unmarried, but does he have "gross income" less than the "exemption amount" for the year in question? And what does this mean? The measuring gross income level of "the exemption amount" is the amount of the personal exemption deduction (e.g., $3,000 for 2002). Tad's gross income for the year is clearly not less than the $3,000 exemption for 2002. We do not, however, stop at this point as the operative word in this part of the step two is "either." Going onto to the next "either" requirement, Tad <u>is</u> Marlo's child, but he is not <u>less than</u> age 19 (as of the end of the year). We then proceed to the last option which Tad also fails. Tad, Marlo's child, is not less than 24 years of age (as of the end of the year) and is a full-time college student. Therefore, with respect to Tad, Marlo is <u>not</u> entitled to get Tad's personal exemption deduction "coupon." This then, answers our question and Tad is entitled to his own personal exemption deduction of $3,000 (for 2002).

As indicated, this question is date sensitive, applicable to the 2002 tax year. This question can easily be modified to accommodate years subsequent to 2002 by incorporating the applicable inflation adjusted personal exemption deduction amount for any particular year.

Answer (a) is incorrect because, as discussed above, Tad, and only Tad, is entitled to his $3,000 personal exemption deduction. **Answer (b) is also incorrect.** While it correctly recognizes that Tad is entitled to take the personal exemption deduction himself, the answer states the wrong amount. $2,000 is the amount listed in IRC § 151(d) as the exemption amount, but it fails to recognize that this number has been adjusted (increased) for inflation each year after 1991. [See IRC § 151(d)(4).] **Answer (d) is also incorrect** but is the source of some confusion among students. The facts indicated that Tad's eyesight is severely impaired (i.e., he is considered blind). Historically, blindness (as well as a taxpayer reaching a certain age) entitled an individual to an "extra" personal exemption – in Tad's case, if this was still the law, he would get two personal exemption deductions of

$3,000 (for 2002) for a total of $6,000. However, in the 1980's this was changed and such factors as eyesight and age no longer give rise to extra personal exemption deductions. Such factors now impact the determination of one's "standard deduction" (see question 22, below). **Answer (e) is incorrect** because, as discussed above, who actually gets to take one's personal exemption deduction is not, as is commonly believed, a matter of choice.

22.   **The correct answer is (e).** Many years ago, the concept of the "standard deduction" was introduced into tax law as a means of reducing an individual's record-keeping needs. The *standard deduction* may be taken in place of a group of deductions known collectively as "itemized deductions." Probably the most commonly known components of this latter group of *itemized deductions* include charitable contributions, deductible interest and taxes, and qualifying medical deductions. Taxpayers have a choice: deduct either 1) the total of itemized deductions (after applying all necessary limits and restrictions as discussed elsewhere in this book), **or** 2) the *standard deduction* amount. In calculating "taxable income," a taxpayer takes as a deduction the greater of these two. [Please see Appendix A for more information about *where* these deductions fit within the framework of calculating taxable income.]

IRC § 63(c) is the focal point for the *standard deduction*. The amount of this *standard deduction* can vary greatly from taxpayer to taxpayer depending on various factors including marital or filing status, age, degree of visual imparity, and whether the taxpayer is a "dependent" of another. In addition, *standard deduction* amounts are subject to change each tax year (and for the most part, do change each year) based on adjustments for "inflation" (i.e., the standard deduction amounts are *indexed* for inflation). The various *standard deduction* amounts listed in the statute (throughout IRC § 63) are not the actual amounts for the current year but, rather, are pre-inflation adjusted "base" amounts (that are well below the actual current amounts). [Appendix B contains the various *standard deduction* amounts for the year 2002 (the most current at the time of this printing).]

For 2002, the "regular" *standard deduction* for a single individual is $4,700 (corresponding to the statutory amount of $3,000 that is unadjusted for inflation). The regular *standard deduction* is **increased** for certain individuals based on age or visual imparity. [IRC § 63(b)(3).] For 2002, single individuals (and heads of households) with severe visual impairment, as defined below, are entitled to an extra $1,150 of *standard deduction*. This $1,150 for 2002 corresponds to the unadjusted for inflation amount of $750 listed in IRC § 63(f)(3). [See Appendix B for the 2002 *standard deduction* "extra amounts" for other classifications of individuals.] The degree of visual impairment that generates this extra amount is defined in the Code as an individual whose "central visual acuity does not exceed 20/200 in the better eye with correcting lenses, or if his visual acuity is greater than 20/200 but is accompanied by a limitation in the fields of vision such that the widest diameter of the visual field subtends an angle no greater than 20 degrees." [IRC § 63(f)(4).] The facts indicate that Tad's eyesight would meet this definition thereby entitling him to an extra $1,150 of *standard deduction*. Barring any other factors, Tad's *standard deduction* is $5,850 ($4,700 + $1,150).

Before concluding that Tad's *standard deduction* for 2002 is $5,850, we need to address one additional item. IRC § 63(c)(5) contains a provision possibly reducing the amount of certain individual's *standard deduction*. For a taxpayer who can be claimed as a "dependent" (and whose personal exemption deduction can be used) by another individual, this provision dictates the use of a formula for determining (and possibly reducing) the taxpayer's *standard deduction*. As discussed in the analysis of question 21, above, while Tad is Marlo's dependent, Marlo is not entitled to claim Tad's personal exemption deduction in computing her taxable income. Therefore, this potentially limiting provision of IRC § 63(c)(5) does not apply, and need not be considered.

In conclusion, Tad's *standard deduction* for 2002 is $5,850. [Please see other questions in this book that address the issue of age vis-à-vis the *standard deduction* amount as well as different or limited *standard deduction* amounts in other instances.]

Of interesting historical note, taxpayers with severely impaired vision (as well as taxpayers age 65 and older) were entitled to an "extra" *personal exemption* deduction (discussed elsewhere in this book) rather than an increase in the *standard deduction*. However, in the 1980's this was changed and such factors as age and eyesight no longer give rise to extra personal exemption deductions but, as discussed above, now impact the determination of one's *standard deduction*.

Answer (a) is incorrect. This answer incorrectly reflects what is the non-applicable special *standard deduction* limiting provision of IRC § 63(c)(5). This provision is not applicable to all dependents, but only those whose personal exemption deduction can be claimed by another pursuant to IRC § 151. **Answer (b) is also incorrect.** While this answer provides a better rendition of the special *standard deduction* limiting provision of IRC § 63(c)(5), this provision is not applicable in Tad's case. In addition, this answer fails to reflect the "extra" amount of standard deduction to which Tad is entitled because of his visual impairment. **Answer (c) is incorrect** because it fails to reflect the "extra" amount of standard deduction to which Tad is entitled due to his visual impairment. **Answer (d) is incorrect** because it utilizes an incorrect number for the "extra" standard deduction. While not at issue in this problem, the "extra" standard deduction amount for a married individual in 2002 is $900. This answer uses this improper amount as Tad's "extra" standard deduction.

23.   **The correct answer is (a).** It goes without saying that this question is very complex. This question, and question 24 below, are the culminating questions for this series and are presented to illustrate how the many components of income and deductions fit together to calculate adjusted gross income (AGI) in this problem (and continuing to "taxable income" in problem 24). Ultimately, we will determine that Tad's AGI for 2002 is <u>$20,000</u>.

This answer to this question (and *taxable income* computation in question 24) draws upon our answers to questions 11 through 13, and 15 through 22. While we are computing Tad's AGI in this question, we will consider the entire *taxable income* framework. The computation framework for taxable income is as follows:

Gross Income

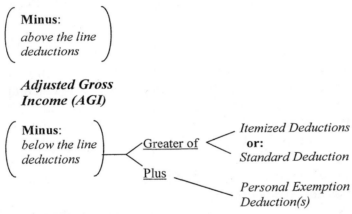

Adjusted Gross Income (AGI)

<u>*Taxable income*</u>

In class, this professor also explains the computation of *taxable income* in a **six-step** approach. AGI, the subject of this question, is the *second* of these steps. To present the material in its logical context, the entire six-step *taxable income* computation is supplied as follows:

Step 1: Determine what is included in the taxpayer's <u>*Gross Income*</u>
    (This reflects all income and exclusions therefrom.)

Step 2: Determine the taxpayer's <u>*Adjusted Gross Income (AGI)*</u>
    (This requires subtracting from *Gross income* any deductions that are allowed *above the line* pursuant to IRC § 62 – see Appendix A for more information.)

Step 3: Determine the total amount of the taxpayer's <u>*Itemized Deductions*</u>

(This requires applying any applicable limitations, floors, or restrictions for certain types of these deductions – see Appendix A for more information.)

Step 4: Determine the amount of the taxpayer's *Standard Deduction*
(This is year-specific and varies by filing status, age, degree of visual impairment, and limitations for certain dependents.)

Step 5: Determine the amount of the taxpayer's *Personal Exemption Deduction(s)*
(This is a year-specific amount per person, and the number of such deductions a taxpayer may claim can vary based on issues of dependency.)

Step 6: Compute *Taxable Income* by subtracting from *AGI* (amount in **Step 2**):
1) Either *itemized deductions* (amount in **Step 3**), or the *standard deduction* (amount in **Step 4**), whichever is the **greater** of the two, **and**
2) The *personal exemption deduction(s)* (amount in **Step 5**)

As indicated, we are concerned with AGI in this question and we begin with step one, determining Tad's "gross income." Tad's *gross income* was calculated in problem 11, above, as $26,000. Recall that this was derived from Tad's $26,000 in wages for 2002. He was not required to include, in gross income, the $20,000 law school scholarship pursuant to IRC § 117.

We now turn to the issue of deductions. In previous questions in this set, we identified the following possible deductions for Tad:

Question 12: Possible IRC § 222 deduction for *qualified tuition and related expenses*.

Question 15: Possible IRC § 221 deduction for *interest on education loans*.

Question 16: Possible IRC § 164 deduction for *taxes paid* (his state income tax of $1,000 and intangibles tax of $800).

Question 17: Possible IRC § 213 deduction for *qualified medical care expenses* (the veterinary fees for his Seeing Eye dog).

Question 18: Possible IRC § 170 deduction for *charitable contributions*.

Question 19: Possible IRC § 162 deduction for *business expenses* (associated with his paralegal job).

Question 20: Possible IRC § 215 deduction for *alimony paid*.

Question 21: Possible IRC § 151 *personal exemption deduction*.

Question 22: Possible IRC § 63 *standard deduction.*

Determination of Tad's *AGI* (step two in our taxable income calculation) requires that we first identify which of the above possible deductions are allowed in its computation. Recall that deductions are basically divided into two camps: the so-called *above the line* deductions (for computing *AGI*) and the *below the line* deductions (subtracted from *AGI* to arrive at *taxable income*). IRC § 62 is the "signpost" section that lists those deductions that are available for computing *AGI*. For Tad, he has three possible *above the line* deductions: IRC § 222 (*qualified tuition and related expenses*), IRC § 221, (*interest on education loans*), and IRC § 215 (*alimony paid*). Calculating Tad's "actual" deductions for these three items is a challenging task, and each of the three possible deductions will be analyzed separately; starting with the easiest of the three: alimony paid.

IRC § 215 Alimony Paid
Tad paid $2,000 in alimony to his ex-wife Nan. We determined, in question 20, above, that this is fully deductible alimony. IRC §215 does not limit the dollar amount of alimony deductions, nor is the deduction "phased-out" for certain taxpayers. Tad will be entitled to an *above the line* $2,000 deduction for the alimony he paid in 2002.

IRC § 221 Interest on Education Loans
In 2002, Tad paid $1,000 in interest on his undergraduate student loans (used for tuition). IRC § 221 is a complex section with many requirements, and was discussed at some length in question 15, above. Recall that once we determined that the loans involved were "qualified educational loans" the statute imposes two important limitations regarding the deduction of this interest: a $2,500 maximum interest deduction, and a "phase-out" of the deduction for taxpayers making over a certain threshold amount of income. Tad's $1,000 in interest paid does not exceed the statutory maximum. At this point, however, we need to determine if Tad's deduction is affected by the "phase-out" mechanism.

Referring to question 15, above, this "phase-out" starts for single individuals with *AGI* (as modified) of $50,000 (for 2002). Recall that the statute uses the term "modified adjusted gross income" because true *AGI* will ultimately reflect any deduction allowed for education interest under IRC § 221. "Modified adjusted gross income" (or MAGI) is defined in IRC § 221(b)(2)(c) as sort of a "pretend" *AGI* amount. *MAGI* is *AGI* before considering this possible IRC § 221 interest deduction and the possible IRC § 222 education expense deduction (which is based on a different *MAGI* permutation). This, by the way, is why we are discussing Tad's possible IRC § 221 deduction before we discuss his possible deduction under IRC § 222. When an individual has both of these possible deductions, as does Tad, the code requires a certain order of computation – different

MAGI's is you prefer – and the IRC § 221 deduction is computed before that in IRC § 222.

Now back to Tad's situation and *MAGI*. Without regard to IRC §§ 221 or 222, his AGI would be $24,000. This is his $26,000 of gross income less the $2,000 alimony deduction. This $24,000 is Tad's *MAGI* for purposes of determining his possible student loan interest deduction under IRC § 221. Again, the phase-out for single individuals (for 2002) starts at $50,000 of *MAGI* (and is fully eliminated when *MAGI* reaches $65,000). Tad's *MAGI* is well below the start of the phase-out range. Therefore, Tad is entitled to an *above the line* deduction for the full $1,000 of student loan interest he paid in 2002.

IRC § 222 Qualified Tuition and Related Expenses
In 2002, Tad paid $4,000 in law school tuition. IRC § 222 is also a complex section with many requirements, and was discussed in question 12, above. Recall that this is a new deduction enacted by the 2001 Tax Act and, for now, is available only for years 2002 through 2005. Like IRC §221 above, the IRC § 222 deduction is fraught with qualifications and limitations. We determined that Tad's $4,000 in tuition were qualifying costs for this deduction. However, the statutory maximum deduction is $3,000 (in 2002 and 2003). Similar to IRC § 221, IRC § 222 has a mechanism limiting the deduction to individuals making less than a certain amount of money. IRC § 222 is unlike IRC § 221, however, in that this mechanism is not a ratable "phase-out" within a certain range of income levels. Rather, the IRC § 222 deduction abruptly evaporates when a certain income level is reached.

Referring to question 12, above, this threshold level, for single individuals, is $65,000 (in 2002 and 2003). Once again, this level of income is a "modified adjusted gross income" or (MAGI). Without going through the entire *MAGI* discussion again, *MAGI* for purposes of IRC § 222, is *AGI* without regard (or before) this section, but after deducting any allowed deduction pursuant to IRC § 221 (discussed above). Tad's *MAGI* for IRC § 222 purposes is $23,000 (his $26,000 of gross income, less the $2,000 in alimony, less the $1,000 in IRC § 221 student loan interest computed above). Clearly, Tad's *MAGI* does not exceed $65,000 and, therefore, he is entitled to a $3,000 deduction under new IRC § 222.

Tad's Real *AGI*

We now have all of the necessary component parts to compute Tad's actual *AGI*. Tad's *AGI*, for 2002, is $20,000 computed as follows:

$26,000	Gross Income
($ 2,000)	Alimony deduction (IRC § 215)
($ 1,000)	Student loan interest deduction (IRC § 221)
($ 3,000)	New higher education expense deduction (IRC § 222)
$20,000	**Adjusted Gross Income (*AGI*)**

Answers (b) through (d) are all incorrect because none of these answers reflects the proper computation of Tad's *AGI*. **Answer (e) is incorrect** because a correct answer (a) is presented.

- **Additional references:** *See* DANIEL Q. POSIN, FEDERAL INCOME TAXATION OF INDIVIDUALS ¶ 6.01 (5th ed. 2000).

24. **The correct answer is this very comprehensive question is (c).** This question represents the culmination for this series of questions: computation of taxable income. Understandably, this is a difficult question to present in a multiple-choice format, as it draws upon the answers to many of the previous questions. It is presented, nonetheless, to illustrate how the many components of income and deductions fit together to calculate *taxable income*. Ultimately, we will determine that Tad's *taxable income* for 2002 is $11,150.

This answer to this question draws upon our answers to questions 11 through 13, and 15 through 23. Reproduced again, is the computational framework for *taxable income*.

Gross Income

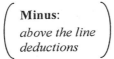

Minus:
above the line deductions

Adjusted Gross Income (AGI)

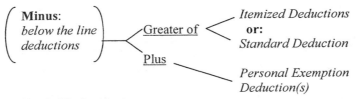

Minus:
below the line deductions Greater of *Itemized Deductions*
or:
Standard Deduction

Plus *Personal Exemption Deduction(s)*

Taxable income

In class, this professor also explains the computation of *taxable income* in a **six-step** approach. This six-step approach is reproduced, again, as follows:

Step 1: Determine what is included in the taxpayer's *Gross Income*
(This reflects all income and exclusions therefrom.)

Step 2: Determine the taxpayer's *Adjusted Gross Income (AGI)*
(This requires subtracting from *Gross income* any deductions that are allowed *above the line* pursuant to IRC § 62 – see Appendix A for more information.)

Step 3: Determine the total amount of the taxpayer's *Itemized Deductions*
(This requires applying any applicable limitations, floors, or restrictions for certain types of these deductions – see Appendix A for more information.)

Step 4: Determine the amount of the taxpayer's *Standard Deduction*
(This is year-specific and varies by filing status, age, degree of visual impairment, and limitations for certain dependents.)

Step 5: Determine the amount of the taxpayer's *Personal Exemption Deduction(s)*
(This is a year-specific amount per person, and the number of such deductions a taxpayer may claim can vary based on issues of dependency.)

Step 6: Compute _Taxable Income_ by subtracting from *AGI* (amount in **Step 2**):
1) Either *itemized deductions* (amount in **Step 3**), or the *standard deduction* (amount in **Step 4**), whichever is the **greater** of the two, **and**
2) The *personal exemption deduction(s)* (amount in **Step 5**)

Question 23, above, addressed the complicated calculation of Tad's *AGI*, "Step Two" in our *taxable income* computation. We determined Tad's *AGI* to be $20.000 computed as follows:

$26,000	Gross Income
($ 2,000)	Alimony deduction (IRC § 215)
($ 1,000)	Student loan interest deduction (IRC § 221)
($ 3,000)	New higher education expense deduction (IRC § 222)
$20,000	**Adjusted Gross Income (*AGI*)**

We will now proceed through the remaining steps (3 through 6) to calculate Tad's *taxable income*.

Step 3 – _Itemized Deductions_

Referring to the computational framework of computing *taxable income*, above, itemized deductions, as a group, are to be compared with the *standard deduction*. The taxpayer, in computing *taxable income* will take the greater of these two, plus any *personal exemption deduction(s)*. All of these deductions are known as *below the line* deductions. Looking back to the analysis of question 23 (and questions 12, 13, 15-22), we identified Tad's possible deductions as follows:

Question 12: Possible IRC § 222 deduction for *qualified tuition and re-lated expenses.*

Question 15: Possible IRC § 221 deduction for *interest on education loans.*

Question 16: Possible IRC § 164 deduction for *taxes paid* (his state income tax of $1,000 and intangibles tax of $800).

Question 17: Possible IRC § 213 deduction for *qualified medical care expenses* (the veterinary fees for his Seeing Eye dog).

Question 18: Possible IRC § 170 deduction for *charitable contributions.*

Question 19: Possible IRC § 162 deduction for *business expenses* (associated with his paralegal job).

Question 20: Possible IRC § 215 deduction for *alimony paid.*

Question 21: Possible IRC § 151 *personal exemption deduction.*

Question 22: Possible IRC § 63 *standard deduction.*

In determining Tad's *AGI*, we dispensed with three deductions: IRC § 215 alimony (from question 20), IRC § 221 student loan interest (from question 15), and IRC § 222 higher education expenses (from question 14). Tad's *standard deduction* (from question 22) and *personal exemption deduction* are addressed below in Steps 4 and 5, respectively. By process of elimination, the deductions that may be part of Tad's *itemized deductions* are the following:

The $1,000 state income tax paid (IRC § 164 – from question 16).
The $800 in state intangibles tax paid (IRC § 164 – from question 16).
The $1,600 in qualified medical care expenses (IRC § 213 – from question 17).
The $3,000 in charitable contributions (IRC § 170 – from question 18).
The $600 in business expenses paid (IRC § 162 – from question 19).

Some of the deductions that comprise *itemized deductions* are subject to various limitations as discussed in each of the questions dealing with a particular deduction. A summary and calculation of each component of Tad's *itemized deductions* follows.

State Income and Intangibles Taxes
These IRC § 164 deductions are not subject to any ceiling or floor limitations and, therefore, the both the $1,000 and $800 that Tad paid (for income and intangibles tax, respectively) will be part of Tad's *itemized deductions* – a total of $1,800.

Qualified Medical Care Expenses
Pursuant to IRC § 213, these expenses are deductible only to the extent that they exceed 7.5% of the taxpayer's *AGI* (see question 17 above). This is known as the 7.5% of AGI "floor" and for Tad, the deduction is:

$1,600	Qualifying medical care expenses
($1,500)	7.5% of Tad's *AGI* (.075 x $20,000)
$ 100	**Tad's Actual Medical Deduction**

Charitable Contributions
As discussed in question 18, above, the deduction for most cash charitable contributions is limited (a ceiling) to 50% of a taxpayer's *AGI*. 50% of Tad's $20,000 AGI is $10,000. Because Tad's $3,000 in charitable con-

tributions do not exceed this ceiling, the full $3,000 will be part of Tad's *itemized deductions*.

Business Expenses
As discussed in question 19, above, IRC § 162 business expenses incurred by an employee are deductible *below the line*, and they are part of a sub-group of *itemized deductions* known as "miscellaneous itemized deductions." The significance of this is that the deduction for items in this sub-group of *miscellaneous itemized deductions* is limited by IRC § 67. In the aggregate, most *miscellaneous itemized deductions* are deductible to the extent that they, in the aggregate, exceed 2% of a taxpayer's *AGI*. Tad's business expense deduction is:

$ 600	Qualifying IRC § 162 business expenses
($ 400)	2% of Tad's *AGI* (.02 x $20,000)
$ 200	**Tad's Actual Business Expense Deduction**

Tad's Total *Itemized Deductions*
His total itemized deductions, after applying any applicable limits and restrictions, is $5,100 computed as follows:

$1,800	State income and intangibles taxes
$ 100	Medical care expense deduction
$3,000	Charitable contributions
$ 200	Business expense deduction
$5,100	**Tad's Itemized deductions Total**

Step 4 – Tad's *Standard Deduction*
Tad's *standard deduction* was computed in question 22, above. Recall that his *standard deduction* for 2002 is **$5,850**. The regular *standard deduction* amount for a single individual (for 2002) is $4,700. However, recall that because of Tad's visual imparity, he is entitled to increase the regular *standard deduction* by $1,150 (for 2002).

Step 5 – Tad's *Personal Exemption Deduction*
In question 13, above, we determined that Tad was entitled to his own *personal exemption deduction* for 2002. This amount, for 2002, is **$3,000**.

Step 6 – Putting it All Together – Tad's *Taxable Income* for 2002

Applying this **six-step** computation approach to Tad, we have the following:

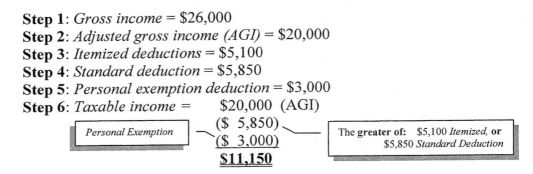

Step 1: *Gross income* = $26,000
Step 2: *Adjusted gross income (AGI)* = $20,000
Step 3: *Itemized deductions* = $5,100
Step 4: *Standard deduction* = $5,850
Step 5: *Personal exemption deduction* = $3,000
Step 6: *Taxable income* = $20,000 (AGI)

Personal Exemption   ($ 5,850)
($ 3,000)   The greater of: $5,100 *Itemized*, **or**
$5,850 *Standard Deduction*
$11,150

A visual depiction of Tad's *taxable income* computation for 2002 is as follows:

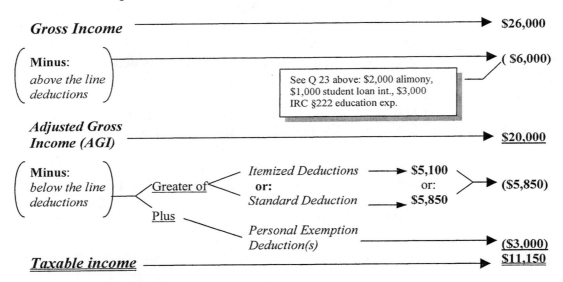

Gross Income ————————————————▶ **$26,000**

Minus:
*above the line
deductions*   ————————————————▶ (**$6,000**)

See Q 23 above: $2,000 alimony,
$1,000 student loan int., $3,000
IRC §222 education exp.

*Adjusted Gross
Income (AGI)* ————————————————▶ **$20,000**

Minus:
*below the line
deductions*   Greater of   *Itemized Deductions* ——▶ **$5,100**
or: or: ($5,850)
Standard Deduction ——▶ **$5,850**

Plus   *Personal Exemption
Deduction(s)* ————————————▶ (**$3,000**)

Taxable income ————————————————▶ **$11,150**

Answers (a), (b) and (d) are all incorrect because none of these answers reflects the proper computation of Tad's *taxable income*. **Answer (e) is incorrect** because a correct answer (a) is presented.

- **Additional references**: *See* DANIEL Q. POSIN, FEDERAL INCOME TAXATION OF INDIVIDUALS ¶ 6.01 (5th ed. 2000).

25.   **The best answer is (a).** IRC § 213 allows for a deduction of certain qualified medical care expenses. Once one makes the determination of what constitutes "qualified" medical care expenses, the subject of this question, the deduction is allowed as an "itemized deduction" only to the extent that the total qualifying ex-

penses exceeds 7.5% of adjusted gross income (AGI). Qualified medical care expenses include typical costs for doctors, dentists, hospital, health insurance, and the like. [See IRC § 213(d).] The section specifically provides that qualifying medical care expenses are those paid by the taxpayer for the taxpayer, his or her spouse, or <u>a dependent (as defined in IRC § 152)</u>.

The costs for Tad's doctor visits clearly qualify as medical care expenses. However, is Marlo entitled to deduct them – is Tad Marlo's "dependent (as defined in IRC § 152)? The answer is yes, as we have already established that Tad qualifies as Marlo's dependent because he is related to her and she provides more than one-half of his support. Therefore, the doctor costs Marlo pays for Tad are qualifying medical care expenses for her. But wait! In question 21, above, did we not say that Marlo could <u>not</u> claim Tad as a dependent for purposes of Marlo taking his personal exemption deduction? Yes, we did. However, recall that there are two steps in determining whether a taxpayer is entitled to take the personal exemption deduction of another. The first step is to determine whether, pursuant to <u>IRC § 152</u>, the person (e.g., Tad) is a dependent of the taxpayer (e.g., Marlo). The second step is to determine whether, pursuant to <u>IRC § 151</u>, the taxpayer is entitled to claim the personal exemption deduction for such dependent. Recall that Tad is Marlo's dependent pursuant to IRC § 152, but that the requirements in IRC § 151 were not met allowing Marlo to take Tad's personal exemption deduction. What does all this mean for purposes of this question? The statute allowing the deduction for medical care expenses paid for a dependent (IRC § 213) requires only that such person be a dependent pursuant IRC § 152, not that in addition, the taxpayer claim such dependent's personal exemption deduction pursuant to IRC § 151.

In summary, Marlo's payments for Tad's doctor bills qualify as medical care expenses for purposes of determining Marlo's medical deduction under IRC § 213.

Answer (b) is not correct because for purposes of IRC § 152 (and deduction of qualifying medical care expenses in IRC § 213) Tad *is* Marlo's dependent. **Answer (c) is not correct** because Tad must qualify as Marlo's dependent (under IRC § 152) in order for Marlo to deduct the medical care expenses she paid for Tad. **Answer (d) is not correct** because Marlo need not be entitled to claim Tad's *personal exemption deduction* in order for Tad to be considered her dependent for purposes of IRC §§ 152 and 213.

- **Additional references:** *See* DANIEL Q. POSIN, FEDERAL INCOME TAXATION OF INDIVIDUALS ¶ 7.01(7) (5th ed. 2000).

**ANSWER KEY
EXAM VIII**

FEDERAL INCOME TAX
MULTIPLE-CHOICE QUESTIONS
ANSWER KEY AND EXPLANATIONS
EXAM VIII

1. **Answer (d) is correct.** *This question is year-specific (2002) and is intended to illustrate a basic calculation of federal income tax liability. [Appendix B, contains relevant, year-specific information applicable to 2002.] This question is easily adaptable to years different than 2002.*

   Sadly, Tiffany lost her spouse at a young age. Computing her "regular" tax liability (ignoring any possible additional taxes and before any tax credits) is a rather straightforward mathematical exercise. IRC § 1 sets out the tax computation rate schedules and as you have most likely studied, the rate schedules vary depending on one's *filing status*. Filing status is determined as of the end of the tax year and Tiffany's status is that of an "unmarried individual (other than a surviving spouse or head of household)." The resulting tax using the 2002 tax rate schedules is $24,315.

   A word of caution about language used on exams. There are many instances where the common use of a term does not necessarily correspond to its official "tax" counterpart. Labels can be deceiving and do not be fooled by their use in lay terms on an exam. In everyday language we would refer to Tiffany as a "surviving spouse." Looking at IRC § 1(a) we see a favorable tax rate schedule (compared to that for unmarried individuals) for certain married individuals and *surviving spouses*. The term *surviving spouse*, however, has a very specific and much narrower definition for federal income tax purposes (and the ability to use the more favorable rate schedule). IRC § 2(a) gives the *tax label* of *surviving spouse* for only the two years after the year in which the taxpayer's spouse died and only if:
   - Such surviving spouse maintains as his or her home a household which constitutes for the taxable year the principal place of abode (as a member of such household) of a dependent
   - Who (within the meaning of IRC § 152) is a son, stepson, daughter, or stepdaughter of the surviving spouse, and
   - With respect to whom the surviving spouse is entitled to a deduction for the taxable year under IRC § 151.

   Distilled, a *surviving spouse* for income tax purposes is an unmarried surviving spouse (for the two years subsequent to his or her spouse's death) who has dependent children living in his or her home. Tiffany is not, for tax purposes, a *surviving spouse* because Robert died too long ago and Tiffany has no children. Even though to the entire non-tax world, Tiffany is a surviving spouse, she is not so considered for federal income tax purposes. Therefore, she is unable to use the more favorable married/surviving spouse rate schedule but, rather, must use the single/unmarried (non heads of households) rate schedule.

Once the proper filing status is determined, the actual calculation of the regular income tax is a simple matter. The rate schedules for individuals are found in IRC § 1, but the schedules that appear in the Code should <u>not</u> be used for actual tax calculations. This is because the rate schedules are "indexed" for inflation and change every year. In addition, the 2001 Tax Act, made changes to various rates and rate brackets that take affect over a period of years. In general, the tax rate schedules reflect a "graduated" nature of the income tax – lower rates for lower levels of taxable income with progressively higher incremental tax rates on higher levels of income. [Please see Appendix B for the various rate schedules applicable to 2002.]

Utilizing the unmarried (single) rate schedule for 2002, $100,000 of taxable income places Tiffany in the 30% "marginal" tax bracket. The progressive nature of the rate schedules insures that only a portion of her $100,000 of taxable income will be taxed at this rate. Other portions of her $100,000 taxable income are taxed, in 2002, at rates of 10%, 15%, and 27%. Applying the 2002 single tax rate schedule to her $100,000, the tax is: $14,625 plus 30% of the difference between her $100,000 taxable income and $67,700. This translates to $14,625 + (30% x ($100,000 - $67,700)), or $14,625 + (30% x $32,300), or $14,625 + $9,690, or **$24,315**. Note that the rate schedules automatically compute the tax on amounts of income at the lower marginal rates. For example, in Tiffany's case, the $14,625 in the rate schedule represents the tax on the first $67,700 of taxable income (applying all of the lower marginal rates to lower levels of income).

Answer (a) is incorrect because this number represents the "regular" income tax using the tax rate schedule for married individuals filing joint returns and *surviving spouse*. Notice that the computed tax using this rate schedule is more favorable than that for single individuals. **Answer (b) is also incorrect**. This answer was computed applying a static 30% tax rate. This is Tiffany's "marginal" rate bracket, but only a portion of her income is taxed at this rate. **Answer (c) is incorrect** because this number represents the "regular" income tax using the tax rate schedule for "heads of households." Tiffany does not qualify for this favorable (compared to single) rate schedule. Qualification as a "head of household" is determined by IRC § 2(b). **Answer (e) is incorrect** because a correct answer (d) is presented.

2.   **The best answer is (d).** The 2001 Tax Act was signed into law in June 2001, and made numerous and major changes to tax laws including many in the "income tax" area. One of the more publicized changes in the income tax area was in the area of tax rate reductions. Prior to the enactment of this major piece of legislation, there were four "marginal tax rates" for individuals: 15%, 28%, 31%, 36% and 39.6%. The progressive nature of the income tax structure was not changed by the 2001 Tax Act (i.e., taxable income is taxed at progressively higher rates as

its level increases). Rather, a new 10% bracket was added for individuals with very low levels of taxable income, and the rates for all but the 15% bracket were reduced based on a scheduled "phase-in" as illustrated below:

Marginal Income Tax Rates for Individuals

Prior to the 2001 Tax Act

15%	28%	31%	36%	39.6%

2001 Tax Act (tax rates)

Year						
2001	10%	15%	27.5%	30.5%	35.5%	39.1%
2002/03	10%	15%	27%	30%	35%	38.6%
2004/05	10%	15%	26%	29%	34%	37.6%
2006 on	10%	15%	25%	28%	33%	35%

The 2001 Tax Act also enacted a provision to "widen" the 15% bracket (to include more income subject to tax at this lower rate), but only for married individuals filing joint returns. This latter "widening" of the 15% bracket for married individuals is scheduled to start in the year 2005, and will continue to widen (based set percentages) each year until 2008 when this bracket (the amount of income taxable at 15%) is twice that of single individuals.

Tax rates, and their changes, are politically volatile and as illustrated above, the changes relating to rates are scheduled to "phase-in" over a period of years. As of this writing, there have been discussions in Congress about altering some aspects of the scheduled changes. However, as of this writing, nothing has been enacted to that effect.

It should be mentioned that the 10% tax rate was effectively enacted in 2001 through an "advance refund" mechanism whereby most taxpayers received pre-"refund" checks in the summer of 2001.

It should also be mentioned that as of this writing, the 2001 Tax Act's "sunset clause" is still part of the law. This sunset clause applies to the entire 2001 Tax Act, and unless affirmatively changed by Congress and enacted into law, all changes made and provisions enacted by the 2001 Tax Act will disappear after December 31, 2010, and tax laws will revert to their status immediately prior to the enactment of the 2001 Tax Act.

Answers (a) and (c) are incorrect because the 2001 Tax Act does not reduce "all other existing" tax rates. As indicated above, the 15% tax *rate* is not reduced. Answer (c) is even more inaccurate because the new 10% bracket effectively became effective for the 2001 tax year. **Answer (b) is incorrect** because, as indicated above, the new 10% tax rate does not replace the 15% tax rate existing prior to the 2001 Tax Act. **Answer (e) in incorrect** because the only accurate answer presented is (d) (although answer (d) is not a complete analysis of the 2001 Tax Act's impact on tax rates).

3.   **The correct answer, as of this writing, is (a).** Hey, sometimes it is very difficult to come up with at least four good answers – the author apologizes for answer (d) above (although it sounds quite nice).

The Economic Growth and Tax Relief Reconciliation Act of 2001 (the "2001 Tax Act") was signed into law in 2001. The 2001 Tax Act made numerous and substantial changes to many areas of tax law including income taxes, and estate and gift taxes. To comply with certain congressional budget rules, the 2001 Tax Act contains a rather unusual provision for a law change of this magnitude: a "sunset clause." Historically, many tax laws (and other laws) have been enacted with *sunset clauses*. For example, a certain provision of the law may change for limited period of time to act as a short-term adjustment or stimulus and then that provision goes away after a certain period of time.

As enacted (and as of this writing) the entire 2001 Tax Act is subject to a *sunset clause*. Unless affirmatively changed by Congress and enacted into law, all changes made and provisions enacted by the 2001 Tax Act will disappear after December 31, 2010, and tax laws will revert to their status immediately prior to the enactment of the 2001 Tax Act.

There are many provisions within the 2001 Tax Act that, pursuant to the Act itself, "phase-in," "phase-out," appear and then disappear. Notwithstanding these provisions, many believe that as a practical matter, Congress will affirmatively act to modify, accelerate, postpone, and remove the *sunset provision* with respect to at least some parts of the 2001 Tax Act. As of this writing, there have been discussions in Congress about altering some aspects of the scheduled changes. However, as of this writing, nothing has been enacted to that effect.

Answer (b) is incorrect because there is no "triggering" mechanism with respect to the Act's *sunset clause*. **Answer (c) is incorrect** because the sunset clause applies to all provisions of the 2001 Tax Act. **No comment about answer (d).**

4.   **The most accurate statement is (e).** To begin with, every living person has, in his or her figurative pocket, a "coupon" good for a personal exemption deduction

for each tax year. There is no real "coupon" involved, but it helps to think of the personal exemption deduction as such. The amount of this exemption deduction is listed in IRC § 151 of the Code as $2,000. However, this amount has been adjusted (increased) each year since 1990, to reflect the general level of inflation. The personal exemption deduction amount at the time of this writing is $3,000 for the year 2002. [Please see Appendix B for other inflation adjusted tax items for the year 2002.] At the outset, Irv and Lorraine filing one return together (a joint return) are entitled to two (2) personal exemption deductions, one for Irv and one for Lorraine – they each get to use their own personal exemption "coupon." They have no dependents, so there is no issue of whether they can claim someone else's personal exemption "coupon" and get the deduction (please see other question in this book addressing such issues).

The primary issue in this question is the potential "phase-out" (reduction or elimination) of the couple's personal exemption deductions because they may have too much income. The "Revenue Reconciliation Act of 1990" enacted IRC § 151(d)(3) that "phases-out" (reduces or totally eliminates) the otherwise allowable personal exemption deduction(s) for certain individuals. The mechanism of this section in how it reduces one's personal exemption deduction(s) is rather bizarre. Trying not to overwhelm with too much detail, if a taxpayer's adjusted gross income (AGI) exceeds a certain "threshold" amount, then the personal exemptions are reduced (or eliminated). This *threshold* amount varies depending on "filing status" (and is indexed for inflation) but, for example, the starting point for 2002 for married individuals filing a joint return, is AGI of $206,000. As mentioned, the mechanism for reduction of the personal exemption deduction(s) is rather bizarre; the deduction reduced by 2% "for each $2,500 (or fraction thereof) by which the taxpayer's adjusted gross income for the taxable year exceeds the threshold amount." Sounds kinda goofy, no? Working the math, if in 2002, for example, a married couple's AGI exceeds $328,500, the personal exemption deductions are **completely** eliminated.

The facts for this question indicate that Irv and Lorraine have income in excess of $500,000 and no real deductions in computing AGI (their charitable contributions deductions are not deductions in computing AGI). [See question 5, below, and Appendix A for more information.] Therefore, at this point, it appears that the personal exemption deductions for Irv and Lorraine will be completely eliminated. While the threshold amounts for this provision are indexed for inflation, it is highly unlikely, given the increases in the thresholds to date, that our couple's level of income will entitle them to any personal exemption deduction. **However,** there is one more pertinent issue to address.

The 2001 Tax Act made changes to the "phase-out" provisions of IRC § 151(d)(3). Pursuant to this new law, the aforementioned phase-out provisions will start to "phase-out" in 2006 with the provisions totally eliminated after 2009. The 2001 Tax Act enacted new IRC § 151(d)(3)(E) which provides a fractional reduction of the phase-out between the years 2006 through 2009. The elimination of the personal exemption phase-out provision of IRC § 151(d)(3) is a favorable change for high-income individuals. Therefore, the answer to our question is that currently (at the time of this writing) Irv and Lorraine probably have no current deduction for personal exemptions because of their level of income. However, the law as currently on the books, will enable them to some personal exemption deduction amount starting in 2006 (with full exemption deductions restored after 2009). As previously mentioned in the preface to this book, at the time of this writing, all of the provisions of the 2001 Tax Act (including this phase-out reduction provision) are set to expire as of 2011 due the Act's rather unique "sunset clause."

Answer (a) is incorrect. Not only does this answer fail to reflect the phase-out provisions discussed above, but it also incorrectly states that they are entitled to four (4) personal exemption deductions. Historically, taxpayers 65 and older (as well as those taxpayers who were blind) were entitled an "extra" personal exemption. However, in the 1980's this was changed and such factors as age and eyesight no longer give rise to extra personal exemption deductions. Such factors now impact the determination of one's "standard deduction" (see other problems in this book addressing such issues). **Answer (b) is incorrect** because it fails to reflect the phase-out provisions discussed above for personal exemption deductions. **Answer (c) is also incorrect.** While it does reflect the phase-out provisions discussed above, it fails to reflect the impact of the 2001 Tax Act with respect to these phase-out provisions. **Answer (d) is incorrect** because it incorrectly states that they are entitled to four (4) potential personal exemption deductions, and it fails to reflect the impact of the 2001 Tax Act with respect to the phase-out provisions.

- **Additional references:** *See* DANIEL Q. POSIN, FEDERAL INCOME TAXATION OF INDIVIDUALS ¶ 7.04 (5th ed. 2000).

5. **The best answer is (b).** An individual's qualified contributions to charity give rise to income tax deductions. [IRC § 170.] In your study of *deductions,* you may cover many deductions including those for interest, taxes, business, medical, moving, etc. expenses. As far as deductions are concerned, there are two major camps of deductions for purposes of computing taxable income. There are deductions that are subtracted from *gross income* to arrive at our intermediary AGI. These are commonly referred to as "above the line" deductions, with AGI representing "the line." The deductions that make up the other camp are those subtracted from AGI to arrive at *taxable income.* These are commonly referred to as "below the line" deductions. The components making up this camp of *below the*

line deductions can include something called the "standard deduction" or, in the alternative, a group of deductions called "itemized deductions." In addition, one or more personal exemption deductions may be included in *below the line* deductions. Deductions for charitable contributions are part of the *itemized deduction* camp. This deduction, pursuant to our facts, is essentially the couple's only *itemized deduction*. [Please see Appendix A for more information about how income and deductions fit together in computing taxable income and AGI.]

Other questions in this book address, in more detail, specific limits or caps for charitable deductions. Generally, for cash contributions to most charities, an individual's charitable deduction is capped at 50% of their adjusted gross income (AGI). [IRC § 170(b).] For Irv and Lorraine, this limitation is not at issue (their potential $30,000 deduction is well below 50% of their approximate $500,000 of adjusted gross income). While this specific charitable deduction limitation would not affect our couple's "itemized" charitable deduction, another more broad special limitation needs to be addressed.

The primary issue in this question is the potential "phase-out" (reduction) of the couple's itemized deductions because they may have too much income. The "Revenue Reconciliation Act of 1990" enacted IRC § 68 that "phases-out" (reduces) the taxpayer's otherwise allowable total *itemized deductions* (with some exceptions). When a taxpayer's adjusted gross income (AGI) exceeds a certain threshold amount, total *itemized deductions* (other than medical expenses, investment interest, and casualty/theft or gambling losses) are reduced by 3% of the amount that their AGI exceeds this threshold amount. This *threshold* amount is indexed for inflation and, for example, the amount is generally $137,300 for 2002. To illustrate this reduction mechanism, let us use the year 2002 for an example. At $500,000 the couple's AGI exceeds the $137,300 threshold by $362,700. Multiplying this amount by 3% equals $10,881. This $10,881 represents the amount that our couple's *itemized deductions* are "phased-out" or reduced. If their $30,000 charitable deduction represents all of their *itemized deductions*, then their total **actual itemized deductions** will only be $19,119 ($30,000 - $10,881). The statute does provide that this phase-out or reduction cannot exceed 80% (i.e., at a minimum, taxpayers are allowed 20% of their *itemized deductions* regardless of their income level). This 80% cap on the reduction is not at issue in our example (their reduction is approximately one-third). There is, however, one last pertinent issue to address.

The 2001 Tax Act made changes to the "phase-out" provisions of IRC § 68. Pursuant to this new law, the aforementioned phase-out provisions will start to "phase-out" in 2006 with the provisions totally eliminated after 2009. The 2001 Tax Act enacted new IRC § 68(f) that provides for a fractional reduction of the phase-out between the years 2006 through 2009, with full elimination of the provisions for years after 2010. However, as previously mentioned in the preface to this book, at the time of this writing, all of the provisions of the 2001 Tax Act (including this phase-out reduction provision) are set to expire as of 2011 due the Act's rather unique "sunset clause."

Note, that for Irv and Lorraine, both their *personal exemption deductions* were phased-out (most likely eliminated) as discussed in problem 4, above, and their *itemized deductions* were reduced, in this problem 5. The two phase-out provisions are completely separate but often both apply to individuals with high-income levels.

Answer (a) is incorrect because it does not reflect the phase-out or reduction of *itemized deductions* pursuant to IRC § 68, as discussed above. **Answer (c) is incorrect** because the couple *will* be entitled to some deduction, albeit reduced, from their charitable contributions. **Answer (d) is incorrect** because for our couple, and most individuals, charitable contributions do not give rise to *above the line* deductions (deductions from gross income in computing adjusted gross income (AGI)). In addition, this answer does not reflect the aforementioned IRC § 68 reduction or phase-out of their itemized deductions.

- **Additional references:** *See* DANIEL Q. POSIN, FEDERAL INCOME TAXATION OF INDIVIDUALS ¶ 7.01(1) (5th ed. 2000).

6. **The best answer is (b).** A deduction serves to reduce *taxable income*. Tax rates are then applied to *taxable income* in order to compute the amount of tax. Tax "credits" then serve to reduce the actual tax liability. In other words, tax credits are a "dollar for dollar" reduction in the amount of tax owed while a deduction only serves to reduce the amount of net income used to compute the tax. Because net income is not taxed at rates anywhere close to 100%, a credit is more valuable.

An illustration might be helpful. Suppose an individual has net or taxable income of $10,000 and, unrealistically, the tax rate is a flat 25%. Let us compare a $2,000 *deduction* with a $2,000 *credit*.

The Deduction
A $2,000 *deduction* would reduce net or taxable income to $8,000 ($10,000 less $2,000). Tax at 25% would be $2,000.

The Credit
Net or taxable income of $10,000 taxed at 25% is $2,500. A $2,000 *credit* would reduce this $2,500 tax by $2,000, resulting in a tax of only $500.

It should be noted that in some instances, an individual might have a choice of taking either a deduction or a credit for a particular item. Although very rare, in such instances a *deduction* may provide for greater overall tax savings when compared to a *credit*.

Answers (a) and (c) are incorrect as discussed above. **Answer (d) is not the best answer** because a credit does not necessarily represent previously paid taxes. Rather, many credits are for current year's expenditures for which a benefit, in the form of a credit, has been granted by the Code.

- **Additional references:** *See* DANIEL Q. POSIN, FEDERAL INCOME TAXATION OF INDIVIDUALS ¶ 10.01 (5th ed. 2000).

7. **The correct answer is (a).** Tax credits are usually quite beneficial to a taxpayer as they serve to reduce the taxpayer's actual tax liability (computed by applying the appropriate tax rates to a taxpayer's *taxable income*). Some tax credits are allowed only to the extent that they reduce tax liability to zero, and are referred to as "nonrefundable credits." In other words, these types of credits do not result in a refund to the taxpayer once tax liability has been reduced to zero. Other tax credits are not so limited and can generate a refund to the taxpayer notwithstanding a zero tax liability. This latter group of tax credits is referred to as "refundable" credits.

Most statutory provisions for "nonrefundable" credits for individuals are contained in Subpart A (of Subtitle A, Chapter 1, Subchapter A, Part IV), beginning IRC § 21 (Expenses for household and dependent care services necessary for gainful employment). Most statutory provisions for "refundable" credits for individuals are contained in Subpart C (of Subtitle A, Chapter 1, Subchapter A, Part IV), beginning IRC § 31 (Tax withheld on wages). IRC § 32 provides for the *earned income credit*, and this credit is "refundable." IRC § 25A contains provisions for the *lifetime learning credit* (and "hope" credit) and this credit is "nonrefundable."

Answers (b), (c), and (d) are all incorrect because they all incorrectly reflect, to some degree the "refundable" or "nonrefundable" nature of the two credits.

- **Additional references:** *See* DANIEL Q. POSIN, FEDERAL INCOME TAXATION OF INDIVIDUALS ¶ 10.01 (5th ed. 2000).

8. **The best answer is (c).** This question (and question 9 below) involves the "childcare" tax credit in IRC § 21. The scope of possible federal income tax issues to address in a semester's income tax course is huge and it is impossible to cover all issues in great depth. Coverage, in class, of the childcare credit ranges from no

mention of it to a full, in-depth analysis. Most likely, Baxter will be entitled to some amount of childcare credit for the amounts he pays for someone to come to his house to look after his daughter Celia.

Basically, IRC § 21 allows a <u>tax credit</u> (reduction of computed tax liability) for amounts paid for the care of certain qualifying individuals that enables the taxpayer to be "gainfully employed" (to work). While the determination of who constitutes a "qualifying individual" can be somewhat involved in certain situations, the most common qualifying individual is: "a dependent of the taxpayer who is under the age of 13 and with respect to whom the taxpayer is entitled to a deduction under section 151(c)." [IRC § 21(b)(1)(A).] Celia qualifies, as she is five years old and is Baxter's dependent (and he is entitled to claim her *personal exemption deduction* pursuant to IRC § 151(c)). Determining what qualifies as childcare expenses can also be much more complex than presented in our facts. Generally, however, they are costs to care for a child that enable the taxpayer to work. [IRC § 21(b)(2).] Baxter's payments for childcare would easily meet this requirement.

While exact numbers are not necessary to answer this question, the maximum amount of childcare expenses that qualify for this credit is $3,000 for one qualifying individual, or $6,000 for two or more qualifying individuals. [IRC § 21(c).] The actual credit, before limitations mentioned below, is equal to 35% of the childcare expenses (limited to the $3,000/$6,000 maximum). This 35% credit percentage is reduced for taxpayer's with adjusted gross income (AGI) in excess of $15,000. [IRC § 21(a)(2).] The actual reduction mechanism is a bit awkward, but the reduction in the credit percentage is gradual for individuals with AGI to $43,000. At that upper level of AGI, the credit percentage remains static at 20%. Therefore, individuals with AGI in excess of $43,000 are still entitled to a credit of 20% of their qualifying childcare expenses.

Based on the limited information that we have in this question, Baxter is entitled to some amount of childcare credit pursuant to IRC § 21.

It should be mentioned that the IRC § 21 childcare credit is a nonrefundable credit (it cannot reduce tax liability below zero resulting in an excess that is refunded to the taxpayer). Also, this credit, along with some other nonrefundable credits, may be otherwise limited for certain individuals. [IRC § 26(a)(1).] It also should be noted that the 2001 Tax Act amended this credit in ways that are generally favorable to taxpayers (qualifying amounts, credit percentages and reductions, etc.) and the discussion above reflects these changes. The changes made by the 2001 Tax Act were effective for years starting in 2002. The *"Job Creation and Worker Assistance Act of 2002"* made some technical changes to this IRC § 21 tax credit that are not applicable to the facts of this problem.

Answer (a) is incorrect. While the amount of the credit percentage declines as one's AGI increases, the credit percentage is not reduced below 20%. **Answer (b) is also incorrect.** A medical care component of childcare is not required for this tax credit. Had the costs actually been for Celia's health care needs, they might give rise to a deduction as a medical care expense under IRC § 213. **Answer (d) is also incorrect.** IRC § 262 provides that "unless expressly provided" in the Code, no deductions are allowed for personal, living and family expenses. While the childcare tax credit is not a deduction, the credit is expressly provided for in IRC § 21.

- **Additional references:** *See* DANIEL Q. POSIN, FEDERAL INCOME TAXATION OF INDIVIDUALS ¶ 10.02 (5th ed. 2000).

9.   **Answer (d) is correct.** This question (and question 8, above) involves the "child-care" tax credit in IRC § 21. The scope of possible federal income tax issues to address in a semester's income tax course is huge, and it is impossible to cover all of the issues in great depth. Coverage, in class, of the childcare credit ranges from no mention of it to a full, in-dept analysis.

Basically, IRC § 21 allows a <u>tax credit</u> (reduction of computed tax liability) for amounts paid for the care of certain qualifying individuals that enables the taxpayer to be "gainfully employed" (to work). While the determination of who constitutes a "qualifying individual" can be somewhat involved in certain situations, the most common qualifying individual is: "a dependent of the taxpayer who is under the age of 13 and with respect to whom the taxpayer is entitled to a deduction under section 151(c)." [IRC § 21(b)(1)(A).] Each of Gerri's three children qualify because they are all less than 13 years old and all three are Gerri's dependents (and she is entitled to claim each of their *personal exemption deductions* pursuant to IRC § 151(c)). Determining what qualifies as childcare expenses can also be much more complex than presented in our facts. Generally, however, they are costs to care for a child that enable the taxpayer to work. [IRC § 21(b)(2).] For "qualifying individuals" of the type described in this question (dependents under 13), costs for day care facilities can qualify as childcare expenses. To qualify, such a facility must "comply with all applicable laws and regulations of a State or unit of local government," and the "qualifying individual(s)" must regularly spend at least eight (8) hours each day in the taxpayer's household. [IRC §§ 21(b)(2)(C) and 21(b)(2)(B).] Gerri's costs for day care most likely qualify (it is assumed that the state licensed facility in our question complies with all applicable laws and that Gerri's three children regularly spend eight hours a day living at home with her.

The maximum amount of childcare expenses that qualify for this credit is $3,000 for one qualifying individual, or $6,000 for two or more qualifying individuals. [IRC § 21(c).] Gerri's expected day care costs of $4,000 per each of her three children will, pursuant to this provision, be limited to a maximum of $6,000 (the limit for two *or more* children). The actual credit, before limitations mentioned below, is equal to 35% of the childcare expenses (limited to the $3,000/$6,000 maximum). This 35% credit percentage is reduced for taxpayer's with adjusted gross income (AGI) in excess of $15,000. [IRC § 21(a)(2).] The actual reduction mechanism is a bit awkward, but the reduction in the credit percentage is gradual for individuals with AGI to $43,000. (The reduction in the credit percentage is 1% for each $2,000, or fraction thereof, that the taxpayer's AGI exceeds $15,000.) At that upper level of AGI, the credit percentage remains static at 20%. Therefore, individuals with AGI in excess of $43,000 are still entitled to a credit of 20% of their qualifying childcare expenses. Gerri's expected AGI of $45,000 would result in a credit percentage of 20%.

Based on Gerri's estimated numbers, her childcare tax credit, pursuant to IRC § 21, will be <u>$1,200</u> ($6,000 x 20%).

It should be mentioned that the IRC § 21 childcare credit is a nonrefundable credit (it cannot reduce tax liability below zero resulting in an excess that is refunded to the taxpayer). Also, this credit, along with some other nonrefundable credits, may be otherwise limited for certain individuals. [IRC § 26(a)(1).] It also should be noted that the 2001 Tax Act amended this credit in ways that are generally favorable to taxpayers (qualifying amounts, credit percentages and reductions, etc.) and the discussion above reflects these changes. The changes made by the 2001 Tax Act were effective for years starting in 2002. The "*Job Creation and Worker Assistance Act of 2002*" made some technical changes to this IRC § 21 tax credit that are not applicable to the facts of this problem.

Answer (a) is incorrect. This number is incorrectly derived as follows: $4,000 costs (which should be limited) x 3 people (credit limit is same for 2 or more) x 20% (the correct credit percentage. **Answer (b) is also incorrect.** This number is incorrectly derived as follows: $3,000 costs (correctly limited) x 2 people (correctly limited) x 35% (the incorrect full credit percentage not allowed because of Gerri's AGI). **Answer (c) is also incorrect.** This number is incorrectly derived as follows: $3,000 costs (correctly limited) x 3 (credit limit is same for 2 or more) x 20% (the correct credit percentage). **Answer (e) is incorrect** because a correct answer (d) is presented.

- **Additional references:** *See* DANIEL Q. POSIN, FEDERAL INCOME TAXATION OF INDIVIDUALS ¶ 10.02 (5th ed. 2000).

10. **The correct answer is (a).** This question involves the "adoption expense" tax credit in IRC § 23. The scope of possible federal income tax issues to address in a semester's income tax course is huge, and it is impossible to cover all other issues in great depth. Coverage, in class, of the adoption tax credit ranges from no mention of it to a more comprehensive analysis.

Basically, IRC § 23 allows a <u>tax credit</u> (reduction of computed tax liability) for amounts paid for certain costs associated with adopting an eligible individual. Qualified costs include reasonable and necessary adoption fees, court costs, attorney fees and other expenses that are directly related to the legal adoption of an eligible individual. [IRC § 23(d).] An eligible individual is generally a child under 18 or who is physically or mentally incapable of caring for himself or herself. There is another category of eligible individuals identified as "special needs" children. Most likely, all of Sonia's adoption related costs listed above would be considered qualified costs. In addition, her new son Adam is an eligible individual.

The basic adoption tax credit is the amount of qualifying costs paid with respect to the adoption up to a maximum of $10,000. [IRC § 23(a)(1).] This $10,000 maximum is indexed for inflation for years after 2002. [IRC § 23(h).] While not applicable in our case, there are slightly different rules relating to adoptions of "special needs" individuals that apply starting in 2003. Like many other tax benefits, this adoption credit "phases-out" or is reduced if the taxpayer has too much income. While not necessary to answer this question, the phase-out begins $150,000 of adjusted gross income (AGI) as modified (by items not pertinent to our facts). [IRC § 23(b)(2).] This $150,000 threshold is also indexed for inflation for years after 2002. The mechanism for computing this "phase-out" is rather complex and need not be discussed with specificity for our problem. Any possible adoption credit is fully "phased-out" (i.e., eliminated) for individuals with AGI (as modified) of $190,000 (adjusted for inflation for years after 2002) or more. Sonia should be entitled to some amount of adoption credit for her adoption related costs assuming her income is not at levels that preclude the tax credit.

It should be noted that there are many issues relating to the adoption credit in IRC § 23 that are not pertinent to our somewhat basic problem on the subject. It should also be mentioned that the IRC § 23 adoption credit is a nonrefundable credit (it cannot reduce tax liability below zero resulting in an excess that is refunded to the taxpayer). Also, this credit, along with some other nonrefundable credits, may be otherwise limited for certain individuals. [IRC § 26(a)(1).] It also should be noted that the 2001 Tax Act amended this credit in ways that are generally favorable to taxpayers (qualifying amounts and threshold) and the above discussion reflects these changes. The changes made by the 2001 Tax Act were effective for years starting in 2002. The "*Job Creation and Worker Assistance Act of 2002*" made some technical changes to this IRC § 23 tax credit that are not applicable to the facts of this problem.

Answer (b) is incorrect. This credit was set to expire at the end of 2001, except as it applied to adoptions of "special needs" individuals. However, the 2001 Tax Act reinstated this credit (and made it more favorable to taxpayers) effective for the 2002 tax year. For adoption of "special needs" individuals, starting in 2003, special (and more beneficial rules) might be applicable for certain taxpayers. **Answer (c) is incorrect** because the answer reflects the prior law's (before 2002) $5,000 limit for qualifying adoption expenses. The pre-2002 limit for adoption of "special needs" individuals was $6,000. **Answer (d) is also incorrect.** As discussed above, IRC § 23 *does* provide a potential credit for adoption related costs. It should be noted that the latter part of this answer, regarding exclusion from income of employer provided adoption costs, is correct under certain conditions and is governed by IRC § 137.

- **Additional references:** *See* DANIEL Q. POSIN, FEDERAL INCOME TAXATION OF INDIVIDUALS ¶ 10.03 (5th ed. 2000).

11. **The best answer is (b).** The area of retirement and pension accounts is vast and an in-depth discussions is well beyond the scope of this book. This question is designed to address some of the basic points relating to one form of retirement accounts: the Individual Retirement Account or IRA.

There are many varieties of individual retirement accounts (IRA's) including traditional IRA's, Roth IRA's, SEP IRA's, and Coverdell Education Savings Accounts (formerly Education IRA's). The traditional IRA (the oldest in the IRA family) is the subject of this question. An IRA is an individuals own personal retirement plan. IRA's have been around for some time, and while the rules and restrictions associated with them have changed many times, the basic concept of them has remained the same. Put money into an IRA now while working, and get a tax deduction for the contribution. The money in the IRA is invested and its earnings are not currently subject to tax (so called "tax free compounding"). Funds are withdrawn from the IRA years later (at retirement). While these later withdrawals are fully taxable, the taxpayer has received the benefit of the "time value of money" along with the advantage of the "tax-free" accumulations in the account. In addition, at the time of withdrawals, the taxpayer is hopefully in a lower income tax bracket (or tax rates have declined). All in all, it makes for a nice deal. However, there are various restrictions and limitations regarding their use and availability. IRC § 219 is the principal section with respect to "traditional" IRA's,

First there is a specific dollar limitation for contributions to an IRA. The amounts vary depending on the year and one's age. For years prior to 2002, the general annual contribution limit was $2,000. The 2001 Tax Act increases this amount to $3,000 for 2002 through 2004, $4,000 for 2005 through 2007, and $5,000 for 2008 and thereafter (with qualification for years after 2010 because of the 2001 Tax Act's "sunset clause"). For individuals 50 and older, there are additional "catch-up" contribution amounts.

The above contribution limits also serve as the maximum deduction amounts for such contributions. The deduction for contributions is fairly simple for an individual (or his or her spouse) who is <u>not</u> a participant in some other qualified employer-sponsored retirement/pension plan. For such individuals, the maximum deduction, in any particular year, is the applicable maximum amount listed above, or the individual's compensation for the year, whichever is less. Unfortunately, these simple deduction rules will not apply to Justin, as he *is* a participant in his company's pension/retirement plan.

If the individual (or his or her spouse) *is* an active participant in a qualified employer-sponsored retirement/pension plan, then the amount of the contribution to an IRA that is deductible may be reduced or eliminated depending on the amount of the taxpayer's adjusted gross income (AGI). As with many other tax benefits, the maximum deductible contribution is "phased-out" (reduced or eliminated) as the level of an individual's income increases. The mechanism of the phase-out for deductible IRA contributions is somewhat complex and the threshold amounts where the phase-out begin and end vary considerably depending on the year, the taxpayer's filing status, and other factors. To give an example, for a single individual in 2002, the phase-out of the deduction for contributions to an IRA begin at AGI levels of $34,000 and the deduction is completely phased-out (i.e., eliminated) for individuals with AGI of $44,000 or more. Justin, in our problem, is a participant in his company's pension/retirement plan, so depending on his AGI, his deductions for contributions to an IRA may be reduced or eliminated. Discussed elsewhere in this book, deductions for "alimony" *are* reflected in the determination of an individual's AGI. Therefore, for IRA contribution deduction purposes, Justin's alimony payments to his ex-wife, Ellen are beneficial (they serve to reduce his AGI and thereby increasing the possibility of some deduction for IRA contributions).

It should be noted that for participants in qualified employer-sponsored pension/retirement plans whose deduction for IRA contributions are reduced or eliminated, contributions can still be made to a "traditional" IRA (subject to the contribution limits previously discussed). There is no immediate tax benefit in such cases and upon withdrawal form the IRA, different tax treatment results.

It should be noted that in addition to the limits and restrictions mentioned above, the timing of withdrawals from an IRA is restricted and severe penalties can apply for noncompliance.

It should also be noted that not all IRA's have the same basic theme as the "traditional" IRA. For example, the Roth IRA is, to some degree, a reversal of the traditional rules – no deduction for current contributions, but the later withdrawals are tax-free.

Answer (a) is incorrect because participation in such a company plan does not necessarily preclude deductible contributions to an IRA. Rather, as discussed above, the deduction may be allowed to some degree depending on the individual's AGI. **Answer (c) is incorrect** because Justin's alimony payments are relevant. They serve to reduce his AGI, which is the determining factor for deductible contributions in his case. **Answer (d) is incorrect** because while there has been discussion about eliminating the restriction of participation in other plans for purposes of deductible IRA contributions, this has not happened as of this writing. It is interesting to note that for a period of time some years ago, this was not a restricting factor for deductible IRA contributions.

- **Additional references:** *See* DANIEL Q. POSIN, FEDERAL INCOME TAXATION OF INDIVIDUALS ¶ 8.04(4) (5th ed. 2000).

12. **The correct answer is (a).** As indicated in the analysis of question 11, above, the area of retirement plans, including the numerous varieties of individual retirement accounts (IRA's) is very complex. This question is designed to illustrate a few basic rules applicable to "traditional" IRA's. IRC § 219 is the primary section applicable to "traditional" IRA's.

As indicated in the analysis of question 11, above, there are various restrictions and limitations relating to contributions and deductions for IRA's. First, there is a specific dollar limitation for contributions to an IRA. The amounts vary depending on the year and one's age. For years prior to 2002, the general annual contribution limit was $2,000. The 2001 Tax Act increases this amount to $3,000 for 2002 through 2004, $4,000 for 2005 through 2007, and $5,000 for 2008 and thereafter (with qualification for years after 2010 because of the 2001 Tax Act's "sunset clause"). For individuals 50 and older, there are additional "catch-up" contribution amounts. Our problem is set in the year 2003 and the maximum contribution that Ellen could make to an IRA would be $3,000.

The above contribution limits also serve as the maximum deduction amounts for such contributions. The deduction for contributions is fairly simple for an individual (or his or her spouse) who is <u>not</u> a participant in some other qualified employer-sponsored retirement/pension plan. For such individuals, the maximum deduction in any particular year is the applicable maximum amount listed above, or the individual's compensation for the year, whichever is less. These are the rules that are applicable to Ellen because she is not a participant in any other pension or retirement plan. At first glance, one may think that while the maximum deduction in 2003 is $3,000, Ellen's compensation of only $1,500 would limit her deduction to that amount. Fortunately, for Ellen, alimony received (and includible in income as is the case here) is considered "compensation" for purposes of determining deductible IRA contributions. [IRC 219(f)(1).] Therefore, Ellen could be entitled to a full $3,000 deduction (in 2003) for her contribution of that amount to a "traditional" IRA.

Because Ellen is not a participant in a company-sponsored retirement/pension plan, we need not be concerned with possible reductions or elimination of the IRA contribution deduction based on the amount of her AGI.

It should be noted that in addition to the limits and restrictions mentioned above, the timing of withdrawals from an IRA is restricted and severe penalties can apply for noncompliance.

It should also be noted that not all IRA's have the same basic theme as the "traditional" IRA. For example, the Roth IRA is, to some degree, a reversal of the traditional rules – no deduction for current contributions, but the later withdrawals are tax-free.

Answer (b) is incorrect because the alimony she receives is also considered compensation for determining deductible contribution limits. **Answer (c) is incorrect** because the amount of her AGI is irrelevant as she is <u>not</u> a participant in another qualified pension/retirement plan. **Answer (d) is incorrect** because full-time employment is not a requirement for deductible IRA contributions.

- **Additional references:** *See* DANIEL Q. POSIN, FEDERAL INCOME TAXATION OF INDIVIDUALS ¶ 8.04(4) (5th ed. 2000).

13. **The most accurate answer is (b).** This is a rather difficult question and may be unanswerable depending on the depth of coverage of certain tax concepts; namely the concepts of "depreciation" and "depreciation recapture." Only after eliminating the possible application of "depreciation recapture" rules can we come to our conclusion that Lucinda's gain from the sale of the property will be a "long-term capital gain."

We do not know the exact amount of Lucinda's realized gain in this problem, but such gain will be recognized. [IRC § 1001(c).] The primary focus of this question is the character of this gain – it is "ordinary income" which is part of the taxpayer's taxable income and taxed at applicable regular income tax rates, or is it accorded "long-term capital gain treatment?" *Long-term capital gains* are included in the taxpayer's taxable income, but if the taxpayer has net *long-term capital gain* (after netting with other capital gains and losses), such gain may be taxed at more favorable (lower) tax rates. [IRC § 1(h).] *Long-term capital gains* are good things when compared to ordinary income. A capital gain analysis requires first determining that we are dealing with a "capital asset" after which, the gain is characterized as having either long-term or short-term status.

IRC § 1221(a) defines a capital asset in a negative fashion but for purposes of this analysis, it includes, by process of elimination, assets held for investment and personal-use purposes. There is little question that Lucinda's rental residence qualifies as a capital asset. Long-term status is reserved for those assets held for more than one year (short-term status for those assets held one year or less). [See IRC § 1222.] Lucinda's purchase of the property "about four years ago" clearly confers "long-term" status to the gain. Although ultimately this is the end result, Lucinda's gain is a *long-term capital gain*, we need to address a few other issues before we can conclude that this is, indeed, the correct answer.

Each year that Lucinda owned the property, she claimed "depreciation" deductions. She benefited from these deductions in prior years as they reduced her net income from the rental activities. These depreciation deductions also reduced her basis (adjusted basis or AB) in the property (IRC § 1016) that, in turn, created a greater gain when sold (gain measured by her selling price less her AB). While this may seem like a wash; deductions in earlier years traded for a larger gain in a later year, Lucinda most likely benefited from this situation. Her depreciation deductions reduced "ordinary" income (thus reducing her tax at regular tax rates) and she benefited from these deductions in earlier years. While she has a larger gain now, when the property is sold, she had the benefit of the use of the taxes saved because of the depreciation deductions. In other words, she benefited from the "time value of money" delaying income to later years. In addition, this larger gain now is favorably taxed *long-term capital gain*. Getting deductions offsetting ordinary income in earlier years in exchange for *long-term capital gain* income in later years is generally a good deal for taxpayers. There is a provision in the law, however, that can affect this later preferential capital-gain treatment and it is known as "depreciation recapture."

Basically, *depreciation recapture*, if it applies, requires that some of the gain that would otherwise be favorable *long-term capital gain*, be reclassified as *ordinary income*. Some of the depreciation taken in prior years is effectively "recaptured" as ordinary income when the property is sold. The *depreciation recapture* provision for real estate is IRC § 1250 (different provisions apply to depreciable personal property). While the rules vary based on numerous factors, the basic theme is that the amount of *depreciation recapture* (the amount of gain classified as *ordinary income*) is a certain percentage of "additional" depreciation that has been deducted by the taxpayer over the years. Depreciation methods are numerous and are very complex, varying by the type and use of assets. Some methods of depreciation are considered favorable or accelerated in that they produce greater depreciation deductions in the early years of the assets use. "Additional" or extra depreciation is this total amount of accelerated depreciation deductions that are in excess of what would have been the total depreciation calculated under a straight pro-rata (or "straight-line") method. How does this apply to our situation? If Lucinda deducted depreciation utilizing a method that accelerated these deductions, then some of her otherwise *long-term capital* gain will be "recaptured" as ordinary income. To make this determination, we need to know what methods of depreciation were available to Lucinda with respect to her rental property.

Over the years, the tax laws have changed many times regarding allowable depreciation. To act as an economic incentive, sometimes the laws have changed to allow shorter depreciation periods for assets and more accelerated methods for computing depreciation. At other times, because of fiscal restraints, depreciation periods have been lengthened and methods producing less acceleration of deductions to earlier years. Lucinda's purchase of the rental property about four years ago places her firmly in the period utilizing a depreciation convention known as the "Modified Accelerated Cost Recovery System" or "MACRS." This system has basically been in place for years after 1986 (it replaced the "Accelerated Cost Recovery System" or "ACRS"). IRC § 168 spells out most of the provisions for MACRS depreciation (although oddly, the statute still uses the term Accelerated Cost Recovery System). Under MACRS, "residential rental real estate" as in Lucinda's rental property, is depreciated over 27.5 years. [IRC § 168(c).] More importantly for our purpose, such property **must** use the "straight-line" method of depreciation. [IRC § 168(b)(3).] What does all this mean for our situation? Lucinda had to have been using the "straight-line" method of depreciation with respect to her rental property. Straight-line depreciation is **not** an accelerated method and, therefore, no "additional" or extra depreciation is created for recapture purposes. Phew!

The bottom line is that all of Lucinda's gain from the sale of her rental property is *long-term capital gain*. The IRC § 1250 *depreciation recapture* provisions do not apply to her, as the depreciation deductions with respect to her property could not have been determined using any sort of accelerated method (thus creating no "additional" or extra recapturable depreciation). Phew!

Answer (a) is incorrect because, as discussed above, Lucinda's rental property qualifies as a capital asset generating a *long-term capital gain* and not *ordinary* income. **Answer (c) is also incorrect.** This would be a logical answer that could not be eliminated as incorrect without a fair amount of knowledge about depreciation methods. The only available method of depreciation for Lucinda's residential rental real estate was the "straight-line" method. This, in turn, does not create any amount of recapturable depreciation, as discussed above. **Answer (d) is incorrect** because the nonrecognition rules applying to houses only apply to a taxpayer's <u>principal residence</u> and not to rental properties.

- **Additional references:** *See* DANIEL Q. POSIN, FEDERAL INCOME TAXATION OF INDIVIDUALS ¶ 4.06(3) (5th ed. 2000).

14. **The best answer is (d).** Like problem 13, above, this question is a bit difficult and may be unanswerable depending on the depth of coverage of certain tax concepts; namely the concepts of "depreciation" and "depreciation recapture." We will conclude that because the furniture is considered "section 1245" property, Lucinda must recapture, as *ordinary* income, the total amount of her depreciation deductions taken with respect to the property.

As indicated in the previous question, *depreciation recapture* provisions are designed to prevent the effective conversion of *ordinary* income (depreciation deductions reducing *ordinary* income) into favorably treated *long-term capital gain* income. The *depreciation recapture* rules vary depending on the nature of the property depreciated and, in some instances, the method of depreciation. Most real property, as Lucinda's rental house in the previous problem, invokes the *depreciation recapture* rules of IRC § 1250. Those rules generally require recapture of only a certain portion of the depreciation taken by the taxpayer (accelerated or "additional" amounts when compared with "straight-line" depreciation). The rules regarding most "personal" property (not personal-use property which is not subject to depreciation, but property other than "real" property) are different and are governed by IRC § 1245. Basically, this section required that the total amount of **all** depreciation taken with respect to such property (regardless of method) is recapturable as ordinary income. [IRC § 1245.] While there are additional issues involving IRC § 1245, the facts of this question requires us to go no further in our analysis.

Lucinda's business furniture is personal property to which IRC § 1245 is applicable. In her sale situation, she is required to recapture as *ordinary* income, the total amount of her depreciation deductions taken with respect to the furniture.

Answer (a) is incorrect because unlike IRC § 1250 that is applicable to most real property, IRC § 1245 recapture (applicable here) does not apply only to excess or accelerated depreciation deductions. Rather, as discussed above, it is more inclusive and generally recaptures all depreciation taken. **Answer (b) is incorrect** because IRC § 1245 *is* applicable regardless to individuals. **Answer (c) is also incorrect.** While it is well beyond the scope of this question, the sale of business assets, such as Lucinda's furniture, can give rise to *capital gain* income. See IRC § 1231.

- **Additional references:** *See* DANIEL Q. POSIN, FEDERAL INCOME TAXATION OF INDIVIDUALS ¶ 4.06(3) (5th ed. 2000).

15. **The best answer is (e).** This question involves the subject that is commonly referred to as the "home office" deduction. Concerned with tax abuses relating to deductions associated with one's personal residence, IRC § 280A was enacted. IRC § 280A covers issues relating to "home offices" as well as "vacation" homes (also perceived as an area of tax abuse). While IRC § 280A does permit business deductions for certain home related expenses under certain qualifying circumstances, the nature of Professor Colleen's work at home will not give rise to business deductions for rent or other operating costs for her home.

Taxpayers are not entitled to deduct as business expenses, any costs of operating their home unless the expense is attributable "to a portion of the dwelling unit which is *exclusively used on a regular basis*:
  (A) as the *principal place of business* for any trade or business of the taxpayer,
  (B) as a place of business which is used by patients, clients, or customers in meeting or dealing with the taxpayer in the normal course of his trade or business, or
  (C) in the case of a separate structure which is not attached to the dwelling unit, in connection with the taxpayer's trade or business." [IRC § 280A(c)(1) (emphasis added).]

For employees, the statute also requires that the business use of the home must be for the convenience of the employer. [IRC § 280A(c)(1).]

Professor Colleen would have problems with these requirements on many levels. First, there would be a problem with the requirement that "a portion of the dwelling unit which is exclusively used on a regular basis." This means that the taxpayer generally must regularly use a *specific* or *designated* portion of the house for business purposes. Working in the family/TV room and their bedroom would not qualify. Next, is the difficult issue of whether she is using her home as her "principal place of business." While there are many interpretive rules regarding this requirement, suffice it to say that Professor Colleen's use of her home as her "principal place of business" would be a stretch. Lastly, as an employee, she would have to show that her working at home is for the convenience of her employer. The only indication that we have from the facts is that working at home is solely for Professor Colleen's convenience.

Therefore, for all three of the reasons discussed, Professor Colleen would be precluded from deducting, as business expenses, for any portion of her rent or other operating costs of her home.

Answer (a) is not the best answer because the failure to use a specific portion of the house on an exclusive and regular basis is not the sole reason for denying deductions. **Answer (b) is incorrect** because merely documenting the time she spends working at home will not be sufficient to generate business deductions for the operating costs of her home. **Answer (c) is not the best answer** because the fact that her working at home is not for the convenience of her employer, is not the sole reason for denying deductions. **Answer (d) is incorrect**. Even if she could show that her working at home was for the convenience of her employer, she would still not qualify for deductions because of the other requirements discussed above.

- **Additional references:** *See* DANIEL Q. POSIN, FEDERAL INCOME TAXATION OF INDIVIDUALS ¶ 6.02(10) (5th ed. 2000).

16. **Answer (b) is correct.** This question raises the very complex issue of the "alternative minimum tax" or AMT. Both in concept and real-world application, the many complex aspects of the AMT can be intimidating and extremely difficult to compute. The study of the AMT varies considerably among law school tax courses: from no mention at all, to a full-blown, in-depth analysis of its provisions and method of computation. For this book, the author has chosen to merely introduce the subject and forego analysis of the many in-depth, analytical rules. This choice was made primarily to leave room for the host of other tax issues that require discussion. The author acknowledges that this level of coverage may be disappointing for those students whose professor more fully covers the AMT in class.

The AMT is a separate calculation of an individual's income tax (using special rates) that is based not on regular *taxable income* but, rather, "alternative minimum taxable income." If the individual's resulting tax utilizing the AMT computations is **greater** than the individual's income tax computed by traditional means, the taxpayer will pay (as a forced alternative) the higher amount. [IRC § 55.] Technically, the amount by which the AMT exceeds the taxpayer's regularly computed tax is an addition to the taxpayer's regular tax. The word "minimum," in "alternative minimum tax" does not have a favorable meaning to the taxpayer and the AMT is not a good thing for taxpayers.

The impetus for the AMT was to prevent taxpayers with "high" levels of income from paying too little income tax, because they took advantage of too many favorable benefits accorded them under the law. The "alternative" tax that such individuals are required to pay at a "minimum" is based on a modification of the taxpayer's *taxable income*. Basically, there are certain items (usually deductions) that are considered "tax preference" items, and if the taxpayer, in computing *taxable income*, has benefited from them, then they will be reflected (in an unfavorable manner) in determining the basis for computing the AMT. In addition, there are certain AMT adjustments that substitute an AMT treatment of a particular item for that item reflected using regular income tax rules. Tax preference items and AMT adjustments encompass such things as depreciation and depletion, certain tax exempt interest, intangible drilling costs, various *itemized deductions*, "passive losses," and many others. As of this writing, Congress was discussing modifications to the scope of AMT tax preference items and its application to certain taxpayers.

Answers (a), (c) and (d) are all incorrect because they do not reflect the nature of the alternative minimum tax.

- **Additional references:** *See* DANIEL Q. POSIN, FEDERAL INCOME TAXATION OF INDIVIDUALS ¶ 7.05 (5th ed. 2000).

17. **The best answer is (c).** This question addresses an income tax doctrine known as the "tax benefit rule." Basically stated, when a taxpayer recovers an amount that was deducted (or credited) in an earlier year, the recovery is included in the taxpayer's gross income in the current year <u>unless, and to the extent</u> the deduction (or credit) did <u>not</u> benefit the taxpayer (reducing his or her tax) in the earlier year. [IRC § 111.] In our facts, if the medical costs Victor incurred and paid last year *benefited him* (reduced his *taxable income*, which, in turn, reduced his income tax) the recovery (to the extent it served to reduce his *taxable income*) will be income in this year. However, if these costs did not benefit him last year tax-wise, the recovery will not be included in income this year.

There is little doubt that Victor's hospital costs were "qualified medical care expenses" pursuant to IRC § 213. Whether his costs qualify as medical care expense is not really at issue in the question. Rather, "how" and "where" these medical care expenses were deductible *is the primary issue*. Figuring out *how* and *where* these expenses were deductible will determine if Victor *benefited* by their deduction (which in turn, determines whether he has to include their refund in gross income in the current year).

The first stop is IRC § 213 itself. A "deduction" for qualified *medical care expenses* is allowed only to the extent that total qualifying expenses for the year exceed 7.5% of adjusted gross income (AGI). Therefore, if Victor's total qualifying medical care expenses last year did not exceed 7.5% of his AGI, he would not have benefited from these expenditures and, therefore, the refund would not be include in his income for this year. However, to the extent his qualifying medical care expenses last year *did* exceed 7.5% of his AGI, we have to continue to the next step of our analysis to see if he benefited from the deduction.

Deducted medical care expenses (those in excess of 7.5% of a taxpayer's AGI) are part of a larger group of deductions known collectively as "itemized deductions." This group of *itemized deductions* also includes such items as deductible taxes (IRC § 164), deductible interest (IRC § 163), charitable deductions (IRC § 170), casualty losses (IRC § 165(h)), and "miscellaneous itemized" deductions (certain IRC § 162 and IRC § 212 deductions). Many of these items that make up *itemized deductions* contain their own "percentage of AGI" floor or ceiling to determine deductibility. In addition, other provisions in the Code may reduce this entire group of itemized deductions. [IRC § 68.] When computing an individual's *taxable income* this group of *itemized deductions* is compared to another major deduction known as the "standard deduction." While other questions in this book explore the *standard deduction* in greater detail, every individual is entitled to a *standard deduction* of some amount (it varies depending on numerous factors). An individual **takes the greater of: the *standard deduction* or *total allowed itemized deductions*** in computing taxable income.

Looking at Victor's situation for last year, in order for him to have benefited from his medical care costs they first would have had to exceed 7.5% of his AGI to make it into the group of *itemized deductions* (and then only the amount exceeding this 7.5% of AGI floor). And then, this entire group of *itemized deductions* (as adjusted if necessary) would have had to exceed Victor's standard deduction. Only to the extent that his medical care expenses made it over both of these hurdles, must Victor include their refund in his income for this year.

[Please see Appendix A for more information on how income and deductions fit together in computing taxable income and AGI. There are also series of questions in this book that explore the comprehensive nature of taxable income.]

Answer (a) is incorrect because the answer fails to recognize the second "hurdle" that Victor's total *itemized deductions* exceeded his *standard deduction*. **Answer (b) is incorrect** because it fails to recognize the first "hurdle" that Victor could have benefited from his medical care costs only to the extent that they exceeded 7.5% of his AGI. **Answer (d) is incorrect** because that is not how the statute deals with this issue. **Answer (e) is incorrect** because the statute does not allow for this choice in handling this issue.

- **Additional references:** *See* DANIEL Q. POSIN, FEDERAL INCOME TAXATION OF INDIVIDUALS ¶¶ 9.02(3) (5th ed. 2000).

18. **The best answer is (e).** The general statute of limitations for an individual amending a prior return to claim a refund or credit is the <u>later</u> of:
    - ➤ Three years from the date the return was filed (or the due date of the return if the return was filed before the due date), or
    - ➤ Two years from the date the tax was paid.

The facts indicate that Elaine has consistently filed her income tax returns on a timely basis. In fact, she consistently files them at least one month prior to the regular April 15th due date for income tax returns. Applying the rule that is applicable to Elaine (the first of the two listed above), she can file amended returns for any years' returns where the due date for filing such returns was in the last three years. The distinction between "filing dates" and "due dates" can be critical. Note that Elaine's "open" period is actually longer than three years from the actual filing dates of her returns.

After a careful reading of the applicable section (IRC § 6511(a)), students logically come away with a different answer, namely (d). IRC § 6511(a) states, in part, that the taxpayer has the later of "3 years from the *time the return was filed*, or 2 years from the time the tax was paid" in which to file a claim for refund or credit (an amended return). With not so much as a clue in IRC §6511, another Code section, IRC § 6513, indicates that for purposes of IRC § 6511, a return that is actually filed before its due date (as is the case for Elaine's prior returns) is considered filed on the due date. This is the reason for the parenthetical comment appearing above in the first of the two rules listed.

Although not required for this question, the appropriate form for most individuals for filing an amended income tax return is *Form 1040X*.

Answer (a) is not the best answer. While it is true that unclaimed benefits in a prior year cannot be claimed in the current year, this answer does not provide the possibility of amending prior income tax returns to claim the missed benefit. **Answer (b) is also not the best answer.** This answer is partially correct but it does not contain necessary information about the periods for which amended returns can be filed. **Answer (c) is incorrect** because claiming the benefits in the current year is not a valid option. **Answer (d) is also incorrect.** This is the most commonly selected answer because it appears to reflect the rules of IRC § 6513. However, IRC § 6511 indicates that if the returns are filed prior to their due dates, the due dates are considered the time of filing for purposes of the three year general rule for filing amended returns.

19.   **The correct answer is (a).** This is a tax procedure question that may or may not be covered in depth in your federal income tax class. However, basic knowledge of the court system, as it relates to federal tax issues, is important if not for anything more than making jurisdictional sense of the cases that you may read. This professor seems to recall learning in the first-year law school civil procedure course that individuals are generally precluded from "forum shopping." This, generally, is not the case with respect to federal tax matters. Most court actions, regarding an individual federal income tax matter, can be brought by the taxpayer in either: 1) the U.S. Tax Court, 2) the U.S. District Court (in the jurisdiction in which the taxpayer resides), or 3) the U.S. Court of Federal Claims (located in Washington D.C.). All three of these "trial" courts generally have "subject matter jurisdiction" with respect to federal income tax issues for individuals.

While not required for this question, the requirements, procedural matters, and adjudication options differ between these three courts. See question 20, below, for a discussion of one such difference.

Answers (b), (c) and (d) are incorrect because all, to varying degrees, identify or fail to identify valid courts in which Terrance can resolve his income tax issue. **Answer (e) is incorrect** because a correct response (a) is presented.

20.   **The best answer is (d).** As indicated in the analysis of question 19, above, an individual contesting a proposed federal income tax deficiency generally has three court options: U.S. Tax Court, U.S. District Court in which the taxpayer resides, and the U.S. Court of Federal Claims. The U.S. Tax Court is unique, among the options, in that the taxpayer need not pay the proposed assessment before litigating the matter. [See IRC § 6213 (regarding petitions to Tax Court).] If Terrance wishes to have his tax matter heard by either the U.S. District or the U.S. Court of Federal Claims, he must first pay the proposed assessment and sue for a refund.

While not required for this question, there are other requirements, procedural matters, and adjudication options that differ depending on the trial court chosen by the taxpayer in which to adjudicate the tax issue in question.

Answer (a) is incorrect because, as discussed above, petitioning to the U.S. Tax Court does not require that the taxpayer first pay the proposed assessment. **Answer (b) is incorrect** because, as discussed above, bringing issue to either the U.S. District Court or U.S. Court of Federal Claims requires that the taxpayer first pay the proposed assessment and then sue for a refund. **Answer (c) is incorrect** and represents an answer that is opposite that of the correct answer.

21.   **The best answer is (c).** An interesting bit of tax history, the first internal-revenue tax was imposed on distilled spirits and stills.

        Answers (a), (b), and (d) are each incorrect because they list items upon which Congress imposed taxes subsequently in order to garner additional revenue.

22.   **The correct answer is (d).** The Revenue Act of 1913 was the first piece of legislation to levy a tax upon individuals.

        Answer (a) is incorrect because the 16th Amendment permitted Congress to "lay and collect taxes on incomes, from whatever source derived." It did not actually impose a tax upon individuals but only allowed such a tax to be imposed. **Answer (b) is incorrect** because Article 1, § 8 of the Constitution merely authorizes Congress "to lay and collect taxes, duties, imposts and excises." It did not actually impose any tax, but only gave Congress this power. **Answer (c) is incorrect** because Article 1, § 9 of the Constitution requires that "direct taxes" be allocated to the states based upon their respective populations. A direct tax is one that is required to be paid by the specific members of the targeted tax group and cannot be shifted to others outside of the group.

23.   **Answer (a) is the most accurate.** Betty could claim that by imposing a tax based upon her income from previous years, Congress violated her Due Process rights under the 5th Amendment. However, the Court held in *Brushaber* that the Due Process clause does not pose such a restriction upon Congress. [*Brushaber v. Union Pac. R. Co.*, 240 U.S. 1, 36 S.Ct. 236 (1916).] Therefore, Congress is able to tax in a retrospective manner despite the taxpayer's lack of foresight that their income will be subjected to a tax in future years. So, Betty will not be successful in making such an argument.

        Answer (b) is incorrect because the Court in *Brushaber* specifically eliminated this argument in such situations. **Answer (c) is incorrect** because the 16th Amendment does not constrain Congress to tax only income earned during the current tax year. **Answer (d) is incorrect** because Congress is permitted to modify the tax structure and there are no restrictions placed upon this power.

24.   **The best answer is (b).** Although the 5th Amendment provides that "no person shall be compelled in any criminal case to be a witness against himself," self-incrimination does not apply with respect to the requirement that each taxpayer file a tax return. Therefore, even though Dave would incriminate himself if he were to file a proper tax return, which would disclose income received from illegal sources, he cannot claim that the 5th Amendment provides any protection in such a situation.

Answer (a) is incorrect because Dave would not prevail if he were to make such an argument since the privilege against self-incrimination does not apply to such a situation. **Answer (c) is incorrect** because the 16th Amendment requires that all income "from whatever source derived" be disclosed upon a tax return even if it is derived from illegal sources. **Answer (d) is incorrect** because state law is not a consideration in such a situation, but federal law governs in order to advance consistency in the application of tax laws from state to state.

25.   **Answer (b) is correct** because higher income individuals would save more under such a regressive structure. Since the consumption tax would simply impose a tax whenever goods are purchased, it would create a heavier burden on lower- and middle- class taxpayers, who would be forced to pay a greater portion of their lower incomes in the form of a tax. Therefore, such a tax has been criticized as unfair.

Answer (a) is incorrect because a consumption tax would actually simplify the administration of taxes by eliminating the various regulations that govern the current tax system. **Answer (c) is incorrect** because increased litigation has not been argued as a major concern. **Answer (d) is incorrect** because such a scheme would inhibit tax evasion since taxpayers would be forced to pay a tax upon purchase rather than being forced to determine the tax based on past events.

Appendix

Appendix A   Overview or framework of taxable income. How income and deductions fit together in computing taxable income and adjusted gross income (AGI).

Appendix B   Tax year 2002 year-specific information. Tax rates, standard deduction amounts, personal exemption deduction amounts, threshold levels for various tax provisions, etc.

Appendix C   "Code Math" – Almost everything you need to know about tax math.

Appendix A

Framework for Taxable Income
How Income and Deductions Fit Together in Computing Taxable Income

The computation of *taxable income* as well as *adjusted gross income (AGI)* requires knowledge of what is includible and excludable from a taxpayer's gross income, as well as what constitute deductible and nondeductible expenses. In addition, a key point in determining a taxpayer's *taxable income* or *AGI* is knowing **where** various deductions are taken. The following is a visual depiction of the *taxable income* and *AGI* calculations showing many of the most common elements of income, exclusion, and deductions. Please be aware that many of the elements listed below are subject to various limitations and restrictions that are discussed throughout the questions in this book.

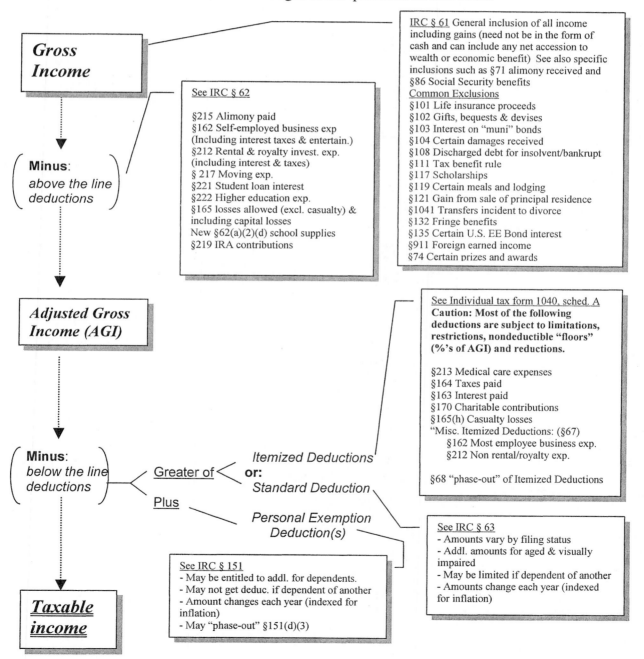

Gross Income

IRC § 61 General inclusion of all income including gains (need not be in the form of cash and can include any net accession to wealth or economic benefit) See also specific inclusions such as §71 alimony received and §86 Social Security benefits
Common Exclusions
§101 Life insurance proceeds
§102 Gifts, bequests & devises
§103 Interest on "muni" bonds
§104 Certain damages received
§108 Discharged debt for insolvent/bankrupt
§111 Tax benefit rule
§117 Scholarships
§119 Certain meals and lodging
§121 Gain from sale of principal residence
§1041 Transfers incident to divorce
§132 Fringe benefits
§135 Certain U.S. EE Bond interest
§911 Foreign earned income
§74 Certain prizes and awards

Minus:
above the line deductions

See IRC § 62

§215 Alimony paid
§162 Self-employed business exp (Including interest taxes & entertain.)
§212 Rental & royalty invest. exp. (including interest & taxes)
§ 217 Moving exp.
§221 Student loan interest
§222 Higher education exp.
§165 losses allowed (excl. casualty) & including capital losses
New §62(a)(2)(d) school supplies
§219 IRA contributions

Adjusted Gross Income (AGI)

Minus:
below the line deductions

Greater of — Itemized Deductions **or:** Standard Deduction

Plus — Personal Exemption Deduction(s)

See Individual tax form 1040, sched. A
Caution: Most of the following deductions are subject to limitations, restrictions, nondeductible "floors" (%'s of AGI) and reductions.

§213 Medical care expenses
§164 Taxes paid
§163 Interest paid
§170 Charitable contributions
§165(h) Casualty losses
"Misc. Itemized Deductions: (§67)
§162 Most employee business exp.
§212 Non rental/royalty exp.

§68 "phase-out" of Itemized Deductions

See IRC § 63
- Amounts vary by filing status
- Addl. amounts for aged & visually impaired
- May be limited if dependent of another
- Amounts change each year (indexed for inflation)

See IRC § 151
- May be entitled to addl. for dependents.
- May not get deduc. if dependent of another
- Amount changes each year (indexed for inflation)
- May "phase-out" §151(d)(3)

Taxable income

Appendix B

Tax Year 2002 – Year-Specific Information

Many Code items, that are pertinent to questions appearing in this book, vary from year to year. Some items, such as *personal exemption deductions* are "indexed for inflation" while others, such as the IRC § 222 deduction for certain "tuition and related expenses," change in certain years pursuant to statutory provisions. Some items, such as tax rates, will be changing each year due to both inflation indexing and statutory changes.

Some of the questions appearing in this book are year-specific. Of these, many are based upon the 2002 tax year, the most current year available at the time of this publication. These questions were included not, necessarily, for the purpose of covering specifically the 2002 tax year but, rather, to provide a computational or "real-world" foundation to explore certain income tax topics. These questions are easily adaptable to years subsequent to 2002.

Provided below, are most of the 2002 year-specific items that have been discussed with respect to questions presented in this book. Please see individual questions for more information about any particular item (and for those not listed).

The *Personal Exemption Deduction* for 2002 (and "Phase-Out" Ranges)

The IRC § 151(d)(1) amount for 2002 is $3,000 per person.

Pursuant to IRC § 151(d)(3), this deduction is "phased-out" over the following ranges:

$206,000 – $328,500 Married filing joint returns (& surviving spouses)
$171,650 – $294,150 Heads of Households
$137,300 – $259,800 Single Individuals
$103,000 – $164,250 Married individuals filing separately

The 2001 Tax Act made changes to this "phase-out" provisions (gradually eliminating it) for years starting in 2006. [See IRC § 151(c)(3)(E).]

The *Standard Deduction(s)* for 2002

Regular *standard deduction* amounts:

$7,850	Married individuals filing joint returns (& surviving spouses)
$6,900	Heads of Household
$4,700	Single individuals
$3,925	Married individuals filing separately

"Extra" *standard deduction* amounts (additions to above) for individuals 65 years of age and older, or severely visually impaired. [See IRC § 63(c)(3).]:

$ 900	Married individuals (& surviving spouses)
$1,150	Single individuals and Heads of Household

Restricted *standard deduction* for individuals who can be claimed as a dependent of another (and who's *personal exemption deduction* is allowable to such other person). [See IRC § 63(c)(5).]:

> The greater of (not to exceed *std deduction* without regard to this provision):
> 1) $750, or
> 2) The individual's "earned income" plus $250.

The IRC § 132(f) "Qualified Parking" Fringe Tax-Free Limit for 2002

The maximum allowed exclusion for 2002 is $185 per month of parking value.

IRC §221 Qualified Student Loan Interest Deduction for 2002

The maximum deduction allowed for 2002 and later years is $2,500.

The "phase-out" ranges of "modified adjusted gross income" (MAGI) for 2002 are:

> $50,000 – $65,000
> ($100,000 – $130,000 for joint filers)

The IRC § 222 Deduction for Certain Higher Education Costs for 2002

The maximum deduction for 2002 and 2003 is $3,000.

This deduction is available only to taxpayers with "modified adjusted gross income" (MAGI) of $65,000 or less ($130,000 or less for joint filers).

The maximum deduction allowed by this provision increases in 2004 and 2005, and for those years, there is a two-tier MAGI threshold calculation.

"Phase-Out" of Itemized Deductions Pursuant to IRC § 68 for 2002

The threshold of *adjusted gross income (AGI)* at which this "phase-out" begins is $137,300 ($68,650 for married filing separately).

"Phase-Out" of IRC § 135 U.S. Savings Bond Interest Used for Education for 2002

The "phase-out" range for the IRC § 135 exclusion for U.S. Savings Bonds used for higher education expenses is "modified adjusted gross income" (MAGI) between $57,600 and $72,600 (between $86,400 and $116,400 for joint filers).

TAX RATES FOR 2002

IRC § 1(a)(2) (Married filing joint returns and surviving spouses)

If **taxable** income is	The tax is
- Not over $12,000	10% of taxable income
- Over $12,000 but not over $46,700	$1,200 plus 15% of excess over $12,000
- Over $46,700 but not over $112,850	$6,405 plus 27% of excess over $46,700
- Over $112,850 but not over $171,950	$24,265.50 plus 30% of excess over $112,850
- Over $171,950 but not over $307,050	$41,995.50 plus 35% of excess over $171,950
- Over $307,050	$89,280.50 plus 38.6% of excess over $307,050

IRC § 1(b) (Head of household)

If **taxable** income is	The tax is
- Not over $10,000	10% of taxable income
- Over $10,000 but not over $37,450	$1,000 plus 15% of excess over $10,000
- Over $37,450 but not over $96,700	$5,117.50 plus 27% of excess over $37,450
- Over $96,700 but not over $156,600	$21,115 plus 30% of excess over $96,700
- Over $156,600 but not over $307,050	$39,085 plus 35% of excess over $156,600
- Over $307,050	$91,742.50 plus 38.6% of excess over $307,050

IRC § 1(c) (Unmarried individuals other than surviving spouse & head of households (i.e., this usually means **Single** individuals)

If **taxable** income is	The tax is
- Not over $6,000	10% of taxable income
- Over $6,000 but not over $27,950	$600 plus 15% of the excess over $6,000
- Over $27,950 but not over $67,700	$3,892.50 plus 27% of excess over $27,950
- Over $67,700 but not over $141,250	$14,625 plus 30% of excess over $67,700
- Over $141,250 but not over $307,050	$36,690 plus 35% of excess over $141,250
- Over $307,050	$94,720 plus 38.6% of excess over $307,050

IRC § 1(d) (Married filing separate returns)
Not reproduced. Rate bracket ranges are one-half those of joint filers (and surviving spouses) for the same applicable tax rate percentages.

Appendix C

Code Math – Almost Everything You Need to Know About Tax Math

Introduction

The study of federal income taxation does involve some math. However, the math utilized is <u>very basic</u> and should not be a source of concern for those of you who do not get excited at the sight of numbers. Actually, the only math skills necessary are those from the four basic "arithmetic" food groups: addition, subtraction, multiplication, and division.

If any difficulty should arise, it will probably not be with the math itself. Rather, it will be interpreting how and when the sections of the Internal Revenue Code ("Code") tell you to add, subtract, multiply and divide. The following is a summary of the necessary math concepts and some samples of how the language of the Code may signal you to use a particular math function.

<u>Addition</u>

Code language: "The sum of [X] plus [Y]."

This means: X + Y

For example, see IRC § 1001(b) discussing computation of "amount realized." It equals "the sum of any money received plus the fair market value of property (other than money) received."

<u>Subtraction</u>

Code language: "The excess of [X] over [Y]." It really should say: "The excess of [X], <u>if any</u>, over [Y]."

This means: X - Y. However, by definition, the result will not be a less than zero.

For example, see IRC § 1001(a) discussing gain realized from the sale of property as "the excess of the amount realized therefrom over the adjusted basis." This means the "amount realized" minus the "adjusted basis." A source of common confusion -- the word "over" in this context does **not** mean the fraction X divided by Y.

Multiplication

Code language: "[X] multiplied by [Y]" or, "the product of [X] and [Y]."

Both of these mean: X multiplied by Y.

For example, see IRC § 68(b)(2) discussing certain inflation adjustments re deductions ". . . shall be increased by an amount equal to -- (A) such dollar amount, multiplied by (B) the cost-of-living adjustment determined . . ."

Sometimes when the Code wants you to multiply something by a percentage, the language will read [X] percent of [Y]. This means [Y] multiplied by [X] percent.

The Code Ratios

This is probably the most dreaded math language of the Internal Revenue Code.

Code language (from IRC §1015(d)(6)(A)): "[The adjustment to basis] shall be an amount which bears the same ratio to the amount of tax so paid as -- (i) the net appreciation in value of the gift, bears to (ii) the amount of the gift."

Here you are solving for an unknown amount [adjustment to basis] which we will call **X**. Expressed in equation form, the above language means:

X / Amount of tax paid = The net appreciation in value of the gift / Amount of gift

Recalling high-school algebra may be uncomfortable, but with only one variable to solve for, the math is usually not too bad. There are various ways to solve for the unknown such as "simplifying the equation and then isolating **X** on one side, "cross-multiplying" (always a neat trick), and the like.

Other Combinations of Math Functions

It is very common that the Code will use a combination of the above math functions in one code provision. The key with these encounters is to make sure you perform each math function separately and in the correct order. These may sound tough at first, but once you see the pattern, it becomes easy.

For an example, see IRC § 68 which says ". . . the amount of the itemized deductions otherwise allowable for the taxable year shall be reduced by the lesser of: (1) 3 percent of the excess of adjusted gross income over the applicable amount, or (2) 80 percent of the amount of the itemized deductions otherwise allowable for such taxable year." This is telling you to first subtract the "applicable amount" from "adjusted gross income" and then (if the result is positive) multiply the result by three percent (.03). Once you have done that, you then must take the amount of "itemized deductions otherwise allowable" and multiply that by 80% (.80). You then take the lesser of those two calculations and subtract it from the amount of the "itemized deductions otherwise allowable."

WOW! Don't worry, it sounds much worse than it is.

Notes

Notes

Notes

Notes

Notes

ANSWER SHEET

	A B C D E		A B C D E		A B C D E		A B C D E		A B C D E
1	① ② ③ ④ ⑤	6	① ② ③ ④ ⑤	11	① ② ③ ④ ⑤	16	① ② ③ ④ ⑤	21	① ② ③ ④ ⑤
2	① ② ③ ④ ⑤	7	① ② ③ ④ ⑤	12	① ② ③ ④ ⑤	17	① ② ③ ④ ⑤	22	① ② ③ ④ ⑤
3	① ② ③ ④ ⑤	8	① ② ③ ④ ⑤	13	① ② ③ ④ ⑤	18	① ② ③ ④ ⑤	23	① ② ③ ④ ⑤
4	① ② ③ ④ ⑤	9	① ② ③ ④ ⑤	14	① ② ③ ④ ⑤	19	① ② ③ ④ ⑤	24	① ② ③ ④ ⑤
5	① ② ③ ④ ⑤	10	① ② ③ ④ ⑤	15	① ② ③ ④ ⑤	20	① ② ③ ④ ⑤	25	① ② ③ ④ ⑤

	A B C D E		A B C D E		A B C D E		A B C D E		A B C D E
1	① ② ③ ④ ⑤	6	① ② ③ ④ ⑤	11	① ② ③ ④ ⑤	16	① ② ③ ④ ⑤	21	① ② ③ ④ ⑤
2	① ② ③ ④ ⑤	7	① ② ③ ④ ⑤	12	① ② ③ ④ ⑤	17	① ② ③ ④ ⑤	22	① ② ③ ④ ⑤
3	① ② ③ ④ ⑤	8	① ② ③ ④ ⑤	13	① ② ③ ④ ⑤	18	① ② ③ ④ ⑤	23	① ② ③ ④ ⑤
4	① ② ③ ④ ⑤	9	① ② ③ ④ ⑤	14	① ② ③ ④ ⑤	19	① ② ③ ④ ⑤	24	① ② ③ ④ ⑤
5	① ② ③ ④ ⑤	10	① ② ③ ④ ⑤	15	① ② ③ ④ ⑤	20	① ② ③ ④ ⑤	25	① ② ③ ④ ⑤

ANSWER SHEET

	A B C D E		A B C D E		A B C D E		A B C D E		A B C D E
1	① ② ③ ④ ⑤	6	① ② ③ ④ ⑤	11	① ② ③ ④ ⑤	16	① ② ③ ④ ⑤	21	① ② ③ ④ ⑤
2	① ② ③ ④ ⑤	7	① ② ③ ④ ⑤	12	① ② ③ ④ ⑤	17	① ② ③ ④ ⑤	22	① ② ③ ④ ⑤
3	① ② ③ ④ ⑤	8	① ② ③ ④ ⑤	13	① ② ③ ④ ⑤	18	① ② ③ ④ ⑤	23	① ② ③ ④ ⑤
4	① ② ③ ④ ⑤	9	① ② ③ ④ ⑤	14	① ② ③ ④ ⑤	19	① ② ③ ④ ⑤	24	① ② ③ ④ ⑤
5	① ② ③ ④ ⑤	10	① ② ③ ④ ⑤	15	① ② ③ ④ ⑤	20	① ② ③ ④ ⑤	25	① ② ③ ④ ⑤

	A B C D E		A B C D E		A B C D E		A B C D E		A B C D E
1	① ② ③ ④ ⑤	6	① ② ③ ④ ⑤	11	① ② ③ ④ ⑤	16	① ② ③ ④ ⑤	21	① ② ③ ④ ⑤
2	① ② ③ ④ ⑤	7	① ② ③ ④ ⑤	12	① ② ③ ④ ⑤	17	① ② ③ ④ ⑤	22	① ② ③ ④ ⑤
3	① ② ③ ④ ⑤	8	① ② ③ ④ ⑤	13	① ② ③ ④ ⑤	18	① ② ③ ④ ⑤	23	① ② ③ ④ ⑤
4	① ② ③ ④ ⑤	9	① ② ③ ④ ⑤	14	① ② ③ ④ ⑤	19	① ② ③ ④ ⑤	24	① ② ③ ④ ⑤
5	① ② ③ ④ ⑤	10	① ② ③ ④ ⑤	15	① ② ③ ④ ⑤	20	① ② ③ ④ ⑤	25	① ② ③ ④ ⑤

ANSWER SHEET

	A B C D E		A B C D E		A B C D E		A B C D E		A B C D E
1	① ② ③ ④ ⑤	6	① ② ③ ④ ⑤	11	① ② ③ ④ ⑤	16	① ② ③ ④ ⑤	21	① ② ③ ④ ⑤
2	① ② ③ ④ ⑤	7	① ② ③ ④ ⑤	12	① ② ③ ④ ⑤	17	① ② ③ ④ ⑤	22	① ② ③ ④ ⑤
3	① ② ③ ④ ⑤	8	① ② ③ ④ ⑤	13	① ② ③ ④ ⑤	18	① ② ③ ④ ⑤	23	① ② ③ ④ ⑤
4	① ② ③ ④ ⑤	9	① ② ③ ④ ⑤	14	① ② ③ ④ ⑤	19	① ② ③ ④ ⑤	24	① ② ③ ④ ⑤
5	① ② ③ ④ ⑤	10	① ② ③ ④ ⑤	15	① ② ③ ④ ⑤	20	① ② ③ ④ ⑤	25	① ② ③ ④ ⑤

	A B C D E		A B C D E		A B C D E		A B C D E		A B C D E
1	① ② ③ ④ ⑤	6	① ② ③ ④ ⑤	11	① ② ③ ④ ⑤	16	① ② ③ ④ ⑤	21	① ② ③ ④ ⑤
2	① ② ③ ④ ⑤	7	① ② ③ ④ ⑤	12	① ② ③ ④ ⑤	17	① ② ③ ④ ⑤	22	① ② ③ ④ ⑤
3	① ② ③ ④ ⑤	8	① ② ③ ④ ⑤	13	① ② ③ ④ ⑤	18	① ② ③ ④ ⑤	23	① ② ③ ④ ⑤
4	① ② ③ ④ ⑤	9	① ② ③ ④ ⑤	14	① ② ③ ④ ⑤	19	① ② ③ ④ ⑤	24	① ② ③ ④ ⑤
5	① ② ③ ④ ⑤	10	① ② ③ ④ ⑤	15	① ② ③ ④ ⑤	20	① ② ③ ④ ⑤	25	① ② ③ ④ ⑤

ANSWER SHEET

	A B C D E		A B C D E		A B C D E		A B C D E		A B C D E
1	① ② ③ ④ ⑤	6	① ② ③ ④ ⑤	11	① ② ③ ④ ⑤	16	① ② ③ ④ ⑤	21	① ② ③ ④ ⑤
2	① ② ③ ④ ⑤	7	① ② ③ ④ ⑤	12	① ② ③ ④ ⑤	17	① ② ③ ④ ⑤	22	① ② ③ ④ ⑤
3	① ② ③ ④ ⑤	8	① ② ③ ④ ⑤	13	① ② ③ ④ ⑤	18	① ② ③ ④ ⑤	23	① ② ③ ④ ⑤
4	① ② ③ ④ ⑤	9	① ② ③ ④ ⑤	14	① ② ③ ④ ⑤	19	① ② ③ ④ ⑤	24	① ② ③ ④ ⑤
5	① ② ③ ④ ⑤	10	① ② ③ ④ ⑤	15	① ② ③ ④ ⑤	20	① ② ③ ④ ⑤	25	① ② ③ ④ ⑤

	A B C D E		A B C D E		A B C D E		A B C D E		A B C D E
1	① ② ③ ④ ⑤	6	① ② ③ ④ ⑤	11	① ② ③ ④ ⑤	16	① ② ③ ④ ⑤	21	① ② ③ ④ ⑤
2	① ② ③ ④ ⑤	7	① ② ③ ④ ⑤	12	① ② ③ ④ ⑤	17	① ② ③ ④ ⑤	22	① ② ③ ④ ⑤
3	① ② ③ ④ ⑤	8	① ② ③ ④ ⑤	13	① ② ③ ④ ⑤	18	① ② ③ ④ ⑤	23	① ② ③ ④ ⑤
4	① ② ③ ④ ⑤	9	① ② ③ ④ ⑤	14	① ② ③ ④ ⑤	19	① ② ③ ④ ⑤	24	① ② ③ ④ ⑤
5	① ② ③ ④ ⑤	10	① ② ③ ④ ⑤	15	① ② ③ ④ ⑤	20	① ② ③ ④ ⑤	25	① ② ③ ④ ⑤

ANSWER SHEET

	A B C D E		A B C D E		A B C D E		A B C D E		A B C D E
1	① ② ③ ④ ⑤	6	① ② ③ ④ ⑤	11	① ② ③ ④ ⑤	16	① ② ③ ④ ⑤	21	① ② ③ ④ ⑤
2	① ② ③ ④ ⑤	7	① ② ③ ④ ⑤	12	① ② ③ ④ ⑤	17	① ② ③ ④ ⑤	22	① ② ③ ④ ⑤
3	① ② ③ ④ ⑤	8	① ② ③ ④ ⑤	13	① ② ③ ④ ⑤	18	① ② ③ ④ ⑤	23	① ② ③ ④ ⑤
4	① ② ③ ④ ⑤	9	① ② ③ ④ ⑤	14	① ② ③ ④ ⑤	19	① ② ③ ④ ⑤	24	① ② ③ ④ ⑤
5	① ② ③ ④ ⑤	10	① ② ③ ④ ⑤	15	① ② ③ ④ ⑤	20	① ② ③ ④ ⑤	25	① ② ③ ④ ⑤

	A B C D E		A B C D E		A B C D E		A B C D E		A B C D E
1	① ② ③ ④ ⑤	6	① ② ③ ④ ⑤	11	① ② ③ ④ ⑤	16	① ② ③ ④ ⑤	21	① ② ③ ④ ⑤
2	① ② ③ ④ ⑤	7	① ② ③ ④ ⑤	12	① ② ③ ④ ⑤	17	① ② ③ ④ ⑤	22	① ② ③ ④ ⑤
3	① ② ③ ④ ⑤	8	① ② ③ ④ ⑤	13	① ② ③ ④ ⑤	18	① ② ③ ④ ⑤	23	① ② ③ ④ ⑤
4	① ② ③ ④ ⑤	9	① ② ③ ④ ⑤	14	① ② ③ ④ ⑤	19	① ② ③ ④ ⑤	24	① ② ③ ④ ⑤
5	① ② ③ ④ ⑤	10	① ② ③ ④ ⑤	15	① ② ③ ④ ⑤	20	① ② ③ ④ ⑤	25	① ② ③ ④ ⑤

ANSWER SHEET

	A B C D E		A B C D E		A B C D E		A B C D E		A B C D E
1	① ② ③ ④ ⑤	6	① ② ③ ④ ⑤	11	① ② ③ ④ ⑤	16	① ② ③ ④ ⑤	21	① ② ③ ④ ⑤
2	① ② ③ ④ ⑤	7	① ② ③ ④ ⑤	12	① ② ③ ④ ⑤	17	① ② ③ ④ ⑤	22	① ② ③ ④ ⑤
3	① ② ③ ④ ⑤	8	① ② ③ ④ ⑤	13	① ② ③ ④ ⑤	18	① ② ③ ④ ⑤	23	① ② ③ ④ ⑤
4	① ② ③ ④ ⑤	9	① ② ③ ④ ⑤	14	① ② ③ ④ ⑤	19	① ② ③ ④ ⑤	24	① ② ③ ④ ⑤
5	① ② ③ ④ ⑤	10	① ② ③ ④ ⑤	15	① ② ③ ④ ⑤	20	① ② ③ ④ ⑤	25	① ② ③ ④ ⑤

	A B C D E		A B C D E		A B C D E		A B C D E		A B C D E
1	① ② ③ ④ ⑤	6	① ② ③ ④ ⑤	11	① ② ③ ④ ⑤	16	① ② ③ ④ ⑤	21	① ② ③ ④ ⑤
2	① ② ③ ④ ⑤	7	① ② ③ ④ ⑤	12	① ② ③ ④ ⑤	17	① ② ③ ④ ⑤	22	① ② ③ ④ ⑤
3	① ② ③ ④ ⑤	8	① ② ③ ④ ⑤	13	① ② ③ ④ ⑤	18	① ② ③ ④ ⑤	23	① ② ③ ④ ⑤
4	① ② ③ ④ ⑤	9	① ② ③ ④ ⑤	14	① ② ③ ④ ⑤	19	① ② ③ ④ ⑤	24	① ② ③ ④ ⑤
5	① ② ③ ④ ⑤	10	① ② ③ ④ ⑤	15	① ② ③ ④ ⑤	20	① ② ③ ④ ⑤	25	① ② ③ ④ ⑤

ANSWER SHEET

	A B C D E		A B C D E		A B C D E		A B C D E		A B C D E
1	① ② ③ ④ ⑤	6	① ② ③ ④ ⑤	11	① ② ③ ④ ⑤	16	① ② ③ ④ ⑤	21	① ② ③ ④ ⑤
2	① ② ③ ④ ⑤	7	① ② ③ ④ ⑤	12	① ② ③ ④ ⑤	17	① ② ③ ④ ⑤	22	① ② ③ ④ ⑤
3	① ② ③ ④ ⑤	8	① ② ③ ④ ⑤	13	① ② ③ ④ ⑤	18	① ② ③ ④ ⑤	23	① ② ③ ④ ⑤
4	① ② ③ ④ ⑤	9	① ② ③ ④ ⑤	14	① ② ③ ④ ⑤	19	① ② ③ ④ ⑤	24	① ② ③ ④ ⑤
5	① ② ③ ④ ⑤	10	① ② ③ ④ ⑤	15	① ② ③ ④ ⑤	20	① ② ③ ④ ⑤	25	① ② ③ ④ ⑤

	A B C D E		A B C D E		A B C D E		A B C D E		A B C D E
1	① ② ③ ④ ⑤	6	① ② ③ ④ ⑤	11	① ② ③ ④ ⑤	16	① ② ③ ④ ⑤	21	① ② ③ ④ ⑤
2	① ② ③ ④ ⑤	7	① ② ③ ④ ⑤	12	① ② ③ ④ ⑤	17	① ② ③ ④ ⑤	22	① ② ③ ④ ⑤
3	① ② ③ ④ ⑤	8	① ② ③ ④ ⑤	13	① ② ③ ④ ⑤	18	① ② ③ ④ ⑤	23	① ② ③ ④ ⑤
4	① ② ③ ④ ⑤	9	① ② ③ ④ ⑤	14	① ② ③ ④ ⑤	19	① ② ③ ④ ⑤	24	① ② ③ ④ ⑤
5	① ② ③ ④ ⑤	10	① ② ③ ④ ⑤	15	① ② ③ ④ ⑤	20	① ② ③ ④ ⑤	25	① ② ③ ④ ⑤

ANSWER SHEET

	A B C D E		A B C D E		A B C D E		A B C D E		A B C D E
1	① ② ③ ④ ⑤	6	① ② ③ ④ ⑤	11	① ② ③ ④ ⑤	16	① ② ③ ④ ⑤	21	① ② ③ ④ ⑤
2	① ② ③ ④ ⑤	7	① ② ③ ④ ⑤	12	① ② ③ ④ ⑤	17	① ② ③ ④ ⑤	22	① ② ③ ④ ⑤
3	① ② ③ ④ ⑤	8	① ② ③ ④ ⑤	13	① ② ③ ④ ⑤	18	① ② ③ ④ ⑤	23	① ② ③ ④ ⑤
4	① ② ③ ④ ⑤	9	① ② ③ ④ ⑤	14	① ② ③ ④ ⑤	19	① ② ③ ④ ⑤	24	① ② ③ ④ ⑤
5	① ② ③ ④ ⑤	10	① ② ③ ④ ⑤	15	① ② ③ ④ ⑤	20	① ② ③ ④ ⑤	25	① ② ③ ④ ⑤

	A B C D E		A B C D E		A B C D E		A B C D E		A B C D E
1	① ② ③ ④ ⑤	6	① ② ③ ④ ⑤	11	① ② ③ ④ ⑤	16	① ② ③ ④ ⑤	21	① ② ③ ④ ⑤
2	① ② ③ ④ ⑤	7	① ② ③ ④ ⑤	12	① ② ③ ④ ⑤	17	① ② ③ ④ ⑤	22	① ② ③ ④ ⑤
3	① ② ③ ④ ⑤	8	① ② ③ ④ ⑤	13	① ② ③ ④ ⑤	18	① ② ③ ④ ⑤	23	① ② ③ ④ ⑤
4	① ② ③ ④ ⑤	9	① ② ③ ④ ⑤	14	① ② ③ ④ ⑤	19	① ② ③ ④ ⑤	24	① ② ③ ④ ⑤
5	① ② ③ ④ ⑤	10	① ② ③ ④ ⑤	15	① ② ③ ④ ⑤	20	① ② ③ ④ ⑤	25	① ② ③ ④ ⑤